PEARSON EDEXCEL A LEVEL

KU-102-882

ECONOMICS A
Fourth Edition

PETER SMITH

 Boost

 HODDER
EDUCATION
AN HACHETTE UK COMPANY

In order to ensure that this resource offers high-quality support for the associated Pearson qualification, it has been through a review process by the awarding body. This process confirms that this resource fully covers the teaching and learning content of the specification or part of a specification at which it is aimed. It also confirms that it demonstrates an appropriate balance between the development of subject skills, knowledge and understanding, in addition to preparation for assessment.

Endorsement does not cover any guidance on assessment activities or processes (e.g. practice questions or advice on how to answer assessment questions), included in the resource nor does it prescribe any particular approach to the teaching or delivery of a related course.

While the publishers have made every attempt to ensure that advice on the qualification and its assessment is accurate, the official specification and associated assessment guidance materials are the only authoritative source of information and should always be referred to for definitive guidance.

Pearson examiners have not contributed to any sections in this resource relevant to examination papers for which they have responsibility.

Examiners will not use endorsed resources as a source of material for any assessment set by Pearson.

Endorsement of a resource does not mean that the resource is required to achieve this Pearson qualification, nor does it mean that it is the only suitable material available to support the qualification, and any resource lists produced by the awarding body shall include this and other appropriate resources.

Every effort has been made to trace all copyright holders, but if any have been inadvertently overlooked, the Publishers will be pleased to make the necessary arrangements at the first opportunity.

Although every effort has been made to ensure that website addresses are correct at time of going to press, Hodder Education cannot be held responsible for the content of any website mentioned in this book. It is sometimes possible to find a relocated web page by typing in the address of the home page for a website in the URL window of your browser.

Hachette UK's policy is to use papers that are natural, renewable and recyclable products and made from wood grown in well-managed forests and other controlled sources. The logging and manufacturing processes are expected to conform to the environmental regulations of the country of origin.

Orders: please contact Hachette UK Distribution, Hely Hutchinson Centre, Milton Road, Didcot, Oxfordshire, OX11 7HH. Telephone: (44) 01235 827827. Email education@hachette.co.uk Lines are open from 9 a.m. to 5 p.m., Monday to Friday. You can also order through our website: www.hoddereducation.co.uk

ISBN: 978 1 5104 4959 6

© Peter Smith 2019

First published in 2008
Second edition published in 2013
Third edition published in 2015
This edition published in 2019 by

Hodder Education,
An Hachette UK Company
Carmelite House
50 Victoria Embankment
London EC4Y 0DZ
www.hoddereducation.co.uk

Impression number   10 9 8 7 6 5 4 3

Year   2022 2021

All rights reserved. Apart from any use permitted under UK copyright law, no part of this publication may be reproduced or transmitted in any form or by any means, electronic or mechanical, including photocopying and recording, or held within any information storage and retrieval system, without permission in writing from the publisher or under licence from the Copyright Licensing Agency Limited. Further details of such licences (for reprographic reproduction) may be obtained from the Copyright Licensing Agency Limited, www.cla.co.uk

Typeset by Aptara in India

Printed and bound by CPI Group (UK) Ltd, Croydon CR0 4YY

A catalogue record for this title is available from the British Library.

Get the most from this book

This textbook provides an introduction to economics. It has been tailored explicitly to cover the content of the Edexcel specification for A level in Economics A. The specification is divided into four themes corresponding to the Edexcel specification.

The text provides the foundation for studying Edexcel Economics, but you will no doubt wish to keep up to date by referring to additional topical sources of information about economic events. This can be done by reading the serious newspapers, visiting key sites on the internet, and reading such magazines as *Economic Review*.

Special features

A statement of the intended learning objectives for each chapter.

Clear, concise definitions of essential key terms where they first appear and a list at the end of each theme.

Short pieces of advice to help you present your ideas effectively and avoid potential pitfalls.

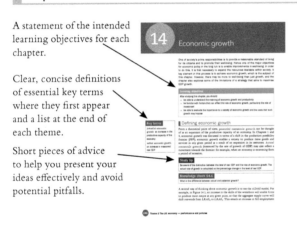

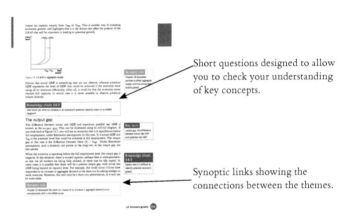

Short questions designed to allow you to check your understanding of key concepts.

Synoptic links showing the connections between the themes.

Worked examples of quantitative skills that you will need to develop.

Bulleted summaries of each topic that can be used as a revision tool.

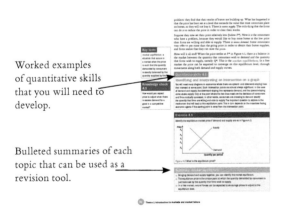

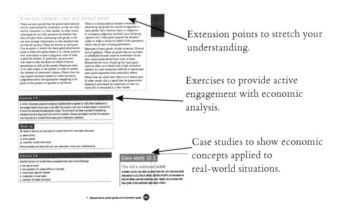

Extension points to stretch your understanding.

Exercises to provide active engagement with economic analysis.

Case studies to show economic concepts applied to real-world situations.

Contents

Introduction vi

Theme 1 Introduction to markets and market failure 1

    Chapter 1 The nature of economics 2

    Chapter 2 The nature of demand 19

    Chapter 3 The nature of supply 39

    Chapter 4 How markets work: price determination and the price mechanism. 51

    Chapter 5 How markets work: the price mechanism in action .68

    Chapter 6 Market failure and externalities 81

    Chapter 7 Market failure: public goods and information gaps 94

    Chapter 8 Government intervention and government failure 104

    Theme 1 key terms 120

Theme 2 The UK economy — performance and policies 123

    Chapter 9 Measures of economic performance: economic growth. 124

    Chapter 10 Measures of economic performance: inflation, unemployment and the
    balance of payments. 141

    Chapter 11 Aggregate demand 160

    Chapter 12 Aggregate supply 170

    Chapter 13 National income and macroeconomic equilibrium 178

    Chapter 14 Economic growth. 190

    Chapter 15 Macroeconomic policy objectives. 204

    Chapter 16 Macroeconomic policies 218

    Theme 2 key terms 240

Theme 3 Business behaviour and the labour market 243

    Chapter 17 Business growth 244

    Chapter 18 Revenues, costs, profits and objectives 253

    Chapter 19 Market structure: perfect competition and monopoly 273

    Chapter 20 Market structure: monopolistic competition and oligopoly 299

    Chapter 21 Pricing strategies and contestable markets 318

    Chapter 22 The labour market 332

    Chapter 23 Government intervention to promote competition 356

    Theme 3 key terms 376

Theme 4 A global perspective 379

    Chapter 24 Globalisation and trade 380

    Chapter 25 Trading blocs and restrictions on trade 404

    Chapter 26 The balance of payments and exchange rates 429

    Chapter 27 Poverty and inequality in developed and developing countries 460

    Chapter 28 Emerging and developing economies 482

    Chapter 29 Strategies influencing growth and development 511

    Chapter 30 The financial sector 539

    Chapter 31 The role of the central bank 550

    Chapter 32 The role of the state in the macroeconomy 564

    Theme 4 key terms 588

    Practice questions 592

    Acknowledgements 606

    Index 607

Introduction

Prior learning, knowledge and progression

Most students who choose to study A level Economics are meeting the subject for the first time, and no prior learning or knowledge of economics is required. The study of economics complements a range of other A level subjects, such as history, geography, business, mathematics and the sciences, and the way of thinking that you will develop as you study economics will help in interpreting issues that you will meet in many of these subjects. Studying economics can provide important employability skills and is a good preparation for those wishing to progress to higher education. If you intend to study economics at university, you may wish to consider studying mathematics as one of your other A level subjects.

Find out more about the Edexcel Economics offering, or other related qualifications, at https://qualifications.pearson.com/en/qualifications/edexcel-a-levels.html.

Assessment objectives

In common with other economics specifications, Edexcel Economics entails four assessment objectives. Candidates will thus be expected to:

- demonstrate knowledge of terms/concepts and theories/models to show an understanding of the behaviour of economic agents and how they are affected by and respond to economic issues
- apply knowledge and understanding to various economic contexts to show how economic agents are affected by and respond to economic issues
- analyse issues within economics, showing an understanding of their impact on economic agents
- evaluate economic arguments and use qualitative and quantitative evidence to support informed judgements relating to economic issues.

Assessment breakdown

The A level in Economics A will be assessed by three examinations. The first two deal respectively with 'markets and business behaviour' and the 'national and global economy'. The third is a synoptic paper ('microeconomics and macroeconomics'), in which you will be required to apply your knowledge and understanding, make connections and transfer higher-order skills across all four themes. Each will be a written paper lasting 2 hours. Further details are provided in the specification on the Edexcel website.

Economics in this book

The study of economics requires a familiarity with recent economic events in the UK and elsewhere, and candidates will be expected to show familiarity with 'recent historical data' — broadly defined as covering the last 7 to 10 years. The following websites will help you to keep up to date with recent trends and events:

- Recent and historical data about the UK economy can be found at the website of the Office for National Statistics (ONS) at: www.ons.gov.uk
- Also helpful is the site of HM Treasury at: www.gov.uk/government/organisations/hm-treasury.
- The Bank of England site is well worth a visit, especially the *Inflation Report* and the Minutes of the Monetary Policy Committee: www.bankofengland.co.uk
- The Institute for Fiscal Studies offers an independent view of a range of economic topics: www.ifs.org.uk

For information about other countries, visit the following:

- www.oecd.org
- http://ec.europa.eu/eurostat
- www.worldbank.org
- www.undp.org

Finally, for answers to the knowledge checks, exercises, case studies and practice questions featured in this book, please visit www.hoddereducation.co.uk/Product? Product= 9781510449596 and click 'Download answers'.

How to study economics

There are two crucial aspects of studying economics. The first stage is to study the theory, which helps us to explain economic behaviour. However, in studying A level Economics it is equally important to be able to apply the theories and concepts that you meet, and to see just how these relate to the real world.

If you are to become competent at this, it is vital that you get plenty of practice. In part, this means working through the exercises and case studies that you will find in this text. However, it also means thinking about how economics helps us to explain news items and data that appear in the newspapers and on the television. Make sure that you practise as much as you can.

In economics, it is also important to be able to produce examples of economic phenomena. In reading this text, you will find some examples that help to illustrate ideas and concepts. Do not rely solely on the examples provided here, but look around the world to find your own examples, and keep a note of these ready for use in essays and exams. This will help to convince the examiners that you have understood economics. It will also help you to understand the theories.

Enjoy economics

Most important of all, I hope you will enjoy your study of economics. I have always been fascinated by the subject, and hope that you will capture something of the excitement and challenge of learning about how markets and the economy operate. I also wish you every success with your studies.

Acknowledgements

I would like to express my gratitude to the reviewer who commented on the previous edition, whose remarks and suggestions have enabled improvements in the content and style of this new edition. I would like to thank James Benefield at Hodder Education, for his detailed reading of the text which helped to further focus the material on the needs of students studying Edexcel Economics.

Many of the data series shown in figures in this book were drawn from the data obtained from the National Statistics website at www.ons.gov.uk, and contain public sector information licensed under the Open Government Licence v3.0.

Other data were from various sources, including the OECD, World Bank, United Nations Development Programme and other sources as specified.

While every effort has been made to trace the owners of copyright material, I would like to apologise to any copyright holders whose rights may have unwittingly been infringed.

Peter Smith

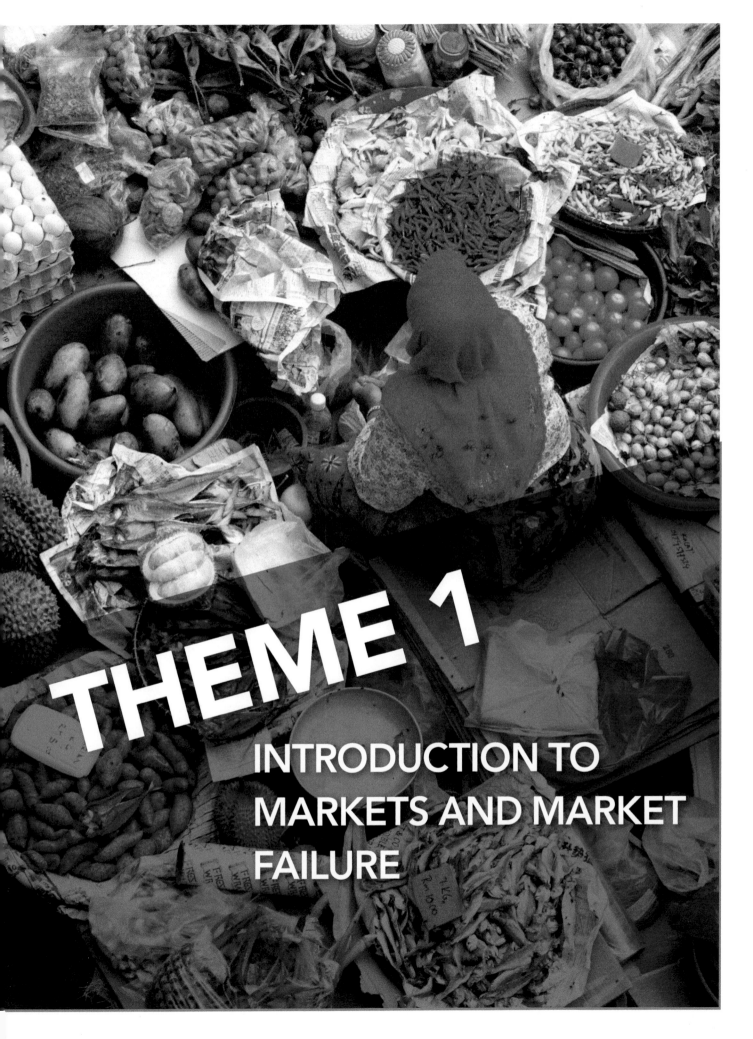

THEME 1

INTRODUCTION TO MARKETS AND MARKET FAILURE

The nature of economics

Welcome to economics. Many of you opening this book will be meeting economics for the first time, and you will want to know what is in store for you as you set out to study the subject. This opening chapter sets the scene by introducing you to some key ideas and identifying the scope of economic analysis. As you learn more of the subject, you will find that economics is a way of thinking that broadens your perspective on the world around you.

Learning objectives

This chapter will introduce you to:
→ the nature and scope of economic analysis
→ the role of models and assumptions in economics
→ positive and normative statements
→ the importance of scarcity and choice
→ the concept of opportunity cost
→ the notion of factors of production
→ the distinction between renewable and non-renewable resources and the idea of sustainability
→ the production possibility frontier
→ the concept of the division of labour
→ how specialisation can improve productivity
→ the role of markets and what is meant by a mixed economy
→ alternative ways of coordinating the allocation of resources in society
→ the distinction between microeconomics and macroeconomics

Economics as a social science

Economics sets out to tackle some complex issues concerning what is a very complex real world. In many of the sciences, investigation can proceed by carrying out experiments, testing hypotheses in the laboratory. Experimental economics is a rapidly expanding area in the subject, but although this allows economists to improve their understanding of individual behaviour, there are still many areas of economics where it is not possible to rely on experiments to advance knowledge. An alternative approach is therefore needed.

If economists are to cope with the complexity of the real world, it is essential to simplify reality in some way; otherwise the task would be overwhelming. Economists thus work with **models**. These are simplified versions of reality that are more manageable for analysis, allowing economists to focus on some key aspects of the world.

Often this works by allowing them to focus on one thing at a time. A model almost always begins with assumptions that help economists to simplify their questions.

Key term

model a simplified representation of reality used to provide insight into economic decisions and events

These assumptions can then be gradually relaxed so that the effect of each one of them can be observed. In this way, economists can gradually move towards a more complicated version of reality.

Chapter 2 considers the demand for a good, and the factors that affect how much of a good is demanded by consumers. Trying to analyse all the possible influences on these decisions would be difficult, so it is common to start by exploring how the price of a good affects the quantity demanded, under the assumption that all other influences stay the same. This is a common assumption in economics, which is sometimes expressed by the Latin phrase **ceteris paribus**, meaning 'other things being equal'. Given the complexity of the real world, it is often helpful to focus on one thing at a time.

To evaluate a model, it is not necessary that it be totally realistic. The model's desired objective may help in predicting future behaviour, or in testing empirical evidence collected from the real world. If a model provides insights into how individuals take decisions, or helps to explain economic events, then it has some value, even if it seems remote from reality.

However, it is always important to examine the assumptions that are made, and to ask what happens if these assumptions do not hold.

Positive and normative economic statements

Economics tries to be objective in analysis. However, some of its subject matter requires careful attention in order to retain an objective distance. In this connection, it is important to be clear about the difference between **positive** and **normative** **statements**.

In short, a positive statement is about *facts* and in principle is testable. A normative statement is about *what ought to be*. Another way of looking at this is that a statement becomes normative when it involves a **value judgement**.

Suppose the government is considering raising the tax on cigarettes. It may legitimately consult economists to discover what effect a higher tobacco tax will have on the consumption of cigarettes and on government revenues. This would be a *positive* investigation, in that the economists are being asked to use economic analysis to forecast what will happen when the tax is increased.

A very different situation will arise if the government asks whether it *should* raise the tax on cigarettes. This moves the economists beyond positive analysis, because it entails a value judgement — so it is now a *normative* analysis. There are some words that betray normative statements, such as 'should' or 'ought to' — watch for these.

Most of this book is about positive economics. However, you should be aware that positive analysis is often called upon to inform normative judgements. If the aim of a policy is to stop people from smoking (which reflects a normative judgement about what *ought* to happen), then economic analysis may be used to highlight the strengths and weaknesses of those alternatives in a purely positive fashion.

Critics of economics often joke that economists always disagree with one another: for example, it has been said that if you put five economists in a room together, they will come up with at least six conflicting opinions. However, although economists may arrive at different value judgements, and thus have differences when it comes to

Knowledge check 1.1

What phrase is used by economists when assuming that some variables are to be held constant?

Key terms

ceteris paribus a Latin phrase meaning 'other things being equal'; it is used in economics when we focus on changes in one variable while holding other influences constant

positive statement a statement about what is (i.e. about facts)

normative statement a statement that involves a value judgement about what *ought to be*

value judgement a statement based on your opinion or beliefs, rather than on facts

Synoptic link

The effect of a tax on cigarettes is examined in Chapter 5.

Increasing taxes on tobacco affects consumption of cigarettes and government revenue

normative issues, there is much greater agreement when it comes to positive analysis. Nonetheless, value judgements do influence economic decision making and policy because different people — and political parties — may have different views about what is desirable for society, even if they agree on how policies may work.

The economic problem

For any society in the world, the fundamental economic problem faced is that of **scarcity**. You might think that this is obvious for some societies in the developing world, where poverty and hunger are rife. But it is also true for relatively prosperous economies such as those of Switzerland, the USA and the UK.

It is true in the sense that all societies have *finite resources*, but people have unlimited wants. A big claim? Not really. There is no country in the world in which all wants can be met, and this is clearly true at the global level.

There are some goods that may be regarded as *free goods*. An example might be the earth's atmosphere, which would not normally be regarded as scarce. Goods that are scarce are known as *economic goods*. Most goods fall into this category.

Talking about scarcity in this sense is not the same as talking about *poverty*. Poverty might be seen as an extreme form of scarcity, in which individuals lack the basic necessities of life; whereas even relatively prosperous people face scarcity, because resources are limited.

Scarcity and choice

The key issue that arises from the existence of scarcity is that it forces people to make choices. Each individual must choose which goods and services to consume. In other words, everyone needs to prioritise the consumption of whatever commodities they need or would like to have, as they cannot satisfy all their wants. Similarly, at the national level, governments have to make choices between alternative uses of resources.

It is this need to choose that underlies the subject matter of economics. Economic analysis is all about analysing those choices made by individual people, firms and governments.

Opportunity cost

This raises one of the most important concepts in all of economic analysis — the notion of **opportunity cost**. When an individual chooses to consume one good, she does so at the cost of the item that would have been next in her list of priorities. For example, suppose you are on a strict diet, and at the end of the day you can 'afford' either one chocolate or a piece of cheese. If you choose the cheese, the opportunity cost of the cheese is the chocolate that you could have had instead.

This important notion can be applied in many different contexts, because whenever you make a decision you reject an alternative in favour of your chosen option. You have chosen to read this book — when instead you could be watching television or meeting friends.

Synoptic link

The meaning and causes of poverty are examined in Chapter 27, where you will see that although absolute poverty may only exist in developing countries, relative poverty also exists in advanced countries such as the UK.

Key terms

scarcity a situation that arises when people have unlimited wants in the face of limited resources

opportunity cost in decision making, the value of the next-best alternative forgone

The notion of opportunity cost is related to an important tool in economics known as **marginal analysis**. This is based on the idea that people take decisions by considering small changes that could be made. For example, in choosing whether to read this book, you may consider if the extra (marginal) benefit you will receive from doing so will exceed the additional benefit you would receive from watching television. Firms may also take decisions in this way, perhaps by checking whether the cost of producing and selling an additional unit of output will exceed the extra (marginal) return they receive from selling it. This approach will become familiar to you as you continue to study economics.

Key term

marginal analysis an approach to economic decision making based on considering the additional (marginal) benefits and costs of a change in behaviour

Exercise 1.1

Andrew has just started his A level subjects, and has chosen to take economics, mathematics and French. Although he was certain about the first two, it was a close call between French and English. What is Andrew's opportunity cost of choosing French?

Study tip

Opportunity cost is a key concept in economics, and is important in a variety of contexts. Similarly, marginal analysis is a key part of economic thinking, so make sure that you understand these fully from the outset.

As you move further into studying economics, you will encounter this notion of opportunity cost again and again. For example, firms take decisions about the sort of economic activity in which to engage. A market gardener has to decide whether to plant onions or potatoes; if he decides to grow onions, he has to forgo the opportunity to grow potatoes. From the government's point of view, if it decides to devote more resources to the National Health Service, then it will have fewer resources available for, say, defence. The need to balance the relative merits of alternative choices is challenging, but crucial. Economic analysis helps to explain how such choices are made, and how they could be improved.

Knowledge check 1.2

How do economists refer to decisions made on the basis of the impact of small changes in behaviour?

Economic agents

In analysing the process by which choices are made, it is important to be aware of the various economic agents that are responsible for making decisions. In economic analysis, there are three key groups of decision makers: consumers, producers and government.

- *Consumers* (individuals and households) make choices about their expenditure. In this role, they are consumers who demand goods and services. In order to be able to buy goods, consumers need income, so they also take decisions about the supply of their labour, which is discussed in the next section.
- *Producers* (firms) exist in order to produce output of goods or services. Producers also make choices, particularly about which goods or services to produce, and the techniques of production to be used. The prices at which they can sell are also important in economic analysis.
- *Government* fulfils several roles in society. It undertakes expenditure, and influences the economy through its taxation and regulation of markets.

Opportunity cost is crucial for each of these economic agents, because they each face constraints on their choices. As soon as they choose one course of action, they forgo the possibility of taking an alternative decision.

Key term

factors of production
resources used in the
production process;
inputs into production,
particularly including
labour, capital, land and
enterprise

Factors of production

People in a society play two quite different roles. On the one hand, they are the consumers, the ultimate beneficiaries of the process of production. On the other, they are a key part of the production process in that they are instrumental in producing goods and services.

More generally, it is clear that both *human resources* and *physical resources* are required as part of the production process. These productive resources are known as the **factors of production**.

The most obvious human resource is labour. Labour is a key input into production. Of course, there are many different types of labour, encompassing different skill levels and working in different ways. *Enterprise* is another key human resource. An entrepreneur is someone who organises production and identifies projects to be undertaken, often bearing the risk of the activity. *Management* might also be classified as a key human resource. *Natural resources* are also inputs into the production process. In particular, all economic activities require some use of land, and most use some raw materials.

Synoptic link

These decisions taken by
producers are discussed
later, in particular in
Chapter 18, but you need
to understand some basics
first.

There are also *produced resources* — inputs that are the product of a manufacturing process. For example, machines are used in the production process; they are resources manufactured for the purpose of producing other goods. These inputs are referred to as capital, which may include things like factory buildings and transport equipment as well as plant and machinery.

The way in which these inputs are combined in order to produce output is another key part of the allocation of resources. Firms need to take decisions about the mix of inputs used in order to produce their output. Such decisions are required in whatever form of economic activity a firm is engaged.

Factors of production — labour (workers), capital (buildings) and land

Knowledge check 1.3

How do we refer to resources such as labour, land, capital and enterprise when they are used in production?

Renewable and non-renewable resources

An important distinction is between **renewable resources** such as forests, and **non-renewable resources** such as oil or coal.

In the case of renewable resources, there have been many debates in recent years about the dangers of depleting such resources at too rapid a rate to allow replacement. One example of this has been the stocks of some fish such as cod, where it has been argued that overfishing may lead to the extinction of the species. Similar arguments have been applied to other resources such as the rainforests. This has highlighted the importance of sustainable development, which has been defined as 'development which meets the needs of the present without compromising the ability of future generations to meet their own needs' (Brundtland Commission, 1987). Applying this to the case of cod fishing, for example, sustainable fishing would be seen in terms of not catching so many cod that the overall population becomes unsustainable.

For non-renewable resources, reserves are finite — by definition — so concern has arisen over their possible exhaustion. Attention has tended to focus on oil, which is much in demand, especially given rapidly rising car ownership. This has led to a search for renewable sources of energy, which would also contribute to sustainability. One economic issue here is whether the prices of resources such as oil will rise as reserves are depleted. This could then have the effect of giving incentives to firms to develop alternative sources of energy. It could also mean that some reserves of oil that are currently uneconomic may become viable. This is one example of how prices can be seen to guide resource allocation.

Key terms

renewable resources natural resources that can be replenished, such as forests that can be replanted, or solar energy that does not get used up

non-renewable resources natural resources that once used cannot be replenished, such as coal or oil

Exercise 1.2

Classify each of the following as human, natural (renewable or non-renewable) or produced resources:

a timber

b services of a window cleaner

c natural gas

d solar energy

e a combine harvester

f a computer programmer who sets up a company to market their software

g a computer

Knowledge check 1.4

Name one example of a renewable energy resource, and one example of a non-renewable energy source.

The three key economic questions

By now you should be getting some idea of the subject matter of economics. The American economist Paul Samuelson (who won the Nobel Prize for Economic Sciences in 1970) identified three key questions that economics sets out to investigate:

1 *What?* What goods and services should be produced in a society from its scarce resources? In other words, how should resources be allocated among producing smartphones, potatoes, banking services and so on?

2 *How?* How should the productive resources of the economy be used to produce these various goods and services?

3 *For whom?* Having produced a range of goods and services, how should these be allocated among the population for consumption?

Exercise 1.3

With which of Samuelson's three questions (what, how, for whom) would you associate the following?

a A firm chooses to switch from producing laptop computers in order to increase its output of tablets.

b The government reduces the highest rate of income tax.

c Faced with increased labour costs, a firm introduces labour-saving machinery.

d There is an increase in social security benefits.

e The owner of a fish-and-chip shop decides to close down and take a job in a local factory.

Summary: key economic ideas

- Positive statements are about what is, whereas normative statements are about what ought to be.
- The fundamental problem faced by any society is scarcity, because resources are finite but wants are unlimited. As a result, choices need to be made.
- Each choice has an opportunity cost — the value of the next-best alternative forgone.
- The amount of output produced in a period depends on the inputs of factors of production.
- The rate at which renewable resources are used needs to be seen in the light of the notion of sustainability.
- Economics deals with the questions of what should be produced, how it should be produced, and for whom.

The production possibility frontier

Key term

production possibility frontier (PPF) a curve showing the maximum combinations of goods or services that can be produced in a given period with available resources

Economists rely heavily on diagrams to help in their analysis. In exploring the notion of opportunity cost, a helpful diagram is the **production possibility frontier (PPF)**. This shows the maximum combinations of goods that can be produced with a given set of resources.

First consider a simple example. In an earlier exercise, Andrew was studying for his A levels. Suppose now that he has got behind with his homework. He has limited time available, and has five economics questions to answer and five maths exercises. An economics question takes the same time to answer as a maths exercise.

What are the options? Suppose he knows that in the time available he can tackle either all of the maths and none of the economics, or all of the economics and none of the maths. Alternatively, he can try to keep both teachers happy by doing some of each.

Quantitative skills 1.1

Drawing and interpreting graphs

An important quantitative skill is to be able to draw and interpret graphs. The diagram showing the *PPF* is a good example to introduce this skill.

Figure 1.1 shows the options that Andrew faces. He can devote all of his efforts to maths, and leave the economics for another day. He will then be at point *A* in the figure, choosing to do 5 maths exercises (which you read off as the value on the vertical axis), but no economics exercises (reading zero on the horizontal axis).

Alternatively, he can do all the economics exercises and no maths, and be at point *B*. The line joining these two extreme points shows the intermediate possibilities. For example, at *C* he does 2 economics exercises and 3 maths problems — again you read off the values from the two axes.

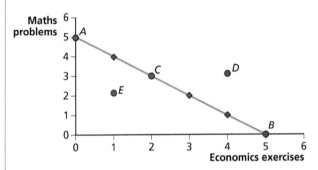

Figure 1.1 The production possibility frontier

The line shows the maximum combinations that Andrew can tackle — which is why it is called a 'frontier'. There is no way he can manage to be beyond the frontier (for example, at point *D*), as to do 3 maths exercises and 4 economics ones would need more time than he has available. However, he could end up inside the frontier, at a point such as *E*. This could happen if he gives up, and squanders his time by watching television; that would be an inefficient use of his resources — at least in terms of tackling his homework.

As Andrew moves down the line from left to right, he is spending more time on economics and less on maths. The opportunity cost of tackling an additional economics question is an additional maths exercise forgone. One way of expressing this is that Andrew faces a trade-off between the time spent on economics and on maths.

Figure 1.2 shows how the *PPF* provides information about opportunity cost. Suppose we have a farmer with 10 hectares of land who is choosing between growing potatoes and onions. The *PPF* shows the combinations of the two crops that could be produced. For example, if the farmer produces 300 tonnes of onions on part of the land, then 180 tonnes of potatoes could be produced from the remaining land. In order to increase production of potatoes by 70 tonnes from 180 to 250, 50 tonnes of onions must be given up. Thus, the opportunity cost of 70 extra tonnes of potatoes is seen to be 50 tonnes of onions.

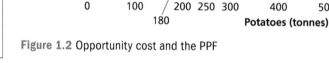

Figure 1.2 Opportunity cost and the PPF

Knowledge check 1.5

In Figure 1.1, which labelled points represent productively efficient positions?

Consumption and investment

Key terms

capital goods goods used as part of the production process, such as machinery or factory buildings

consumer goods goods produced for present use (consumption)

To move from thinking about an individual to thinking about an economy as a whole, it is first necessary to simplify reality. Assume an economy that produces just two types of good: **capital goods** and **consumer goods**. Consumer goods are for present use, whereas the capital goods are to be used to increase the future capacity of the economy — in other words, for investment.

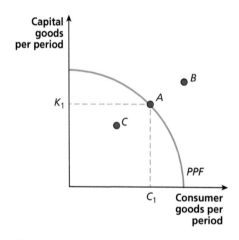

Figure 1.3 Capital and consumer goods

Figure 1.3 illustrates society's options in a particular period. Given the resources available, society can produce any combination of capital and consumer goods along the *PPF* line. Thus, point *A* represents one possible combination of outputs, in which the economy produces C_1 consumer goods and K_1 capital goods.

As with the simpler example, if society were to move to the right along the *PPF*, it would produce more consumer goods — but at the expense of capital goods. Thus, it can be seen that the opportunity cost of producing consumer goods is forgone opportunities to produce capital goods. Notice that this time the *PPF* has been drawn as a curve instead of a straight line. This is because not all factors of production are equally suited to the production of both sorts of good. When the economy is well balanced, as at *A*, the factors can be allocated to the uses for which they are best equipped. However, as the economy moves towards complete specialisation in one of the types of good, factors are no longer being best used, and the opportunity cost changes. For example, if nearly all of the workers are engaged in producing consumer goods, it becomes more difficult to produce still more of these, whereas those workers producing machinery find they have too few resources with which to work. In other words, the more consumer goods are being produced, the higher is their opportunity cost.

It is now possible to interpret points B and C. Point B is unobtainable given present resources, so the economy cannot produce that combination of goods. This applies to any point outside the *PPF*. On the other hand, at point C society is not using its resources efficiently. In this position there is *unemployment* of some resources in the economy. By making better use of the resources available, the economy can move towards the frontier, reducing unemployment in the process. However, at any point on the frontier, production is productively efficient in the sense that all resources are being fully utilised.

> ### Knowledge check 1.6
>
> If a firm buys a computer to use in its production process, is this an example of a consumer or a capital good?

▌Economic growth or decline

Figure 1.3 focuses on a single period. However, if the economy is producing capital goods, then in the following period its capacity to produce should increase, as it will have more resources available for production. How can this be shown on the diagram? An expansion in the available inputs suggests that in the next period the economy should be able to produce more of both goods. This is shown in Figure 1.4.

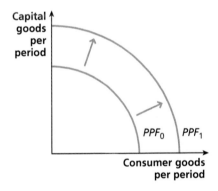

Figure 1.4 Economic growth

In the initial period the production possibility frontier is at PPF_0. However, in the following period the increased availability of capital resources enables greater production, and the frontier moves to PPF_1. This is a process of **potential economic growth**, an expansion of the economy's productive capacity through the increased availability of inputs. If the economy were to go into decline, such that less output could be produced, the frontier would shift inwards.

Notice that the decision to produce more capital goods today means that fewer consumer goods will be produced today. People must choose between 'more jam today' or 'more jam tomorrow'.

> ### Key term
>
> **potential economic growth** an expansion in the productive capacity of the economy

Total output in an economy

Remember that the *PPF* is a model: a much simplified version of reality. In a real economy, many different goods and services are produced by a wide range of different factors of production — but it is not possible to draw diagrams to show all of them.

The total output of an economy like the UK is measured by its **gross domestic product (GDP)**.

By calculating the *average* level of GDP per person in a country, it is possible to derive a measure of the average amount of resources per person — or average income per head.

Key term

gross domestic product (GDP) a measure of the economic activity carried out in an economy over a period

Exercise 1.4

Megan has been cast away on a desert island, and has to survive by spending her time either fishing or climbing trees to get coconuts. The *PPF* in Figure 1.5 shows the maximum combinations of fish and coconuts that she can gather during a day. Which of the points A to E represents each of the following?

a a situation where Megan spends all her time fishing
b an unobtainable position
c a day when Megan goes for a balanced diet — a mixture of coconuts and fish
d a day when Megan does not fancy fish, and spends all day collecting coconuts
e a day when Megan spends some of the time trying to attract the attention of a passing ship

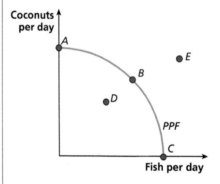

Figure 1.5 Fish and coconuts

Summary: the production possibility frontier

- The production possibility frontier shows the maximum combinations of goods or services that can be produced in a period by a given set of resources.
- At any point on the frontier, society is making full use of all resources.
- At any point inside the frontier, there is unemployment of some resources.
- Points beyond the frontier are unobtainable.
- In a simple society producing two goods (consumer goods and capital goods), the choice is between consumption and investment for the future.
- As society increases its stock of capital goods, the productive capacity of the economy increases, and the production possibility frontier moves outwards: this may be termed 'economic growth'.

Specialisation and the division of labour

Key term

division of labour a process whereby the production procedure is broken down into a sequence of stages, and workers are assigned to a particular stage

How many workers does it take to make a pin? The eighteenth-century economist Adam Smith figured that 10 was about the right number. He argued that when a worker was producing pins on their own, carrying out all the various stages involved in the production process, the maximum number of pins that could be produced in one day was 20 — given the technology of his day, of course. This would imply that 10 workers could produce about 200 pins if they worked in the same way as the lone worker. However, if the pin production process were broken into 10 separate stages, with one worker specialising in each stage, the maximum production for a day's work would be a staggering 48,000. This is known as **division of labour**.

The division of labour is effective because individual workers become skilled at performing specialised tasks. By focusing on a particular stage, they can become highly adept, and thus more efficient, at carrying out that task. In any case, people are not all the same, so some are better at certain activities. Furthermore, this specialisation is more efficient because workers do not spend time moving from one activity to another. Specialisation may also enable firms to operate on a larger scale of production. You will see later that this may be advantageous.

This can be seen in practice in many businesses today, where there is considerable specialisation of functions. Workers are hired for particular tasks and activities. You do not see Harry Kane pulling on the goalkeeper's jersey at half time because he fancies a change. Earlier in the chapter, it was argued that 'labour' is considered a factor of production. This idea can be developed further by arguing that there are different types of labour, having different skills and functions.

Advantages and disadvantages of division of labour

Specialisation therefore means that workers can focus on the tasks that they perform well and hence become more productive. Training can also be provided more cost-effectively when it can be focused on specific tasks that workers need to perform. Furthermore, working as a team allows more overall output to be produced. However, it is possible to take specialisation too far. A worker who spends all their time on a narrow and repetitive task may find that it becomes tedious or that they becomes bored and careless. Over-specialisation may also mean that a team of workers becomes inflexible: if a worker specialising in a key part of the production process becomes ill, it may be difficult to find cover.

Employees at a BMW factory. Each worker specialises in a particular task, creating an efficient assembly line

Specialisation between firms and nations

Although we refer to the division of labour, we can extend these arguments to consider specialisation among firms. For example, consider car manufacturing. The process of mass producing cars does not all take place within a single firm. One firm may specialise in producing tyres; another may produce windscreens; another may focus on assembling the final product. Here again, specialisation enables efficiency gains to be made.

Specialisation also takes place among nations, simply because some countries are better equipped to produce some products than others. For example, it would not make sense for the UK to go into commercial production of pineapples or mangoes. There are other countries with climatic conditions that are much more suitable for producing these products. On the other hand, most Formula 1 racing teams have their headquarters in the UK, and there are benefits from this specialisation.

Synoptic link

The possible gains from specialisation and trade are discussed more fully in Chapter 24 in the context of international trade.

Knowledge check 1.7

Name a possible disadvantage of over-specialisation in production.

Summary: specialisation and the division of labour

- Adam Smith introduced the notion of division of labour.
- This suggests that workers can become more productive by specialising in stages of the production process.
- This enables more output to be produced.
- There may be limits to specialisation, as performing repetitive tasks may become tedious and induce errors.

Markets

You will find that in economics the term **market** is used frequently, so it is important to be absolutely clear about what is meant by it.

A market need not be a physical location (although it could be — you might regard the local farmers' market as an example of 'a set of arrangements that allows transactions to take place'). With the growth of the internet, everyone is becoming accustomed to ways of buying and selling that do not involve direct physical contact between buyer and seller, so the notion of an abstract market should not be too alien a concept.

In relation to a particular product, a market brings together potential buyers and sellers. This is explored in the coming chapters.

Markets are important in the process of resource allocation, with prices acting as a key signal to potential buyers and sellers. If a firm finds that it cannot sell its output at the price it has chosen, this is a signal about the way that buyers perceive the product. Price is one way that firms find out about consumers and their willingness to pay for a particular product. This is explored more carefully in Chapter 5.

Key term

market a set of arrangements that allows transactions to take place

The functions of money

Imagine a world without money. It is lunchtime, and you fancy a banana. In your bag you have an apple. Perhaps you can find someone with a banana who fancies an apple? But the only person with a banana available fancies an ice cream. The problem with such a *barter economy* is that you need to find someone who wants what you have and who has what you want — a *double coincidence of wants*. If this problem were to be faced by a whole economic system, undertaking transactions would be so inefficient as to be impossible. Hence the importance of *money* as a *medium of exchange*.

In order to fulfil this role, money must be something that is acceptable to both buyers and sellers. Nobody would accept money in payment for goods or services if they did not trust that they could proceed to use money for further transactions. Money must thus also act as a *store of value*: it must be possible to use it for future transactions. This quality of money means that it can be used as one way of storing wealth for future purchases.

Money also allows the value of goods, services and other assets to be compared — it provides a *unit of account*. In this sense, prices of goods reflect the value that society places on them, and must be expressed in money terms. So, money is also a *measure of value*.

A further role for money is that it acts as a *method of deferred payment*. For example, a firm may wish to agree a contract for the future delivery of a good, or may wish to hire a worker to be paid at the end of the month. Such contracts are typically agreed in terms of a money value.

Knowledge check 1.8

Name the four key functions of money.

All of these *functions of money* are important to the smooth operation of markets, and are crucial if prices are to fulfil their role in allocating resources within society. This will become apparent as you learn more about economics.

The coordination problem

With so many different individuals and organisations (consumers, firms, governments) all taking decisions, a major question is how it all comes together. How are all these separate decisions coordinated so that the overall allocation of resources in a society is coherent? In other words, how can it be ensured that firms produce the commodities that consumers wish to consume? And how can the distribution of these products be organised? These are some of the basic questions that economics sets out to answer.

Market economy

A **free market economy** is one in which market forces are allowed to guide the allocation of resources within a society without intervention from government. Prices play a key role in this sort of system, providing signals and incentives to producers and consumers. Adam Smith argued that in such a system resources would be allocated effectively (and fairly) through the operation of an 'invisible hand'. This operates when individuals are free to pursue their own interests. Firms would produce the goods and services that consumers wish to consume.

Key term

free market economy an economy in which market forces are allowed to guide the allocation of resources

Synoptic link

The role of prices in influencing resource allocation is explored in Chapter 4.

Karl Marx argued that in a capitalist society in which there is private ownership of productive resources, the owners of capital would exploit their position at the expense of labour, eventually resulting in revolution. Although this did not transpire in the way that Marx expected, there was a move in some countries away from private ownership of capital and towards state control of resource allocation through central planning.

Key terms

command economy
an economy in which
decisions on resource
allocation are guided by
the state

mixed economy an
economy in which
resources are allocated
partly through price signals
and partly on the basis of
intervention by the state

Command economy

A **command economy** is one in which the government undertakes the coordination role, planning and directing the allocation of resources. Given the complexity of modern economies, reliance on central planning poses enormous logistical problems. In order to achieve a satisfactory allocation of resources across the economy, the government needs to make decisions on thousands of individual matters.

One example of this emerges from the experience of central planning in Russia after the revolution in 1917. Factories were given production targets to fit in with the overall plan for the development of the economy. These targets then had to be met by the factory managers, who faced strong incentives to meet those targets. Factories producing nails were given two sorts of target. Some factories were given a target to produce a certain number of nails, whereas others were given targets in weight terms. The former responded by producing large numbers of very small nails; the latter produced a very small number of very big nails. Neither was what the planners had in mind!

Micromanagement on this sort of scale proved costly to implement administratively. The collapse of the Soviet bloc in the 1990s largely discredited this approach, although a small number of countries (such as North Korea and Cuba) continue to stick with central planning. China has moved away from pure central planning by beginning to allow prices to be used as signals.

Mixed economy

Another influential economist was Friedrich von Hayek, who came from what became known as the neo-Austrian School. He saw that in the period after the Second World War, there was a move towards more intervention in the economy by governments which perceived that markets were not working effectively. For example, John Maynard Keynes had argued for a more active government in times of high unemployment, such as occurred in many countries in the inter-war period. Hayek argued that such intervention would be damaging, because governments are faced with imperfect information, especially in a command economy. Markets would be more effective because they rely on people responding to signals and incentives.

Today, most economies operate a **mixed economy** system, in which market forces are complemented by some state intervention. This may be important because free markets can lead to inequality in the distribution of resources in society. It has been argued that any such state intervention should be *market-friendly*: in other words, when governments do intervene in the economy, they should do so in a way that helps markets to work, rather than trying to have the government replace market forces. In such an economy, the government plays a minimal role by setting the framework in which markets can operate: for example, by securing property rights.

Incentives

Another important concept that is at the heart of economic analysis is the notion that individuals respond to *incentives*. The coordination problem is handled in different forms of economy through the operation of different forms of incentive that influence decision making. In a market economy, prices and profits provide incentives, whereas in a centrally planned economy these incentives are replaced by state directives.

Knowledge check 1.9

Name one example of a mixed economy.

Microeconomics and macroeconomics

The discussion so far has focused sometimes on individual decisions, and sometimes on the decisions of governments, or of 'society' as a whole. Economic thinking is applied in different ways, depending on whether the focus is on the decisions taken by individual agents in the economy or on the interaction between economic variables at the level of the whole economy:

- **Microeconomics** deals with individual decisions taken by households or firms, or in particular markets.
- **Macroeconomics** examines the interactions between economic variables at the level of the aggregate economy.

In some ways the division between the two types of analysis is artificial. The same sort of economic reasoning is applied in both types, but the focus is different.

Key terms

microeconomics the study of economic decisions taken by individual economic agents, including households and firms

macroeconomics the study of the interrelationships between economic variables at an aggregate (economy-wide) level

Exercise 1.5

Think about the following, and see whether you think each represents a microeconomic or macroeconomic phenomenon:

a the overall level of prices in an economy
b the price of ice cream
c the overall rate of unemployment in the UK
d the unemployment rate among catering workers in Aberdeen
e the average wage paid to construction workers in Southampton

Summary: free market, mixed and command economies

- Decisions about resource allocation need to be coordinated within a society.
- This may happen by allowing markets to guide decisions, through direct intervention by the state, or through a combination of the two in a mixed economy.
- Microeconomics deals with individual decisions made by consumers and producers, whereas macroeconomics analyses the interactions between economic variables in the aggregate — but both use similar ways of thinking.

Case study 1.1

Plantains and tobacco

Jacob is a subsistence farmer who lives in Nangare, a village in the west of Uganda. He lives in a mud hut and owns two sheep, two chickens and one mattress for his household of ten people. He farms a small piece of land, on which he grows plantains (a staple food crop in Uganda, related to the banana) and some tobacco. One of the key decisions that Jacob faces is how to allocate his land between plantains and tobacco. If he chooses to plant more tobacco in his field, he faces a cost, as growing more tobacco means growing fewer plantains.

A number of factors are likely to influence this decision. For example, the prices of plantains and tobacco may be important, and it may be that the costs involved in growing the two crops are different. Or it may be that some parts of the land are more suitable for growing one of the crops. There may also be other crops that could be grown on the land. All of these factors could affect Jacob's decisions.

Plantains or tobacco? How will Jacob allocate his land?

Follow-up questions

a With reference to Jacob's choice between growing plantains and tobacco, explain the concept of **opportunity cost**.

b Draw a possible **production possibility frontier** to illustrate Jacob's choice of producing plantains and tobacco.

c Identify a point on the diagram that you drew for part (b) to illustrate a situation in which:
  i Jacob uses his land to produce only plantains.
  ii Jacob uses his land to produce a combination of plantains and tobacco.
  iii Jacob does not use all of the land available, but produces a combination of the two crops.

2 The nature of demand

The demand and supply model is perhaps the most famous of all pieces of economic analysis; it is also one of the most useful. It has many applications that help explain the way markets work in the real world. It is thus central to understanding economics. This chapter introduces the 'demand' side of the model. Chapter 3 will introduce supply.

Learning objectives

After studying this chapter, you should:

→ be aware of the assumptions of rational economic decision making
→ be familiar with the notion of the demand for a good or service
→ be aware of the relationship between the demand for a good and its price
→ be familiar with the demand curve and the law of demand
→ understand the distinction between a movement along the demand curve and a shift in its position
→ be aware of the distinction between normal and inferior goods and between substitutes and complements
→ understand the other influences that affect the position of the demand curve
→ understand the concept of elasticity measures and appreciate their importance and applications

▌ Rational decision making

Before trying to analyse the way in which economic agents take decisions, it is important to make assumptions about what it is that they are aiming to achieve. This is the case for consumers and for firms.

Consider an individual consumer, taking a decision about which products to consume. What motivates that decision? A simple assumption is that the individual wants to gain as much satisfaction as possible from the combination of products that are consumed. Economists refer to satisfaction in this context as *utility*, so the assumption that is made is that rational consumers set out to maximise their utility.

The corresponding assumption for firms is that they aim to make as much profit as possible: in other words, they aim to maximise profits.

Why is it important to assume rational decision making by economic agents such as consumers and firms? The simple reason is that unless we do this, we cannot analyse how consumers or firms will act. In other words, if we know that a consumer sets out to maximise satisfaction, we can build a model to show under what conditions they would achieve this. On the other hand, if we do not know what they want to achieve, we have no way of understanding their behaviour.

This assumption of rational behaviour has underpinned economic analysis from its beginnings. It enables economists to further our understanding of human behaviour and to identify situations in which people seem to depart from rationality.

Do people always act rationally? Not necessarily — or not in the way that economists think about rational behaviour. Later, we explore situations in which consumers or firms may choose to pursue other objectives, and analyse how this affects the economic analysis of behaviour.

> ### Synoptic link
>
> Behavioural economics is a rapidly growing branch of economics that analyses how consumers and producers may take decisions that seem to contradict rational decision making. The behaviour of consumers in this context is explored in Chapter 5. Ways in which firms may depart from profit-maximising behaviour and pursue alternative objectives are discussed in Chapter 18.

Demand

Key term

demand the quantity of a good or service that consumers are willing and able to buy at any given price in a given period of time

Consider an individual consumer. Think of yourself, and a product that you consume regularly. What factors influence your **demand** for that product? Put another way, what factors influence how much of the product you choose to buy?

When thinking about the factors that influence your demand for your chosen product, common sense will probably mean that you focus on a range of different points. You may think about why you enjoy consuming the product. You may focus on how much it will cost to buy the product, and whether you can afford it. You may decide that you have consumed a product so much that you are ready for a change; or perhaps you will decide to try something advertised on television, or being bought by a friend.

Whatever the influences you come up with, they can probably be categorised under four headings that ultimately determine your demand for a good.

- The *price of the good* is an important influence on your demand for it, and will affect the quantity of it that you choose to buy.
- The *price of other goods* may be significant.
- Your *income* will determine how much of the good you can afford to purchase.
- Almost any other factors that you may have thought of can be listed as part of your *preferences*.

This reasoning is based on the assumption that consumers act rationally, by seeking to take decisions that will produce the best result possible given the constraints that they face. The 'best' result in this context is judged in terms of the utility (satisfaction) gained from consuming a good or service. The additional utility gained from consuming an extra unit of a good is known as the *marginal utility*.

> ### Knowledge check 2.1
>
> How do economists refer to the additional satisfaction gained by a consumer from an extra unit of a good?

This provides the basis for the economic analysis of demand. A lot of economic analysis begins in this way, by constructing a model rooted in how we expect rational people or firms to behave.

Individual and market demand

A similar line of argument may apply if we think in terms of the demand for a particular product — say, tablet computers. The market for tablets can be seen as bringing together all the potential buyers (and sellers) of the product, and market demand can be analysed in terms of the factors that influence all potential buyers of that good or service. In other words, market demand can be seen as the total quantity of a good or service that all potential buyers are willing and able to buy at any given price in a given period of time. The same four factors that influence your own individual decision to buy will also influence the total market demand for a product. In addition, the number of potential buyers in the market will clearly influence the size of total demand at any price.

What factors influence the demand for tablets?

Demand and the price of a good

Assume for the moment that the influences mentioned above, other than the price of the good, are held constant, so that the focus is only on the extent to which the price of a good influences the demand for it. Given the complexity of the real world, it is often helpful to focus on one thing at a time.

For an individual, the marginal utility that you gain from consuming a product is likely to decline the more of it you consume, although your total utility may increase. You may gain lots of utility from the first chocolate bar that you eat, but the tenth bar will add less satisfaction. In other words, the additional (marginal) utility that you receive from consuming a good is likely to decline as you consume more of it. This is referred to as **diminishing marginal utility**, and suggests that you will place a lower value on a product, the more of it you have already consumed. This influences the shape of the demand curve, as the price that you would pay for relatively large amounts of a product would be correspondingly low.

The law of demand and the demand curve

How is the demand for tablets influenced by their price? Other things being equal (ceteris paribus), you would expect the demand for tablets in the market as a whole to be higher when the price is low and lower when the price is high. In other words, you would expect an inverse relationship between the price and the quantity demanded. This is such a strong phenomenon that it is referred to as the **law of demand**.

Synoptic link

This common sort of assumption in economics was introduced in Chapter 1, using the Latin phrase ceteris paribus.

Key terms

diminishing marginal utility describes the situation where an individual gains less additional utility from consuming a product, the more of it is consumed

law of demand a law that states that there is an inverse relationship between quantity demanded and the price of a good or service, ceteris paribus

Key term

demand curve a graph showing how much of a good will be demanded by consumers at any given price

If you were to compile a list that showed how many tablets would be bought at any possible price and plot these on a diagram, this would be called the **demand curve**. Figure 2.1 shows what this might look like. As it is an inverse relationship, the demand curve slopes downwards. Notice that this need not be a straight line: its shape depends on how consumers react at different prices.

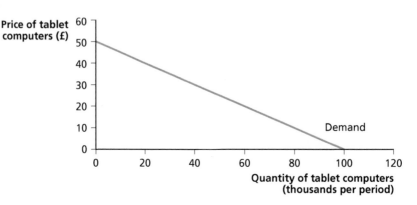

Figure 2.1 A demand curve for tablet computers

Synoptic link

We discuss the market for tablet computers again in Chapter 4.

Knowledge check 2.2

What is the law of demand?

Quantitative skills 2.1

Reading a graph

An important skill is to be able to read off numerical values from a graph such as Figure 2.1. If you wanted to see what the quantity demanded would be at a particular price, you would select the price on the vertical axis, and then read off the value on the horizontal axis at that price. For example, in this figure, if price were to be set at £40, the quantity demanded would be 20,000 per period. However, if the price were only £20, the demand would be higher, at 60,000.

Exercise 2.1

Table 2.1 shows how the demand for oojits varies with their price. Draw the demand curve.

Table 2.1 The demand for oojits

Price (£)	100	90	80	70	60	50	40	30	20
Quantity	0	3	7	15	25	40	60	85	120

Extension material: the demand curve

An analysis of why the demand curve should be downward sloping would reveal that there are two important forces at work. At a higher price, a consumer buying a tablet computer has less income left over. This is referred to as the *real income effect* of a price increase. In addition, if the price of tablets goes up, consumers may find other goods more attractive and choose to buy something else instead of tablets. This is referred to as the *substitution effect* of a price increase.

Movements along and shifts in the demand curve

As the price of a good changes, a movement along the demand curve can be observed as consumers adjust their buying pattern in response to the price change.

Notice that the demand curve has been drawn under the ceteris paribus assumption. In other words, it was assumed that all other influences on demand were held constant in order to focus on the relationship between demand and price. There are two important implications of this procedure.

- First, the price drawn on the vertical axis of a diagram such as Figure 2.1 is the relative price — it is the price of tablets under the assumption that all other prices are constant.
- Second, if any of the other influences on demand change, you would expect to see a shift of the whole demand curve. It is very important to distinguish between factors that induce a movement along a curve (known as an extension or contraction of demand), and factors that induce a shift of a curve (an increase or decrease). This applies not only in the case of the demand curve — there are many other instances where this distinction is important.

The two panels of Figure 2.2 show this difference. In panel (a), the demand curve has shifted to the right because of a change in one of the factors that influence demand. In panel (b), the price of tablets falls from P_0 to P_1, inducing a movement along the demand curve as demand expands from Q_0 to Q_1.

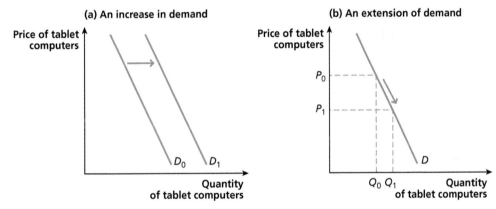

Figure 2.2 A shift in the demand curve and a movement along it

Study tip

In order to emphasise the difference between a shift of the demand curve and a movement along it, the convention is adopted to use an *extension* (or *contraction*) of demand for a movement along the demand curve, and to use an *increase* (or *decrease*) to denote a shift of the curve. Such shifts are caused by factors sometimes known as the *conditions* of demand.

Knowledge check 2.3

Explain the difference between an extension of demand and an increase in demand.

Extension material: snob effects

It is sometimes argued that for some goods a 'snob effect' may lead to the demand curve sloping upwards. The argument is that some people may value certain goods more highly simply because their price is high, especially if they know that other people will observe them consuming these goods; an example might be Rolex watches. In other words, people gain value from having other people notice that they are rich enough to afford to consume a particular good. This *conspicuous consumption* effect was first pointed out by Thorstein Veblen at the end of the nineteenth century. Indeed, it is sometimes known as the *Veblen effect*.

However, although there may be some individual consumers who react to price in this way, there is no evidence to suggest that there are whole markets that display an upward-sloping demand curve for this reason. In other words, most consumers would react normally to the price of such goods.

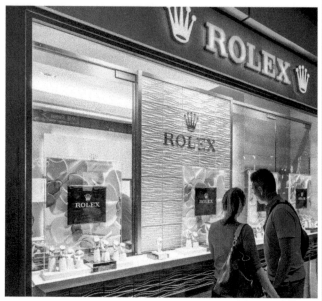

Rolex watches may benefit from the conspicuous consumption effect

Key term

normal good one where the quantity demanded increases in response to an increase in consumer incomes

Demand and consumer incomes

The second influence on demand is consumer incomes. For a **normal good**, an increase in consumer incomes will, ceteris paribus, lead to an increase in the quantity demanded at any given price. Foreign holidays are an example of a normal good because, as people's incomes rise, they will tend to demand more foreign holidays at any given price.

Figure 2.3 illustrates this. D_0 here represents the initial demand curve for foreign holidays. An increase in consumers' incomes causes demand to be higher at any given price, and the demand curve shifts to the right — to D_1.

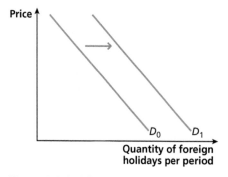

Figure 2.3 A shift in the demand curve following an increase in consumer incomes (a normal good)

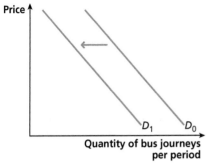

Figure 2.4 A shift in the demand curve following an increase in consumer incomes (an inferior good)

However, demand does not always respond in this way. For example, think about bus journeys. As incomes rise in a society, more people can afford to have a car, or to use taxis. This means that, as incomes rise, the demand for bus journeys may tend to fall. Such goods are known as **inferior goods**.

This time an increase in consumers' incomes in Figure 2.4 causes the demand curve to shift to the left, from its initial position at D_0, to D_1 where less is demanded at any given price.

The relationship between quantity demanded and income (QDI) can be shown more directly on a diagram. Panel (a) of Figure 2.5 shows how this would look for a normal good. The income–demand curve is upward sloping, showing that the quantity demanded is higher when consumer incomes are higher. In contrast, the income–demand curve for an inferior good, shown in panel (b) of the diagram, slopes downwards, indicating that the quantity demanded will be lower when consumer incomes are relatively high.

Key term

inferior good one where the quantity demanded decreases in response to an increase in consumer incomes

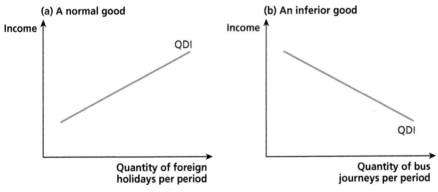

Figure 2.5 Demand and income

Exercise 2.2

Identify each of the following products as being either a normal good or an inferior good:

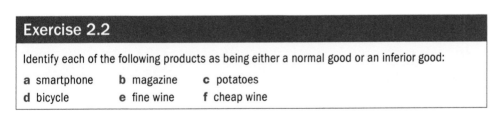

a smartphone   b magazine   c potatoes

d bicycle   e fine wine   f cheap wine

Knowledge check 2.4

What is meant by a 'normal good'?

Extension material: Giffen goods

Remember that a consumer's response to a change in the price of a good is made up of a substitution effect and a real income effect (see the extension material on page 22). The substitution effect always acts in the opposite direction to the price change: in other words, an increase in the price of a good always induces a switch *away* from the good towards other goods. However, it can now be seen that the real income effect may operate in either direction, depending on whether it is a normal good or an inferior good that is being considered.

Suppose there is a good that is very inferior. A fall in the price of a good induces a substitution effect towards the good, but the real income effect works in the opposite direction. The fall in price is equivalent to a rise in real income, so consumers will consume less of the good. If this effect is really strong, it could overwhelm the substitution effect, and the fall in price could induce a *fall* in the quantity demanded: in other words, for such a good the demand curve could be upward sloping.

Such goods are known as *Giffen goods*, after Sir Robert Giffen, who pointed out that this could happen. However, in spite of stories about the reaction of demand to a rise in the price of potatoes during the great Irish potato famine in the late 1840s, there have been no authenticated sightings of Giffen goods. The notion remains a theoretical curiosity.

Key terms

substitutes two goods are said to be substitutes if the demand for one good is likely to rise if the price of the other good rises

complements two goods are said to be complements if an increase in the price of one good causes the demand for the other good to fall

Demand and the price of other goods

The demand for a good may respond to changes in the price of other related goods, of which there are two main types. On the one hand, two goods may be **substitutes** for each other. For example, consider two different (but similar) breakfast cereals. If there is an increase in the price of one of the cereals, consumers may switch their consumption to the other, as the two are likely to be close substitutes for each other. Not all consumers will switch, of course — some may be deeply committed to one particular brand — but some of them are certainly likely to change over.

On the other hand, there may also be goods that are **complements** — for example, products that are consumed jointly, such as breakfast cereals and milk, or cars and petrol. Here a fall in the price of one good may lead to an increase in demand for *both* products.

Whether goods are substitutes or complements determines how the demand for one good responds to a change in the price of another. Figure 2.6 shows the demand curves (per period) for two goods that are substitutes — tea and coffee. If there is an increase in the price of tea from P_0 to P_1 in panel (a), more consumers will switch to coffee and the demand curve in panel (b) will shift to the right — say, from D_{c0} to D_{c1}.

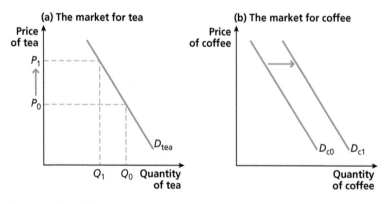

Figure 2.6 A shift in the demand curve following an increase in the price of a substitute good

For complements the situation is the reverse: in Figure 2.7 an increase in the price of tea from P_0 to P_1 in panel (a) causes the demand curve for milk to shift leftwards, from D_{m0} to D_{m1}.

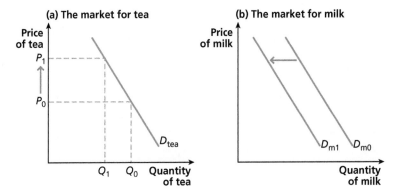

Figure 2.7 A shift in the demand curve following an increase in the price of a complementary good

Demand, consumer preferences and other influences

Consumer preferences

The discussion has shown how the demand for a good is influenced by the price of the good, the price of other goods and consumer incomes. It was stated earlier that almost everything else that determines demand for a good can be represented as 'consumer preferences'. In particular, this refers to whether you like or dislike a good. There may be many things that influence whether you like or dislike a product. In part it simply depends on your own personal inclinations — some people like dark chocolate, others prefer milk chocolate. However, firms may try to influence your preferences through advertising or branding, and sometimes they succeed. Or you might be one of those people who get so irritated by television advertising that you compile a blacklist of products that you will never buy! Even this is an influence on your demand.

In some cases, your preferences may be swayed by other people's demand — again, this may be positive or negative. Fashions may influence demand, but some people like to buck (or lead) the trend.

You may also see a movement of the demand curve if there is a sudden surge in the popularity of a good — or, indeed, a sudden collapse in demand.

Study tip

As you proceed through your study of economics, it is useful to keep track of some key issues. An example is the key influences on the demand for a good, which are:

- the price of the good
- the prices of other goods — in particular, the substitutes and complements
- consumer incomes
- consumer preferences
- the time period over which demand is being considered

Keep a note of these and be ready to make use of them.

Exercise 2.3

Sketch some demand curves for the following situations, and think about how you would expect the demand curve to change (if at all):

a the demand for chocolate following a campaign highlighting the dangers of obesity

b the demand for oranges following an increase in the price of apples

c the demand for oranges following a decrease in the price of oranges

d the demand for Blu-ray discs following a decrease in the price of Blu-ray players

e the demand for private transport following an increase in consumer incomes

f the demand for public transport following an increase in consumer incomes

The effect of time

The above discussion has covered most of the factors that influence the demand for a good. However, in some cases it is necessary to take a time element into account. Not all of the goods bought are consumed instantly. In some cases, consumption is spread over long periods of time. Indeed, there may be instances where goods are not bought for consumption at all, but are seen by the buyer as an investment, perhaps for resale at a later date. In these circumstances, expectations about future price changes may be relevant. For example, people may buy fine wine or works of art in the expectation that prices will rise in the future. There may also be goods whose prices are expected to fall in the future. This has been common with many high-tech products, such as the latest smartphones; initially a newly launched product may sell at a high price, but as production levels rise, costs may fall, and prices too. People may therefore delay purchase in the expectation of future price reductions.

Knowledge check 2.5

Are people likely to respond more or less strongly to a change in price as time passes?

Summary: markets and demand

- A market is a set of arrangements that enables transactions to take place.
- The market demand for a good depends on the price of the good, the price of other goods, consumers' incomes and preferences, and the number of potential consumers.
- The demand curve shows the relationship between demand for a product and its price, ceteris paribus.
- The demand curve is downward sloping, as the relationship between demand and price is an inverse one.
- A change in price induces a movement along the demand curve, whereas a change in the other determinants of demand induces a shift in the demand curve.
- When the demand for a good rises as consumer incomes rise, that good is referred to as a normal good; when demand falls as income rises, the good is referred to as an inferior good.
- A good or service may be related to other goods by being either a substitute or a complement.
- For some products, demand may be related to expected future prices.

Elasticity: the sensitivity of demand

Key term

elasticity a measure of the sensitivity of one variable to changes in another variable

Both the demand for and the supply of a good or service can be expected to depend on its price as well as other factors. It is often interesting to know just how sensitive demand and/or supply will be to a change in either price or one of the other conditions of demand — for example, in predicting how market equilibrium will change in response to a change in the market environment. The sensitivity of demand to a change in one of its determining factors can be measured by its **elasticity**.

The price elasticity of demand

The most common elasticity measure is the **price elasticity of demand (PED)**. This measures the sensitivity of the quantity demanded of a good or service to a change in its price.

The elasticity is defined as the percentage change in quantity demanded divided by the percentage change in the price. There are two important things to notice about this. First, because the demand curve is downward sloping, the elasticity will always be negative. This is because the changes in price and quantity are always in the opposite direction. Economists often ignore the minus sign when discussing the *PED*. Second, you should try to calculate the elasticity only for a relatively small change in price, as it becomes unreliable for very large changes.

When the demand is highly price sensitive, the percentage change in quantity demanded following a price change will be large relative to the percentage change in price. In this case, *PED* will take on a value that is greater than 1 (ignoring the minus sign). For example, suppose that a 2% change in price leads to a 5% change in quantity demanded; the elasticity is then −5 divided by 2 = −2.5. When the price elasticity is greater than 1, demand is referred to as being **elastic**.

When demand is not very sensitive to price, the percentage change in quantity demanded will be smaller than the original percentage change in price, and the elasticity will then be less than 1. For example, if a 2% change in price leads to a 1% change in quantity demanded, then the value of the elasticity will be −1 divided by 2 = −0.5. In this case, demand is referred to as being **inelastic**.

We define the percentage change in price as $100 \times \Delta P/P$ (where Δ means 'change in' and P stands for price). Similarly, the percentage change in quantity demanded is $100 \times \Delta Q/Q$. Then the formula for the elasticity is:

$$PED = \frac{100 \times \Delta Q/Q}{100 \times \Delta P/P}$$

This phenomenon is true for any straight-line demand curve: in other words, demand is relatively elastic at higher prices and relatively inelastic at lower prices. At the halfway point the elasticity is exactly −1, and demand is referred to as **unitary elastic**.

Why should this happen? The key is to remember that elasticity is defined in terms of the percentage changes in price and quantity. Thus, when price is relatively high, a 1p change in price is a small percentage change, and the percentage change in quantity is relatively large — because when price is relatively high, the initial quantity is relatively low. The reverse is the case when price is relatively low. Notice that the *PED* is infinity when quantity is zero, and zero when price is zero. Figure 2.8 shows how the elasticity of demand varies along a straight-line demand curve.

Key terms

price elasticity of demand (PED) a measure of the sensitivity of quantity demanded to a change in the price of a good or service. It is measured as:

% change in quantity demanded
―――――――――――
% change in price

elastic a term used when the price elasticity of demand is greater than 1 but less than infinity

inelastic a term used when the price elasticity of demand is less than 1 but greater than zero

unitary elastic a term used when the price elasticity of demand is equal to 1

Knowledge check 2.6

Why is the *PED* always negative?

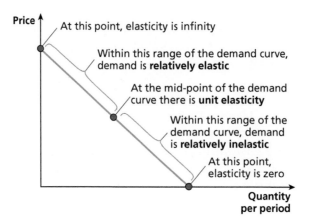

Figure 2.8 The price elasticity of demand varies along a straight line

Quantitative skills 2.2

Calculating an elasticity

Figure 2.8 shows a demand curve for pencils. When the price of a pencil is 40p, the quantity demanded will be 20. If the price falls to 35p, the quantity demanded will rise to 30. The percentage change in quantity is $100 \times 10/20 = 50$ and the percentage change in price is $100 \times -5/40 = -12.5$. Thus, the elasticity can be calculated as $(50/-12.5) = -4$. At this price, demand is highly price elastic.

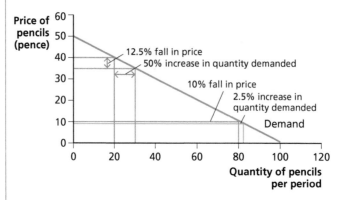

Figure 2.9 A demand curve for pencils

At a lower price, the result is quite different. Suppose that price is initially 10p, at which price the quantity demanded is 80. If the price falls to 9p, demand increases to 82. The percentage change in quantity is now $100 \times 2/80 = 2.5$, and the percentage change in price is $100 \times -1/10 = -10$, so the elasticity is calculated as $2.5/-10 = -0.25$, and demand is now price inelastic.

Extension material: elasticity

An alternative way of looking at this is to notice that, because the demand curve is drawn as a straight line, the ratio of the change in quantity to the change in price ($\Delta Q/\Delta P$) is always the same. (In fact, this is the slope of the demand curve.)

However, the ratio of the level of quantity to price varies along the demand curve. When price is relatively high, quantity is relatively low, so P/Q is high and elasticity is high. Conversely, when price is low, quantity is high and P/Q is low.

An example

A study by the Institute for Fiscal Studies for the UK found that the price elasticity of demand for wine was −1.69. This means that demand for wine is relatively elastic. If the price of wine were to increase by 10% (ceteris paribus), there would be a fall of 16.9% in the quantity of wine demanded.

The price elasticity of demand and total revenue

One reason why firms may have an interest in the price elasticity of demand is that, if they are considering changing their prices, they will be eager to know the extent to which demand will be affected. For example, they may want to know how a change in price will affect their total revenue. As it happens, there is a consistent relationship between the price elasticity of demand and total revenue.

Total revenue is given by price multiplied by quantity. In Figure 2.10, if price is at P_0, quantity demanded is at Q_0 and total revenue is given by the area of the rectangle OP_0AQ_0. If price falls to P_1 the quantity demanded rises to Q_1, and you can see that total revenue has increased, as it is now given by the area OP_1BQ_1. This is larger than at price P_0, because in moving from P_0 to P_1 the area P_1P_0AC is lost, but the area Q_0CBQ_1 is gained, and the latter is the larger. As you move down the demand curve, total revenue at first increases like this, but then decreases — try sketching this for yourself to check that it is so.

Knowledge check 2.7

Suppose that a good has a *PED* of −0.3. Would you describe this as being relatively elastic or relatively inelastic?

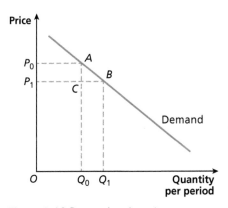

Figure 2.10 Demand and total revenue

Quantitative skills 2.3

Elasticity and total revenue

Quantitative skills box 2.2 showed how to calculate the price elasticity of demand at different points along a demand curve for pencils. When the price of a pencil fell from 40 to 35, the quantity demanded rose from 20 to 30, and elasticity was calculated to be −4.

Total revenue before and after the price change can be calculated. Total revenue is equal to price multiplied by quantity, so at the original price revenue was $40 \times 20 = 800$. At the new lower price, total revenue was $35 \times 30 = 1,050$. We can therefore see that when the price elasticity of demand is elastic, a fall in price leads to a rise in revenue.

When the price of a pencil fell from 10 to 9, and quantity demanded rose from 80 to 82, demand was inelastic (−0.25). At the original price, revenue was $10 \times 80 = 800$, and at the lower price it was $9 \times 82 = 738$. This time, total revenue has fallen with a fall in price and inelastic demand.

For the case of a straight-line demand curve the relationship is illustrated in Figure 2.11. Remember that demand is price elastic when price is relatively high. This is the range of the demand curve in which total revenue rises as price falls. This makes sense, as in this range the quantity demanded is sensitive to a change in price and increases by more (in percentage terms) than the price falls. This implies that as you move to the right in this segment, total revenue rises. The increase in quantity sold more than compensates for the fall in price. However, when the mid-point is reached and demand becomes unit elastic, total revenue stops rising — it is at its maximum at this point. The remaining part of the curve is inelastic: that is, the increase in quantity demanded is no longer sufficient to compensate for the decrease in price, and total revenue falls. Table 2.2 summarises the situation.

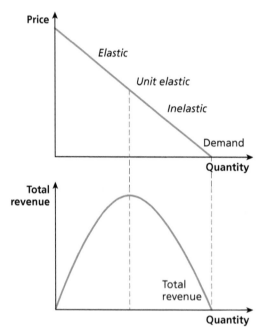

Figure 2.11 Elasticity and total revenue

Synoptic link

This relationship appears again in the discussion of firm behaviour in Chapter 19.

Table 2.2 Total revenue, elasticity and a price change

Price elasticity of demand	For a price increase, total revenue...	For a price decrease, total revenue...
Elastic	falls	rises
Unit elastic	does not change	does not change
Inelastic	rises	falls

Thus, if a firm is aware of the price elasticity of demand for its product, it can anticipate consumer response to its price changes, which may be a powerful strategic tool.

One very important point must be made here. If the price elasticity of demand varies along a straight-line demand curve, such a curve cannot be referred to as either elastic or inelastic. To do so is to confuse the elasticity with the slope of the demand curve. It is not only the steepness of the demand curve that determines the elasticity, but also the point on the curve at which the elasticity is measured.

Perfectly elastic and inelastic demand

Two extreme cases of the *PED* should also be mentioned. Demand may sometimes be totally insensitive to price, so that the same quantity will be demanded whatever price is set for it. In such a situation, demand is said to be *perfectly inelastic*. The demand curve in this case is vertical — as in D_i in Figure 2.12. In this situation, the numerical value of the price elasticity is zero, as quantity demanded does not change in response to a change in the price of the good.

The other extreme is shown on the same figure, where D_e is a horizontal demand curve and demand is *perfectly elastic*. The numerical value of the elasticity here is infinity. Consumers demand an unlimited quantity of the good at price P_e. No firm has any incentive to lower price below this level, but if price were to rise above P_e, demand would fall to zero.

Knowledge check 2.8

What would happen to a firm's total revenue if it were to increase the price of its product when demand is elastic?

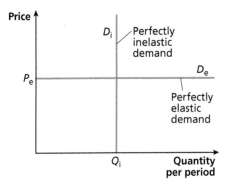

Figure 2.12 Perfectly elastic and inelastic demand

Influences on the price elasticity of demand

A number of important influences on the price elasticity of demand can now be identified. The most important is the *availability of substitutes* for the good or service under consideration. For example, think about the demand for cauliflower. Cauliflower and broccoli are often seen as being very similar, so if the price of cauliflower is high one week, people might quite readily switch to broccoli. The demand for cauliflower can be said to be price sensitive (relatively elastic), as consumers can readily substitute an alternative product. On the other hand, if the price of all vegetables rises, demand will not change very much, as there are no substitutes for vegetables in the diet. Thus, goods that have close substitutes available will tend to exhibit relatively elastic demand, whereas the demand for goods for which there are no substitutes will tend to be more inelastic.

Cauliflower and broccoli are easily substituted, so demand will be elastic

Associated with this is the question of whether an individual regards a good or service as a *necessity* or as a *luxury* item. If a good is a necessity, then demand for it will tend to be inelastic, whereas if a good is regarded as a luxury, consumers will tend to be more price sensitive. This is closely related to the question of substitutes, as by labelling a good as a necessity one is essentially saying that there are no substitutes for it.

A third influence on the *PED* is the *relative share of the good or service in overall expenditure*. You may not notice small changes in the price of an inexpensive item that is a small part of overall expenditure, such as salt or sugar. This tends to mean that demand for that good is relatively inelastic. On the other hand, an item that figures large in the household budget will be seen very differently, and consumers will tend to be much more sensitive to price when a significant proportion of their income is involved.

Finally, the *time period* under consideration may be important. Consumers may respond more strongly to a price change in the long run than in the short run. An increase in the price of petrol may have limited effects in the short run; however, in the long run, consumers may buy smaller cars or switch to diesel. Thus, the elasticity of demand tends to be more elastic in the long run than in the short run. Habit or commitment to a certain pattern of consumption may dictate the short-run pattern of consumption, but people do eventually adjust to price changes.

Study tip

Be ready to identify the four key influences on the *PED*:

- the availability of close substitutes for the good
- whether the good is perceived as a necessity
- the proportion of income or expenditure devoted to the good
- the time period over which elasticity is considered

Summary: price elasticity of demand

- The price elasticity of demand (*PED*) measures the sensitivity of the quantity of a good demanded to a change in its price.
- As there is an inverse relationship between quantity demanded and price, the price elasticity of demand is always negative.
- Where consumers are sensitive to a change in price, the percentage change in quantity demanded will exceed the percentage change in price. The elasticity of demand then takes on a value that is numerically greater than 1, and demand is said to be relatively elastic.
- Where consumers are not very sensitive to a change in price, the percentage change in quantity demanded will be smaller than the percentage change in price. Elasticity of demand then takes on a value that is numerically smaller than 1, and demand is said to be relatively inelastic.
- When demand is elastic, a fall (rise) in price leads to a rise (fall) in total revenue.
- When demand is inelastic, a fall (rise) in price leads to a fall (rise) in total revenue.
- The size of the price elasticity of demand is influenced by the availability of substitutes for a good, the relative share of expenditure on the good in the consumer's budget and the time that consumers have to adjust.

Exercise 2.4

Examine Table 2.3, which shows the demand for a particular red wine at different prices.

a Draw the demand curve.
b Calculate the price elasticity of demand when the initial price is £8.
c Calculate the price elasticity of demand when the initial price is £6.
d Calculate the price elasticity of demand when the initial price is £4.

Table 2.3 Demand for Château Econ

Price (£)	10	8	6	4	2
Quantity demanded (bottles per week)	20	40	60	80	100

The income elasticity of demand

Elasticity is a measure of the sensitivity of a variable to changes in another variable. In the same way as the price elasticity of demand is determined, an elasticity measure can be calculated for any other influence on demand or supply. **Income elasticity of demand (*YED*)** is therefore defined as:

$$YED = \frac{\%\ \text{change in quantity demanded}}{\%\ \text{change in consumer income}}$$

Unlike the price elasticity of demand, the income elasticity of demand may be either positive or negative. Remember the distinction between normal and inferior goods? For normal goods the quantity demanded will increase as consumer income rises, whereas for inferior goods the quantity demanded will tend to fall as income rises. Thus, for normal goods the *YED* will be positive, whereas for inferior goods it will be negative.

For normal goods, the size of the elasticity indicates the extent to which a good is regarded as a necessity. A **necessity** is a good with a *YED* that is positive but less than 1, as the quantity demanded tends to rise less than proportionately with income, such that consumers spend a lower proportion of their income on it as income rises.

Suppose you discover that the *YED* for cheese is 0.2. How do you interpret this number? If consumer incomes were to increase by 10%, the demand for cheese would increase by 10 × 0.2 = 2%. This example of a normal good may be helpful information for cheese sellers, if they know that consumer incomes are rising over time. Notice that this value of the *YED* implies that cheese is a necessity, as demand is income inelastic.

In some cases, the *YED* may be very strongly positive. For example, suppose that the *YED* for smartphones is +2. This implies that the quantity demanded of such phones will increase by 20% for every 10% increase in incomes. An increase in income is encouraging people to devote more of their incomes to this product, which increases its share in total expenditure. Such a good is referred to as a **luxury good**.

On the other hand, if the *YED* for coach travel is −0.3, that means that a 10% increase in consumer incomes will lead to a 3% fall in the demand for coach travel — perhaps because more people are travelling by car or train. In this instance, coach travel would be regarded as an inferior good.

Key terms

income elasticity of demand (*YED*) a measure of the sensitivity of quantity demanded to a change in consumer incomes

necessity a good for which the income elasticity of demand is positive, and less than 1, such that as income rises, consumers spend proportionally less on the good

luxury good one for which the income elasticity of demand is positive, and greater than 1, such that as income rises, consumers spend proportionally more on the good

Knowledge check 2.9

What would be the value of the *YED* if a 5% in consumer income leads to a 10% fall in quantity demanded?

Key term

cross elasticity of demand (*XED*) a measure of the sensitivity of quantity demanded of a good or service to a change in the price of some other good or service

When interpreting the *YED* in this way, notice that not all consumers will view goods in the same way. A good that is regarded as a luxury by some people (such as a second car) might be viewed differently by wealthy households.

Cross elasticity of demand

Another useful measure is the **cross elasticity of demand (*XED*)**. This is helpful in revealing the interrelationships between goods. Again, this measure may be either positive or negative, depending on the relationship between the goods. It is defined as:

$$XED = \frac{\% \text{ change in quantity demanded of good X}}{\% \text{ change in price of good Y}}$$

If the *XED* is seen to be positive, it means that an increase in the price of good Y leads to an increase in the quantity demanded of good X. For example, an increase in the price of apples may lead to an increase in the demand for pears. Here apples and pears are regarded as substitutes for each other; if one becomes relatively more expensive, consumers will switch to the other. A high value for the *XED* indicates that two goods are very close substitutes. This information may be useful in helping a firm to identify its close competitors.

On the other hand, if an increase in the price of one good leads to a fall in the quantity demanded of another good, this suggests that they are likely to be complements. The *XED* in this case will be negative. An example of such a relationship would be that between coffee and sugar, which tend to be consumed together. If the *XED* were seen to be zero, this would indicate that the goods concerned were unrelated — neither substitutes nor complements.

Extension material: cross elasticity of demand

Does this notion of the cross elasticity of demand have any relevance in the real world? One part of government policy that you will meet later in your study of economics is competition policy. The Competition and Markets Authority has the responsibility of safeguarding consumer interests by ensuring that firms do not exploit excessive market power. An important part of their investigations entails an evaluation of whether firms face competition in their markets. The cross elasticity of demand can reveal whether two products are regarded as substitutes for each other. If they are shown to be, then this implies that the firms do face competition. This is an important application of this concept, as it can affect the judgement of whether a firm is in a position to exploit its market position.

Knowledge check 2.10

If the *XED* for a good is negative, would this suggest that the goods are substitutes or complements?

Examples

A study by the Institute for Fiscal Studies using data for the UK found that the cross elasticity of demand for wine with respect to a change in the price of beer was −0.60, whereas the cross elasticity with respect to the price of spirits was +0.77. The negative cross elasticity with beer suggests that wine and beer are complements: a 10% increase in the price of beer would lead to a 6% fall in the quantity demanded of wine. In contrast, the cross elasticity of demand for wine with respect to the price of spirits is positive, suggesting that wine and spirits are substitutes. An increase in the price of spirits leads to an increase in the quantity demanded of wine.

Using elasticities

The various elasticity measures can be useful to firms and to the government as part of their decision making. For example, suppose you are responsible for choosing the price to charge for a product sold by your firm. The *PED* will be informative about how buyers of the good are likely to respond to a price change. If you know they will be sensitive to a price increase, you might hesitate about raising price because this would affect revenues. Furthermore, the *YED* will help to forecast changing demand if real incomes are increasing, or if the economy is heading into a recession. The *XED* helps in anticipating changes in demand if the prices of other products are changing.

From the government perspective, imposing an indirect tax will raise the price and lead to a fall in demand, so knowing the *PED* helps to forecast the tax revenues expected. This is explored in Chapter 8. Introducing a subsidy would reduce the selling price of a good, and knowing the *PED* allows the government to assess the impact of such a move.

Summary: income and cross elasticities of demand

- The income elasticity of demand (*YED*) measures the sensitivity of quantity demanded to a change in consumer incomes. It serves to distinguish between normal, luxury and inferior goods.
- The cross elasticity of demand (*XED*) measures the sensitivity of the quantity demanded of one good or service to a change in the price of some other good or service. It can serve to distinguish between substitutes and complements.

Case study 2.1

Burgers

The fast-food and takeaway sector has been a feature of the UK since Charles Dickens referred to a 'fried fish warehouse' in *Oliver Twist* in 1839. In 1910, it was thought that there were 25,000 chippies in Britain, rising to 35,000 in 1929.

Of course, the fast-food sector has changed enormously since then, becoming a firmly entrenched part of British life, although the number of chippies fell to only 10,000 by 2009, serving some 229 million fried fish takeaways. But by that time, other products had come onto the scene, with 749 million burgers being served, and by the mid-2010s, McDonald's had 1,249 outlets in the UK.

In recent years, there have been changes in the market environment. The government has run a number of campaigns in an attempt to combat a perceived problem with obesity, especially among younger generations. At the same time, people's incomes have risen, albeit more slowly during the recession and slow recovery of the early 2010s. There have

been social changes too, with many workers in the service industries feeling pressures on their time.

There has also been a rise in alternative sources of fast food, with pre-prepared sandwiches and wraps being readily available, and delivery service firms increasing in number.

One particular development has been the rise of Gourmet Burger Kitchen, founded in 2001. This company has grown dramatically since then, offering a quality product — large burgers using fresh produce and an innovative range of fillings.

Follow-up questions

a Which of the conditions of demand would be affected by government campaigns about healthy eating?

b How would you expect a rise in consumer incomes to affect the demand for fast food?

c How would you expect companies like McDonald's to respond to the rise of competitors such as Gourmet Burger Kitchen and other changes to market conditions?

Bicycles

If you had visited Shanghai in the early 1990s, one thing that would have struck you is that the roads were dominated by bicycles. Cars were relatively few in number, and in busy streets in the city centre, cars had to thread their way through the mass of bicycles.

Now, things are different. True, you would still find many more bicycles on the streets than you would find in the UK, but they have their own part of the road. This still causes mayhem at junctions, when cars need to turn across the cycle tracks, but things are more orderly. The number of cars has increased significantly.

In the period since the early 1990s, China's economy has gone through a period of rapid economic growth and transformation. As part of this process, real incomes have risen, and many households have become much better off, especially in the urban areas where much of the change has been concentrated.

Follow-up questions

a What reasons might help to explain the change in the pattern of traffic between cars and bicycles in China over the period described in the passage?

b What would you expect to be the nature of the income elasticity of demand for bicycles in China?

c What would you expect to be the nature of the income elasticity of demand for cars in China?

3 The nature of supply

The previous chapter introduced you to the demand curve. The other key component of the demand and supply model is, of course, supply. For any market transaction, there are two parties, buyers and sellers. The question this chapter considers is what determines the quantity that sellers wish to supply to the market.

Learning objectives

After studying this chapter, you should:
→ be familiar with the notion of the supply of a good or service
→ be aware of the relationship between the supply of a good and its price in a competitive market
→ understand what is meant by the supply curve and the factors that influence its shape and position
→ be able to distinguish between shifts of the supply curve and movements along it
→ be aware of the effect of taxes and subsidies on the supply curve
→ understand what is meant by the price elasticity of supply

Supply

In discussing demand, the focus of attention was on consumers, and on their willingness to pay for goods and services. In thinking about **supply**, attention switches to firms, as it is firms that take decisions about how much output to supply to the market. It is important at the outset to be clear about what is meant by a 'firm'. A **firm** exists to organise production: it brings together various factors of production, and organises the production process in order to produce output.

There are various forms that the organisation of a firm can take. A firm could be a *sole proprietor*: probably a small business, such as a newsagent, where the owner of the firm also runs the firm. A firm could be in the form of a *partnership* — for example, a dental practice in which profits (and debts) are shared between the partners in the business. Larger firms may be organised as private or public *joint stock companies*, owned by shareholders. The difference between private and public joint stock companies is that the shares of a public joint stock company are traded on the stock exchange, whereas this is not the case with a private company.

In order to analyse how firms decide how much of a product to supply, it is necessary to make an assumption about what it is that firms are trying to achieve. A common assumption under rational choice is that they aim to maximise their profits, where 'profits' are defined as the difference between a firm's total revenue and its total costs.

Key terms

supply the quantity of a good or service that producers are willing and able to sell at any given price in a given period of time

firm an organisation that brings together factors of production in order to produce output

Knowledge check 3.1

What assumption is often made by economists about the objective that underpins firms' decisions under rational decision making?

The supply curve

As discussed in Chapter 2, the demand curve shows a relationship between quantity demanded and the price of a good or service. A similar relationship between the quantity supplied by firms and the price of a good can be identified in relation to the behaviour of firms in a **competitive market** — that is, a market in which individual firms cannot influence the price of the good or service that they are selling, because of competition from other firms.

As with the demand curve, there is a distinction between the supply curve of an individual firm, and the supply curve for a *market*. The individual supply curve shows the amount that an individual firm is willing and able to supply at any given price in a given period of time. The market supply curve shows the total amount of a product that firms are willing and able to supply at any given price in a given time period.

In such a market it may well be supposed that firms will be prepared to supply more goods at a high price than at a lower one (ceteris paribus), as this will increase their profits. The **supply curve** illustrates how much the firms in a market will supply at any given price, as shown in Figure 3.1. As firms are expected to supply more goods at a high price than at a lower price, the supply curve will be upward sloping, reflecting this positive relationship between quantity and price.

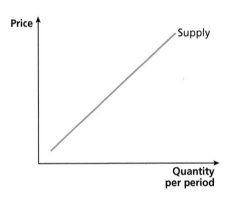

Figure 3.1 A supply curve

Key terms

competitive market a market in which individual firms cannot influence the price of the good or service they are selling, because of competition from other firms

supply curve a graph showing the quantity supplied at any given price

Knowledge check 3.2

Explain why firms in a competitive market will be prepared to supply more output at a higher price, ceteris paribus.

Quantitative skills 3.1

Interpreting lines on a graph

Be clear about why the upward-sloping nature of the supply curve reflects the fact that firms are willing to supply more output at a higher price, whereas the downward-sloping nature of the demand curve reflects the way that consumers are willing to purchase more of a good when the price is relatively low. This is bound up with the way in which we interpret the supply (or demand) curve. In Figure 3.1, think about how firms behave when the price is relatively low — that is, when you pick a price low down on the vertical axis. The quantity that firms are willing to supply is read off from the supply curve — and is relatively low. However, if you read off the quantity from a higher price level, the quantity is also higher. You need to become accustomed to interpreting lines and curves on a diagram in this way. The shape of the line (or curve) shows the extent to which firms respond at different prices.

A movement along the supply curve

A change in the price of a good will induce firms to change their supply decision. For example, consider Figure 3.2. Suppose that initially the price of the good is at P_0. Firms will choose to supply the quantity Q_0 of the good. Ceteris paribus, if the price then falls to P_1, firms will find it less profitable to supply the good, and will reduce their supply, causing a movement along the supply curve to a new quantity at Q_1.

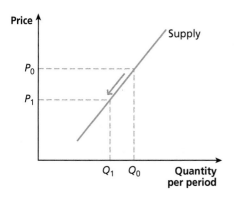

Figure 3.2 A contraction of supply

Notice that the focus of the supply curve is on the relationship between quantity supplied and the price of a good in a given period, ceteris paribus — that is, holding other things constant. As with the demand curve, there are other factors affecting the quantity supplied. These other influences on supply (the conditions of supply) will determine the position of the supply curve: if any of them changes, the supply curve can be expected to shift.

▋ What influences supply?

We can identify five important influences on the quantity that firms will be prepared to supply to the market at any given price:

- production costs
- the technology of production
- taxes and subsidies
- the price of related goods
- firms' expectations about future prices
- the number of firms operating in the market

Study tip

Be sure that you are familiar with the various factors that can influence the quantity that firms will be prepared to supply to the market at any given price.

Costs and technology

If firms are aiming to maximise profits, an important influence on their supply decision will be the costs of production that they face. In order to produce output, firms need to use inputs of the factors of production — labour, capital, land, etc. If the cost of those inputs increases, firms will in general be expected to supply less output at any given price. The effect of this is shown in Figure 3.3, where an increase in production costs induces firms to supply less output at each price. The curve shifts

Knowledge check 3.3

Under what conditions would there be a movement down along the supply curve?

Exercise 3.1

The following table shows how the supply of oojits varies with their price. Draw the supply curve.

Table 3.1 The supply of oojits

Price (£)	Quantity
100	98
90	95
80	91
70	86
60	80
50	70
40	60
30	50
20	35
10	18

from its initial position at S_0 to a new position at S_1. For example, suppose the original price was £10 per unit; before the increase in costs, firms would have been prepared to supply 100 units of the product to the market. An increase in costs of £6 per unit that shifted the supply curve from S_0 to S_1 would mean that, at the same price, firms would now supply only 50 units of the good. Notice that the vertical distance between S_0 and S_1 is the amount of the change in cost per unit.

Synoptic link

Chapter 1 introduced the factors of production and their importance to firms.

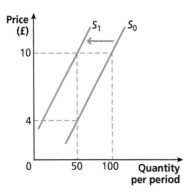

Figure 3.3 The supply curve shifts to the left if production costs increase

In contrast, if a new technology of production is introduced, which means that firms can produce more cost-effectively, this could have the opposite effect, shifting the supply curve to the right. This is shown in Figure 3.4, where improved technology induces firms to supply more output at any given price, and the supply curve shifts from its initial position at S_0 to a new position at S_1. Thus, if firms in the initial situation were supplying 50 units with the price at £10 per unit, then a fall in costs of £6 per unit would induce firms to increase supply to 100 units (if the price remained at £10).

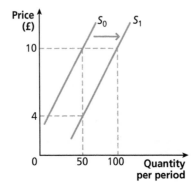

Figure 3.4 The supply curve shifts to the right if production costs fall

Taxes and subsidies

Suppose the government imposes a sales tax such as VAT on a good or service. The price paid by consumers will be higher than the revenue received by firms, as the tax has to be paid to the government. This means that firms will (ceteris paribus) be prepared to supply less output at any given market price. Again, the supply curve shifts to the left. This is shown in panel (a) of Figure 3.5, which assumes a fixed per unit tax. Such a tax is known as a specific tax. The supply curve shifts, as firms supply less at any given market price. On the other hand, if the government pays firms a subsidy to produce a particular good, this will reduce their costs, and induce them to supply more output at any given price. The supply curve will then shift to the right, as shown in panel (b).

> **Synoptic link**
>
> The effect of an indirect tax is discussed in more detail in Chapter 5, after we have developed the demand and supply model.

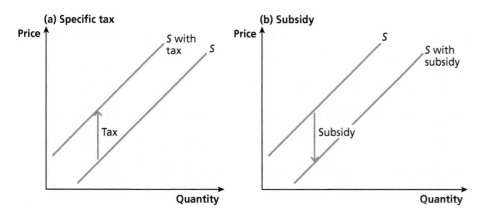

Figure 3.5 The effects of taxes and subsidies on supply

Prices of other goods

It was shown earlier that from the consumers' perspective, two goods may be substitutes for each other, such that if the price of one good increases, consumers may be induced to switch their consumption to substitute goods. Similarly, there may be substitution on the supply side. A firm may face a situation in which there are alternative uses to which its factors of production may be put: in other words, it may be able to choose between producing a range of different products. A rise in the price of a good raises its profitability, and therefore may encourage a firm to switch production from other goods. This may happen even if there are high switching costs, provided the increase in price is sufficiently large. For example, a change in relative prices of potatoes and organic swedes might encourage a farmer to stop planting potatoes and grow organic swedes instead.

In other circumstances, a firm may produce a range of goods jointly. Perhaps one good is a by-product of the production process of another. An increase in the price of one of the goods may mean that the firm will produce more of both goods. This notion of joint supply is similar to the situation on the demand side where consumers regard two goods as complements.

Expected prices

Because production takes time, firms often take decisions about how much to supply on the basis of expected future prices. Indeed, if their product is one that can be stored, there may be times when a firm will decide to allow stocks of a product to build up in anticipation of a higher price in the future, perhaps by holding back some of its production from current sales. In some economic activities, expectations about future prices are crucial in taking supply decisions because of the length of time needed in order to increase output. For example, a firm producing palm oil, rubber or wine needs to be aware that newly planted trees or vines need several years to mature before they are able to yield their product.

Wine producers have to take supply decisions based on expected future prices

Key term

cartel an agreement between firms in a market on price and output with the intention of maximising their joint profits

Synoptic link

The operation of cartels is discussed more fully in Chapter 20.

Market power

In some markets, firms may be able to use market power in order to influence the supply of a commodity. For example, think about the oil industry. Here, the oil-exporting nations work together as a **cartel** to influence the quantity supplied. One motivation for this is to influence price and hence the profits of the members of the cartel.

Movements along and shifts of the supply curve: a reminder

As with the demand curve, it is important to remember that there is a distinction between *movements along* the supply curve and *shifts of* the supply curve. If there is a change in the market price, this induces a movement along the supply curve. After all, the supply curve is designed to reveal how firms will react to a change in the price of the good. For example, in Figure 3.6, if the price is initially at P_0 firms will be prepared to supply the quantity Q_0, but if the price then increases to P_1 this will induce a movement along the supply curve as firms increase supply to Q_1.

In contrast, as seen in the previous section, a change in any of the other conditions of supply will induce a shift of the whole supply curve, as this affects the firm's willingness to supply at any given price.

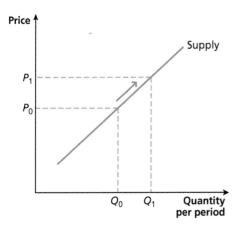

Figure 3.6 A movement along a supply curve in response to a price change

Knowledge check 3.4

If a producer finds that the market price of its product has increased, would this induce an extension of or an increase in supply?

Study tip

As with the discussion of demand, it is important to be clear about the difference between a shift of the supply curve and a movement along it. Again, the convention is adopted to use an *extension* (or *contraction*) of supply for a movement along the supply curve, and to use an *increase* (or *decrease*) to denote a shift of the curve. It is also helpful to distinguish between those factors that affect the position of the supply curve and those that affect the position of the demand curve. The factors that affect the position of the supply curve are:

- production costs
- the technology of production
- taxes and subsidies
- the price of related goods
- firms' expectations about future prices
- the number of firms in the market

Exercise 3.2

For each of the following, decide whether the demand curve or the supply curve will move, and in which direction:

a Consumers are convinced by arguments about the benefits of organic vegetables.
b A new process is developed that reduces the amount of inputs that firms need in order to produce bicycles.
c There is a severe frost in Brazil that affects the coffee crop.
d The government increases the rate of value added tax.
e Real incomes rise.
f The price of tea falls: what happens in the market for coffee?
g The price of sugar falls: what happens in the market for coffee?

Summary: the supply curve

- Other things being equal, firms in a competitive market can be expected to supply more output at a higher price.
- The supply curve traces out this positive relationship between price and quantity supplied.
- Changes in the costs of production, technology, taxes and subsidies or the prices of related goods may induce shifts of the supply curve, with firms being prepared to sell more (or less) output at any given price.
- Expectations about future prices may affect current supply decisions.

Price elasticity of supply

In the previous chapter, the concept of elasticity was introduced as a way of measuring the sensitivity of quantity demanded to any of the components that affect demand. As elasticity is a measure of sensitivity, its use need not be confined to influences on demand, but can also be turned to evaluating the sensitivity of quantity *supplied* to a change in its determinants — price in particular.

It has been argued that the supply curve is likely to be upward sloping, so the price elasticity of supply can be expected to be positive. In other words, an increase in the market price will induce firms to supply more output to the market. The **price elasticity of supply (PES)** is defined as:

$$PES = \frac{\% \text{ change in the quantity supplied}}{\% \text{ change in price}}$$

Key term

price elasticity of supply (PES) a measure of the sensitivity of quantity supplied of a good or service to a change in the price of that good or service

Quantitative skills 3.2

Calculating the elasticity of supply

Suppose that the price of a good increases from £10 to £12, and that in response, firms increase the quantity supplied from 2,000 units to 2,200 units. What is the price elasticity of supply?

To find out, we need first to calculate the percentage changes in price and quantity. Price has changed by $100 \times 2/10 = 20\%$; the quantity supplied has changed by $100 \times 200/2{,}000 = 10\%$. The price elasticity of supply is therefore $10/20 = 0.5$.

Knowledge check 3.5

Why is the *PES* a positive number?

The interpretation of the elasticity of supply is straightforward. If the *PES* is 0.8, an increase in price of 10% will encourage firms to supply 8% more. As with the *PED*, if the elasticity is greater than 1, supply is referred to as being relatively elastic, whereas if the value is between 0 and 1, supply is considered relatively inelastic. Unit elasticity occurs when the *PES* is exactly 1, so that a 10% increase in price induces a 10% increase in quantity supplied.

The value of the price elasticity of supply will depend on how willing and able firms are to respond to a change in price. If a firm is currently running below full capacity, then it may be able to respond quickly to an increase in price. Similarly, if the firm is holding stockpiles of goods ready to be sold, then it may be able to respond quickly to the increase in the selling price of the good. On the other hand, if the firm needs to pay overtime to its workers, or to rent new buildings or hire additional machinery in order to expand production, then the increase in costs may not justify responding to the increase in price. The willingness of the firm to expand output may also depend on whether the firm expects the change in price to be permanent or temporary.

The short run and the long run

An issue that arises in many areas of economic analysis is the importance of time. For example, economic agents often need time to adjust to a changing market environment. A higher price may induce firms to want to supply more of a good, but how quickly will they change? A firm may choose to wait in order to see whether a change is permanent or temporary. Even if a firm wants to change immediately, it may take time to adjust, especially if it needs to obtain new machinery or other equipment in order to expand, or if it needs to hire more skilled labour. This provides the important distinction between the short run and the long run.

It is thus important to realise that it may be more feasible for firms to change their supply decision in the long run than in the short run. For example, if firms are operating close to the capacity of their existing plant and machinery or factory space, they may be unable to respond to an increase in price, at least in the short run. So here again, supply can be expected to be more elastic in the long run than in the short run. Figure 3.7 illustrates this. In the short run, firms may be able to respond to an increase in price only in a limited way, and so supply may be relatively inelastic, as shown by S_s in the figure. An important issue here is whether the nature of the good is such that it is possible for firms to hold stocks of the good, which might allow them to expand sales in the short run even if it takes time to expand production. The extent to which goods can be stored in this way will reflect the nature of the good concerned: for example, depending on whether or not the good is perishable, or costly to store.

Synoptic link

The distinction between the short run and the long run is more fully discussed in Chapter 18, when we explore how producers face costs that may be fixed in the short run.

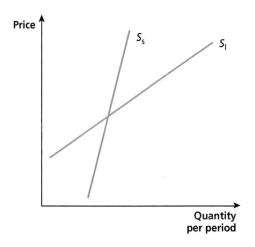

Figure 3.7 Short- and long-run supply

However, firms can become more flexible in the long run by installing new machinery or building new factories, so supply can then become more elastic, moving to S_l. When analysing the theory of the firm, economists define the short run and the long run in this way, seeing the short run as a period in which the firm is not able to vary its inputs of all factors of production, and the long run as the period in which this becomes possible. In particular, it is often supposed that capital inputs are relatively difficult to vary in the short run, whereas firms may be more able to vary the amount of labour input.

Knowledge check 3.6

Will a firm's supply curve be steeper or shallower in the long run as compared with the short run?

Key terms

perfectly inelastic supply
a situation in which
firms can supply only a
fixed quantity, so cannot
increase or decrease the
amount available: elasticity
of supply is zero

perfectly elastic supply
a situation in which firms
will supply any quantity
of a good at the going
price: elasticity of supply
is infinite

Two special cases

There are two limiting cases of supply elasticity. For some reason, supply may be fixed such that, no matter how much price increases, firms will not be able to supply any more. For example, it could be that a certain amount of fish is available in a market, and however high the price goes, no more can be obtained. Equally, if the fishermen know that the fish they do not sell today cannot be stored for another day, they have an incentive to sell, however low the price goes. In these cases, there is **perfectly inelastic supply**. At the other extreme is **perfectly elastic supply**, where firms would be prepared to supply any amount of the good at the going price.

These two possibilities are shown in Figure 3.8. Here S_i represents a perfectly inelastic supply curve: firms will supply Q_i whatever the price, perhaps because that is the amount available for sale. Supply here is vertical. At the opposite extreme, if supply is perfectly elastic then firms are prepared to supply any amount at the price P_e, and the supply curve is given by the horizontal line S_e.

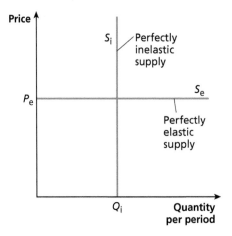

Figure 3.8 Perfectly elastic and inelastic supply

Exercise 3.3

Imagine the following scenario. You are considering a pricing strategy for a bus company.
The economy is heading into recession, and the company is running at a loss. Your local rail
service provider has announced an increase in rail fares. How (if at all) do you use the following
information concerning the elasticity of bus travel with respect to various variables to inform
your decision on price? Do you raise or lower price?

■ price elasticity of demand	−1.58
■ income elasticity of demand	−2.43
■ cross-price elasticity of demand with respect to rail fares	+2.21
■ your price elasticity of supply	+1.15

Summary: the elasticity of supply

- The price elasticity of supply (*PES*) measures the sensitivity of the quantity supplied to a change in the price of a good or service.
- The price elasticity of supply can be expected to be greater in the long run than in the short run, as firms have more flexibility to adjust their production decisions in the long run.

Case study 3.1

Champagne

The market for champagne has been changing in recent years. Champagne has always commanded a premium price compared with other sparkling wines because of its reputation and status as the wine for celebrations of all kinds. Christmas is one such focus for drinking champagne, and major events such as the millennium celebrations cause blips in demand, with no party being complete without a few bottles of champagne. However, the increased availability of good-quality alternatives to champagne at competitive prices has affected champagne producers. It has even been known for some English sparkling wines to fare well at blind tastings compared with some champagnes. Nonetheless champagne production has remained profitable as consumer incomes have risen. Mechanisation of some parts of the production process has benefited producers.

There are strict rules governing the production of champagne. Indeed, champagne can only be called by that name if it comes from a particular designated area in France, and this has effectively limited the amount that can be produced. In early 2008, it was announced that consideration was being given to expanding the area that could be recognised as producing champagne. The proposal was accepted, and although there had been considerable resistance from existing growers, the first vines were expected to be planted in 2015.

More affordable alternatives have affected the market for champagne

This will not affect the market for some period, as it takes time for newly planted vines to produce grapes that can be used to make wine — it is unlikely that any champagne from the expanded region will come to market before 2021.

Follow-up questions

a From the passage, identify factors that would be expected to affect the demand curve for champagne.

b From the passage, identify factors that would be expected to affect the supply curve for champagne.

Case study 3.2

Rice

In 2007/08, sudden and unexpected food prices hit the headlines. There were riots on the streets of cities in many countries around the world, with protestors demonstrating against massive increases in the prices of some staple foods, especially wheat and rice.

The increases affected some countries especially severely. In much of South East Asia, rice is a staple commodity, forming a part of most people's daily diet. For some countries, such as the Philippines, much of the rice consumed has to be imported, so the price rises caused particular difficulties. The demonstrators wanted governments to intervene to control the prices and protect the poor.

It was reported that in some countries, poor households were coping with the price rises by changing their eating habits, by consuming less meat, or by finding other ways of cutting down. The United Nations called for worldwide action to prevent hunger and malnutrition from spreading.

Follow-up questions

a Would you expect the demand for rice to be price elastic or inelastic?

b Explain your answer to part (a), referring to the passage to provide evidence to support your explanation.

c Do you think that government intervention to control prices would be an effective answer to the problem?

Fish

Imagine a remote island in the South Seas. Some of the islanders own canoes which they use to go fishing, selling their catch on the beach when they return each day. Some islanders only go fishing occasionally, as they find it more worthwhile to spend their time on other activities. The island has no electricity, so there is no way of storing the fish that are caught — if they are not consumed on the day of the catch, they must be thrown away.

The market for fish on the island is limited by the size of the population. Fortunately for the fishermen, the islanders enjoy fish, and regard it as an important part of their diet, although they also grow vegetables and raise goats and chickens. Fruit and coconuts are also abundant.

Follow-up questions

a What would you expect to be the nature of the price elasticity of supply in the short run (that is, on any given day)?

b Suppose that, on one particular day, fishing conditions are so good that all fishermen return with record catches. How would this affect the price of fish?

c How might the situation in (b) affect the supply of fish on the following day?

d How would you expect the supply of fish to be affected by the invention of a new style of canoe that makes it easier to catch fish?

e How would the market be affected if this new-style canoe also enabled fish to be traded with a neighbouring island?

4 How markets work: price determination and the price mechanism

The previous chapters introduced the notions of demand and supply, and it is now time to bring these together in order to meet the key concept of market equilibrium. The model can then be further developed to see how it provides insights into how markets operate. Indeed, it is also time to take a wider view of the process of resource allocation within society. An important question is whether markets can be relied on to guide this process, or whether there are times when markets will fail. This chapter begins to address this by examining how prices can act as market signals to guide resource allocation.

Learning objectives

After studying this chapter, you should:
- → understand the notion of equilibrium and its relevance in the demand and supply model
- → be aware of how market equilibrium changes in the face of shifts in demand and supply
- → have an overview of how the price mechanism works to allocate resources
- → be able to see how prices provide incentives to producers
- → understand the meaning and significance of consumer surplus
- → understand the meaning and significance of producer surplus
- → be aware of the effects of the entry and exit of firms into and out of a market
- → be familiar with the way in which resources are allocated in a free market economy

Market equilibrium

Demand and supply curves begin to tell us about the behaviour of consumers and firms, but the power of the demand and supply model comes to the fore when we bring the curves together. Figure 4.1 shows the demand for and supply of butter.

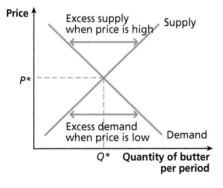

Figure 4.1 Bringing demand and supply together

Synoptic link

The demand curve was explained in Chapter 2 and supply was discussed in Chapter 3.

Suppose that the price were to be set relatively high (above $P\star$). At such a price, firms wish to supply lots of butter to the market. However, consumers are not very keen on butter at such a high price, so demand is not strong. Firms now have a problem: they find that their stocks of butter are building up. What has happened is that the price has been set at a level that exceeds the value that most consumers place on butter, so they will not buy it. There is *excess supply*. The only thing that the firms can do is to reduce the price in order to clear their stocks.

Suppose they now set their price relatively low (below $P\star$). Now it is the consumers who have a problem, because they would like to buy more butter at the low price than firms are willing and able to supply. There is *excess demand*. Some consumers may offer to pay more than the going price in order to obtain their butter supplies, and firms realise that they can raise the price.

How will it all end? When the price settles at $P\star$ in Figure 4.1, there is a balance in the market between the quantity that consumers wish to demand and the quantity that firms wish to supply, namely $Q\star$. This is the **market equilibrium**. In a free market the price can be expected to converge on this equilibrium level, through movements along both demand and supply curves.

Key term

market equilibrium a situation that occurs in a market when the price is such that the quantity demanded by consumers is exactly balanced by the quantity supplied by firms

Knowledge check 4.1

How would you expect price to adjust when there is excess demand for a good in a competitive market?

Quantitative skills 4.1

Identifying and interpreting an intersection on a graph

You will meet many diagrams in economics where there are upward- and downward-sloping lines that intersect at some point. Such intersection points are almost always significant. In the case of demand and supply, the downward-sloping line represents demand, and the upward-sloping curve shows supply. Only at the point where the two lines meet are the decisions of consumers and firms mutually consistent. In other words, consumers are choosing to demand exactly the quantity that firms are willing and able to supply. The important question to explore is the mechanism that will lead to this equilibrium point. This in turn depends on the incentives facing economic agents if the starting point is away from the intersection point.

Exercise 4.1

Identify the equilibrium market price if demand and supply are as in Figure 4.2.

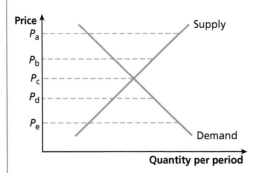

Figure 4.2 What is the equilibrium price?

Summary: market equilibrium

- Bringing demand and supply together, you can identify the market equilibrium.
- The equilibrium price is the unique point at which the quantity demanded by consumers is just balanced by the quantity that firms wish to supply.
- In a free market, natural forces can be expected to encourage prices to adjust to the equilibrium level.

Changes to market equilibrium

You have seen the way in which a market moves towards equilibrium between demand and supply through price adjustments and movements along the demand and supply curves. Now consider what happens if there is a change in one of the conditions of demand or supply. What will then happen to the market equilibrium?

Knowledge check 4.2

What factors could affect the position of the demand curve?

A market for dried pasta

Begin with a simple market for dried pasta, a basic staple foodstuff obtainable in any supermarket. Figure 4.3 shows the market in equilibrium. D_0 represents the demand curve in this initial situation, and S_0 is the supply curve. The market is in equilibrium with the price at P_0, and the quantity being traded is Q_0. It is equilibrium in the sense that pasta producers are supplying just the amount of pasta that consumers wish to buy at that price. This is the 'before' position. Some experiments will now be carried out with this market by disturbing the equilibrium.

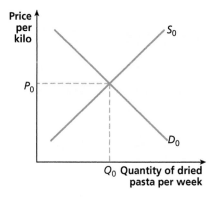

Figure 4.3 A market for dried pasta

A change in consumer preferences

Suppose that a study is published highlighting the health benefits of eating pasta, backed up with an advertising campaign. The effect of this is likely to be an increase in the demand for pasta at any given price. In other words, this change in consumer preferences will shift the demand curve to the right, as shown in Figure 4.4.

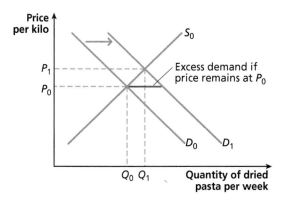

Figure 4.4 A change in consumer preferences for dried pasta

The market now adjusts to a new equilibrium, with a new price P_1 and a new quantity traded at Q_1. In this case, both price and quantity have increased as a result of the change in preferences. There has been a movement along the supply curve (an extension of supply).

Changes in consumer preferences are just one factor affecting the market for dried pasta

A change in the price of a substitute

A second possibility is that there is a fall in the price of fresh pasta. This is likely to be a close substitute for dried pasta, so the probable result is that some former consumers of dried pasta will switch their allegiance to the fresh variety. This time the demand curve for dried pasta shifts in the opposite direction, as can be seen in Figure 4.5. Here the starting point is the original position, with market equilibrium at price P_0 and a quantity traded Q_0. After the shift in the demand curve from D_0 to D_2, the market settles again with a price of P_2 and a quantity traded of Q_2. Both price and quantity traded are now lower than in the original position.

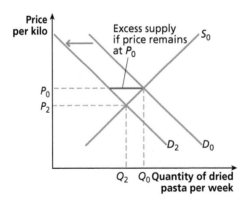

Figure 4.5 A change in the price of a substitute for dried pasta

Study tip

Economists use diagrams a lot to analyse how equilibrium is affected by external changes — in this case, a change in market conditions that induces a shift in the demand curve. Remember that practice makes perfect, so watch in the news for examples of events that are likely to affect a market, and sketch demand and supply curves to analyse what is expected to happen next. For example, in the heatwave in 2018, the media highlighted a shortage of carbon dioxide (used in manufacturing fizzy drinks and in storing food products). What effect would this have on the market?

An improvement in pasta technology

Next, suppose that a new pasta-making machine is produced, enabling dried pasta makers to produce at a lower cost than before. This technical advance reduces firms' costs, and consequently they are willing to supply more dried pasta at any given price. The starting point is the same initial position, but now it is the supply curve that shifts — to the right. This is shown in Figure 4.6.

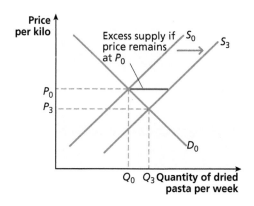

Figure 4.6 New pasta-making technology

The new market equilibrium is now at price P_3, which is lower than the original equilibrium, but the quantity traded is higher at Q_3.

An increase in labour costs

Finally, suppose that pasta producers face an increase in their labour costs. Perhaps the Pasta Workers' Union has negotiated higher wages, or the pasta producers have become subject to stricter health and safety legislation, which raises their production costs. Figure 4.7 starts as usual with equilibrium at price P_0 and quantity Q_0.

The increase in production costs means that pasta producers are prepared to supply less dried pasta at any given price, so the supply curve shifts to the left — to S_4. This takes the market to a new equilibrium at a higher price than before (P_4), but with a lower quantity traded (Q_4).

Knowledge check 4.3

What factors could affect the position of the supply curve?

Knowledge check 4.4

In a competitive market, suppose that the equilibrium price and quantity traded are both seen to increase. What shifts in the demand and supply curves could have taken place?

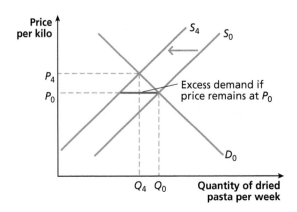

Figure 4.7 An increase in labour costs

Summary: analysing changes in market equilibrium

- You can analyse the way in which markets respond to external shocks by comparing market equilibrium before and after a shock.
- All you need to do is to figure out whether the shock affects demand or supply, and in which direction.
- The size and direction of the shifts of the demand and supply curves determine the overall effect on equilibrium price and quantity traded.

Exercise 4.2

For each of the following market situations, sketch a demand and supply diagram, and see what happens to the equilibrium price and quantity. Explain your answers.

a An increase in consumer incomes affects the demand for bus travel.

b New regulations on environmental pollution force a firm making paint to increase outlay on reducing its emission of toxic fumes.

c A firm of accountants brings in new, faster computers, which have the effect of reducing the firm's costs.

d An outbreak of bird flu causes consumers of chicken to buy burgers instead. What is the effect on both markets?

Prices and resource allocation

The coordination problem

As Chapter 1 indicated, all societies face the fundamental economic problem of scarcity. Because there are unlimited wants but finite resources, it is necessary to take decisions on which goods and services should be produced, how they should be produced and for whom they should be produced. For an economy the size of the UK, there is thus an immense coordination problem. Another way of looking at this is to ask how consumers can express their preferences between alternative goods so that producers can produce the best mix of goods and services.

In a completely free market economy, market forces are allowed to allocate resources. At the other extreme, in a centrally planned economy the state plans and directs resources into a range of uses. In between there is the mixed economy. In order to evaluate these alternatives, it is necessary to explore how each of them operates. In a free market economy, prices play the key role; this is sometimes referred to as the laissez-faire approach to resource allocation.

Consumer surplus

Think a little more carefully about what the demand curve represents. Figure 4.8 shows the demand curve for smartphones. Suppose that the price is set at $P\star$ and quantity demanded is thus $Q\star$. $P\star$ can be seen as the value that the last customer places on a smartphone. In other words, if the price were even slightly above $P\star$, there would be one consumer who would choose not to buy: this individual will be referred to as the *marginal consumer*.

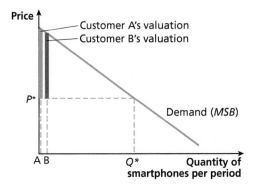

Figure 4.8 Price as a marginal benefit

To that marginal consumer, $P\star$ represents the satisfaction derived from consuming this good — it is the price that just reflects the consumer's benefit from a smartphone, as it is the price that just induces them to buy. It is their willingness to pay for a smartphone.

In most markets, all consumers face the same prices for goods and services. This leads to an important concept in economic analysis. $P\star$ may represent the value of smartphones to the marginal consumer, but what about all the other consumers who are also buying smartphones at $P\star$? They would all be willing to pay a higher price for a smartphone. Indeed, consumer A in Figure 4.8 would pay a very high price indeed, and thus values a smartphone much more highly than $P\star$. When consumer A pays $P\star$ for a smartphone, they get a great deal, as they value the good so much more highly — as represented by the vertical green line on Figure 4.8. Consumer B also gains a surplus above their willingness to pay (the red line).

If all these surplus values are added up, they sum to the total surplus that society gains from consuming smartphones. This is known as the **consumer surplus**, represented by the shaded triangle in Figure 4.9. It can be interpreted as the welfare that society gains from consuming the good, over and above the price that has to be paid for it.

Key term

consumer surplus the value that consumers gain from consuming a good or service over and above the price paid

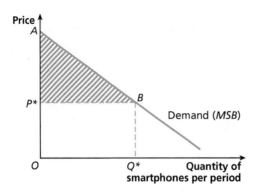

Figure 4.9 Consumer surplus

Indeed, thinking of the society as a whole, we can think of the price $P\star$ as the benefit that society gains from consuming the last unit of the good. This will be known as the **marginal social benefit (MSB)** derived from consuming the good. The same argument could be made about any point along the demand curve, so the curve itself can be interpreted as the marginal social benefit to be derived from consuming smartphones.

Knowledge check 4.5

Explain why consumer surplus can be interpreted as representing the welfare that society gains from consuming a good.

Quantitative skills 4.2

Interpreting areas on a graph

In using diagrams like Figure 4.9, it is important to be able to interpret *areas* on the graph as well as lines and positions. In this case, the area of interest is the total amount of consumer surplus. The area under the demand curve up to the quantity sold (Q^*) represents the total value of the good that is sold. In total, consumers spend an amount on this which is the price multiplied by the quantity sold, namely P^* multiplied by Q^*. In Figure 4.9 this is the area of the rectangle OP^*BQ^*. The surplus is then the shaded triangle P^*AB.

Key terms

marginal social benefit (MSB) the additional benefit that society gains from consuming an extra unit of a good

producer surplus the difference between the price received by firms for a good or service and the price at which they would have been prepared to supply that good or service

Producer surplus

Parallel to the notion of consumer surplus is the concept of **producer surplus**. Think about the nature of the supply curve: it reveals how much output firms are prepared to supply at any given price in a competitive market. Figure 4.10 depicts a supply curve. Assume the price is at $P\star$ and that all units are sold at that price. $P\star$ represents the value to firms of the marginal unit sold. In other words, if the price had been set slightly below $P\star$, the last unit would not have been supplied, as firms would not have found this profitable.

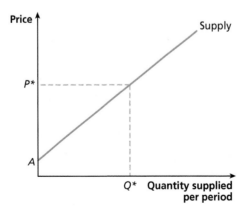

Figure 4.10 A supply curve

Notice that the threshold at which a firm will decide it is not profitable to supply is the point at which the price received by the firm reaches the cost to the firm of producing the last unit of the good. The supply curve shows that, in the range of prices between point A and $P^\star$, firms would have been willing to supply positive amounts of this good or service. So at $P^\star$, they would gain a surplus value on all units of the good supplied below $Q^\star$. The total area is shown in Figure 4.11 — it is the area above the supply curve and below $P^\star$, shown as the shaded triangle.

One way of defining this producer surplus is as the surplus earned by firms over and above the minimum that would have kept them in the market. It is the *raison d'être* of firms.

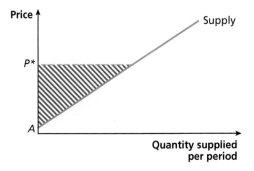

Figure 4.11 Producer surplus

Consumer and producer surplus can be shown on the same diagram. Figure 4.12 shows a market in equilibrium, with price at $P^\star$ and quantity traded at $Q^\star$. The green shaded area shows consumer surplus, while the pink area represents producer surplus.

Knowledge check 4.6

Explain why producer surplus may be considered as the *raison d'être* of firms.

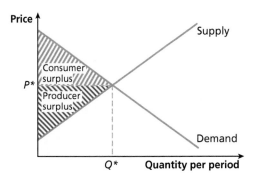

Figure 4.12 Consumer and producer surplus

A change in the conditions of demand or supply will affect the size of consumer and producer surplus. Figure 4.13 illustrates the effect of an increase in demand, in other words, where consumers are now willing to buy more of a good an any given price. In Figure 4.13, the initial demand curve is given by D_0 and the supply curve is S. The initial equilibrium price is P_0 and the quantity traded is Q_0. In this situation, consumer surplus is the area ABP_0 and producer surplus is P_0BC. If demand shifts to D_1, equilibrium price increases to P_1 and the quantity increases to Q_1. Consumer surplus is now XYP_1 and producer surplus is P_1YC. In other words, both consumers and producers receive a higher surplus, which makes sense because consumers now value the good more highly.

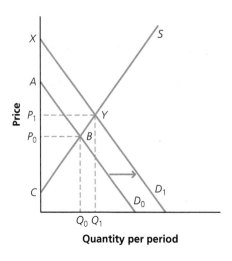

Figure 4.13 Consumer and producer surplus with an increase in demand

Exercise 4.3

Figure 4.14 shows the effect on consumer and producer surplus before and after a decrease in supply, caused by an increase in production costs.

a Identify the areas representing consumer surplus before and after the change.
b Identify the areas representing producer surplus before and after the change.
c Comment on the relative size of the surpluses before and after the change.

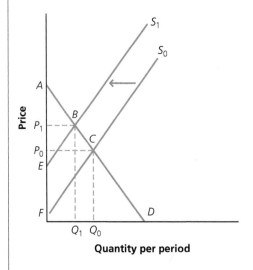

Figure 4.14 Consumer and producer surplus with a decrease in supply

Extension material: consumer and producer surplus

The notions of producer and consumer surplus are important when we come to think about the total welfare that economic agents receive from their economic activities. For consumers, the consumer surplus represents the surplus that they receive over and above what they are willing to pay for a good or service. For firms, the producer surplus represents the surplus that they receive over and above their costs of production. There is thus a sense in which we interpret the sum of these two surpluses as being the net welfare that society as a whole gains from the production and consumption of this good or service. It could be argued that efficient resource allocation is achieved when this is maximised.

Summary: consumer and producer surplus

- The demand curve shows the valuation that consumers place on a good, reflecting the satisfaction they gain from consuming it.
- Consumer surplus represents the benefit that consumers gain from consuming a product over and above the price they pay for that product.
- Producer surplus represents the benefit gained by firms over and above the price at which they would have been prepared to supply a product.

Prices and preferences

How can consumers signal their preferences to producers? Demand and supply analysis provides the clue. Figure 4.15 shows the demand and supply for smartphones. Over time there has been a rightward shift in the demand curve — in the figure, from D_0 to D_1. This simply means that consumers are placing a higher value on these goods; they are prepared to demand more at any given price. The result is that the market will move to a new equilibrium, with price rising from P_0 to P_1 and quantity traded from Q_0 to Q_1: there is a movement along the supply curve.

The shift in the demand curve is an expression of consumers' preferences; it embodies the fact that they value smartphones more highly now than before. The price that consumers are willing to pay represents their valuation of smartphones.

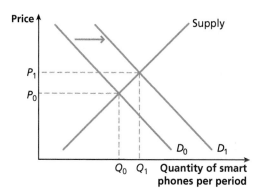

Figure 4.15 The market for smartphones

The price mechanism

Resource allocation is influenced by the operation of the **price mechanism** through rationing, incentives and signalling.

In a free market, where there is excess demand, consumers are rationed because the equilibrium price will rise to choke off the excess demand — so some consumers will not get to buy the good.

Key term

price mechanism a process by which resource allocation is influenced through rationing, incentives and signalling

Signalling and incentives

From the producers' perspective, the question is how they receive signals from consumers about their changing preferences. Price is the key. Figure 4.15 showed how an increase in demand for smartphones leads to an increase in the equilibrium market price. The shift in the demand curve leads to an increase in the equilibrium price, which encourages producers to supply more smartphones — there is an extension of supply. This is really saying that producers find it profitable to expand their output of smartphones at that higher price. The price level is thus a signal to producers about consumer preferences.

Notice that the **price signal** works equally well when there is a decrease in the demand for a good or service. Figure 4.16, for example, shows the market for desktop PCs. With the growth of tablets, there has been a fall in the demand for desktop PCs, so the demand for them has shifted to the left — consumers are demanding fewer desktop PCs at any price. Thus, the demand curve shifts from D_0 to D_1. Producers of desktop PCs are beginning to find that they cannot sell as many desktop PCs at the original price as before, so they have to reduce their price to avoid an increase in their unsold stocks. They have less incentive to produce desktop PCs, and will supply less. There is a movement along the supply curve to a lower equilibrium price at P_1, and a lower quantity traded at Q_1.

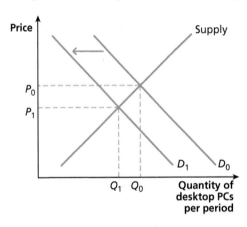

Figure 4.16 The market for desktop PCs

Thus, you can see how existing producers in a market receive signals from consumers in the form of changes in the equilibrium price, and have the incentive to respond to these signals by adjusting their output levels. Notice that the threshold at which a firm will decide it is not profitable to supply is the point at which the price received by the firm reaches the cost to the firm of producing the last unit of the good. If the price is higher than the cost of an extra unit, the firm will make a profit by producing it. The cost of producing an additional unit of a good is known by economists as the **marginal cost**. In a competitive market, the supply curve reflects that marginal cost.

Notice that the price signal works both ways. Firms receive signals from consumers about changing preferences, but in similar fashion, prices act as a rationing device if firms are unable to supply the goods that consumers want to buy. For example, suppose there is a poor harvest of coffee because of weather conditions in Brazil. The equilibrium price will rise, and consumers will find themselves rationed.

Entry and exit of firms

The discussion so far has focused on the reactions of existing firms in a market to changes in consumer preferences. However, this is only part of the picture. Think back to Figure 4.15, where there was an increase in demand for smartphones following a change in consumer preferences. The equilibrium price rose, and

Key terms

price signal where the price of a good carries information to producers or consumers that guides the market towards equilibrium and assists in resource allocation

marginal cost the cost of producing an additional unit of output

Knowledge check 4.7

What would happen to the equilibrium price if there was a good harvest, creating a glut?

existing firms expanded the quantity supplied in response. Those firms are now earning a higher producer surplus than before. Other firms not currently in the market will be attracted by these surpluses, perceiving this to be a profitable market in which to operate.

If firms are free to enter the market, they will do so. This in turn will tend to shift the supply curve to the right, as there will then be more firms prepared to supply. As a result, the equilibrium market price will tend to drift down again, until the market reaches a position in which there is no further incentive for new firms to enter the market. This will occur when the rate of return for firms in the smartphone market is no better than in other markets.

Figure 4.17 illustrates this situation. The original increase in demand leads, as before, to a new equilibrium with a higher price P_1. As new firms join the market in quest of producer surplus, the supply curve shifts to the right to S_2, pushing the price back down to P_0, but with the quantity traded now up at Q_2.

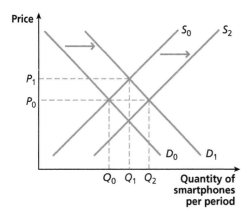

Figure 4.17 The market for smartphones revisited

If the original movement in demand is in the opposite direction, as it was for desktop PCs in Figure 4.16, a similar long-run adjustment takes place. As the market price falls, some firms in the market may decide that they no longer wish to remain in production, and will exit from the market altogether. This will shift the supply curve to the left in Figure 4.18 (to S_2) until only firms that continue to find it profitable will remain in the market. In the final position, price is back to P_0 and quantity traded has fallen to Q_2.

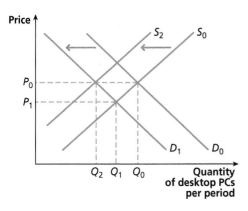

Figure 4.18 The market for desktop PCs

Exercise 4.4

a Sketch a demand and supply diagram and mark on it the areas that represent consumer and producer surplus when the market is in equilibrium.

b Using a demand and supply diagram, explain the process that provides incentives for firms to adjust to a decrease in the demand for fountain pens in a competitive market.

c Think about how you could use demand and supply analysis to explain recent movements in the world price of oil.

Summary: signals and incentives

■ If market forces are to allocate resources effectively, consumers need to be able to express their preferences for goods and services in such a way that producers can respond.

■ Consumers express their preferences through prices, as prices will adjust to equilibrium levels following a change in consumer demand.

■ Producers have an incentive to respond to changes in prices. In the short run this occurs through output adjustments of existing firms (movements along the supply curve), but in the long run firms will enter the market (or exit from it) until there are no further incentives for entry or exit.

Aspects of efficiency

In tackling the fundamental economic problem of scarcity, a society needs to find a way of using its limited resources as effectively as possible. In normal parlance it might be natural to refer to this as a quest for efficiency. From an economist's point of view there are two key aspects of efficiency, both of which are important in evaluating whether markets in an economy are working effectively.

Consider these aspects in relation to the production possibility frontier (*PPF*). Figure 4.19 shows a country's *PPF*. One of the choices to be made in allocating resources in this country is between producing agricultural or manufactured goods.

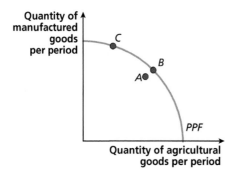

Figure 4.19 Efficiency in production

Synoptic link

The production possibility frontier was explained in Chapter 1.

At a production point such as *A* the economy would not be using its resources fully, since by moving to a point on the *PPF* it would be possible to produce more of both types of good. For example, if production took place at point *B*, then more of both agricultural and manufactured goods could be produced, so that society would be better off than at *A*.

A similar claim could be made for any point along the *PPF*: it is more efficient to be at a point on the frontier than at some point within it. However, if you compare point *B* with point *C*, you will notice that the economy produces more manufactured goods at *C* than at *B* — but only at the expense of producing fewer agricultural goods.

This draws attention to the trade-off between the production of the two sorts of goods. It is difficult to judge whether society is better off at *B* or at *C* without knowing more about the preferences of consumers.

This discussion highlights the two aspects of efficiency. On the one hand, there is the question of whether society is operating on the *PPF*, and thus using its resources effectively. On the other hand, there is the question of whether society is producing the balance of goods that consumers wish to consume. This aspect of efficiency is known as **allocative efficiency**.

It has been argued that one way of viewing the demand curve for a good is that it represents the willingness of consumers to pay for a good, so it can be regarded as the *marginal benefit* from consuming the good. If the marginal benefit were higher than the extra (marginal) cost of producing it, then it could be argued that society would be better off if more of the good were produced — as this would add more to benefit than to costs. This implies that society would be well-off in situations where the price of a good was equal to its marginal cost.

Key term

allocative efficiency
achieved when society is producing an appropriate bundle of goods relative to consumer preferences

Study tip

This idea that allocative efficiency is achieved when price is equal to marginal cost is really important, and you will come across it in many different contexts. Make sure that you understand and remember it — and are ready to use it.

Knowledge check 4.8

Name the two key aspects of efficiency.

Exercise 4.5

Consider Figure 4.20, which shows a production possibility frontier (*PPF*) for an economy that produces consumer goods and investment goods.

Identify each of the following (Hint: in some cases more than one answer is possible):

a a point of productive inefficiency
b a point of productive efficiency
c a point of allocative efficiency
d an unreachable point (Hint: think about what would need to happen for society to reach such a point)

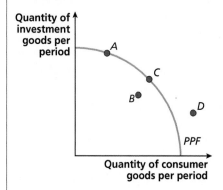

Figure 4.20 A production possibility frontier

The working of a market economy

The previous section showed that the price mechanism allows a society to allocate its resources effectively if firms respond to changes in prices. Consumers express changes in their preferences by their decisions to buy (or not to buy) at the going price, which leads to a change in the equilibrium price. Firms thus respond to changes in consumer demand, given the incentive of profitability, which is related to price. In the short run, existing firms adjust their output levels along the supply curve. In the long run, firms enter into markets (or exit from them) in response to the relative profitability of the various economic activities that take place in the economy. But how does this work out in practice in a 'real-life' economy?

Opportunity cost

One way of viewing this system is through the notion of opportunity cost, introduced in Chapter 1. For example, in choosing to be active in the market for desktop PCs, a firm faces an opportunity cost. If it uses its resources to produce desktop PCs, it is not using those resources to produce something else. There may come a point at which the cost of producing desktop PCs becomes too high, if the profitability of other goods is so much higher than that for desktop PCs because of changes in the pattern of consumer demand. When the firm finds that it is not covering its opportunity costs, it will transfer production away from the desktop PC market.

The government's role

The government's role in a free economy is relatively limited, but nonetheless important. A basic framework of *property rights* is essential, together with a basic legal framework. However, the state does not intervene in the production process directly. Secure property rights are significant, as this assures the incentives for the owners of capital.

Within such a system, consumers try to maximise the satisfaction (utility) they gain from consuming a range of products, and firms seek to maximise their profits by responding to consumer demand through the medium of price signals.

> ### Synoptic link
>
> This goes back to Adam Smith's notion of the 'invisible hand', which was introduced in Chapter 1.

It is worth noting that Adam Smith also sounded a word of warning. He felt that there were too many factors that interfered with the free market system, such as over-protectionism and restrictions on trade. At the same time, he was not utterly convinced that a free market economy would be wholly effective, noting also that firms might at times collude to prevent the free operation of the market mechanism:

> *People of the same trade seldom meet together, even for merriment and diversion, but the conversation ends in a conspiracy against the public, or in some contrivance to raise prices...*
>
> (Adam Smith, *The Wealth of Nations*, Vol. I)

So there may be situations in which consumer interests need to be protected, if there is some sort of market failure that prevents the best outcome from being achieved.

Adam Smith was not convinced that a free market economy would be wholly effective

Summary: allocative efficiency

- A society needs to find a way of using its limited resources as efficiently as possible.
- Allocative efficiency occurs when firms produce an appropriate bundle of goods and services, given consumer preferences.
- An individual market exhibits aspects of allocative efficiency when the marginal benefit received by society from consuming a good or service matches the marginal cost of producing it — that is, when price is equal to marginal cost.
- Free markets do not always lead to the best possible allocation of resources: there may be market failure.

Synoptic link

Types of market failure are explored in Chapters 6 and 7.

Case study 4.1

A healthy diet?

Hardly a week seems to go by without scientists or nutritionists coming up with some new finding about the healthiness of our diets. Real butter is more healthy than margarine. Smoked salmon from farmed fish may contain more fat than a pizza. Red wine is good for you — or is it bad for you? In March 2018, a judge in Los Angeles ruled that coffee sold in California must carry a cancer warning because the chemical acrylamide which is created in part of the roasting process is regarded as carcinogenic.

A growing obsession has focused on the health and environmental benefits of organic foods. The overuse of chemical fertilisers and pesticides is seen as damaging for the environment, and potentially damaging to our health. This has resulted in a premium price for certified organic foods, notably vegetables. Wine producers in some regions have also become involved in organic (and biodynamic) production methods. However, converting to organic production and gaining authentication is a long-winded and costly process.

Follow-up questions

Suppose people become convinced of the benefits of consuming organic foods.

a Sketch a demand and supply diagram to analyse how this would affect the market for non-organic products in the short run.

b Now use a demand and supply diagram to show how the market for certified organic foods would be affected in the short run.

c With the help of more diagrams, explain how these interdependent markets will adjust in the longer term, remembering that achieving certified organic status is slow and costly.

5 How markets work: the price mechanism in action

In the previous chapters, you have seen how the demand and supply model can be used in order to analyse market situations. It is now time to begin to apply this model in a variety of circumstances to see how it provides insights into how different markets operate at local, national and global level. You will encounter demand and supply in a wide variety of contexts, and begin to glimpse some of the ways in which the model can help to explain how the economic world works. You will also see how government intervention in the form of indirect taxation and subsidies can affect markets. We will also explore the question of whether consumers always act rationally.

Learning objectives

After studying this chapter, you should be able to:
→ apply demand and supply analysis in a variety of different market situations
→ analyse the effect of taxes and subsidies in a market, using demand and supply analysis
→ evaluate the extent to which a sales tax is borne by buyers and sellers
→ use demand and supply analysis to interpret economic events in the real world
→ be aware that consumers may not always act rationally

All the examples of demand and supply discussed so far were consumer goods of some sort — smartphones, butter, pencils and so on. However, it would be wrong to think that demand and supply analysis is of relevance only in that sort of market. So, this chapter broadens the horizons, looking beyond consumer goods markets.

Agricultural markets

The markets for agricultural produce have some interesting characteristics that can be analysed with the demand and supply model. One particular characteristic of many such markets is that the supply side of the market can be strongly affected by weather and climate, sometimes in random or unpredictable ways. This can create conditions in which it is difficult to forecast market outcomes in advance. In particular, this means that prices can vary quite widely from year to year, making conditions in agricultural markets difficult to predict. For some commodities, attempts can be made to stabilise prices by storing surplus produce in good years to sell in bad years.

Knowledge check 5.1

What would be the effect on equilibrium price and quantity if there is an especially good harvest of strawberries one year?

Exercise 5.1

When South East Asia was suffering from an outbreak of the SARS virus which had spread around the region, one of the main wholesale fruit and vegetable markets in Singapore, at Pasir Panjang, had to be closed when workers were found to have been infected. Sketch a demand and supply diagram to predict how the retail market for vegetables was affected.

Commodity markets

Another category of market that is of particular interest is the one for commodities. This encompasses markets for various types of raw material used in the production process of many manufacturing industries. Prices in these markets too can be volatile, but this time the volatility arises from the demand side of the market.

The market for bauxite

Figure 5.1 shows the market for bauxite, a commodity used as a raw material in the production of aluminium. Many countries experience fluctuations in the overall level of economic activity over time. There are periods of boom and periods of recession. The demand for aluminium (and hence for bauxite) tends to vary with these cycles of activity. D_{av} here represents the average position of the demand curve for bauxite. At the peak of the cycle demand is high and the price rises to P_{peak}, but at the trough of the cycle prices fall to P_{trough}. The quantity traded does not vary very much. This is because the figure has been drawn showing supply to be relatively inelastic, so the main burden of adjustment to market equilibrium takes place through the price level.

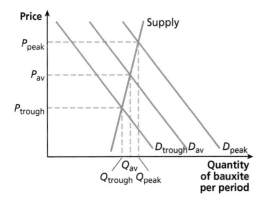

Figure 5.1 The market for bauxite

Such markets are sometimes complicated by the existence of futures markets, in which commodities can be bought in the present period for delivery at a future date at prices agreed now. This adds a speculative element to the demand.

Exercise 5.2

Bauxite is a mineral which is the principal source of aluminium. It is in plentiful supply in many countries around the world. The largest importer of bauxite is China, which has greatly increased its refining of bauxite into aluminium as part of its recent economic growth. Indonesia is an exporter of bauxite, but was keen to expand its own aluminium refining capacity. In 2014, it banned exports of bauxite, most of which had previously gone to China.

On the basis of this information, sketch a demand and supply diagram to show the market situation. From your diagram, would you expect price to increase or decrease? How about quantity?

The market for oil

A commodity market that has been much discussed in recent years is the market for oil. This is seen as being especially significant for the global economy because oil is so important for the functioning of other markets, especially transport. The market for oil is inevitably a global one. All countries use oil, but oil reserves are concentrated in only some countries. The price of oil over time has followed something of an erratic path, as you can see in Figure 5.2.

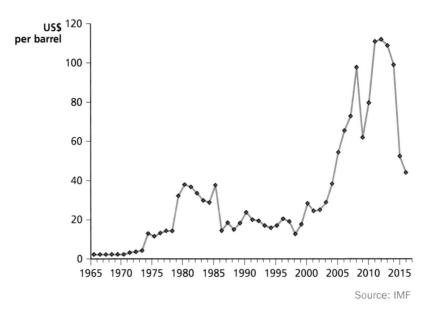

Figure 5.2 The price of oil, 1965-2016

Key term

cartel an agreement between firms in a market on price and output with the intention of maximising their joint profits

The Organisation of the Petroleum Exporting Countries (OPEC) has played an influential role in the way that prices have evolved over time, but other factors have also been important. OPEC is an organisation that operates as a producer **cartel**. A cartel is an agreement between firms in a market on price and output with the intention of maximising their joint profits. Although such agreements are illegal in countries such as the UK and the USA, OPEC is an agreement between nation producers, so is less easy to regulate. Cartel agreements can interfere with the free working of the price mechanism.

Although the market for oil may not be a freely operating competitive market, demand and supply analysis can still help in the interpretation of how it has evolved over time. Before the first so-called 'oil-price crisis' of 1973–74, the price of oil had been stable over a long period. Two events occurred in the early 1970s that affected the supply side of the oil market. One was the Yom Kippur War (1973), which interrupted the supply of oil from the Middle East. The second was a decision by OPEC to restrict supply. With demand being relatively inelastic, the disruption to supply resulted in a substantial increase in the price of oil.

Demand was inelastic in the short run because consumers had become accustomed to relatively low prices, and could not adjust demand quickly. For example, in the UK many houses were heated through oil-fired central heating. In addition, cars of the day were relatively fuel-inefficient. As time went by, new houses were no longer built with oil-fired heating, and cars became more efficient in their use of petrol. In other words, demand was less inelastic in the longer term.

You can see, therefore, that the first major oil price increase was supply driven. This was also the case for the second crisis, which took place in 1979–80 when OPEC again decided to reduce supply. Looking at Figure 5.2, the sudden fall in oil prices in the mid-1980s was also the result of an oil supply shock, when Saudi Arabia increased its supply of oil, leading to a fall in the price of oil.

The rises in the price of oil in the early 2000s arose in a rather different way. There were again some supply-side influences, such as the Iraq War. However, there were also effects on the demand side, particularly with the rapid economic growth that was taking place in China. The financial crisis of the late 2000s caused a downward spike in prices as demand fell during the global recession. The fall in price after 2014 reflects a number of factors, including the slowdown of China's economy, moves to increase capacity in the USA and Canada, and Saudi Arabia's wish to maintain market share in the face of weakening demand.

You may find it helpful to sketch some demand and supply diagrams to analyse the effects of these changes in the oil market for yourself.

Knowledge check 5.2

How would you expect the supply of oil to adjust in the long run if OPEC continued to hold the price at an artificially high level?

Synoptic link

As the process of globalisation has proceeded, the price of oil has become a key variable affecting economies. This is discussed in Chapter 24. The operations of a cartel are discussed in Chapter 20.

The destruction of oil wells during the Iraq War disrupted the supply of oil in the early 2000s

The housing market

Everyone needs somewhere to live, and housing makes up a large part of the household budget. This makes the housing market particularly important in any economy. Here too, demand and supply can be used to explain how the market operates. Although people do move around the country, housing markets tend to operate at a relatively local level, responding to specific characteristics of the local area.

> ### Study tip
>
> The housing market can be seen as an example of a local market, because of the local conditions that affect both demand and supply of housing. However, it will also be influenced by some national aspects of the market environment. In the exam, you may be asked to discuss examples of markets at local, national or global level, so you need to think about whether a market primarily depends on influences at those three levels.

The housing market is not in fact a single market, as there are different segments that may operate in quite different ways. There are the owner-occupier market and the private and public rental sectors. Of course, these segments interact in some ways, but they may be influenced by different factors.

The owner-occupier market

The owner-occupier housing market often features in the news. The purchase of a house is the largest single transaction that most people will make in their lifetimes, and is normally funded through borrowing (apart from the occasional lottery win!) The demand for houses to buy is thus influenced partly by the cost of borrowing — in other words, the interest rate. Later chapters of this book will cover the way in which interest rates are used as a policy instrument to stabilise the overall economy. In the early part of the twenty-first century, interest rates have been relatively low by historical standards, and this has encouraged borrowing, which has fed into the demand for houses, pushing the demand curve to the right.

> ### Synoptic link
>
> The interest rate became a key instrument of policy at the economy-wide level, being used to influence the rate of inflation. However, it also had side-effects on markets such as the housing market. The use of interest rates is discussed in Chapters 16, 31 and 32.

At the same time, the supply of houses has been expanding only slowly — at least in some regions. Building takes time, of course, but also there have been environmental concerns, and the resulting regulation has limited the growth of the housing stock by restricting the amount of new stock being built.

> ### Synoptic link
>
> Even by 2017 the UK economy was still operating below trend, as is discussed in Chapter 14.

Figure 5.3 sketches how this might be seen in terms of demand and supply. Demand increases rapidly, but supply expands relatively slowly. The result is an increase in the equilibrium price, from P_0 to P_1, with only a modest expansion of supply, from Q_0 to Q_1. The late 1990s and the early 2000s did indeed see a rapid increase in house prices, and there was much speculation that they were rising too rapidly to be sustainable. This proved to be the case and house prices fell between 2007 and 2009 with the onset of recession and the financial crisis. There was a mild recovery in 2010 but this was followed by a period of stagnation. The significant role of housing in everyone's lives makes this an important issue.

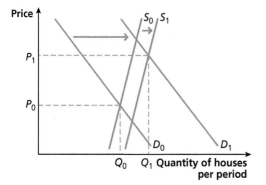

Figure 5.3 The market for houses for owner occupation

Demand and supply may help to explain why house prices have been rising. However, there are other factors to be considered before arriving at a complete explanation of the market.

Knowledge check 5.3

Why should there be so much variation in house prices in different parts of the UK?

The foreign exchange market

When you take your holidays in Spain you need to buy euros. Equally, when German tourists come to visit London they need to buy pounds. If there is buying going on, then there must be a market — remember from Chapter 1 that a market is a set of arrangements that enable transactions to be undertaken. So here is another sort of market to be considered. The exchange rate is the price at which two currencies exchange, and it can be analysed using demand and supply.

Consider the market for pounds, and focus on the exchange rate between pounds and euros, as shown in Figure 5.4. Think first of all about what gives rise to a demand for pounds. It is not just German tourists who need pounds to spend on holiday: anyone holding euros who wants to buy British goods needs pounds in order to pay for them. So the demand for pounds comes from people in the euro area who want to buy British goods or services — or assets. When the exchange rate for the pound in euros is high, potential buyers of British goods get relatively few pounds per euro so the demand will be relatively low, whereas if the euros per pound rate is relatively low, they get more for their money. Hence the demand curve is expected to be downward sloping.

Synoptic link

The foreign exchange market is discussed in more detail in Chapter 26.

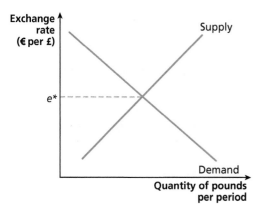

Figure 5.4 The market for pounds sterling

Foreign exchange as a derived demand

One point to notice from this is that the foreign exchange market is an example of a *derived demand*, in the sense that people want pounds not for their own sake, but for the goods or services that they can buy. This notion of a derived demand is explored more fully in Chapter 22, as it is important in explaining the demand for labour. One way of viewing the exchange rate is as a means by which to learn about the international competitiveness of British exports. When the exchange rate is high, British goods are less competitive in Europe, ceteris paribus. Notice the ceteris paribus assumption there. This is important, because the exchange rate is not the only determinant of the competitiveness of British goods: they also depend on the relative price levels in the UK and Europe.

What about the supply of pounds? Pounds are supplied by UK residents wanting euros to buy goods or services from Europe. From this angle, when the euros per pound rate is high, UK residents get more euros for their pounds, and therefore will tend to supply more pounds.

If the exchange market is in equilibrium, the exchange rate will tend to $e^\star$, where the demand for pounds is matched by the supply.

Pounds are traded for euros on the foreign exchange market

Knowledge check 5.4

Give another example of a derived demand.

The stock market

Another important financial market is the stock market. Firms that want to raise funds for investing in new machinery or other projects can do so by issuing 'stocks', which are then sold on the stock market. People wanting a good return on their savings may then purchase stocks and shares in the hope of receiving good dividends (sharing in the profits of the firm), or capital gains as the value of the firm (hopefully) rises with success.

Although it may sound as if the stock market is a quite different sort of market, it too can be analysed by using demand and supply analysis. The demand for stocks comes from savers looking for a return, so the strength of demand will depend on their expectations of the future success of the firm, and future movements in the price of the stock, which will affect the capital gain. The supply of stocks will depend on firms' expectations of the future demand for the product, which will determine whether or not they are keen to invest in new capital goods.

The interaction of demand and supply will thus determine the price of the stock in the market. However, notice how important expectations are on both sides of the market. This suggests that there will be substantial uncertainty surrounding market conditions. One result of this is that there could be some instability in the positions of both demand and supply, especially where people react strongly to news about the markets. If people suddenly come to believe that stock prices are about to tumble, perhaps because of gloomy forecasts about the economy, then demand is likely to fall as savers move their funds to alternative financial assets. Demand and supply analysis then predicts that prices will fall — all because people expect this to happen. In other words, the stock market could be characterised by self-fulfilling expectations.

Financial markets

Chapter 1 highlighted the importance of money in enabling exchange to take place through the operation of markets. This implies that people have a *demand for money*. This demand for money is associated with the functions of money set out on pages 14–15 — as a medium of exchange, store of value, unit of account and standard of deferred payment. If there is a demand for money, then perhaps there should also be a market for money?

The demand for and supply of money

We can think of the demand for money depending on a number of factors — in particular, on the number of transactions that people wish to undertake — which probably depends on income. But is there a price of money? The price of money can be viewed in terms of opportunity cost. When people choose to hold money, they incur an opportunity cost, which can be seen as the next best alternative to holding money. For example, instead of holding money, you could decide to purchase a financial asset that would provide a rate of return, represented by the rate of interest. This rate of interest can thus be interpreted as the price of holding money.

How about the supply of money? This will be discussed much later in the course, but for now, it can be assumed that the supply of money is determined by the Bank of England, and it can be assumed that this money supply will not depend on the rate of interest. Figure 5.5 illustrates the market for money. The demand for money is shown to be downward sloping, as the higher the rate of interest, the greater the return that is sacrificed by holding money, so the smaller will be the demand for money. The supply of money does not depend on the rate of interest (by assumption), so is shown as a vertical line. The market is in equilibrium when the rate of interest is at $r^\star$, the level at which the demand and supply of money are equal.

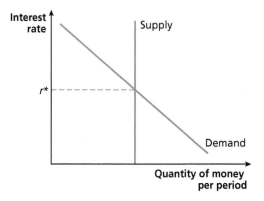

Figure 5.5 The market for money

Synoptic link

The significance of money supply and interest rates is examined in Chapter 30.

Summary: examples of markets

- In agricultural markets, supply can fluctuate between seasons because of weather conditions. This causes volatility in prices.
- In commodity markets, demand may fluctuate across the business cycle, again causing volatility in prices.
- The oil market has been highly influential because of the importance of oil as a source of energy.
- The housing market can be analysed using demand and supply analysis. The level of demand may be influenced by government policy on interest rates.
- Demand and supply enables you to examine how the foreign exchange rate is determined.
- The stock market is another market to which demand and supply analysis can be applied.

Indirect taxes and subsidies

Key terms

indirect tax a tax levied on expenditure on goods or services (as opposed to a direct tax, which is a tax charged directly to an individual based on a component of income)

specific tax a sales tax that is set at a constant amount per unit of sales

One final application of the demand and supply model in this chapter is to analyse the effect on a market of the imposition of **indirect taxes** and subsidies. These are important ways in which the government may intervene to influence a market.

Indirect taxes

In the UK, value added tax (VAT) is the most prominent example of an indirect tax, although other levies, such as excise duties on alcohol and tobacco, are also indirect taxes. An indirect tax is paid by the seller, so it affects the supply curve for a product.

Figure 5.6 illustrates the case of a fixed-rate, or **specific tax** — a tax that is set at a constant amount per pack of cigarettes. Without the tax, the market equilibrium is at the intersection of demand and supply, with price P_0 and quantity traded Q_0. The effect of the tax is to reduce the quantity that firms are prepared to supply at any given price; to put it another way, for any given quantity of cigarettes, firms need to receive the amount of the tax over and above the price at which they would have been prepared to supply that quantity. The effect is thus to move the supply curve upwards by the amount of the tax, as shown in the figure. A new equilibrium is reached with a higher price at P_1 and a lower quantity traded at Q_1.

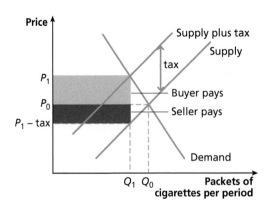

Figure 5.6 The effects of an indirect tax on cigarettes

An important question is: who bears the burden of the tax? If you look at the diagram, you will see that the price difference between the with- and without-tax situations (i.e. $P_1 - P_0$) is less than the amount of the tax, which is the vertical distance between the with and without supply curves. So, although the seller (producer) may be responsible for the mechanics of paying the tax, part of the tax is effectively passed on to the buyer (consumer) in the form of the higher price. So the **incidence of the tax** falls partly on the seller, but in Figure 5.6 most of the tax is borne by the buyer.

The price elasticity of demand determines the incidence of the tax. If demand were perfectly inelastic, sellers would be able to pass the whole burden of the tax on to buyers through an increase in price equal to the value of the tax, knowing that this would not affect demand. However, if demand were perfectly elastic, sellers would not be able to raise the price at all, so they would have to bear the entire burden of the tax.

If the tax is not a constant amount, but a percentage of the price (known as an *ad valorem* tax), the supply curve is still affected; but now it steepens, as shown in Figure 5.7.

Key terms

incidence of a tax the way in which the burden of paying a sales tax is divided between buyers and sellers

***ad valorem* tax** a sales tax that is set at a percentage of the price

subsidy a grant given by the government to producers to encourage production of a good or service

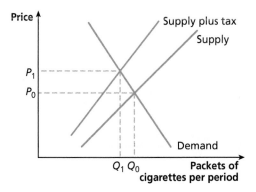

Figure 5.7 The effects of an *ad valorem* tax on cigarettes

Exercise 5.3

Sketch diagrams to investigate the incidence of a tax when demand is perfectly inelastic and perfectly elastic.

Knowledge check 5.5

Explain what is meant by the 'incidence of a tax'.

Subsidies

In some situations the government may wish to encourage production of a particular good or service, perhaps because it views the good as having strategic significance to the country. One way it can do this is by giving **subsidies**.

Such subsidies have been especially common in agriculture, which is often seen as being of strategic significance. In the early years of this century, the USA came under pressure to reduce the subsidies that it grants to cotton producers. Analytically, a subsidy can be regarded as a sort of negative indirect tax that shifts the supply curve down, as shown in Figure 5.8. Without the subsidy, market equilibrium is at price

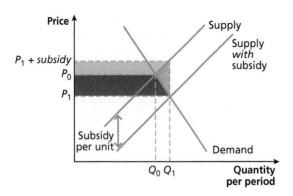

Figure 5.8 The effects of a subsidy

P_0 and quantity traded Q_0. With the subsidy in place, the equilibrium price falls to P_1 and the quantity traded increases to Q_1.

Again, notice that, because the price falls by less than the amount of the subsidy, the benefits of the subsidy are shared between buyers and sellers, depending on the elasticity of demand. Consumer surplus increases as a result of the subsidy, shown by the purple shaded area. Producer surplus increases by the blue area. The cost to the government of the subsidy is the sum of the blue, purple and orange areas, but the orange area cannot be recovered.

If the aim of the subsidy is to increase production, it is only partially successful — the degree of success also depends on the elasticity of demand.

Study tip

Remember that if you are asked to discuss an indirect tax or a subsidy in the exam, the effect is to shift the *supply curve* to the left/upwards (for a tax) or to the right/downwards (for a subsidy).

Do consumers always act rationally?

In discussing the way that markets work, it has been assumed that consumers act rationally, aiming to maximise their utility. Recent research in experimental and behavioural economics suggests that this may not always be the case, and that there may be situations in which consumers seem to take decisions that are economically irrational.

Economically irrational behaviours

Key terms

habitual behaviour where consumers persist in acting in a particular way even when conditions have changed

herding where people take decisions based on the actions of others, rather than on a rational evaluation of the situation that they face

One example is where it is observed that consumers may not react to a price change. One reason for this may be that people display **habitual behaviour**, which may lead to persistence, even if this is costly. This does not only apply to products that are addictive, such as tobacco, although that is an extreme example of persistence.

An example of persistence can be seen in relation to gym membership. An individual may take out a gym membership based on good intentions of getting and remaining fit. However, they have other things to do, or they cannot be bothered to go to the gym — but they may continue to pay the subscriptions anyway, through inertia, or because they still have the good intentions, even if they are not reflected in action. Similarly, people may not bother to switch their bank account or energy suppliers, even if there are cheaper options available.

It has also been observed that individual consumers may exhibit **herding** behaviour, buying a product because others are doing so, rather than because of its intrinsic merits. For example, they may purchase goods that are known to be popular, or which their friends have raved about.

People may also take decisions on impulse. For example, they may reach for a chocolate bar cunningly displayed beside the supermarket checkout queue.

People are also seen to take decisions that are altruistic in nature, such as giving to charity, or behaving in a way that is perceived to be socially responsible, but costly. For example, avoiding buying goods that involve unrecyclable plastic could be costly, but could help to conserve the environment, so you may be prepared to incur the extra cost out of a sense of social responsibility.

Knowledge check 5.6

Give an example of how a sense of social responsibility may influence behaviour.

Bounded rationality

In some cases, seemingly irrational behaviour may reflect information overload. There may be more information about consumption possibilities than consumers are able to absorb and interpret. Or, indeed, it may be that information about products is difficult to gather or to analyse. People may then take decisions based on the best information that they can find, or the most information that they are capable of analysing. For example, it may be that consumers are weak at undertaking calculations, or do not have the information needed to undertake calculations. This is sometimes referred to as **bounded rationality**, where economic agents do the best that they can, given the information available.

These are all ways in which consumers can be perceived as irrational in their behaviour — in the sense that they are not acting to maximise their utility.

Nudge theory

Firms and government have become aware of this sort of behaviour, and have tried to exploit it, realising that people's choices can be influenced by making decisions easy. This has become known as **nudge theory**. For example, people may be enticed into socially responsible behaviour by appealing to their sense of justice. An example would be where signs are provided in motorway service stations encouraging people to take their litter home by saying that 'others do' — or by reminding them that there are CCTV cameras observing them.

Another example of nudge theory is where legislation is passed that allows people to opt-out, rather than opt-in to some desirable action. For example, the rules under which individuals are automatically enrolled in workplace pension schemes unless they consciously opt out. Research has shown that people are more likely to remain opted-in than to take the trouble to opt out. Robert Thaler was awarded the Nobel Prize for Economic Sciences in 2017 for his work in this area.

Key terms

bounded rationality a situation in which people's ability to make rational decisions is limited by a lack of information or an inability to interpret the information that is available, perhaps because of weakness at computation

nudge theory analysis that suggests that people's behaviour can be influenced by making desirable decisions easy to make

---

Summary: taxes, subsidies and behavioural theories

- An indirect tax levied on a good or service will be seen as a shift in the supply curve. The incidence of the tax (whether the burden is borne by buyers or sellers) is determined by the elasticity of demand.
- Subsidies may be used by governments to encourage domestic production of a good.
- It is important to remain aware that consumers may not always act rationally, and may take decisions that are more difficult to capture in an economic model.

Case study 5.1

Jewellery

A local craft market is populated by a variety of stalls selling a range of items — antiques, football memorabilia, second-hand books, hand-made jewellery and other items. The same sellers are present at the market every time it opens, each with their regular place, but there are some vacant stalls. The stall holders just make enough profit to make it worth their while.

One week, the craft market is featured in the local newspaper, and an item appears on local television highlighting the quality of design and value for money of the jewellery on sale at the market. The jewellery sellers suddenly find that their stock is moving very rapidly, and realise that they can increase their prices. As word gets around, some of the vacant stalls are taken up by new jewellery makers and, although the number of buyers remains high, prices drift back to their original level.

Follow-up questions

a Sketch a demand and supply diagram to track these changes in the market for jewellery.

b Would you expect other (non-jewellery) stalls to be affected by this process?

c How might established jewellers in the area respond to the popularity of the craft market?

New jewellery stalls have come into the market

6 Market failure and externalities

Earlier chapters have shown that prices can act as signals that help to guide the allocation of resources. However, there are situations in which markets fail to produce the ideal outcome for society, as the free market equilibrium may depart from the socially optimum position. This chapter and the next discuss some key ways in which market failure can occur. The main focus of this chapter is to explore what happens if market prices are not able to reflect the full costs and benefits associated with market transactions. There are many situations in which there are costs or benefits that are external to the workings of the market mechanism.

Learning objectives

After studying this chapter, you should:
→ recognise situations in which the free market mechanism may fail to take account of costs or benefits that are associated with market transactions
→ be familiar with situations in which there may be a divergence between private and social costs or benefits, such that price is not set equal to marginal cost
→ be able to use diagrams to analyse positive and negative externalities in either production or consumption
→ be familiar with a wide range of examples of externalities

▌Causes of market failure

This chapter and the next explore a number of ways in which markets may fail to bring the best result for society as a whole. In each case, the failure arises because a market settles in a position in which marginal social cost diverges from marginal social benefit. When this occurs, the market equilibrium will not reach the socially optimum position. This chapter introduces the most important reasons for **market failure** and examines one common form — externalities. Some other forms of market failure are discussed in Chapter 7.

Externalities

If market forces are to guide the allocation of resources, it is crucial that the costs that firms face and the prices to which they respond fully reflect the actual costs and benefits associated with the production and consumption of goods. However, there are situations and markets in which this does not happen because of **externalities**. In the presence of such externalities, a price will emerge that is not equal to the 'true' marginal cost.

Information gaps

If markets are to perform a role in allocating resources, it is essential that all relevant economic agents (buyers and sellers) have good information about market conditions; otherwise they may not be able to take rational decisions.

> **Key terms**
>
> **market failure** a situation in which the free market equilibrium does not lead to a socially optimal allocation of resources, such that too much or too little of a good is being produced and/or consumed
>
> **externality** a cost or a benefit that is external to a market transaction, and is thus not reflected in market prices, which may affect third parties not involved in the transaction

It is important that consumers can clearly perceive the benefits of consuming particular goods or services, in order to determine their own willingness to pay. Such benefits may not always be clear. For example, people may not fully perceive the benefits to be gained from education — or they may fail to appreciate the harmfulness of smoking tobacco.

In other market situations, economic agents on one side of the market may have different information from those on the other side: for example, sellers may have information about the goods that they are providing that buyers cannot discern.

Public goods

There is a category of goods known as public goods, which because of their characteristics cannot be provided by a purely free market. Street lighting is one example: there is no obvious way in which a private firm could charge all the users of street lighting for the benefits that they receive from it.

Synoptic link

Chapter 7 explains the market failure caused by information gaps and public goods.

Knowledge check 6.1

Name three possible causes of market failure.

Summary: market failure

- Free markets do not always lead to the best possible allocation of resources: there may be market failure, causing the market equilibrium to diverge from the socially optimum position.
- When there are costs or benefits that are external to the price mechanism, the economy will not reach allocative efficiency.
- Markets can operate effectively only when participants in the market have full information about market conditions.
- Public goods have characteristics that prevent markets from supplying the appropriate quantity.

Study tip

Market failure is often used as a justification for government intervention in markets, so it is important to be aware of its various causes and to be able to recognise situations in which market failure may occur. At the heart of this is whether the free market equilibrium coincides with the socially optimum position.

Externalities

Externality is one of those ugly words invented by economists, which says exactly what it means. It simply describes a cost or a benefit that is external to the market mechanism.

An externality will lead to a form of market failure because if the cost or benefit is not reflected in market prices, it cannot be taken into consideration by all parties to a transaction. In other words, there may be costs (or benefits) resulting from a transaction that are borne (or enjoyed) by some third party not directly involved in that transaction. This in turn implies that decisions will not be aligned with the best interests of society.

For example, if there is an element of costs that is not borne by producers, it is likely that 'too much' of the good will be produced. Conversely, where there are benefits that are not included, it is likely that too little will be produced. Later in the chapter, you will see that this is exactly what does happen. Externalities can affect either demand or supply in a market: that is to say, they may arise either in **consumption** or in **production**.

Another way of expressing this is that the total cost of producing a good or service is made up of two components: the **private costs** faced by producers and the additional **external costs** that producers do not perceive. In other words, the costs to society (the **social costs**) are equal to private costs plus external costs. Similarly, **social benefits** are equal to **private benefits** that accrue to individuals plus the **external benefits** received by third parties.

Knowledge check 6.2

What is meant by an 'externality'?

In approaching this topic, begin by tackling Exercise 6.1, which offers an example of two types of externality.

Exercise 6.1

Each of the following situations describes a type of externality. Do they affect production or consumption?

1 A factory situated in the centre of a town, and close to a residential district, emits toxic fumes through a chimney during its production process. Residents living nearby have to wash their clothes more frequently, and incur higher medical bills as a result of breathing in the fumes.
2 Residents living along a main road festoon their houses with lavish Christmas lights and decorations during the month of December, helping passers-by to capture the festive spirit.

Key terms

consumption externality an externality that affects the consumption side of a market, which may be either positive or negative

production externality an externality that affects the production side of a market, which may be either positive or negative

private cost a cost incurred by an individual (firm or consumer) as part of its production or other economic activities

external cost a cost associated with an individual's (a firm or household's) production or other economic activities, which is borne by a third party and is not reflected in market prices

social cost the sum of private and external costs

social benefit the sum of private benefits and external benefits

private benefit the benefit from an individual's (a firm or household's) economic activity that accrue to that individual

external benefit the benefit that society receives over and above those that accrue to the individual engaged in an economic activity

Pollution from toxic fumes is an example of an externality

Toxic fumes

Example 1 in Exercise 6.1 is a negative production externality. The factory emits toxic fumes that impose costs on the residents (third parties) living nearby, who incur high washing and medical bills. The households face costs as a result of the production activities of the firm, so the firm does not face the full costs of its activity.

Key term

marginal social cost
the cost to society of producing an extra unit of a good

Thus, the private costs faced by the producer are lower than the costs faced by society as a whole. The producer will take decisions based only on its private costs, ignoring the external costs it imposes on society. In other words, the social cost of producing a good includes both private and external costs. In looking at decisions, we will often focus on **marginal social cost**, which is the cost to society of producing an extra unit of a good.

Figure 6.1 illustrates this situation under the assumption that firms operate in a competitive market (i.e. there is not a monopoly). Here, D (MSB) represents the demand curve, which was characterised in Chapter 4 as representing the marginal social benefit derived from consuming a good. In other words, the demand curve represents consumers' willingness to pay for the good, and thus reflects their marginal valuation of the product.

Producers face marginal private costs given by the line MPC, but in fact impose higher costs than this on society. Thus MSC represents the total costs imposed on society in the production of this good.

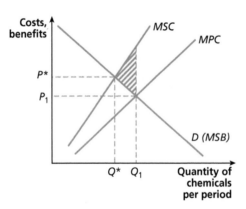

Figure 6.1 A negative productive externality

If the market is unregulated by the government, firms will choose how much to supply on the basis of the marginal (private) cost they face, shown by MPC in Figure 6.1. The market equilibrium will thus be at quantity traded Q_1, where firms just break even on the marginal unit sold. Price will be set at P_1.

This is not a good outcome for society, as it is clear that there is a divergence between the price in the market and the 'true' marginal cost — in other words, a divergence between marginal social benefit and marginal social cost. This divergence is at the heart of the market failure. The last unit of this good sold imposes higher costs on society than the marginal benefit derived from consuming it. Too much is being produced at the market equilibrium.

In fact, the socially optimum position is at $Q^\star$, where marginal social benefit is equal to marginal social cost. This will be reached if the price is set equal to (social) marginal cost at $P^\star$. Less of the good will be consumed, but also less pollution will be created, and society will be better off than at Q_1.

Knowledge check 6.3

Does the presence of a negative production externality cause over-production or under-consumption?

Quantitative skills 6.1

Identifying welfare loss in a diagram

The extent of the welfare loss that society suffers can be identified: it is shown by the shaded triangle in Figure 6.1. Each unit of output that is produced above Q^* imposes a cost equal to the vertical distance between MSC and MPC. The shaded area thus represents the difference between marginal social cost and marginal benefit (MSB) over the range of output between the optimum output and the free market level of output.

Study tip

Externalities are a common topic, so be ready to respond if questioned. Be very careful when drawing the diagram, especially in identifying the area representing welfare loss. If you understand *why* this area represents welfare loss, you should be able to check whether you have identified it correctly.

Christmas lights

Example 2 in Exercise 6.1 is an example of a positive consumption externality. Residents of this street decorate their homes in order to share the Christmas spirit with passers-by. The benefit they gain from the decorations spills over and adds to the enjoyment of others. In other words, the social benefits from the residents' decision to provide Christmas decorations go beyond the private enjoyment that they receive.

Figure 6.2 illustrates this situation. MPB represents the marginal private benefits gained by residents from the Christmas lights; but MSB represents the full marginal social benefit that the community gains, which is higher than the MPB. Residents will provide decorations up to the point Q_2, where their marginal private benefit is just balanced by the marginal cost of the lights. However, if the full social benefits received are taken into account, $Q^\star$ would be the optimum point: the residents do not provide enough décor for the community to reach the optimum. The shaded triangle in Figure 6.2 shows the welfare loss: that is, the amount of social benefit forgone if the outcome is at Q_2 instead of $Q^\star$. Again, there is a divergence between the free market equilibrium and the socially optimum position.

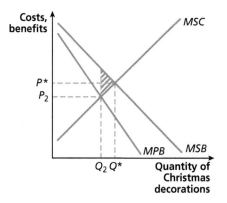

Figure 6.2 A positive consumption externality

Knowledge check 6.4

Does the presence of a positive consumption externality cause over-production or under-consumption?

Positive and normative revisited

Example 2 is a reminder of the distinction between positive and normative analysis, which was introduced in Chapter 1. Economists would agree that Figure 6.2 shows the effects of a beneficial consumption externality. However, probably not everyone would agree that the lavish Christmas decorations are providing such benefits. This is where a *normative judgement* comes into play. It could equally be argued that the lavish Christmas decorations are unsightly and inappropriate, or that they constitute a distraction for drivers and are therefore likely to cause accidents. After all, not everyone enjoys these lavish (and sometimes garish) displays.

Extension material: other externalities

Discussion has centred on two examples of externalities: a production externality that had negative effects, and a consumption externality that was beneficial to society. In fact, there are two other possibilities.

Think about a factory that produces chemicals and is located on the banks of a river. It installs a new water purification plant that improves the quality of water discharged into the river. A trout farm located downstream finds that its productivity increases, so it has to spend less on filtering the water. This is an example of a positive production externality, so that marginal social cost is lower than marginal private cost.

In contrast, think about Liz, a 'metal' enthusiast, who enjoys playing her music at high volume late at night, in spite of the fact that she lives in a flat with inadequate sound insulation. The neighbours prefer rock, but cannot escape the metal. This would be an example of a negative consumption externality, in which marginal social benefit is lower than marginal private benefit.

Knowledge check 6.5

Explain how to identify the area of welfare loss in a diagram showing the effect of a negative production externality.

Summary: externalities

- Markets can operate effectively only if all relevant costs and benefits are taken into account in decision making.
- Some costs and benefits are external to the market mechanism, and are thus neglected, causing a distortion in resource allocation.
- Such external costs and benefits are known as 'externalities'.
- Externalities may occur in either production or consumption, thereby affecting either demand or supply.
- Externalities may be either positive or negative, but either way resources will not be optimally allocated if they are present.

Exercise 6.2

Discuss examples of some externalities that you meet in everyday situations, and classify them as affecting either production or consumption.

Examples of markets with externalities

Externalities occur in a wide variety of market situations, and constitute an important source of market failure. This means that externalities may hinder the achievement of good resource allocation from society's perspective. The rest of this chapter explores some examples of markets in which externalities may be present.

Externalities and the environment

Concern for the environment has been growing, with 'green' lobbyist groups drawing attention to the issues, sometimes through demonstrations. There are so many different facets to environmental concern that it is sometimes difficult to isolate the core issues. Externalities lie at the heart of much of the debate.

Global warming

Some of the issues are international in nature, such as global warming. At the heart of this concern is the way in which emissions of greenhouse gases are said to be warming up the planet. Sea levels are rising and major climate change seems imminent — if it is not already happening.

One reason why global warming is especially difficult to tackle is that actions taken by one country can have effects on other countries. Scientists argue that the problem is caused mainly by pollution created by transport and industry, especially in the richer countries. However, poorer nations suffer the consequences as well, especially countries such as Bangladesh. Here much of the land is low-lying and prone to severe flooding almost every year. In some years up to three-quarters of the land area is under water at the height of the flooding.

In principle, this is similar to example 1 in Exercise 6.1: it is an example of a negative production externality, in which the nations causing most of the damage face only part of the costs caused by their lifestyles and production processes. The inevitable result in an unregulated market is that too much pollution is produced.

When externalities cross international borders in this way, the problem can be tackled only through international cooperation. For example, at the Kyoto World Climate Summit held in Japan in 1997, almost every developed nation agreed to cut greenhouse gas emissions by 6% by 2010. The USA, the largest emitter of carbon dioxide, did not ratify the agreement, fearing the consequences of such a restriction for the US economy. The Kyoto Protocol was discussed at the 2012 Doha climate change talks and it was agreed to begin a new round of negotiations. In December 2015, 196 countries adopted the Paris Agreement, a new framework designed as a coordinated effort to tackle climate change. This seemed to be a major step forward in tackling climate change, but the agreement suffered a setback in 2017, when Donald Trump announced that the USA would withdraw from the agreement as soon as it was legal to do so. He argued that the deal reached had been unfair to the USA, threatening to cost the USA US$3 trillion in lost GDP and 6.5 million jobs. He kept open the possibility that the USA could re-join the agreement, if a new deal could be reached. The withdrawal would mean that the USA was effectively the only country in the world not to be signed up — and the USA is the second-largest emitter of carbon dioxide.

Acid rain

Global warming is not the only example of international externality effects. Scandinavian countries have suffered from acid rain caused by pollution in other European countries, including the UK. Forest fires left to burn in Indonesia have caused air pollution in the neighbouring countries of Singapore and Malaysia.

River water

Another environmental issue concerns rivers. Some of the big rivers of the world, such as the Nile in Africa, pass through several countries on their way to the sea.

> **Synoptic link**
>
> The impact of economic growth on the environment is discussed further in Chapter 14.

The Nile runs through Egypt at the end of its journey, and it is crucial for the economy. If countries further upstream were to increase their usage of the river, perhaps through new irrigation projects, this could have disastrous effects on Egypt. Again, the actions of one set of economic agents would be having damaging effects on others, and these effects would not be reflected in market prices, in the sense that the upstream countries would not have to face the full cost of their actions. In this example, Egypt is a third party.

Part of the problem here can be traced back to the difficulty of enforcing property rights. If the countries imposing the costs could be forced to make appropriate payment for their actions, this would help to bring the costs back within the market mechanism. Such a process is known in economics as 'internalising the externality'.

Biodiversity

Concern has also been expressed about the loss of *biodiversity*, a word that is shorthand for 'biological diversity'. The issue here is that when a section of rainforest is cleared to plant soya beans or for timber, it is possible that species of plants, insects or even animals whose existence is not even known at present may be wiped out. Many modern medicines are based on chemicals that occur naturally in the wild. By eradicating species before they have been discovered, possible scientific advances will be forgone. Notice that when it comes to measuring the value of what is being destroyed, biodiversity offers particular challenges — namely, the problem of putting a value on something that might not even be there.

Externalities and transport

The London authorities use the congestion charge to control traffic within the city. When traffic on the roads reaches a certain volume, congestion imposes heavy costs on road users. This is another example of an externality.

Figure 6.3 illustrates the situation. Suppose that D (MSB) represents the demand curve for car journeys along a particular stretch of road. When deciding whether or not to undertake a journey, drivers will balance the marginal benefit gained from making the journey against the marginal cost that they face. This is given by MPC — the marginal private cost of undertaking journeys. When the road is congested, a motorist who decides to undertake the journey adds to the congestion, and slows the traffic. The MPC curve incorporates the cost to the motorist of joining a congested road, and the chosen number of journeys will be at Q_1.

Synoptic link

Possible ways of dealing with the problems caused by externalities are discussed in Chapter 8.

Knowledge check 6.6

What sort of externality would be present if forests are cleared for timber in Indonesia or Brazil?

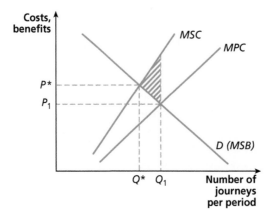

Figure 6.3 Traffic congestion

However, in adding to the congestion the motorist not only suffers the costs of congestion, but also imposes some marginal increase in costs on all other users of the road. Thus, the marginal social costs (MSC) of undertaking journeys are higher than the cost faced by any individual motorist. MSC is therefore higher than MPC. Society would be better off with lower congestion: that is, with the number of journeys undertaken being limited to $Q\star$, where marginal social benefit equals marginal social cost. By imposing a charge on motorists entering central London, the authorities are trying to ensure that drivers face at least part of the external costs they impose on others by using congested roads.

Knowledge check 6.7

All vehicles on UK roads must pay an annual road tax. Why might this not be an effective way of controlling congestion?

The congestion charge in London is an attempt to make drivers face some of the social costs of their journeys

Externalities and health

Healthcare is a sector in which there is often public provision, or at least some state intervention in support of the health services. In the UK, the National Health Service is the prime provider of healthcare, but private healthcare is also available, and the use of private health insurance schemes is on the increase. Again, externalities can help to explain why there is a need for government to intervene.

Consider the case of vaccination against a disease such as measles. Suppose an individual is considering whether or not to be vaccinated. Being vaccinated reduces the probability of that individual contracting the disease, so there are palpable potential benefits to that individual. However, these benefits must be balanced against the costs. There may be a direct charge for the vaccine, some individuals may have a phobia against needles, or they may be concerned about possible side-effects. Individuals will opt to be vaccinated only if the marginal expected benefit to them is at least as large as the marginal cost.

From society's point of view, however, there are potential benefits that individuals will not take into account. After all, if they do contract measles, there is a chance of their passing it on to others. Indeed, if lots of people decide not to be vaccinated, there is the possibility of a widespread epidemic, which would be costly and damaging to many.

Figure 6.4 illustrates this point. The previous paragraph argues that the social benefits to society of having people vaccinated against measles exceed the private benefits that will be perceived by individuals, so that marginal social benefits exceed marginal private benefits. Private individuals will choose to balance marginal private benefit against marginal private cost at Q_1, whereas society would prefer more people to be vaccinated at $Q^\star$. This parallels the discussion of a positive consumption externality.

Synoptic link

Another aspect of healthcare provision is explored in Chapter 7.

Knowledge check 6.8

Why might there be externality effects associated with smoking tobacco?

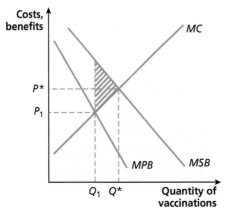

Figure 6.4 Vaccination

Externalities and education

As you are reading this textbook, it is reasonably safe to assume that you are following a course in economics. You have decided to demand education. This is yet another area in which externalities may be important.

When you decided to take A levels (including economics), there were probably a number of factors that influenced your decision. Perhaps you intend to demand even more education in the future, by going on to study at university. Part of your decision process probably takes into account the fact that education improves your future earnings potential. Your expected lifetime earnings depend in part on your level of qualifications. Research has shown that, on average, graduates earn more during their lifetimes than non-graduates. This is partly because there is a productivity effect: by becoming educated, you cultivate a range of skills that in later life will make you more productive, and this helps to explain why you can expect higher lifetime earnings than someone who chooses not to demand education. There is also a signalling effect, as having a degree signals to potential employers that you have the ability to cope with university study and have gained a range of skills.

What does society get out of this? Evidence suggests that, not only does education improve productivity, but a *group* of educated workers cooperating with each other become even more productive. This is an externality effect, as it depends on interaction between educated workers — but each individual perceives only the individual benefit, and not the benefits of cooperation.

In other words, when you decide to undertake education, you do so on the basis of the expected private benefits that you hope to gain from education. However, you do not take into account the external benefits through cooperation that society will reap. So here is another example of a positive consumption externality. As with healthcare, some other aspects of education will be discussed in Chapter 7.

Knowledge check 6.9

School drop-out rates tend to be high in some developing countries. What sort of externality effect might be at work here?

Waste disposal and recycling

A major problem faced by twenty-first-century society and governments is waste disposal. Landfill is one way of dealing with waste, but it has long-term effects on the environment, and imposes negative externalities on people living near landfill sites. Recycling is an alternative, but also suffers from externality effects. There are positive consumption externalities associated with recycling, in the sense that the benefits to society exceed the benefits to individuals (i.e. $MSB > MPB$). In such a situation, there will be 'too little' recycling relative to the best outcome for society, and the government or local authorities may need to find ways of encouraging households to recycle more.

Externalities and tourism

As international transport has become easier and cheaper, more people are wanting to travel to new and different destinations. For developing countries, this offers an opportunity to earn much-needed foreign exchange.

There has been some criticism of this. The building of luxury hotels in the midst of the poverty that characterises many developing countries is said to have damaging effects on the local population by emphasising differences in living standards.

However, constructing the infrastructure that tourists need may have beneficial effects on the domestic economy. Improved roads and communication systems can benefit local businesses. This effect can be interpreted as an externality, in the sense that the local firms will face lower costs as a result of the facilities provided for the tourist sector.

Knowledge check 6.10

What sort of externality is present if improved infrastructure yields benefits to local firms?

Summary: examples of externalities

- Externalities arise in many aspects of economic life.
- Environmental issues are especially prone to externality effects, as market prices do not always incorporate impacts on the environment, especially where property rights are not assigned.
- Congestion on the roads can also be seen as a form of externality.
- Externalities also arise in the areas of healthcare provision and education, where individuals do not always perceive the full social benefits that arise.

Exercise 6.3

Table 6.1 shows the situation in a market where pollution is generated by the production process.

Table 6.1 A market with pollution

Quantity produced (thousands per week)	Marginal social benefit (£)	Marginal private cost (£)	Marginal social cost(£)
10	80	5	10
20	75	10	20
30	70	20	35
40	60	32	60
50	48	48	90
60	30	75	125
70	8	110	175

a At what level of output would marginal social benefit be equal to marginal private cost? (Note: this is the quantity of output that would be produced by firms in an unregulated competitive market.)

b By how much would marginal social cost exceed marginal private cost at this level of output?

c At what level of output would marginal social benefit be equal to marginal social cost?

d What amount of tax would induce firms to supply this quantity of output?

Case study 6.1

Healthcare: public or market?

The NHS was founded in 1948. Seventy years on, it faces crisis, with much talk in the media about failures in providing care and long waiting lists. This has revitalised the debate about whether healthcare should be state-provided, or whether market forces should be given a greater role. In the UK, market forces have played an increasing part in allocating resources within the public health sector through the operation of internal markets, but the debate over public vs private provision continues. So far, the proportion of health expenditure that is undertaken by the public sector has changed little.

What does economic analysis have to say about the matter? The justification for public provision of healthcare rests on the existence of **market failure**. There are a number of reasons why there might be some form of market failure in the provision of healthcare, whether we consider the provision of preventative or curative measures.

In the case of preventative healthcare, there may be other factors at work. Take the case of vaccination against disease. If vaccinations are provided by a private competitive market, an individual faces costs of the treatment, both financial and perhaps in the unpleasantness and possible risks of being vaccinated. The benefits of having been vaccinated may be perceived to be relatively low, if the individual sees a low probability of being infected. However, the benefits of vaccination from the point of view of society may be greater,

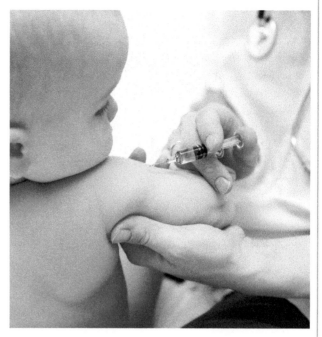

A vaccination programme has palpable benefits for society

because a widespread vaccination programme not only reduces the risk of infection for each individual, but also reduces the likelihood of an epidemic.

Follow-up questions

a Explain what is meant by **market failure**.

b Draw a diagram to help to explain the possible market failure outlined in relation to a vaccination programme.

Case study 6.2

Plastic oceans

The contamination of the natural marine environment by plastics has been increasing, causing a range of negative effects. These include endangering marine life, damaging maritime industries and infrastructure, and potentially having an impact on human wellbeing. This issue has been prominent in the media, and a succession of studies have sought to analyse the impact of plastics on the environment. A prime source of the contamination is litter — about 70% of litter in the oceans is made of plastic. In particular, much of this litter comprises single-use packaging, as well as rope, netting and sewage-related debris. A government report published in 2017 noted that if plastic litter continues to enter the marine environment at current rates, this would far exceed the possibility of clean-up removal.

Packaged goods have become a way of life, as any visit to the supermarket will demonstrate. It is cheap and convenient, and firms under pressure to keep their costs low in order to remain competitive are naturally reluctant to use more expensive but more environmentally friendly materials. This leads to a divergence between private and social costs.

Follow-up questions

a Draw a diagram to show the economic effect of plastic pollution on society.

b Discuss the problems in tackling this problem given that plastic in the ocean is occurring on a global scale.

Market failure: public goods and information gaps

Externalities are not the only form of market failure. There are also situations where the characteristics of a good or service can affect the effective operation of a market, causing the free market equilibrium to diverge from the socially optimum position. This chapter explores goods with unusual economic characteristics and markets that may fail as a result of problems with information.

Learning objectives

After studying this chapter, you should:

→ be aware of the distinction between private and public goods
→ understand the nature of public goods and problems that arise in their provision
→ be able to identify examples of public goods
→ appreciate how imperfect market information may be a source of market failure and a misallocation of resources

---

Key terms

private good a good that, once consumed by one person, cannot be consumed by somebody else; such a good has excludability and is rivalrous

non-excludability a situation in which it is not possible to provide a product to one person without allowing others to consume it as well

non-rivalry a situation in which one person's consumption of a good does not prevent others from consuming it as well

public good a good that is non-exclusive and non-rivalrous in consumption — consumers cannot be excluded from consuming the good, and consumption by one person does not affect the amount of the good available for others to consume

Private and public goods

Private goods

Most of the goods that individuals consume are **private goods**. You buy a can of Diet Coke, you drink it, and it's gone. You may choose to share it with a friend, but you do not have to: by drinking it you can prevent anyone else from doing so. Furthermore, once it is gone, it's gone: nobody else can subsequently consume that Coke.

The two features that characterise a private good are:

■ other people can be excluded from consuming it
■ once consumed by one person, it cannot be consumed by another

The first feature can be described as *excludability*, whereas the second feature might be described by saying that consumption of a private good is *rivalrous*: the act of consumption uses up the good.

Public goods

Not all goods and services have these two characteristics. There are goods that, once provided, are available to all. In other words, people cannot be excluded from consuming such goods. There are other goods that do not diminish through consumption, so they are non-rivalrous in consumption. Goods that have the characteristics of **non-excludability** and **non-rivalry** are known as **public goods**.

Examples of public goods that are often cited include street lighting, a lighthouse and a nuclear deterrent. For example, once street lighting has been provided in a particular street, anyone who walks along that street at night benefits from the lighting — no one can be excluded from consuming it. So street lighting is non-exclusive. In addition, the fact that one person has walked along the street does not mean that there is less street lighting left for later walkers. So street lighting is also non-rivalrous. Public goods may also be non-rejectable. If your government provides a nuclear deterrent, it will be there for you whether you want it or not.

The key feature of such a market is that, once the good has been provided, there is no incentive for anyone to pay for it — so the market will fail, as no firm will have an incentive to supply the good in the first place. This is often referred to as the **free-rider problem**, as individual consumers can free-ride and avoid having to pay for the good if it is provided.

Key term

free-rider problem when an individual cannot be excluded from consuming a good, and thus has no incentive to pay for its provision

Knowledge check 7.1

Name the two key characteristics of a public good.

Extension material: public goods

A key question is how well the market for a public good is likely to operate. In particular, will a free market reach a position where there is allocative efficiency, i.e. where price equals marginal social cost?

Think about the supply and demand curves for a public good such as street lighting. To simplify matters, suppose there are just two potential demanders of the good, person A and person B. Consider Figure 7.1. If it is assumed that the supply is provided in a competitive market, S represents the supply curve, reflecting the marginal cost of providing street lighting. The curves d_a and d_b represent the demand curves of the two potential demanders. For a given quantity Q_1, A would be prepared to pay P_a and B would pay P_b. If these prices are taken to be the value that each individual places on this amount of the good, then $P_a + P_b = P_T$ represents the social benefit derived from consuming Q_1 units of street lighting. Similarly, for any given quantity of street lighting, the marginal social benefit derived from consumption can be calculated as the vertical sum of the two demand curves. This is shown by the curve MSB. So, the optimal provision of street lighting is given by $Q^\star$, at which point the marginal social benefit is equated with the marginal cost of supplying the good.

However, if person A were to agree to pay P_a for the good, person B could then consume Q_1 of the good free of charge, but would not be prepared to pay in order for the supply to be expanded beyond this

point — as person B's willingness to pay is below the marginal cost of provision beyond this point. So the social optimum at $Q^\star$ cannot be reached. Indeed, when there are many potential consumers, the likely outcome is that none of this good will be produced: why should any individual agree to pay if he or she can free-ride on others?

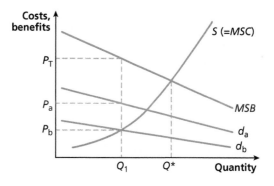

Figure 7.1 Demand and supply of a public good

The free-rider problem helps to explain why these sorts of goods have typically been provided through state intervention. This begs the question of how the state can identify the optimal quantity of the good to be provided — in other words, how the government determines $Q^\star$. The extent to which individuals value a particular good cannot be directly observed. However, by including statements about the provision of public goods in their election manifestos, politicians can collect views about public goods provision via the medium of the ballot box. This is an indirect method, but it provides some mandate for the government to take decisions.

Knowledge check 7.2

Explain the free-rider problem in the context of the provision of national defence.

Synoptic link

For developing countries, a key issue is how to improve their transport and communications infrastructure. This is discussed in Chapter 28, where it is argued that infrastructure may share some of the characteristics of a public good.

Knowledge check 7.3

Is it necessarily the case that a public good can only be provided directly by the government?

The free-rider problem makes it difficult to charge for a public good, so the private sector will be reluctant to supply such goods. In fact, pure public goods are relatively rare, but there are many goods that have some but not all of the required characteristics.

Other examples of public goods

In fact, there are many goods that are either non-rivalrous or non-excludable, but not both. One example of this is a football match. If I go to watch a premiership football match, my 'consumption' of the match does not prevent the person sitting next to me from also consuming it, so it is non-rivalrous; at least, for those attending the match. However, if I go along without my season ticket (or do not have a ticket), I can clearly be excluded from consuming the match, so it is *not* non-exclusive.

A stretch of road may be considered non-excludable, as road users are free to drive along it. However, it is not non-rivalrous, in the sense that as congestion builds up consumption is affected. This example is also imperfect as a public good because, by installing toll barriers, users can be excluded from consuming it.

Where goods have some features of a public good, the free market may fail to produce an ideal outcome for society. Exercise 7.1 provides some examples of goods: to what extent may each of these be considered to be non-rivalrous or non-excludable?

Exercise 7.1

For each of the following goods, think about whether they have elements of non-rivalry, non-excludability, both or neither:

a a national park

b a playground

c a theatre performance

d an apple

e a television programme

f a firework display

g police protection

h a lecture

i a DVD recording of a film

j the national defence

Tackling the public goods problem

For some public goods, the failure of the free market to ensure provision may be regarded as a serious problem — for example, in such cases as street lighting or law and order. Some government intervention may thus be needed to make sure that a sufficient quantity of the good or service is provided. Notice that this does not necessarily mean that the government has to provide the good itself. It may be that the government will raise funds through taxation in order to ensure that street lighting is provided, but could still make use of private firms to supply the good through some sort of subcontracting arrangement. In the UK, it may be that the government delegates the responsibility for provision of public goods to local authorities, which in turn may subcontract to private firms.

In some other cases, it may be that changes in technology may alter the economic characteristics of a good. For example, in the case of television programmes, originally provision was entirely through the BBC, funded by the licence fee. Subsequently, ITV set up in competition, using advertising as a way of funding its supply. The advent of satellite and digital broadcasting has reduced the degree to which television programmes are non-excludable, allowing private firms to charge for transmissions. For example, films and many sports events are available from Sky or BT only by subscription.

Summary: public goods

- A private good is one that, once consumed by one person, cannot be consumed by anyone else — it has characteristics of excludability and rivalry.
- A public good is non-exclusive and non-rivalrous.
- Because of these characteristics, public goods tend to be underprovided by a free market.
- One reason for this is the free-rider problem, whereby an individual cannot be excluded from consuming a public good, and thus has no incentive to pay for it.
- Public goods, or goods with some of the characteristics of public goods, must be provided with the assistance of the government or its agents.

Information gaps

If markets are to be effective in guiding resource allocation, it is important that economic decision-makers receive full and accurate information about market conditions. Ideally, all traders in a market should have the same information about market conditions — a situation known as **symmetric information**. Consumers need information about the prices at which they can buy and the quality of the products for sale. Producers need to be able to observe how consumers react to prices. Information is thus of crucial significance if markets are to work. However, there are some markets in which not all traders have access to good information, or in which some traders have more or better access to it than others. This is known as a situation of **asymmetric information**, and can be a source of market failure.

Healthcare

One example of asymmetric information is in healthcare. Suppose you go to your dentist for a check-up. He tells you that you have a filling that needs to be replaced, although you have had no pain or problems with it. In this situation the seller in a market has much better information about the product than the buyer. You as the buyer have no idea whether or not the recommended treatment is needed, and without going to another dentist for a second opinion you have no way of finding out. You might think this is an unsatisfactory situation, as it seems to give a lot of power to the seller relative to the consumer. The situation is even worse where the dentist does not even publish the prices for treatment until after it has been carried out! The Office of Fair Trading criticised private dentists for exactly this sort of practice when it reported on this market. Indeed, dentists are now required by law to publish prices for treatment.

The same argument applies in the case of other areas of healthcare, where doctors have better information than their patients about the sort of treatment that is needed.

Key terms

symmetric information a situation in which all participants in a market (buyers and sellers) have the same information about market conditions

asymmetric information a situation in which some participants in a market have better information about market conditions than others

Synoptic link

The responsibilities of the Office of Fair Trading are now part of the role of the Competition and Markets Authority, which is discussed in Chapter 23.

Knowledge check 7.4

To what extent does the 5 A Day campaign address the problem of obesity?

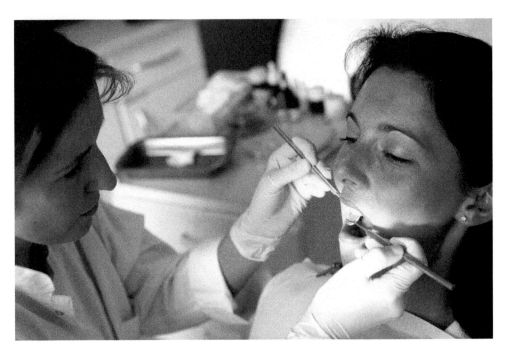

Dentists have better information than their patients about what treatments are needed

Tobacco

The market for tobacco is an interesting example of how imperfect market information can contribute to market failure. Chapter 5 discussed the effects of imposing an indirect tax on cigarettes (see Figure 5.6 on page 76). If you look back at the diagram, you will see that the impact of the tax is to raise the price of cigarettes significantly, with the incidence of the tax falling mainly on consumers. The problem with using a tax in this case is that the demand for cigarettes is inelastic, so a substantial tax has only a modest effect on the consumption of cigarettes.

Knowledge check 7.5

Explain why the demand for tobacco should be so inelastic.

One reason for this is that tobacco is addictive, but there is also an information gap present. The government took the view that, although the link between tobacco and ill health was proven, smokers had not fully assimilated the dangers, or were prepared to discount the future damage to their health in the short run. As a result, cigarette companies are required to add health warnings to cigarette packets in an attempt to correct the information gap. The controls on information became more and more stringent over time, with bans on advertising and open sales of cigarettes, not to mention the banning of smoking in public buildings — all because smokers failed to take heed of the information about the dangers of smoking and continued to rate the benefits of smoking more highly than was good for society.

Exercise 7.2

Ethel, an old-age pensioner, is sitting quietly at home when the doorbell rings. At the door is a stranger called Frank, who tells her that he has noticed that her roof is in desperate need of repair, and if she does not get something done about it very soon, there will be problems in the next rainstorm. Fortunately, he can help — for a price. Discuss whether there is a market failure in this situation, and what Ethel (or others) could do about it.

Education

The market for education is another example. Teachers or government inspectors may know more about the subjects and topics that students need to study than the students do themselves. This is partly because teachers are able to take a longer view and can see education provision in a broader perspective. Students taking economics at university may have to take a course in mathematics and statistics in their first year, and some will always complain that they have come to study economics, not maths. It is only later that they come to realise that competence in maths is crucial these days for the economics that they will study later in their course.

How could this problem be tackled? The answer would seem to be obvious — if the problem arises from an information gap, then the answer should be to improve the information flow, in this case to students. This might be achieved by providing a convincing explanation of why the curriculum has been designed in a particular way. It may also be necessary to provide incentives for students to study particular unpopular subjects, perhaps by making success a requirement for progression to the next stage of the course. By understanding the economic cause of a problem, it is possible to devise a strategy that should go some way towards removing the market failure.

There are also externality effects present in relation to education. As explained earlier, research has shown that educated workers are better able to cooperate and work together, becoming jointly more productive than they would be if they were working individually. Furthermore, there are other external benefits. Education has health spillovers because it brings a better understanding of nutrition and hygiene. It is also seen that when education levels in a society are high, crime rates tend to be lower and there is better-informed political debate and decision making. More schooling may enable more technological progress to be made. In other words, the social benefits of education may exceed the private benefits to the individuals who receive it.

Knowledge check 7.6

Students whose parents or relatives have attended university are much more likely to take up a university place than those from families where nobody has ever attended. To what extent could this be a result of an information gap?

Synoptic link

The externality effects of education were discussed in Chapter 6.

Second-hand cars

One of the most famous examples of asymmetric information relates to the second-hand ('pre-owned') car market. This is because the first paper that drew attention to the problem of asymmetric information, by Nobel laureate George Akerlof, focused on this market.

Akerlof argued that there are two types of car. Some cars are good runners and are totally reliable, whereas some are continually breaking down and needing parts and servicing; the latter are known as 'lemons' in the USA (allegedly from fruit machines, where lemons offer the lowest prize). The problem in the second-hand car market arises because the owners of cars (potential sellers) have better information about their cars than the potential buyers. In other words, when a car owner decides to sell a car, he or she knows whether it is a lemon or a good-quality car — but a buyer cannot tell.

In this sort of market, car dealers can adopt one of two possible strategies. One is to offer a high price and buy up all the cars in the market, knowing that the lemons will be sold on at a loss. The problem is that, if the lemons make up a large proportion of the cars in the market, this could generate overall losses for the dealers. The alternative is to offer a low price, and just buy up all the lemons to sell for scrap. In this situation, the market for good-quality used cars is effectively destroyed because owners of good-quality cars will not accept the low price — an extreme form of market failure!

Again, the solution may be to tackle the problem at its root, by finding a way to provide information. In the case of second-hand cars, AA inspection schemes or the offering of warranties may be a way of improving the flow of information about the quality of cars for sale.

Pensions

The market for pensions is another that is fraught with information problems by its very nature. Information gaps here arise from uncertainty and risk. Individuals face uncertainty in predicting their need for an adequate pension in the future, which depends on their state of health in the future, their longevity and so on. There is risk involved in the sense that pension funds depend critically on movements in the stock market. There is also the fact that there is a vast array of alternative pension schemes available, many of them very complex. This makes it very difficult for individuals to know how to take a rational decision — especially when their need for a pension is many years in the future. If people make bad decisions about pensions, this creates problems for the future, and society may find that it needs to cope with care for the elderly, especially when improvements in health mean that more people are living for longer. Regulations introduced in the UK requiring workers to be automatically enrolled in a workplace pension scheme (unless they consciously opt out) are one attempt to tackle this issue.

> ### Knowledge check 7.7
> Given that workers can opt out of workplace pensions schemes if they wish to, why would regulations about automatic enrolment be effective?

The insurance market

Key terms

adverse selection a situation in which a person at risk is more likely to take out insurance

moral hazard a situation in which a person who has taken out insurance is prone to taking more risk

People take out insurance to cover themselves against the risk of uncertain future events. Asymmetric information can cause problems with this market in two different ways. Suppose an individual approaches an insurance company wanting health insurance. The individual knows more about his or her health and health history than the insurance company. After all, the individual knows whether they are prone to illness or if they are accident-prone. This could mean that the people most likely to take out health insurance are the ones most likely to fall ill or be involved in accidents. This is known as **adverse selection**. A second type of information gap in terms of insurance is known as **moral hazard**. An individual who has taken out insurance may be more likely to take risks, knowing that he or she is covered by insurance. For example, if someone has taken out insurance against the loss of their mobile phone, they may be less careful about leaving it around.

> ### Synoptic link
> The insurance market and the notions of adverse selection and moral hazard are revisited in Chapter 30 in the context of financial markets, especially in Case study 30.1.

> ### Knowledge check 7.8
> A bank makes risky loans believing that it will be bailed out if it gets into trouble. Is this an example of adverse selection or moral hazard?

Extension material: merit and demerit goods

There are some goods that the government believes will be undervalued by consumers, so that too little will be consumed in a free market. In other words, individuals do not fully perceive the benefits that they will gain from consuming such goods, or do not have enough information to take decisions that are best for society. These are known as *merit goods*. One situation in which the merit good phenomenon arises is where the government is in a better position than individuals to take a long-term view of what is good for society. In particular, governments may need to take decisions on behalf of future generations as well as the present. Resources need to be used wisely in the present in order to protect the interests of tomorrow's citizens. Notice that this may require decision-makers to make normative judgements about the appropriate weighting to be given to the present as opposed to the future.

There is a strong political element involved in identifying the goods that should be regarded as merit goods: this is because there is a subjective or normative judgement involved, since declaring a good to be a merit good requires the decision-maker to make a choice on behalf of the population, which may be seen as being paternalistic.

Examples of merit goods include museums, libraries and art galleries. These are goods that are provided or subsidised because someone somewhere thinks that communities should have more of them. Economists are wary of playing the merit good card too often, as it entails such a high normative element. It is also sometimes difficult to disentangle merit good arguments from externality effects.

Notice that we could view tobacco as a *demerit good*. In other words, this is a good that the government believes is overvalued by consumers, so that too much of it is consumed in a free market.

Exercise 7.3

In 2012, the pharmaceutical company GlaxoSmithKline agreed to a $3 billion settlement in the largest health fraud case in the USA. This arose in part from a lawsuit about a clinical trial of one of its leading antidepressant drugs. The company had been accused of concealing evidence that the drug could be harmful to children. Discuss the extent to which this situation may have led to a market failure because of information problems.

Study tip

Be ready to discuss the key types of market failure that have been discussed:

- externalities
- public goods
- imperfect market information

Where possible, be ready with your own examples to show your understanding.

Exercise 7.4

Identify the form of market failure associated with each of the following:

a illegal fly-tipping
b the provision of a police officer on the beat
c vaccination against measles
d investment in new roads
e provision of higher education

Summary: information gaps

- Information gaps can lead to market failure in certain situations: for example, where some participants in a market have better information about some aspect(s) of the market than others.
- Examples of this include healthcare, education and second-hand cars.
- Asymmetric information can also result in problems of adverse selection and moral hazard.

Case study 7.1

The BBC in a digital world

A survey undertaken in the UK in 2015 found that the most popular leisure activity for people aged 8 years and over was consuming mass media (watching television, listening to music or reading). This activity outstripped all other leisure pursuits.

From an early stage, the UK government has been intimately involved in television broadcasting. At several points, there were calls for the government to take over the BBC (notably during the General Strike of 1926 and the Suez Crisis of 1956).

The major part of the BBC's income comes through a mandatory licence, which came to £3.8 billion in 2017. The government grants licences (via its regulator) to broadcasters. In exchange for the right to broadcast, these companies have to fulfil a number of obligations.

Why should the government be so involved in broadcasting? The basic reason is the existence of market failure: the idea that a freely functioning market in broadcasting will not produce the most socially desirable outcome. The issue is: why won't the free market, left unregulated, inform, educate and entertain? There are three main types of market failure relevant for broadcasting:

- broadcasting may have some characteristics of a public good
- the broadcasting market is highly concentrated, leading to market power
- consumption of broadcasting is subject to externalities

The broadcasting market has become even more complex with the growth of satellite and cable providers, not to mention the streaming services available. Nonetheless, the BBC continues to operate under its 2017 Charter which sets out its mission to 'act in the public interest, serving all audiences through the provision of impartial, high-quality and distinctive output and services which inform, educate and entertain'. This charter runs until 2027.

The BBC is publicly funded by the television licence fee

Follow-up questions

a Discuss the forms of market failure mentioned, and evaluate the extent to which they are potentially relevant to broadcasting.

b To what extent do you think that recent developments in the technology of broadcasting have affected these forms of market failure?

Case study 7.2

A common problem

In mediaeval times, it was not unusual for areas of land to be designated as a 'common'. The name still persists today in some regions — Wimbledon Common, for example. Before enclosure in the sixteenth century, many villages had areas of common land that could be used for grazing free of charge by the villagers. This land was thus non-excludable for the villagers, but not non-rivalrous, as there would be no limit on the amount of livestock that could be put to graze. Such conditions still exist in some developing countries today.

Follow-up questions

a How would you expect a market to develop if the good has these characteristics of being non-excludable but rivalrous?

b Give another example of where this problem could arise.

Case study 7.3

Paying for lighthouses

On the face of it, the lighthouse service seems to be a good example of a public good. In spite of the availability of accurate GPS systems that enable ships to know exactly where they are in relation to potential hazards, lighthouses continue to contribute significantly to marine safety.

Once a lighthouse has been constructed and is sending out its signal, all boats and ships that pass within the range of its light can benefit from the service. Furthermore, the fact that one ship has seen the lighthouse signal does not reduce the amount of light available to the next ship. This suggests that a lighthouse is a classic example of a public good.

As with all public goods, this raises the question of how to finance the lighthouse service. Of course, it could simply be taken into public ownership, and be funded by the taxpayer. However, this could be seen to be inequitable.

A levy system has thus been devised to pay for the lighthouse service. Ships must pay 'light dues' every time they enter or leave UK ports, and the fees collected (by Trinity House) are used to fund lighthouses, buoys and beacons around the coast. The level of the light dues is related to the size of individual ships, such that larger vessels pay a higher levy. Tugs and fishing vessels with a length below 10 metres and pleasure craft weighing less than 20 tons are exempt from the charges.

In principle, it could be argued that the existence of the light dues renders lighthouses excludable, as ships can be prevented from sailing if they have not paid their dues, and so could not consume the lighthouse services. However, there have been complaints from the shipping companies that small leisure craft that do not have to pay the charges make more use of the lighthouses than the larger vessels.

Nonetheless, this is one example of a charging system designed to try to overcome the free-rider problem associated with the provision of public goods.

Follow-up questions

a Explain why the second paragraph indicates that a lighthouse should be seen as a 'classic example of a public good'.

b Why would it be seen as inequitable to rely on general taxation to fund the lighthouse service?

c Discuss the effectiveness of the light dues system as a way of overcoming the free-rider problem.

Government intervention and government failure

The previous two chapters have examined forms of market failure, and have discussed the sorts of policy intervention that might be used to try to correct these market failures. This chapter reminds us of some of these interventions and explores how some well-intentioned interventions by government can sometimes produce unintended results — a situation that may be tantamount to government failure.

Learning objectives

After studying this chapter, you should:
→ be familiar with ways in which governments intervene in an attempt to address market failure
→ appreciate the role of government expenditure and state provision of goods and services
→ be able to identify areas in which government actions may have unintended distortionary effects
→ be aware of some sources of government failure
→ be familiar with the effects of price controls such as minimum alcohol prices and rent controls
→ be able to analyse the effects of sales taxes and subsidies

---

▌Correcting market failure

Key terms

market-based policy an approach to tackling market failure by using the market mechanism

regulation intervention to tackle market failure by direct action to command and control behaviour

Markets fail when the price mechanism causes an inefficient allocation of resources within a society. This occurs when price is not set equal to marginal cost, or where marginal social benefit is not equal to marginal social cost. In such circumstances, it seems apparent that by improving the way in which resources are allocated, the society could become better off. In other words, market failure is often viewed as a valid reason for governments to intervene in the economy. The focus in this chapter is on the ways in which governments may intervene to tackle market failure. Typically, such intervention takes one of two forms. One possibility is to is to adopt a **market-based policy**, influencing the behaviour of producers or consumers through the market mechanism. The alternative is to use **regulation**, influencing behaviour through direct controls.

Synoptic link

Chapters 6 and 7 explored what is meant by market failure and hinted at some possible solutions. Here, we explore government interventions in more detail, together with some possible unintended consequences.

Externalities

Chapter 6 looked at the problems caused by externalities, and discussed how these can occur in various different contexts. An externality occurs where the price mechanism fails to reflect the true costs or benefits associated with a product, thus imposing costs on (or providing benefits to) third parties. A market-based approach to tackling this problem is to internalise the externality, by bringing its effects into the market mechanism. For example, this might be done by making sure that firms that cause pollution face the true costs of their production activities. An alternative approach is to impose direct regulation that ensures that the appropriate level of output of a good is produced, perhaps by imposing limits on emissions of toxic gases, and imposing penalties or fines on firms that do not comply.

Public goods

The problem with public goods arises from the free-rider problem. When goods are non-exclusive and non-rivalrous, no individual has the incentive to pay. In such circumstances, some form of intervention is needed to ensure that a sufficient quantity of such public goods is produced. This intervention need not involve direct production by the government, but could include subsidies to local authorities or other bodies, funded by tax revenue.

Imperfect market information

A natural approach to tackling information problems is by providing information. This may take the form of government campaigns to spread information, or some form of regulation that requires firms to reveal information about their products. One example might be the regulations that require firms to specify ingredient lists on processed food products.

Study tip

When preparing your revision on government intervention and government failure, notice that governments intervene in markets in a variety of ways, and that you may need to look back at earlier chapters to draw together the material on these interventions. Do not forget that you may be called upon to evaluate such interventions as well as explaining them.

▌Government failure

Most governments see it as their responsibility to try to correct some of the failures of markets to allocate resources efficiently. As outlined above, this has led to a wide variety of policies being devised to address issues of market failure, such as taxes on polluting firms, levies to enable funding of public goods, or campaigns to combat information gaps. However, some policies have unintended effects that may not culminate in successful elimination of market failure. Indeed, in some cases government intervention may introduce new market distortions, leading to a phenomenon known as **government failure**. The remainder of this chapter examines some examples of such government failure.

Many of the measures outlined at the beginning of this chapter can cause problems if they are not carefully implemented, or if the government itself does not have sufficient information to take good decisions. For example, in the case of externalities, the government may choose to tackle pollution by a tax, or by regulation. However, if it is not possible to identify the appropriate amount of the tax that is needed to correct the market failure, or if it is not known how much pollution represents the optimum outcome for society, then it will not be possible to get the policy exactly right. Similar implementation problems may arise with other attempts to deal with market failure. However, government failure may arise in many other ways.

Knowledge check 8.1

What is meant by a negative production externality?

Synoptic link

Public goods were discussed in Chapter 7. Figure 5.8 on page 78 illustrates the effect of a subsidy on a market.

Knowledge check 8.2

What are the two key characteristics of a public good?

Key term

government failure a misallocation of resources arising from government intervention to correct a market failure that causes a less efficient allocation of resources and imposes a welfare loss on society

How would the imposition
of an *ad valorem* tax be
shown on a demand and
supply diagram?

Synoptic link

The effects of a sales tax
were discussed briefly in
Chapter 5. We now revisit
this discussion in order to
analyse the consequences
of this policy action.

Key term

indirect tax a tax levied
on expenditure on goods
or services (as opposed
to a direct tax, which is
a tax charged directly to
an individual based on a
component of income)

Sales taxes

Governments need to raise funds to finance the expenditure that they undertake. One way of doing this is through expenditure taxes such as value added tax (VAT) or excise duties on such items as alcohol or tobacco. You might think that raising money in this way to provide goods and services that would otherwise not be provided would be a benefit to society. But there is a downside to this action, even if all the funds raised by a sales tax are spent wisely. This is another example of government failure.

The effects of a sales tax can be seen in a demand and supply diagram. An **indirect tax** is paid by the seller, so it affects the supply curve for a product. Figure 8.1 illustrates the case of a fixed-rate or specific tax — a tax that is set at a constant amount per litre of petrol. Without the tax, the market equilibrium is at the intersection of demand and supply with a price of P_0 and a quantity traded of Q_0. The effect of the tax is to reduce the quantity that firms are prepared to supply at any given price — or, to put it another way, for any given quantity of petrol, firms need to receive the amount of the tax over and above the price at which they would have been prepared to supply that quantity. The effect is thus to move the supply curve upwards by the amount of the tax, as shown in the figure. We get a new equilibrium with a higher price at P_1 and a lower quantity traded at Q_1.

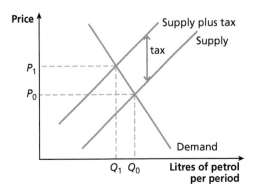

Figure 8.1 The effects of an indirect tax on petrol

To what extent is this good for society? The government has raised revenue as a result of the tax, so we might argue that the funds raised can be used in a way that benefits society as a whole. However, the picture is not quite so straightforward. Recall from Chapter 4 that an efficient allocation of resources is achieved when a market reaches an equilibrium such that the price of a product is equal to the marginal cost of producing it. This suggests that the market for petrol shown in Figure 8.1 has been moved away from this ideal state of affairs. It may thus arise that by imposing a tax to raise funds for correcting market failure in one part of the economy, the government introduces a misallocation of resources elsewhere.

Of course, it may be that in this particular market, the government has some other reason for wanting to reduce the consumption of petrol — perhaps because of congestion or pollution. However, this argument cannot be applied to many other markets in which indirect taxes are levied. After all, VAT is applied to almost all goods and services sold in the UK.

Knowledge check
8.4

If the government imposes
a specific tax on a good,
would consumption of
the good decrease or
increase?

Indirect taxes on petrol can be used to reduce consumption

Extension material: sales taxes

Is it possible to identify how a sales tax will affect total welfare in society? Consider Figure 8.2, which shows the market for games consoles. Suppose that the government imposes a specific tax on games consoles. This would have the effect of taking market equilibrium from the free market position at $P\star$ with quantity traded at $Q\star$ to a new position, with price now at P_t and quantity traded at Q_t. Remember that the price rises by less than the amount of the tax, implying that the incidence of the tax falls partly on buyers and partly on sellers. In Figure 8.2 consumers pay more of the tax (the area $P\star P_t BE$) than the producers (who pay $FP\star EG$). The effect on society's overall welfare will now be examined.

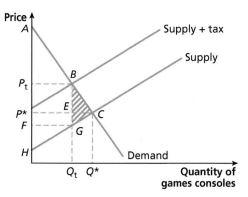

Figure 8.2 A sales tax and economic welfare

Remember that the total welfare that society receives from consuming a product is the sum of consumer and producer surplus. The situation before and after the sales tax is as follows. Before the tax, consumer surplus is given by the area $AP\star C$ and producer surplus is given by the triangle $P\star CH$. How about afterwards? Consumer surplus is now the smaller triangle $AP_t B$, and producer surplus is FGH. The area $P_t BGF$ is the revenue raised by the government from the tax, which should be included in total welfare on the assumption that the government uses this wisely. The total amount of welfare is now $ABGH$. If you compare these total welfare areas before and after the tax, you will realise that they differ by the area BCG. This triangle represents a deadweight loss that arises from the imposition of the tax. It is sometimes referred to as the excess burden of the tax.

So, even where the government intervenes to raise funding for its expenditure — and spends wisely — a distortion is introduced to resource allocation, and society must bear a loss of welfare.

A subsidy also entails a welfare loss. If you look back at Figure 5.8 on page 78, the welfare loss is represented by the orange shaded triangle. This is part of the cost of providing the subsidy that cannot be recovered by either producers or consumers.

Key terms

internalising an externality an attempt to deal with an externality by bringing an external cost or benefit into the price system

'polluter pays' principle an argument that a firm causing pollution should be charged the full external cost that they inflict on society

Dealing with externalities

Chapter 6 showed how externalities arise in situations where there are items of cost or benefit associated with transactions that are not reflected in market prices. In these circumstances a free market will not lead to an optimum allocation of resources. One approach to dealing with such market situations is to bring those externalities into the market mechanism — a process known as **internalising an externality**. The London congestion charge may be seen as an attempt to internalise the externality effects of traffic congestion. In the case of pollution, this principle would entail forcing the polluting firms to face the full social cost of their production activities. This is sometimes known as the **'polluter pays' principle**.

Pollution: an example of an externality

Imposing a tax

Figure 8.3 illustrates a negative production externality: pollution. Suppose that firms in the market for chemicals use a production process that emits toxic fumes, thereby imposing costs on society that the firms themselves do not face. In other words, the marginal private costs faced by these firms are less than the marginal social costs that are inflicted on society. As explained in Chapter 6, firms in a market in this situation will choose to produce up to point Q_1 and charge a price of P_1 to consumers. At this point, marginal social benefit is below the marginal cost of producing the chemicals, so it can be claimed that 'too much' of the product is being produced — that society would be better off if production were at $Q^\star$, with a price charged at $P^\star$.

Synoptic link

As explained in Chapter 6, this is a situation in which the free market equilibrium results in too much output relative to the socially optimum position.

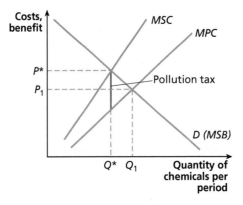

Figure 8.3 Pollution

Note that this optimum position is not characterised by zero pollution. In other words, from society's point of view it pays to abate pollution only up to the level where the marginal benefit of reducing pollution is matched by the marginal cost of doing so. Reducing pollution to zero would be too costly.

Knowledge check 8.5

What would be the effect if the government overestimated the size of the tax needed to discourage pollution?

How can society reach the optimum output of chemicals at $Q^\star$? The 'polluter pays' principle argues that polluters should face the full external costs caused by their actions. One approach would be to impose a tax on firms in line with this principle. In Figure 8.3, if firms were required to pay a tax equivalent to the vertical distance between marginal private cost (*MPC*) and marginal social cost (*MSC*), they would choose to produce at $Q^\star$, paying a tax equal to the pink line on the figure.

Emissions reduction

An alternative way of looking at this question is via a diagram showing the marginal benefit and marginal cost of emissions reduction. In Figure 8.4 *MB* represents the marginal social benefits from reducing emissions of some pollutant and *MC* is the marginal costs of reducing emissions. The optimum amount of reduction is found where marginal benefit equals marginal cost, at e^*. Up to this point, the marginal benefit to society of reducing emissions exceeds the marginal cost of the reduction, so it is in the interest of society to reduce pollution. However, beyond that point the marginal cost of reducing the amount of pollution exceeds the benefits that accrue, so society will be worse off. Setting a tax equal to t^* in Figure 8.4 will induce firms to undertake the appropriate amount of emission reduction.

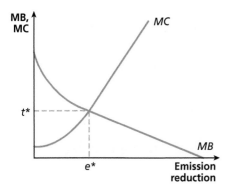

Figure 8.4 Reducing the emission of toxic fumes

This is not the only way of reaching the objective, however. Figure 8.4 suggests that there is another possibility — namely, to impose environmental standards, and to prohibit emissions beyond e^*. This amounts to controlling quantity rather than price; and, if the government has full information about marginal costs and marginal benefits, the two policies will produce the equivalent result.

Measuring benefits and costs

Either of the approaches outlined above will be effective — *if* the authorities have full information about the marginal costs and benefits. But how likely is this? There are many problems with this proviso. The measurement of both marginal benefits and marginal costs is fraught with difficulties.

The marginal social benefits of reducing pollution cannot be measured with great precision, for many reasons. It may be argued that there are significant gains to be made in terms of improved health and lower death rates if pollution can be reduced, but quantifying this is not straightforward. Even if it were possible to evaluate the saving in resources that would need to be devoted to future medical care resulting from the pollution, there are other considerations: quantification of the direct improvements to quality of life; whether or not to take international effects into account when formulating domestic policy; and the appropriate discount rate for evaluating benefits that will be received in the future. Moreover, the environmentalist and the industrialist may well arrive at different evaluations of the benefits of pollution control, reflecting their different viewpoints.

The measurement of costs may also be problematic. For example, it is likely that there will be differences in efficiency between firms. Those using modern technology may face lower costs than those using relatively old capital equipment. Do the authorities try to set a tax that is specific to each firm to take such differences into account? If they do not, but instead set a flat-rate tax, then the incentives may be inappropriate. This would mean that a firm using modern technology would face the same tax as one using old capital. The firm using new capital would then tend to produce too little output relative to those using older, less efficient capital.

Tradable pollution permits

Key term

tradable pollution permit system a system for controlling pollution based on a market for permits that allow firms to pollute up to a limit

Another approach is to use a **tradable pollution permit system**, under which the government issues or sells permits to firms, allowing them to pollute up to a certain limit. These permits are then tradable, so that firms that are relatively 'clean' in their production methods and do not need to use their full allocation of permits can sell their polluting rights to other firms, whose production methods produce greater levels of pollution.

Advantages

One important advantage of such a scheme lies in the incentives for firms. Firms that pollute because of their relatively inefficient production methods will find they are at a disadvantage because they face higher costs. Rather than continuing to purchase permits, they will find that they have an incentive to produce less pollution — which, of course, is what the policy is intended to achieve. In this way, the permit system uses the market to address the externality problem — in contrast to direct regulation of environmental standards, which tries to solve pollution by overriding the market.

A second advantage is that the overall level of pollution can be controlled by this system, as the authorities control the total amount of permits that are issued. After all, the objective of the policy is to control the overall level of pollution, and a mixture of 'clean' and 'dirty' firms may produce the same amount of total emissions as uniformly 'slightly unclean' firms.

Disadvantages

However, the permit system may not be without its problems. In particular, there is the question of enforcement. For the system to be effective, sanctions must be in place for firms that pollute beyond the permitted level, and there must be an operational and cost-effective method for the authorities to check the level of emissions.

Furthermore, it may not be a straightforward exercise for the authorities to decide on the appropriate number of permits to issue in order to produce the desired reduction in emission levels. Some alternative regulatory systems share this problem, as it is not easy to measure the extent to which marginal private and social costs diverge.

One possible criticism that is unique to a permit form of regulation is that the very different levels of pollution produced by different firms may seem inequitable — as if those firms that can afford to buy permits can pollute as much as they like. On the other hand, it might be argued that those most likely to suffer from this are the polluting firms, whose public image is likely to be tarnished if they acquire a reputation as heavy polluters. This possibility might strengthen the incentives of such firms to clean up their production. Taking the strengths and weaknesses of this approach together, it seems that on balance such a system could be effective in regulating pollution.

The EU Emissions Trading System

An example of a permit system is the EU Emissions Trading System (EU ETS), which has been in operation since 2005. It now operates in 31 countries, and limits carbon emissions from more than 11,000 energy-using installations. The system works on a 'cap and trade' system. A cap is set on the total amount of greenhouse gases that can be emitted by installations that are part of the scheme, with the cap being reduced over time. Companies in the scheme receive or buy emission allowances that can then be traded with other firms. The scheme is seen as having had success in reducing emissions. By 2020 emissions are expected to be 21% lower compared with 2015.

Global warming

Global warming is widely seen to require urgent and concerted action at a worldwide level. The Kyoto summit of 1997 laid the foundations for action, with almost all developed nations agreeing to take action to reduce emissions of carbon dioxide and other 'greenhouse' gases that are seen to be causing climate change. This was discussed in Chapter 6 (see page 87), where it was noted that although virtually every country in the world had signed up to the Paris Agreement by 2018, the USA announced that it was withdrawing until it could negotiate a fairer deal. This demonstrates the difficulties of tackling externalities where the effects cross international borders.

The NIMBY syndrome

One problem that arises in trying to deal with externalities is that you cannot please all of the people all of the time. For example, it may well be that it is in society's overall interests to relocate unsightly facilities — it may even be that everyone would agree about this; but such facilities have to be located somewhere, and someone is almost bound to object because they are the ones to suffer. This is the **NIMBY (not in my back yard)** syndrome.

For example, many people would agree that it is desirable for the long-run sustainability of the economy that cleaner forms of energy are developed. One possibility is to build wind farms. People may well be happy for these to be constructed — as long as they do not happen to be living near them.

Exercise 8.1

You discover that your local authority has chosen to locate a new landfill site for waste disposal close to your home. What costs and benefits for society would result? Would these differ from your private costs and benefits? Would you object?

Property rights

The existence of a system of secure property rights is essential as an underpinning for the economy. The legal system exists in part to enforce property rights, and to provide the set of rules under which markets operate. When property rights fail, there is a failure of markets.

One of the reasons underlying the existence of some externalities is that there is a failing in the system of property rights. For example, think about the situation

Knowledge check 8.6

Why is international cooperation so important in tackling climate change?

Study tip

Try to keep up to date with recent developments in environmental policy, as it is good to show examiners that you can apply your economic thinking to events in the world around us.

Key term

NIMBY (not in my back yard) a syndrome under which people are happy to support the construction, of an unsightly or unsocial facility, so long as it is not in their back yard

Knowledge check 8.7

Provide another example of the NIMBY syndrome.

in which a factory is emitting toxic fumes into a residential district. One way of viewing this is that the firm is interfering with local residents' clean air. If those residents could be given property rights over clean air, they could require the firm to compensate them for the costs it was inflicting. However, the problem is that, with such a wide range of people being affected to varying degrees, (according to prevailing winds and how close they live to the factory), it is impossible in practical terms to use the assignment of property rights to internalise the pollution externality. This is because the problem of coordination requires high transaction costs in order for property rights to be individually enforced. It may also be difficult to introduce property rights into a situation where none has previously existed. Therefore, the government effectively takes over the property rights on behalf of the residents, and acts as a collective enforcer.

Nobel Prize winner Ronald Coase argued that externality effects could be internalised in conditions where property rights could be enforced, and where the transaction costs of doing so were not too large.

Summary: tackling externalities

- In seeking to counter the harmful effects of externalities, governments look for ways of internalising the externality, by bringing external costs and benefits within the market mechanism.
- For example, the 'polluter pays' principle argues that the best way of dealing with a pollution externality is to force the polluter to face the full costs of its actions.
- Attempts have been made to tackle pollution through taxation, the regulation of environmental standards and the use of pollution permits.
- In some cases the allocation of property rights can be effective in curbing the effects of externalities — so long as the transaction costs of implementing it are not too high.

Government expenditure and state provision

Expenditure taxes are not only imposed to address perceived market failure, but also to help finance the government's expenditure. This includes expenditure on the administration of government, but also to enable transfer payments to be made in order to affect the distribution of income in a society — protecting the vulnerable and addressing poverty that may exist.

Chapter 7 discussed public goods, and argued that the free-rider problem would prevent the provision of public goods by the private sector in a free market. This does not mean that the government itself needs to provide such goods, but expenditure may be needed to encourage the private sector to provide public goods.

Maintaining an appropriate balance between the public and private sectors is one of the fundamental dilemmas of government. For private firms to operate effectively and to compete in international markets, they need access to public goods such as a good transport and communications infrastructure. If the government does not put sufficient resources into road maintenance, or the development of the rail network, then firms may face higher costs, and be disadvantaged relative to their international competitors. On the other hand, if the government over-invests, then there is an opportunity cost, because more resources used for infrastructure implies that fewer resources are available for private sector investment.

Knowledge check 8.8

What is the free-rider problem?

HS2 is a project designed to provide a high-speed rail link between London and Birmingham, which will be extended to Manchester, Sheffield and Leeds. The first passengers to use HS2 are expected in 2026. Estimates of the cost have varied — the budget for the project in late 2017 was £55.7 billion, but some critics have claimed that it could cost £200 billion. The project has been highly contentious, raising questions about value for money as well as specifics about the route — and whether this is the best way of using the funds. The whole debate provides an example of the tension that can arise when the government seeks to invest heavily in specific projects.

Government plans to invest in the HS2 rail link has sparked large-scale protests

Price controls

In some markets, governments have been seen to intervene to regulate price directly. This could be viewed as a response to market failure — for example, if it were apparent that price was not being set equal to marginal cost. Some governments in developing countries have at times intervened to control food prices in urban areas in response to civil unrest. This can create a form of government failure if it provides weak incentives for farmers to raise production or improve their crops.

Regulation of prices has also been introduced in other contexts, notably in the housing market, where rent controls have been used to prevent exploitation of tenants by landlords. There have also been proposals to set minimum prices for alcohol in an attempt to control drinking.

A minimum price for alcohol

Can problems caused by excessive drinking of alcohol be tackled by setting minimum prices for alcoholic drinks? Figure 8.5 represents the market.

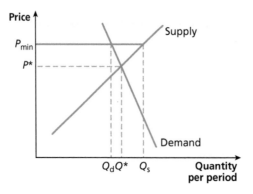

Figure 8.5 A minimum price for alcohol?

In equilibrium, the market price would be at $P\star$, and the quantity traded would be $Q\star$. If the government want to discourage heavy drinking, they could introduce a minimum price, so that sellers were not able to charge a price below P_{min}.

Quantitative skills 8.1

Interpreting quantities on a graph

Figure 8.5 shows a market in disequilibrium, and it is helpful to be able to read off the relevant quantities. The equilibrium position is of course at the point where demand and supply intersect, at $P*$, $Q*$. However, if the price is set by government to be at least P_{min}, the market is held away from that equilibrium. Buyers and sellers now want different things. Buyers are only prepared to buy Q_d at this price, whereas suppliers would be prepared to sell Q_s.

One effect of the minimum price is therefore that there is excess supply, given by the distance $Q_s - Q_d$.

What is happening here is that, with the minimum price in effect, *some* consumers reduce their consumption: alcohol consumption falls by the distance $Q* - Q_d$.

Whether this would be seen as a successful policy is a different matter. As Figure 8.5 has been drawn the demand for alcohol is relatively inelastic with respect to the increase in price. If demand had been relatively more elastic, the impact would have been greater.

Rent controls

Another market in which governments have been tempted to intervene is the housing market. Figure 8.6 represents the market for rented accommodation. The free market equilibrium would be where demand and supply intersect, with the equilibrium rent being $R\star$ and the quantity of accommodation traded being $Q\star$.

If the government regards the level of rent as excessive, to the point where households on low incomes may be unable to afford rented accommodation, then, given that housing is one of life's necessities, it may regard this as unacceptable.

The temptation for the government is to move this market away from its equilibrium by imposing a maximum price (level of rent) that landlords are allowed to charge their tenants. Suppose that this level of rent is denoted by R_{max} in Figure 8.6. Again, there are two effects that follow. First, landlords will no longer find it profitable to supply as much rental accommodation, and so will reduce supply to Q_s. Second, at this lower rent there will be more people looking for accommodation, so that demand for rented accommodation will move to Q_d. The upshot of the rent controls, therefore, is that there is less accommodation available, and there are more homeless people.

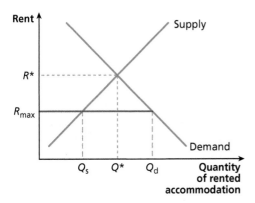

Figure 8.6 Rent controls

It can be seen that the well-meaning rent control policy, intended to protect low-income households from being exploited by landlords, merely has the effect of reducing the amount of accommodation available. This is not what was supposed to happen.

Exercise 8.2

The markets for rented and owner-occupied dwellings are likely to be interrelated, at least to some extent. Use demand and supply diagrams to examine how a rent control policy would affect the two markets in the short and long run.

Legislation and regulation

In some markets, the government chooses to intervene directly through legislation and regulation, rather than by influencing prices. For example, it may limit the market power of large firms to protect consumers, or place direct controls on the emission of pollution.

Prohibition

An extreme form of this is to declare some goods illegal. This may also have unintended effects. Consider the situation in which action is taken to prohibit the consumption of a good. Consider the case of a hard drug, such as cocaine. It can be argued that there are substantial social disbenefits arising from the consumption of hard drugs, and that addicts and potential addicts are in no position to make informed decisions about their consumption of them. One response to such a situation is to consider making the drug illegal — that is, to impose **prohibition**.

Figure 8.7 shows how the market for cocaine might look. You may wonder why the demand curve takes on this shape. The argument is that there are two types of cocaine user. There are the recreational users, who will take cocaine if it is available

Key term

prohibition an attempt to prevent the consumption of a good by declaring it illegal

at a reasonable price, but who are not addicts. In addition, there is a hard core of habitual users who are addicts, whose demand for cocaine is highly inelastic. Thus, at low prices demand is relatively elastic because of the presence of the recreational users, who are relatively price sensitive. At higher prices the recreational users drop away, and demand from the addicts is highly price inelastic. Suppose that the supply in free market equilibrium is given by S_0; the equilibrium will be with price P_0 and quantity traded Q_0. If the drug is made illegal, this will affect supply. Some dealers will leave the market to trade in something else, and the police will succeed in confiscating a certain proportion of the drugs in the market. However, they are unlikely to be totally successful, so supply could move to, say, S_1.

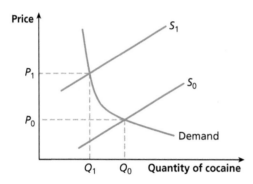

Figure 8.7 Prohibition

In the new market situation, price rises substantially to P_1, and quantity traded falls to Q_1. However, what has happened is that the recreational users have dropped out of the market, leaving a hard core of addicts who will pay any price for the drug, and who may resort to muggings and robberies in order to finance their habit. Smuggling and illicit production may also be encouraged. This behaviour clearly imposes a new sort of externality on society. And the more successful the police are in confiscating supplies, the higher the price will be driven. There may thus be disadvantages in using prohibition as a way of discouraging consumption of a good where its consumption is seen as damaging society.

Tackling information gaps

Asymmetric information

Knowledge check 8.9

What is meant by 'asymmetric information'?

Market failure can arise from information gaps, especially where there is asymmetric information or where economic agents lack information or the capacity to process the information available. In such circumstances, the solution would seem to be to find a way of providing the information to remedy the situation.

One example discussed in Chapter 7 was that of second-hand cars, where car dealers may find that they cannot find buyers for good-quality cars at a fair price if potential buyers cannot distinguish quality. The solution here may be to tackle the problem at its root, by finding a way to provide information about quality. In the case of second-hand cars, AA inspection schemes or the offering of warranties may be a way of improving the flow of information about the quality of cars for sale. Buyers may then have confidence that they are not buying a lemon.

Similarly, in the case of the insurance market, the asymmetric information problem helps to explain why insurance companies try to cover themselves by insisting on comprehensive health histories of those who take out health insurance, and include exclusion clauses that entitle them to refuse to pay out if past illnesses have not been disclosed. It also helps to explain why banks may insist on collateral to back up loans.

Smoking

Information problems may also be present in respect of some goods. Think back to the tobacco example discussed in Chapter 7. Tobacco is seen by government as a 'demerit' good on the grounds that smokers underestimate the damaging effects of smoking. There may also be negative externalities caused by passive smoking. At first, taxes were used to try to discourage smoking, but given the inelastic demand for tobacco, this proved ineffective. The taxes were reinforced by extensive campaigns to spread information about the damaging effects of smoking. When even this did not solve the problem, the government had to introduce regulation by prohibiting smoking in public buildings. The spread of e-cigarettes adds a new dimension to the situation.

The negative externalities caused by passive smoking led the government to introduce a no-smoking ban in public places

▌Costs of intervention

Some roles are critical for a government to perform if a mixed economy is to function effectively. A vital role is the provision by the government of an environment in which markets can operate effectively. There must be stability in the political system if firms and consumers are to take decisions with confidence about the future. And there must be a secure system of property rights, without which markets could not be expected to work.

In addition, there are sources of market failure that require intervention. This does not necessarily mean that governments need to substitute markets with direct action. However, it does mean that they need to be more active in markets that cannot operate effectively, while at the same time performing an enabling role to encourage markets to work well whenever this is feasible.

Such intervention entails costs. There are costs of administering and of monitoring the policy to ensure that it is working as intended. This includes the need to look out for the unintended distortionary effects that some policies can have on resource allocation in a society. It is therefore important to check that the marginal costs of implementing and monitoring policies do not exceed their marginal benefits.

Summary: government failure

- Government failure can occur when well-meaning intervention by governments has unintended effects.
- Rent controls may have the effect of reducing the amount of accommodation available.
- A sales tax imposes an excess burden on society.
- Prohibition may also have unintended effects.
- Governments have often regarded it as desirable to intervene in agricultural markets to sustain food production and stabilise prices.

Case study 8.1

Who pays taxes?

This may sound like a simple question, but many politicians do not seem to know the answer. Nor do a great many journalists. In fact, if there is one important economic concept that almost no one seems to understand, it is tax incidence — the economic study of who really pays taxes.

You might think it is easy to work out who pays tax — just look at who is handing over the money. Beer drinkers pay alcohol duties when they buy a pint, businesses pay corporation tax when they file their accounts (unless they can find a way of avoiding doing so, as highlighted by the media in some high-profile cases in the mid 2010s). It all seems so straightforward. But this is where an economist has to dig a little deeper. Consider the case of indirect taxes like VAT or the tax on alcohol. Who pays this tax?

To understand who is really paying a tax, we have to understand that both sides of the market (producers and consumers, or employers and employees) are trying to shift the burden of the tax on to the other side.

Suppose the government is worried about drunkenness in society, and introduces a new tax on vodka, intended to be paid by the consumer when they buy their bottle of Smirnoff at the off-licence. Will the vodka drinker have to bear the whole burden of the tax?

An alternative approach was adopted by Russia in the mid-1980s, when the newly elected leader Mikhail Gorbachev launched a sobriety campaign. The majority of liquor shops were closed, alcohol was completely banned at wedding parties, and individuals found to be drunk at work or in public were prosecuted.

Follow-up questions

a Draw a demand and supply diagram to examine how much of the new vodka tax will be paid by the consumer, and how much by the producer. How would your answer differ if the demand for vodka were perfectly inelastic?

b How would you expect the market for vodka to react to reforms such as those introduced by Gorbachev?

Case study 8.2

A bitter-sweet tax?

In his 2016 Budget, George Osborne, the then chancellor of the exchequer, announced a new tax intended to tackle the growing problem of childhood obesity. This soon became popularly known as the 'sugar tax', although the levy targets the producers and importers of sugary soft drinks, not sugar and other products that contain sugar. The Soft Drinks Industry Levy came into effect on 6 April 2018.

According to the government:

'This is not a tax on consumers. The government is not increasing the price of products; companies don't have to pass the charge on to their customers. If companies take the right steps to make their drinks healthier they will pay less tax, or even nothing at all.'

(www.gov.uk/government/news/soft-drinks-industry-levy-12-things-you-should-know)

The levy is charged at different rates according to the total sugar content, with companies having to pay 18p per litre of drink if the product contains more than 5 grams of sugar per 100 millilitres, and 24p per litre if it contains more than 8 grams per millilitre. Pure fruit juices and drinks with a high milk content are exempt.

When originally announced, it was thought that revenue from the levy would be in the region of £520 million, which was intended to be used to encourage children to participate in sport. However, on the day the levy came into effect, this estimate had been reduced to £240 million.

Some firms had taken action before the introduction of the levy, by cutting the sugar content of their drinks — in some cases attracting complaints from their consumers.

Several other countries have also introduced similar levies. For example, in Mexico it was found that a 10% tax led to a 6% reduction in sales of sugar-sweetened drinks in 2014 (the figure for lower income households was a reduction of 9%). The Danish experience of a so-called 'fat tax' was less successful, and was repealed after just a year of operation.

Follow-up questions

a Would you expect the manufacturers of sugary drinks to absorb all of the levy, or would they pass some of the cost on to consumers? Explain your answer.

b Discuss the sort of market failure that the government was trying to tackle through the levy.

c The estimated revenue from the levy was much lower at the time of its launch than had been originally been envisaged. Discuss whether this is an indication that the levy was not working.

Theme 1 key terms

ad valorem tax a sales tax that is set at a percentage of the price

adverse selection a situation in which a person at risk is more likely to take out insurance

allocative efficiency achieved when society is producing an appropriate bundle of goods relative to consumer preferences

asymmetric information a situation in which some participants in a market have better information about market conditions than others

bounded rationality a situation in which people's ability to take rational decisions is limited by a lack of information or an inability to interpret the information that is available, perhaps because of weakness at computation

capital goods goods used as part of the production process, such as machinery or factory buildings

cartel an agreement between firms in a market on price and output with the intention of maximising their joint profits

ceteris paribus a Latin phrase meaning 'other things being equal'; it is used in economics when we focus on changes in one variable while holding other influences constant

command economy an economy in which decisions on resource allocation are guided by the state

competitive market a market in which individual firms cannot influence the price of the good or service they are selling, because of competition from other firms

complements two goods are said to be complements if an increase in the price of one good causes the demand for the other good to fall

consumer goods goods produced for present use (consumption)

consumer surplus the value that consumers gain from consuming a good or service over and above the price paid

consumption externality an externality that affects the consumption side of a market, which may be either positive or negative

cross elasticity of demand (XED) a measure of the sensitivity of quantity demanded of a good or service to a change in the price of some other good or service

demand the quantity of a good or service that consumers are willing and able to buy at any given price in a given period of time

demand curve a graph showing how much of a good will be demanded by consumers at any given price

diminishing marginal utility describes the situation where an individual gains less additional utility from consuming a product, the more of it is consumed

division of labour a process whereby the production procedure is broken down into a sequence of stages, and workers are assigned to a particular stage

elastic a term used when the price elasticity of demand is greater than 1 but less than infinity

elasticity a measure of the sensitivity of one variable to changes in another variable

external benefit the benefit that society receives over and above those that accrue to the individual engaged in an economic activity

external cost a cost associated with an individual's (a firm or household's) production or other economic activities, which is borne by a third party and is not reflected in market prices

externality a cost or a benefit that is external to a market transaction, and is thus not reflected in market prices, which may affect third parties not involved in the transaction

factors of production resources used in the production process; inputs into production, particularly including labour, capital, land and enterprise

firm an organisation that brings together factors of production in order to produce output

free market economy an economy in which market forces are allowed to guide the allocation of resources

free-rider problem when an individual cannot be excluded from consuming a good, and thus has no incentive to pay for its provision

government failure a misallocation of resources arising from government intervention to correct a market failure that causes a less efficient allocation of resources and imposes a welfare loss on society

gross domestic product (GDP) a measure of the economic activity carried out in an economy over a period

habitual behaviour where consumers persist in acting in a particular way even when conditions have changed

herding where people take decisions based on the actions of others, rather than on a rational evaluation of the situation that they face

incidence of a tax the way in which the burden of paying a sales tax is divided between buyers and sellers

income elasticity of demand (YED) a measure of the sensitivity of quantity demanded to a change in consumer incomes

indirect tax a tax levied on expenditure on goods or services (as opposed to a direct tax, which is a tax charged directly to an individual based on a component of income)

inelastic a term used when the price elasticity of demand is less than 1 but greater than zero

inferior good one where the quantity demanded decreases in response to an increase in consumer incomes

internalising an externality an attempt to deal with an externality by bringing an external cost or benefit into the price system

law of demand a law that states that there is an inverse relationship between quantity demanded and the price of a good or service, ceteris paribus

luxury good one for which the income elasticity of demand is positive, and greater than 1, such that as income rises, consumers spend proportionally more on the good

macroeconomics the study of the interrelationships between economic variables at an aggregate (economy-wide) level

marginal analysis an approach to economic decision making based on considering the additional (marginal) benefits and costs of a change in behaviour

marginal cost the cost of producing an additional unit of output

marginal social benefit (MSB) the additional benefit that society gains from consuming an extra unit of a good

marginal social cost the cost to society of producing an extra unit of a good

market a set of arrangements that allows transactions to take place

market-based policy an approach to tackling market failure by using the market mechanism

market equilibrium a situation that occurs in a market when the price is such that the quantity demanded by consumers is exactly balanced by the quantity supplied by firms

market failure a situation in which the free market equilibrium does not lead to a socially optimal allocation of resources, such that too much or too little of a good is being produced and/or consumed

microeconomics the study of economic decisions taken by individual economic agents, including households and firms

mixed economy an economy in which resources are allocated partly through price signals and partly on the basis of intervention by the state

model a simplified representation of reality used to provide insight into economic decisions and events

moral hazard a situation in which a person who has taken out insurance is prone to taking more risk

necessity a good for which the income elasticity of demand is positive, and less than 1, such that as income rises, consumers spend proportionally less on the good

NIMBY (not in my back yard) a syndrome under which people are happy to support the construction of an unsightly or unsocial facility, so long as it is not in their back yard

non-excludability a situation in which it is not possible to provide a product to one person without allowing others to consume it as well

non-renewable resources natural resources that once used cannot be replenished, such as coal or oil

non-rivalry a situation in which one person's consumption of a good does not prevent others from consuming it as well

normal good one where the quantity demanded increases in response to an increase in consumer incomes

normative statement a statement that involves a value judgement about what *ought to be*

nudge theory analysis that suggests that people's behaviour can be influenced by making desirable decisions easy to make

opportunity cost in decision making, the value of the next-best alternative forgone

perfectly elastic supply a situation in which firms will supply any quantity of a good at the going price: elasticity of supply is infinite

perfectly inelastic supply a situation in which firms can supply only a fixed quantity, so cannot increase or decrease the amount available: elasticity of supply is zero

'polluter pays' principle an argument that a firm causing pollution should be charged the full external cost that they inflict on society

positive statement a statement about what is (i.e. about facts)

potential economic growth an expansion in the productive capacity of the economy

price elasticity of demand (PED) a measure of the sensitivity of quantity demanded to a change in the price of a good or service

price elasticity of supply (PES) a measure of the sensitivity of quantity supplied of a good or service to a change in the price of that good or service

price mechanism a process by which resource allocation is influenced through rationing, incentives and signalling

price signal where the price of a good carries information to producers or consumers that guides the market towards equilibrium and assists in resource allocation

private benefit the benefit from an individual's (a firm or household's) economic activity that accrue to that individual

private cost a cost incurred by an individual (firm or consumer) as part of its production or other economic activities

private good a good that, once consumed by one person, cannot be consumed by somebody else; such a good has excludability and is rivalrous

producer surplus the difference between the price received by firms for a good or service and the price at which they would have been prepared to supply that good or service

production externality an externality that affects the production side of a market, which may be either positive or negative

production possibility frontier (PPF) a curve showing the maximum combinations of goods or services that can be produced in a given period with available resources

prohibition an attempt to prevent the consumption of a good by declaring it illegal

public good a good that is non-exclusive and non-rivalrous in consumption – consumers cannot be excluded from consuming the good, and consumption by one person does not affect the amount of the good available for others to consume

regulation intervention to tackle market failure by direct action to command and control behaviour

renewable resources natural resources that can be replenished, such as forests that can be replanted, or solar energy that does not get used up

scarcity a situation that arises when people have unlimited wants in the face of limited resources

social benefit the sum of private benefits and external benefits

social cost the sum of private and external costs

specific tax a sales tax that is set at a constant amount per unit of sales

subsidy a grant given by the government to producers to encourage production of a good or service

substitutes two goods are said to be substitutes if the demand for one good is likely to rise if the price of the other good rises

supply the quantity of a good or service that producers are willing and able to sell at any given price in a given period of time

supply curve a graph showing the quantity supplied at any given price

symmetric information a situation in which all participants in a market (buyers and sellers) have the same information about market conditions

tradable pollution permit system a system for controlling pollution based on a market for permits that allow firms to pollute up to a limit

unitary elastic a term used when the price elasticity of demand is equal to 1

value judgement a statement based on your opinion or beliefs, rather than on facts

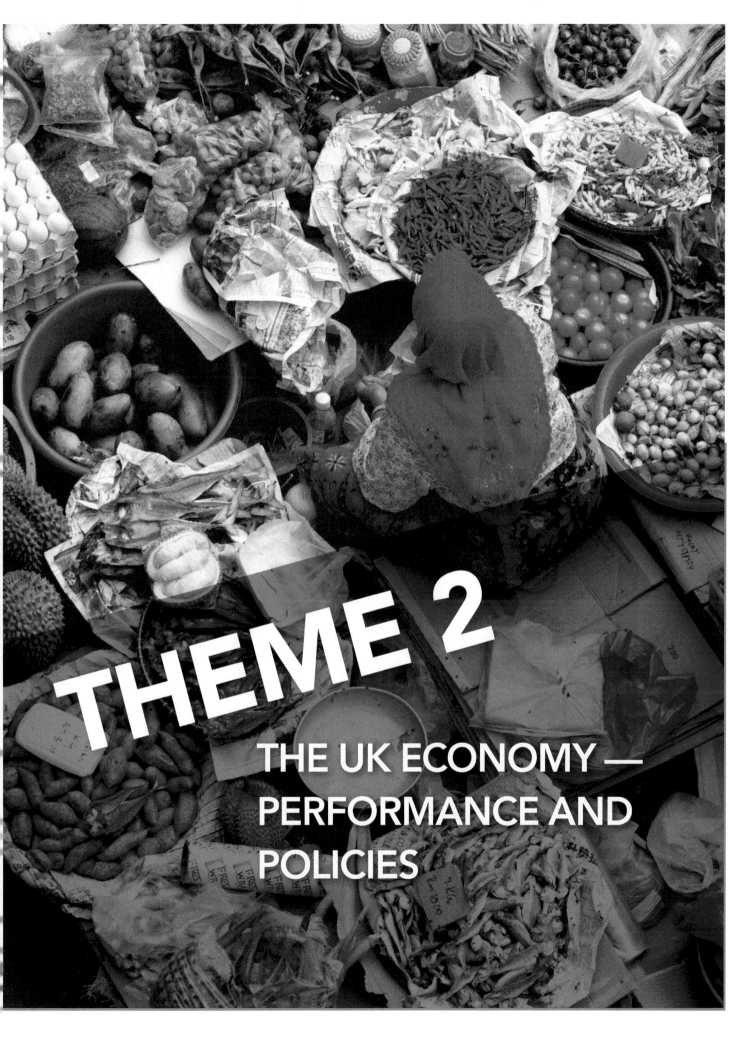

THEME 2

THE UK ECONOMY — PERFORMANCE AND POLICIES

9 Measures of economic performance: economic growth

This part of the book switches our attention to macroeconomics. Macroeconomics has much in common with microeconomics, but focuses on the whole economy, rather than on individual markets and how they operate. Although the way of thinking about issues is similar, and although similar tools are used, now it is interactions between economic variables at the level of the whole economy that are studied. This chapter will introduce economic growth; the following chapter will discuss other major concerns of the media — inflation, unemployment and the balance of payments.

Learning objectives

After studying this chapter, you should:
- → be aware of the main economic aggregates in a modern economy
- → understand the distinction between real and nominal variables
- → be familiar with the use of index numbers and the calculation of growth rates
- → understand how economic growth is measured and its limitations
- → appreciate the inadequacy of economic growth as a measure of the standard of living
- → be aware of problems of comparison between developed and developing countries

Economic performance

The first part of the book emphasised the importance of individual markets in achieving allocative and productive efficiency. In a modern economy, there are so many separate markets that it is difficult to get an overall picture of how well the economy is working. When it comes to monitoring its overall performance, the focus thus tends to be on the **macroeconomic** aggregates. 'Aggregates' here means 'totals' — for example, total unemployment in an economy, or total spending on goods and services — rather than, say, unemployed workers in a particular occupation, or spending on a particular good.

There are a number of dimensions on which the economy as a whole can be monitored. One prime focus of economic policy in recent years has been the inflation rate, as it has been argued that maintaining a stable economic environment is crucial to enabling markets to operate effectively. A second focus has been unemployment, which has been seen as an indicator of whether the economy is using its resources to the full — in other words, whether there are factors of production that are not being fully utilised. In addition, of course, there may be concern that the people who are unemployed are being disadvantaged.

More fundamentally, there is an interest in economic growth (an increase in GDP over time). Is the economy expanding its potential capacity as time goes by, thereby making more resources available for members of society? In fact, it might be argued that this is the most fundamental objective for the economy, and the most important indicator of the economy's performance.

Key term

macroeconomics
the study of the interrelationships between economic variables at an aggregate (macroeconomic) level

Synoptic link

The notions of allocative and productive efficiency were discussed in Chapter 4.

Synoptic link

Inflation and unemployment are discussed more fully in Chapter 10.

Other concerns may also need to be kept in mind. In particular, there is the question of how the economy interacts with the rest of the world. The UK is an 'open' economy — one that actively engages in international trade — and this aspect of UK economic performance needs to be monitored too, especially in the light of the Brexit situation.

The importance of data

To monitor the performance of the economy, it is crucial to be able to observe how the economy is functioning, and for this you need data. Remember that economics, especially macroeconomics, is a non-experimental discipline. It is not possible to conduct experiments to see how the economy reacts to various stimuli in order to learn how it works. Instead, it is necessary to observe the economy, and to come to a judgement about whether or not its performance is satisfactory, and whether macroeconomic theories about how the economy works are supported by the evidence.

Study tip

Although data are important in economics, notice that it is not necessary to learn lots of detailed facts and statistics about the UK economy. However, it is of course important to be familiar with recent events and general trends in the performance of the economy.

So, a reliable measure is needed for tracking each of the variables mentioned above, in order to observe how the economy is evolving through time. The key indicators of the economy's performance will be introduced as we proceed.

Sources of data

Most of the economic statistics used by economists are collected and published by various government agencies. Such data in the UK are published mainly by the Office for National Statistics (ONS). Data on other countries are published by the International Monetary Fund (IMF), the World Bank and the United Nations, as well as national sources. There is little alternative to relying on such sources because the accurate collection of data is an expensive and time-consuming business.

Care needs to be taken in the interpretation of economic data. It is important to be aware of how the data are compiled, and the extent to which they are indicators of what economists are trying to measure. It is also important to remember that the economic environment is ever changing, and that single causes can rarely be ascribed to the economic events that are observed. This is because the ceteris paribus condition that underlies so much economic analysis is rarely fulfilled in reality. In other words, you cannot rely on 'other things remaining constant' when using data about the real world.

It is also important to realise that even the ONS cannot observe with absolute accuracy. Indeed, some data take so long to be assembled that early estimates are provisional in nature and subject to later revision as more information becomes available. Data used in international comparisons must be treated with even greater caution.

Knowledge check 9.1

What is measured by GDP? (Hint: this term was first introduced in Chapter 1.)

Knowledge check 9.2

What is meant by an 'open' economy?

Knowledge check 9.3

Explain what is meant by the 'ceteris paribus' assumption.

Real and nominal measurements

The measurement of economic variables poses many dilemmas for statisticians. Not least is the fundamental problem of what to use as units of measurement. Suppose economists wish to measure total output produced in an economy during successive years. In the first place, they cannot use volume measures. They may be able to count how many computers, passenger cars, tins of paint and cauliflowers the economy produces — but how do they add all these different items together to produce a total?

An obvious solution is to use the *money values*. Given prices for all the items, it is possible to calculate the money values of all these goods and thus produce a measurement of the total output produced in an economy during a year in terms of pounds sterling. However, this is just the beginning of the problem because, in order to monitor changes in total output between 2 years, it is important to be aware that not only do the volumes of goods produced change, but so too do their prices, and thus their value in money terms. In effect, this means that if the pound sterling is used as the unit of measurement, the unit of measurement will change from one year to the next as prices change.

This is a problem that is not faced by most of the physical sciences. After all, the length of a metre does not alter from one year to the next, so if the length of something is being measured, the unit is fixed. Economists, however, have to make allowance for changing prices when measuring in pounds sterling or US dollars.

When GDP is measured using current prices, the resulting measure is a *value* measure; this is known as **nominal GDP**. However, when prices are rising over time, this measure will always overstate the extent to which the *volume* of GDP is growing through time. By removing the effect of changing prices, an estimate of this underlying volume of GDP is produced, which is known as **real GDP**. A similar distinction between nominal and real values applies for other macroeconomic variables that are observed over time.

One way in which these real measures can be obtained is by taking the volumes produced in each year and valuing these quantities at the prices that prevailed in some base year. This then enables allowance to be made for the changes in prices that take place, permitting a focus on the real values. These can be thought of as being measured at constant prices.

Key terms

nominal GDP the *value* of GDP based on current prices, taking no account of changing prices through time

real GDP an estimate of the *volume* of GDP taking account of changing prices through time

Knowledge check 9.4

Would GDP at current prices be known as real GDP or as nominal GDP?

How can we add together all the different items an economy produces?

For example, suppose that last year you bought a tub of ice cream for £3, but that inflation has been 10%, so that this year you had to pay £3.30 for the same tub. Your volume of consumption of the item has not changed, but your spending has increased. If you were to use the value of your spending to measure changes in consumption through time, it would be misleading, as you know that your real consumption has not changed at all (so is still £3), although its *nominal* value has increased to £3.30.

Quantitative skills 9.1

Converting nominal measurements to real

It is worth being aware that the ratio of the current (nominal) value of a variable to its constant price (real) value (multiplied by 100) is a price index. For example:

$$100 \times \frac{\text{nominal GDP}}{\text{real GDP}} \quad \text{is a price index}$$

So, if we know GDP at current prices and we know the relevant price index, we can calculate the real value of GDP.

For example, in 2017, GDP for the UK in current prices was estimated to be £2.038 billion, and the underlying price index was 104 (based on 2015 = 100). The real value of GDP can thus be calculated as:

$$100 \times \frac{2.038}{104} = £1.960 \text{ billion}$$

Quantitative skills 9.2

Calculating a percentage change

In macroeconomics it is often important to be able to calculate the percentage change in a variable. For example, it may be that there is interest in knowing how rapidly prices are changing, or in calculating the rate of economic growth. In the previous paragraph, the price of a tub of ice cream was supposed to have increased from £3 to £3.30. To calculate the percentage change in the price, calculate the change in price (3.30 − 3 = 0.30) and express that as a percentage of the original value. In other words, the percentage change is:

$$100 \times (3.30 - 3) \div 3 = 10\%$$

Notice that the change in the variable is always expressed as a percentage of the initial value, not the final value.

Knowledge check 9.5

If a country's real GDP was $120 billion and the underlying price index was 105, what would be the value of nominal GDP?

Index numbers

In some cases there is no apparent unit of measurement that is meaningful. For example, if you wished to measure the general level of prices in an economy, there is no meaningful unit of measurement that could be used. In such cases the solution is to use **index numbers**, which are a form of ratio that compares the value of a variable with some base point.

For example, suppose the price of a 250g pack of butter last year was 1.20p, and this year it is 1.80p. How can the price between the two periods be compared? One way of doing it is to calculate the percentage change using the formula introduced above:

$$100 \times (1.80 - 1.20) \div 1.20 = 50\%$$

Key term

index number a device for comparing the value of a variable in one period or location with a base observation (e.g. the consumer price index measures the average level of prices relative to a base period)

Quantitative skills 9.3

Creating an index number

An alternative way of doing this is to calculate an index number. In the above example, the current value of the index could be calculated as the current value divided by the base value, multiplied by 100. In other words, this would be $100 \times 1.80 \div 1.20 = 150$. The resulting number gives the current value relative to the base value. This turns out to be a useful way of expressing a range of economic variables where you want to show the value relative to a base period. Index numbers can also be used to compare between regions or to compare variables measured in different units — anything where you want to compare with some base level.

Summary: measurement issues

- Macroeconomics is the study of the interrelationships between economic variables at the level of the whole economy.
- Some variables are of particular interest when monitoring the performance of an economy — for example, inflation, unemployment and economic growth.
- As economists cannot easily conduct experiments in order to test economic theory, they rely on the use of economic data: that is, observations of the world around them.
- Data measured in money terms need to be handled carefully, as prices change over time, thereby affecting the units in which many economic variables are measured.
- Index numbers are helpful in comparing the value of a variable with a base date or unit.

Economic growth

If the ultimate aim of a society is to improve the well-being of its citizens, then in economic terms this means that the resources available within the economy need to expand through time in order to widen people's choices. This requires a process of economic growth.

Potential economic growth

From a theoretical point of view, **potential economic growth** can be thought of as an expansion of the productive capacity of an economy. If you like, it is an expansion of the potential output of the economy.

The notion of economic growth was introduced in Chapter 1 using the production possibility frontier. Figure 9.1 is a reminder (reproducing Figure 1.4). Economic growth is characterised as an outward movement of the production possibility frontier from PPF_0 to PPF_1. In other words, economic growth enables a society to produce more goods and services in any given period as a result of an expansion in its resources.

Synoptic link

Chapter 1 introduced the idea of economic growth, describing it as an increase in the productive capacity of the economy.

Key term

potential economic growth an expansion in the productive capacity of the economy

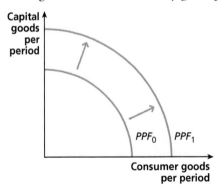

Figure 9.1 Economic growth

Chapter 1 also briefly introduced the notion of **gross domestic product (GDP)** as representing the total output of an economy during a period of time. GDP can be seen as the total value added produced by firms in the domestic economy during a period, but it can also be measured by adding up total expenditures in the period, or by totalling the amount of income earned. In principle, these should all give the same answer, but in practice GDP is calculated as the average of the three measures.

GDP focuses on the domestic economy. However, it is also important to recognise that residents of the economy also receive some income from abroad — and some income earned in the domestic economy is sent abroad. **Gross national income (GNI)** takes into account these income flows between countries, and for some purposes is a more helpful measure — indeed, this is the standard measure used by the World Bank to compare average incomes across countries. This measure was formerly known as gross national product (GNP).

> ### Knowledge check 9.6
> What is the difference between GNI and GDP?

Key terms

gross domestic product (GDP) a measure of the economic activity carried out in the domestic economy over a period

gross national income (GNI) GDP plus net income from abroad

actual economic growth the rate of growth of real GDP in a period

trade (business) cycle a phenomenon whereby GDP fluctuates around its underlying trend, following a regular pattern

Actual economic growth

Actual economic growth is measured by the percentage rate of growth of real GDP (or GNI) in a period. This may differ from potential economic growth because the economy is not always operating at full capacity. Economies tend to go through a **trade or business cycle**, with the level of economic activity fluctuating around an underlying trend.

Figure 9.2 shows real GDP since 1948. You can see that during this period, real GDP grew in almost every year, but that there are some years where real GDP dipped. In particular, notice how real GDP fell after 2007 before rising again.

It is important to note that this shows the *level* of real GDP, so to calculate growth it is necessary to compute the annual rate of change. This is done in Figure 9.3, which shows the annual growth rate of real GDP in the UK since 1949. You can see that it is quite difficult to determine the underlying trend because the year-to-year movements are so volatile. Figure 9.4 takes 5-yearly average growth rates over the same period, with the horizontal red line showing the underlying trend rate of growth. Again, you can see that the recession of the late 2000s was well out of line with previous experience.

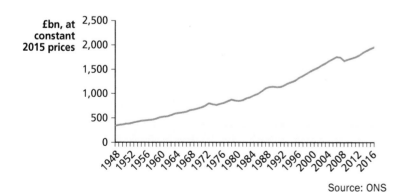

Source: ONS

Figure 9.2 Real GDP, 1948–2017 (£ billion)

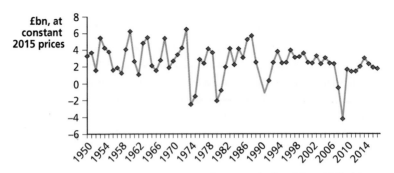

Source: calculated from ONS data

Figure 9.3 Growth of real GDP, 1950–2017 (% change over previous year)

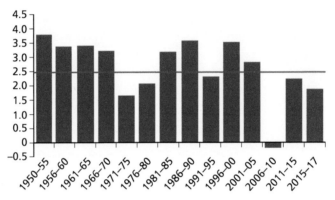

Source: calculated from ONS data

Figure 9.4 Average annual growth rates in the UK since 1950

Key term

seasonal adjustment a process by which seasonal fluctuations in a variable are smoothed to reveal the underlying trend

The data for GDP are also provided on a quarterly (i.e. four times per year) basis. Like many other macroeconomic variables, the level of real GDP tends to fluctuate with the seasons of the year. For example, GDP tends to be higher in the Christmas quarter (from October to December), but then falls in the following period. These regular fluctuations also occur for things like inflation and unemployment, and can distract from the overall pattern through time. For this reason, a process of **seasonal adjustment** is undertaken. This is a process of smoothing out these regular fluctuations through the year. Figure 9.5 illustrates this using quarterly data from 2012 to 2017. You can see how the seasonally adjusted series focuses on the underlying trend, removing the distractions of the seasonal variations.

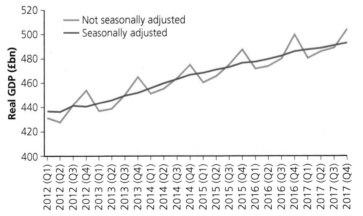

Source: based on data from ONS

Figure 9.5 Real GDP in the UK with and without seasonal adjustment, 2012–17

Summary: economic growth

- Economic growth is a fundamental aspect of the overall performance of an economy, as it is through growth that the citizens of a country can become better off.
- From a theoretical point of view, potential economic growth is an increase in the productive capacity of an economy — in other words, an increase in the potential output of an economy.
- GDP is a measure of the total economic activity carried out in an economy during a period by residents living on its territory.
- The rate of growth of real GDP informs about actual economic growth, but not necessarily about the growth of potential output, which is much more difficult to measure.
- Economies tend not to grow according to a constant trend, but to fluctuate around the underlying trend, creating a business cycle.

Exercise 9.1

Table 9.1 provides data on real GDP for the period 2005–17. Convert the series to an index based on 2005 = 100. Calculate the growth rate of GDP for each year from 2005/06 to 2016/17. In which year was growth at its highest and in which year was it at its lowest?

Table 9.1 Real GDP in the UK, 2005–17 (£bn)

2005	1,676
2006	1,717
2007	1,758
2008	1,749
2009	1,676
2010	1,704
2011	1,729
2012	1,755
2013	1,791
2014	1,845
2015	1,889
2016	1,925
2017	1,960

GDP, GNI and the standard of living

GDP is a way of measuring the total output of an economy over a period of time. Although this measure can provide an indicator of the quantity of resources available to citizens of a country in a given period, as an assessment of the standard of living it has its critics.

A first point to notice is that if the intention is to monitor the standard of living in a country — in other words, the quality of life that is enjoyed by the country's residents — GNI is to be preferred to GDP, as it more closely reflects the incomes of the residents, including net flows of income between countries. This would be important for some countries such as Pakistan or the Philippines, where there are relatively large inflows of income from people working abroad and remitting income to their families.

Advantages of GNI

GNI does have some things going for it. First, it is relatively straightforward and thus is widely understood. Second, it is a well-established indicator and one that is available for almost every country in the world, so that it can be used to compare

Key term

GNI per capita the average level of GNI per head of population

income levels across countries. A first point to notice is that if we want to compare across countries, we need to recognise that different countries have differently sized populations, and we need to take this into account. This is done by calculating the average level of GNI per head of population, which is known as **GNI per capita**.

Quantitative skills 9.4

Calculating GNI per capita

Suppose you want to compare living standards in China and Malaysia. In 2016, GNI in China was US$11,393,571 billion, whereas in Malaysia it was US$307,242 billion. However, China's population was 1,379 million, compared to Malaysia's 31 million. It is more meaningful to compare average GNI per capita. For China this was US$11,393,570/1,379 = US$8,260. Notice that because GNI was measured in billions, but population was in millions, it was necessary to convert GNI into millions for this calculation to be correct. For Malaysia, GNI per capita was US$9,911.

Figure 9.6 provides data on GNI per capita for a range of countries around the world. The extreme differences that exist around the globe are immediately apparent from the data. GNI per capita in Burundi was just $280 in 2016, whereas in the USA the figure was $56,180.

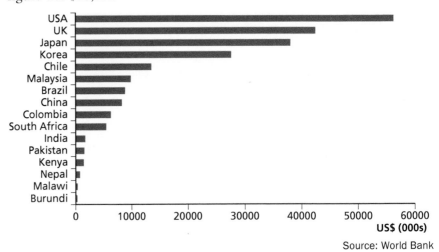

Source: World Bank

Figure 9.6 GNI per capita, 2016, in US$

In trying to interpret these data, there are a number of issues that need to be borne in mind, as the comparison is not as straightforward as it looks.

Knowledge check 9.7

Why is it important to consider per capita values of GNI when undertaking international comparisons?

Inequality in income distribution

One important point to notice is that looking at the average level of income per person may be misleading if there are wide differences in the way in which income is distributed within countries. In other words, it cannot be assumed that every person living in Burundi receives $280, or that every US citizen receives $56,180. If income is more unequally distributed in some countries, this will affect one's perception of what the term 'average' means. For example, Chile and Hungary had broadly similar GNI per capita levels in 2016, but the income distribution in Hungary was more equitable than in Chile.

The informal sector and the accuracy of data

A further problem with undertaking international comparisons is that it is never absolutely certain that the accuracy with which data are collected is consistent across

Study tip

As said already, it is good to be familiar with generalised facts about regions and countries of the world, but you will *not* be expected to produce lots of facts and figures about individual countries in the exam.

countries. Definitions of GNI and other variables are set out in a clear, internationally agreed form, but even when countries are working to the same definitions, some data collection agencies may be more reliable than others.

In many developing countries, substantial economic activity may take place without an exchange of money

One particular area in which this is pertinent relates to the informal sector. In every economy there are some transactions that go unrecorded. In most economies, there are economic activities that take place that cannot be closely monitored because of their informal nature. This is especially prevalent in many developing countries, where substantial amounts of economic activity often take place without an exchange of money. For example, in many countries subsistence agriculture remains an important facet of economic life. If households are producing food simply for their own consumption, there is no reason for a money transaction to take place with regard to its production, and thus such activity will not be recorded as a part of GNI. Equally, much economic activity within the urban areas of developing countries comes under the category of the 'informal sector'.

Where such activity varies in importance between countries, comparing incomes on the basis of measured GNI may be misleading, as GNI will be a closer indicator of the amount of real economic activity in some countries than in others.

Knowledge check 9.8

Give some examples of economic activity in the UK that are not captured by the measurement of GNI.

Exchange rate problems

The data presented in Figure 9.6 were expressed in terms of US dollars. This allows economists to compare average incomes using a common unit of measurement. At the same time, however, it may create some problems.

Economists want to compare average income levels so that they can evaluate the standard of living, and compare standards across countries. In other words, it is important to be able to assess people's command over resources in different societies, and to be able to compare the purchasing power of income in different countries.

GNI is initially calculated in terms of local currencies, and subsequently converted into US dollars using official exchange rates. Will this provide information about the relative local purchasing power of incomes? Not necessarily.

One reason for this is that official exchange rates are sometimes affected by government intervention. Indeed, in many of the developing countries, exchange rates are pegged to an international currency — usually the US dollar. In these circumstances, exchange rates are more likely to reflect the government's policy and actions than the relative purchasing power of incomes in the countries under scrutiny.

Where exchange rates are free to find their own equilibrium level, they are likely to be influenced strongly by the prices of *internationally traded* goods — which are likely to be very different from the prices of the goods that are typically consumed by residents in these countries. Again, it can be argued that the official exchange rates may not be a good reflection of the relative purchasing power of incomes across countries.

Knowledge check 9.9

Give reasons why official exchange rates may not be ideal for comparing purchasing power across countries.

Key term

purchasing power parity (PPP) exchange rate an exchange rate adjusted to reflect the relative purchasing power of incomes in different countries

Purchasing power parity

The United Nations International Comparison Project has been working on this problem for many years. It now produces an alternative set of international estimates of GNI based on **purchasing power parity (PPP) exchange rates**, which are designed to reflect the relative purchasing power of incomes in different societies more accurately. Figure 9.7 shows estimates for the same set of countries.

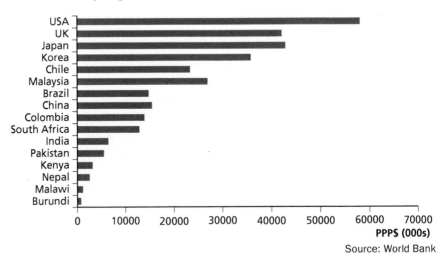

Source: World Bank

Figure 9.7 GNI per capita, 2016, in PPP$

Comparing this with Figure 9.6, you will notice that the gap between the low-income and high-income countries seems a bit less marked when PPP dollars are used as the unit of measurement, although it remains wide. In other words, the US dollar estimates exaggerate the gap in living standards between rich and poor countries. This is a general feature of these measurements — that measurements in US dollars tend to understate real incomes for low-income countries and overstate them for high-income countries compared with PPP-dollar data. Put another way, people in the lower-income countries have a stronger command over goods and services than is suggested by US-dollar comparisons of GNI per capita. You can also see that the relative levels of GNI per capita of countries in PPP dollars are different in some cases — for example, compare Malaysia with Chile, or Japan with the UK.

Social indicators

A final question that arises is whether GNI can be regarded as a reasonable indicator of a country's standard of living. You have seen that GNI provides an indicator of the total resources available within an economy in a given period, calculated from data about total output, total incomes or total expenditure. This focus on summing the transactions that take place in an economy over a period can be seen as a rather narrow view of what constitutes the 'standard of living'. After all, it may be argued that the quality of people's lives depends on more things than simply the material resources that are available.

Health and education

For one thing, people need to have knowledge if they are to make good use of the resources that are available. Two societies with similar income levels may nonetheless provide very different quality of life for their inhabitants, depending on the education levels of the population. Furthermore, if people are to benefit from consuming or using the available resources, they need a reasonable lifespan coupled with good health. So, good standards of health are also crucial to a good quality of life.

It is important to remember that different societies tend to set different priorities on the pursuit of growth and the promotion of education and health. This needs to be taken into account when judging relative living standards through a comparison of GNI per capita, as some countries have higher-than-average levels of health and education as compared with other countries with similar levels of GNI per capita.

Environmental factors

A reasonable environment in which to live may be seen as another important factor in one's quality of life, and there may be a trade-off between economic growth and environmental standards.

There are some environmental issues that can distort the GNI measure of resources. Suppose there is an environmental disaster — perhaps an oil tanker breaks up close to a beautiful beach. This reduces the overall quality of life by degrading the landscape and preventing enjoyment of the beach. However, it does not have a negative effect on GNI; on the contrary, the money spent on clearing up the damage actually adds to GNI, so that the net effect of an environmental disaster may be to *increase* the measured level of GNI!

Synoptic link

The United Nations produce an indicator known as the Human Development Index, which takes education and health levels into account as well as GNI per capita. This is discussed in Chapter 28.

Knowledge check 9.10

Give some examples of aspects of the standard of living that are not captured in the measurement of GNI.

Exercise 9.2

Below are some indicators for two countries, A and B. Discuss the extent to which GNI per capita (here measured in PPP$) provides a good indication of relative living standards in the two countries.

Table 9.2 Social indicators for countries A and B

Indicators	Country A	Country B
GNI per capita (PPP$)	11,578	11,445
Life expectancy (in years at birth)	56.1	75.2
Adult literacy rate (%)	93.0	98.0
Infant mortality rate (per 1,000 live births)	33.3	5.7
% of population living on less than $1 per person per day	13.77	0.21

Discuss what other indicators might be useful in this evaluation.

Economic growth: international experience

The growth performance of different regions around the world has shown contrasting patterns in recent years. As early as the 1950s, a gap had opened up between the early developing countries in North America, Western Europe and Japan and the late developers in sub-Saharan Africa and Latin America.

From the 1960s this gap began to widen, except for a small group of countries, mainly in East Asia, that had begun to close it. Figure 9.8 gives some data for countries in different regions. These data relate to GDP per capita rather than GNI, as GNI data are not available for all countries back to 1960.

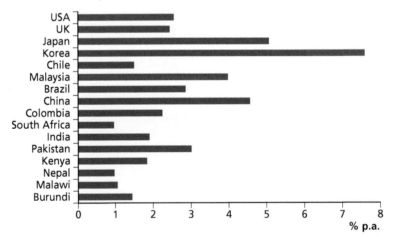

Source: calculated from World Bank data

Figure 9.8 Growth of GDP per capita, selected countries, 1960-90 (annual average)

Countries in sub-Saharan Africa such as Burundi, Malawi and Kenya, together with Nepal and India (in South Asia) had started with low levels of GDP per capita, and they experienced relatively low growth in this period. South Africa also grew slowly over this period, partly because of the period in which sanctions were applied in protest against apartheid. Latin America showed a diverse experience: the examples shown in the figure are Colombia, which grew at 2.25% per annum, and Brazil, which achieved growth of nearly 3% per annum. However, China and some other

East Asian economies (Korea and Malaysia) took off during this period, achieving rapid growth partly through exporting to world markets. Japan also grew rapidly at this time, while the UK and the USA grew at a more sedate pace of between 2 and 3% per annum.

Since 1990, patterns of growth have changed somewhat. Figure 9.9 shows how growth in GDP per capita developed from 1990 to 2007 (on the eve of the financial crisis), and how it has evolved since then.

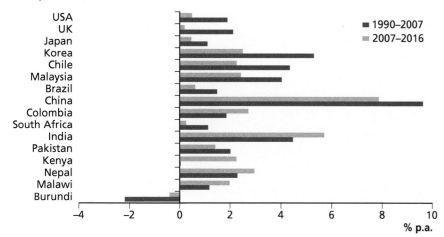

Source: calculated from World Bank data

Figure 9.9 Growth of GDP per capita, 1990–2007 and 2007–16 (annual averages)

In the period 1990–2007, the stand-out feature is the performance of China's economy, growing at an unprecedented rate of almost 10% per annum, becoming a major player in the global economy. Korea, Chile, Malaysia and India also showed strong growth in the period. In some of the lower-income economies, the picture was less bright, with Burundi experiencing negative growth and Kenya having about the same level of GDP per capita in 2007 as it had in 1990. Japan's economy slowed considerably, and the UK and USA continued to growth at around 2% per annum.

The period since the financial crisis of 2008–09 saw the UK, USA and Japan with average growth rates well below trend, reflecting a slow recovery from the recession that affected most developed countries. China continued to show relatively strong growth, and India improved its position. Lower-income countries seemed to have suffered rather less, even showing higher growth in the recent period.

Knowledge check 9.11

Looking at Figure 9.9, which countries fared better in terms of the growth of GDP per capita in 2007–16 than in 1990–2007?

Can we measure happiness?

If the intention is to measure the standard of living that is achieved by people in a society, is there a different approach that could be adopted? Many attempts have been made to do this. For example, an alternative indicator was proposed by William Nordhaus and James Tobin in 1972, known as the *Measure of Economic Welfare (MEW)*. This began with GNP (GNI) and then made various adjustments so that it only included the consumption and investment items that contribute positively to economic well-being. For example, they argued that the value of informal production should be added, but that there should be deductions for negative externalities such as environmental damage. An attempt was made to re-launch this as the *Index of Sustainable Economic Welfare (ISEW)*. It was hoped that this indicator would be able to capture key issues relating to the sustainability of economic growth, but it has yet to gain widespread support.

Gross national happiness and well-being

The fourth dragon king of Bhutan, Jigme Singye Wangchuck, went further when he came to the throne in 1972. He was intent on building an economy based on Buddhist values, so turned his back on the idea of GNI, shifting the focus of attention to GNH, gross national happiness. Can this be measured? One possibility is to ask people whether they are happy or not. The percentage of people answering positively could then be used as an indicator, and it would be possible to track how this changes through time, or across countries.

The 2007 OECD World Forum issued a declaration calling for fact-based information that could be used by a society to formulate a shared valuation of national well-being. In the UK, the ONS launched its Measuring National Well-Being Programme in 2010, to bring together a range of indicators across ten dimensions of the quality of life that would allow the monitoring of well-being through time. These indicators include measures of personal well-being, relationships, health, education and the environment, as well as some relating to the economy and personal finance. Again, these measures have not yet become fully embedded in the process of monitoring the economy, but they do allow some comparisons to be made across Europe, as similar measures are being produced for other countries.

Happiness and income

Key term

Easterlin paradox the hypothesis that happiness increases with average incomes, but only up to a point

To what extent is happiness likely to be correlated with incomes? The relationship is not likely to be very close, as people's subjective perception of happiness will be related to a whole range of different things in addition to their material prosperity. Figure 9.10 takes data from the *World Happiness Report* of 2018 and produces a scatter plot of happiness against GNI per capita for 148 countries for which data were available. The values for happiness for each country represent the average values from interviews with individuals based on a scale of 0 to 10. Economist Richard Easterlin has argued that happiness increases with average incomes, but only up to a point. This is known as the **Easterlin paradox**.

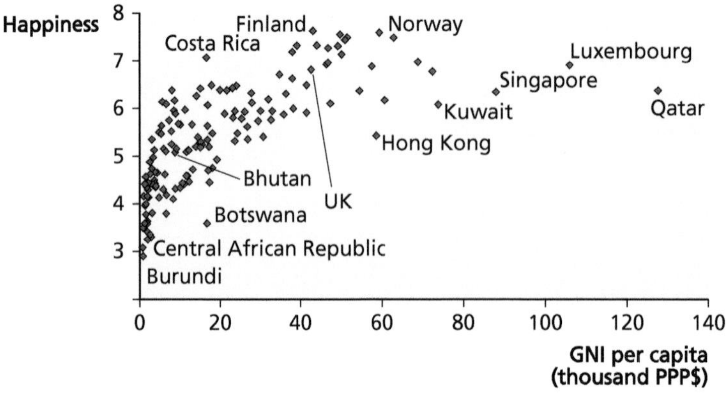

Sources: World Bank, http://worldhappiness.report/ed/2018/

Figure 9.10 Happiness and GNI per capita

Interpreting a scatter diagram

Scatter diagrams are useful in providing a visual impression of the degree of association between two variables. In Figure 9.10, we are trying to evaluate the extent to which happiness and GNI per capita are related. The way to interpret each point of the graph is to read off values from each axis. For example, look at the point labelled as Qatar. From the x-axis, we see that GNI per capita is about PPP$128,000 and the happiness index is about 6.4.

If the two variables were very closely related, we would expect to see the scatter of points approximating to an upward-sloping straight line. However, this is not the case, as the relationship between the variables seems to be a curve (non-linear). It is steep at low levels per capita income, but flatter towards the right of the graph. This could suggest that average income levels are a more important influence on happiness when income is low, than when income levels reach a certain point. This provides some support for the Easterlin paradox.

You will see some of the points are labelled. This may help in interpreting the pattern. Notice that Finland achieved the highest level of happiness in 2018, although it did not display the highest average income by any means. Burundi and the Central African Republic were the two lowest countries in terms of both GNI per capita and happiness. In spite of its emphasis on gross national happiness, Bhutan is in the centre of the cluster of points. However, people surveyed in Costa Rica seem to be more happy than would be expected from their per capita GNI levels.

Knowledge check 9.12

Comment on Botswana's position in Figure 9.10.

Summary: GNI, the standard of living and happiness

- GNI is a widely understood and widely available measure, but it does have some drawbacks.
- Average GNI per capita neglects the important issue of income distribution.
- There may be variation in the effectiveness of data collection agencies in different countries, and variation in the size of the informal sector.
- Converting from a local currency into US dollars may distort the use of GNI as a measure of the purchasing power of local incomes.
- GNI may neglect some important aspects of the quality of life.
- Recent research has begun to explore alternative ways of measuring well-being.

China's economic growth

Since China adopted market reforms in the late 1970s, its economy has enjoyed a period of rapid economic growth that is unprecedented by historical standards. One of the characteristics of this period of rapid growth has been the gradual move towards allowing market forces to operate after a long period of central planning. This would be expected to have benefits for the economy in terms of the efficiency of resource allocation.

Although China's success in achieving such rapid economic progress has been much admired, it has also been much criticised, for a number of reasons.

One source of criticism centres on the environmental damage that results from a rapid rate of economic growth. A key ingredient of the growth process — especially in terms of industrialisation — is an expansion in energy supplies. Factories cannot operate without reliable electricity and other energy sources. Proposals to double China's production of hydroelectric power caused concerns about the effects of new dams on river levels in downstream countries in South East Asia and in India.

Air pollution has become a severe problem, with heavy smog levels in Beijing and other cities. The problem is not confined to China's boundaries, and neighbours Japan and South Korea have suffered from pollution spreading from China into their territories.

Booming car ownership raises further concerns: the number of cars in China had reached 173 million by 2015 (from just 4 million in 2000). This number continues to rise rapidly, and China is the largest car producer in the world. The effect of this on the demand for oil has already been reflected in higher world prices — China is already the world's second biggest oil importer (behind the USA). China is also the world's biggest producer of coal, which accounts for some 80% of China's energy use.

All of this means that China has now overtaken the USA as the largest emitter of carbon dioxide. It seems unlikely that environmental damage on this sort of scale is sustainable from a global perspective.

China is building hydroelectric dams at an unprecedented rate, raising environmental concerns

Follow-up questions

a Explain why a move towards a market-based system would be expected to 'have benefits for the economy in terms of the efficiency of resource allocation'.

b Discuss how the cross-border externalities caused by pollution could be tackled.

c Discuss whether China should seek to restrain the growing car ownership that is a by-product of rapid economic growth, which has led to rising real incomes.

The previous chapter introduced one of the most important macroeconomic indicators — economic growth. In trying to evaluate the performance of the economy at the macroeconomic level, it is also important to monitor other indicators, particularly inflation, unemployment and the balance of payments. The economy needs to perform well in these areas if economic growth is to be possible and sustainable.

Learning objectives

After studying this chapter, you should:
→ appreciate the significance of inflation for the modern economy
→ be familiar with alternative measurements of inflation in the context of the UK economy
→ be aware of the meaning and significance of unemployment, and ways in which it is measured in the UK
→ be familiar with the role and importance of the balance of payments

Inflation

Although economic growth may be seen as the most fundamental objective of macroeconomic policy, attention focuses strongly on the control of **inflation**, principally because it is feared that instability of prices will deter firms from undertaking investment and thus hinder economic growth. Indeed, it would seem that the government's performance in guiding the economy at the macroeconomic level has often been judged in terms of inflation. This being so, it is important to understand how inflation is defined and measured.

Inflation is defined as a change in the overall level of prices in an economy. The first step in measuring inflation is therefore to measure the average level of prices in the economy. Inflation can then be calculated as the percentage rate of change of prices over time.

Index numbers are crucial when it comes to monitoring how prices change through time, or when you want to show the average level of prices at different points in time. For such a general price index, one procedure is to define a typical basket of commodities that reflects the spending pattern of a representative household. The cost of that bundle can be calculated in a base year, and then in subsequent years. The cost in the base year is set to equal 100, and in subsequent years the index is measured relative to that base date, thereby reflecting the change in prices since then. For example, if in the second year the weighted average increase in prices were 2.5%, then the index in year 2 would take on the value 102.5 (based on year 1 = 100). Such a general index of prices could be seen as an index of the cost of living for the representative household, as it would give the level of prices faced by the average household relative to the base year.

Key term

inflation the rate of increase in the average price level in an economy

Synoptic link

Chapter 15 explains the consequences of inflation, which shows why inflation has been considered to be so important as a policy target.

Synoptic link

Index numbers were introduced in Chapter 9.

Knowledge check 10.1

If a bundle of goods costs 4% higher in year 2 than in year 1, what would be the value of an index for year 2 based on year 1 = 100?

Exercise 10.1

Table 10.1 contains data on oil and petrol prices.

Table 10.1 Prices of oil and petrol

Date	Oil price ($ per barrel)	Average petrol price, South East region (£ per litre)	Average supermarket petrol price (£ per litre)
March 2015	61.2	1.118	1.099
March 2016	39.5	1.031	1.003
March 2017	51.4	1.204	1.116
March 2018	65.5	1.206	1.168

Source: Automobile Association

a Construct index numbers based on March 2015 = 100 and compare the movements in the price of petrol in the South East region with the price of oil during this period.

b Construct index numbers to compare petrol prices in the South East with the average supermarket price for each of the periods.

Key terms

consumer price index (CPI) a measure of the general level of prices in the UK, the rate of change of which has been used as the government's inflation target since January 2004

CPIH a version of the CPI that takes into account the housing costs of owner-occupiers and the council tax

retail price index (RPI) a measure of the average level of prices in the UK

Knowledge check 10.2

Why is CPIH inflation a more helpful measure than that based on CPI?

The consumer price index

The most important general price index in the UK is the **consumer price index (CPI)**, which has been used by the government in setting its inflation target since the beginning of 2004. This index is based on the prices of a bundle of goods and services measured at different points in time. A total of 180,000 individual price quotes on more than 700 different products are collected by the ONS each month, by visits to shops, telephone and using the internet. Data on spending from the *Household Final Monetary Consumption Expenditure* survey is used to compile the weights for the items included in the index. These weights are updated each year, as changes in the consumption patterns of households need to be accommodated if the index is to remain representative.

The index was much criticised because it excluded housing costs of owner-occupiers and council tax, and a new index was launched in March 2013 to remedy this. The index is known as **CPIH** and its rate of change became the ONS's headline measure of inflation in March 2017.

As noted above, it is important to remember that the CPI or CPIH provide a measurement of the *level* of prices in the economy. This is not inflation: inflation is the *rate of change* of prices, and the percentage change in the CPI provides one estimate of the inflation rate. Notice that the CPI sets out to measure the way that inflation affects the 'average' or representative family, but individual households whose consumption patterns differs from the norm may experience inflation in different ways — for example, pensioners may have different patterns of consumption and may experience inflation in a different way.

Alternative measurements of inflation

The retail price index

The traditional measure of inflation in the UK for many years was the **retail price index (RPI)**, which was first calculated (under another name) in the early twentieth century to evaluate the extent to which workers were affected by price changes during the First World War. When Tony Blair's government was elected in 1997, one of its first steps was to set an explicit inflation target. It chose to use the RPIX as the target, which is the RPI excluding mortgage interest payments. This was felt to be a better measure of the effectiveness of macroeconomic policy. It was argued that if interest rates are to be used to curb inflation, then including mortgage interest payments in the inflation measure would be misleading.

The CPI replaced RPIX partly because it is believed to be a more appropriate indicator for evaluating policy effectiveness. In addition, it has the advantage of being calculated using the same methodology as is used in other countries within the European Union, so that it is more useful than the RPIX for making international comparisons of inflation.

The CPI and RPI are based on a similar approach, although there are some significant differences in the detail of the calculation. Both measures set out to calculate the overall price level at different points in time. Each is based on calculating the overall cost of a representative basket of goods and services at different points in time relative to a base period. Both are produced from the same raw data, but use different formulae to produce the index. The result of these calculations is an index that shows how the general level of prices has changed relative to the base year. The rate of inflation is then calculated as the percentage rate of change of the price index, whether it be the CPI, CPIH or the RPI.

The indexes share a common failing, arising from the fixed weights used in calculating the overall index. Suppose the price of a particular item rises more rapidly than other prices during the year. One response by consumers is to substitute an alternative, cheaper, product. As the indexes are based on fixed weights, they do not pick up this substitution effect, and therefore tend to overstate the price level in terms of the cost of living. Some attempt is made to overcome this problem by changing the weights on an annual basis in order to limit the impact of major changes. This includes incorporating new items when appropriate — for example, several new items were included in the CPI in 2018, including a digital media player, body moisturising lotion and chilled mashed potato, to improve coverage and to reflect changes in consumer spending patterns.

The CPI and the RPI are based on a representative bundle of goods and services, reflecting consumption patterns in the UK

Knowledge check 10.3

Give reasons why pensioner households might display a different pattern of consumption than other households.

Differences between the CPI and RPI

The CPI and RPI differ for a number of reasons, partly because of differences in the content of the basket of goods and services that are included, and partly in terms of the population of people who are covered by the index. For example, in calculating the weights, the RPI excludes pensioner households and the highest-income households, whereas the CPI does not. There are also some other differences in the ways that the calculations are carried out.

Source: based on data from ONS

Figure 10.1 Alternative inflation measures in the UK, 2007–18

Figure 10.1 shows data for the rates of change of the CPI, RPI and CPIH since 2007. These rates have been calculated on a monthly basis, computing the percentage rate of change of each index relative to the value 12 months previously. Notice that by calculating the inflation rate with reference to the index 12 months previously, seasonal variations are smoothed out — this is an alternative approach to the seasonal adjustment process outlined in Chapter 9.

A noticeable characteristic of Figure 10.1 (apart from in 2009) is that for much of the period the CPI and CPIH have shown a lower rate of change than the RPI. In part this reflects the way in which the prices are combined, but it also reflects the fact that different items and households are covered.

Until the end of 2003, the government's target for inflation was set at 2.5% per annum in the RPIX. After that date, the target for CPI was set at 2% per annum. Since 1997, the Bank of England has had the responsibility of ensuring that inflation remains within one percentage point of this target. You can see from Figure 10.1 that inflation accelerated (on all three measures) during 2008, partly because of rising food prices in world markets, before plummeting in the global financial crisis that hit in late 2009. Notice how RPI inflation actually went negative at this time. This partly reflected the fact that interest rates were at an all-time low, which affected mortgage interest payments, causing RPI to fall for a period. Inflation then accelerated again, remaining above the target rate until 2015.

Synoptic link

Inflation is such an important topic in macroeconomics that we will revisit it in a number of places. Chapter 15 looks at the causes and consequences of inflation; Chapter 16 puts inflation in the context of monetary policy; Chapter 30 discusses how very high inflation hinders transactions; and Chapter 31 explores inflation targeting.

Table 10.2 provides data on consumer prices for the UK, USA and Brazil.

a Calculate the annual inflation rate for each of the countries from 2007 to 2016.

b Plot these three inflation series on a graph against time.

c By what percentage did prices increase in each country over the whole period — that is, between 2006 and 2016?

d Which economy do you judge to have experienced most stability in the inflation rate?

Table 10.2 Consumer prices for the UK, USA and Brazil

	Consumer price index (2011 = 100)		
	UK	USA	Brazil
2006	89.4	94.4	82.9
2007	91.5	95.1	85.9
2008	94.8	96.7	90.8
2009	96.8	98.4	95.2
2010	100.0	100.0	100.0
2011	104.5	103.2	106.6
2012	107.4	105.3	112.4
2013	110.2	106.8	119.4
2014	111.8	108.6	126.9
2015	111.8	108.6	138.4
2016	112.6	110.1	150.5

Source: IMF

Deflation

The recession that began to affect many advanced countries in the late 2000s raised the possibility that the overall level of prices in an economy might fall. This situation of negative inflation is known as **deflation**. Figure 10.1 showed that the UK experienced falling prices according to the RPI for a period. This is not to be confused with **disinflation**, which refers to a period in which inflation falls relative to the previous period.

Deflation is sometimes perceived to be bad for the economy on the grounds that economic agents will see this as a sign that the economy is in terminal decline. Indeed, if people expect prices to continue to fall, they may postpone purchases in the expectation of being able to buy at a lower price in the future. This would then mean a fall in demand in the economy, perpetuating the recession. However, central banks have ways of intervening to prevent deflation being long-lived, and it is not clear that consumers would actually act in the way described.

Key terms

deflation a fall in the average level of prices (negative inflation)

disinflation a fall in the rate of inflation

Knowledge check 10.4

If the rate of change of prices decelerates but remains positive, would this be described as deflation or disinflation?

Exercise 10.3

Table 10.3 shows annual inflation in the UK between 2007 and 2011, as measured by changes in the RPI. Identify years in which there was inflation, deflation and disinflation.

Table 10.3 RPI inflation in the UK, 2007–11

	RPI inflation (% p.a.)
2007	4.3
2008	4.0
2009	−0.5
2010	4.6
2011	5.2

Inflation in the UK and throughout the world

UK inflation in context

Figure 10.2 shows a time path for the rate of change in price levels since 1949, using data for the annual change in the RPI. The figure provides the backdrop to understanding the way the UK economy evolved during this period. Apart from the period of the Korean War, which generated inflation in 1951–52, the 1950s and early 1960s were typified by a low rate of inflation, with some acceleration becoming apparent in the early 1970s. This helps to provide some context for inflation in recent years.

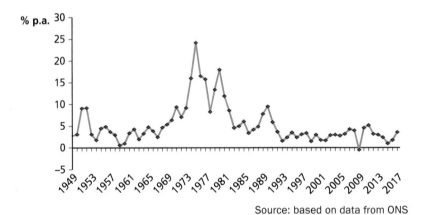

Source: based on data from ONS

Figure 10.2 RPI inflation, 1949–2017 (% change over previous year)

Synoptic link

The pattern of inflation in recent years is discussed in Chapter 15 and in Chapter 31.

Study tip

Although Figure 10.2 shows inflation right back to 1949, you do not need to learn about this whole period in detail. The data are provided to give you some background and context for what has happened more recently. However, it is helpful to be aware of changes and trends in the last few years.

The instability of the 1970s was due to a combination of factors. Oil prices rose dramatically in 1973–74 and again in 1979–80, which certainly contributed to rising prices, not only in the UK but worldwide. However, inflation was further fuelled by the abandonment of the fixed exchange rate system under which sterling had been tied to the US dollar until 1972. Under a fixed exchange rate system, the government must dedicate the use of monetary policy to maintaining the value of the currency. However, the transition to a floating exchange rate system freed up monetary policy in a way that was perhaps not fully understood by the government of the day. As you can see in Figure 10.2, prices were allowed to rise rapidly — by nearly 25% in 1974/75. The diagram also shows how inflation was gradually reined in during the 1980s, and underlines the relative stability that has since been achieved, with inflation keeping well within the target range set by the government until the late 2000s, as noted above.

Worldwide pattern of inflation

Figure 10.3 shows something of the extent to which the UK's experience is typical of the pattern of inflation worldwide. You can see from this how inflation in the industrial countries followed a similar general pattern, with a common acceleration in the early 1970s, and a period of gradual control after 1980. However, you can also see that the developing countries in the world experienced inflation at a much higher average level after 1974 because they proved to be less able to bring prices under control after the oil price shocks. Much of this reflects events in Latin America, which suffered especially high rates of inflation in the 1980s and 1990s. This instability in the macroeconomic environment has almost certainly hindered development in the countries affected, and makes it important to understand how inflation is generated and how to curb it.

Knowledge check 10.5

Why would rising oil prices lead to an increase in other prices?

Study tip

It is useful to be familiar with the costs of inflation, given that policy makers and commentators on the economy have regarded it as one of the most important evils that can afflict an economy, even if in recent years the onset of recession has somewhat switched the main focus of attention in other directions.

Synoptic link

The causes and consequences of inflation are discussed in Chapter 15, after we have learnt some new tools of analysis.

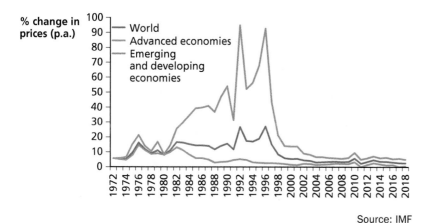

Source: IMF

Figure 10.3 World inflation since 1972 (% change in the consumer price index)

Summary: inflation

- The retail price index (RPI) is one measure of the average price level in the UK.
- In December 2003 the government adopted the consumer price index (CPI) as its preferred measure of the price level, and inflation is monitored through the rate of change of CPI.
- A version of the CPI known as CPIH is now the ONS's headline measure of inflation; this includes housing costs of owner-occupiers and council tax.
- The control of inflation has been the major focus of macroeconomic policy in the UK since about 1976.
- Low inflation reduces uncertainty, and may encourage investment by firms.
- Deflation is negative inflation, and may need corrective action by the central bank to avoid perpetuating a recession.

in employment people who are either working for firms or other organisations, or self-employed

economically inactive those people of working age who are not looking for work, for a variety of reasons

discouraged workers people who have been unable to find employment and who are no longer looking for work

workforce people who are economically active — either in employment or unemployed

unemployed people who are economically active but are not in employment

Employment and the UK workforce

In 2017, there were 42.4 million people living in the UK aged between the ages of 16 and 64. These are those considered to be of working age, although 65 is no longer seen as the normal retirement age. Figure 10.4 shows how they were distributed between three key economic categories: the employed, the unemployed and the economically inactive. Those **in employment** in this context include both those who are employed by firms or other organisations (such as government) and also the self-employed. The **economically inactive** include students, and those who have retired, are sick or are looking after family members. Also included are **discouraged workers** — people who have failed to find work and have given up looking. In other words, the economically inactive category includes all those people in the age range who are not considered to be active in the **workforce**. The **unemployed** are those who are in the workforce, but who are without jobs (a more precise definition will be provided soon).

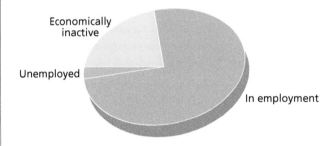

Source: ONS

Figure 10.4 The structure of the UK population aged between 16 and 64 years, 2017

Knowledge check 10.6

Would the unemployed be classified as being economically active or inactive?

The number of those employed is an important indicator, given that they contribute to the production process in their role as the factor of production: labour. Figure 10.5 shows the number of those in employment in each year since 1971. You can see that the number employed has increased substantially over this period, from just over 24 million in 1971 to 32 million in 2017. It is also interesting to note that, although the number employed fell in 2009 as recession began to bite, the number employed recovered quite quickly, with employment in 2017 being higher than it had been in 2008.

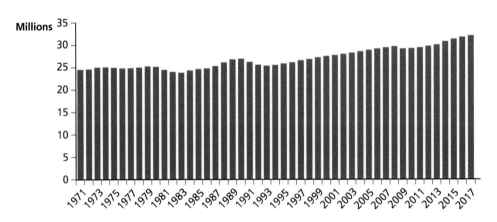

Source: ONS

Figure 10.5 Employment in the UK, 1971–2017

Full employment

Full employment is seen as one of the core macroeconomic policy objectives. Having large numbers of people without jobs means that the economy is not making the best use of its labour resources, and is thus sacrificing potential output that could be produced. It is also undesirable from the perspective of the individuals who find themselves unemployed.

However, does this mean that everyone should have a job or be self-employed? Setting aside those who are economically inactive, there will always be some unemployment in a society, if only because there will be some people between jobs or engaging in job search. Furthermore, if the economy were to be operating very close to full capacity, this would be likely to put upward pressure on wages and thus prices. In other words, there may be a conflict between achieving full employment and maintaining the stability of prices.

So full employment does not mean that unemployment will be zero. But it is difficult to specify a particular percentage that would constitute full employment. This may vary in different periods, and in different countries, partly reflecting the degree of flexibility in the labour market.

Measuring employment

The measurement of unemployment in the UK has also been contentious over the years, and the standard definition used to monitor performance has altered several times, especially during the 1980s, when a number of rationalisations were introduced.

Historically, unemployment was measured by the number of people registered as unemployed and claiming unemployment benefit (the Jobseeker's Allowance (JSA)). This measure of employment is known as the **claimant count of unemployment**. People claiming the JSA must declare that they are out of work, capable of, available for and actively seeking work, during the week in which their claim is made.

One of the problems with the claimant count is that, although people claiming the JSA must declare that they are available for work, it nonetheless includes some people who are claiming benefit, but are not actually available or prepared to work. It also excludes some people who would like to work, and who are looking for work, but who are not eligible for unemployment benefit, such as women returning to the labour force after child birth. The introduction of Universal Credit has made the JSA less reliable as an indicator.

Because of these problems, the claimant count has been superseded for official purposes by the so-called **ILO unemployment rate**, a measure based on the UK *Labour Force Survey*. This identifies the number of people available for work, and seeking work, but without a job. This definition corresponds to that used by the International Labour Organisation (ILO), and is closer to what economists would like unemployment to measure. It defines as being unemployed those people who are:

— *without a job, want a job, have actively sought work in the last four weeks and are available to start work in the next two weeks; or*

— *out of work, have found a job and are waiting to start it in the next two weeks*

(Labour Market Statistics)

Key terms

full employment a situation where people who are economically active in the workforce and are willing and able to work (at going wage rates) are able to find employment

claimant count of unemployment the number of people claiming the Jobseeker's Allowance each month

ILO unemployment rate a measure of the percentage of the workforce who are without jobs, but are available for work, willing to work and looking for work

Knowledge check 10.7

Why will unemployment not be zero if there is full employment?

The ILO employment rate is higher than the claimant count

Quantitative skills 10.1

Calculating the percentage rate of unemployment

When calculating the percentage rate of unemployment, the key question concerns the portion of the active workforce who are unemployed at any point in time. This is calculated by expressing the number of unemployed as a percentage of the active workforce (i.e. employed plus unemployed). At the end of 2017 it was estimated that there were 31.054 million people in employment and 1.338 million people unemployed. The percentage rate was thus: $100 \times 1.338 \div (31.054 + 1.338) = 4.13\%$.

Figure 10.6 shows the ILO unemployment rate since 1971, expressed as a percentage of the workforce. The surge in unemployment in the early 1980s stands out on the graph, when the percentage of the workforce registered as unemployed more than doubled in a relatively short period. Although this seemed to be coming under control towards the end of the 1980s, unemployment rose again in the early 1990s before a steady decline into the new millennium, rising again in the financial crisis and recession of the late 2000s and tailing off towards the end of the 2010s.

Study tip

If you are confronted with a graph such as Figure 10.6, showing unemployment over an extended period, and you need to describe the trends over that period, do not think that you have to work through picking out every observation, but focus on the main periods in which there were divergences from the norm.

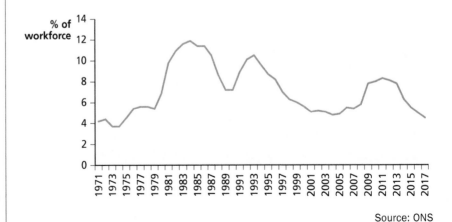

Source: ONS

Figure 10.6 ILO unemployment rate, 1971–2017

Problems of measurement

It is important to be aware of the difficulties in measuring unemployment accurately. The claimant count is unreliable because it only captures those people who are eligible for the Jobseeker's Allowance, so it excludes some people who might be validly recognised as being unemployed. As mentioned earlier, it excludes people returning to the workforce after raising children or for other reasons of absence. It also excludes those who are on government training schemes and a range of other categories of people. The ILO unemployment data are based on sample evidence, and extrapolated up to give the picture for the UK as a whole. The sample cannot be guaranteed to be fully representative. From the perspective of economic analysis, it would also be helpful to know how many people are unemployed in the sense of not being able to find employment at their desired wage, but this is not covered in the definition.

Measuring unemployment in developing countries becomes even more difficult. If there is no social security system, then unemployed workers have no incentive to register as being unemployed. Furthermore, there may be people who cannot find jobs for which they are qualified, and who take jobs in second-choice occupations. This is a form of **underemployment**: for example, where qualified lawyers or doctors find themselves working as taxi drivers. In the UK context, underemployment could take the form of workers being unable to work for as many hours as they would like.

Causes of unemployment

Frictional unemployment

There will always be some unemployment in a dynamic economy. At any point in time, there will be workers transferring between jobs. Indeed, this needs to happen if the pattern of production is to keep up with changing patterns of consumer demand and relative opportunity cost. In other words, in a typical period of time there will be some sectors of an economy that are expanding and others that are in decline. It is crucial that workers are able to transfer from those activities that are in decline to those that are booming. Accordingly, there will be some unemployment while this transfer takes place, and this is known as **frictional unemployment**.

Structural unemployment

In some cases, this transfer of workers between sectors may be quite difficult to accomplish. For example, coal mining may be on the decline in an economy, but international banking may be booming. It is clearly unreasonable to expect coal miners to turn themselves into international bankers overnight. In this sort of situation there may be some longer-term unemployment while workers retrain for new occupations and new sectors of activity. Indeed, there may be workers who find themselves redundant at a relatively late stage in their career and for whom the retraining is not worthwhile, or who cannot find firms that are prepared to train them for a relatively short payback time. Such unemployment is known as **structural unemployment**. It arises because of the mismatch between the skills of workers leaving contracting sectors and the skills required by expanding sectors in the economy.

> ## Key terms
>
> **underemployment** where an individual is employed in a second-choice occupation or is only able to work part-time but would like to work full-time
>
> **frictional unemployment** unemployment associated with job search (i.e. people who are between jobs)
>
> **structural unemployment** unemployment arising because of changes in the pattern of economic activity within an economy

Key terms

cyclical unemployment
unemployment that arises during the downturn of the economic cycle, such as a recession

demand-deficient unemployment
unemployment that arises because of a deficiency of aggregate demand in the economy, so that the equilibrium level of output is below full employment

seasonal unemployment
unemployment that arises in seasons of the year when demand is relatively low

real wage inflexibility an argument that if real wages do not adjust downwards the result would be persistent unemployment

voluntary unemployment
situation arising when an individual chooses not to accept a job at the going wage rate

Synoptic link

Chapter 22 considers the labour market and explains what determines labour demand and supply.

Synoptic link

The ideas of the Keynesian school of macroeconomists are introduced in Chapter 12.

Low demand for workers

Unemployment could also arise in a period of recession, when the demand for workers is low. This is sometimes referred to as **cyclical unemployment**. In addition, there may be periods when the economy is in equilibrium below full employment because of a deficiency in aggregate demand, which is known as **demand-deficient unemployment**. A solution to this might be to boost aggregate demand, but not all economists believe that this is appropriate, as will be discussed later. There may also be times of the year when the demand for labour varies because of seasonal effects: for example, the tourist sector experiences quiet periods during the winter. This may give rise to **seasonal unemployment**.

Knowledge check 10.8

In Figure 10.6 you can see how unemployment was affected in the recession that followed the financial crisis. What sort of unemployment was this?

Wage levels

A further reason for unemployment concerns the level of wages, which can be analysed on the assumption that both the demand for and the supply of labour depend on the wage. Figure 10.7 shows a labour market in which a free market equilibrium would have wage $W\star$ and quantity of labour $L\star$. If for some reason wages were set at W_0, there would be disequilibrium between labour supply (at L_s) and labour demand (at L_d). Expressing this in a different way, here is a situation in which there are more workers seeking employment at the going wage (L_s) than there are firms prepared to hire at that wage (L_d). The difference is unemployment.

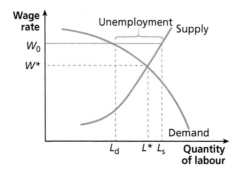

Figure 10.7 Unemployment in a labour market

There is a number of reasons why this situation might arise. Trade unions may have been able to use their power and influence to raise wages above the equilibrium level, thereby ensuring higher wages for their members who remain in employment, but denying jobs to others. Alternatively, it could be argued that real wages will be inflexible downwards. Thus, a shock that reduced firms' demand for labour could leave wages above the equilibrium, and they may adjust downwards only slowly. This argument that unemployment could be caused by **real wage inflexibility** was advanced by economists in the Keynesian school as a reason why unemployment might be persistent.

Finally, if unemployment benefits are set at a relatively high level compared with wages in low-paid occupations, some people may choose not to work, thereby creating some **voluntary unemployment**. From the point of view of those individuals, they are making a rational choice on the basis of the options open to them. However, from society's point of view there needs to be a balance between providing appropriate social protection for those unable to obtain jobs and trying to make the best use of available resources for the benefit of society as a whole.

Migration and unemployment

A contentious issue in recent years has been the question of migration, and the effect of an inflow of migrants on the domestic labour market. From the point of view of economic analysis, this issue turns on the characteristics of immigrant workers, especially in relation to skills. If immigrant workers have skills that are complementary to those of native workers, then a flow of in-migration can have beneficial effects on the domestic economy, by raising national income, resulting in an increase in the demand for workers. The situation is different where in-migrants are substitutes for domestic workers, such that the result may be a decrease in the equilibrium wage.

Synoptic link

The effects of migration are analysed in Chapter 22 as part of the discussion of the labour market.

Costs of unemployment

The consequences of unemployment are mainly negative, affecting consumers, firms, workers, government and society as a whole. This stems from the fact that if there is unemployment, then the economy is operating within its production possibility frontier, and is therefore not making the best possible use of its resources. In other words, there is an opportunity cost to unemployment.

- *Effect on consumers:* consumers are affected because the economy is operating below its capacity, so resources are in shorter supply than could have been. This means that overall, consumers will experience a lower standard of living than could be achieved. Of course, it may be that some consumers will suffer more than others.
- *Effect on firms:* because fewer people are employed, firms will face lower demand for their products, resulting in lower sales and revenues. This in turn is likely to mean lower profits than could have been made. On the other hand, there may be less pressure on firms to pay higher wages.
- *Effect on workers:* the burden of unemployment falls heavily on those workers who lose their jobs — or are unable to find a job. These workers will most obviously experience a lower standard of living. There are also costs to the individual unemployed worker in the sense that **involuntary unemployment** carries a cost in terms of forgone earnings and the need to rely on social security support. At the same time, the inability to find work and to contribute to the family budget may impose a cost in terms of personal worth and dignity.
- *Effect on government:* the government is affected in two key ways. With fewer people in employment, earnings will be lower and income tax revenues will be lower as a result. Indirect tax revenues will also fall if people are spending less on goods and services. At the same time, there will be an increase in the number of people claiming social security benefits, so government spending will rise.
- *Effect on society as a whole:* all of these effects impact society as a whole in a negative way. In addition, there may be additional effects, such as gloomy expectations that may intensify the recession. There may also be an increase in social unrest that may lead to an increase in criminal activity.

Key terms

involuntary unemployment situation arising when an individual who would like to accept a job at the going wage rate is unable to find employment

Exercise 10.4

Classify each of the following types of unemployment as arising from frictional, structural, demand-deficient or other causes, and decide whether they are voluntary or involuntary:

a unemployment arising from a decline of the manufacturing sector and the expansion of financial services

b a worker leaving one job to search for a better one

c unemployment that arises because the real wage rate is held above the labour market equilibrium

d unemployment arising from slow adjustment to a fall in aggregate demand

e unemployment arising because workers find that low-paid jobs are paying less than can be obtained in unemployment benefit

Summary: unemployment

- The population of working age is made up of the employed, the unemployed and the economically inactive.
- Full employment is an objective of macroeconomic policy, as unemployment is costly to those who are unemployed and to society as a whole.
- Unemployment is measured in two ways. The claimant count is based on the number of people claiming Jobseeker's Allowance. The ILO measure is based on a sample of the population through the Labour Force Survey.
- Unemployment arises for a variety of reasons, and there will always be some unemployment in the economy, even when the economy is in equilibrium.

Exercise 10.5

Visit the website of the Office for National Statistics (at www.ons.gov.uk) and find out the latest data for inflation and unemployment. Has the performance of the economy in respect of these two variables improved or deteriorated in the last year?

The balance of payments

Another important dimension over which the macroeconomy needs to be monitored is in relation to a country's transactions with the rest of the world. Such transactions involve exports and imports of goods and services, but also assets, not to mention the flow of factor incomes. All of these transactions are monitored through the **balance of payments**, which is a set of accounts designed to identify international transactions between the UK economy and the rest of the world.

It is important to be able to monitor these transactions because of the increasing interconnectedness of economies through the process of international trade — a process known as *globalisation*. Economies have become more and more connected as a result of rapid changes in communications and transport technology, and with the increasing deregulation of markets. The UK's decision to reduce its dependence on the EU through Brexit would go against this trend, but its success would depend on being able to develop new links with economies elsewhere in the world.

Key term

balance of payments a set of accounts showing the transactions conducted between residents of a country and the rest of the world

Synoptic link

This process of globalisation, by which economies have become increasingly interconnected, is discussed in Chapter 24.

The transactions in the balance of payments are separated into three categories. Transactions in goods and services, together with income payments and transfers, comprise the **current account**. The **capital account** reflects transactions in fixed assets and is relatively small; it refers mainly to transactions involving migrants. The **financial account** records transactions in financial assets.

The current account

Commentators often focus on the current account. Three main items appear on this account. First, there is the balance of trade in goods and services — in other words, the balance between UK exports and imports of such goods and services. If UK residents buy German cars, this is an import and counts as a negative entry on the current account; on the other hand, if a German resident buys a British car, this is an export and constitutes a positive entry. In the UK, the trade in goods is normally negative overall. However, this is partly balanced by a normally positive flow in trade in services, where the UK earns strong credits from its financial services.

The process of trading with other countries creates important connections across national borders. After all, UK exports become the imports of its trading partners. In principle, this suggests that overall the sum of all countries' trade balances should be zero. In practice, this will not be the case — if only because of data inaccuracies and misrecordings. However, it is important to realise that the demand for UK exports depends in part on economic conditions in its trading partners.

Key terms

current account of the balance of payments an account identifying transactions in goods and services between the residents of a country and the rest of the world

capital account of the balance of payments an account identifying transactions in (physical) capital between the residents of a country and the rest of the world

financial account of the balance of payments an account identifying transactions in financial assets between the residents of a country and the rest of the world

Synoptic link

Net exports comprise an important part of aggregate demand, as will be discussed in Chapter 11.

BMW cars waiting to be exported at Bremerhaven harbour, Germany

The second item in the current account is (primary) income. Part of this represents employment income from abroad, but the major item of income is made up of profits, dividends and interest receipts arising from UK ownership of overseas assets.

Finally, there are international transfers (secondary income) — either transfers through central government or transfers made or received by private individuals. This includes transactions and grants with international organisations or with the EU. The current balance combines these items together into an overall balance.

The overall balance of payments

Overall, the balance of payments must always be zero, as in some way or other we have to pay for all we consume and receive payment for all we sell. However, because data can never be entirely accurate, the accounts also incorporate a 'net errors and omissions' item, which ensures that everything balances at the end of the day.

What this really means is that any deficit in the current and capital accounts will always be balanced by a surplus on the financial account. Notice that the financial account incorporates official foreign exchange transactions undertaken by the government. In other words, if British residents buy more goods and services than they sell (i.e. if there is a current account deficit), then they must pay for them by selling financial assets or foreign exchange (i.e. there must be a financial account surplus).

There is a number of ways in which the overall balance can be achieved. 'Balance' could mean that both current and financial accounts are small, or it could mean that a deficit on one is balanced by a surplus on the other. The media tend to focus on the current balance, and a deficit on current account is sometimes seen as a matter of concern. A persistent deficit on the current account may pose long-term problems that need to be addressed, as it may not be desirable to continue selling UK assets indefinitely.

Table 10.4 presents the components of the balance of payments accounts for 2017. This was a year in which the current account was in substantial deficit. The financial account was in surplus.

Table 10.4 The UK balance of payments, 2017 (£ million at current prices)

Trade in goods and services	−23,933
Primary income (investment income)	−23,571
Secondary income (including transfers)	−20,861
Current balance	**−68,365**
Capital account	**−1,724**
Financial account	**89,864**
Net errors and omissions	−19,775
Overall balance of payments	**0**

Source: ONS

Imagine a situation in which inflation accelerates, so that the Bank of England needs to take action. It would do this by raising the rate of interest. High UK interest rates would tend to attract financial inflows from abroad, as investors would find the UK an attractive home for their funds. These flows are sometimes known as 'hot money'. This implies a surplus on the financial account — and hence a deficit on the current account. The downside of such a structure is that UK assets would be sold abroad, which might not be in the best interest of the economy in the long run.

Monitoring the components of the balance of payments

It is this potential long-run difficulty that makes it important to monitor the overall balance over time. Figure 10.8 shows the main components of the balance of payments since 1980, in current price (nominal) terms, which is the form in which the data are published by the ONS. This is in the form of a stacked bar chart, and

Knowledge check 10.9

Explain why the balance of payments must always balance overall.

the nature of the balance of payments is that the positive and negative components exactly balance each year. The clear picture that emerges is that the current account has been negative (in deficit) for most of the period since 1980, and that this has been balanced by a positive balance (surplus) on the financial account. In other words, the UK has been importing more goods and services than it has been exporting; but this has been counterbalanced by the surplus on the financial account (i.e. of UK assets sold abroad).

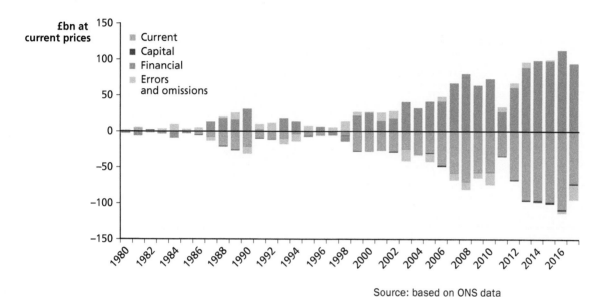

Source: based on ONS data

Figure 10.8 The UK balance of payments, 1980–2017

The data in Figure 10.8 are measured in current prices, which means that they are nominal measurements, which make no attempt to allow for the effects of inflation. It would thus be misleading to infer too much about the magnitude of the quantities shown. A better perspective on this is provided by Figure 10.9, which shows the current account balance expressed as a percentage of nominal GDP. This helps to put the more recent data into perspective.

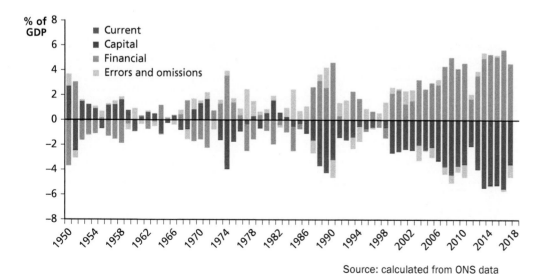

Source: calculated from ONS data

Figure 10.9 The current account of the UK balance of payments, 1950–2017

Knowledge check 10.10

Explain why looking at the balance of payments measured in current prices could be misleading.

Closely associated with the balance of payments is the **exchange rate** — the price of domestic goods in terms of foreign currency. Chapter 5 introduced the notion of the demand and supply of foreign currency, as shown in Figure 10.10. The demand for pounds arises from overseas residents (e.g. in the euro area) wanting to purchase UK goods, services or assets, whereas the supply of pounds emanates from domestic residents wanting to purchase overseas goods, services or assets. The connection is that the balance of payments accounts itemise these transactions, which entail the demand for and supply of pounds.

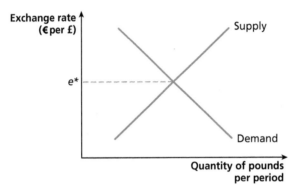

Figure 10.10 The market for pounds sterling

Key term

exchange rate the price of one currency in terms of another

Synoptic link

Chapter 15 discusses macroeconomic objectives (including issues surrounding the balance of payments) and how they are interrelated. The way in which economies are interconnected through international trade is discussed in Chapter 24. The balance of payments and the exchange rate are explored in more detail in Chapter 26.

Summary: the balance of payments

- The balance of payments is a set of accounts which itemises transactions that take place between an economy and the rest of the world, including goods, services, income and assets.
- The current account sets out transactions in goods, services, investment income and transfers.
- The capital account itemises transactions in fixed assets and is relatively small.
- The financial account covers transactions in financial assets and includes direct investment and official intervention in the foreign exchange market ('official financing').
- The overall balance of payments is always zero.
- However, this overall balance has often been achieved in the UK through a persistent deficit on the current account, balanced by a corresponding surplus on the financial account.
- This may be a matter for concern in the long run.

Case study 10.1

The UK economy in mid-2008

Figures 10.11 and 10.12 respectively show monthly inflation and unemployment in the UK between the beginning of 2004 and March 2008. Imagine that you are the chancellor of the exchequer considering the state of the economy.

Follow-up question

Discuss whether these two indicators give cause for concern about the performance of the economy. What other information would you need in order to come to a judgement?

After you have thought about this, look back at Figures 10.1 and 10.6 to see what happened next.

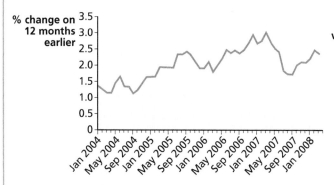

Source: ONS

Figure 10.11 Inflation in the UK, 2004–08

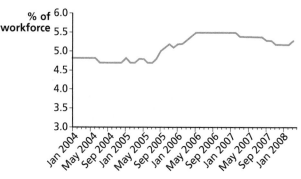

Source: ONS

Figure 10.12 Unemployment in the UK, 2004–08

Case study 10.2

The UK balance of trade

Figure 10.13 shows the UK's balance of trade in goods since 1990, measured in current prices. The picture is startling, showing a steady increase in the deficit since 1997, following a period of relative stability.

There are several possible causes underpinning this picture. One relates to the production of North Sea oil and gas, which peaked in the late 1990s, and has declined steadily since then. Second, the structure of economic activity has been changing, such that the trade balance in services has increased steadily, which partly offsets the decline in the goods trade balance.

Overall, the negative trade balance has contributed to the overall deficit on the current account of the balance of payments, which has meant that the overall balance of payments has only been maintained by surpluses on the financial account.

Follow-up questions

a What is the significance of the fact that the trade balance as shown in Figure 10.13 is measured in current prices?
b Why is the changing structure of the economy pertinent in trying to understand why the trade deficit has declined so rapidly?
c To what extent does the increasing deficit in the trade balance raise concerns for the authorities?

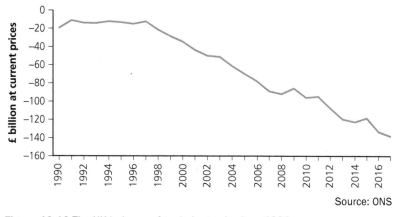

Source: ONS

Figure 10.13 The UK balance of trade in goods since 1990

11 Aggregate demand

Now that you have been introduced to the main macroeconomic aggregates, it is time to start thinking about how economic analysis can be used to explore the ways in which these variables interact. The starting point is to consider the components of aggregate demand. The way in which the levels of these components are determined in practice is an important key to the operation of the economy when considered at the aggregate level.

Learning objectives

After studying this chapter, you should:
→ understand what is meant by aggregate demand
→ be able to identify the components of aggregate demand and their determinants
→ be familiar with the notion of the aggregate demand curve

The components of aggregate demand

Key term

aggregate demand the total amount of spending on goods and services produced in an economy during a period of time

Aggregate demand is the total amount of spending on goods and services produced in an economy during a period of time. Understanding the factors that influence this is an important step in analysing the operation of the economy at the aggregate level.

It is helpful to separate aggregate demand into its key components, according to which economic agents are undertaking the spending. It is then possible to analyse how each component will be determined. The key economic agents in this context are households, firms and government. However, for an economy that engages in international trade, it is also important to take account of spending in and by the rest of the world.

From this perspective, aggregate demand comprises the combined spending of households on consumer goods and firms on investment goods, together with government expenditure (including current and capital spending). Exports (spending by the rest of the world on domestically produced goods) add to aggregate demand, but spending by residents on goods and services from the rest of the world (imports) must be deducted. The full version of aggregate expenditure can thus be written as:

$$AD = C + I + G + (X - M)$$

where AD denotes aggregate demand, C is consumption, I is investment, G is government spending, X is exports and M is imports.

Knowledge check 11.1

In thinking about the components of aggregate demand, which economic agent or agents undertake investment expenditure?

Figure 11.1 shows the expenditure-side breakdown of real GDP in the UK in 2017. This highlights the relative size of the components of aggregate demand. Consumption is by far the largest component, amounting to about 66% of real GDP in 2017. Government current expenditure accounted for 18.6%, but you should realise that this somewhat understates the importance of government in overall spending, as it excludes public spending on investment, which is treated together with private sector investment in the data. Combined public and private sector investment made up just under 17% of total GDP; this includes changes in the inventory holdings of firms. Notice that imports were rather higher than exports, indicating a negative balance of trade in goods and services.

Knowledge check 11.2

What is the largest component of aggregate demand?

Exercise 11.1

Suppose there is an economy in which the values in Table 11.1 apply.

a Calculate the level of aggregate demand.

b Calculate the trade balance.

Table 11.1 Values in an economy (all measured in £ million)

Consumption	75
Profits	60
Investment	30
Government expenditure	25
Exports	50
Private saving	50
Imports	55

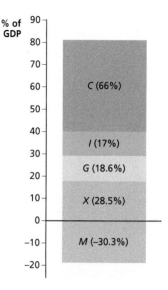

Note: C includes spending by non-profit institutions serving households; I includes changes in inventory holdings; the statistical discrepancy is not shown.

Source: ONS

Figure 11.1 The breakdown of real GDP in 2017

Consumption

Consumption is the largest single component of aggregate demand. What factors could be expected to influence the size of total spending by households? John Maynard Keynes, in his influential book *The General Theory of Employment, Interest and Money*, published in 1936, suggested that the most important determinant is **disposable income**. Disposable income here refers to the income that households have to devote to consumption and saving, taking into account payments of direct taxes and transfer payments.

In other words, as real incomes rise, households will tend to spend more. However, he also pointed out that they would not spend all of an increase in income, but would save some of it. Keynes defined the **average propensity to consume** as the ratio of consumption to income, and the **marginal propensity to consume (MPC)** as the proportion of an increase in disposable income that households would devote to consumption. Similarly, the **marginal propensity to save (MPS)** is the proportion of an increase in disposable income that households would devote to saving.

Synoptic link

The significance of the marginal propensity to consume (and other marginal propensities) is set out in Chapter 13.

Key terms

consumption total planned household spending

disposable income the income that households have to devote to consumption and saving, taking into account payments of direct taxes and transfer payments

average propensity to consume the proportion of income that households devote to consumption

marginal propensity to consume (MPC) the proportion of additional income devoted to consumption

marginal propensity to save (MPS) the proportion of an increase in disposable income that households would devote to saving

J. M. Keynes's hugely influential book *The General Theory of Employment, Interest and Money* was published in 1936

Quantitative skills 11.1

Calculating the average and marginal propensities to consume

Suppose that in an economy, household consumption (*C*) is $80 and disposable income (*Y*) is $100. The average propensity to consume is calculated as $C/Y = 80/100 = 0.8$. If disposable income increases to 110 and consumption rises to 87, we can calculate the marginal propensity to consume as the proportion of the increase in income that is devoted to consumption. We need to divide the change in consumption by the change in income. In other words, it is $(87 - 80)/(110 - 100) = 0.7$.

Knowledge check 11.3

Define the 'marginal propensity to consume'.

Exercise 11.2

Suppose that in an economy, household consumption (*C*) is 160 and disposable income (*Y*) is 200. Suppose that disposable income increases to 220 and consumption rises to 174.

Calculate the average propensity to save in the initial year and the marginal propensity to save out of the additional income in the second year.

Extension material: other consumption hypotheses

Later writers argued that consumption does not necessarily depend on current income alone. For example, Milton Friedman put forward the *permanent income hypothesis*, which suggested that consumers take decisions about consumption based on a notion of their permanent, or normal, income levels — that is, the income that they expect to receive over a 5- or 10-year time horizon. This suggests that households do not necessarily vary their consumption patterns in response to changes in income that they perceive to be only transitory.

An associated theory is the *life-cycle hypothesis*, developed by Ando Modigliani, who suggested that households smooth their consumption over their lifetimes, on the basis of their expected lifetime incomes. Thus, people tend to borrow in their youth against future income; then in middle age, when earning more strongly, they pay off their debts and save in preparation to fund their consumption in retirement. Consumption thus varies by much less than income, and is based on expected lifetime earnings rather than on current income.

Other influences on consumption

Key term

wealth effects where changes in household wealth induce changes in consumer expenditure

However, income will not be the only influence on consumption. There may also be **wealth effects**. It is important to realise that income and wealth are not the same: wealth is the accumulation of assets, which is different in concept from the flow of income received by households per period. Wealth can be thought of in terms of the asset holdings of households. If households experience an increase in the value of their asset holdings, this may influence their spending decisions. In particular, changes in house prices that affect the wealth of households may influence their expenditure: if house prices increase, households may be more prepared to consume rather than save, having the security of their property. The general state of the economy may also be a factor, as households may spend more if they have confidence in the future. Of course, in times of recession or falling house prices, the reverse may happen.

Furthermore, if part of household spending is financed by borrowing, the rate of interest may be significant in influencing the total amount of consumption spending. An increase in the rate of interest that raises the cost of borrowing may deter consumption. At the same time it may encourage saving, as the return on saving is higher when the interest rate is higher. The rate of interest may also have an indirect effect on consumption through its effect on the value of asset holdings. In addition, households may be influenced in their consumption decisions by their expectations about future inflation. Notice that some of these effects may not be instantaneous: that is, consumption may adjust to changes in its determinants only after a time lag.

Finally, consumer spending may be influenced by expectations about the overall health of the economy, and the confidence of individual consumers. This confidence (or lack of it) may be influenced by trends in house or share prices, or uncertainty caused by the global environment.

Knowledge check 11.4

What is the most important influence on consumer expenditure?

Extension material: the consumption function

The relationship between consumption and income is known as the *consumption function*. This is shown in Figure 11.2, which focuses on the relationship between consumption and household income, ceteris paribus: in other words, in drawing the relationship between consumption and income, it is assumed that the other determinants of consumption, such as wealth and the interest rate, remain constant. A change in any of these other influences will affect the *position* of the line. Notice that the marginal propensity to consume (*MPC*) is the slope of this line.

In practice, it is not expected that the empirical relationship between consumption and income will reveal an exact straight line, if only because over a long time period there will be changes in the other influences on consumption, such as interest rates and expected inflation. However, Figure 11.3

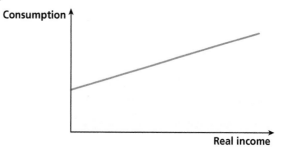

Figure 11.2 The consumption function

shows that the hypothesis is not totally implausible, as indicated by the fact that most of the scatter points are quite close to the fitted line. However, there are some points that diverge from the pattern towards the end of the period, suggesting that the relationship was affected by the recession that followed the financial crisis of the late 2000s.

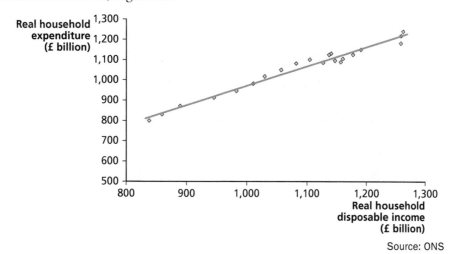

Source: ONS

Figure 11.3 Real consumption and disposable income in the UK, 1997–2017

Key terms

investment expenditure undertaken by firms on capital goods

gross investment net investment plus depreciation

depreciation (of capital equipment) the fall in the value of capital goods due to wear and tear

net investment investment net of the replacement of existing capital (depreciation)

Study tip

In economics 'investment' relates to a firm buying new capital, such as machinery or factory buildings. If you put money into a bank account, that is an act of saving, not investment. Do not confuse these different concepts.

Quantitative skills 11.2

Interpreting the marginal propensity to consume

If the *MPC* is 0.7, this means that for every additional £100 of income received by households, £100 × 0.7 = £70 would be consumer expenditure and the remaining £30 would be saved.

Investment

The second major component of aggregate demand is spending by firms on **investment**. Investment leads to an increase in the productive capacity of the economy, by increasing the stock of capital available for production. This capital stock comprises plant and machinery, vehicles and other transport equipment, and buildings, including new dwellings, which provide a supply of housing services over a long period.

Gross investment (i.e. total investment) is made up of two components. Part of investment by firms is to replace capital that has worn out: this component of investment relates to the **depreciation** of old capital. The second component (**net investment**) is investment undertaken to increase a firm's productive capacity. In exploring aggregate demand, it is important to consider what will induce firms to undertake such productive investment.

Net investment includes machinery and factory buildings, critical factors in the production process

Expectations about future demand

The overall state of the economy may be an important influence. If the economy is going through a period of rapid economic growth, and this is expected to continue, then firms are likely to be optimistic about the future prospects for demand for their products, and will wish to be able to exploit the opportunities for profit. On the other hand, when the economy heads into recession, the prospects for the future will be less robust, and firms may hesitate to invest in new capacity.

This suggests that business expectations and confidence in the future path of the economy will be important in shaping their willingness to undertake investment expenditure. Keynes argued that the 'animal spirits' of firms would influence them in this situation. This could result in instability in the economy. If recession dampens the confidence with which firms view the future, such that investment expenditure falls, this will deepen the recession — or at least delay the recovery.

Expectations about future demand depend not only on the state of the domestic economy. International competitiveness is also important where firms are involved in exporting activity. There may be firms where a buoyant demand for exports can offset the effects of low domestic demand. However, in the case of a global recession that affects many economies simultaneously, the dampening effects on confidence could be severe. The recession that followed the financial crisis of the late 2000s was a case in point, affecting many of the world's advanced countries.

Government incentives

Decisions on investment may also be influenced by government, which has an interest in encouraging investment because of its beneficial impact on expanding the economy's productive capacity and hence on economic growth. It may do this by providing incentives for firms to invest, in the form of tax concessions. It may also use regulation to influence the pattern or location of investment: for example, by targeting EU funding towards parts of the country that have found it difficult to attract private investment.

It has also been argued that inflation is damaging for an economy, as a high rate of inflation increases uncertainty about the future and may dampen firms' expectations about future demand, thereby discouraging investment.

These influences on investment focus on reasons why firms may wish to undertake investment expenditure. However, it is also important to consider how such expenditure is to be financed, given that firms must spend in the present but will reap the returns in the future. This suggests that the cost and availability of finance for investment will also affect the amount of investment that takes place.

Investment and the interest rate

Consider the cost of obtaining finance for investment. The rate of interest represents the cost of borrowing, so if firms need to borrow in order to undertake investment, they may be discouraged from spending on investment goods when the rate of interest is relatively high. Notice that not all investment has to be funded from borrowing — firms may be able to use past profits for this purpose. However, if firms choose to do this, they face an opportunity cost. In other words, profits can be used to buy financial assets that will provide a rate of return dependent on the rate of interest. The rate of interest is thus important, as it represents the opportunity cost of an investment project.

Synoptic link

The significance of investment for developing countries is discussed in Chapter 28.

Knowledge check 11.5

What are the main influences on investment expenditure by firms?

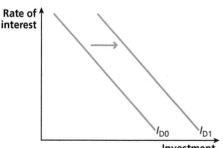

Figure 11.4 Investment and the rate of interest

Figure 11.4 shows the relationship between investment and the rate of interest. The investment demand function I_{D0} is downward sloping because investment is relatively low when the rate of interest is relatively high. An improvement in business confidence for the future would result in more investment being undertaken at any given interest rate, so the investment function would move from I_{D0} to I_{D1}.

Firms' willingness to borrow in order to finance their investment expenditure is only part of the story. Access to credit is also crucial. In order for firms to be able to borrow, it is necessary that financial institutions are prepared to lend and that they have funds available to lend. In the aftermath of the financial crisis, one manifestation of which was the failure of some banks, the commercial banks appeared unwilling to lend, having become more averse to taking risk. The ability of banks to provide credit also depends on the behaviour of households, who provide bank deposits through their saving activity. With rates of interest at the low levels seen during and after the crisis, the returns on saving have been correspondingly low.

Government expenditure

By and large, you might expect government expenditure to be decided by different criteria from those influencing private sector expenditures.

From the point of view of investigating macroeconomic equilibrium, government expenditure can be regarded as mainly *autonomous*: that is, independent of the variables in the model that will be constructed in this chapter and the following ones. In some situations, the government may choose to manipulate its spending in order to influence the path of the economy.

It is also important to be aware that some parts of government expenditure are likely to vary with fluctuations in the level of overall economic activity. Think about what happens if the economy moves into a period of recession. Some workers lose their jobs, and start to claim the Jobseeker's Allowance — which affects government expenditure. Furthermore, workers who are no longer in work cease to pay income tax, so government revenue falls. The reverse effect occurs during the recovery period, so net government expenditure can be seen to vary with the business cycle.

Net trade (X – M)

Finally, there are the factors that may influence the level of exports and imports. Most imports into the UK are normal goods, so as real incomes rise over time, there will be an increase in demand for imported goods. However, the demand for exports will depend on changes in income in the UK's trade partners. If there is slow economic growth in the countries that are customers for the UK's exports, then this will have an impact on aggregate demand in the UK. The global recession that set in during the late 2000s had a noticeable effect on world trade.

Another factor that will affect both exports and imports is the exchange rate between sterling and other currencies. This affects the relative prices of UK goods and those produced overseas. Other things being equal, an increase in the sterling exchange rate makes UK exports less competitive and imports into the UK more competitive.

The volume of international trade can also be affected by protectionist policies introduced by countries to protect their own industries. Historically, many countries imposed tariffs on imports of goods. A tariff is a tax on imports, and the period after the Second World War showed substantial reductions in tariff rates to allow

Synoptic link

Chapter 32 returns to the issue of how government expenditure will vary across the business cycle.

Knowledge check 11.6

What is meant by the statement that government expenditure is 'autonomous'?

countries to benefit from specialisation and trade. However, some tariffs remain, and countries have also imposed non-tariff barriers to limit their dependence on trade. This might be in the form of regulations that impose restrictive quality controls on imported goods. In 2018, a trade war threatened, with President Trump raising tariffs against some imports from China, later also extended to EU countries. This brought retaliatory action from China and the EU.

The demand for exports and imports will also depend on the relative prices of goods produced in the UK and the rest of the world. If UK inflation is high relative to elsewhere, again this will tend to make UK exports less competitive and imports more competitive. Movements in the exchange rate can thus tend to counteract changes in relative prices between countries.

▌The aggregate demand curve

The key relationship to carry forward from this discussion is the **aggregate demand curve**, which shows the relationship between aggregate demand and the overall price level. Formally, this curve shows the total amount of goods and services demanded in an economy at any given overall level of prices.

It is important to realise that this is a very different sort of demand curve from the microeconomic demand curves that were introduced in Chapter 2, where the focus was on an individual product and its relationship with its own price. Here the relationship is between the total demand for goods and services and the overall price level. Thus, aggregate demand is made up of all the components discussed above, and price is an average of all prices of goods and services in the economy.

Figure 11.5 shows an aggregate demand curve. The key question is why it slopes downwards. To answer this, it is necessary to determine the likely influence of the price level on the various components of aggregate demand that have been discussed in this chapter, as prices have not been mentioned explicitly (except for how expectations about inflation might influence consumer spending). First, however, the discussion needs to be cast in terms of the price *level*.

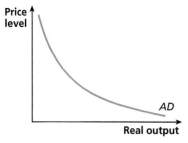

Figure 11.5 An aggregate demand curve

The position of the *AD* curve

When the overall level of prices is relatively low, the purchasing power of income is relatively high. In other words, low overall prices can be thought of as indicating relatively high real income. Furthermore, when prices are low, this raises the real value of households' wealth. For example, suppose a household holds a financial asset such as a bond with a fixed money value of £100. The relative (real) value of that asset is higher when the overall price level is relatively low. From the above discussion, this suggests that, ceteris paribus, a low overall price level means relatively high

Synoptic link

Protectionist policies are discussed more fully in Chapter 25 following the explanation of why countries engage in international trade.

Knowledge check 11.7

What would be the effect on net exports if there is a fall in the sterling exchange rate?

Key term

aggregate demand (AD) curve the relationship between the level of aggregate demand and the overall price level; it shows planned expenditure at any given possible overall price level

Study tip

It is important to remember this difference between the aggregate demand curve and the microeconomic demand curve for a product. In the macroeconomic context, always label the vertical axis as 'Price level' as a reminder.

real balance effect an
effect by which an increase
in the average price level
reduces purchasing power
and thus the quantity of
real output demanded

Study tip

As with the microeconomic
demand curve, the
distinction between a shift
of the *AD* curve and a
movement along it is very
important. A change in the
overall price level induces
a movement along the *AD*
curve, while a change in
any of the components of
aggregate demand leads
to a shift of the curve.

consumption. Conversely, an increase in the average price level reduces purchasing power, thus reducing the quantity of real output demanded: this is the **real balance effect**.

A second argument relates to interest rates. When prices are relatively low, interest rates also tend to be relatively low, which, it was argued, would encourage both investment and consumption expenditure, as interest rates can be seen as representing the cost of borrowing.

A third argument concerns exports and imports. It has been argued that, ceteris paribus, when UK prices are relatively low compared with the rest of the world, this will increase the competitiveness of UK goods, leading to an increase in foreign demand for UK exports, and a fall in the demand for imports into the UK as people switch to buying UK goods and services.

All of these arguments support the idea that the aggregate demand curve should be downward sloping. In other words, when the overall price level is relatively low, aggregate demand will be relatively high, and when prices are relatively high, aggregate demand will be relatively low.

Other factors discussed above will affect the position of the *AD* curve. It is again very important to be aware of the distinction between a movement along and a shift of the aggregate demand curve. A change in the overall price level induces a movement along the *AD* curve, but a change in any of the components of aggregate demand will result in a shift of the *AD* curve. For example, an increase in government expenditure would lead to a rightward shift of the *AD* curve. The effects of this on the macroeconomy will be analysed after we have explored the aggregate supply curve.

Knowledge check 11.8

What factors would induce a shift of the aggregate demand curve, and what would induce a movement along it?

Summary: aggregate demand

- Aggregate demand is the total demand in an economy, made up of consumption, investment, government spending and net exports.
- Consumption is the largest of these components and is determined by income and other influences, such as interest rates, wealth and expectations about the future.
- Investment leads to increases in the capital stock and is influenced by interest rates, past profits and expectations about future demand.
- Government expenditure may be regarded as largely autonomous.
- Trade in goods and services (exports and imports) is determined by the competitiveness of domestic goods and services compared with the rest of the world, which in turn is determined by relative inflation rates and the exchange rate. Imports are also affected by domestic income, and exports are affected by incomes in the rest of the world.
- The aggregate demand curve shows the relationship between aggregate demand and the overall price level.

Investment and the financial crisis

Investment in capital goods includes expenditure by firms on plant and machinery, buildings and transport equipment. In other words, this is expenditure on produced resources that will be used in the future production of goods and services. Firms also need to spend on depreciation to replace old capital goods. Government also contributes to investment, in particular by expenditure on infrastructure that contributes to the smooth running of the economy. This means that investment is very important for the economy, as it contributes to economic growth by providing the capital resources needed to increase the productive capacity of the economy.

The amount of investment expenditure that firms undertake depends on many factors. For firms to remain viable they need to make profits, and investment is one way of improving their profit prospects. Indeed, in a competitive market environment, investment may be needed just to keep up with competitors by remaining cost-effective in their production methods. Investment expenditure now is to bring benefits in the future, although the costs come in the present. For example, investment in a new factory must be paid for in the present, although the benefits will not accrue until some future period.

(The same reasoning applies to government expenditure on a high-speed train link or a tunnel under Stonehenge, which will only bring benefits in the future.) Firms' expectations about their future prospects will thus figure heavily in their decision making.

Another key factor to take into account is how firms will finance their spending in the period before the investment begins to provide a return. Firms may be able to finance investment expenditure from their existing resources, such as past profits. Otherwise, they may need to borrow now against the future returns.

Figure 11.6 shows investment in the UK as a percentage of GDP from 2005–17. (Note that 'gross fixed capital formation' is the term used by the ONS to describe 'investment' in the national accounts.) This covers the period of the global financial crisis of the late 2000s and its aftermath.

Follow-up questions

a What factors could explain the percentage of GDP devoted to investment in the 2005–17 period shown in Figure 11.6?

b From 2009 onwards, interest rates were at an all-time low. How would this be expected to affect firms' willingness to undertake investment?

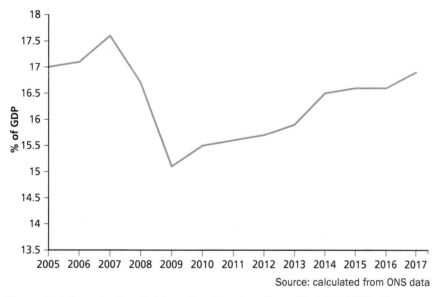

Source: calculated from ONS data

Figure 11.6 Gross fixed capital formation (investment) as a % of GDP 2005–17

12 Aggregate supply

Having seen what is meant by aggregate demand, it is now time to investigate aggregate supply and the factors that influence it in both the short run and the long run. The different approaches adopted by the Keynesian and classical/monetarist schools of thought will be discussed.

Learning objectives

After studying this chapter, you should:
→ understand what is meant by aggregate supply
→ be able to identify the factors that influence aggregate supply in the short and long run
→ be familiar with the notion of the aggregate supply curve
→ be familiar with alternative Keynesian and classical views of the long-run aggregate supply curve

The aggregate supply curve

The previous chapter discussed the notion of aggregate demand and introduced the aggregate demand curve. The next stage of building a model of the macroeconomy is to derive a second relationship: that between aggregate supply and the price level.

Aggregate supply covers the output of all sorts of goods and services that is produced within an economy during a period of time. However, it is not simply a question of adding up all the individual supply curves from individual markets. Within an individual market, an increase in price may induce higher supply of a good because firms will switch from other markets in search of higher profits. What we now need to be looking for is a relationship between the *overall* price level and the total amount supplied, which is a different kettle of fish given the interrelated nature of markets at the microeconomic level.

The total quantity of output supplied in an economy in a period of time depends on the quantities of inputs of factors of production employed: that is, the total amounts of labour, capital and other factors used. The ability of firms to vary output in the short run will be influenced by the degree of flexibility the firms have in varying inputs. It is thus necessary to distinguish between short-run and long-run aggregate supply.

Aggregate supply in the short run

In the short run, firms may have relatively little flexibility to vary their inputs. Money wages are likely to be fixed, and if firms wish to vary output, they may need to do so by varying the intensity of utilisation of existing inputs. For example, if a firm wishes to expand output, the only way of doing so in the short run may be by paying its existing workers overtime, or paying a premium price for quick delivery of raw materials. Firms may only be prepared to incur these costs if they can pass on the cost in the form of higher prices. This suggests that in the short run, aggregate supply may be upward sloping, as shown in Figure 12.1, where *SRAS* represents **short-run aggregate supply.**

Figure 12.1 Aggregate supply in the short run

Firms will not want to operate in this way in the long run. It is not good practice to be permanently paying workers overtime. In the long run, therefore, firms will adjust their working practices and hire additional workers to avoid this situation.

As always, it is important to be aware of the distinction between shifts *of* the aggregate supply curve, and movements *along* it. If the overall price level changes, this will induce a movement along the curve, but if something changes to affect the position of the curve, it will shift. So what factors affect the position of the short-run aggregate supply curve?

The position of the short-run aggregate supply curve

Underlying the aggregate supply curve are the decisions taken by firms about production levels at any given price. Firms are assumed to choose how much output to produce in order to maximise profits. In the short run, the strongest influence on these decisions is likely to be the costs faced by firms, as these can change quite rapidly in the short run, whereas other factors such as technological change are more significant in the long run. So, a change in the costs faced by firms may induce them to choose to supply more (or less) output.

The cost of inputs
There are several factors that could influence costs in the short run. For example, suppose there is a change in the cost of raw materials. If a key raw material becomes more limited in supply, perhaps because reserves are exhausted, then prices will tend to rise, thus raising firms' costs of production. They may then choose to supply less output at any given price — and the aggregate supply curve would shift to the left.

The price of oil has been subject to significant variations over time. Oil is a key input for many firms, and an increase in the price of oil affects the cost of energy and transport. It also affects the economy in many other ways, as oil is a key input in the production of many fertilisers used in the agricultural sector. The price of oil may therefore have a significant impact on the position of aggregate supply in the short run.

Another key input for firms is labour, so an increase in labour costs will also cause a leftward shift of the short-run aggregate supply curve.

Key term

short-run aggregate supply curve (SRAS) a curve showing how much output firms would be prepared to supply in the short run at any given overall price level

Knowledge check 12.1

Explain why the short-run aggregate supply curve (SRAS) is upward-sloping.

Study tip

This distinction between shifts of a curve and movements along it keeps cropping up — this is because it is really important to distinguish between the two sorts of change.

Knowledge check 12.2

What would induce a movement up along the SRAS?

Synoptic link

You can see the extent to which the price of oil has fluctuated over time by looking back at Figure 5.2 on page 70.

Variations in the price of oil can have an impact on aggregate supply in the short run

The exchange rate

Where firms rely on imported inputs of raw materials, energy or component parts used in production, then a change in the exchange rate could affect aggregate supply, by affecting the domestic price of imported inputs. This could be favourable, of course, depending on the direction in which the exchange rate changes. It could be that the exchange rate rises (appreciates), thus reducing the domestic price of imports. Firms may then be prepared to supply more output at any given price, so the aggregate supply curve would shift to the right.

The exchange rate can change in the short run for a variety of different reasons, so firms may face some quite sudden changes in their costs. One way that firms can guard against this is through the nature of the contracts drawn up with their foreign suppliers, if future prices can be specified in a way that hedges against possible exchange rate fluctuations.

Government intervention

There are some forms of government intervention that can affect firms' costs in the short run. An increase in regulation that forced firms to spend more on health and safety measures would raise costs, and result in a leftward shift of the aggregate supply curve in the short run. An increase in the rate of corporation tax would have similar effects.

Exercise 12.1

For each of the following, state whether the short-run aggregate supply curve would shift to the left or to the right:

a the discovery of a new source of a raw material, reducing its price

b an increase in the exchange rate

c an increase in labour costs

d a fall in the price of oil

Summary: short-run aggregate supply

- The short-run aggregate supply (*SRAS*) curve shows the relationship between aggregate supply and the overall price level.
- A change in the overall price level induces a movement along the short-run aggregate supply curve.
- Changes in the costs faced by firms result in a shift of the short-run aggregate supply curve.

Aggregate supply in the long run

The discussion so far has focused on short-run aggregate supply. However, it is also important to consider how aggregate supply can be seen in the longer term. This is an area where different groups of economists have held different views. The **classical/monetarist school** argued that the economy would always converge on an equilibrium level of output that they referred to as the **natural rate of output**. Associated with this long-run equilibrium was a **natural rate of unemployment**. If this were the case, then the long-run relationship between aggregate supply and the price level would be vertical, as shown in Figure 12.2. Here Y_{FE} is the natural rate of output: that is, the full employment level of aggregate output. In other words, a change in the overall price level does not affect aggregate output, because the economy always readjusts rapidly back to full employment — a position in which the aggregate economy is operating at its potential full capacity level.

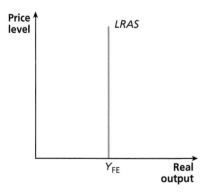

Figure 12.2 Aggregate supply in the long run (the classical/monetarist view)

An opposing school of thought (known as the **Keynesian school**) held that the macroeconomy was not sufficiently flexible to enable continuous full employment. They argued that the economy could settle at an equilibrium position below full employment, at least in the medium term. In particular, inflexibilities in labour markets would prevent adjustment. For example, if firms had pessimistic expectations about aggregate demand, and thus reduced their supply of output, this would lead

Key terms

classical/monetarist school economists who believed that the macroeconomy always adjusts rapidly to the full employment level of output, and that monetary policy should be the prime instrument for stabilising the economy

natural rate of output the long-run equilibrium level of output to which monetarists believe the macroeconomy will always tend

natural rate of unemployment the unemployment rate that will exist when the economy is in long-run equilibrium

Keynesian school economists who believed that the macroeconomy could settle at an equilibrium that was below full employment

Knowledge check 12.4

Which group of economists would argue that the long-run aggregate supply curve (*LRAS*) is perfectly inelastic?

to lower incomes because of the workers being laid off. This would then mean that aggregate demand was indeed deficient, so firms' pessimism was self-fulfilling.

These sorts of argument led to a belief that there would be a range of output over which long-run aggregate supply would be upward sloping. Figure 12.3 illustrates such an aggregate supply curve, in which Y_{FE} represents full employment; however, when the economy is operating below this level of output, aggregate supply is somewhat sensitive to the price level, becoming steeper as full employment is approached.

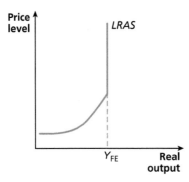

Figure 12.3 Aggregate supply in the long run (the 'Keynesian' view)

The shape of the long-run aggregate supply curve has significant implications for policy. If the *LRAS* is indeed vertical, so that the economy always returns to its long-run equilibrium, then there would seem to be little scope for trying to use policy to affect the path of the economy. This is especially the case if the adjustment to the long-run equilibrium is rapid, which is what the classical/monetarist school have argued. On the other hand, the Keynesian economists argued that the economy could find itself trapped in a position below full employment, and that intervention would be needed to get back to full employment.

Synoptic link

The operation of macroeconomic policy is discussed in Chapter 16.

The position of the long-run aggregate supply curve

Whatever the shape of the long-run aggregate supply curve, it is important to understand the factors that may affect its position. Both classical/monetarist and Keynesian versions identify a capacity level of aggregate output, so the question here centres on what affects this.

The quantity of inputs

The first obvious way in which aggregate output could be increased is if there is an increase in the availability of the factors of production. In particular, an increase in labour and/or capital inputs would lead to an increase in the amount of output that can be produced.

Synoptic link

The effect of an increase in the size of the workforce on economic growth is examined in Chapter 14.

As far as labour input is concerned, an increase in the size of the workforce will affect the position of aggregate supply. In practice, the size of the labour force tends to change relatively slowly, which is why this affects long-run rather than short-run aggregate supply. One way in which the workforce expands is through migration. For example, the expansion of membership of the EU in May 2004 led to significant migration into the UK. This expansion of the workforce can lead to an increase in potential output.

Demographic changes and migration can also affect the size of the workforce in the long run. The UK and many other advanced economies have been characterised by an ageing population in recent years. As more people live longer into retirement, the working population falls as a proportion of the total, and the *LRAS* may shift to the left. One response to this pattern has been the changes to the retirement age. Until 2011, the default retirement age in the UK was 65 years, but this was abolished so that those who wished to continue to work beyond 65 could do so. In many developing countries in sub-Saharan Africa, the HIV/AIDS epidemic was especially devastating to people of working age, so reduced the size and effectiveness of the labour force. In-migration can also affect the size of the workforce.

An increase in the quantity of capital will also have the effect of increasing the capacity of the economy to produce. However, such an increase requires firms to have undertaken investment activity. In other words, the balance of spending between consumption and investment may affect the position of the aggregate supply curve in future periods.

The effective use of inputs

The effectiveness with which inputs are utilised is another important influence on the position of the aggregate supply curve. Advances in technology are one route through which inputs can be more effectively utilised. New machinery can improve the efficiency with which other inputs are used, and the development of new materials can also have an impact. Such developments can reduce firms' costs and increase the amount of aggregate output that can be produced, leading to a shift in the long-run aggregate supply curve. This is shown in Figure 12.4, where aggregate supply was originally at $LRAS_0$. Technological change that improves efficiency in the use of capital and other inputs means that firms are prepared to supply more output at any given overall price level, so the aggregate supply curve shifts to $LRAS_1$.

Figure 12.4 A shift in aggregate supply

Labour as a factor of production can also become more effective and productive, and can be seen as a form of human capital. Improvements to education and the provision of skills training can improve the productivity of labour, again leading to a rightward shift of long-run aggregate supply. Training and education may be especially important for an economy that is undergoing structural change, so

Synoptic link

The effects of demographic changes and migration are analysed in Chapter 22, which deals with labour market issues.

Synoptic link

The significance of the shape of aggregate supply for macroeconomic policy is revisited in Chapter 32.

that workers need to be prepared to move between occupations. Government encouragement or provision of such training can improve the flexibility of the labour market and affect aggregate supply.

An increase in congestion on the roads would raise transport costs, and lead to a less efficient use of inputs, raising the costs faced by firms. These effects would tend to result in a leftward shift of the aggregate supply curve. On the other hand, improvements to infrastructure in the domestic economy, such as improvements to the transport system, would have the opposite effect of reducing the costs faced by firms, which could then lead to a rightward shift of the aggregate supply curve.

Synoptic link

There are situations (analysed in Chapters 19 and 20), in which firms may act to restrict output in order to increase their profits. In such situations, attempts by government to influence firms' behaviour through competition policy can shift the *AS* curve. This is discussed in Chapter 23.

Summary: long-run aggregate supply

- It is useful to distinguish between classical/monetarist and Keynesian views about the shape of the long-run aggregate supply curve.
- Monetarist economists have argued that the economy always converges rapidly on equilibrium at the natural rate of output, implying that policies affecting aggregate demand have an impact only on prices, leaving real output unaffected. The aggregate supply curve in this world is vertical.
- The Keynesian view is that the economy may settle at an equilibrium that is below full employment, and that there is a range over which the aggregate supply curve slopes upwards.
- The position of the long-run aggregate supply curve depends on the quantity of inputs available, and on the efficiency with which they are utilised.

Knowledge check 12.5

Name the factors that affect the position of the *LRAS* curve.

Exercise 12.2

For each of the following, identify whether the change described will affect short-run or long-run aggregate supply, and whether the result is a leftward or rightward shift.

a a fall in the exchange rate that affects the price of imported inputs

b an increase in the rate of in-migration

c an increase in the price of oil

d a reduction in corporation tax

e the introduction of new super-computers

The importance of expectations

In mid-2008, the UK economy was seen to be in a state of crisis. Economic growth had slowed (although it was still positive, so technically the economy had not yet entered into recession). Inflation had been affected by a number of world events. China's economy was continuing to expand at an unprecedented rate, and was having an impact on world prices by its strong demand for oil, foodstuffs and other commodities. The growth in demand for biofuels was fuelling a rise in the prices of some key food items, including rice and wheat. This was partly because land previously used to grow food was being turned over to grow crops to be made into biofuels. These effects were beginning to take their toll on the UK economy. Surveys of business confidence showed that firms were expecting a recession, and house prices were falling.

Follow-up questions

a Explain how the events described above would be expected to affect aggregate demand and/or short-run and long-run aggregate supply.

b The Brexit process would affect the UK economy in many ways. How do you think these effects can be portrayed in the *AD/AS* framework?

Demand for biofuels affected the price of crops such as rice and wheat

13

National income and macroeconomic equilibrium

Gross domestic product (GDP) has been discussed as a way of measuring total income in an economy, and some of its limitations have been analysed. Income can be seen as a flow of resources in the economy. As a concept, it can be seen to be closely associated with total expenditure and total output, and this chapter begins by exploring the relationship between these three notions. There is also some discussion of the important distinction to be drawn between income and wealth. The chapter also brings together aggregate demand and aggregate supply curves to explore the nature of macroeconomic equilibrium.

Learning objectives

After studying this chapter, you should:
→ understand that national income can be represented as a circular flow of income, expenditure and output
→ be aware of the distinction between income and wealth
→ be familiar with the notion of injections and withdrawals within the circular flow
→ appreciate the potential impact and importance of investment in productive capacity
→ understand the nature of equilibrium in the macroeconomy
→ be able to analyse external shocks affecting aggregate demand and aggregate supply
→ be familiar with the multiplier and its significance

The circular flow of income, expenditure and output

It is now time to examine the concept of gross domestic product (GDP) as a measure of total output produced in an economy, which can help to highlight the way that macroeconomic variables interact.

Synoptic link

GDP was first mentioned in Chapter 1, and further discussed in Chapter 9, when economic growth was seen in terms of changes in real GDP. We need to think more closely about it in the context of the *AD/AS* model.

The circular flow model

Consider a much simplified model of an economy. Assume for the moment that there are just two types of economic agent in an economy: households and firms. In other words, ignore the government and assume there is no international trade. (These agents will be brought back into the picture soon.) We also assume that all factors of production are owned and supplied to firms by households.

In this simple world, assume that firms produce goods and use factors of production (labour, capital, etc.), which are supplied by households. In return for supplying factors of production households receive income, which they spend on consumer goods.

If you examine the monetary flows in this economy, you can see how the economy operates. In Figure 13.1 the blue arrow shows the flow of income that goes from firms to households. The orange arrow shows that output produced by firms goes to households in the form of consumer goods. The green arrow shows that the expenditure flows back to firms. This model is sometimes known as the **circular flow model**.

Key term

circular flow of income, expenditure and output a model of the economy which shows the movement of goods and services between households and firms and their corresponding payments in money terms

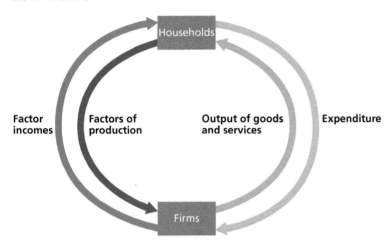

Figure 13.1 The circular flow of income, expenditure and output

Knowledge check 13.1

Explain what is represented by the red line in Figure 13.1.

The three measures of economic activity

As this is a closed system, these flows must balance. This means that there are three ways in which the total amount of economic activity in this economy can be measured: by the incomes that firms pay out, by the total amount of output that is produced, or by total expenditure. Whichever method is chosen, it should give the same result.

An economy such as the UK's is more complicated than this, so it is also necessary to take into account the economic activities of government and the fact that the UK engages in international trade, so that some of the output produced is sold abroad and some of the expenditure goes on foreign goods and services. Furthermore, some of the output produced by firms is made up of investment goods purchased by firms, and some household income is used for saving. However, the principle of measuring total economic activity is the same: GDP can be measured in three ways. These issues of government and international trade are considered later in the chapter.

In practice, when the Office for National Statistics (ONS) carries out the measurements by collecting data, the three answers are never quite the same, as it is impossible to measure with complete accuracy. The published data for GDP are therefore calculated as the average of these three measures, each of which gives information about different aspects of a society's total resources.

Knowledge check 13.2

What is meant by saying that this simple version of the circular flow model is a 'closed system'?

What the three measures tell us

The expenditure-side estimate describes how those resources are being used, so that it can be seen what proportion of society's resources is being used for consumption and what for investment, etc.

The income-side estimate reports on the way in which households earn their income. In other words, it tells something about the balance between rewards to labour (e.g. wages and salaries), capital (interest), land (rents), enterprise (profits) and so on.

The output-side estimate focuses on the economic structure of the economy. One way in which countries differ is in the balance between primary production such as agriculture, secondary activity such as manufacturing, and tertiary activity such as services. Service activity has increased in importance in the UK in recent years, with financial services in particular emerging as a strong part of the UK's comparative advantage.

Summary: the circular flow

- The circular flow of income, expenditure and output describes the relationship between these three key variables.
- The model suggests that there are three ways in which the total level of economic activity in an economy during a period of time can be measured: by total income, by total expenditure and by total output produced.
- In principle, these should give the same answers, but in practice data measurements are not so accurate.

Key terms

withdrawals where money flows out of the circular flow in the form of savings, taxation and imports

injections where money flows into the circular flow in the form of investment, government spending and exports

▌Injections and withdrawals

The circular flow diagram in Figure 13.1 was a simple model of the economy that analysed the three-way flow of resources around an economy. Households supplied factors of production in exchange for income, which was then spent on goods and services produced by firms. This model has limited applicability from a real-world perspective because it is a *closed* system, whereas in practice this is not the case, as there are **withdrawals** (or leakages) from the system and **injections** into it. These arise because of the economic activities of government and through an economy's international trade with the rest of the world.

Injections into the circular flow

The government affects the circular flow in two important ways. First, the government spends money on goods and services. For example, it may spend on the provision of public goods, and has to spend in order to carry out its other governmental obligations. In order to finance these activities, the government must raise revenue — which it can do through taxation.

International trade also affects the circular flow. Part of the expenditure on goods and services in the economy comes from abroad in the form of exports. In addition, part of the expenditure undertaken by households is on imported goods and services.

The saving activity of households also affects the circular flow, as there is a part of household income that is saved instead of being spent on goods and services. It is also important to realise that firms contribute to expenditure when they buy investment goods to add to their productive capacity.

Figure 13.2 adds all of these effects on to the circular flow diagram. The flow of expenditure is no longer just made up of household consumption expenditure on consumer goods, but is augmented by investment expenditure by firms (I), export expenditure from overseas (X) and government expenditure (G). These can be regarded as injections into the circular flow.

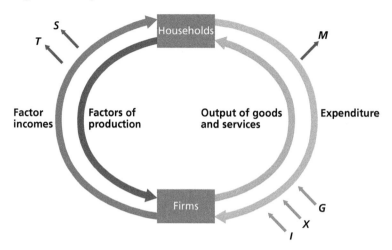

Figure 13.2 Injections and withdrawals in the circular flow

Notice that investment in the form of expenditure by firms on machinery, buildings and other productive resources plays an important role within the macroeconomy. By undertaking investment expenditure, firms add to the productive capacity of the economy, and thus enable economic growth to take place. A change in the balance between investment and consumption activity therefore affects the long-run path of the economy.

An increase in expenditure on investment by firms may have other effects as well. In order to meet the additional demand for machinery, other firms need to expand production. This means that they need to hire extra workers — and pay them, of course. The additional workers will then spend part of their income on consumer goods, thus unleashing a second round of expenditure. This phenomenon is examined later in the chapter.

Withdrawals from the circular flow

On the other side of the coin, there are withdrawals from the circular flow, made up of spending on imports from the rest of the world (M), household savings (S) and taxes raised by the government from households (T). The overall economy will be in balance when planned injections are equal to planned withdrawals. Notice that there are connections between the injections and withdrawals — for example, household savings may enter financial markets, and firms borrow from financial markets in order to finance their investment expenditure.

Knowledge check 13.3

Suppose that an increase in the rate of interest causes a fall in investment expenditure by firms. How would this effect the circular flow?

Study tip

There may be occasions when you will find it helpful to be able to draw the circular flow to illustrate your response to a question. As with other diagrams, practise doing this *before* you go into the exam.

Knowledge check 13.4

If a rise in the rate of interest encourages people to save more, how would this affect the circular flow?

Summary: injections into and withdrawals from the circular flow

■ The circular flow diagram needs to be expanded to accommodate injections and withdrawals.
■ The government affects the circular flow through expenditure (an injection) and taxation (a withdrawal).
■ International trade is important because of exports (an injection) and imports (a withdrawal).
■ The circular flow is also affected by household savings (a withdrawal) and by firms' investment expenditure (an injection).
■ Investment is also important because it affects the productive capacity of the economy in the long run, and is thus important for economic growth.

Income and wealth

Key terms

income a flow concept — the amount of income that is earned during a period

wealth a stock concept — the accumulation of assets, such as property or shares

In everyday parlance, it is not uncommon to use 'income' and 'wealth' interchangeably. In economic analysis, it is important to realise that the two things are very different. **Income** has been described as a *flow*; it is the amount of income that is earned during a period. **Wealth** is a *stock* — it is the accumulated amount of assets that have been built up from past income.

Wealth is considerably less evenly distributed than income. In 2014–16, households in the top 10% of the income distribution in Great Britain owned 43.8% of total wealth, compared with 8.7% owned by households in the bottom 50%. Wealth is affected by changing house prices and strongly influenced by the value of pension funds.

Notice that, although wealth and income are not the same thing, inequality in wealth can lead to inequality in income, as wealth (the ownership of assets) creates an income flow — from rents and profits — which then feeds back into a household's income stream.

A significant change in the pattern of ownership of assets in recent decades has been the increase in home ownership and the rise in house prices. For those who continue to rent their homes this is a significant source of rising inequality.

The rise in home ownership has led to increasing inequality

Summary: income and wealth

- Income is a flow, but wealth is a stock.
- Wealth is less evenly distributed than income in the UK.
- Inequality in wealth can lead to inequality in income.

Macroeconomic equilibrium

The circular flow model notes that total expenditure should be the same as total income and total output if all were measured fully. This might seem to suggest that the macroeconomy is always in a sort of equilibrium, in the sense that expenditure and output are always the same. However, this is misleading. When you observe the economy, you should find that expenditure and output are the same *after* the event, but this does *not* mean that equilibrium holds in the sense that all economic agents will have found that their plans were fulfilled. In other words, it is not necessarily the case that *planned* expenditure equals *planned* output.

This is the significance of the inclusion of inventory changes as part of investment. If firms find that they have produced more output than is subsequently purchased, their inventory holdings increase. Thus, although after-the-event expenditure always equals output, this is because any disequilibrium is reflected in unplanned inventory changes.

The circular flow diagram is useful in emphasising the importance of the interactions between households, firms and other economic factors in the macroeconomy. The next step in building a model of the macroeconomy is to analyse macroeconomic equilibrium by bringing together aggregate demand and aggregate supply. The equilibrium will be seen in terms of real national output and the overall price level.

First consider the short-run equilibrium. In Figure 13.3, with aggregate supply given by *SRAS* and aggregate demand by *AD*, equilibrium is reached at the real national output level *Y*, with the price level at *P*.

This is an equilibrium, in the sense that if nothing changes then firms and households will have no reason to alter their behaviour in the next period. At the price *P*, aggregate supply is matched by aggregate demand.

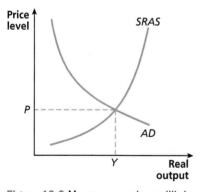

Figure 13.3 Macroeconomic equilibrium

An increase in aggregate demand

Having identified macroeconomic equilibrium, it is possible to explore what happens if there is a change in market conditions. The position of the aggregate demand curve depends on the components of aggregate demand: consumption, investment, government spending and net exports. Factors that affect these components will affect the position of aggregate demand.

Consider Figure 13.4. Suppose that the economy begins in equilibrium with aggregate demand at AD_0. The equilibrium output level is Y_0, and the price level is at P_0. An increase in government expenditure will affect the position of the aggregate demand curve, shifting it to AD_1. The economy will move to a new equilibrium position, with a higher output level Y_1 and a higher price level P_1.

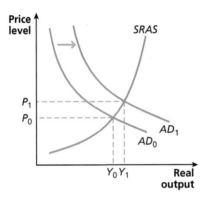

Figure 13.4 A shift in aggregate demand

An important question is whether this new equilibrium is sustainable. Suppose that the original level of real output at Y_0 had been the full employment level. Firms react in the short run by increasing their prices and raising output. However, in order to raise output in the short run, they may need to pay their workers overtime, or to hire additional office space. They will not want to continue to do this, and may also find that their suppliers are also increasing their prices. Firms then realise that their costs are rising, and will be prepared to supply less output at any given price. The short-run aggregate supply curve shifts back to the left, and the higher level of real output at Y_1 will not be sustained. This is another reason why this is an analysis of short-run equilibrium.

> ### Knowledge check 13.5
> Explain why the effect of an increase in aggregate demand cannot be sustained if the economy begins at full employment.

The effect of a supply shock

The *AD/AS* model can also be used to analyse the effects of an external shock that affects aggregate supply. For example, suppose there is an increase in oil prices arising from a disruption to supplies in the Middle East. This raises firms' costs, and leads to a reduction in aggregate supply.

Figure 13.5 analyses the situation. The economy begins in equilibrium with output at Y_0 and the overall level of prices at P_0. The increase in oil prices causes a movement of the aggregate supply curve from $SRAS_0$ to $SRAS_1$, with aggregate demand unchanged at AD. After the economy returns to equilibrium, the new output level has fallen to Y_1 and the overall price level has increased to P_1.

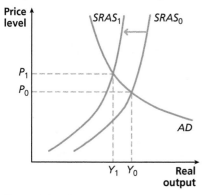

Figure 13.5 A supply shock

At the time of the first oil price crisis back in 1973–74, the UK government of the day tried to maintain the previous level of real output by stimulating aggregate demand. This had the effect of pushing up the price level, but did not have any noticeable effect on real output. Such a result is not unexpected, given the steepness of the aggregate supply curve.

Long-run equilibrium

Long-run equilibrium is analysed in the same way, as shown in Figure 13.6 with a Keynesian long-run aggregate supply curve.

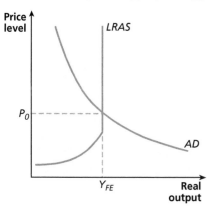

Figure 13.6 Macroeconomic equilibrium at full employment

Equilibrium occurs at the intersection of AD and $LRAS$, with price at P_0 and real output at Y_{FE}. The figure has been drawn with equilibrium real output occurring at the full employment level, where the $LRAS$ is vertical. But can it be guaranteed that the macroeconomic equilibrium will always occur at the full employment level of output? For example, suppose that the intersection of AD and $LRAS$ had occurred at a level of real output below Y_{FE}. Keynesians would argue that this is possible, as shown in Figure 13.7, but monetarists would hold that the $LRAS$ is vertical at Y_{FE}, so that equilibrium is always at full employment.

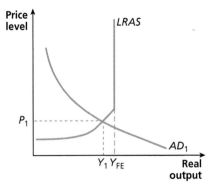

Figure 13.7 Macroeconomic equilibrium below full employment

Summary: macroeconomic equilibrium

- The aggregate supply (*SRAS*) curve shows the relationship between aggregate supply and the overall price level.
- Macroeconomic equilibrium in the short run is reached at the intersection of *AD* and *SRAS*.
- An increase in the equilibrium level of real output and the price level may not be sustainable if real output moves beyond the full employment level in the short run.
- Shifts in aggregate demand and aggregate supply curves lead to a new equilibrium price level and real output.
- Long-run equilibrium is found at the intersection of *AD* and *LRAS*.

The multiplier

Key term

multiplier the ratio of a change in equilibrium real income to the autonomous change that brought it about; it is defined as 1 divided by the marginal propensity to withdraw

In his *General Theory*, Keynes pointed out that there may be **multiplier** effects in response to certain types of expenditure. Suppose that the government increases its expenditure by £1 billion, perhaps by increasing its road-building programme. The effect of this is to generate incomes for households — for example, those of the contractors hired to build the road. Those contractors then spend part of the additional income (and save part of it). By spending part of the extra money earned, an additional income stream is generated for shopkeepers and café owners, who in turn spend part of *their* additional income, and so on. Thus, the original increase in government spending sparks off further income generation and spending, causing the multiplier effect. In effect, equilibrium output may change by more than the original increase in expenditure.

Government spending on road building may increase spending in other areas of the economy due to the multiplier effect

Withdrawals and injections

The size of this multiplier effect depends on a number of factors. Most importantly, it depends on the size of *withdrawals* or *leakages* from the system. In particular, it depends on how much of the additional income is saved by households, how much is spent on imported goods, and how much is returned to the government in the form of direct taxes. These withdrawals detract from the multiplier effect. For example, if households save a high proportion of their additional income, then this clearly reduces the multiplier effect, as the next round of spending will be that much lower. This seems to go against the traditional view that saving is good for the economy.

In the same way that the marginal propensity to consume (MPC) was defined as the proportion of additional income devoted to consumer expenditure, the **marginal propensity to import (MPM)** is the proportion of additional income that is spent on imported goods and services, and the **marginal propensity to tax (MPT)** is the proportion of additional income that is taxed. The sum of the marginal propensities to save, import and tax is the **marginal propensity to withdraw (MPW)**. The eventual size of the multiplier effect is given by 1 divided by the marginal propensity to withdraw.

However, there are also *injections* into the system in the form of autonomous government expenditure, investment and exports. One condition of macroeconomic equilibrium is that total withdrawals equal total injections. The fact that injections can have this multiplied effect on equilibrium output and income seems to make the government potentially very powerful, as by increasing its expenditure it can have a multiplied effect on the economy.

Key terms

marginal propensity to import (MPM) the proportion of additional income that is spent on imports of goods and services

marginal propensity to tax (MPT) the proportion of additional income that is taxed

marginal propensity to withdraw (MPW) the proportion of additional income that is withdrawn from the circular flow — the sum of the marginal propensities to save, import and tax

Knowledge check 13.6

How would the multiplier be affected if there is an increase in the marginal propensity to consume?

Quantitative skills 13.1

Calculating the multiplier

A numerical value for the multiplier can be calculated with reference to the withdrawals from the circular flow. Suppose that the marginal propensity to save is 0.25, the marginal propensity to import is 0.1 and the marginal propensity to tax is 0.15. The marginal propensity to withdraw is then $0.25 + 0.1 + 0.15 = 0.5$. The multiplier formula is 1 divided by the marginal propensity to withdraw ($1/MPW$). If the MPW is 0.5, then the value of the multiplier is 2, so for every £100 million injection into the circular flow, there will be a £200 million increase in equilibrium output.

It is worth noting that the size of the withdrawals may depend in part on the domestic elasticity of supply. If domestic supply is inflexible, and therefore unable to meet an increase in demand, more of the increase in income will spill over into purchasing imports, and this will dilute the multiplier effect.

Exercise 13.1

Identify each of the following as an injection or a withdrawal, and state whether it increases or decreases the impact of the multiplier:

a saving by households

b expenditure by central government

c spending by UK residents on imported goods and services

d expenditure by firms on investment

e spending by overseas residents on UK goods and services

f income tax payments

The multiplier and aggregate demand (*AD*)

What does the existence of the multiplier imply for aggregate demand? The multiplier is the idea that an increase in autonomous expenditure, such as government expenditure or investment expenditure by firms, will have *multiplier* effects through successive rounds of additional expenditure. In the context of the *AD/AS* model, this will affect the extent to which the *AD* curve shifts to the right following an increase in autonomous expenditure. In other words, the initial shift of *AD* will be augmented in following periods by further shifts as the successive rounds of additional expenditure work themselves through the system.

All of this seems to suggest that the government can always reach full employment, simply by increasing its expenditure. However, you should be a little cautious in reaching such a conclusion, as the effect on equilibrium output and the price level will depend on how close the economy is to the full employment level. Notice that the aggregate supply curve becomes steeper as output and the price level increase. In other words, the closer the economy is to the full employment level, the smaller is the elasticity of supply, so an increase in aggregate demand close to full employment will have more of an effect on the price level (and hence potentially on inflation) than on the level of real output. Indeed, if the economy is in equilibrium at the full employment level of real output before the increase in aggregate demand, the multiplier simply means more upward pressure on the equilibrium price level.

Synoptic link

In the case of an increase in government expenditure, the way it is financed is also important. This is discussed in Chapter 32.

Exercise 13.2

State whether each of the following statements about aggregate demand and/or the aggregate demand curve is true or false.

a The aggregate demand curve shows the relationship between the level of aggregate demand and the overall price level in an economy.

b The aggregate demand curve shows planned expenditure in an economy at any given possible overall price level.

c As the aggregate price level falls, the demand for goods and services in the economy rises and more of each good or service will be demanded.

d Government expenditure is regarded as autonomous, and affects the shape of the aggregate demand curve.

e The value of the multiplier depends on the level of government spending.

f An increase in government spending may induce a multiplier effect.

g The way in which consumption and investment respond to changes in the interest rate affects the shape of the aggregate demand curve.

h Investment expenditure by firms is the largest component of aggregate demand in an economy.

Exercise 13.3

For each of the following, decide whether the change affects aggregate demand or aggregate supply, and sketch a diagram to illustrate the effects on equilibrium real output and overall price level. Undertake this exercise first for a starting position in the steep part of the *AS* curve, and then for an initial position further to the left, where *LRAS* is upward sloping under Keynesian assumptions:

a an advancement in technology that improves the efficiency of capital

b a financial crisis in Asia that reduces the demand for UK exports

c an improvement in firms' expectations about future demand, such that investment expenditure increases

d the introduction of new health and safety legislation that raises firms' costs

For each of these changes, indicate whether the result is a shift of or a movement along the *AD* and *AS* curves.

Summary: the multiplier

- Autonomous spending, such as government expenditure, may give rise to a magnified impact on equilibrium output through the multiplier effect.
- The magnitude of the multiplier effect depends on the marginal propensity to withdraw.
- The presence of the multiplier affects the impact of an increase in autonomous expenditure on the resulting shift of the aggregate demand curve.

Case study 13.1

The HS2 project and the macroeconomy

The quality of a nation's infrastructure provides important support for business. If a country's transport and communication system is inefficient, firms will find it difficult to compete with foreign firms. However, in 2010 the Organisation for Economic Cooperation and Development (OECD) ranked Britain as only 33rd in the world for the quality of its infrastructure.

One project being undertaken by the UK government is HS2, designed to provide a new high-speed rail link between London and Birmingham, which will later be extended in two directions: to northwest England (Manchester) and Yorkshire (Sheffield and Leeds). This will be the largest infrastructure construction project in Europe.

The project involves large-scale expenditure in the short run; in 2013, the total cost was estimated at £42.6 billion at 2011 prices, but the estimate has since been revised upwards, and the budget was stated as £55.7 billion in late 2017. However, some critics of the project suggest that the final cost could be as much as £200 billion. The first passengers are expected to travel on HS2 in 2026. Costs include the capital costs of purchasing land and constructing railway lines, stations, depots and rolling stock. There will be some multiplier effects of these expenditures while the project is being undertaken. When completed, the project will ease existing capacity constraints and allow more rapid travel between London and the destinations in the north. It is claimed that for each £1 spent on the project, the UK will receive £2.30 in benefits.

Follow-up questions

a Use an *AD/AS* diagram to analyse the short-run effects of this project.

b With reference to another *AD/AS* diagram, discuss the expected long-run impact of the project.

One of society's prime responsibilities is to provide a reasonable standard of living for its citizens and to promote their well-being. Hence one of the major objectives for economic policy in the long run is to enable improvements in well-being. In order to do this, it is first necessary to expand the resources available within society. A key element in this process is to achieve economic growth, which is the subject of this chapter. However, there may be more to well-being than just growth, and the chapter also explores some of the limitations of a strategy that aims to maximise GDP growth.

Learning objectives

After studying this chapter, you should:
→ be able to understand the meaning of economic growth and productivity
→ be familiar with factors that can affect the rate of economic growth, particularly the role of investment
→ be able to evaluate the importance to a society of economic growth and the costs that such growth may impose

Key terms

potential economic growth an increase in the productive capacity of the economy

actual economic growth an increase in measured real GDP

Defining economic growth

From a theoretical point of view, **potential economic growth** can be thought of as an expansion of the productive capacity of an economy. In Chapters 1 and 9, economic growth was discussed in terms of a shift in the production possibility frontier (*PPF*); economic growth enables a society to produce more goods and services in any given period as a result of an expansion in its resources. **Actual economic growth** (measured by the rate of growth of real GDP) may also reflect a movement towards the frontier: for example, when an economy is recovering from a period of recession.

Study tip

Be aware of the distinction between the *level* of real GDP and the rate of economic growth. The actual rate of growth is calculated as the percentage change in the level of real GDP.

Knowledge check 14.1

What is the difference between actual and potential growth?

A second way of thinking about economic growth is to use the *AD/AS* model. For example, in Figure 14.1, an increase in the skills of the workforce will enable firms to produce more output at any given price, so that the aggregate supply curve will shift outwards from $LRAS_0$ to $LRAS_1$. This entails an increase in full employment output (or capacity output) from Y_{FE0} to Y_{FE1}. This is another way of analysing economic growth, and highlights that it is the factors that affect the position of the $LRAS$ that will be important in leading to potential growth.

Figure 14.1 A shift in aggregate supply

Notice that actual GDP is something that we can observe, whereas potential GDP represents the level of GDP that could be achieved if the economy were using all its resources effectively. After all, it could be that the economy never reaches full capacity, in which case it is never possible to observe potential output directly.

Synoptic link

Chapter 16 discusses policies to affect aggregate supply and thus encourage growth.

Knowledge check 14.2

How would you show an increase in an economy's potential capacity output in an *AD/AS* diagram?

The output gap

The difference between actual real GDP and maximum possible real GDP is known as the **output gap**. This can be illustrated using an *AD/AS* diagram. If you look back at Figure 13.7, you will see an economy that is in equilibrium below full employment, under Keynesian assumptions. In this case, Y_1 is actual GDP and Y_{FE} is the potential level that could be achieved at full employment. The output gap in this case is the difference between them ($Y_1 - Y_{FE}$). Under Keynesian assumptions, such a situation can persist in the long run, so the output gap can also persist.

When the economy is operating below the full employment level, the output gap is negative. In this situation, there is unused capacity: perhaps there is unemployment, so that not all workers are being fully utilised, or there may be idle capital. In some cases, it is possible that there will be a positive output gap, with actual real GDP being beyond its capacity level. For example, this could occur if firms have responded to an increase in aggregate demand in the short run by asking workers to work overtime. However, this will only be a short-run phenomenon, as it will not be sustainable.

Key term

output gap the difference between actual real GDP and potential real GDP

Knowledge check 14.3

Explain why it is difficult to identify potential economic growth.

Synoptic link

Chapter 13 discussed the short-run impact of an increase in aggregate demand as an unsustainable shift in the *SRAS* curve.

Figure 14.2 shows an economy with a classical (vertical) *LRAS*. When aggregate demand is relatively low, at AD_1, there is a negative output gap of $Y_1 - Y_{FE}$. If aggregate demand were to move to AD_2, there would be a movement along the *SRAS* in the short run, so a positive output gap ($Y_2 - Y_{FE}$) would emerge. Under classical assumptions, this would be short-lived, and the economy would soon move back to the full employment level of output at Y_{FE}.

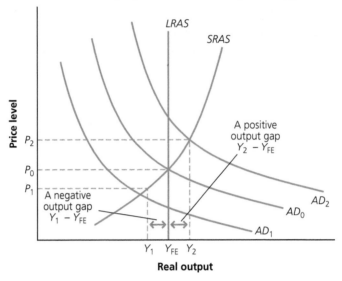

Figure 14.2 Positive and negative output gaps

Knowledge check 14.4

If an economy is operating with output below its full capacity output, would there be a positive or negative output gap?

Exercise 14.1

In Figure 14.3, which of the following represent(s) potential economic growth?

a a shift from *A* to *B*

b a shift from *B* to *C*

c a shift from *C* to *A*

d a shift from *C* to *D*

e none of the above

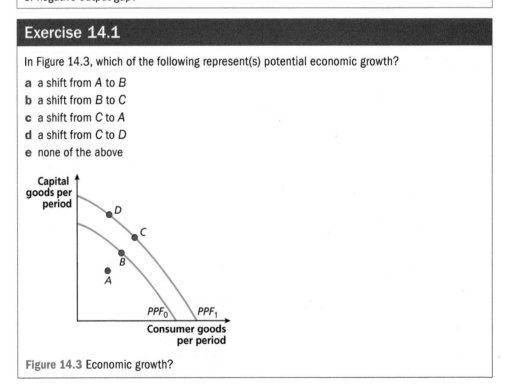

Figure 14.3 Economic growth?

Sources of economic growth

At a basic level, production arises from the use of factors of production — capital, labour, enterprise and so on. Capacity output is reached when all factors of production are fully and efficiently utilised. From this perspective, an increase in capacity output can come either from an increase in the quantity of the factors of production, or from an improvement in their efficiency or productivity.

Productivity is a measure of the efficiency of a factor of production. For example, **labour productivity** measures output per worker, or output per hour worked. The latter is the more helpful measure, as clearly total output is affected by the number of hours worked, which does vary somewhat across countries. **Capital productivity** measures output per unit of capital. **Total factor productivity** refers to the average productivity of all factors, measured as the total output divided by the total amount of inputs used.

An increase in productivity raises aggregate supply and the potential capacity output of an economy, and thus contributes to economic growth.

Synoptic link

The measurement of productivity, together with some international comparisons, are discussed more fully in Chapter 26.

Capital

Capital is a critical factor in the production process. An increase in capital input is thus one source of economic growth. In order for capital to accumulate and increase the capacity of the economy to produce, **investment** needs to take place.

In the national accounts, the closest measurement that economists have to investment is 'gross fixed capital formation'. This covers net additions to the capital stock, but it also includes *depreciation*, as explained in Chapter 11.

Figure 14.4 shows the time path for gross investment in the UK since 1950, expressed as a percentage of GDP. You can see that the share of investment in GDP has fluctuated a little over the years, but it settled at about 17% in recent years, which is relatively high by historical standards, before falling with the onset of recession in the late 2000s, then beginning to recover.

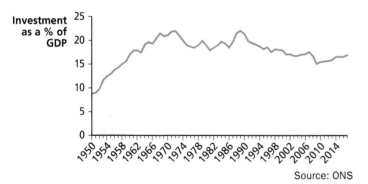

Source: ONS

Figure 14.4 Gross fixed capital formation in the UK, 1950–2017

Knowledge check 14.6

What is the difference between gross and net investment?

Knowledge check 14.5

Name the two key ways in which productive capacity can increase.

Key terms

productivity a measure of the efficiency of a factor of production

labour productivity a measure of output per worker, or output per hour worked

capital productivity a measure of output per unit of capital

total factor productivity the average productivity of all factors, measured as the total output divided by the total amount of inputs used

Key term

investment expenditure undertaken by firms on capital goods

The choice that any society makes here is between using resources for current consumption and using resources for investment. Investment thus entails sacrificing present consumption in order to have more resources available in the future.

Different countries give investment very different priorities. Something of this can be seen in Figure 14.5, which shows gross capital formation in a selection of countries around the world in 2015. The diversity is substantial, ranging from just 13.7% in Malawi to 45.4% in China. Given its high rate of investment, it is perhaps not surprising to discover that China is among the fastest-growing economies in the world in the early twenty-first century — but it must also be remembered that there is a cost to this, as it means sacrificing present consumption in China.

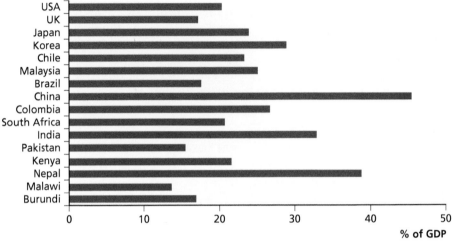

Note: countries are in descending order of GNI per capita.   Source: World Bank

Figure 14.5 Gross capital formation in 2015

The contribution of capital to growth is reinforced by technological progress, as the productivity of new capital is greater than that of old capital that is being phased out. For example, the speed and power of computers has increased enormously over recent years, which has had a great impact on productivity. Effectively, this means that technology is increasing the contribution that investment can make towards enlarging capacity output in an economy.

Innovation can also contribute, through the invention of new forms of capital and new ways of using existing capital, both of which can aid economic growth.

Labour

Capital has sometimes been seen as the main driver of growth, but labour too has a key contribution to make. There is little point in installing a lot of high-tech equipment unless there is the skilled labour to operate it.

There is relatively little scope for increasing the size of the labour force in a country, except through international migration. (Encouraging population growth is a rather long-term policy!) Nonetheless, the size of the workforce does contribute to the size of capacity output. For example, the expansion of the European Single Market in 1992 allowed an increase in migration to the UK, which many saw as having enabled economic growth.

A number of sub-Saharan African countries have seen this effect in reverse in recent years, with the impact of HIV/AIDS. The spread of this epidemic had a devastating impact in a number of countries in the region. It had a serious effect on capacity output because the disease affects people of working age disproportionately, diminishing the size of the workforce and the productivity of workers. The effects have persisted although the epidemic has passed its peak.

The quality of labour input is more amenable to policy action. Education and training can improve the productivity of workers, and can be regarded as a form of investment in **human capital**.

Synoptic link

Aspects of education and healthcare were discussed in Chapters 6 and 7, which argued that there may be elements of market failure that justify government intervention.

For many developing countries, the provision of healthcare and improved nutrition can be seen as additional forms of investment in human capital, since such investment can lead to future improvements in productivity.

Key term

human capital the stock of skills and expertise that contribute to a worker's productivity; it can be increased through education and training

A mobile clinic in rural Uganda – investing in healthcare can lead to improvements in productivity

Growth and international trade

International trade can contribute to economic growth. Indeed, for many relatively small countries, international trade is a key part of achieving economic growth. If the domestic market is not sufficiently large, effective demand may not allow economies of scale to be reaped. By engaging in international trade, a country is able to specialise, and thus produce goods more efficiently, reaping the gains from large-scale production.

For many developing countries, this is especially important, as not only is it crucial to be able to reach a large market, but also it is important to be able to earn the foreign exchange needed to import physical capital that cannot be produced domestically.

The countries that have been most successful in achieving economic growth in the last few decades are all countries that have relied on being able to expand rapidly through promoting exports — a process known as **export-led growth**. Examples include the east Asian 'Tiger' economies that enjoyed rapid growth from the 1960s onwards — countries like South Korea, Singapore, Hong Kong and Taiwan. More recently, China has enjoyed unprecedented success in economic growth, founded upon the rapid expansion of exports, showing that it is not only small countries that can achieve export-led growth. The export-led growth in China has created one of the most dramatic examples of sustained economic growth in history. This growth could not have been based on the domestic market alone. The high level of investment suggests that growth in China came from a combination of rightward shifts in both aggregate demand and aggregate supply.

> **Key term**
>
> **export-led growth** a strategy for achieving rapid economic growth through the promotion of export activity

> ### Knowledge check 14.7
>
> China's economic growth has been enabled by high investment and exports. What is the opportunity cost of this?

Growth and aggregate demand

Notice that this discussion of the sources of economic growth has focused on potential economic growth and the factors that affect aggregate supply, as in Figure 14.1. This is because the productive capacity of the economy can increase only when the *AS* curve shifts to the right. But how does aggregate demand affect the picture?

An increase in aggregate demand can lead to higher real output in the economy if the initial equilibrium is below full capacity output, but this is equivalent to a move *towards* the *PPF*. In other words, this is actual economic growth that does not affect overall productive capacity in the economy. An exception to this is where the increase in aggregate demand is due to an increase in investment expenditure that will later enable an increase in productive capacity. This will be considered in Chapter 16, which analyses policy instruments available to the government.

> ### Summary: economic growth
>
> - Economic growth is the expansion of an economy's productive capacity.
> - This can be envisaged as a movement outwards of the production possibility frontier, or as a rightward shift of the aggregate supply curve.
> - Economic growth can be seen as the underlying trend rate of growth in real GDP.
> - Economic growth can stem from an increase in the inputs of factors of production, or from an improvement in their productivity: that is, the efficiency with which factors of production are utilised.
> - Investment contributes to growth by increasing the capital stock of an economy, although some investment is to compensate for depreciation.
> - The contribution of capital is reinforced by the effects of technological progress.
> - Labour is another critical factor of production that can contribute to economic growth: for instance, education and training can improve labour productivity. This is a form of human capital formation.

Exercise 14.2

Which of the following represent potential economic growth, and which may just mean a move towards the *PPF*?

a an increase in the rate of change of potential output

b a fall in the unemployment rate

c improved work practices that increase labour productivity

d an increase in the proportion of the population joining the labour force

e an increase in the utilisation of capital

f a rightward shift in the aggregate supply curve

The trade (business) cycle

The process of actual economic growth is not always smooth, as real GDP tends to be subject to fluctuations over time. The fluctuation of real GDP around an underlying trend is known as the **trade or business cycle**. At any point in time, GDP may be below or above its trend value.

Consider an economy at point *A* on Figure 14.6. At this stage in the cycle, the economy is entering a period of recession, in which GDP is falling. This continues until point *B*, the trough of the cycle, at which point GDP stops falling and begins to grow again. At point *C*, the economy is showing growth in actual GDP, but GDP is still below its trend value, but recovery has set in; only at point *D* does the economy hit the trend. In other words, between points *A* and *D*, the output gap is negative. Beyond point *D* the economy moves into a **boom** period (as at point *E*), where GDP grows more rapidly than its trend value, and the level of GDP is above its trend value. At point *F*, the cycle reaches its peak and stops increasing; beyond this point actual GDP again begins to fall in the slowdown phase, and then the story repeats.

Key terms

trade (business) cycle
a phenomenon whereby GDP fluctuates around its underlying trend, following a regular pattern

boom the expansionary phase of the trade (business) cycle

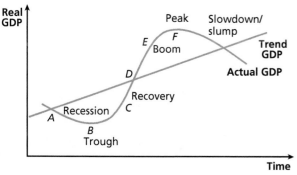

Figure 14.6 The business cycle

From a policy perspective, it is important to know at what stage of the trade (business) cycle the economy is. When the output gap is negative, and the level of output is below trend, then it may be tempting for policy-makers to try to 'fill the gap' by stimulating aggregate demand. However, this would be dangerous when the output gap is positive, as the effect would be to put upward pressure on the price level.

Knowledge check 14.8

Which phase of the trade (business) cycle would be characterised by upward pressure on prices and falling unemployment?

Real GDP in the UK and elsewhere

Figure 14.7 shows the actual time path of real GDP in the UK since 1960, together with its underlying trend. The trend shown is based on the average growth rate between 1960 and 2007 (the year before recession set in). Although the two series do not diverge by very much for most of the period, you can see the way in which the actual path of real GDP fluctuates around the trend, especially in the middle part of the period. Also very apparent in the figure is the recession that started in 2008, when GDP dipped significantly below its trend value.

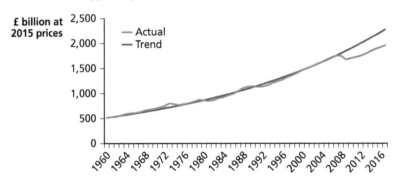

Source: calculated from ONS data

Figure 14.7 Real GDP, 1960–2017 (£ billion)

Key term

recession occurs when GDP falls for two or more consecutive quarters

One classic example of a cycle occurred from 1984 to 1993, as shown in Figure 14.8; here the output gap was positive from 1985 to 1988, but then GDP fell below its trend value (shown by the horizontal line) as the economy went into recession. Notice that the term **recession** is only used in practice when GDP falls for two or more consecutive quarters.

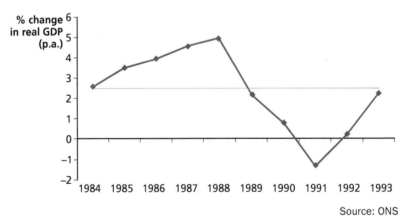

Source: ONS

Figure 14.8 A classic business cycle

Knowledge check 14.9

Looking at the path of GDP after 2008 in Figure 14.7, would you say that the economy has returned to its previous trend growth rate?

In mid-2008, the chancellor of the exchequer took the unprecedented step of stating publicly that the UK was heading for its biggest recession since the Second World War. This was unprecedented because most chancellors shy away from saying anything that will damage expectations about the economy. Figure 14.9 shows quarterly data for the period 2003 to 2008, showing the information that was available to the chancellor when he made this claim. He was right — as you can see in Figure 14.7.

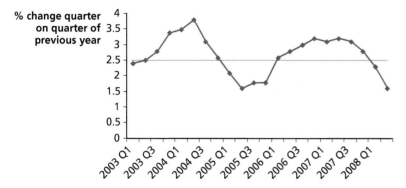

Source: ONS

Figure 14.9 The UK economy heading for recession?

Figure 14.10 shows the growth rates of GDP per capita in selected countries from 1971 to 2016. Although the graph looks a little congested, it is useful because it shows that there are some periods when fluctuations occur simultaneously across countries. For example, look at what happened in 1974/75, when all countries shown were negatively affected by the oil price shock of 1973/74. Notice that all countries enjoyed a more stable period of growth between about 1984 and 1990. So there are periods in which there are common cycles across countries. On the other hand, there are also exceptions to this — for example, Japan's negative growth in 1998 and 1999, which was not shared by the other countries in the graph.

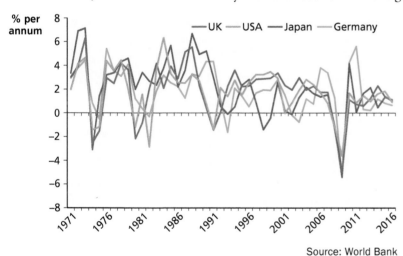

Source: World Bank

Figure 14.10 Growth of real GDP per capita in selected countries, 1971–2016

It is important to be aware that if countries do follow common patterns — at least in some periods — then this implies that domestic economic policy may not be the only influence on an economy's performance.

Synoptic link

If you look back at Figures 9.3 and 9.4 you can see the growth path of GDP in the UK in more detail.

Summary: the trade (business) cycle

- Economies are subject to regular fluctuations in GDP around its trend, known as the business or trade cycle.
- The cycle displays a series of phases, from recession through recovery, boom to a peak, after which there tends to be a slowdown.
- The business cycle may affect different countries simultaneously, and its effects may spread across countries.

The benefits of economic growth

Expanding the availability of resources in an economy enables the standard of living of the country to increase. In the industrial economies, populations have come to expect steady improvements in incomes and resources. For households, economic growth may bring higher incomes and more employment opportunities; for firms it may bring higher profits; for governments it may bring higher tax revenue and an improved capacity to provide public goods. If there is a buoyant economy, this is likely to be accompanied by an increase in confidence among consumers and businesses, which may encourage further investment. For developing countries this may facilitate the easing of poverty, and may allow investment in human capital that will improve standards of living further in the future.

Knowledge check 14.10

How does the control of inflation facilitate economic growth?

Thus for any society economic growth is likely to be seen as a fundamental objective — perhaps even the most important one. It may be argued that other policy objectives should be regarded as subsidiary to the growth target. In other words, the control of inflation, the maintenance of full employment and the achievement of stability in the current account of the balance of payments are seen as important short-run objectives because their achievement facilitates long-run economic growth.

Extension material: growth vs basic needs

In some developing countries the perspective may be different, and there has been a long-running debate about whether a society in its early stages of development should devote its resources to achieving the growth objective or to catering for basic needs. By making economic growth the prime target of policy, it may be necessary in the short run to allow inequality of incomes to continue in order to provide the incentives for entrepreneurs to pursue growth. With such a 'growth-first' approach, it is argued that eventually, as growth takes place, the benefits will trickle down: in other words, growth is necessary in order to tackle poverty and provide for basic needs. However, others have argued that the first priority should be to deal with basic needs, so that people gain in human capital and become better able to contribute to the growth process. It is also important to realise that economic growth does not necessarily translate into improvements in living standards: for example, where the benefits from growth are concentrated in certain groups within a society, rather than being spread widely.

Recession in the late 2000s

For the industrial countries, the importance of economic growth has been brought into sharp focus through the crisis of the late 2000s. After a period of relative stability during the 2000s, the onset of financial crisis initiated not only a slowdown in the growth of GDP, but the most severe recession of recent times.

Figure 14.11 shows how recession affected the UK in late 2008, with GDP growth being negative for six consecutive quarters. The UK was not the only economy affected by recession, and many advanced countries followed a similar pattern — indeed, countries like Greece were more severely hit in this period. The consequences of such a recession are significant. If output is falling, and firms are reducing their production, it is likely that they are laying off workers, so that unemployment rises. This then leads to falling incomes, which reduce aggregate demand and may lead to further drops in output, prolonging the recession. You can see from Figure 14.11 that the recovery from recession has been sluggish. If you look back at Figure 14.7 you can see that the time path of real GDP has remained well below what might have been had the recession has not happened.

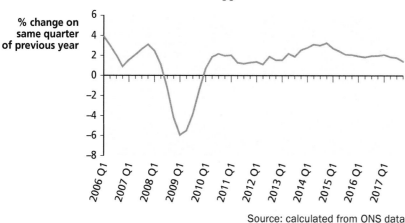

Source: calculated from ONS data

Figure 14.11 Economic growth in the UK since 2006

> **Study tip**
>
> Notice that it is *negative* growth that defines a recession: in Figure 14.11 the *growth rate* of GDP fell in the first quarter of 2008, but it did not go negative, so this would not formally count as a recession. The UK was not officially in recession until the last quarter of 2008, which was the second successive quarter in which growth had been negative.

The costs of economic growth

Economic growth also brings costs, perhaps most obviously in terms of pollution and degradation of the environment. In designing long-term policy for economic growth, governments need to be aware of the importance of maintaining a good balance between enabling resources to increase and safeguarding the environment. Pollution reduces the quality of life, so pursuing economic growth without regard to this may be damaging. This means that it is important to consider the long-term effects of economic growth — it may be important to consider the effects not only for people today, but also for future generations.

These costs have been highlighted in recent years by the growing concerns that have been expressed about global climate change and the pressures on non-renewable resources such as oil and natural gas. For example, the rapid growth rates being achieved by large emerging economies such as China and India have raised questions about the sustainability of economic growth in the long run. China in particular has experienced a period of unprecedented growth since about 1978, which is shown in Figure 14.12. This shows the average growth in China over 5-year periods since 1978. No other economy in recent history has been able to achieve an average growth rate of 8% per annum over such a long period.

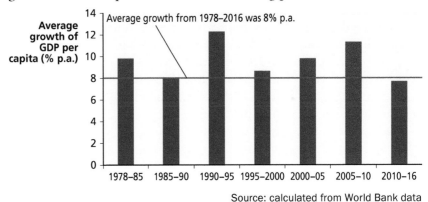

Source: calculated from World Bank data

Figure 14.12 China's economic growth

Key term

sustainable development
'development that meets the needs of the present without compromising the ability of future generations to meet their own needs' (Brundtland Commission, 1987)

Economic growth may thus have important effects on the environment, and in pursuing growth, countries must bear in mind the need for **sustainable development**, safeguarding the needs of future generations as well as the needs of the present. In other words, today's generation has a responsibility to safeguard the standard of living of people in the future.

Extension material: the environment as a factor of production

One way of viewing the environment is as a factor of production that needs to be used effectively, just like any other factor of production. In other words, each country has a stock of *environmental* capital that needs to be utilised in the best possible way.

However, if environmental capital is to be used appropriately, it must be given an appropriate value and this can be problematic. If property rights are not firmly established — as they are not in many developing countries — it is difficult to enforce legislation to protect the environment.

Furthermore, if the environment (as a factor of production) is underpriced, then 'too much' of it will be used by firms.

There are externality effects at work here too, in the sense that the loss of biodiversity is a global loss, and not just something affecting the local economy. In some cases there have been international externality effects of a more direct kind, such as when forest fires in Indonesia caused the airport in Singapore to close down because of the resulting smoke haze.

Trade-offs with other objectives

Figure 14.3 reminds us that there is an opportunity cost involved in pursuing economic growth. Devoting more resources to investment in capital goods has an opportunity cost in terms of the consumption that must be sacrificed in the present. This an important consideration for developing countries, where consumption today is needed to help to alleviate poverty. Indeed, poverty levels may increase if economic growth primarily benefits richer members of society, thus increasing inequality in the distribution of income.

Synoptic link

Achieving an equitable distribution of income is an objective of governments. Inequality is thus an important topic, and is discussed in Chapter 27.

There may be concerns about the desirability of economic growth. If economic growth entails structural change in the economy, there may be workers who are displaced from declining sectors who find that they do not have the right skills for redeployment in expanding sectors. In other words, there may be structural unemployment, although hopefully this could be a transitional problem. There may also be times when economic growth has an effect on the balance of payments, if the marginal propensity to import is high — in other words, if rising incomes lead to a rapid increase in imports. It is also possible that a focus on economic growth could have social effects if people feel stressed or find that leisure time is coming under pressure.

So, although economic growth is important to a society, the drive for growth must be tempered by an awareness of the possible trade-offs with other important objectives. In other words, we need to balance the possible benefits from economic growth against the associated costs.

Knowledge check 14.11

Explain what is meant by 'structural unemployment'.

Exercise 14.3

Discuss with your fellow students the various benefits and costs associated with economic growth, and evaluate their relative importance.

Summary: benefits and costs of economic growth

- The experience of economic growth has varied substantially in different regions of the world.
- There is a gap in living standards between countries that industrialised early and countries that are now classified as developing.
- A few countries, mainly in east Asia, went through a period of rapid growth from the 1960s that has allowed them to close the gap. This was achieved partly through export-led growth, although other factors were also important.
- However, countries in sub-Saharan Africa have stagnated, and remain on very low incomes.
- Economic growth remains important for all countries, at whatever stage of development.
- There may be costs attached to economic growth, particularly in respect of the environment.

Case study 14.1

Deforestation and biodiversity

In discussions about climate change, many commentators point to deforestation of the rainforests as contributing to the problem. The World Bank has estimated that in 1990, 65.4% of Indonesia's land area was given over to forest; by 2015, this had fallen to 50.2%. Concern has also been expressed at the rate at which the Amazonian rainforest is being destroyed.

Plantations in Indonesia that have replaced areas of rainforest supply raw materials to produce toilet paper, biofuels and vegetable oil (used for foodstuffs such as margarine, cream cheese and chocolate). In other cases, the land has been cleared to enable mining companies to move in. This has meant that many indigenous people have been forced off their land and have migrated to the cities.

Another aspect of environmental degradation concerns *biodiversity*. This refers to the way in which misuse of the environment is contributing to the loss of plant species — not to mention those of birds, insects and mammals — which are becoming extinct as their natural habitat is destroyed. Some of the lost species may not even have been discovered yet. Given the natural healing properties of many plants, this could mean the destruction of plants that might provide significant new drugs for use in medicine. But how can something be valued when its very existence is as yet unknown?

Follow-up questions

a Discuss who benefits and who suffers from deforestation occurring in the pursuit of economic growth.

b Identify examples of externalities associated with economic growth through its impact on deforestation.

15 Macroeconomic policy objectives

Inevitably, there is a policy dimension to the study of the performance of the macroeconomy. Indeed, in evaluating such performance, it is the success of macroeconomic policy that is under scrutiny. However, the success of macroeconomic policy can be judged only if you are aware of what it is that the policy is trying to achieve. This chapter introduces and analyses the main objectives of policy at the macroeconomic level and explores the possibility that there may be conflict between some of the targets.

Learning objectives

After studying this chapter, you should:
→ be familiar with the principal objectives of macroeconomic policy
→ understand the reasons for setting these policy objectives
→ be aware of some potential obstacles that may inhibit the achievement of the targets

Targets of policy

Chapters 9 and 10 introduced a number of ways in which economists try to monitor and evaluate the performance of the economy at the macroeconomic level. If macroeconomic performance is found to be wanting in some way, then it is reasonable to ask whether some policy intervention might improve the situation. This chapter considers aspects of the macroeconomy that might be regarded as legitimate targets for policy action. Chapter 16 analyses the policy actions that might be introduced, and evaluates their possible effectiveness.

Synoptic link

Chapter 9 discussed the importance of economic growth for an economy and Chapter 10 explored inflation, unemployment and the balance of payments.

As well as the potential policy targets discussed earlier, it is pertinent to ask whether governments should be concerned about inequality of income distribution within a society. The government may also need to be aware of the need to control public sector debt. Furthermore, there is a growing concern about the need to preserve the environment in which we live; Chapter 6 pointed out that an externality element in connection with the environment may be a cause of market failure, and commented that there may be international externalities that need to be considered. Chapter 14 noted that this issue has a macroeconomic dimension to it, so it will also need to be analysed in conjunction with the discussion of macroeconomic policy. Each of these objectives will now be considered in turn.

Study tip

When considering (or revising) macroeconomic policy, structure your thinking around these seven key objectives:

- increased economic growth
- a reduction in unemployment
- control of inflation
- restoration of equilibrium in the balance of payments
- making the distribution of income more equal
- balancing the government budget
- protection of the environment

Economic growth

If the ultimate aim of a society is to improve the well-being of its citizens, then in economic terms this means that the resources available within the economy need to expand through time in order to widen people's choices. This requires a process of economic growth, which as we saw in Chapter 14 is an increase in the productive capacity of the economy. If you like, it is an expansion of the potential output of the economy.

This is such an important policy objective for an economy that the whole of Chapter 14 was devoted to it. Recall that the nearest measure that economists have of the resources available to members of a society is GDP; so in looking for economic growth, they are looking for sustained growth in real GDP over time.

As has been argued, economic growth may be regarded as the most fundamental of all macroeconomic policy objectives, with other policy objectives being subsidiary to it. For example, one of the key reasons for maintaining low inflation is to encourage firms to undertake investment — because this enables economic growth. Maintaining full employment ensures the best possible use of a society's resources, enabling it to reach the production possibility frontier — and failure to do this may have indirect consequences for economic growth. Running a sustained current account deficit on the balance of payments that requires the sale of UK assets may limit the future growth prospects of the economy.

Knowledge check 15.1

Explain why economic growth may be regarded as the most fundamental of all macroeconomic policy objectives.

Full employment (low unemployment)

For an economy to be operating on the production possibility frontier, the factors of production need to be fully employed. From society's point of view, surplus capacity in the economy represents waste. In the macroeconomic policy arena, attention in

A wide choice of goods for shoppers is a sign of economic growth

this context focuses on achieving low unemployment. For example, Figure 15.1 shows that it is possible for the economy to be in macroeconomic equilibrium at a level of output Y_1 that is below the potential full employment level at Y_{FE}. This may be seen as an unnecessary waste of potential output. In addition, there may be a cost suffered by the people who are unemployed in this situation and who could have been productively employed.

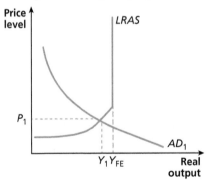

Figure 15.1 Macroeconomic equilibrium below full employment

Knowledge check 15.2

Which group of economists argued that it was possible for an economy to be in equilibrium below the full employment level?

Synoptic link

The causes and consequences of unemployment were discussed in Chapter 10.

Summary: full employment

- Full employment occurs when an economy is operating on the production possibility frontier, with full utilisation of factors of production.
- An economy operating below full capacity is characterised by unemployment.

Price stability

One of the most prominent objectives of macroeconomic policy in recent years has been the need to control inflation. Indeed, this has been at the heart of governments' stated policy objectives since 1976.

Knowledge check 15.3

What is the UK's favoured measure of inflation?

Causes of inflation

Cost-push inflation

Inflation is a rise in the general price level. However, it is important to distinguish between a one-off increase in the price level and a sustained rise over a long period of time. For example, a one-off rise in the price of oil may have an effect on the price level by shifting aggregate supply, thus affecting the equilibrium price level — as shown in Figure 15.2. However, this takes the economy to a new equilibrium price level, and if nothing else were to change, there would be no reason for prices to continue to rise beyond P_1.

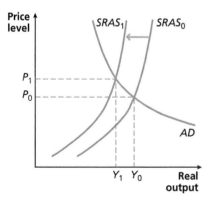

Figure 15.2 A supply shock

Synoptic link

Inflation was introduced in Chapter 10, together with some explanation of how it is measured. The issues explored in this chapter are to do with the causes and costs of inflation — in other words, why the control of inflation should be an objective for policy. Chapter 16 will look at the policy options for dealing with it.

Nonetheless, this is one reason why prices may begin to increase. Inflation thus may be initiated on the supply side of the macroeconomy, arising from an increase in the costs faced by firms, perhaps through an increase in the price of oil, or increases in wage costs. This is sometimes referred to as **cost-push inflation**, as the increase in the overall level of prices is cost driven.

Demand-pull inflation

In terms of the *AD/AS* model, it is clear that an alternative explanation of a rise in the general price level could come from the demand side, where an increase in aggregate demand leads to a rise in prices, especially if the *AS* curve becomes so steep in the long run as to become vertical, as some macroeconomists believe. An increase in aggregate demand could come, for example, from an expansion of money supply that causes interest rates to be lower than would have been the case, thus encouraging higher consumption and investment expenditure. This is shown in Figure 15.3, where the increase in aggregate demand from AD_0 to AD_1 leads to a rise in the overall price level from P_0 to P_1 with no change at all in real output. An increase in the price level emanating from the demand side of the macroeconomy is sometimes referred to as **demand-pull inflation**.

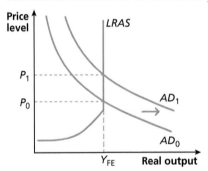

Figure 15.3 An increase in aggregate demand

Knowledge check 15.4

Would cost-push inflation be initiated by demand- or supply-side factors?

The money supply

But why should there be *persistent* increases in prices over time? One-off movements in either aggregate demand or aggregate supply may lead to one-off changes in the overall price level, but unless the movements continue in subsequent periods there is no reason to suppose that inflation will continue. One explanation for continuing inflation is provided by changes in the supply of money circulating in an economy.

Persistent inflation can take place only when the **money supply** grows more rapidly than real output. This can be shown in terms of aggregate demand and aggregate supply. If the money supply increases, firms and households in the economy find they have excess cash balances: that is, for a given price level they have more purchasing power than they expected to have, and are holding more money than they intended. Their impulse will thus be to increase their spending, which will cause the aggregate demand curve to move to the right. They will probably also save some of the excess, which will tend to result in lower interest rates — which will then reinforce the increase in aggregate demand. However, as the *AD* curve moves to the right, the equilibrium price level will rise, returning the economy to equilibrium.

If the money supply continues to increase, the process repeats itself, with prices then rising persistently. One danger of this is that people will get so accustomed to the process that they speed up their spending decisions, which accelerates the whole process.

> ### Synoptic link
>
> The relationship between money supply and prices is explored in more detail in Chapter 16.

To summarise, the analysis suggests that, although a price rise can be triggered on either the supply side or the demand side of the macroeconomy, persistent inflation can arise only through persistent excessive growth in the money stock, which can be seen in terms of persistent movements of the aggregate demand curve.

Costs of inflation

A crucial question is why it matters if an economy experiences inflation. The answer is that very high inflation gives rise to a number of costs.

Menu and shoe-leather costs

When inflation is relatively high, firms have to keep amending their price lists, which raises the costs of undertaking transactions. These costs are often known as the *menu costs* of inflation; however, these should not be expected to be significant unless inflation really is very high. A second cost of very high inflation is that it discourages people from holding money because, at the very high nominal interest rates that occur when inflation is high, the opportunity cost of holding money becomes great. People therefore try to keep their money in interest-bearing accounts for as long as possible, even if it means making frequent trips to the bank — for which reason these are known as the *shoe-leather costs* of inflation.

> ### Knowledge check 15.5
>
> What is meant by the 'menu costs' of inflation?

Ineffective markets

This reluctance to use money for transactions may inhibit the effectiveness of markets. For example, there was a period in the early 1980s when inflation in Argentina was so high that some city parking fines had to be paid in litres of petrol rather than in cash. Markets will not work effectively when people do not use money and the economy begins to slip back towards a barter economy. The situation may be worsened if taxes or pensions are not properly indexed, so that they do not keep up with inflation. If pensions do not keep up with inflation, this means that pensioners lose out, and income inequality worsens. If tax revenue fails to keep up with government expenditure, then the authorities may be drawn into printing even more money in order to finance their spending plans.

These costs are felt mainly when inflation reaches the *hyperinflation* stage. This has been rare in developed countries in recent years, although many Latin American economies were prone to hyperinflation for a period in the 1980s, and some of the transition economies also went through very high inflation periods as they began to introduce market reforms; one example of this was the Ukraine, where inflation reached 10,000% per year in the early 1990s. Another example of hyperinflation is the African country of Zimbabwe, where inflation became almost impossible to measure because it was so rapid. The BBC claimed that inflation had reached 231,000,000% in 2008.

A Zimbabwean looks at a new 50 billion dollar bank note issued in 2009

Uncertainty

However, there may be costs associated with inflation even when it does not reach these heights, especially if inflation is volatile. If the rate of change of prices cannot be confidently predicted by firms, the increase in uncertainty may be damaging, and firms may become reluctant to undertake the investment that would expand the economy's productive capacity. This is important for economic growth.

Unreliable price signals

Furthermore, as Chapter 5 emphasised, prices are very important in allocating resources in a market economy. Inflation may consequently inhibit the ability of prices to act as reliable signals in this process, leading to a wastage of resources and lost business opportunities.

Study tip

The key costs of inflation are:

- menu costs
- shoe-leather costs
- reluctance to use money for transactions
- redistribution of income away from those on fixed incomes
- uncertainty reduces incentives for investment
- prices fail to be reliable signals for resource allocation

It is these last reasons that elevated the control of inflation to being one of the central planks of UK government macroeconomic policy. However, it should be noticed that the target for inflation has not been set at zero. During the period when the inflation target was set in terms of RPIX (as explained in Chapter 10), the target was 2.5%; from 2004 the target for CPI inflation was 2%. The reasoning here is twofold. One argument is that it has to be accepted that measured inflation will overstate actual inflation, partly because it is so difficult to take account of quality changes in products such as PCs or smartphones, where it is impossible to distinguish accurately between a price change and a quality change. Second, wages and prices tend to be sticky in a downward direction: in other words, firms may be reluctant to reduce prices and wages. A modest rate of inflation (e.g. 2%) thus allows relative prices to change more readily, with prices rising by more in some sectors than in others. This may help price signals to be more effective in guiding resource allocation.

Summary: causes and costs of inflation

- The control of inflation has been the major focus of macroeconomic policy in the UK since about 1976.
- Inflation can be initiated on either the supply side of an economy or the demand side.
- However, sustained inflation can take place only if there is also a sustained increase in money supply.
- High inflation imposes costs on society and reduces the effectiveness with which markets can work.
- Low inflation reduces uncertainty, and may encourage investment by firms.

Exercise 15.1

Suppose that next year inflation in the UK economy suddenly takes off, reaching 60% per annum — in other words, prices rise by 60% — but so do incomes. Discuss how this would affect your daily life. Why would it be damaging for the economy in the future?

The balance of payments

Lists of macroeconomic policy objectives invariably include equilibrium on the balance of payments as a key item. Unlike inflation and unemployment, it is not so obvious why disequilibrium in the balance of payments is a problem that warrants policy action.

Figure 15.4 shows the market for pounds relative to euros. Here the demand for pounds arises from residents in the euro area wanting to buy UK goods, services and assets, whereas the supply arises from UK residents wanting to buy goods, services and assets from the euro area. If the exchange rate is at its equilibrium level, this implies that the demand for pounds (i.e. the foreign demand for UK goods, services and assets) is equal to the supply of pounds (i.e. the domestic demand for goods, services and assets from the euro area).

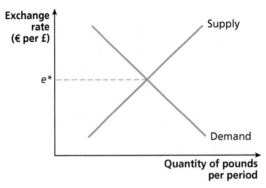

Figure 15.4 The market for pounds sterling

In a free foreign exchange market, the exchange rate can be expected to adjust to bring about this equilibrium position. Even under a fixed exchange rate system in which the government pledges to hold the exchange rate at a particular level, any discrepancy between the demand for and supply of pounds would have to be met by the monetary authorities buying or selling foreign exchange reserves. Thus, the overall balance of payments is always in equilibrium. So why might there be a problem?

The problem arises not with the *overall* balance of payments, but with an imbalance between components of the balance of payments. In particular, attention focuses on the balance of the current account, which shows the balance of the trade in goods and services together with investment income flows and current transfers.

A deficit on current account

If the current account is in deficit, UK residents are spending more on imports of goods and services than the economy is exporting. Another way of expressing this is that UK earnings from exports are not sufficient to pay for UK imports. This is a bit like a household spending beyond its income, which can be sustained only by selling assets or by borrowing.

The concern for the economy is that a large and sustained deficit on the current account implies that the financial account must be experiencing a large and sustained surplus. This in turn means that the UK is effectively exporting assets. And this means that overseas residents are buying up UK assets, which in turn may mean a leakage of investment income in the future. Alternatively, overall balance could be achieved through the sale of foreign exchange reserves. This soaks up the excess supply of pounds that arises because UK residents are supplying more pounds in order to buy imports than overseas residents are demanding in order to buy UK exports.

Knowledge check 15.6

Why is a sustained financial account surplus a potential issue for an economy in the long run?

However the current account deficit is financed, a large deficit cannot be sustained indefinitely. This begs the question of what is meant by a 'large' deficit. Figure 10.9 on page 157 showed the current account balance as a percentage of GDP, which gives some idea of the relative magnitude of the deficit. This shows that, although the current account has been in deficit every year since 1984, the deficit has been a relatively small proportion of GDP, although the recent period has seen a significant increase in the size of the deficit.

Investment from abroad

A critical issue is whether UK assets remain attractive to foreign buyers. Running a sustained deficit on current account requires running a surplus on financial account. If foreign buyers of UK assets become reluctant to buy, UK interest rates might have to rise in order to make UK assets more attractive. A by-product of this would be a curb in spending by UK firms and consumers. Given that part of this reduction in spending would have an impact on imports, this would begin to reduce the current account deficit.

One way in which the balance of payments is important from a policy perspective occurs when a government wishes to stimulate the economy, perhaps because it regards the level of unemployment as being excessive. An expansionary policy may be intended to increase domestic aggregate demand. However, in designing such a policy it is vital to remember that some of the increased demand will go not on domestic goods, but on imports, which is likely to dilute the effect of the expansion.

The initial effect of the financial crisis that began in the late 2000s was a reduction in the current account deficit for the UK, falling to 2.4% of GDP in 2011. However, since then, the deficit has increased, reaching 5.8% in 2016, the highest since records began in 1946. According to the ONS, this was partly attributable to a decline in investment income from abroad.

Causes of a deficit on current account

Synoptic link

The factors affecting international competitiveness are discussed in Chapter 26.

The quantity of exports of goods and services from the UK depends partly on income levels in the rest of the world and partly on the competitiveness of UK goods and services, which in turn depends partly on the sterling exchange rate and partly on relative price levels in the UK and elsewhere. Similarly, the level of imports depends partly on domestic income and partly on the international competitiveness of UK and foreign goods and services.

This suggests that a fundamental cause of a deficit on the current account is a lack of competitiveness of UK goods and services, arising from an overvalued exchange rate or from high relative prices of UK goods and services. Alternatively, UK incomes may be rising more rapidly than those in the rest of the world.

Summary: the current account of the balance of payments

- If the exchange rate is free to reach its equilibrium value, the overall balance of payments will always be zero.
- However, a deficit on the current account of the balance of payments must always be balanced by a corresponding surplus on the financial account.
- A persistent deficit on the current account means that in the long run domestic assets are being sold to overseas buyers, or that foreign exchange reserves are being run down. Neither situation can be sustained in the long run.
- A key cause of a deficit on the current account is the lack of competitiveness of domestic goods and services.

A balanced government budget

The financial crisis of the late 2000s focused attention on the government budget position. If the government spends more than it raises in revenue, the resulting deficit has to be financed in some way. The government deficit is the difference between public sector spending and revenues, and is known as the *public sector net cash requirement* (PSNCR). Part of the PSNCR is covered by borrowing, and the government closely monitors its *net borrowing*. Over time, such borrowing leads to *net debt*, which is the accumulation of past borrowing. The Labour government that was in power from 1997 to 2010 aimed to keep this below 40% — and was successful in achieving this until the financial crisis hit.

A major argument in favour of controlling the level of public sector net debt arose from a concern for the long-run effects of policy on spending and borrowing. It was argued that sustainable economic growth has to take into account the needs of future generations. The Labour government thus took the view that its current spending should be met out of current revenues, and that only investment for the future should be met through borrowing. In other words, future generations should not have to meet the cost of the consumption of the present population.

While public sector debt was stable at less than 40% of GDP, it was not seen as being of major concern. However, the financial crisis led to a refocusing of macroeconomic policy. Figure 15.5 shows the impact of the crisis on this policy target. The crisis was first manifest in the banking system. In the UK, this began with the failure of Northern Rock in 2008, followed by problems in other commercial banks. The bailout for these banks needed to safeguard the financial system led to the enormous increase in public sector net debt evident in Figure 15.5. The government's stake in bailed-out banks has been gradually reduced, so that from 2017 the banks involved have been returned to the private sector. However, the legacy of the crisis is evident, as public sector debt remains at more than 80% of GDP, and the need to bring down the level of debt has coloured policy design.

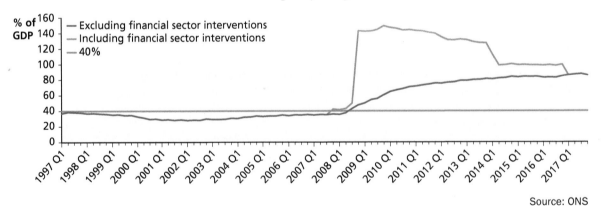

Source: ONS

Figure 15.5 Public sector net debt in the UK, 1997–2017

Concern for the environment

International externalities pose problems for policy design because they require coordination across countries. If pollution caused by the UK manufacturing sector causes acid rain elsewhere in Europe, the UK is imposing costs on other countries that are not fully reflected in market prices. Furthermore, there may be effects that are felt across generations. If the environment today is damaged, it may not be enjoyed by future generations — in other words, there may be intergenerational externality effects.

The growing concerns about global warming have drawn attention to the possible harm caused by rapid economic growth. It is this relationship between the environment and the rate of economic growth that has highlighted the macroeconomic dimension to concern for the environment, and led to growing calls for growth to be sustainable — as was pointed out in the previous chapter.

Knowledge check 15.7

Why should a government be concerned about intergenerational externality effects?

Income redistribution

The final macroeconomic policy objective to be considered concerns attempts to influence the distribution of income within a society. These may entail transfers of income between groups in society — that is, from richer to poorer — in order to protect the latter. Income redistribution may work through progressive taxation (whereby those on high incomes pay a higher proportion of their income in tax) or through a system of social security benefits such as the Jobseeker's Allowance and Universal Credit.

Synoptic link

The use of taxation to affect the distribution of income is examined in Chapter 27.

Causes of inequality

Some degree of inequality in the income distribution within a society is inevitable. People have different innate talents and abilities, and choose to undergo different types and levels of education and training, such that they acquire different sets of skills. Market forces imply that different payments will be made to people in different sectors of economic activity and different occupations. Income inequality also arises because of inequality in the ownership of assets. However, people in identical circumstances and with identical skills and abilities *may* receive identical income. This notion is sometimes known as *horizontal equity*, which most people would agree is desirable.

One category of policy measures is designed to encourage horizontal equity. Equal opportunities legislation tries to ensure that members of society do not suffer discrimination that might deny them equal pay for equal work, or equal access to employment. Nonetheless, there remain significant differences in earnings and employment between ethnic groups and between men and women.

Knowledge check 15.8

Why is horizontal equity seen as a desirable outcome?

Setting this aside, the key question remaining is the extent to which the government needs to intervene at the macroeconomic level to influence the distribution of income and protect vulnerable groups by redistributing from richer to poorer. Indeed, are there economic effects of inequality which suggest that redistribution of income is needed for reasons other than the purely humanitarian objective of alleviating poverty and protecting the vulnerable?

Women demonstrating for equal pay in London in 2014 — there still remain significant differences in earnings between men and women

The costs of inequality

In a society where there is substantial inequality in the distribution of income, there are likely to be groups of people who are disadvantaged in various ways: for example, they may find it more difficult to obtain education for themselves or for their children. In the UK it remains the case that a lower proportion of students from low-income families go to university. It may also be that some potential entrepreneurs find it more difficult to obtain the credit needed to launch their business ideas.

If this is so, it suggests that there are people in society who are inhibited from developing their productive potential — which in turn implies that economic growth in the future will be lower than it could be. This could provide a justification for redistributing income — or at least for trying to ensure that there is equality of opportunity for all members of society. However, it might be argued that redistribution can be taken too far. If the higher-income groups in society face too high a marginal tax rate on their income — in other words, if additions to income are very heavily taxed for the rich — this could remove their incentive to exploit income-earning opportunities, which could have a damaging impact on economic growth. Getting the right balance between protecting the vulnerable and providing appropriate incentives for enterprise is a tricky task for policy-makers.

Too much inequality may also lead to high crime rates and social discontent, which in turn may lead to political instability in a society. This could affect the security of property rights and inhibit economic growth.

There is some evidence that inequality has been widening in many countries in recent years. In particular, the way that technology has been progressing places a higher premium on skills, so that the gap between the earnings of skilled and unskilled workers has been widening.

Summary: other objectives of policy

- A balanced government budget is needed to avoid increases in the stock of public sector debt.
- There may be a need to moderate the pursuit of economic growth in order to protect the environment.
- Macroeconomic policy may also encompass the redistribution of income within society, on grounds of equity and also because extreme inequality may inhibit economic growth.

Exercise 15.2

Discuss which of the objectives of macroeconomic policy *you* think to be of most importance.

Case study 15.1

Policy dilemmas

Imagine you are the economic dictator of a country called Nowhere. The economy has been experiencing a period of prosperity, with low inflation and unemployment and steady economic growth. However, you are aware that you soon face re-election, and there are some problems on the horizon. Imports of consumer goods from China are growing rapidly, and unemployment has begun to creep up as some firms go out of business. Global commodity prices are rising,

putting additional pressures on the prices of some key strategic imports. There is a growing environmental lobby putting pressure on you to reduce the environmental impact of economic growth and tackle carbon dioxide emissions. Inflation is towards the top end of the acceptable range. A house price bubble is threatening to burst.

Follow-up question

Discuss to which objective you should give top priority.

16 Macroeconomic policies

Previous chapters have shown that there may be a range of macroeconomic policy objectives, including economic growth, full employment, the control of inflation and equilibrium on the current account of the balance of payments. There may also be concerns for the environment, the government budget and for the distribution of income. Attention now turns to the sorts of policy that might be implemented to try to meet these targets. Policies at the macroeconomic level are designed to affect either aggregate demand or aggregate supply, and each will be examined in turn.

> ### Learning objectives
>
> After studying this chapter, you should:
> → understand and be able to evaluate policies that affect aggregate demand, including fiscal, monetary and exchange rate policies
> → understand and be able to evaluate policies that affect aggregate supply
> → be able to appraise the relative merits of policies applied to the demand and supply sides of the macroeconomy
> → be familiar with how macroeconomic policy has been conducted in the UK in recent years

Macroeconomic policy instruments

The government has three main types of policy instrument with which to attempt to meet its macroeconomic objectives:

1 *Fiscal policy*: the term 'fiscal policy' covers a range of policy measures that affect government expenditures and revenues through the decisions made by the government on its expenditure, taxation and borrowing. Fiscal policy is used to influence the level and structure of aggregate demand in an economy. As this chapter unfolds, you will see that the effectiveness of fiscal policy depends crucially on the whole policy environment in which it is utilised, and on the interrelationship between the three types of policy.

2 *Monetary policy*: this entails the use of monetary variables such as money supply and interest rates to influence aggregate demand. Under a fixed exchange rate system, monetary policy becomes wholly impotent, as it has to be devoted to maintaining the exchange rate. So here again, the effectiveness of monetary policy will depend on the policy environment in which it is used.

3 *Supply-side policies*: such policies comprise a range of measures intended to have a direct impact on aggregate supply — specifically, on the potential capacity output of the economy. These measures are often microeconomic in character and are designed to increase output and hence economic growth.

Knowledge check 16.1

List the main targets of macroeconomic policy.

Fiscal policy

The term **fiscal policy** covers a range of policy measures that affect government expenditures, revenues and borrowing. For example, an expansionary fiscal policy would be seen as an increase in government spending (or reduction in taxes) that shifts the aggregate demand curve to the right.

Key term

fiscal policy decisions made by the government on its expenditure, taxation and borrowing

Government expenditure

Government undertakes spending on a wide range of goods and services. For example, expenditure on the National Health Service and education takes a significant portion of the budget. Government also spends on infrastructure projects such as Crossrail or HS2. Such projects are intended to facilitate economic growth.

In Figure 16.1 macroeconomic equilibrium is initially at the intersection of aggregate supply ($LRAS$) and the initial aggregate demand curve (AD_0), so that real output is at Y_0, which is below the full employment level of output at Y_{FE}. As government expenditure is one of the components of aggregate demand, an increase in such expenditure moves the aggregate demand curve from AD_0 to AD_1. In response, the economy moves to a new equilibrium, in which the overall price level has risen to P_1 but real output has moved to Y_1, which is closer to the full employment level Y_{FE}.

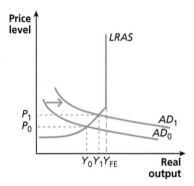

Figure 16.1 The use of fiscal policy

In this scenario, government expenditure is treated as an injection into the circular flow, and it will be reinforced by the multiplier effect. In Figure 16.1, an increase in government expenditure is effective in raising the level of real output in the economy, although some of the increase is dissipated in the form of an increase in the overall level of prices. Notice that, if the multiplier is relatively low, the reinforcement of fiscal policy through this route will also be relatively weak. Remember that the strength of the multiplier effect depends on the size of withdrawals from the circular flow. For example, if consumers have a high propensity to import, this will weaken the impact of the multiplier.

Knowledge check 16.2

Give an example of a fiscal measure that would increase aggregate demand.

The importance of aggregate supply

This kind of policy is effective only if the aggregate demand curve intersects the aggregate supply curve in the upward-sloping segment of $LRAS$. If the economy is already at the full employment level of output, an increase in aggregate demand merely results in a higher overall level of prices. This would also be the case with a vertical (monetarist) $LRAS$ curve. The effective use of such policy thus requires policy-makers to have good information about the current state of the economy; in particular, they need to know whether the economy is at or below full employment.

Knowledge check 16.3

Explain why the multiplier effect is weakened if the marginal propensity to import is relatively high.

Otherwise, the results could be damaging for the price stability target. In other words, there is a danger that an expansionary fiscal policy will lead to price increases, but not affect output very much if the *LRAS* curve is relatively steep.

The effect on the balance of payments must also be borne in mind. Part of an increase in aggregate demand is likely to be spent on imports, but there is no immediate reason for exports to change, so in the short run there is likely to be an increase in the current account deficit on the balance of payments.

Taxation and the government budget

Although the focus of the discussion so far has been on government expenditure, fiscal policy also refers to taxation. In fact, the key issue in considering fiscal policy is the balance between government expenditure and government revenue, as it is this balance that affects the position of aggregate demand directly.

An increase in the **government budget deficit** (or a decrease in the **government budget surplus**) moves the aggregate demand curve to the right. The budget deficit may arise either from an increase in expenditure or from a decrease in taxation, although the two have some differential effects.

Key term

government budget deficit (surplus) the balance between government expenditure and revenue

Knowledge check 16.4

If government expenditure is greater than revenue from taxation, would there be a budget deficit or budget surplus?

Synoptic link

The effectiveness of fiscal policy is considered in Chapter 32.

> **Exercise 16.1**
>
> Use *AD/AS* analysis to consider the effect of an expansionary fiscal policy on the equilibrium level of real output and the overall price level. Undertake this exercise with different initial positions along the long-run aggregate supply curve, first analysing an economy that begins at full employment and then one in which aggregate demand creates an equilibrium that is below full employment. Discuss the differences in your results.

Fiscal policy in the UK

If the government spends more than it raises in revenue, the resulting deficit has to be financed in some way. When the deficit is covered by net borrowing, the result is an accumulation of debt. The global financial crisis led to a substantial increase in public sector net debt in the late 2000s, which required a rethinking of fiscal policy. Decisions had to be taken in awareness of the need to bring down the level of outstanding debt, so spending had to be lower than it might otherwise have been.

Synoptic link

You can see what happened to public sector net debt during the crisis in Chapter 15, Figure 15.5 on page 214.

Balance between the public and private sectors

Even if the size of the budget deficit limits the government's actions in terms of fiscal policy, there are still decisions to be made about the overall balance of activity in the economy. A neutral government budget can be attained either with high expenditure and high revenues, or with relatively small expenditure and revenues. Such decisions affect the overall size of the public sector relative to the private sector. Over the years, different governments in the UK have taken different decisions on this issue — and different countries throughout the world have certainly adopted different approaches.

Chancellor of the Exchequer Phillip Hammond announcing the 2018 budget — fiscal policy is used to influence aggregate demand in an economy

In part, such issues are determined through the ballot box. In the run-up to an election, each political party presents its overall plans for taxation and spending, and typically they adopt different positions as to the overall balance. It is then up to those voting to give a mandate to whichever party offers a package that most closely resembles their preferences.

Direct and indirect taxes

Fiscal policy, and taxation in particular, has not only been used to establish a balance between the public and private sectors of an economy. In addition, taxation remains an important weapon against some forms of market failure, and it also influences the distribution of income. In this context, the choice between using direct and indirect taxes is important.

Direct taxes are taxes levied on income of various kinds, such as personal income tax. Income tax can be effective in redistributing income, as a higher income tax rate can be charged to those earning high incomes. In contrast, indirect taxes — taxes on expenditure, such as VAT and excise duties — fall more heavily on those on lower incomes. Poorer households tend to spend a higher proportion of their income on items that are subject to excise duties, so a greater share of their income is taken up by indirect taxes. VAT can have similar effects if higher-income households save a greater proportion of their incomes.

Indirect taxes can be targeted at specific instances of market failure; hence the high excise duties on such goods as tobacco (seen to cause significant negative externality effects) and petrol (seen as damaging to the environment because of the externality of greenhouse gas emissions).

Knowledge check 16.5

Is VAT an example of a direct or an indirect tax?

Synoptic link

The use of indirect taxes to address market failure is discussed in Chapter 8, which also explores the effectiveness of such taxes. Aspects of both direct and indirect taxes are also discussed in Chapter 27.

Summary: fiscal policy

- Fiscal policy is concerned with the decisions made by government about its expenditure, taxation and borrowing.
- As government expenditure is an autonomous component of aggregate demand, an increase in expenditure will shift the *AD* curve to the right.
- If *AD* intersects *LRAS* in the vertical segment of *LRAS*, the effect of the increase in aggregate demand is felt only in prices.
- However, if the initial equilibrium is below the full employment level, the shift in *AD* will lead to an increase in both equilibrium real output and the overall price level.
- In fact, it is net spending that it is important, so government decisions on taxation are also significant.
- The government budget deficit (surplus) is the difference between government expenditure and revenue.
- If the government runs a budget deficit, it may need to undertake net borrowing, which over time affects the net debt position.
- Direct taxes help to redistribute income between groups in society, but if too progressive they may dampen incentives to provide effort.

Key term

monetary policy the decisions made by government regarding monetary variables such as the money supply or the interest rate

Synoptic link

The functions of money (which underpin the demand for money) were discussed in Chapter 1.

Knowledge check 16.6

Explain why the interest rate can be regarded as the opportunity cost of holding money.

Synoptic link

The measurement and significance of the money supply is discussed in Chapter 30.

Monetary policy

Monetary policy is the approach currently favoured by the UK government to stabilise the macroeconomy. It entails the use of monetary variables such as the money supply or interest rates to influence aggregate demand.

It is important at the outset to realise that it is not possible to control money supply and interest rates simultaneously and independently. Firms and households choose to hold some money. They may do this in order to undertake transactions, or as a precaution against the possible need to undertake transactions at short notice. In other words, there is a *demand for money*. However, in choosing to hold money they incur an opportunity cost, in the sense that they forgo the possibility of earning interest by purchasing some form of financial asset.

Money and the interest rate

This means that the interest rate can be regarded as the opportunity cost of holding money; put another way, it is the price of holding money. At high rates of interest, people can be expected to choose to hold less money, as the opportunity cost of holding money is high. *MD* in Figure 16.2 represents such a money demand curve. It is downward sloping.

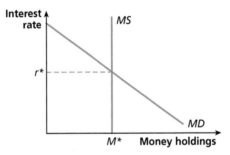

Figure 16.2 The demand for money

Suppose the government wants to set the money supply (*MS*) at *M*★ in Figure 16.2. This can be achieved in two ways. If the government controls the supply of money at *M*★, then equilibrium will be achieved only if the interest rate is allowed to adjust to *r*★. An alternative way of reaching the same point is to set the interest rate at *r*★ and then allow the money supply to adjust to *M*★. The government can do one or the other — but it cannot set money supply at *M*★ and hold the interest rate at any value *other than r*★ without causing disequilibrium.

A problem with attempting to control the money supply directly is that the complexity of the modern financial system makes it quite difficult to pin down a precise definition or measurement of money. For this and other reasons, the chosen instrument of monetary policy is the interest rate.

Monetary policy and aggregate demand

Through the interest rate, monetary policy affects aggregate demand. At higher interest rates, firms undertake less investment expenditure and households undertake less consumption expenditure. This is partly because when the interest rate is relatively high, the cost of borrowing becomes high and firms and people are discouraged from borrowing for investment or consumption purposes. There are reinforcing effects that operate through the exchange rate if UK interest rates are high relative to elsewhere in the world. If the exchange rate rises because of high interest rates, this will reduce the competitiveness of UK goods, and attract inflows of financial capital ('hot money'). This interaction of the money supply, interest rates and the exchange rate makes policy design a complicated business.

Suppose the government believes that the economy is close to full employment and is in danger of overheating. Overheating could push prices up without any resulting benefit in terms of higher real output. An increase in the interest rate will lead to a fall in aggregate demand, thereby relieving the pressure on prices. This is illustrated in Figure 16.3, where the initial position has aggregate demand relatively high at AD_0, real output at the full employment level Y_{FE} and the overall price level at P_0. The increase in interest rates shifts aggregate demand to the left, to AD_1. Real output falls slightly to Y_1 and the equilibrium price level falls to P_1.

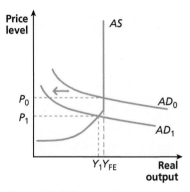

Figure 16.3 The use of monetary policy

Monetary policy in the UK

All developed and most developing countries have a **central bank**, fulfilling a range of roles, including being banker to the government. The central bank may also be responsible for the issue of coins and banknotes, for acting as banker to commercial banks and for regulating the financial system. In the UK, this role is taken by the **Bank of England**.

Since 1997, the responsibility for monetary policy has been devolved to the Bank of England, which was given the task of achieving the government's stated inflation target, initially set at 2.5% for RPIX inflation. As noted in Chapter 10, the target was amended in 2004, when it became 2% per annum as measured by the CPI.

The Monetary Policy Committee

According to this arrangement, the **Monetary Policy Committee** (MPC) of the Bank of England sets interest rates in such a way as to keep inflation within 1 percentage point (either way) of the 2% target for CPI inflation. If it fails to achieve this, the Bank has to write an open letter to the chancellor of the exchequer to explain why the target has not been met. Such a letter became necessary for the first time in March 2007, when CPI inflation touched 3.1%. This was to become the norm in the early 2010s, although inflation came back into the target range in mid-2012, as will be discussed later.

Operationally, the MPC sets the interest rate which it pays on commercial bank reserves. This is known as the **bank rate**. The commercial banks tend to use this rate as their own base rate, from which they calculate the rates of interest that they

Knowledge check 16.7

Why would the exchange rate rise if UK interest rates were high compared with rates in other countries?

Key terms

central bank the banker to the government, performing a range of functions, which may include issue of coins and banknotes, acting as banker to commercial banks and regulating the financial system

Bank of England the UK's central bank

Monetary Policy Committee the body within the Bank of England responsible for the conduct of monetary policy

bank rate the interest rate that is set by the Monetary Policy Committee of the Bank of England in order to influence inflation

Synoptic link

The role of the central bank (and the Bank of England in particular) is the topic of Chapter 31.

Key term

transmission mechanism of monetary policy the process by which a change in the bank rate affects inflation

Knowledge check 16.8

Would an increase in interest rates lead to a leftward or rightward shift of the *AD* curve?

charge to their borrowers. Thus, if the MPC changes the bank rate, the commercial banks soon adjust the rates they charge to borrowers. These will vary according to the riskiness of the loans — for example, credit cards are charged at a higher rate than mortgages — but all the rates are geared to the base rate set by the commercial banks, and hence indirectly to the bank rate set by the Bank of England.

Figure 16.4 summarises the **transmission mechanism of monetary policy**. The Bank of England sets the official bank rate, which affects both market rates of interest and the exchange rate. These in turn influence other asset prices and expectations about the future, and the degree of confidence among economic agents. These factors then affect both domestic and net external demand, and hence aggregate demand. An increase (decrease) in aggregate demand puts upward (downward) pressure on prices, thus affecting the amount of domestic inflationary pressure, while at the same time changes in the exchange rate have an effect on import prices, which also affect inflation. As you can see, there is a long and complicated chain of linkages that enables a change in monetary policy to affect inflation.

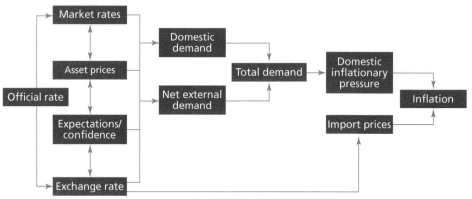

Source: Bank of England

Note: For simplicity, this figure does not show all interactions between variables, but these can be important.

Figure 16.4 The transmission mechanism of monetary policy

Although inflation remained within the 1% band from 1997 right through until March 2007, the following period showed a much more unstable pattern. Figure 16.5 shows bank rate and the inflation rate since 2004.

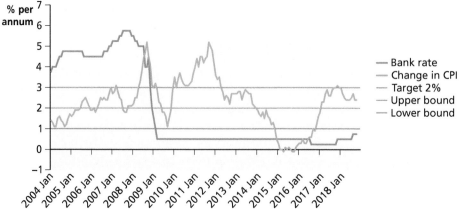

Sources: ONS, Bank of England

Figure 16.5 UK bank rate and the inflation target, 2004-18

Monetary policy from 2004 to 2007

In the first part of this period, inflation seemed under control. The association between the bank rate and movements in the inflation rate in this period is not easy to distinguish. This is partly because the relationship between them is obscured by other influences. It also reflects the fact that the MPC takes into account a wide range of factors when deciding whether to move the bank rate or to leave it as it was in the previous month. At a typical meeting, the MPC discusses financial market developments, the international economy, money, credit, demand and output, and costs and prices. In other words, the inflation target is considered within the broad context of developments in various aspects of the economy. All of these factors are discussed in some detail before a decision on the bank rate is taken. In the interests of transparency, the minutes of the regular MPC meetings are published on the internet — you can see them at www.bankofengland.co.uk/news. This means that you can readily check recent developments in the economy.

The underlying idea is that by influencing the level of aggregate demand, the MPC could affect the rate of inflation so as to keep it within the target range, although the effects of a change in the bank rate are not likely to happen immediately. A key reason for giving the Bank of England such independence was that it increases the credibility of the policy. If firms and households realise that the government is serious about controlling inflation, they will have more confidence in its actions, and will be better able to form expectations about the future path the economy will take. In particular, firms will be encouraged to undertake more investment, and this will have a supply-side effect, shifting the aggregate supply curve to the right in the long run.

When inflation began drifting towards 3% in early 2007, you can see that bank rate was increased in an attempt to bring inflation down — and you can also see that this did indeed happen during 2007, with inflation coming back down to around 2%.

A Monetary Policy Committee briefing led by Mark Carney, Governor of the Bank of England

Monetary policy from 2008

Inflation accelerated during 2008, but the MPC considered that this was likely to be a temporary surge. The financial crisis began to bite, and with many commercial banks finding themselves in trouble and being bailed out, the MPC was all too aware that credit in the economy was tight. Instead of raising bank rate in order to curb inflation, the MPC reduced bank rate, and by early 2009 bank rate had reached 0.5%, which was almost as low as it could go.

Quantitative easing

Key term

quantitative easing a process by which liquidity in the economy is increased when the Bank of England purchases assets from banks

Knowledge check 16.9

How does quantitative easing lead to an increase in money supply?

With the economy heading into recession, reducing bank rate in order to boost aggregate demand was no longer an option, and the Bank of England instead turned to a policy that became known as **quantitative easing**. This was a process by which the Bank of England purchased assets (mainly government securities) from the banks, thus affecting the banks' liquidity positions. The aim of this was to encourage lending by the banks, which had dried up during the credit crunch, thus making it difficult for firms to borrow. Quantitative easing was effectively a way in which the Bank of England could increase money supply in order to boost aggregate demand and help to counter the recession. Bank rate remained at 0.5%, even though inflation accelerated beyond its target during parts of 2011, as you can see very clearly in Figure 16.5.

So, how does quantitative easing work? The starting point is that the Bank of England uses electronically created money to buy high-quality financial assets, with the stated aim of improving the flow of credit in the economy, thus allowing firms to obtain finance for investment. Figure 16.6 shows the transmission mechanism from asset purchases to bank lending.

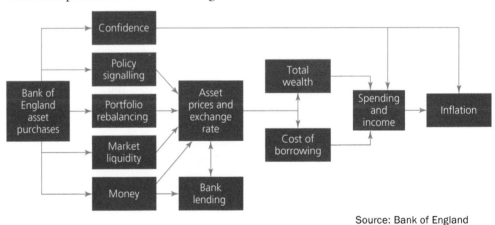

Source: Bank of England

Figure 16.6 The transmission mechanism for quantitative easing

The initial impact of asset purchases is intended to give economic agents confidence that action was being undertaken and to provide clear signals of policy intent. This would also encourage a rebalancing of portfolios, provide market liquidity and increase the supply of money.

The improvement in confidence would affect asset prices and the exchange rate, as well as spending and income in the economy. This could also affect inflation, but this was considered less important than the recession that was building — indeed inflation was decelerating anyway. These other effects of the asset purchases would work together to reinforce the impact on asset prices and the exchange rate, with the increase in money supply operating through the impact on bank lending. The adjustment in asset prices and the exchange rate would also affect total wealth and the cost of borrowing, in turn affecting spending and income.

In this way, monetary policy can be used to mitigate the effects of recession, even with the bank rate at its lowest point. The key part of this is the provision of credit to allow the economy to function more effectively.

Meanwhile, in the USA, the Federal Reserve (the USA's central bank) also took measures to safeguard its financial system, by expanding the amount of credit provided to the banking system and by increasing the money supply by purchasing long-term securities. The crisis had begun in the housing market, and mortgage lenders Fannie Mae and Freddie Mac were nationalised in 2008.

The late 2010s

The UK's recovery from recession was slow, and the time path of real GDP remained stubbornly below trend. You can see in Figure 16.5 that inflation fell below the target range in 2015 and 2016, even turning negative in some months. In August 2016, the MPC agreed to cut bank rate to 0.25% in an attempt to bring inflation back towards the target — and in recognition of the weakening prospects for growth following the EU referendum result. Inflation began to move back into the target range, and in late 2017 the MPC brought bank rate back up to 0.5% as inflation hit the top of its target range. Bank rate was raised to 0.75% in August 2018.

Evaluation of demand-side policies

Both fiscal and monetary policy operate through the demand-side of the economy, affecting the position of the *AD* curve in order to influence the path of the economy. Whether intervention is needed in response to an external shock depends on whether the economy adjusts rapidly back to equilibrium at the natural rate, or whether the adjustment process can be long and persistent.

The financial crisis represented one of the greatest external shocks to hit developed economies since the Second World War. So how effective were demand-side policies in responding to the crisis? In both the UK and the USA, a combination of fiscal and monetary policy measures were introduced.

■ *Fiscal policy:* governments on both sides of the Atlantic launched fiscal stimulus packages in the form of increased expenditure. In the UK, the government also introduced changes to direct taxes and implemented a temporary reduction in the rate of VAT. The strength of this approach is that the measures take effect quite quickly, and help to safeguard employment. However, the downside is that running a budget deficit in this way adds to public sector net debt, as the expenditures need to be financed.

■ *Monetary policy:* this was also used in an attempt to stimulate aggregate demand, with cuts in interest rates and quantitative easing also designed to stimulate aggregate demand. The need to bailout failing banks further added to public sector debt.

Looking back at Figure 14.10 on page 199, you can see that economic growth was restored in both the UK and the USA, although growth remained below the long-run trend value.

The message from *AD/AS* analysis is that stimulating aggregate demand is not a solution to long-run economic growth, except insofar as it entails investment expenditure that adds to a nation's productive capacity. Although the measures taken through demand-side policy during the financial crisis may have cushioned the impact, in the long run it is by supply-side policies that economic growth can be restored.

The Great Depression of the interwar years

Some parallels can be drawn with the Great Depression of the period between the two world wars. A stock market crash in New York in 1929 spread rapidly to the UK. World trade contracted and unemployment in the UK rose to 3 million. Figure 16.7 shows the unemployment rate in the UK in this period. Unemployment rose after the First World War, and the process of recovery and adjustment to peace was slow. Unemployment through much of the 1920s was around 10%. However, this rocketed as the depression took hold, and only fell below the level of the early 1920s as the Second World War approached.

Knowledge check 16.10

How would the onset of the Second World War have affected aggregate demand?

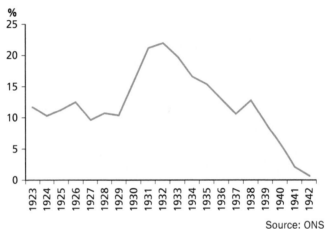

Source: ONS

Figure 16.7 Unemployment in the UK during the Great Depression

The government of the day was committed to classical economic ideas, and was determined to maintain balance in the government budget. In order to achieve this, it cut government spending. In addition, the theory suggested that unemployment would only fall if labour costs were reduced so that employers would be prepared to hire labour. They thus encouraged people to take wage cuts. This had the effect of reducing aggregate demand. As these measures took effect, the economy fell further into depression. It was in this context that Keynes published his *General Theory*, which pointed to the multiplier effects of autonomous spending, and suggested that a boost to aggregate demand could assist the recovery. This debate was renewed in the late 2000s, when some commentators argued for cuts in public expenditure in order to reduce the burden of public sector debt, while others advocated a stimulus to aggregate demand to speed the recovery.

In the USA, a different approach was adopted. President Roosevelt launched his 'New Deal' in 1933, a substantial fiscal expansion programme designed to improve the country's infrastructure and bring people into employment. Unemployment had peaked at 23.6% in 1932, but by 1938 it was still relatively high at 19.0%, so the extent to which the fiscal expansion had an effect is not clear. Spending on the Second World War may have done the trick, as unemployment in 1942 was down to 4.7%.

Exercise 16.2

Visit the Bank of England website and check whether the MPC chose to change the interest rate at its most recent meeting. Take a look at the minutes of the meeting to see the factors that were considered in taking this decision.

Study tip

Make sure that you practise drawing the *AD/AS* diagram and manipulating the curves to illustrate the alternative policy approaches, using both monetarist and Keynesian shapes for the *LRAS* curve.

Summary: monetary policy

- Monetary policy is concerned with the decisions made by government on monetary variables such as money supply and the interest rate.
- A change in the interest rate influences the level of aggregate demand through the investment expenditure of firms, the consumption behaviour of households and (indirectly) net exports.
- In 1997, the Bank of England was given independent responsibility to set interest rates in order to meet the government's inflation target.
- The Monetary Policy Committee (MPC) of the Bank sets the bank rate, which is then used as a base rate by the commercial banks and other financial institutions.
- Giving independence to the Bank of England in this way increases the credibility of monetary policy.
- If this encourages investment, there may be a long-run impact on aggregate supply.
- With the financial crisis of the late 2000s a new approach was needed.
- Quantitative easing was introduced to help manage an economy in recession.

Policies affecting aggregate supply

Demand-side policies have been aimed primarily at stabilising the macroeconomy in the relatively short run, but with the hope of affecting aggregate supply in the long run, by influencing firms' and households' confidence in the future path of the economy. However, there are also policies that can be used to influence the aggregate supply curve directly. These **supply-side policies** can take two forms. The classical economists recommend **market-based policies**, based on freeing up markets, providing improved incentives for enterprise and initiative. Others advocate **interventionist policies** by which the authorities should intervene directly in ways that stimulate aggregate supply.

Chapter 12 indicated that the position of the long-run aggregate supply curve depends primarily on the quantity of factor inputs available in the economy, and on the efficiency of those factors. Supply-side policies thus focus on affecting these determinants of aggregate supply in order to shift the *LRAS* curve to the right.

Investment is central to this in the long run, and we have seen how demand-side policies that stabilise the macroeconomy in the short run may also have long-run effects on aggregate supply by encouraging investment.

Key terms

supply-side policies
a range of measures intended to have a direct impact on aggregate supply — and specifically the potential capacity output of the economy

market-based policies
policies that rely on allowing markets to work more freely and providing incentives for enterprise and initiative

interventionist policies
policies by which the government intervenes to stimulate aggregate supply

Market-based policies

Incentive effects

Incentive effects are important in economic analysis. In this context, questions have been raised about the extent to which the tax system provides appropriate incentives to supply work effort.

There are dangers in having a taxation system that is too progressive. Most people accept that income tax should be progressive — that is, that those on relatively high incomes should pay a higher rate of tax than those on low incomes — as a way of redistributing income within society and preventing inequality from becoming extreme. However, there may come a point at which marginal tax rates are so high that a large proportion of additional income is taxed away, reducing incentives for individuals to supply additional effort or labour. This could also have an effect on aggregate supply. Again, however, it is important to balance these incentive effects against the distortion caused by having too much inequality in society.

Supply-side policies can be important in shifting aggregate supply and enabling an increase in the productive capacity of the economy. However, it is important to remember that these are policies for the long term, and many of them take time to become effective. For each of the policies discussed, there may be problems in evaluating the magnitude of the effects that can be anticipated.

Privatisation and deregulation

Synoptic link

Privatisation and deregulation are discussed fully in Chapter 23, following an analysis of how firms behave in Chapters 19 and 20.

In the past, some industries were taken into public ownership in the belief that this would protect consumers from being exploited. However, it was later realised that this was leading to inefficiency, because incentives and accountability for managers of these publicly owned enterprises were inadequate. Such enterprises have been sold back into the private sector through a process known as *privatisation*. This was intended to stimulate aggregate supply by improving efficiency.

There are other situations in which industries have been over-regulated, and again, deregulation has been put forward as a supply-side policy.

Reforming the labour market

An important supply-side approach is to find ways of improving the flexibility of the labour market.

One possibility is to limit the power of the trade unions, whose actions can sometimes lead to inflexibility, either through resistance to new working practices that could improve productivity or by pushing up wages so that the level of employment is reduced. It has also been argued that abolishing the minimum wage would improve flexibility. However, this must be balanced against the need to protect low-paid workers.

Maintaining the flexibility of markets is one way in which the macroeconomic stability promoted by disciplined fiscal and monetary policy can improve aggregate supply. Macroeconomic stability enables price signals to work more effectively, as producers are better able to observe changes in relative prices. This can promote allocative efficiency.

Reforming the benefit system

Synoptic link

The effect of unemployment benefits on the labour market is discussed in Chapter 22, together with more analysis of the flexibility of the labour market.

An important influence on labour supply, particularly for low-income workers, is the level of unemployment benefit. If unemployment benefit is provided at too high a level, it may inhibit labour force participation, in that some workers may opt to live on unemployment benefit rather than take up low-skilled (and low-paid) employment. In such a situation, a reduction in unemployment benefit may induce an increase in labour supply, which again will move the aggregate supply curve to the right.

Such a policy needs to be balanced against the need to provide protection for those who are unable to find employment. It is also important that unemployment benefit is not reduced to such a level that workers are unwilling to leave their jobs to search for better ones, as this may inhibit the flexibility of the labour market.

Interventionist policies

Education and training

An important interventionist supply-side policy takes the form of encouraging workers (and potential workers) to undertake education and training to improve their human capital and thus their productivity.

This takes place partly through education in schools and colleges in preparation for work. It is important, therefore, that the curriculum is designed to provide key skills that will be useful in the workplace. However, this does not mean that all education has to be geared directly to providing skills. For example, problem-solving and analytical skills can be developed through the study of a wide range of disciplines.

Adult education is also important. When the structure of the economy is changing, retraining must be made available to enable workers to move easily between sectors and occupations. This is crucial if structural unemployment is not to become a major problem. For any society, education and skills are necessary to enable workers to switch into new activities in response to structural changes in the economy. For example, workers displaced from manufacturing industry are likely to need retraining if they are to find jobs in the service sector. Workers released from agriculture in a developing country will need training before they can become productive members of the industrial workforce.

Knowledge check 16.11

Explain what is meant by 'human capital'.

Synoptic link

The meaning and significance of human capital was discussed in Chapter 14; we now need to consider how policy can affect it.

An apprentice working on the wing of an Airbus A320 — education and training is an investment in human capital

The market may not deliver the training that is necessary, as firms will not invest in training workers unless they can be sure that they will not be poached by competitors once they have completed their training. The government may thus need to provide incentives. One particular concern has been the number of young people aged between 16 and 18 who are not in education, employment or training (known as 'NEETs'). At the end of 2016 it was estimated that 6% of 16–18-year-olds were in this category. The Department for Education has piloted a number of initiatives to tackle this problem.

Knowledge check 16.12

Why might the government need to intervene to encourage firms to train their workers?

Figure 16.8 shows how such a policy can affect the aggregate supply curve, moving it from $LRAS_0$ to $LRAS_1$. This move enables an increase in the potential output capacity of the economy, and it need not be inflationary. Indeed, in the figure the overall price level falls from P_0 to P_1 following the shift in aggregate supply, with real output increasing from Y_{FE0} to Y_{FE1}.

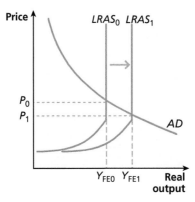

Figure 16.8 A shift in aggregate supply

Infrastructure

Synoptic link

The market failure arising for public goods is discussed in Chapter 7.

An important area of government expenditure relates to the provision of infrastructure. Firms need there to be efficient transport and communication networks, and other types of infrastructure than enable markets to operate effectively. The public goods aspects of infrastructure means that they will not be adequately provided by the free market mechanism, so government intervention is needed.

Promotion of competition

A recurrent theme in many policy statements from governments and international organisations like the World Bank and IMF has been the importance of promoting competition. There are several reasons why this might be important in influencing aggregate supply. One possibility is that a monopoly firm in a market may be able to use its market power to maximise profits by restricting output and raising price. If such a firm is forced to confront competition from other firms, it may have to temper its use of that market power, and reduce price in order to sell more output and protect its market share. The intensity of competition may also affect firms' willingness to improve productivity. It is possible that in some markets the lack of competition will produce complacency, depriving firms of the incentive to operate at maximum efficiency. This was especially true in the UK for the formerly nationalised industries such as electricity and gas supply, which were widely believed to have operated with widespread productive inefficiency. Policies that promote competition may thus lead to improvements in both allocative and productive efficiency.

Synoptic link

Government intervention to promote competition is discussed in Chapter 23.

Plugging information gaps

Information gaps are a form of market failure. One area in which this may be a problem is in the labour market, where workers may not have adequate information about job opportunities — especially in other regions of the economy. By providing information abut job vacancies, the authorities may be able to encourage mobility of workers, thus improving the way in which the labour market operates. Subsidies for key workers in regions where housing and transport costs are high may also be a useful interventionist strategy to encourage labour mobility.

Evaluation of supply-side policies

The strengths of supply-side policies are that they are targeted on specific problems that can inhibit economic growth by limiting the productive capacity of the economy. They may not always be fast-acting — after all, education and training or investing in infrastructure tend to be long-term projects. Nonetheless, there tends to be less uncertainty than with demand-side policies.

A weakness is the need for careful balancing of the effects of some policies. For example, lowering unemployment benefits to encourage more people into work may cause suffering for those unable to work, unless the policy is carefully designed.

Study tip

Be prepared to evaluate each of the alternative supply-side policies. In other words, be aware of their strengths and weaknesses.

Exercise 16.3

For each of the following policies, identify whether it is an example of fiscal, monetary or supply-side policy. Discuss how each policy affects either aggregate demand or aggregate supply (or both), and examine its effects on equilibrium real output and the overall price level:

a an increase in government expenditure

b a decrease in the rate of unemployment benefit

c a fall in the rate of interest

d legislation limiting the power of trade unions

e encouragement for more students to attend university

f provision of retraining in the form of adult education

g a reduction in the highest rate of income tax

h measures to break up a concentrated market

i an increase in the bank rate

Summary: supply-side policies

- Policies to shift the aggregate supply curve may be used to encourage economic growth.
- Supply-side policies may be market-based or interventionist.
- Incentive effects are an important influence on aggregate supply. For example, if unemployment benefits are set too high, this may discourage labour force participation. An over-progressive income taxation structure can also have damaging incentive effects.
- Measures to improve the flexibility of labour and product markets may lead to an overall improvement in productivity and thus may affect aggregate supply.
- Education and training can be viewed as a form of investment in human capital, which is designed to improve the productivity of workers.
- Government expenditure on improving the country's infrastructure may enable efficiency gains.
- Promoting competition can also improve the effectiveness of markets in the economy.

Conflicts in the implementation of policy

Having reviewed the main macroeconomic policy objectives, it should be clear that designing economic policy is likely to be something of a juggling act. This is especially so because there may be conflicts and trade-offs between some of the targets of policy and the instruments used to address them.

Unemployment and inflation

One example of a trade-off was discovered by the New Zealand-born economist Bill Phillips. In 1958, Phillips claimed that he had found an 'empirical regularity' that had existed for almost a century and that traced out a relationship between the rate of unemployment and the rate of change of money wages. This was rapidly generalised into a relationship between unemployment and inflation (by arguing that firms pass on increased wages in the form of higher prices).

Key term

Phillips curve an empirical relationship suggesting that there is a trade-off between unemployment and inflation

The Phillips curve

Figure 16.9 shows what became known as the **Phillips curve**. Although Phillips began with data, he also came up with an explanation of why such a relationship should exist. At the heart of his argument was the idea that, when the demand for labour is high (and unemployment is low), firms will be prepared to bid up wages in order to attract labour. To the extent that higher wages are then passed on in the form of higher prices, this would imply a relationship between unemployment and inflation: when unemployment is low, inflation will tend to be higher, and vice versa.

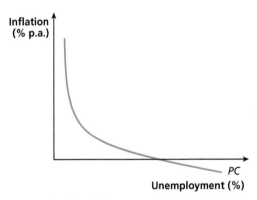

Figure 16.9 The Phillips curve

The Phillips curve trade-off

From a policy perspective, this suggests a trade-off between unemployment and inflation objectives. If the Phillips curve relationship holds, attempts to reduce the rate of unemployment are likely to raise inflation. On the other hand, a reduction in inflation is likely to result in higher unemployment. This suggests that it might be difficult to maintain full employment and low inflation at the same time. For example, Figure 16.10 shows a Phillips curve that is drawn such that to achieve an unemployment rate of 5%, inflation would need to rise to 15% per annum; this would not be acceptable these days, when people have become accustomed to much lower inflation rates.

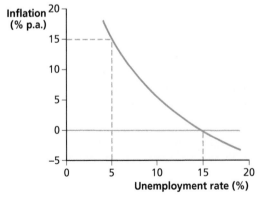

Figure 16.10 The Phillips curve inflation–unemployment trade-off

Nonetheless, the Phillips curve trade-off offers a tempting prospect to policy-makers. For example, if an election is imminent, it should be possible to reduce unemployment by allowing a bit more inflation, thereby creating a feel-good factor. After the election the process can be reversed. This suggests that there could be a political business cycle induced by governments seeking re-election. In other words, the conflict between policy objectives could be exploited by politicians who see that in the short run an electorate is concerned more about unemployment than inflation.

Knowledge check 16.13

Why might a government want to exploit the Phillips curve relationship in the run-up to an election?

The 1970s provided something of a setback to this theory, when suddenly the UK economy started to experience both high unemployment and high inflation simultaneously, suggesting that the Phillips curve had disappeared. This combination of stagnation and inflation became known as **stagflation**. One possibility that was put forward was that the Phillips curve had not in fact disappeared, but had moved. Suppose that wage bargaining takes place on the basis of *expectations* about future rises in retail prices. As inflation becomes embedded in an economy, and people come to expect it to continue, those expectations will be built into wage negotiations. Another way of viewing this is that expectations about price inflation will influence the *position* of the Phillips curve.

Figure 16.11 shows some empirical data for the UK to explore whether there is evidence of the Phillips curve trade-off. The scatter of points joined by the red line plots inflation and unemployment between 1986 and 1995, showing a negative relationship between these variables. The green scatter shows data for the later period 2006 to 2017. This does not connect well with the earlier trade-off, and appears to show a much flatter relationship (especially if we ignore the 2009 observation, which was an abnormal year in which inflation went negative). The relationship also seems to have shifted to the left, with unemployment being appreciably lower. This could be interpreted as a shift of the curve as well as a flattening.

Key term

stagflation a situation describing an economy in which both unemployment and inflation are high at the same time

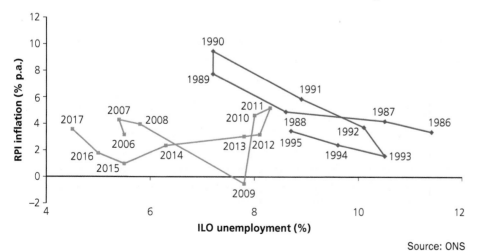

Source: ONS

Figure 16.11 Unemployment and inflation in the UK, 1986–1995 and 2006–2017

Extension material: the Phillips curve in the short and long run

You may have wondered how this notion of the Phillips trade-off can be reconciled with the notion of the natural rate of unemployment. One interpretation is that the Phillips curve is a short-run relationship showing how there can be short-run departures from the natural rate.

We could view the Phillips curve described above as the short-run Philips curve (SRPC). Suppose that $SRPC_0$ represents an initial Phillips curve, and that we start with the economy at the *natural rate of unemployment* , U_{nat}. If the economy is at point A, with inflation at π_0 and unemployment at U_{nat}, the economy is in equilibrium. If the economy always moves back to the natural rate (i.e. the LRAS is vertical), then the long-run Phillips curve (LRPC) is also vertical at the natural rate of unemployment.

If the government tries to exploit the Phillips curve by allowing inflation to rise to π_1, the economy moves in the short run to point B. However, as people realise that inflation is now higher, they adjust their expectations. This eventually begins to affect wage negotiations; the Phillips curve then moves to $SRPC_1$, and unemployment returns to the natural rate. The economy settles at C and is again in equilibrium, but now with higher inflation than before — and the same initial rate of unemployment. For this reason, the natural rate of unemployment is sometimes known as the

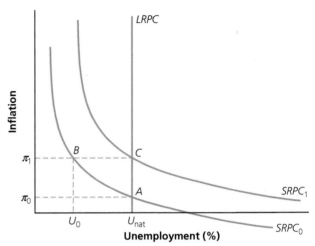

Figure 16.12 The long-run Phillips curve

non-accelerating-inflation rate of unemployment (NAIRU).

The problem that arises with this is how to get back to the original position with a lower inflation rate. This can happen only if people's expectations adjust so that lower inflation is expected. This means that the economy has to move down along $SRPC_1$, pushing up unemployment in order to reduce inflation. Then, once expectations adjust, the Phillips curve will move back again until the natural rate of unemployment is restored. If this takes a long time, the cost in terms of unemployment will be high.

Economic growth and the current account of the balance of payments

In some circumstances, conflict can arise between achieving economic growth and attaining equilibrium on the current account of the balance of payments. An increase in economic growth resulting in higher real incomes could lead to an increase in imports of goods and services, if UK residents spend a high proportion of their additional income abroad. This was seen as a major problem during the fixed exchange rate era of the 1950s and 1960s, when any deficit on the current account had to be met by running down foreign exchange reserves. This led to a 'stop–go' cycle of macroeconomic policy, where every time growth began to accelerate, the current account went into deficit, and policy then had to be adjusted to slow down the growth rate to deal with the deficit.

> **Knowledge check 16.14**
>
> Explain why the current account of the balance of payments might act as a constraint on economic growth when the government is committed to supporting the exchange rate.

Economic growth and environmental sustainability

The previous chapter noted the potential environmental effects of pursuing economic growth. Nowhere is this better seen than in the case of China in the early part of the twenty-first century. China's persistently rapid growth has had consequences for the quality of the environment. Figure 16.13 shows one aspect of this — the emissions of carbon dioxide, which is one of the key so-called greenhouse gases that contribute to the process of global warming. The acceleration of emissions in China in the early 2000s is very apparent in the figure, and China became the largest emitter of carbon dioxide in 2005.

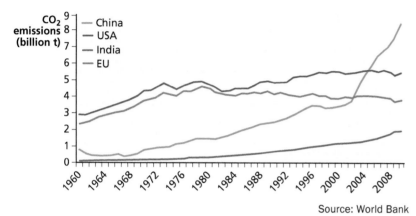

Source: World Bank

Figure 16.13 Carbon dioxide emissions

The link between economic growth and environmental degradation is a clear one. In the case of China, there are several aspects to notice. During the process of industrialisation, it is crucial to ensure that energy supplies keep pace with demand, as factories cannot operate effectively without reliable electricity and other energy sources. China has become the world's second biggest oil importer (behind the USA), and is the world's largest producer of coal, which is not the cleanest of energy technologies. China has recognised the problem, and has been making attempts to reduce its dependence on coal.

For economic growth to be sustainable, these environmental effects must be taken into account, or there is a real danger that the improved standard of living that flows from the growth process will be obtained only at the expense of the quality of life of future generations. This may require growth to be slowed in the short run in order to devote resources to the development of renewable and cleaner energy sources. However, it is politically and morally difficult to impose this on newly emerging societies in which there is widespread poverty, especially when the richer nations of the world continue to enjoy high standards of living while causing pollution of their own.

Fiscal and monetary policy

It was seen earlier that fiscal policy may have implications for the interest rate. If the government increases its expenditure, perhaps with the intention of improving infrastructure or subsidising education and training, one side-effect could be to require higher borrowing and push up interest rates. This could in turn lead to an inflow of hot money, affecting the exchange rate and the competitiveness of domestic goods in international markets. This suggests that there may be circumstances in which fiscal and monetary policy may come into conflict, given that interest rates are a key part of the transmission of monetary policy. Consequently, a way must be

Knowledge check 16.15

Why is the independence of the Bank of England important for macroeconomic policy?

found of coordinating fiscal and monetary policy. This is naturally difficult to do, given the way that the Bank of England acts independently of the government in conducting monetary policy in order to meet the inflation target.

Exercise 16.4

Discuss how giving the Bank of England independence in using monetary policy to meet an inflation target is likely to affect the expectations of economic agents. Why is this potentially significant?

Summary: conflicts and trade-offs

- There may be conflict and trade-offs between policy objectives.
- The Phillips curve describes a trade-off between unemployment and the inflation rate, which suggests that in the short run, lower unemployment can be achieved only at the expense of a higher rate of inflation.
- There may also be a conflict between attaining a high rate of economic growth and sustainability, although some forms of growth may be less problematic in this respect.
- Economic growth may also lead to problems with the current account of the balance of payments in some circumstances.

Designing the policy mix

In the context of the *AD/AS* model, it is clear that demand- and supply-side policies are aimed at achieving rather different objectives.

The primary rationale for monetary and fiscal policies is to stabilise the macroeconomy. In this, fiscal policy has come to take on a subsidiary role, supporting monetary policy. This was not always the case, and there have been periods in which fiscal policy has been used much more actively to try to stimulate the economy. There are still some countries in which such policies are very much the vogue: for example, it has been suggested that much of Latin America's problem with high inflation has stemmed from fiscal indiscipline, although not all Latin American economists accept this argument. The fact that fiscal policy has not always been well implemented does not mean that such policies cannot be valuable tools — but it does warn against their misuse.

In the UK, the use of monetary policy with the support of fiscal policy seemed to be working reasonably effectively in the early years of the twenty-first century, at least until the global financial crisis pushed the economy into recession.

Supply-side policies aim to influence aggregate supply directly, either raising the supply of factor inputs or improving productivity and efficiency.

The design and conduct of economic policy may therefore be seen as an elaborate balancing act. Differing policy objectives need to be prioritised, as in many cases there may be conflict between them. Choices have to be made about the balance to be achieved between fiscal, monetary and supply-side policies.

The consensus view in the early part of the twenty-first century was that fiscal policy should be used to achieve the desired balance between the public and private sectors. Monetary policy should be devoted to meeting the government's inflation target in order to create a stable macroeconomic environment; this would then encourage growth and enable improvements in the standard of living. Problems arose when fiscal policy was forced into action in order to protect the financial system, resulting in an escalation of public debt.

In the long run, supply-side policies are perhaps the most important, as these contribute to raising efficiency and increasing the productive capacity of the economy. The keynote in policy design lies in enabling markets to operate as effectively as possible.

Summary: the policy mix

- Demand-side and supply-side policies have different objectives.
- Demand-side policies such as fiscal and monetary policy are aimed primarily at stabilising the economy.
- Supply-side policies are geared more towards promoting economic growth.
- There are situations in which different policies have conflicting impacts on the economy.
- The financial crisis and the recession that it triggered have led to some rethinking of the relationship between monetary and fiscal policy, with fiscal policy being invoked to protect the financial system.

Case study 16.1

Macroeconomic policy instruments

Governments in a modern economy have three main types of policy instrument for affecting the macroeconomy — monetary policy, fiscal policy and supply-side policy. Monetary policy is dedicated to ensuring the stability of the economy by influencing aggregate demand. Fiscal policy is used to maintain balance in the economy between public and private sectors and between present and future generations of citizens. Supply-side policies are dedicated to affecting the productive capacity of the economy, operating primarily through microeconomic incentives.

Follow-up question

Explain these distinctions between the types of policy instrument. Which type do you consider to be of most importance?

Case study 16.2

Macroeconomic policy conflicts

Imagine that you are a policy-maker in a country and are considering some of the issues involved in designing macroeconomic policy.

Suppose that the central bank has been given the task of achieving the inflation target, so is intent on achieving low inflation within the target range. The minister responsible for employment issues insists that a high priority must be given to reaching full employment. The trade secretary is concerned about the deficit on the current account of the balance of payments. The green lobby insists that more resources need to be devoted to protecting the environment. The health minister demands more funding for the health service, and the defence secretary points out the need to reinforce military spending. As if this wasn't enough, there is also pressure to reduce income inequality in the country. You are also keen to promote economic growth in order to improve the standard of living for your citizens. The Office for Budget Responsibility is insistent that the level of public sector net debt needs to be reduced.

Follow-up questions

a To what extent are these competing policy objectives valid and mutually consistent?
b Is it possible to create a policy package to achieve all of these demands simultaneously?

Theme 2 key terms

actual economic growth the rate of growth of real GDP in a period

aggregate demand the total amount of spending on goods and services produced in an economy during a period of time

aggregate demand (*AD*) curve the relationship between the level of aggregate demand and the overall price level; it shows planned expenditure at any given possible overall price level

average propensity to consume the proportion of income that households devote to consumption

balance of payments a set of accounts showing the transactions conducted between residents of a country and the rest of the world

Bank of England the UK's central bank

bank rate the interest rate that is set by the Monetary Policy Committee of the Bank of England in order to influence inflation

boom the expansionary phase of the trade (business) cycle

capital account of the balance of payments an account identifying transactions in (physical) capital between the residents of a country and the rest of the world

capital productivity a measure of output per unit of capital

central bank the banker to the government, performing a range of functions, which may include issue of coins and banknotes, acting as banker to commercial banks and regulating the financial system

circular flow of income, expenditure and output a model of the economy which shows the movement of goods and services between households and firms and their corresponding payments in money terms

claimant count of unemployment the number of people claiming the Jobseeker's Allowance each month

classical/monetarist school economists who believed that the macroeconomy always adjusts rapidly to the full employment level of output, and that monetary policy should be the prime instrument for stabilising the economy

consumer price index (CPI) a measure of the general level of prices in the UK, the rate of change of which has been used as the government's inflation target since January 2004

consumption total planned household spending

cost-push inflation inflation initiated by an increase in the costs faced by firms, arising on the supply side

CPIH a version of the CPI that takes into account the housing costs of owner-occupiers and the council tax

current account of the balance of payments an account identifying transactions in goods and services between the residents of a country and the rest of the world

cyclical unemployment unemployment that arises during the downturn of the economic cycle, such as a recession

deflation a fall in the average level of prices (negative inflation)

demand-deficient unemployment unemployment that arises because of a deficiency of aggregate demand in the economy, so that the equilibrium level of output is below full employment

demand-pull inflation inflation initiated by an increase in aggregate demand

depreciation (of capital equipment) the fall in the value of capital goods due to wear and tear

discouraged workers people who have been unable to find employment and who are no longer looking for work

disinflation a fall in the rate of inflation

disposable income the income that households have to devote to consumption and saving, taking into account payments of direct taxes and transfer payments

Easterlin paradox the hypothesis that happiness increases with average incomes, but only up to a point

economically inactive those people of working age who are not looking for work, for a variety of reasons

exchange rate the price of one currency in terms of another

export-led growth a strategy for achieving rapid economic growth through the promotion of export activity

financial account of the balance of payments an account identifying transactions in financial assets between the residents of a country and the rest of the world

fiscal policy decisions made by the government on its expenditure, taxation and borrowing

frictional unemployment unemployment associated with job search (i.e. people who are between jobs)

full employment a situation where people who are economically active in the workforce and are willing and able to work (at going wage rates) are able to find employment

GNI per capita the average level of GNI per head of population

government budget deficit (surplus) the balance between government expenditure and revenue

gross domestic product (GDP) a measure of the economic activity carried out in the domestic economy over a period

gross investment net investment plus depreciation

gross national income (GNI) GDP plus net income from abroad

human capital the stock of skills and expertise that contribute to a worker's productivity; it can be increased through education and training

ILO unemployment rate a measure of the percentage of the workforce who are without jobs, but are available for work, willing to work and looking for work

in employment people who are either working for firms or other organisations, or self-employed

income a flow concept – the amount of income that is earned during a period

index number a device for comparing the value of a variable in one period or location with a base observation (e.g. the consumer price index measures the average level of prices relative to a base period)

inflation the rate of increase in the average price level in an economy

injections where money flows into the circular flow in the form of investment, government spending and exports

interventionist policies policies by which the government intervenes to stimulate aggregate supply

investment expenditure undertaken by firms on capital goods

involuntary unemployment situation arising when an individual who would like to accept a job at the going wage rate is unable to find employment

Keynesian school economists who believed that the macroeconomy could settle at an equilibrium that was below full employment

labour productivity a measure of output per worker, or output per hour worked

macroeconomics the study of the interrelationships between economic variables at an aggregate (macroeconomic) level

marginal propensity to consume (MPC) the proportion of additional income devoted to consumption

marginal propensity to import (MPM) the proportion of additional income that is spent on imports of goods and services

marginal propensity to save (MPS) the proportion of an increase in disposable income that households would devote to saving

marginal propensity to tax (MPT) the proportion of additional income that is taxed

marginal propensity to withdraw (MPW) the proportion of additional income that is withdrawn from the circular flow – the sum of the marginal propensities to save, import and tax

market-based policies policies that rely on allowing markets to work more freely and providing incentives for enterprise and initiative

monetary policy the decisions made by government regarding monetary variables such as the money supply or the interest rate

Monetary Policy Committee the body within the Bank of England responsible for the conduct of monetary policy

money supply the quantity of money in the economy

multiplier the ratio of a change in equilibrium real income to the autonomous change that brought it about; it is defined as 1 divided by the marginal propensity to withdraw

natural rate of output the long-run equilibrium level of output to which monetarists believe the macroeconomy will always tend

natural rate of unemployment the unemployment rate that will exist when the economy is in long-run equilibrium

net investment investment net of the replacement of existing capital (depreciation)

nominal GDP the *value* of GDP based on current prices, taking no account of changing prices through time

output gap the difference between actual real GDP and potential real GDP

Phillips curve an empirical relationship suggesting that there is a trade-off between unemployment and inflation

potential economic growth an expansion in the productive capacity of the economy

productivity a measure of the efficiency of a factor of production

purchasing power parity (PPP) exchange rate an exchange rate adjusted to reflect the relative purchasing power of incomes in different countries

quantitative easing a process by which liquidity in the economy is increased when the Bank of England purchases assets from banks

real balance effect an effect by which an increase in the average price level reduces purchasing power and thus the quantity of real output demanded

real GDP an estimate of the *volume* of GDP taking account of changing prices through time

real wage inflexibility an argument that if real wages do not adjust downwards the result would be persistent unemployment

recession occurs when GDP falls for two or more consecutive quarters

retail price index (RPI) a measure of the average level of prices in the UK

seasonal adjustment a process by which seasonal fluctuations in a variable are smoothed to reveal the underlying trend

seasonal unemployment unemployment that arises in seasons of the year when demand is relatively low

short-run aggregate supply curve (SRAS) a curve showing how much output firms would be prepared to supply in the short run at any given overall price level

stagflation a situation describing an economy in which both unemployment and inflation are high at the same time

structural unemployment unemployment arising because of changes in the pattern of economic activity within an economy

supply-side policies a range of measures intended to have a direct impact on aggregate supply — and specifically the potential capacity output of the economy

sustainable development 'development that meets the needs of the present without compromising the ability of future generations to meet their own needs' (Brundtland Commission, 1987)

trade (business) cycle a phenomenon whereby GDP fluctuates around its underlying trend, following a regular pattern

total factor productivity the average productivity of all factors, measured as the total output divided by the total amount of inputs used

transmission mechanism of monetary policy the process by which a change in the bank rate affects inflation

underemployment where an individual is employed in a second-choice occupation or is only able to work part-time but would like to work full-time

unemployed people who are economically active but are not in employment

voluntary unemployment situation arising when an individual chooses not to accept a job at the going wage rate

wealth a stock concept — the accumulation of assets, such as property or shares

wealth effects where changes in household wealth induce changes in consumer expenditure

withdrawals where money flows out of the circular flow in the form of savings, taxation and imports

workforce people who are economically active — either in employment or unemployed

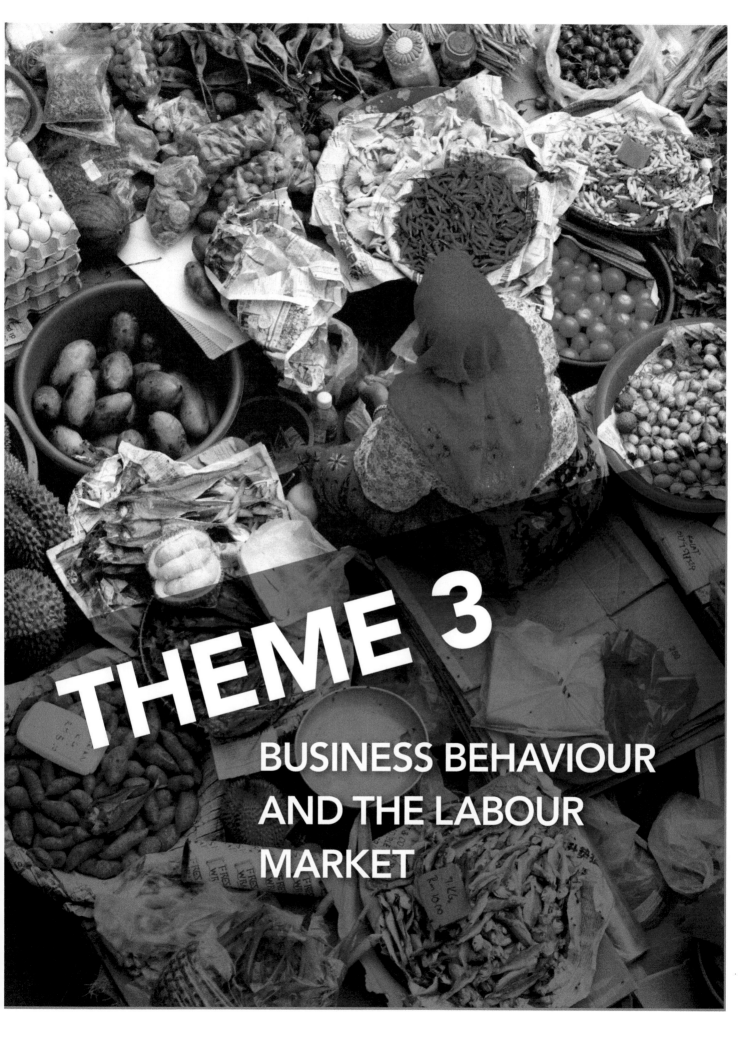

THEME 3

BUSINESS BEHAVIOUR AND THE LABOUR MARKET

Business growth

From earlier discussions, you will have come to realise the importance of firms in the operation of markets. Business economics looks more closely at the decisions made by firms, and the implications of those decisions for the effectiveness of markets in allocating resources within an economy. This chapter examines the nature of firms and the way in which they may grow.

Synoptic link

The material relating to Theme 3 builds on the microeconomic analysis in Theme 1. Chapter 3 is especially important, as this laid the foundations for analysing the theory of the firm.

Learning objectives

After studying this chapter, you should:
→ be aware of the reason for the birth of firms, and the desire for their growth
→ be familiar with alternative ways in which firms grow
→ be able to distinguish between horizontal, vertical and conglomerate mergers
→ be aware of the need for firms to grow if they wish to compete in global markets

Key terms

firm an organisation that brings together factors of production in order to produce output

private sector made up of firms that are privately owned

public sector made up of state-owned organisations, including those that run central and local government activities and some enterprises in public ownership

not-for-profit organisations organisations such as charities that operate on a non-profit-making basis

Synoptic link

Not all firms may seek to maximise profits, and Chapter 18 examines alternative motivations that firms may have.

Sizes and types of firms

In Chapter 3, the notion of the supply curve in a competitive market was introduced. This is a key component of the demand and supply model, which was seen to be powerful in enabling the interpretation of changes in market conditions. In order to construct the supply curve, it was argued that a **firm** will respond to price in taking decisions about how much output to produce. This was based on the assumption that the main motivation of firms is to make profits.

Private and public sector firms

The main focus will be on decisions taken by privately owned firms, that is, firms that comprise the **private sector**. However, it is also important to be aware of organisations in the **public sector**, which take decisions in a different way. The public sector includes the organisations that are part of central and local government (including such organisations as the National Health Service) and some other enterprises that have been taken into state ownership (such as Network Rail Ltd). It is also important to be aware that some organisations operate on a **not-for-profit** basis, such as charities. These may also take decisions based on rather different criteria.

Internally, firms may be organised in various ways, from small, sole proprietors (such as a corner shop) to mega-sized, transnational companies such as Google (also known as multinational corporations).

Firms that operate in the private sector and are run on a commercial basis are often assumed to set out to maximise their profits, and this underpins much of the traditional theory of the firm in economic analysis. In other words, they are assumed to take decisions that make as much surplus of revenue over costs as possible. It will be seen later that this may not always be the case, but it is a helpful working assumption.

It is important to recognise that not all private firms may operate in this way. Charities and other enterprises may work on a not-for-profit basis, aiming to cover their costs but not make a surplus above that level. Firms in the public sector may also have other objectives. For example, they may be established in order to provide services rather than to earn a profit, perhaps aiming for efficiency in provision and customer coverage rather than monetary profit. Their decisions will therefore be taken with these alternative objectives in mind.

Scale of operations

A key decision that all firms face concerns the scale of their operations. This decision turns partly on the nature of the market that they are serving, but it also depends on the technology of the sector in which they operate and the structure of costs that they face.

Some firms may need to grow in order to compete with other large-scale competitors in global markets. There may be many reasons why firms wish to expand their operations. This chapter will begin to explain why this is so.

In some sectors, there are examples of both large and small firms. For example, your local gymnasium may be a relatively small enterprise, but there are also some big players in the sport market, such as Chelsea FC or Sky. There may be small local taxi firms that are part of the transport sector, but there are also large firms such as British Airways.

The nature of the activity being undertaken by the firm and its scale of operation will help to determine its most efficient form of organisation. For firms to operate successfully, they must minimise the transaction costs of undertaking business. Some firms may not wish to grow into large organisations — nor may it be profitable for them to do so.

> ### Synoptic link
>
> The way that costs vary with the scale of production is important; Chapter 18 explains the nature of the costs that firms face and how this influences their behaviour.

Exercise 17.1

Identify firms that are operating in your town or city. Which of them would you classify as being relatively small-scale enterprises, and which operate on a more national or international basis?

▌ The growth of firms

A feature of the economic environment in recent years has been the increasing size of firms. Some, such as Facebook, Walmart and Google, have become giants. Why is this happening?

Firms may wish to increase their size in order to gain market power within the industry in which they are operating. A firm that can gain market share, and perhaps become dominant in the market, may be able to exercise some control over the price of its product, and thereby influence the market.

Organic growth

Some firms grow simply by being successful. For example, a successful marketing campaign may increase a firm's market share, and provide it with a flow of profits that can be reinvested to expand the firm even more. Some firms may choose to borrow in order to finance their growth, for example by taking out loans from a bank.

Key term

organic growth when a firm grows internally by reinvesting profits or borrowing from banks

Such **organic growth** may encounter limits. A firm may find that its product market is saturated, so that it can grow further only at the expense of other firms in the market. If its competitors are able to maintain their own market shares, the firm may need to diversify its production activities by finding new markets for its existing product, or perhaps offering new products.

There are many examples of growth through diversification. Tesco, a leading UK supermarket, launched itself into new markets by opening branches overseas, and it has also introduced a range of new products, including financial services, to its existing customers. Microsoft has famously used this strategy in the past, by selling first its internet browser and later its media player as part of its Windows operating system, in an attempt to persuade existing customers to buy its new products. This aggressive approach attracted the attention of the regulatory authorities in the USA and Europe.

Knowledge check 17.1

If a firm expands its market share by using funds from past profits, would this be classified as 'organic growth'?

Diversification may be a dangerous strategy: moving into a market in which the firm is inexperienced and existing rival firms already know the business may pose quite a challenge. In such circumstances, much may depend on the quality of the management team. However, diversification may reduce risk if the firm's products do not follow the same cycle of activity through time.

Knowledge check 17.2

Explain what is meant by 'diversification' in this context.

A Tesco store in China — diversifying into new markets is one way to maintain growth

Mergers and acquisitions

Instead of growing organically — that is, based on the firm's own resources — many firms choose to grow by merging with, or acquiring, other firms. The distinction here is that an *acquisition* (or takeover) may be hostile, whereas a *merger* may be the coming together of equals, with each firm committed to forming a single entity.

Growth in this way has a number of advantages: for example, it may allow some rationalisation to take place within the organisation. On the other hand, firms tend to develop their own culture, or way of doing things, and some mergers have foundered because of an incompatibility of corporate cultures.

Horizontal mergers

Mergers (or acquisitions) can be of three different types. A **horizontal merger** is a merger between firms operating in the same industry and at the same stage of the production process: for example, the merger of two car assembly firms. The car industry has been characterised by such mergers in the past, including the takeover of Rover by BMW in 1994 and the merger of Daimler-Benz with Chrysler in 1998. A more recent example was the acquisition of Kerry Foods by Pork Farms: both firms produce chilled savoury pastry products (pork pies, sausage rolls, pasties and slices, quiches and scotch eggs). The result of such a merger is known as **horizontal integration**.

A horizontal merger can affect the degree of market concentration, because after the merger takes place there are fewer independent firms operating in the market. This may increase the market power held by the new firm.

Vertical mergers

A car assembly plant merging with a tyre producer, on the other hand, is an example of the second type of merger: a **vertical merger**. Vertical mergers may be either upstream or downstream. If a car company merges with a component supplier, that is known as **backward integration**, as it involves merging with a firm that is involved in an earlier part of the production process. **Forward integration** entails merging in the other direction, as for example if the car assembly plant decided to merge with a large distributor. An example of backward integration is when Hotel Chocolat acquired its own cocoa plantation in St Lucia.

Knowledge check 17.3

Give another example of forward integration.

Vertical integration may allow rationalisation of the process of production. Car producers often work on a just-in-time basis, ordering components for the production line only as they are required. This creates a potential vulnerability, because if the supply of components fails then production has to stop. If a firm's component supplier is part of the firm rather than an independent operator, this may improve the reliability of, and confidence in, the just-in-time process, and in consequence may make life more difficult for rival firms. However, vertical mergers have different implications for concentration and market power.

Conglomerate mergers

The third type of merger — **conglomerate merger** — involves the merging of two firms that are operating in quite different markets or industries. For example, companies like Unilever, Tata and Nestlé operate in a range of different markets, partly as a result of acquisitions. Sainsbury's acquired Argos in 2016, thus expanding their non-food business. In 2018, Nestlé announced a global coffee alliance, whereby it would pay Starbucks $7.1 billion to sell its coffee, thus extending its supply chain downwards.

Synoptic link

The meaning and significance of market concentration requires some understanding of market structure, and is examined in Chapter 20.

Key terms

horizontal merger a merger between two firms at the same stage of production in the same industry

horizontal integration the result of a horizontal merger

vertical merger a merger between two firms in the same industry, but at different stages of the production process

backward integration a process under which a firm merges with a firm that is involved in an earlier part of the production chain

forward integration a process under which a firm merges with a firm that is involved in a later part of the production chain

conglomerate merger a merger between two firms operating in different markets

Knowledge check 17.4

Give another example of a conglomerate firm.

Study tip

Make sure that you are familiar with the three types of merger (horizontal, vertical and conglomerate) and be ready with examples of each to illustrate your answers.

Synoptic link

The impact of the globalisation process is discussed in more detail in Chapter 24.

Key term

transnational company a firm that conducts its operations in a number of countries

Knowledge check 17.5

Why is it an advantage for a firm to have greater control over its supply chain after a vertical merger?

One argument in favour of conglomerates is that they reduce the risks faced by firms. Many markets follow fluctuations that are in line with the business cycle but are not always fully synchronised. By operating in a number of markets that are on different cycles, the firm can even out its activity overall. However, this is not necessarily an efficient way of doing business, as the different activities undertaken may require different skills and specialisms.

Exercise 17.2

Categorise each of the following as a horizontal, vertical or conglomerate merger:

a the merger of a firm operating an instant coffee factory with a coffee plantation
b the merger of a brewer and a bakery
c the merger of a brewer and a crisp manufacturer
d the merger of a soft drinks manufacturer with a chain of fast-food outlets
e the merger of an internet service provider with a film studio
f a merger between two firms producing tyres for cars

Globalisation and transnational companies

Since the 1980s, advances in the technology of transport and communications and deregulation of international markets have led to a process known as *globalisation*. This has had a significant effect on the growth of firms. The whole process of marketing goods and services has been revolutionised with the spread of the internet and e-commerce. Amazon is a prime example of a firm that has been built on online technology.

Transnational companies will make a number of appearances in the following chapters of the book, and their increasing role in the global economy will be evaluated. One motive for mergers and acquisitions has been defensive — that is, to try to compete with other large firms in the global market. However, there are many firms that aspire to operate as transnationals in order to have access to larger international markets, to obtain competitively priced resources or to become more efficient by outsourcing parts of their production chain.

Evaluation of mergers and acquisitions

Mergers and acquisitions seem at first glance to be an attractive option for a firm wishing to expand. Organic growth may offer a more controlled environment for growth, as it builds on the known existing strengths of the growing firm. However, it may be a slower process, as the rate of growth may be constrained by the availability of finance, whereas a merger offers an instant expansion of market share and of the expertise available within the merged firm. It also seems to offer the potential for cost savings through rationalisation of key functions within the internal organisation of a firm.

In the case of a horizontal merger, the advantages may be seen as providing instant access to increased economies of scale, and an increase in market share, perhaps leading to increased market power. In practice, this may also be a disadvantage, because such gains in market share may attract the attention of the regulator, as will be discussed in Chapter 23.

A vertical merger, whether forward or backward, offers greater control over the supply chain. If the firm after the merger now has its own suppliers of components, or its own distribution chain, it is clearly less subject to interruptions in supply, and has more control over the margins at each stage of the production process.

A conglomerate merger may also offer advantages because a diversified portfolio of production activities may leave the firm less vulnerable to recession, if different activities are affected to different degrees by fluctuations in the general level of economic activity. There may also be possibilities for cost savings, if the merged firms can find synergies in core business functions such as financial accounting or marketing. It is thus likely to consolidate these functions, shedding staff and perhaps relocating some functions. On the other hand, there may be managerial diseconomies if the management team do not understand all aspects of the new diversified business.

Constraints on the growth of firms

In practice, there may be constraints on the growth of firms. The size of the market may be an important factor here. If a firm is operating in a niche market, then there may be clear limits on the size to which the firm can grow. It may also be that the market for a good or service is localised, so that there may be limited scope for expansion. An example might be hairdressing salons, which tend to have a local and loyal clientele. The technology of the production process may also limit the extent to which a firm is able to grow.

Some firms may choose to remain small-scale, perhaps because the owner does not feel the need to expand. A sole proprietor of a small business may prefer to stay in charge, rather than handing over to a management team. Small businesses may also find it more difficult to raise finance for expansion, and be limited by their own resources. For example, the owner of a market stall or greengrocery shop may not be able to obtain a bank loan to expand — and may not wish to do so. Having reached a certain size, firms may not wish to grow further for fear of attracting the attention of the regulator.

> **Synoptic link**
>
> Firms may grow to the point where they can exert market power in ways that damage consumers. In such cases, they may become subject to regulation (in the UK by the Competition and Markets Authority). This is discussed in Chapter 23.

The principal–agent problem

One issue for many larger firms — especially public limited companies — is that the owners may not be directly involved in running the business. This gives rise to the **principal–agent** (or **agency) problem**. In a public limited company, the shareholders delegate the day-to-day decisions concerning the operation of the firm to managers who act on their behalf. In this case the shareholders are the *principals*, and the managers are the *agents* who run things for them. The degree of accountability of managers to the owners may be weak when the shareholders are a disparate group of individuals.

> **Key term**
>
> **principal–agent (agency) problem** a problem arising from conflict between the objectives of the principals and those of the agents who take decisions on their behalf

If the agents are fully in sympathy with the objectives of the owners, there is no problem and the managers will take exactly the decisions that the owners would like. Problems arise when there is conflict between the aims of the owners and those of the managers. Shareholders (the owners) are likely to want the firm to maximise its profits, but the managers may have other motivations.

> **Synoptic link**
>
> The objectives that firms (or their managers) pursue are discussed in Chapter 18.

One simple explanation of why this problem arises is that the managers like a quiet life, and therefore do not push to make as much profit as possible, but do just enough to keep the shareholders off their backs. Herbert Simon referred to this as 'satisficing' behaviour, where managers aim to produce satisfactory profits rather than maximum profits.

Another possibility is that managers become negligent because they are not fully accountable. One manifestation of this may be *organisational slack* in the

Knowledge check 17.6

Why might there be conflict between a firm's owners and its managers?

organisation: costs will not be minimised, as the firm is not operating as efficiently as it could.

The principal–agent problem arises primarily from an information asymmetry. This arises because the agents have better information about the effects of their decisions than the owners (the principals), who are not involved in the day-to-day running of the business. In order to overcome this, the owners need to overcome the information problem by improving their monitoring of the managers' actions, or to provide the managers with an incentive to take decisions that would align with the owners' objectives. For example, by offering bonuses related to profit, the managers would be more likely to try to maximise profits.

Exercise 17.3

The principal-agent distinction is applicable in many different contexts. In each of the following cases, identify which is the principal and which is the agent:

a the owners of a firm and the managers hired to run it

b a department store and its employees

c a department store and its customers

d an electricity supplier and consumers of electricity

e a dentist and his or her patients

Demergers

In practice, not all mergers turn out to be as successful as had been expected. In some cases, it may be that the costs of integrating the managements of two different firms are underestimated before the event. Computer or production systems may not be compatible, and it may not be as easy as expected to make staff cuts. Corporate cultures may collide, especially where the merger takes place across national borders. This may mean that the expected gains in market share or profits do not materialise. Once two firms have merged, reversing the process by separating can turn out to be costly and acrimonious.

If the expected cost savings do not seem to be reaped, or if shareholder value does not seem to be enhanced as a result of the merger or acquisition then it could be that the firm has to admit failure and seek to reverse the process by demerging. This may simply be a case of the firm realising that the merger was a mistake, or it may be that the regulator steps in and insists that the firms demerge. For example, in 2008, the British Airports Authority was forced by the regulator to sell some of the airports that had come under its control, including Gatwick. In early 2018, Whitbread announced its decision to spin off Costa Coffee.

A demerger is potentially disruptive for the firm and for the workers who have been displaced or discharged. It may also be confusing for the consumers. Where the original merger was effectively an acquisition, in which a large firm took over a smaller firm and tried to assimilate it, there may be little possibility of the smaller firm recovering the position it held before the merger.

From the perspective of the firm, a demerger may allow a renewed focus on the core business, or may simply enable the firm to remove loss-making sections of the firm. From the workers' point of view, those that remain with the firm after the demerger may have enhanced job security. For consumers, a more focused company may be better able to provide the products that they wish to buy.

Summary: growth of firms and mergers

- A firm is an organisation that exists to bring together factors of production in order to produce goods or services.
- Firms range, in the complexity of their organisation, from sole proprietors to public limited companies.
- Firms may undergo organic growth, building on their own resources and past profits.
- If limited by the size of their markets, firms may diversify into new markets or products.
- Firms may also grow through horizontal, vertical or conglomerate mergers and acquisitions.
- Globalisation has enabled the growth of giant firms operating on a global scale.
- There may be constraints on the growth of firms in some market situations.
- For many larger firms, where day-to-day control is delegated to managers, a principal–agent problem may arise if there is conflict between the objectives of owners (principals) and those of the managers (agents).
- The process of demerging will have an impact on businesses, workers and consumers, which may be positive or negative.

Case study 17.1

A failed merger

This case study examines an episode in which a merger did not turn out the way that the firms involved anticipated.

In 2001 negotiations began between two firms in the telecoms-equipment business — the French firm Alcatel and Lucent Technologies of America — and 5 years later, in April 2006, an agreement was reached that the two firms would merge.

There seemed to be good commercial reasons for coming together. Alcatel, the bigger of the two firms, would gain entry into the lucrative American market, and the merger would make the combined firm one of the world's largest in the market. The combined revenue of the two firms from sales of network equipment would be slightly larger than that of Cisco Systems, the market leader at the time.

It was expected that the merger would not only give the firm a higher profile in the two key markets of America and Europe, but also enable the exploitation of economies of scale. By combining the companies, it was expected that about 10% of the existing workforce could be cut, saving $1.7 billion. This would be achieved by eliminating overlapping administrative, procurement and marketing costs, as well as reducing the workforce.

However, things did not work out as expected, and the merged company ran into problems. The firm found cost savings difficult to realise, in spite of 16,500 job losses from a workforce of 88,000 — and found that prices in the market were falling, squeezing profitability. The firm faced competition from new entrants, particularly from Chinese firms, and found difficulty in keeping up with the pace of technological change. It was also reported that the firm was suffering from a clash of cultures between the French and American parts of the business.

The result of all this was that in July 2008 it was announced that the French chairman (who was formerly the boss of Alcatel) and the American chief executive (formerly the boss of Lucent) were leaving the company and being replaced by a new executive team charged with the task of taking the company forward. The new chairman was neither French nor American, but Dutch.

The company continued trading as Alcatel-Lucent until it was acquired by Nokia in 2016.

Even the most carefully planned mergers can end up as failures

Follow-up questions

a What factors contributed to the merger not working out as expected?
b Why might a clash of cultures be a challenge to the success of the merger?

Case study 17.2

Acquiring Homebase

Homebase is a British home improvement retailer and garden centre, founded in 1979 as Sainsbury's Homebase. In 1995, the company tripled in size through the acquisition of Texas Homecare. Sainsbury's sold Homebase in 2000 in a £969 million deal. Homebase changed hands again in 2002, before becoming part of the Home Retail Group plc (HRG) in 2006. HRG was the parent company of Argos and Habitat.

By 2015/16, Homebase was facing a difficult time. It had underperformed for a number of years, and was set to close several stores. Sainsbury's were interested in acquiring HRG to gain control of Argos, but did not want to re-acquire Homebase.

Wesfarmers is an Australian conglomerate, one of its companies being Bunnings, the number one garden centre chain in Australia. Bunnings were keen to gain a foothold in the UK market, which was seen to have a large number of old houses, high home ownership and keen gardeners. Homebase looked to be a good match. Wesfarmers bought Homebase for £340 million in February 2016, claiming to have saved hundreds of workers from redundancy.

One of the first steps taken by Bunnings was to axe the entire Homebase senior management team and about 160 middle managers, replacing them with an Australian leadership team, assuming that the UK market would welcome the Bunnings warehouse style of retailing. The Australian DIY chain had been famous for low prices and sausage sizzlers. The firm also ditched its previously popular kitchen and bathroom ranges, and ousted concessions such as Laura Ashley, Habitat and Argos.

Sainsbury's subsequently acquired Argos through its takeover of HRG. Homebase under the Bunnings management made a pre-tax loss of £28 million in the 6 months to the end of 2016, followed by a loss of £54 million in the first 6 months of 2017 and an expected £97 million loss in the second half of 2017. Competition from Screwfix and other incumbent firms may have contributed to the situation.

Follow-up questions

a Why did Homebase seem to be a good match for Bunnings?

b Do you think that the acquisition could have worked for Bunnings?

c What strategy might have enabled greater success for the acquisition?

Revenues, costs, profits and objectives

Firms need to make key decisions about production and price. Revenues and costs are an important influence on these decisions, and we begin our analysis by exploring them. The chapter also examines some of the key concepts that are needed to analyse the behaviour of firms, and considers the objectives that firms may choose to pursue.

Learning objectives

After studying this chapter, you should:
→ be familiar with short- and long-run cost curves and their characteristics
→ understand the significance of economies of scale in the context of the growth of firms
→ understand the profit maximisation motive and its implications for firms' behaviour
→ be aware of the principal–agent issue, and its influence on the motivations of firms
→ be familiar with alternative motivations for firms and how these affect decision making, such as revenue and sales maximisation
→ be aware of behavioural approaches to the theory of the firm

Costs facing firms

Firms have to make key decisions about the quantity of output that they wish to produce. This also involves taking decisions about the inputs of factors of production needed to produce this output, and the ways in which those factors are combined. An important element in taking these decisions concerns the way in which the costs of production vary with the level of output to be produced, which depends on the prices of the factors of production and the way in which they are combined.

This section focuses on the relationship between costs and the level of output produced by a firm. For simplicity, assume that the firm produces a single product using two factors of production — labour and capital.

In exploring the firm's decisions, it is important to distinguish between the **short run** and the **long run**. In the short run, the firm faces limited flexibility. Varying the quantity of labour input that the firm uses may be relatively straightforward — it can increase the use of overtime, or hire more workers, fairly quickly. However, varying the amount of capital that the firm has at its disposal may take longer. For example, it takes time to commission a new piece of machinery, or to build a new factory — or a Channel Tunnel! Hence labour is regarded as a variable factor and capital as a fixed factor. The short run is defined as the period over which the firm is free to vary the input of variable factors, but not of the fixed factors. In the long run, the firm is able to vary inputs of both variable and fixed factors.

In considering the various items of costs, it will be necessary to talk about the *total* cost of producing a certain level of output, together with the *average* cost per unit of output and the *marginal* cost of producing additional units of output.

Synoptic link

The notion of factors of production was introduced in Chapter 1.

Key terms

short run the period over which a firm is free to vary the input of one of its factors of production (labour), but faces a fixed input of the other (capital)

long run the period over which the firm is able to vary the inputs of all its factors of production

Knowledge check 18.1

When considering the decisions made by firms, how do we define the 'long run'?

The law of diminishing returns

The nature of technology in an industry will determine the way in which output varies with the quantity of inputs. However, one thing is certain. If the firm increases the amount of inputs of the variable factor (labour) while holding constant the input of the other factor (capital), it will gradually derive less additional output per unit of labour for each further increase. This is known as the **law of diminishing returns**, and is one of the few 'laws' in economics. It is a *short-run* concept, as it relies on the assumption that capital is fixed.

It can readily be seen why this should be the case. Suppose a firm has 10 computer programmers working in an office, using 10 computers. The 11th worker may add some extra output, as the workers may be able to 'hot-desk' and take their coffee breaks at different times. The 12th worker may also add some extra output, perhaps by keeping the printers stocked with paper. However, if the firm keeps adding programmers without increasing the number of computers, each extra worker will be adding less additional output to the office. Indeed, the 20th worker may add nothing at all, being unable to get access to a computer. In other words, as the input of a variable factor is increased, there is diminishing marginal productivity, as the additional output produced by each additional unit of input falls.

Knowledge check 18.2

Why is the law of diminishing returns regarded as a short-run concept?

Additional computer programmers increase production provided they have machines to use

Total costs in the short run

Because the firm cannot vary some of its inputs in the short run, some costs may be regarded as fixed, and some as variable. For example, a firm may have contracted to lease a piece of machinery or rent a factory for a period of time, so cannot vary this. In this short run, some **fixed costs** are **sunk costs**: that is, costs that the firm cannot avoid paying even if it chooses to produce no output. **Variable costs** are those such

Key terms

law of diminishing returns law stating that if a firm increases its inputs of one factor of production while holding inputs of the other factor fixed, it will eventually derive diminishing marginal returns from the variable factor

total fixed costs costs that do not vary with the level of output

sunk costs short-run costs that cannot be recovered if the firm closes down

total variable costs the sum of costs that vary with the level of output

as operating costs, or wages paid to short-term contract staff. Total costs are the sum of fixed and variable costs:

total cost = total fixed costs + total variable costs

Knowledge check 18.3

Give an example of a sunk cost.

Total costs will increase as the firm increases the volume of production, because more of the variable input is needed to increase output. A common assumption made by economists is that in the short run, at very low levels of output, total costs will rise more slowly than output, but that as diminishing returns set in, total costs will accelerate, as shown in Figure 18.1.

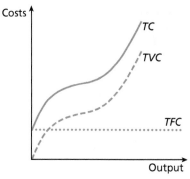

Figure 18.1 Costs in the short run

Average and marginal costs

Average total cost (total cost divided by the amount of output produced) varies with the level of output, importantly because of diminishing marginal returns. Firms may often take decisions at the margin: for example, by checking whether or not producing an additional (marginal) unit of output will add to profit. **Marginal cost** is the cost of producing an additional unit of output. More generally, marginal cost is defined as the change in costs divided by the additional quantity produced. Average and marginal costs are closely related.

Key terms

average total cost total cost divided by the quantity produced

marginal cost the cost of producing an additional unit of output

To summarise, the key formulae are:

$$\text{average total cost (ATC)} = \frac{\text{total cost}}{\text{quantity of output produced}}$$

$$\text{average fixed cost (AFC)} = \frac{\text{total fixed costs}}{\text{quantity of output produced}}$$

$$\text{average variable cost (AVC)} = \frac{\text{total variable costs}}{\text{quantity of output produced}}$$

$$\text{marginal cost (MC)} = \frac{\text{change in cost}}{\text{change in quantity}}$$

Knowledge check 18.4

A firm produces 50 units of a good. What is the firm's average total cost if it faces fixed costs of £4,000 and total variable costs of £2,500?

The relationship between output and costs

Table 18.1 provides an arithmetic example to illustrate the relationship between these different aspects of costs. The firm represented here faces fixed costs of £225 per week (column 2). The table shows the costs of production for up to 6,000 units of the firm's product per week. Column 3 shows total variable costs of production: you can see that these rise quite steeply as the volume of production increases. Adding fixed and variable costs gives the total costs (TC) at each output level. This is shown in column 4, which is the sum of columns 2 and 3.

Table 18.1 The short-run relationship between output and costs (in £s)

(1) Output (000 units per week)	(2) Fixed costs (TFC)	(3) Total variable costs (TVC)	(4) Total costs (2) + (3) (TC)	(5) Average total cost (4)/(1) (SATC)	(6) Marginal cost Δ(4)/Δ(1) (MC)	(7) Average variable cost (3)/(1) (AVC)	(8) Average fixed cost (2)/(1) (AFC)
1	225	85	310	310		85	225
2	225	150	375	187.5	65	75	112.5
3	225	210	435	145	60	70	75
4	225	300	525	131.25	90	75	56.25
5	225	475	700	140	175	95	45
6	225	870	1,095	182.5	395	145	37.5

Short-run average total cost (SATC – column 5) is calculated as total cost divided by output. To calculate marginal cost, you need to work out the additional cost of producing an extra unit of output at each output level. This is calculated as the change in costs divided by the change in output (Δ column 4 divided by Δ column 1, where Δ means 'change in').

Finally, average variable costs (AVC, i.e. column 3/column 1) and average fixed costs (AFC, i.e. column 2/column 1) can be calculated.

Notice that SATC falls as output increases, but after 4,000 units of output it begins to increase. Notice that SATC is composed of average variable and average fixed costs (AVC and AFC). AFC falls continuously as output increases, because the fixed costs are being spread out across more units of output. This helps to explain why SATC initially falls. However, as diminishing marginal returns set in, average variable costs begin to increase, and this helps to explain the way that SATC varies with output.

Graphing short-run costs

Quantitative skills 18.1 showed the arithmetic relationship between the components of short-run costs. The short-run average and marginal curves based on these data are plotted in Figure 18.2. First, notice that the short-run average total cost curve (SATC) takes on a U-shape. This form is often assumed in economic analysis. SATC is the sum of average fixed and variable costs (SAFC and SAVC, respectively). The average fixed cost curve slope downwards throughout – this is because fixed costs do not vary with the level of output, so as output increases, AFC must always get smaller, as the fixed costs are spread over more and more units of output. However, SAVC also shows a U-shape, and it is this that gives the U-shape to SATC.

A very important aspect of Figure 18.2 is that the short-run marginal cost curve (SMC) cuts both SAVC and SATC at their minimum points. This is always the case. If you think about this for a moment, you will realise that it makes good sense. If you are adding on something that is greater than the average, the average must always increase. For a firm, when the marginal cost of producing an additional unit of a good is higher than the average cost of doing so, the average cost must rise. If the marginal cost is the same as the average cost, then average cost will not change.

An example can show how general this rule is. Suppose that a team newly promoted to football's premier league brings in a new striker, whose wage far exceeds that of existing players. What happens to the average wage? Of course it must increase, as the marginal wage of the new player is higher than the previous average wage. This is quite simply an arithmetic property of the average and the marginal, and always holds true.

Another feature of the figure is that the AVC curve gets closer to SATC at higher levels of output. This is because the difference between them is AFC, which gets smaller as output increases.

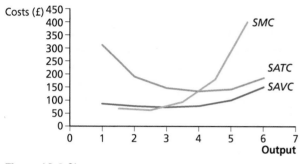

Figure 18.2 Short-run cost curves

Study tip

Whenever you draw average and marginal cost curves, always remember that the MC curve must pass through the minimum point of the AC curve. Note that another way of viewing marginal cost is as the slope or gradient of the total cost curve.

Costs in the long run

In the long run, a firm is able to vary both capital and labour. It is thus likely to choose the level of capital that is appropriate for the level of output that it expects to produce. Figure 18.3 shows a number of short-run average total cost curves corresponding to different expected output levels, and thus different levels of capital. With the set of SATC curves in Figure 18.3, the long-run average cost curve (LAC) can be seen to take on a U-shape.

Knowledge check 18.5

When drawing average and marginal cost curves, what is the key relationship between them?

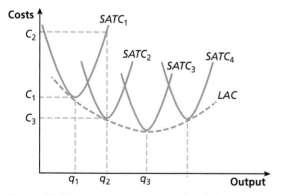

Figure 18.3 Short-run cost curves with different levels of capital input

For the firm in Figure 18.3, the choice of capital is important. Suppose the firm wants to produce the quantity of output q_1. It would choose to install the amount of capital corresponding to the short-run average total cost curve $SATC_1$, and could then produce q_1 at an average cost of C_1 in the short run. However, if the firm finds that demand is more buoyant than expected, and so wants to increase output to q_2, in the short run it has no option but to increase labour input and expand output along $SATC_1$, taking cost per unit to C_2.

In the longer term, the firm will be able to adjust its capital stock and move on to $SATC_2$, reducing average total cost to C_3. Thus, as soon as the firm moves away from the output level for which capital stock is designed, it incurs higher average total cost in the short run than is possible in the long run.

In this way a long-run average total cost curve can be derived to illustrate how the firm chooses to vary its capital stock for any given level of output. The dashed line in Figure 18.3 shows what such a curve would look like for the firm. The long-run average cost curve (LAC) just touches each of the short-run average total cost curves, and is known as the 'envelope' of the $SATC$ curves.

Economies of scale

Key term

economies of scale occur for a firm when an increase in a firm's scale of production leads to production at lower long-run average cost

Knowledge check 18.6

Will firms always benefit from economies of scale if they increase production?

One of the reasons why firms find it beneficial to be large is the existence of **economies of scale**. These occur when a firm finds that it is more efficient in cost terms to produce on a larger scale.

It is not difficult to imagine industries in which economies of scale are likely to arise. For example, recall the notion of the division of labour, which you encountered earlier. When a firm expands, it reaches a certain scale of production at which it becomes worthwhile to take advantage of division of labour. Workers begin to specialise in certain stages of the production process, and their productivity increases. Because this is only possible for relatively large-scale production, this is an example of economies of scale. It is the size of the firm (in terms of its output level) that enables it to produce more efficiently — that is, at lower average cost.

Although the division of labour is one source of economies of scale, it is by no means the only source, and there are several explanations of cost benefits from producing on a large scale. Some of these are industry-specific, and thus some sectors of the economy exhibit more significant economies of scale than others — it is in these activities that the larger firms tend to be found. There are no hairdressing salons that come into the top ten largest firms, but there are plenty of oil companies.

Technology

One source of economies of scale is in the technology of production. There are many activities in which the technology is such that large-scale production is more efficient.

One source of technical economies of scale arises from the physical properties of the universe. There is a physical relationship between the volume and surface area of an object, whereby the storage capacity of an object increases proportionately more than its surface area. Consider the volume of a cube. If the cube is 2 metres each way, its surface area is $6 \times 2 \times 2 = 24$ square metres, while its volume is

$2 \times 2 \times 2 = 8$ cubic metres. If the dimension of the cube is 3 metres, the surface area is 54 square metres (more than double the surface area of the smaller cube) but the volume is 27 cubic metres (more than three times the volume of the smaller cube). Thus the larger the cube, the lower the average cost of storage. A similar relationship applies to other shapes of storage containers, whether they be barrels or ships.

What this means in practice is that a large ship can transport proportionally more than a small ship, or that large barrels hold more wine relative to the surface area of the barrel than small barrels. Hence there may be benefits in operating on a large scale.

Furthermore, some capital equipment is designed for large-scale production, and would only be viable for a firm operating at a high volume of production. Combine harvesters cannot be used in small fields; a production line for car production would not be viable for small levels of output. In other words, there may be *indivisibilities* in the production process.

The importance of fixed costs

In addition to indivisibilities, there are many economic activities in which there are high *overhead* expenditures. Such components of a firm's costs do not vary directly with the scale of production. For example, having built a factory, the cost of that factory is the same regardless of the amount of output that is produced in it. Expenditure on research and development could be seen as such an overhead, which may be viable only when a firm reaches a certain size.

Notice that there are some economic activities in which these overhead costs are highly significant. For example, think about the Channel Tunnel. The construction (overhead) costs were enormous compared to the costs of running trains through the tunnel. Thus the overhead cost element is substantial — and the economies of scale will also be significant for such an industry.

There are other examples of this sort of cost structure, such as railway networks and electricity supply. The largest firm in such a market will always be able to produce at a lower average cost than smaller firms. This could prove such a competitive advantage that no other firms will be able to become established in that market, which may therefore constitute what is known as a **natural monopoly**. Intuitively, this makes sense. Imagine having several underground railway systems operating in a single city, all competing against each other on the same routes!

Key term

natural monopoly
monopoly that arises
in an industry in which
there are such substantial
economies of scale that
only one firm is viable

Synoptic link

The characteristics of
a natural monopoly are
discussed in Chapter 19,
after we have explored
the characteristics of a
monopoly market.

The Channel Tunnel — the construction costs were enormous compared to the costs of running trains through the tunnel

Management and marketing

A second source of economies of scale pertains to the management of firms. One of the key factors of production is managerial input. A certain number of managers are required to oversee the production process. As the firm expands, there is a range of volumes of output over which the management team does not need to grow as rapidly as the overall volume of the firm, as a large firm can be managed more efficiently. Notice that there are likely to be limits to this process. At some point, the organisation begins to get so large and complex that management finds it more difficult to manage. At this point **diseconomies of scale** are likely to cut in — in other words, average costs may begin to rise with an increase in output at some volume of production.

Similarly, the cost of marketing a product may not rise as rapidly as the volume of production, leading to further scale economies. One interpretation of this is that we might see marketing expenses as a component of fixed costs — or at least as having a substantial fixed cost element.

Finance and procurement

Large firms may have advantages in a number of other areas. For example, a large firm with a strong reputation may be able to raise finance for further expansion on more favourable terms than a small firm. This, of course, reinforces the market position of the largest firms in a sector and makes it more difficult for relative newcomers to become established.

Once a firm has grown to the point where it is operating on a relatively large scale, it will also be purchasing its inputs in relatively large volumes. In particular, this relates to raw materials, energy and transport services. When buying in bulk in this way, firms may be able to negotiate good deals with their suppliers, and thus again reduce average cost as output increases.

It may even be the case that some of the firm's suppliers will find it beneficial to locate in proximity to the firm's factory, which would reduce costs even more.

External economies of scale

The factors listed so far that may lead to economies of scale arise from the internal expansion of a firm. If the firm is in an industry that is itself expanding, there may also be **external economies of scale**.

> ### Key terms
>
> **diseconomies of scale** occur for a firm when an increase in the scale of production leads to higher long-run average costs
>
> **internal economies of scale** economies of scale that arise from the expansion of a firm
>
> **external economies of scale** economies of scale that arise from the expansion of the industry in which a firm is operating

> ### Knowledge check 18.7
>
> List factors that may result in economies of scale for a firm when it expands its scale of production.

Some of the most successful firms of recent years have been involved in activities that require high levels of technology and skills. Web design is one example of an economic activity that has expanded rapidly. As the sector expands, a pool of skilled labour is built up that all the firms can draw on. The very success of the sector encourages people to acquire the skills needed to enter it, colleges may begin to find it viable to provide courses and so on. Each individual firm benefits in this way from the overall expansion of the sector. The greater availability of skilled workers reduces the amount that individual firms need to spend on training.

Web design is by no means the only example of this. Formula 1 development teams, pharmaceutical companies and others similarly enjoy external economies of scale.

If the firm is operating at the lowest possible level of long-run average costs, it is said to be in a position of **productive efficiency** because at this point, the firm has chosen the appropriate combination of the factors of production and is producing the maximum output possible from those inputs. The level of output at which long-run average cost stops falling as output rises is known as the **minimum efficient scale**.

Extension material: economies of scope

There are various ways in which firms expand their scale of operations. Some do so within a relatively focused market, but others are multi-product firms that produce a range of different products, sometimes in quite different markets.

For example, look at Nestlé. You may immediately think of instant coffee, and indeed Nestlé produces 200 different brands of instant coffee worldwide. However, Nestlé also produces baby milk powder, mineral water, ice cream and pet food, and has diversified into hotels and restaurants.

Such conglomerate companies can benefit from *economies of scope*, whereby there may be benefits of size across a range of different products. These economies may arise because there are activities that can be shared across the product range. For example, a company may not need a finance or accounting section for each different product, nor human resource or marketing departments.

Shape of the long-run average cost curve

In Figure 18.4, if the firm expands its output up to $q^\star$, long-run average cost falls. Up to $q^\star$ of output is the range over which there are economies of scale. To the right of $q^\star$, however, long-run average cost rises as output continues to be increased, and the firm experiences diseconomies of scale. The output $q^\star$ itself is at the intermediate state of **constant returns to scale**.

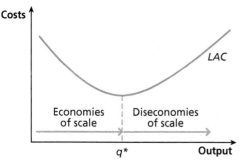

Figure 18.4 The long-run average cost curve

The long-run average cost curve (*LAC*) in Figure 18.4 is drawn as a U-shape because of the assumptions that were made about the technology of production. The underlying assumption here is that the firm faces economies of scale at relatively low levels of output, so that *LAC* slopes downwards. However, at some point decreasing returns to scale set in, and *LAC* then begins to slope upwards.

This turns out to be a convenient representation, but in practice the *LAC* curve can take on a variety of shapes. Figure 18.5 shows some of these. LAC_1 is the typical U-shape, which has already been discussed. LAC_2 shows an example of a situation in which there are economies of scale up to a point, after which long-run average cost levels out and there is a long flat range over which the firm faces constant returns to scale. LAC_3 is a bit similar, except that the constant returns to scale (flat) segment eventually runs out and diseconomies of scale set in. In LAC_4 the economies of scale

Key terms

productive efficiency occurs when firms have chosen appropriate combinations of factors of production and produce the maximum output possible from those inputs, thus producing at minimum long-run average cost

minimum efficient scale the level of output at which long-run average cost stops falling as output increases

constant returns to scale found when long-run average cost remains constant with an increase in output, i.e. when output and costs rise at the same rate

continue over the whole range of output shown. This could occur in a market where the fixed costs are substantial, dominating the influence of variable costs.

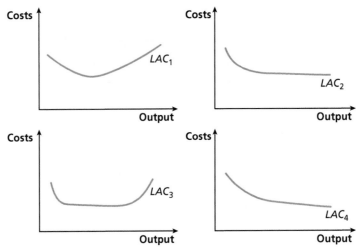

Figure 18.5 Possible shapes of the *LAC* curve

Exercise 18.1

Which of the following reflects a movement *along* a long-run average cost curve, and which would cause a shift *of* a long-run average cost curve?

a A firm becomes established in a market, learning the best ways of utilising its factors of production.

b A firm observes that average cost falls as it expands its scale of production.

c The larger a firm becomes, the more difficult it becomes to manage, causing average cost to rise.

d A firm operating in the financial sector installs new, faster computers, enabling its average cost to fall for any given level of service that it provides.

Summary: costs in the short and long run

- A firm may face inflexibility in the short run, with some factors being fixed in quantity and only some being variable.
- The short run is defined in this context as the period over which a firm is free to vary some factors but not others.
- The long run is defined as the period over which the firm is able to vary the input of all of its factors of production.
- The law of diminishing returns states that, if a firm increases the input of a variable factor while holding input of the fixed factor constant, eventually the firm will get diminishing marginal returns from the variable factor.
- Short-run costs can be separated into fixed, sunk and variable costs.
- There is a clear and immutable relationship between total, average and marginal costs.
- For a U-shaped average total cost curve, marginal cost always cuts the minimum point of average total cost.
- The minimum efficient scale is the point at which the long-run average cost curve stops sloping downwards.
- In practice, long-run average cost curves may take on a variety of shapes, according to the technology of the industry concerned.

A firm faces long-run total cost conditions as in Table 18.2.

Table 18.2 Output and long-run costs

Output (000 units per week)	Total cost (£000)
0	0
1	32
2	48
3	82
4	140
5	228
6	352

a Calculate long-run average cost and long-run marginal cost for each level of output.
b Plot long-run average cost and long-run marginal cost curves on a graph. (Hint: don't forget to plot *LMC* at points that are halfway between the corresponding output levels.)
c Identify the output level at which long-run average cost is at a minimum.
d Identify the output level at which *LAC* = *LMC*.
e Within what range of output does this firm enjoy economies of scale?
f Within what range of output does the firm experience diseconomies of scale?
g If you could measure the nature of returns to scale, what would characterise the point where *LAC* is at a minimum?

A firm's revenues

Synoptic link

You are advised to remind yourself of the discussion in Chapter 2, which explored the relationship between average and total revenue and the price elasticity of demand.

Chapter 2 introduced the notion of the demand curve and its relationship with the revenues received by a firm from selling different levels of output. Indeed, ignoring indirect taxes, the price of a good is the average revenue received by the firm, and the total revenue is the price multiplied by the quantity sold. You saw earlier that there is a fixed mathematical relationship between total, average and marginal costs. The same applies to total, average and marginal revenue. Marginal revenue is the additional revenue received by the firm when it sells an additional unit of output.

The formulae for these are:

total revenue = price × quantity sold

$$\text{average revenue} = \frac{\text{total revenue}}{\text{quantity sold}}$$

$$\text{marginal revenue} = \frac{\text{change in revenue}}{\text{change in quantity sold}}$$

Knowledge check 18.8

What is the relationship between average revenue and price? How would total revenue be affected if there is an increase in price when demand is elastic?

The relationship between sales and revenue

Table 18.3 provides an arithmetic example to illustrate the relationship between these different aspects of revenue.

Table 18.3 The relationship between sales and revenue

(1) Quantity sold	(2) Average revenue (Price, £)	(3) Total revenue (TR)	(4) Marginal revenue (MR)
0	12	0	
			10
20	10	200	
			6
40	8	320	
			2
60	6	360	
			−2
80	4	320	
			−6
100	2	200	
			−10
120	0	0	

Columns 1 and 2 plot out the demand curve for this product, showing the quantities sold at each price. Column 3 calculates total revenue (TR) as column 1 multiplied by column 2. Marginal revenue is shown in column 4. This is calculated by taking the change in revenue between the points on the demand curve, expressed per unit. For example, if price goes from £10 to £8, the quantity sold increases from 20 to 40, and total revenue goes from £200 to £320, so revenue increases by £(320 − 200) = £120, which is £6 per unit sold. In the table the values for marginal revenue are shown halfway between the values in the other columns, as we are looking at the change between the successive points.

Figure 18.6 plots these values (I have not plotted all of the negative values of MR). This shows the relationship between AR and MR. The two lines (curves) share the same intercept with the y-axis, and the MR curve is exactly twice as steep as the AR line (curve). This relationship always holds.

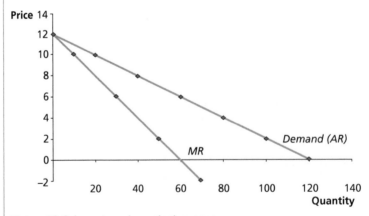

Figure 18.6 Average and marginal revenue

Notice that the MR line cuts the x-axis at the quantity 60, which is the point at which TR is at a maximum. This is also a mathematical feature of the relationship.

Extension material: the mathematical relationship between *AR*, *MR* and *PED*

If you are studying mathematics alongside your economics, you will know that the formula for a straight line is:

$$P = a - bQ$$

This shows the inverse of the demand curve, which is what is plotted in Figure 18.6, where a and b are positive parameters.

The equation for the *MR* curve is then:

$$P = a - 2bQ$$

Chapter 2 also explored the way in which the price elasticity of demand (*PED*) varies along a linear demand curve. The formula that expresses this is that:

$$MR - P(1 + (1/PED))$$

Summary: a firm's revenue

- Ignoring indirect taxes, the price of a good is the average revenue that the firm receives from selling its good.
- The demand curve reflects average revenue.
- Marginal revenue is the additional revenue received by the firm when it sells an additional unit of output.
- Total revenue is the price multiplied by the number of units sold.
- There is a fixed mathematical relationship between average revenue and marginal revenue.

Business objectives

The previous chapter stated that firms exist to organise production, by bringing together the factors of production in order to produce output. This begs the question of what motivates them to produce particular *levels* of output, and at what price. In the remainder of this chapter, consideration will be given to alternative objectives that firms may set out to achieve.

Profit maximisation

Traditional economic analysis has tended to start from the premise that firms set out with the objective of maximising profits. It is important to be clear about what is meant by 'profits' in this context.

All firms need to make enough profit to cover the cost of being in business. If a firm does not cover the opportunity cost of operating in a market, it has no incentive to remain in the market. This normal rate of return is known as **normal profit**. It can be seen as the opportunity cost of capital: the rate of return that is sufficient to prevent the firm from exiting from the market. Normal profit is viewed by economists as being part of the total cost faced by the firm. Profits made by a firm above that level are known as **supernormal profits**, or **abnormal profits**.

How does a firm choose its output level if it wishes to maximise profits? Suppose a firm is a relatively small player in a big market, and thus has no influence over the price of its product. Its total revenue is then proportional to the amount of output it sells. If it faces a total cost curve like the one that was introduced earlier in the chapter, its output decision can be analysed by reference to Figure 18.7. To

Synoptic link

The assumption that firms would maximise profits was first introduced in Chapter 3, but we now need to explore this more carefully.

Key terms

normal profit profit that covers the opportunity cost of capital and is just sufficient to keep the firm in the market

supernormal profits/ abnormal profits/ economic profit terms referring to profits that exceed normal profit

maximise profits, the firm needs to choose the output level at which total revenue is as far above the total cost curve as possible. This happens at $q^\star$.

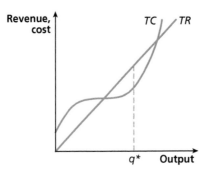

Figure 18.7 Profit maximisation

The *MR* = *MC* rule

An alternative way of looking at the profit-maximising decision is to draw the marginal cost and marginal revenue curves. In this case, the firm has no influence over the price of the product, as it was assumed that the firm is a small player in the market. This means that the firm receives the same revenue from the sale of each unit of the good. In other words, the **marginal revenue** that it receives from selling each unit of output is the same. Consider Figure 18.8. Marginal revenue (*MR*) is shown as a horizontal straight line, and marginal cost is given by *MC*, having a U-shape as before.

Key term

marginal revenue the additional revenue gained by a firm from selling an additional unit of output

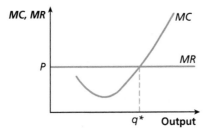

Figure 18.8 Profit maximisation again

It turns out that the level of output that maximises profit will be found where $MC = MR$. If the firm is producing less output than this, it will find that the marginal revenue from selling an additional unit of output is higher than the marginal cost of producing it, so the firm can add to its profits by increasing output. In contrast, if the firm is producing more than $q^\star$, it will find that the marginal revenue from selling an extra unit fails to cover the cost of producing the unit, so it will not pay the firm to produce beyond $q^\star$. Therefore, $q^\star$ can be seen as the level of output that maximises the firm's profits.

The $MC = MR$ rule is a general rule for firms that want to maximise profits, and it holds in all market situations. For example, suppose the firm faces a downward-sloping demand curve for its product, such that it can sell more by reducing the price. You may recall that a linear demand curve is associated with a total revenue curve like that shown in Figure 18.9. Assume that the firm faces the usual shape of short-run total cost curve *TC*. Profits are again maximised where the distance of *TR* above *TC* is as large as possible. This occurs at q_π.

Knowledge check 18.9

What is the significance of the level of output at which $MR = MC$?

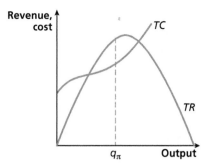

Figure 18.9 Profit maximisation with a downward-sloping demand curve

Study tip

The $MR = MC$ rule for profit maximisation is an important one, as it applies in any market situation where a firm sets out to maximise profits, so make sure you understand and remember it.

Exercise 18.3

Figure 18.10 shows a firm in short-run equilibrium. The firm is operating in a market in which it has no influence over price, so it gains the same marginal revenue from the sale of each unit of output. Marginal revenue and average revenue are thus the same. P_1, P_2 and P_3 represent three possible prices that could prevail in the market.

a For each price level, identify the output level that the firm would choose in order to maximise profits.

b For each of these output levels, compare the level of average revenue with that of average cost, and consider what this means for the firm's profits.

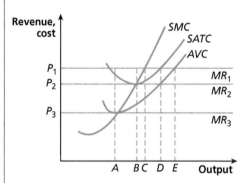

Figure 18.10 Profit maximisation in the short run

The shut-down price

Notice that in the short run, a firm may choose to remain in a market even if it is not covering its opportunity costs, provided its revenues are covering its variable costs. Since the firm has already incurred fixed costs, if it can cover its variable costs in the short run, it will be better off remaining in business and paying off part of the fixed costs than exiting the market and losing all of its fixed costs. Thus, the level of average variable costs represents the **shut-down price**, below which the firm will exit from the market in the short run.

If the firm were to be charging a price of P_3 in Figure 18.10, it would be making a loss, because its average revenue is well below short-run average costs. Does it pay for the firm to continue to produce in this situation? Indeed, the firm makes losses with the price at any level between P_3 and P_2, because of the need to cover its fixed costs. These fixed costs cannot be avoided in the short run, but in this range of prices, the firm is at least contributing to its average variable costs, so it is better off continuing to produce. Only if the price falls below P_3 will it choose to exit from the market immediately. P_3 is the shut-down price.

Key term

shut-down price the price below which a firm will cease production in the short run, as it is not covering its variable cost

Of course, this situation would not be sustained in the long run. The firm will only remain in the market in the long run if it is making at least normal profit. In other words, if long-run average costs exceed average revenues, the firm will exit the market.

Knowledge check 18.10

Why would a firm continue in business in the short run if it is operating below short-run average costs?

X-inefficiency

Will a firm always operate as efficiently as it can? Chapter 17 introduced the notion of the principal–agent phenomenon, and it was noted that this could lead to some managerial slack, if management are not fully accountable to the owners of the firm. This is an example of what is called **X-inefficiency**. For example, in Figure 18.11 $LAC^\star$ represents the long-run average cost curve showing the most efficient cost positions for the firm at any output level. With X-inefficiency, a firm could end up producing on a long-run average cost curve such as LAC_1 that is above the most efficient that could be achieved. For example, at output q_1, the firm would produce at an average cost of AC_1, although it could have produced at $AC^\star$ if it were not for the X-inefficiency. Thus, in the presence of X-inefficiency the firm will be operating *above* its lowest possible long-run average cost curve.

Key term

X-inefficiency situation arising when a firm is not operating at minimum cost, perhaps because of organisational slack

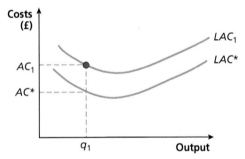

Figure 18.11 X-inefficiency

Some writers have argued that the managers may be pursuing other objectives. For example, some managers may enjoy being involved in the running of a *large* business, and may prefer to see the firm gaining market share — perhaps beyond the profit-maximising level. Others may like to see their status rewarded and so will want to divert part of the profits into managerial perks — large offices, company cars and so on. Or they may feel that having a large staff working for them increases their prestige inside the company. These sorts of activity tend to reduce the profitability of firms.

Revenue maximisation

William Baumol argued that managers may set out with the objective of maximising revenue. The effects of such action can be seen in Figure 18.12. As before, q_π represents the profit-maximising level of output. However, you can see that total revenue is maximised at the peak of the TR curve at q_r. Thus, a revenue-maximising firm will produce more output than a profit-maximising one, and will need to charge a lower price in order to sell the extra output. Notice that the revenue maximisation point occurs at the level of output at which marginal revenue is equal to zero ($MR = 0$).

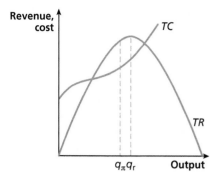

Figure 18.12 Revenue maximisation

Baumol pointed out that the shareholders might not be too pleased about this. The way the firm behaves then depends on the degree of accountability that the agents (managers) have to the principals (shareholders). For example, the shareholders may have sufficient power over their agents to be able to insist on some minimum level of profits. The result may then be a compromise solution between the principals and the agents, with output being set somewhere between q_π and q_r.

Sales maximisation

In some cases, managers may focus more on the volume of sales than on the resulting revenues. This could lead to output being set even higher, as shown in Figure 18.13. The firm would now push for higher sales up to the point where it just breaks even at q_s. This is the point at which total revenue only just covers total cost and where average cost equals average revenue. Remember that total cost includes normal profit — the opportunity cost of the resources tied up in the firm. The firm would have to close down if it did not cover this opportunity cost.

Synoptic link

The levels of output at which a firm will maximise sales or revenue is shown diagrammatically in Chapter 19.

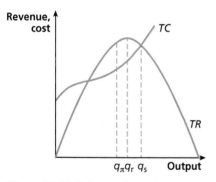

Figure 18.13 Sales maximisation

Again, the extent to which the managers will be able to pursue this objective without endangering their positions with the shareholders depends on how accountable the managers are to the shareholders. Remember that the managers are likely to have much better information about the market conditions and the internal functioning of the firm than the shareholders, who view the firm only remotely. This may be to the managers' advantage if they want to pursue their own objectives.

Long-run profit maximisation

Firms may be prepared to take a long-term view of their situation. There may be times when the decision to maximise profits in the short run may damage their long-run prospects. For example, firms may undertake costly investment now in

Knowledge check 18.11

What is the difference between 'sales maximisation' and 'revenue maximisation'?

Synoptic link

In some markets, firms will need to take the actions and reactions of rivals into account when taking their own decisions on price or output. The way that firms may act strategically in their pricing decisions is explored in Chapter 20.

Synoptic link

Bounded rationality was discussed in the context of rational decision making by consumers in Chapter 5.

Knowledge check 18.12

Explain what is meant by 'satisficing' behaviour.

Key terms

satisficing behaviour under which the managers of firms aim to produce satisfactory results for the firm, e.g. in terms of profits, rather than trying to maximise them

bounded rationality a situation in which a firm's ability to take rational decisions is limited by a lack of information or an inability to interpret the information that is available

corporate social responsibility actions that a firm takes in order to demonstrate its commitment to behaving in the public interest

order to reap higher profits in the long term. Or firms may delay adjusting price to an increase in costs so that they maintain customer loyalty. In other words, short-run profit maximisation may not always be in the best long-run interests of the firm.

Behavioural theories

Businesses may not set out to maximise anything, either consciously because they have other motivations, or as a result of the principal–agent issue. For example, it might be that managers simply prefer a quiet life, and therefore do not push for the absolute profit-maximising position, but do just enough to keep the shareholders off their backs. Herbert Simon referred to this as '**satisficing**' behaviour, where managers aim to produce satisfactory profits rather than maximum profits.

Although firms may set out to take rational decisions, they may not have all the relevant information about market conditions that is needed, or might not have the capacity to analyse the information that they have. It might be that the information is costly to acquire, or costly to analyse fully. In such a situation firms do the best that they can to take good decisions, but without full information they may not achieve a fully rational outcome. This is known as a situation of **bounded rationality**.

Firms may wish to develop a favourable reputation by demonstrating a commitment to acting in ways that benefit society at large, or that improve the welfare of their employees and the community in which they are located. This notion of **corporate social responsibility** (CSR) has become widespread, with firms devoting resources to promoting community programmes of various kinds and encouraging their employees to engage in volunteering activities.

Exercise 18.4

Google 'corporate social responsibility' with the name of some large firms with which you are familiar, and check out the range of activities in which firms engage under this banner.

Has this now become a prerequisite for firms' survival? If it is perceived that failure to engage with CSR has a major impact on firms' sales, then it becomes crucial for a firm to be able to demonstrate its commitment in order to compete with its rivals. Devoting resources to CSR then becomes part of a firm's strategy to safeguard its market position.

Knowledge check 18.13

Give another example of an action taken by a firm to demonstrate a commitment to behaving responsibly.

▌Why assume profit maximisation?

The discussion has revealed a range of reasons explaining why firms may depart from profit maximisation. Does this mean that it should be abandoned as an assumption?

It could be argued that some of the strategies adopted by firms seem to diverge from profit maximisation in the short run, but may result in the maximisation of profits in the long run. For example, if all firms in a market are engaging in CSR in order to improve their credibility with their customers, then it could be argued that this expenditure becomes part of operating costs, and a necessary part of maintaining the market share needed to maximise profits in the long term.

From an economic modelling perspective, being able to assume that firms maximise profits allows the economist to come to an understanding of firms' behaviour under a simple and clear assumption. This offers much more straightforward insights into firms' behaviour than trying to implement some of the more complex assumptions that could be made about what motivates firms' decisions. Profit maximisation then provides a benchmark for other more complex models that enables an evaluation of how differently firms may behave under alternative assumptions. So even if it is not the case that firms always act to maximise profits, it is a useful starting point to ask how they would behave if they did maximise profits, and then explore alternative theories using profit maximisation as the benchmark against which to compare other models of behaviour.

Summary: profit maximisation and other aims of firms

- Traditional economic analysis assumes that firms set out to maximise profits.
- The opportunity cost of a firm's resources is viewed as a part of fixed costs. This is known as normal profit.
- Profits above this level are known as supernormal profits.
- A firm maximises profits by choosing output such that marginal revenue is equal to marginal cost.
- When managers are free to pursue alternative objectives, this may lead to satisficing behaviour and to X-inefficiency.
- William Baumol suggested that managers may set out to maximise revenue rather than profits; others have suggested that sales or the growth of the firm may be the managers' objectives.
- For an individual firm, productive efficiency can be regarded as having been achieved when the firm is operating at minimum long-run average cost.

Case study 18.1

The costs of a hypothetical firm

In producing 100 units of output, a firm incurs average fixed costs per unit (AFC) of £15 and total variable costs (TVC) of £1,700.

Follow-up questions

a Calculate total fixed cost (TFC), total cost (TC) and average total cost (ATC).

b The firm sees that the marginal cost per unit (MC) of producing 100 more units of output is £14. Calculate total cost (TC), total variable cost (TVC), average fixed cost (AFC) and average total cost (ATC).

c The firm knows that the total cost of producing 300 units is £5,700. Calculate the marginal cost (MC) of producing the last 100 units. Also calculate average fixed cost (AFC) and average total cost (ATC).

d Is the firm experiencing economies of scale at this level of output? Explain your answer and comment on the pattern shown by the way that AFC varies with output.

e What additional information would you need in order to identify the profit-maximising level of output?

Coke vs Pepsi in India

In the mid-2000s it was reported that Coca-Cola and PepsiCo were fighting to increase their sales in India. A pesticide scare in the previous year had caused sales to plummet, and the two firms were anxious to recover the situation.

The tactics they adopted were to reduce the size of the bottles for sale in order to appeal to consumers with low incomes, to cut prices, to increase the availability of the products in rural areas, and to encourage more at-home consumption in the urban areas.

It was seen that there was plenty of scope for growth in the market, as India showed one of the lowest average levels of consumption of fizzy drinks in the world, and was substantially below the Asian average. This may partly reflect the fact that children have been discouraged from drinking colas by their teachers at school.

The prices being charged were rated as being the world's lowest price for cola as the two firms battled to increase their market shares. However, in consequence the firms faced reductions in their profit margins, and continued to face competition from local producers. The logistics of supplying such a geographically large and diverse region, given the need to ensure refrigeration, added significantly to costs. Attempts were made to counter this by reducing the weight of the bottles and by making use of cheap transport in the form of bullock carts and cycle rickshaws in the rural areas.

Market analysts said that soft-drink companies should be able to improve profits, but executives remained bent on boosting volumes. The vice-president of Coca-Cola marketing in India was quoted as saying that 'any affordability strategy will put pressure on margins, but it is critical to build the market'.

The pesticide issue proved to be a long-lasting controversy, and the Kerala government filed a criminal complaint against PepsiCo over its environmental impact, although this was rejected by the Supreme Court of India in 2010. Indeed, the US Department of State named PepsiCo as one of the 12 transnational companies that displayed 'the most impressive corporate social responsibility credentials in emerging markets'.

Coke and Pepsi compete for market share in India

Follow-up questions

a Given the statements in the passage, do you think that Coca-Cola and PepsiCo were trying to maximise short-run profits?

b Explain your answer to (a) and comment on what the firms were trying to achieve by their strategies.

c Identify ways in which the firms were seeking to influence their costs.

d How do you think PepsiCo's record on CSR will have affected its position in the market?

e Discuss what you think the firms would want to achieve in the long run.

19 Market structure: perfect competition and monopoly

Chapters 6 and 7 introduced the notion of market failure — describing situations in which free markets may not produce the best outcome for society in terms of efficiency. One of the reasons given for this concerned what is termed 'imperfect competition'. It was argued that, if firms can achieve a position of market dominance, they may distort the pattern of resource allocation. It is now time to look at market structure more closely in order to evaluate the way that markets work, and the significance of this for resource allocation. The fact that firms try to maximise profits is not in itself bad for society. However, the structure of a market has a strong influence on how well the market performs. 'Structure' here is seen in relation to a number of dimensions, but in particular to the number of firms operating in a market and the way in which they interact. This chapter considers two extreme forms of market structure: perfect competition and monopoly. It begins with a discussion of efficiency.

Learning objectives

After studying this chapter, you should:
- be familiar with the economist's notions of efficiency
- understand what is meant by market structure, and why it is important for firms
- appreciate the significance of barriers to entry in influencing the market structure
- be familiar with the assumptions of the model of perfect competition
- understand how a firm chooses profit-maximising output under perfect competition
- appreciate how a perfectly competitive market reaches long-run equilibrium
- understand how the characteristics of long-run equilibrium under perfect competition affect the performance of the market in terms of productive and allocative efficiency
- be familiar with the assumptions of the model of monopoly
- understand how a monopoly firm chooses output and sets price
- understand why a monopoly can arise in a market
- understand how the characteristics of equilibrium under monopoly affect the performance of the market in terms of productive and allocative efficiency
- be aware of the relative merits of perfect competition and monopoly in terms of market performance
- be aware of the conditions under which price discrimination may be possible

Efficiency

The extent to which markets will deliver productive and allocative efficiency will be explored in the following chapters, but it is also important to refine these notions further since they were first introduced. Indeed, it has already been noted that the principal–agent problem can lead to X-inefficiency, which is one reason why the ideal combination of productive and allocative efficiency will not be achieved.

Synoptic link

The ideas underlying productive and allocative efficiency were first introduced in Chapter 4; X-inefficiency appeared in Chapter 18.

Key terms

productive efficiency occurs when firms have chosen appropriate combinations of factors of production and produce the maximum output possible from those inputs, thus producing at minimum long-run average cost

static efficiency efficiency at a particular point in time

allocative efficiency achieved when society is producing the appropriate bundle of goods and services relative to consumer preferences

dynamic efficiency a view of efficiency that takes into account the effect of innovation and technical progress on productive and allocative efficiency in the long run

Knowledge check 19.1

Under what conditions would a firm be productively efficient?

Knowledge check 19.2

Why is allocative efficiency a desirable outcome?

Productive efficiency

The notion of **productive efficiency** is closely tied to the costs faced by firms, particularly in relation to the average total cost of production. Productive efficiency can be seen in terms of the minimum average cost at which output can be produced, recognising that average cost is likely to vary at different scales of output. For example, in Figure 18.4 the point $q^\star$ may be regarded as the optimum level of output, in the sense that it minimises average cost per unit of output.

From the firm's perspective, the decision process can be viewed as a three-stage procedure. First, the firm needs to decide how much output it wants to produce. Second, it chooses an appropriate combination of factors of production, given that intended scale of production. Third, it attempts to produce as much output as possible, given those inputs. Another way of expressing this is that, having chosen the intended scale of output, the firm tries to minimise its costs of production.

Notice that when the firm starts this decision process, it is likely to choose its desired output level on the basis of current or expected market conditions and the prevailing state of technology. However, remember the distinction between the short and the long run. Once the firm has chosen its desired scale of production, and installed the necessary capital, it is tied into that level of capital stock in the short run. If it needs to change its decision in the future, it will take time to implement the changes. In the short run, a firm may thus be in a situation of **static efficiency**, choosing the minimum average cost, given the conditions at that point in time.

Allocative efficiency

The notion of **allocative efficiency** relates to the issue of whether an economy allocates its resources in such a way as to produce a balance of goods and services that matches consumer preferences. In an individual market, this would mean that firms were producing the ideal amount of a good that consumers wish to buy. This is related to the notion of equilibrium in the demand and supply model, in which prices act as signals to consumers and producers to bring demand and supply into equilibrium. For an individual market, allocative efficiency would occur when the price charged is equal to marginal cost.

Synoptic link

Although prices may bring demand and supply into equilibrium, you should also remember that market failure may prevent the best allocation of resources for society from being achieved. This was discussed in Chapters 6 and 7.

Dynamic efficiency

The discussion of efficiency so far has been conducted in terms of how to make the best use of existing resources, producing an appropriate mix of goods and services and using factor inputs as efficiently as possible, given existing knowledge and technology. This is good as far as it goes, but it does represent a relatively static view of efficiency.

Dynamic efficiency goes one step further, recognising that the state of knowledge and technology changes over time. For example, investment in research and development today means that production can be carried out more efficiently at some future date. Furthermore, the development of new products may also mean that a different mix of goods and services may serve consumers better in the long term.

The notion of dynamic efficiency stemmed from the work of Joseph Schumpeter, who argued that a preoccupation with static efficiency may sacrifice opportunities for greater efficiency in the long run. In other words, there may be a trade-off between achieving efficiency today and improving efficiency tomorrow.

Summary: productive and allocative efficiency

- A society needs to find a way of using its limited resources as efficiently as possible.
- Productive efficiency occurs when firms have chosen appropriate combinations of factors of production and produce the maximum output possible from those inputs.
- Allocative efficiency occurs when firms produce an appropriate bundle of goods and services, given consumer preferences.
- An individual market exhibits aspects of allocative efficiency when the marginal benefit received by society from consuming a good or service matches the marginal cost of producing it — that is, when price is equal to marginal cost.
- Dynamic efficiency recognises that there may be a trade-off between efficiency in the short run and in the long run.

Knowledge check 19.3

Explain the difference between 'static' and 'dynamic' efficiency.

Study tip

These notions of efficiency are important, and will be central to the discussion of market structures, so make sure that you understand them before moving on.

Market structure

Firms cannot take decisions without having some awareness of the market in which they are operating. In some markets, firms find themselves to be such small players that they cannot influence the price at which they sell. In others, a firm may find itself to be the only firm, which clearly gives it much more discretion in devising a price and output strategy. There may also be many intermediate situations where the firm has some control over price, but needs to be aware of rival firms in the market.

Economists have devised a range of models that allow such different **market structures** to be analysed. Before looking carefully at the most important types of market structure, the key characteristics of alternative market structures will be introduced. The main models are summarised in Table 19.1. In many ways, we can regard these as a spectrum of markets with different characteristics.

Key term

market structure the market environment within which firms operate

Table 19.1 A spectrum of market structures

	Perfect competition	**Monopolistic competition**	**Oligopoly**	**Monopoly**
Number of firms	Many	Many	Few	One
Freedom of entry	Not restricted	Not restricted	Some barriers to entry	High barriers to entry
Firm's influence over price	None	Some	Some	Price maker, subject to the demand curve
Nature of product	Homogeneous	Differentiated	Varied	No close substitutes
Examples	Cauliflowers Carrots	Fast-food outlets Travel agents	Cars Mobile phones	PC operating systems Local water supply

Perfect competition

At one extreme of the market spectrum is *perfect competition*. This is a market in which each individual firm is a *price taker*. This means that no individual firm is large enough to be able to influence the price, which is set by the market as a whole.

This situation arises where there are many firms operating in a market, producing a product that is much the same whichever firm produces it. You might think of a market for a particular sort of vegetable, for example. One cauliflower is very much like another, and it would not be possible for a particular cauliflower-grower to set a premium price for its product.

Such markets are also typified by freedom of entry and exit. In other words, it is relatively easy for new firms to enter the market, or for existing firms to leave it to produce something else. The market price in such a market will be driven down to that at which the typical firm in the market just makes enough profit to stay in business. If firms make more than this, other firms will be attracted in, and thus supernormal profits will be competed away. If some firms in the market do not make sufficient profit to want to remain in the market, they will exit, allowing price to drift up until again the typical firm just makes enough to stay in business.

Synoptic link

The model of perfect competition is fully analysed later in this chapter.

Monopoly

At the other extreme of the spectrum of market structures is *monopoly*. This is a market where there is only one firm in operation. Such a firm has some influence over price, and can choose a combination of price and output in order to maximise its profits. The monopolist is not entirely free to set any price that it wants, as it must remain aware of the demand curve for its product. Nonetheless, it has the freedom to choose a point along its demand curve.

The nature of a monopolist's product is that it has no close substitutes — either actual or potential — so it faces no competition. An example might be Microsoft, which for a long time held a global monopoly for operating systems for PC computers. At the time of the famous trial in 1998, Microsoft was said to supply operating systems for about 95% of the world's PCs. In early 2018, Google's share of the UK search engine market was estimated to have reached about 85% (which was in fact slightly down on the previous year).

Synoptic link

We will return to analyse the monopoly model and barriers to entry later in this chapter, after we have discussed perfect competition.

Knowledge check 19.4

What form of market structure could be regarded as being at the opposite extreme of the spectrum to monopoly?

Another condition of a monopoly market is that there are barriers to the entry of new firms. This means that the firm is able to set its price such as to make profits that are above the minimum needed to keep the firm in business, without attracting new rivals into the market.

On trial in 1998, Microsoft was found to have a global monopoly on PC operating systems

Monopolistic competition

Between the two extreme forms of market structure are many intermediate situations in which firms may have some influence over their selling price, but still have to take account of the fact that there are other firms in the market. One such market is known as *monopolistic competition*. This is a market in which there are many firms operating, each producing similar but not identical products, so that there is some scope for influencing price, perhaps because of brand loyalty. However, firms in such a market are likely to be relatively small. Such firms may find it profitable to make sure that their own product is differentiated from other goods, and may advertise in order to convince potential customers that this is the case. For example, small-scale local restaurants may offer different styles of cooking.

Oligopoly

Another intermediate form of market structure is *oligopoly*, which literally means 'few sellers'. This is a market in which there are just a few firms that supply the market. Each firm will take decisions in close awareness of how other firms in the market may react to their actions. In some cases, the firms may try to *collude* — to work together in order to behave as if they were a monopolist — thus making higher profits. In other cases, they may be intense rivals, which will tend to result in supernormal profits being competed away. The question of whether firms in an oligopoly collude or compete has a substantial impact on how the overall market performs in terms of resource allocation, and whether consumers will be disadvantaged as a result of the actions of the firms in the market.

Synoptic link

The characteristics of monopolistic competition and oligopoly are examined in Chapter 20.

Barriers to entry

It has been argued that if firms in a market are able to make supernormal profits, this will act as an inducement for new firms to try to gain entry into that market in order to share in those profits. A **barrier to entry** is an obstacle that makes it difficult for new firms to join a market. The existence of such barriers is thus of great importance in influencing the market structure that will evolve.

For example, if a firm holds a patent on a particular good, this means that no other firm is permitted by law to produce the product, and the patent-holding firm thus has a monopoly. The firm may then be able to set price such as to make supernormal profits without fear of rival firms competing away those profits. On the other hand, if there are no barriers to entry in a market, and if the existing firms set price to make supernormal profits, new firms will join the market, and the increase in market supply will push price down until no supernormal profits are being made.

Key term

barrier to entry a characteristic of a market that prevents new firms from readily joining the market

Knowledge check 19.5

Why is the existence of barriers to entry significant for market structure?

Summary: alternative market structures

- The decisions made by firms must be taken in the context of the market environment in which they operate.
- Under conditions of perfect competition, each firm must accept the market price as given, but can choose how much output to produce in order to maximise profits.
- In a monopoly market, where there is only one producer, the firm can choose output and price (subject to the demand curve).
- Monopolistic competition combines some features of perfect competition, and some characteristics of monopoly. Firms have some influence over price, and will produce a differentiated product in order to maintain this influence.
- Oligopoly exists where a market is occupied by just a few firms. In some cases, these few firms may work together to maximise their joint profits; in other cases, they may seek to outmanoeuvre each other.

Exercise 19.1

For each of the market situations listed below, select the form of market structure that is most likely to apply. In each case, comment on the way in which the firm's actions may be influenced by the market structure.

Forms of market structure:

A perfect competition

B monopoly

C monopolistic competition

D oligopoly

a A fairly large number of fast-food outlets in a city centre, offering various different styles of cooking (Indian, Chinese, fish and chips, burgers, etc.) at broadly similar prices.

b An island's only airport.

c A large number of farmers selling parsnips at the same price.

d A small number of large firms that between them supply most of the market for commercial vans.

The model of perfect competition

Key term

perfect competition a form of market structure that produces allocative and productive efficiency in long-run equilibrium

The model of **perfect competition** has a special place in economic analysis, because if all its assumptions were fulfilled, and if all markets operated according to its precepts, the best allocation of resources would be ensured for society as a whole. Although it may be argued that this ideal is not often achieved, perfect competition nonetheless provides a yardstick by which all other forms of market structure can be evaluated.

Assumptions

The assumptions of the model of perfect competition are as follows:

1 Firms aim to maximise profits.

2 There are many participants (both buyers and sellers), none of whom is large enough to influence price.

3 The product is homogeneous.

4 There are no barriers to entry to or exit from the market.

5 There is perfect knowledge of market conditions.

6 There are no externalities.

Knowledge check 19.6

What are the key differences between perfect competition and monopolistic competition?

Profit maximisation

The first assumption is that firms act to maximise their profits. You might think that this means that firms, acting in their own self-interest, are unlikely to do consumers any favours. However, it transpires that this does not interfere with the operation of the market. Indeed, it is the pursuit of self-interest by firms and consumers which ensures that the market works effectively.

Many participants

This is an important assumption of the model: that there are so many buyers and so many sellers that no individual trader is able to influence the market price. The market price is thus determined by the operation of the market.

On the sellers' side of the market, this assumption is tantamount to saying that there are limited economies of scale in the industry. If the minimum efficient scale is small relative to market demand, then no firm is likely to become so large that it will gain influence in the market.

A homogeneous product

This assumption means that buyers of the good see all products in the market as being identical, and will not favour one firm's product over another. If there were brand loyalty, such that one firm was more popular than others, then that firm would be able to charge a premium on its price. By ruling out this possibility the previous assumption is reinforced, and no individual seller is able to influence the selling price of the product.

No barriers to entry or exit

By this assumption, firms are able to join the market if they perceive it to be a profitable step, and they can exit from the market without hindrance. This assumption is important when it comes to considering the long-run equilibrium towards which the market will tend.

Perfect knowledge

It is assumed that all participants in the market have perfect information about trading conditions in the market. In particular, buyers always know the prices that firms are charging, and thus can buy the good at the cheapest possible price. Firms that try to charge a price above the market price will get no takers. At the same time, traders are aware of the product quality.

Knowledge check 19.7

Why is the assumption of perfect knowledge important in perfect competition?

No externalities

Chapter 6 described externalities as a form of market failure that prevents the attainment of allocative efficiency. Here externalities are ruled out in order to explore the characteristics of the perfect competition model.

Perfect competition in the short run

The firm under perfect competition

With the above assumptions, it is possible to analyse how a firm will operate in the market. An important implication of these assumptions is that no individual trader can influence the price of the product. In particular, this means that the firm is a **price taker**, and has to accept whatever price is set in the market as a whole.

As the firm is a price taker, it faces a perfectly elastic demand curve for its product, as is shown in Figure 19.1. In this figure, P_1 is the price set in the market, and the firm cannot sell at any other price. If it tries to set a price above P_1 it will sell nothing, as buyers are fully aware of the market price and will not buy at a higher price, especially as they know that there is no quality difference between the products offered by different firms in the market. What this also implies is that the firm can sell as much output as it likes at that going price — which means there is no incentive for any firm to set a price below P_1. Thus, all firms charge the same price, P_1.

Key term

price taker a firm that must accept whatever price is set in the market as a whole

Knowledge check 19.8

What shape would the demand curve take if demand is perfectly elastic?

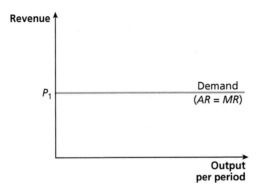

Figure 19.1 The firm's demand curve

Extension material: competition and the internet

The assumption of perfect knowledge of market conditions can seem to be unrealistic in some situations, but it is necessary for the model of perfect competition to work. This is because if some traders have better information than others, they may be able to exploit the situation, and firms may not all face the same price. Chapter 7 explored some of the implications of asymmetric information for a market.

If you think about it, the internet has had an enormous impact on the information available

to buyers — and to sellers in relation to their competitors. The proliferation of price comparison sites makes it easy to look for good deals when buying goods and services. In this context, the assumption of perfect knowledge begins to appear rather less unrealistic. So, we might argue that the arrival of the internet has made it more likely that firms in some markets will indeed be price takers, less able to charge high prices because consumers are better informed.

Study tip

Remember from the previous chapter that SMC cuts the minimum points of SAVC and SATC.) As the demand curve is horizontal, the firm faces constant average and marginal revenue and will choose output at q_1, where $MR = MC$.

The firm's short-run supply decision

If the firm can sell as much as it likes at the market price, how does it decide how much to produce?

Chapter 18 explained that to maximise profits a firm needs to set output at such a level that marginal revenue is equal to marginal cost. Figure 19.2 illustrates this rule by adding the short-run cost curves to the demand curve.

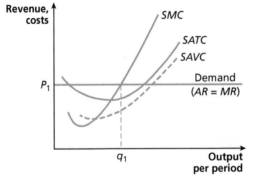

Figure 19.2 The firm's short-run supply decision

If the market price were to change, the firm would react by changing output, but always choosing to supply output at the level at which $MR = MC$. This suggests that the short-run marginal cost curve represents the firm's short-run supply curve: in other words, it shows the quantity of output that the firm would supply at any given price.

However, there is one important proviso to this statement. If the price falls below short-run average variable cost, the firm's best decision will be to exit from the market, as it will be better off just incurring its fixed costs. So the firm's **short-run supply curve** is the *SMC* curve above the shut-down point where it cuts *SAVC*.

Industry equilibrium in the short run

One crucial question not yet examined is how the market price comes to be determined. To answer this, it is necessary to consider the industry as a whole. In this case there is a conventional downward-sloping demand curve, of the sort met in Chapter 2. This is formed according to preferences of consumers in the market and is shown in Figure 19.3.

On the supply side, it has been shown that the individual firm's supply curve is its marginal cost curve above *SAVC*. If you add up the supply curves of each firm operating in the market, the result is the industry supply curve, also shown in Figure 19.3. The price will then adjust to P_1 at the intersection of demand and supply. The firms in the industry will between them supply Q_1 output, and the market will be in equilibrium.

Key term

short-run supply curve for a firm operating under perfect competition, the curve given by its short-run marginal cost curve above the price at which $MC = SAVC$; for the industry, the horizontal sum of the supply curves of the individual firms

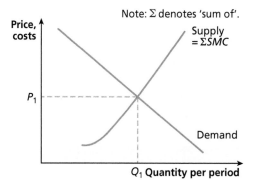

Figure 19.3 A perfectly competitive industry in short-run equilibrium

The firm in short-run equilibrium revisited

As this seems to be a well-balanced situation, with price adjusting to equate market demand and supply, the only question is why it is described as just a *short-run equilibrium*. The clue to this is to be found back with the individual firm.

Figure 19.4 returns to the position facing an individual firm in the market. As before, the firm maximises profits by accepting the price P_1 as set in the market and producing up to the point where $MR = MC$, which is at q_1. However, now the firm's average revenue (which is equal to price) is greater than its average cost (which is given by AC_1 at this level of output). The firm is thus making supernormal profits at this price. (Remember that 'normal profits' are included in average cost.) Indeed, the amount of total profits being made is shown as the shaded area on the graph. Notice that average revenue minus average costs equals profit per unit, so multiplying this by the quantity sold determines total profit.

This is where the assumption about freedom of entry becomes important. If firms in this market are making profits above opportunity cost, the market is generating more profits than other markets in the economy. This will prove attractive to other firms, which will seek to enter the market — and the assumption is that there are no barriers to prevent them from doing so.

Knowledge check 19.9

Which curve represents the individual firm's short-run supply curve under perfect competition?

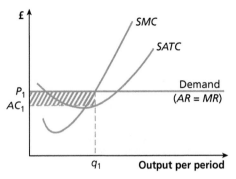

Figure 19.4 The firm in short-run equilibrium

This process of entry will continue for as long as firms are making supernormal profits. However, as more firms join the market, the *position* of the industry supply curve, which is the sum of the supply curves of an ever-larger number of individual firms, will be affected. As the industry supply curve shifts to the right, the market price will fall. At some point the price will have fallen to such an extent that firms are no longer making supernormal profits, and the market will then stabilise.

If the price were to fall even further, some firms would choose to exit from the market, and the process would go into reverse. Therefore, price can be expected to stabilise such that the typical firm in the industry is just making normal profits.

Figure 19.5 shows a situation in which a firm also tries to maximise profits by setting $MC = MR$, but finds that its average cost exceeds the price. It makes losses shown by the shaded area, and in the long run will choose to leave the market. As this and other firms exit from the market, the market supply curve shifts to the left, and the equilibrium price will drift upwards until firms are again making normal profits.

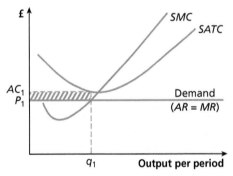

Figure 19.5 The firm in short-run equilibrium again

Knowledge check 19.10

What is the long-run shutdown price for a firm under perfect competition?

Perfect competition in long-run equilibrium

Figure 19.6 shows the situation for a typical firm and for the industry as a whole once long-run equilibrium has been reached and firms no longer have any incentive to enter or to exit the market. The market is in equilibrium, with demand equal to supply at the going price. The typical firm sets marginal revenue equal to marginal cost to maximise profits, and just makes normal profits.

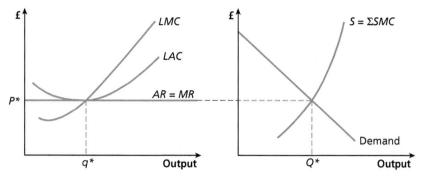

Figure 19.6 Long-run equilibrium under perfect competition

The long-run supply curve

Suppose there is an increase in the demand for this product. Perhaps, for some reason, everyone becomes convinced that the product is really health promoting, so demand increases at any given price. This disturbs the market equilibrium, and the question then is whether (and how) equilibrium can be restored.

Figure 19.7 reproduces the long-run equilibrium that was shown in Figure 19.6. Thus, in the initial position market price is at $P\star$, the typical firm is in long-run equilibrium producing $q\star$, and the industry is producing $Q\star$. Demand was initially at D_0, but with the increased popularity of the product it has shifted to D_1. In the short run this pushes the market price up to P_1 for the industry because, as market price increases, existing firms have the incentive to supply more output: that is, they move along their short-run supply curves. So in the short run a typical firm starts to produce q_1 output. The combined supply of the firms then increases to Q_1.

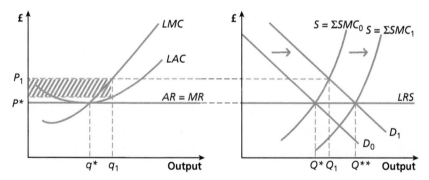

Figure 19.7 Adjusting to an increase in demand under perfect competition

However, at the higher price the firms start making supernormal profits (shown by the shaded area in Figure 19.7). Under the assumptions underpinning perfect competition, firms have perfect knowledge of market conditions, so the fact that firms in the market are making supernormal profits is known. Furthermore, there are no barriers to entry that prevent new firms joining the market. The fact that the product is homogeneous simplifies entry further. This means that in time more firms will be attracted into the market, pushing the short-run industry supply curve to the right. This process will continue until there is no further incentive for new firms to enter the market — which occurs when the price has returned to $P\star$, but with increased industry output at $Q\star\star$. In other words, the adjustment in the short run is borne by existing firms, but the long-run equilibrium is reached through the entry of new firms.

This suggests that the **industry long-run supply curve (LRS)** is horizontal at the price $P\star$, which is the minimum point of the long-run average cost curve for the typical firm in the industry.

Key term

industry long-run supply curve (LRS) under perfect competition, the curve that, for the typical firm in the industry, is horizontal at the minimum point of the long-run average cost curve

Knowledge check 19.11

What level of profits is made by a firm operating under perfect competition in long-run equilibrium?

Extension material: different cost conditions

If firms are not identical, but face different cost conditions, then the *LRS* may slope upwards. This could happen because some firms face a more favourable environment than others. Perhaps their location confers some advantage because they are closer to the market, or to some raw material. This would then allow some firms to survive for longer if the market price falls. In this case, as price falls, the least efficient firms would exit from the market until the marginal firm just makes normal profits. Notice that this also suggests that the most efficient firms in the market are able to make some supernormal profits even in long-run equilibrium, and it is only the marginal firm that just breaks even.

Quantitative skills 19.1

Interpreting points and areas on a diagram

Figure 19.8 shows the short-run cost curves for a firm that is operating in a perfectly competitive market. We can use a graph like this to analyse some key aspects of the firm's situation. Think carefully about what follows, and make sure you understand the points and areas mentioned.

A first question is to consider at what price the firm would just make 'normal' profits. This point would be where the price (average revenue) is just equal to average total costs, which would be at a price *OA* in the figure.

If the price were indeed at *OA*, then we could find areas of the figure to represent fixed and variable costs. With the price at *OA* the firm would produce *OQ* output (where *MC* = *MR*), so average variable costs would be given by *OE*, and total variable costs would be the area *OEHQ*. We can then infer that total fixed costs are the area *EADH*.

Chapter 18 considered the conditions under which a firm would choose to exit the market. In the short run, if the firm is getting a sufficiently high price to cover its variable cost then it will stay in business, as it is at least covering a part of its fixed costs. However, the firm would exit if the price were to fall below *OI* (the shut-down price). In other words, when the price is between OI and *OA*, the firm makes a loss in the short run as it is not fully covering its fixed costs, but it continues in the market. but continues in the market.

Notice that as the price varies, the firm effectively moves along its *SMC* curve, so we can interpret the *SMC* curve (above *OI*) as showing the short-run supply curve of the firm.

Notice also that if the price is above *OA*, the firm makes supernormal profits.

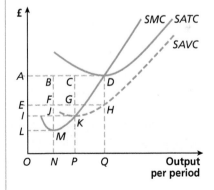

Figure 19.8 A firm operating under short-run perfect competition

Study tip

These diagrams can be quite confusing until you get used to them, and you would be well advised to practise both interpreting and drawing them, so you can be confident in using them when you need to do so.

Efficiency under perfect competition

Having reviewed the characteristics of the long-run equilibrium of a perfectly competitive market, you may wonder what is so good about such a market in terms of productive and allocative efficiency.

Productive efficiency

For an individual market, productive efficiency is reached when a firm operates at the minimum point of its long-run average cost curve. Under perfect competition, this is indeed a feature of the long-run equilibrium position. So productive efficiency is achieved in the long run — but not in the short run, when a firm is not necessarily operating at minimum average cost.

Allocative efficiency

For an individual market, allocative efficiency is achieved when price is set equal to marginal cost. This was explained in Chapter 4. Again, the process by which supernormal profits are competed away through the entry of new firms into the market ensures that price is equal to marginal cost within a perfectly competitive market in long-run equilibrium. So allocative efficiency is also achieved. Indeed, firms set price equal to marginal cost even in the short run, so allocative efficiency is a feature of perfect competition in both the short run and the long run.

Evaluation of perfect competition

A criticism sometimes levelled at the model of perfect competition is that it is merely a theoretical ideal, based on a sequence of assumptions that rarely holds in the real world. Perhaps you have some sympathy with that view.

It could be argued that the model does hold for some agricultural markets. One study in the USA estimated that the elasticity of demand for an individual farmer producing sweetcorn was −31,353, which is pretty close to perfect elasticity.

However, to argue that the model is useless because it is unrealistic is to miss a very important point. By allowing a glimpse of what the ideal market would look like, at least in terms of resource allocation, the model provides a measure against which alternative market structures can be compared. Furthermore, economic analysis can be used to investigate the effects of relaxing the assumptions of the model, which can be another valuable exercise. For example, it is possible to examine how the market is affected if firms can differentiate their products, or if traders in the market are acting with incomplete information.

So, although there may be relatively few markets that display all the characteristics of perfect competition, that does not destroy the usefulness of the model in economic theory. It will continue to be a reference point when examining alternative models of market structure.

Extension material: a word of warning

Some writers, such as Nobel prize winner Friedrich von Hayek, have disputed the idea that perfect competition is the best form of market structure. Hayek argued that supernormal profits can be seen as the basis for investment by firms in new technologies, research and development (R&D) and innovation. If supernormal profits are always competed away, as happens under perfect competition, such activity will not take place. Similarly, Joseph Schumpeter argued that only in monopoly or oligopoly markets can firms afford to undertake R&D. Under this sort of argument, it is not quite so clear that perfect competition is the most desirable market structure.

Summary: perfect competition

- The model of perfect competition describes an extreme form of market structure. It rests on a sequence of assumptions.
- Its key characteristics include the assumption that no individual trader can influence the market price of the good or service being traded, and that there is freedom of entry and exit.
- In such circumstances, each firm faces a perfectly elastic demand curve for its product, and can sell as much as it likes at the going market price.
- A profit-maximising firm chooses to produce the level of output at which marginal revenue (*MR*) equals marginal cost (*MC*).
- The firm's short-run marginal cost curve, above its short-run average variable cost curve, represents its short-run supply curve.
- The industry's short-run supply curve is the horizontal summation of the supply curves of all firms in the market.
- Firms may make supernormal profits in the short run, but because there is freedom of entry these profits will be competed away in the long run by new firms joining the market.
- The long-run industry supply curve is horizontal, with price adjusting to the minimum level of the typical firm's long-run average cost curve.
- Under perfect competition in long-run equilibrium, both productive efficiency and allocative efficiency are achieved.

The model of monopoly

Key term

monopoly a form of market structure in which there is only one seller of a good or service

A **monopoly** is a market with a single seller of a good. There is a bit more to it than that, and economic analysis of monopoly rests on some important assumptions. In the real world, the Competition and Markets Authority (CMA), the official body in the UK with responsibility for monitoring monopoly markets, is empowered to investigate a merger if it results in the combined firm having more than 25% of a market. The operations of the CMA will be discussed in Chapter 23.

Assumptions

The assumptions of the monopoly model are as follows:

1 There is a single seller of a good.

2 There are no substitutes for the good, either actual or potential.

3 There are barriers to entry into the market.

It is also assumed that the firm aims to maximise profits. You can see that these assumptions all have their counterparts in the assumptions of perfect competition, and that in one sense this model can be described as being at the opposite end of the market structure spectrum.

If there is a single seller of a good, and if there are no substitutes for the good, the monopoly firm is insulated from competition. Furthermore, any barriers to entry into the market will ensure that the firm can sustain its market position into the future. The assumption that there are no potential substitutes for the good reinforces the situation. (Chapter 21 explores what happens if this assumption does not hold.)

Knowledge check 19.12

What is the significance of the assumption that there are no substitutes for the product of a monopolist?

A monopoly in equilibrium

The first point to note is that a monopoly firm faces the market demand curve directly. Thus, unlike in perfect competition, the demand curve slopes downwards. For the monopolist, the demand curve may be regarded as showing average revenue. Unlike a firm under perfect competition, therefore, the monopolist has some influence over price, and can make decisions regarding price as well as output. This is not to say that the monopolist has complete freedom to set the price, as the firm is still constrained by market demand. However, the firm is a *price maker* and can choose a location *along* the demand curve.

Elasticity and total revenue

As a preliminary piece of analysis, recall from Chapter 2 that there is a relationship between the price elasticity of demand along a straight-line demand curve and total revenue. The key graphs are reproduced here as Figure 19.9. The price elasticity of demand is elastic above the mid-point of the demand curve and inelastic in the lower half, with total revenue increasing with a price fall when demand is elastic and falling when demand is inelastic.

The marginal revenue curve (*MR*) has been added to the figure. This has a fixed relationship with the average revenue curve (*AR*). This is for similar mathematical reasons as those that explained the relationship between marginal and average costs in the previous chapter. *MR* shares the intercept point on the vertical axis (point *A* in Figure 19.9) and has exactly twice the slope of *AR*.

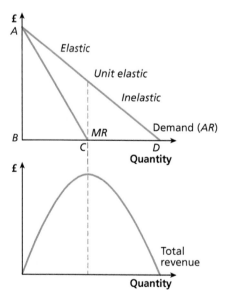

Figure 19.9 Elasticity and total revenue

Study tip

Whenever you have to draw this figure, remember that *MR* and *AR* have this relationship — meeting at *A*, and with the distance *BC* being the same as the distance *CD*. *MR* is zero (meets the horizontal axis) at the maximum point of the total revenue curve.

As with the firm under perfect competition, a monopolist aiming to maximise profits will choose to produce at the level of output at which marginal revenue equals marginal cost. This is at Q_m in Figure 19.10. Having selected output, the monopolist then identifies the price that will clear the market for that level of output — in Figure 19.10 this is P_m. Notice that a monopoly will always produce in the segment of the demand curve where MR is positive, which implies that demand is price elastic.

This choice allows the monopolist to make supernormal profits, which can be identified as the shaded area in the figure. As before, this area is average revenue minus average cost (profit per unit) multiplied by the quantity.

Barriers to entry

It is at this point that barriers to entry become important. Other firms may see that the monopoly firm is making healthy supernormal profits, but the existence of barriers to entry will prevent those profits from being competed away, as would happen in a perfectly competitive market.

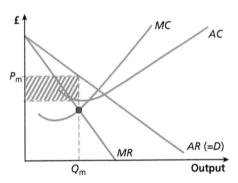

Figure 19.10 Profit maximisation and monopoly

It is important to notice that the monopolist cannot be guaranteed always to make such substantial profits as are shown in Figure 19.10. The size of the profits depends on the relative position of the market demand curve and the position of the cost curves. For example, if the cost curves in the diagram were higher, as in Figure 19.11, the monopoly would actually incur losses, as if the monopoly tries to maximise profits by choosing the output at which $MR = MC$, it will charge a price (P_m) that is below average cost (AC_m).

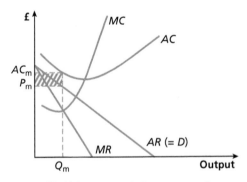

Figure 19.11 Losses made by a monopoly

Knowledge check 19.13

Will a profit-maximising monopoly firm always make supernormal profits? Briefly explain your answer.

Exercise 19.3

Table 19.2 shows the demand curve faced by a monopolist.

a Calculate total revenue and marginal revenue for each level of demand.
b Plot the demand curve (*AR*) and marginal revenue on a graph.
c Plot total revenue on a separate graph.
d Identify the level of demand at which total revenue is at a maximum.
e At what level of demand is marginal revenue equal to zero?
f At what level of demand is there unit price elasticity of demand?
g If the monopolist maximises profits, will the chosen level of output be higher or lower than the revenue-maximising level?
h What does this imply for the price elasticity of demand when the monopolist maximises profits?

Table 19.2 Demand curve for a monopolist

Demand (000 units per week)	Price (£)
0	80
1	70
2	60
3	50
4	40
5	30
6	20
7	10

A monopoly and an increase in demand

If a monopoly experiences (or can induce) an increase in the demand for its product, it will benefit. In Figure 19.12, suppose that initially the monopoly faces the demand curve D_0. It maximises profits by setting $MR = MC$, producing Q_0 output and charging a price P_0. If the demand curve shifts to the right, notice that the MR curve will also shift, as this has a fixed relationship with the demand curve. After the increase in demand, the monopoly chooses to produce Q_1 output, where $MR = MC$, and now sets a higher price at P_1, making higher profits.

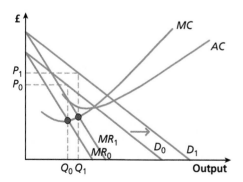

Figure 19.12 A monopoly and an increase in demand

How do monopolies arise?

Monopolies may arise in a market for a number of reasons. In a few instances, a monopoly is created by the authorities. For example, for 150 years the UK Post Office held a licence giving it a monopoly on delivering letters. This service was opened to some competition in the 2000s, although any company wanting to deliver packages weighing less than 350 grams and charging less than £1 could do so only by applying for a licence. The Post Office monopoly formerly covered a much wider range of services, but its coverage was eroded over the years, and competition in delivering larger packages has been permitted for some time. It was fully privatised (transferred into private ownership) in 2013. Nonetheless, it remains an example of one way in which a monopoly can be created.

The patent system offers a rather different form of protection for a firm. The patent system was designed to provide an incentive for firms to innovate through the development of new techniques and products. By prohibiting other firms from copying the product for a period of time, a firm is given a temporary monopoly.

A natural monopoly

In some cases, the technology of the industry may create a monopoly situation. In a market characterised by substantial economies of scale, there may not be room for more than one firm in the market. This could happen where there are substantial fixed costs of production but low marginal costs. For example, building a high-speed rail link such as HS2 entails substantial expenditure in the form of fixed costs to create new track, upgraded stations and new rolling stock. However, once it is in operation, the marginal cost of carrying an additional passenger is very low.

Figure 19.13 illustrates this point. The firm in this market enjoys economies of scale right up to the limit of market demand. Any new entrant into the market will be operating at a lower scale, so will inevitably face higher average costs. The existing firm will always be able to price such firms out of the market. Here the economies of scale act as an effective barrier to the entry of new firms and the market is a **natural monopoly**. A profit-maximising monopoly would thus set $MR = MC$, produce at quantity Q_m and charge a price P_m.

> ### Key term
>
> **natural monopoly**
> monopoly that arises in an industry in which there are such substantial economies of scale that only one firm is viable

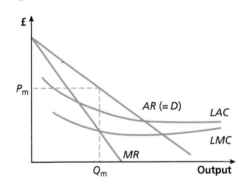

Figure 19.13 A natural monopoly

Such a market poses particular problems regarding allocative efficiency. Notice in the figure that marginal cost is below average cost over the entire range of output. If the firm were to charge a price equal to marginal cost, it would inevitably make a loss, so such a pricing rule would not be viable. This problem is analysed in Chapter 23.

Examples of natural monopoly

The sort of market where a natural monopoly may emerge is one in which there may be substantial fixed costs of operation but relatively low marginal cost. An example might be an underground railway system in a city or a Channel Tunnel. The setup costs of building a rail network under a city or a tunnel under the Channel are enormous compared with the marginal cost of carrying an additional passenger. Some cities (e.g. Kuala Lumpur) do have more than one underground railway system, but they do not compete on the same routes. It would not make economic sense to have parallel rail systems competing for the same passengers on a particular route, any more than it would be sensible to have two Channel Tunnels close to each other. Notice that although the Channel Tunnel may seem an obvious natural monopoly, this does not mean that the firm operating it faces no competition. The tunnel has to compete with ferry companies and airlines.

Knowledge check 19.14

Explain why the rail network (that is, the track) might be regarded as a natural monopoly.

The London Underground is an example of a natural monopoly

Another example of a natural monopoly might seem to be the manufacture of passenger aircraft. Building a plane capable of carrying large numbers of passengers on long-haul routes has large economies of scale. There are indivisibilities in the production process, and any firm producing such aircraft has to make substantial investment in research and development upfront. Thus there are large economies of scale in the production process. Furthermore, the market is relatively small, in the sense that the number of aircraft sold in a year is modest. However, looking at the market, it is clear that it is not a monopoly as there are two firms operating in the market — Boeing and Airbus. These are the only effective global competitors.

Does this negate the natural monopoly theory? The answer is no. In fact, this market has aroused much transatlantic debate and contention. Boeing, the US producer, has accused European governments of unfairly subsidising Airbus's R&D programme. In return, Airbus has responded by pointing to the benefits that Boeing has received from the US military research programme. Without being drawn into this debate at this stage, the net effect of the interventions has been to create a duopoly situation (a market with just two firms) in which Boeing and Airbus compete for market share. Later discussion will examine why such competition is regarded as being more favourable for consumers than allowing an unregulated natural monopoly to develop.

Synoptic link

Many natural monopolies formerly operated as nationalised industries (i.e. they were state-owned). Transferring these industries into private ownership raised the need for regulation. This is discussed in Chapter 23.

Competitive monopoly

There are markets in which firms have risen to become monopolies by their actions in the market. Such a market structure is sometimes known as a *competitive monopoly*.

Firms may get into a monopoly position through effective marketing, through a process of merger and acquisition, or by establishing a new product as a widely accepted standard. For example, by the mid-2010s, Google had come to control some 90% of the search engine market in Europe.

Exercise 19.4

When Sainsbury's merged with the Home Retail Group (which owned Argos and Habitat), this brought together food and non-food retailers. Think about the possible synergies from such a merger, and the sorts of costs entailed. Would the combined firm be expected to gain a monopoly position in its operations?

Monopoly and efficiency

The characteristics of the monopoly market can be evaluated in relation to productive and allocative efficiency (see Figure 19.10).

Productive efficiency

A firm is said to be productively efficient if it produces at the minimum point of its long-run average cost curve. It is clear from the figure that this is extremely unlikely for a monopoly. The firm will produce at its minimum long-run average cost only if it so happens that the marginal *revenue* curve passes through this exact point — and this would happen only by coincidence. Furthermore, if a monopoly is protected by barriers to entry, the incentive to become and remain productively efficient may be lacking. In this case, complacency could lead to X-inefficiency, which was discussed in Chapter 18.

Allocative efficiency

For an individual firm, allocative efficiency is achieved when price is set equal to marginal cost. It is clear from Figure 19.10 that this will not be the case for a profit-maximising monopoly firm. The firm chooses output where MR equals MC; however, given that MR is below AR (i.e. price), price will always be set above marginal cost.

Perfect competition and monopoly compared

It is possible to identify the extent to which a monopoly by its behaviour distorts resource allocation, by comparing the monopoly market with the perfectly competitive market. To do this, the situation can be simplified by setting aside the possibility of economies of scale. This is perhaps an artificial assumption to make, but it can be relaxed later.

Suppose that there is an industry with no economies of scale, which can be operated either as a perfectly competitive market with many small firms, or as a monopoly firm running a large number of small plants.

Figure 19.14 shows the market demand curve ($D = AR$), and the long-run supply curve under perfect competition (LRS). If the market is operating under perfect competition, the long-run equilibrium will produce a price of P_{pc}, and the firms in the industry will together supply Q_{pc} output. Consumer surplus is given by the area $AP_{pc}E$, which represents the surplus that consumers gain from consuming this product. In other words, it is a measure of the welfare that society receives from consuming the good, as was explained in Chapter 4.

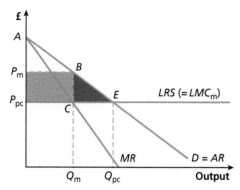

Figure 19.14 Comparing perfect competition and monopoly

Now suppose that the industry is taken over by a profit-maximising monopolist. The firm can close down some of the plants to vary its output over the long run, and the *LRS* can be regarded as the monopolist's long-run marginal cost curve. As the monopoly firm faces the market demand curve directly, it will also face the *MR* curve shown, so will maximise profits at quantity Q_m and charge a price P_m.

Thus, the effect of this change in market structure is that the profit-maximising monopolist produces less output than a perfectly competitive industry and charges a higher price.

It is also apparent that consumer surplus is now very different, as in the new situation it is limited to the area AP_mB. Looking more carefully at Figure 19.14, you can see that the loss of consumer surplus has occurred for two reasons. First, the monopoly firm is now making profits shown by the shaded area P_mBCP_{pc}. This is a redistribution of welfare from consumers to the firm, but, as the monopolist is also a member of society, this does not affect overall welfare. However, there is also a deadweight loss, which represents a loss to society resulting from the monopolisation of the industry. This is measured by the area of the triangle *BCE*. Chapter 23 examines whether the authorities need to worry about this situation and explores the sort of policy that could be adopted to tackle the issue.

Synoptic link

Remember that there are some key concepts (such as consumer surplus, mentioned in this section) that you will have learned in Chapter 4 which are important here as well.

Summary: monopoly

- A monopoly market is one in which there is a single seller of a good.
- The model of monopoly used in economic analysis also assumes that there are no substitutes for the goods or services produced by the monopolist, and that there are barriers to the entry of new firms.
- The monopoly firm faces the market demand curve, and is able to choose a point along that demand curve in order to maximise profits.
- Such a firm may be able to make supernormal profits, and sustain them in the long run because of barriers to entry and the lack of substitutes.
- A monopoly may arise because of patent protection or from the nature of economies of scale in the industry (a 'natural monopoly').
- A profit-maximising monopolist does not achieve allocative efficiency, and is unlikely to achieve productive efficiency in the sense of producing at the minimum point of the long-run average cost curve.
- A comparison of perfect competition with monopoly reveals that a profit-maximising monopoly firm operating under the same cost conditions as a perfectly competitive industry will produce less output, charge a higher price and impose a deadweight loss on society.

▍Price discrimination

Are there any conditions in which a monopoly firm would produce the level of output that is consistent with allocative efficiency?

Consider Figure 19.15. Suppose this market is operated by a monopolist who faces constant marginal cost LMC. (This is to simplify the analysis.) Under perfect competition the market outcome would be at price $P\star$ and quantity $Q\star$. What would induce the monopolist to produce at $Q\star$?

One of the assumptions made throughout the analysis so far is that all consumers in a market get to pay the same price for the product. In Figure 19.15, if the market were operating under perfect competition and all consumers were paying the same price, consumer surplus would be given by the area $AP\star B$. If the market were operated by a monopolist, also charging the same price to all buyers, then profits would be maximised where $MC = MR$: that is, at quantity Q_m and price P_m.

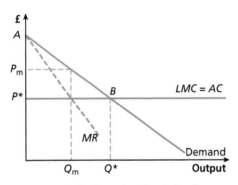

Figure 19.15 Perfect price discrimination

But suppose this assumption is now relaxed; suppose that the monopolist is able to charge a different price to each individual consumer. A monopolist is then able to charge each consumer a price that is equal to his or her willingness to pay for the good. In other words, the demand curve effectively becomes the marginal revenue curve, as it represents the amount that the monopolist will receive for each unit of the good. It will then maximise profits at point B in Figure 19.15, where MR (i.e. AR) is equal to LMC. The difference between this situation and that under perfect competition is that the area $AP\star B$ is no longer consumer surplus, but producer surplus: that is, the monopolist's profits. The monopolist has hijacked the whole of the original consumer surplus as its profits.

First-degree price discrimination

From society's point of view, total welfare is the same as it is under perfect competition (but more than under monopoly without discrimination). However, now there has been a redistribution, from consumers to the monopoly — and presumably to the shareholders of the firm. This situation is known as **perfect price discrimination**, or **first-degree price discrimination**.

Perfect price discrimination is fairly rare in the real world, although it might be said to exist in the world of art or fashion, where customers may commission a painting, sculpture or item of designer jewellery and the price is a matter of negotiation between the buyer and supplier.

Key terms

perfect/first-degree price discrimination situation arising in a market whereby a monopoly firm is able to charge each consumer a different price

third-degree price discrimination situation in which a firm is able to charge groups of consumers a different price for the same product

Third-degree price discrimination

There are situations in which only partial price discrimination is possible. For example, students or old-age pensioners may get discounted bus fares, the young and/or old may get cheaper access to sporting events or theatres etc. In these instances, individual consumers are paying different prices for what is in fact the same product. This is known as **third-degree price discrimination**.

There are three conditions under which a firm may be able to price discriminate:

1 The firm must have market power.

2 The firm must have information about consumers and their willingness to pay — and there must be identifiable differences between consumers (or groups of consumers).

3 The consumers must have limited ability to resell the product.

Knowledge check 19.15

Why would a firm not be able to use price discrimination if consumers could resell the product?

Perfect price discrimination exists in the art world

Market power

Clearly, price discrimination is not possible in a perfectly competitive market, where no seller has the power to charge other than the going market price. So price discrimination can take place only where firms have some ability to vary the price.

Information

From the firm's point of view, it needs to be able to identify different groups of consumers with different willingness to pay. What makes price discrimination profitable for firms is that different consumers display different sensitivities to price: that is, they have different price elasticities of demand.

Ability to resell

If consumers could resell the product easily, then price discrimination would not be possible, as consumers would engage in **arbitrage**. In other words, the group of consumers who qualified for the low price could buy up the product and then turn a profit by reselling to consumers in the other segment(s) of the market. This would mean that the firm would no longer be able to sell at the high price, and would no longer try to discriminate in pricing.

In the case of student discounts and OAP concessions, the firm can identify particular groups of consumers; and such 'products' as bus journeys and dental treatment cannot be resold. But why should a firm undertake this practice?

Key term

arbitrage a process by which prices in two market segments are equalised by the purchase and resale of products by market participants

The simple answer is that, by undertaking price discrimination, the firm is able to increase its profits. This is shown in Figure 19.16, which separates two distinct groups of consumers with differing demand curves. Thus, panel (a) shows market A and panel (b) shows market B, with the combined demand curve being shown in panel (c), which also shows the firm's marginal cost curve.

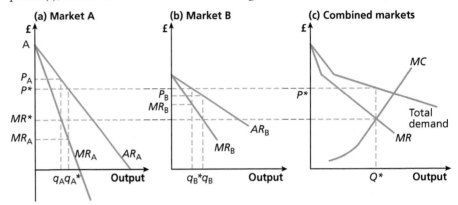

Figure 19.16 A price-discriminating monopolist

If a firm has to charge the same price to all consumers, it sets marginal revenue in the combined market equal to marginal cost, and produces $Q\star$ output, to be sold at a price of $P\star$. This maximises profits when all consumers pay the same price. The firm sells $q_A\star$ in market A, and $q_B\star$ in market B.

However, if you look at panels (a) and (b), you will see that marginal revenue in market A is much lower (at MR_A) than that in market B (at MR_B). It is this difference in marginal revenue that opens up a profit-increasing opportunity for the firm. By taking sales away from market A and selling more in market B, the firm gains more extra revenue in B than it loses in A. This increases its profit. The optimal position for the firm is where marginal revenue is equalised in the two markets. In Figure 19.16 the firm sells q_A in market A at the higher price of P_A. In market B sales increase to q_B with price falling to P_B. Notice that in both situations the amounts sold in the two sub-markets sum to $Q\star$.

Benefits for consumers?

The consumers in market B seem to do quite well by this practice, as they can now consume more of the good. Indeed, it is possible that with no discrimination the price would be so high that they would not be able to consume the good at all.

In 2016, the Competition and Markets Authority reported on an investigation of the energy market. One of their findings was that there was wide variation in the prices paid by domestic customers for energy, although electricity and gas are homogenous products. Potentially, most customers could have made savings by switching suppliers, tariffs or payment methods. Indeed, average potential gains from switching were equivalent to more than 20% of customers' bills. A number of remedies were recommended to address this situation.

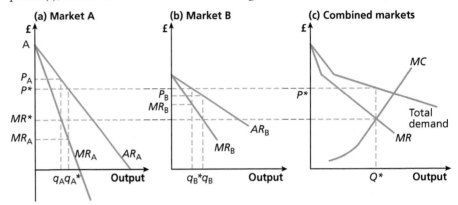

Knowledge check 19.16

What incentive would a firm have to practise price discrimination?

Study tip

Be ready with the three conditions necessary for a firm to be able to use price discrimination:

- The firm must have market power.
- The firm must be able to identify different consumers (or groups of consumers) and differences in their elasticities of demand.
- There must be limited ability for consumers to resell the product.

Exercise 19.5

In which of the following products might price discrimination be possible? Explain your answers.

a hairdressing
b peak and off-peak rail travel
c apples
d air tickets

e newspapers
f plastic surgery
g beer

Summary: price discrimination

- In some markets a monopolist may be able to engage in price discrimination by selling its product at different prices to different consumers or groups of consumers.
- This enables the firm to increase its profits by absorbing some or all of the consumer surplus.
- Under first-degree price discrimination, the firm is able to charge a different price to each customer and absorb all consumer surplus.
- The firm can practise price discrimination only where it has market power, where consumers have differing elasticities of demand for the product, and where consumers have limited ability to resell the product.

Evaluation of monopoly

A profit-maximising monopoly firm produces less output at a higher price than under perfect competition. As the price is set above marginal cost, allocative efficiency is not achieved. However, a monopoly may be able to exploit economies of scale that would not be available to smaller firms, so although there will not be productive efficiency in the sense that the firm will not produce at minimum average cost, nonetheless, the firm may be producing at lower cost than could be the case under perfect competition. By producing at lower cost, a firm with a monopoly in the home market may be in a position to compete with firms in a global market environment.

As the firm can make supernormal profits, it may be able to undertake research and development activity that will lead to dynamic efficiency. On the other hand, in the absence of competition, the firm may become complacent, and allow X-inefficiency to creep in.

If a monopoly firm is able to practise price discrimination, some consumers may be able to have access to products that would otherwise be out of their price range. The use of monopoly power has the effect of transferring consumer surplus into producer surplus, so there are distributional effects.

Exercise 19.6

Discuss the potential costs and benefits of monopoly for firms, consumers, employees, suppliers and society as a whole.

Case study 19.1

Of cabbages and rings

Ted Greens has a farm on which he grows a variety of crops, including cabbages that grow well on his south field, which seems especially suited to the crop. When Ted takes his cabbage crop to market, hoping to make as much profit as possible, he finds that the price he can charge for cabbages depends on market conditions — after all, one cabbage is very much like any other. He thus has to accept the price that he can get, which is the same as that charged by his many rival producers. If he tries to set a higher price, he sells nothing as all traders in the market have good awareness of market conditions, but as he can sell as much as he likes at the going price, there is no need to drop price below that prevailing in the market. Price tends to fluctuate from one harvest season to the next, and in some years when cabbages are plentiful, Ted finds that he barely covers his costs.

Edward de Vere owns a diamond mine — the only such mine in the country. His company cuts the stones and uses them to produce diamond rings. In selling the rings, Edward takes into account the strength of demand, choosing a price that will clear the market. He finds that by restricting the number of rings that he produces, he is able to charge a higher price. By doing so he is able to increase the profits that he makes. As he controls the only source of diamonds, Edward does not have to worry about other producers entering the market, and there are no acceptable substitutes for diamonds that people are prepared to accept.

Follow-up questions

a Which of the two producers appears to operate under conditions of perfect competition, and which is a monopoly?

b Explain your answer to part (a), referring to the assumptions that underlie the two theories of market structure.

c Under what conditions would Ted Greens decide to give up growing cabbages?

d Can you think of steps that Ted Greens might take in order to improve his profits on cabbages?

e Draw a diagram to explain how Edward de Vere would react to an increase in the demand for diamond rings.

f Suppose that a foreign firm starts to import diamond rings into the country in competition with Edward de Vere. How would you expect him to react?

Case study 19.2

Pricing rail travel

Travelling between Southampton and Cambridge by train to get to a meeting, I faced a choice between five different prices for a single journey, ranging from £26.30 to £89.30. Potential passengers can also acquire one of the 14 railcards, that offer discounts, so the range with a railcard goes from £16.25 to £89.30 (depending on which railcard you own). Choosing a slightly different route and travelling half-an-hour later, the cheapest fare with a senior railcard becomes £36.85 instead of £17.35. This is because only a limited number of 'advance' tickets are available.

In other words, when travelling by train, passengers find themselves paying a different price for what is effectively the same product (although you get a more comfortable seat in first class). There is also a maze of complexity surrounding the choices — indeed, it took quite some time for the booking office clerk to work out the cheapest price for the passenger in the queue in front of me.

This is an example of price discrimination at work. There are some identifiable groups of passengers that might be expected to have different characteristics. For example, there may be significant differences between commuters who need to use the train to travel to work at a specific time and passengers who are going out for the day on a pleasure trip. These two groups may have different elasticities of demand. The commuter group need to travel at a specific time, whereas the pleasure trippers will have more flexibility about when they travel. This may suggest that there is a rationale for charging lower prices at off-peak periods. To put it another way, commuters may be less sensitive to price because they cannot choose to travel off-peak.

Similarly, some people who commute for long distances may need to make productive use of their journey, which may be more possible by travelling first class, rather than in a congested carriage.

Follow-up questions

a Explain why groups of passengers with different characteristics may have differing elasticities of demand, and under what conditions this enables the train companies to charge different prices for the same journey.

b What is the incentive for the train companies to practise price discrimination?

c Do passengers benefit from price discrimination?

20 Market structure: monopolistic competition and oligopoly

The previous chapter introduced the models of perfect competition and monopoly, describing them as being at the extreme ends of a spectrum of forms of market structure. In between those two extremes are other forms of market structure, which have some but not all of the characteristics of either perfect competition or monopoly. It is in this sense that there is a spectrum of structures. Attention in this chapter is focused on some of these intermediate forms of market structure.

Learning objectives

After studying this chapter, you should:
- → be familiar with the range of market situations that exists between the extremes of perfect competition and monopoly
- → understand the meaning of product differentiation and its role in the model of monopolistic competition
- → understand the significance of concentration in a market and how to measure it
- → understand the notion of oligopoly and be familiar with approaches to modelling firm behaviour in an oligopoly market
- → understand the benefits that firms may gain from forming a cartel — and the tensions that may result
- → be familiar with the characteristics of a monopsony market

▌Monopolistic competition

If you consider the characteristics of the markets that you frequent on a regular basis, you will find that few (if any) of them display all of the characteristics associated with perfect competition. However, there may be some that show a few of these features. In particular, you will find some markets in which there appears to be intense competition among many buyers, but in which the products for sale are not identical. For example, think about restaurants. In cities, you will find a wide range of restaurants, cafés and pubs that compete with each other for business, but do so by offering slightly different products.

The theory of **monopolistic competition** was devised by Edward Chamberlin, writing in the USA in the 1930s, and his name is often attached to the model, although Joan Robinson published her book on imperfect competition in the UK at the same time. The motivation for the analysis was to explain how markets worked when they were operating neither as monopolies nor under perfect competition.

The model describes a market in which there are many firms producing similar, but not identical, products, such as travel agents, hairdressers or fast-food outlets. In the case of fast-food outlets, the high streets of most cities are characterised by large numbers of different types of takeaway — burgers, fish and chips, Indian, Chinese, fried chicken and so on.

Key term

monopolistic competition a market that shares some characteristics of monopoly and some of perfect competition

Synoptic link

The models of perfect competition and monopoly were discussed in Chapter 19 as being at the opposite ends of a spectrum of market structures. The models explored in this chapter are intermediate models that fall between those extremes.

The monopolistic competition model describes the fast-food market in many cities

Model characteristics
Three important characteristics of the model of monopolistic competition distinguish this sort of market from others.

Product differentiation
First, firms produce differentiated products, and face downward-sloping demand curves. In other words, each firm competes with the others by making its product slightly different. This allows the firms to build up brand loyalty among their regular customers, which gives them some influence over price. It is likely that firms will engage in advertising in order to maintain such brand loyalty, and heavy advertising is a common characteristic of a market operating under monopolistic competition.

Because other firms are producing similar goods, there are substitutes for each firm's product, which means that demand will be relatively price elastic. However, it is not perfectly price elastic, as was the case with perfect competition. These features — that the product is not homogeneous and demand is not perfectly price elastic — represent significant differences from the model of perfect competition.

Freedom of entry
Second, there are no barriers to entry into the market. Firms are able to join the market if they observe that existing firms are making supernormal profits. New entrants to the market will be looking for some way to differentiate their product slightly from the others — perhaps the next fast-food restaurant will be Nepalese, or Peruvian.

This characteristic distinguishes the market from the monopoly model, as does the existence of fairly close substitutes.

Many firms
Third, there are many firms operating in the market. For this reason, a price change by one of the firms will have negligible effects on the demand for its rivals' products.

This characteristic means that the market is also different from an oligopoly market, where there are a few firms that interact strategically with each other.

Overview
Taking these three characteristics together, it can be seen that a market of monopolistic competition has some of the characteristics of perfect competition and some features of monopoly; hence its name.

Key term

product differentiation a strategy adopted by firms that marks their product as being different from their competitors'

Synoptic link

Oligopoly models are discussed later in this chapter.

Study tip

Remember these three characteristics, and why they are important in making the model of monopolistic competition distinct from either perfect competition or monopoly.

Short-run equilibrium

Figure 20.1 represents short-run equilibrium under monopolistic competition. D_s is the demand curve, and MR_s is the corresponding marginal revenue curve. AC and MC are the average and marginal cost curves for a representative firm in the industry. If the firm is aiming to maximise profits, it will choose the level of output such that $MR_s = MC$. This occurs at output Q_s, and the firm will then choose the price that clears the market at P_s.

Knowledge check 20.1

Why is product differentiation an important characteristic of the model of monopolistic competition?

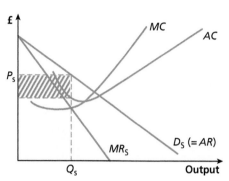

Figure 20.1 Short-run equilibrium under monopolistic competition

This closely resembles the standard monopoly diagram that was introduced in Chapter 19. As with monopoly, a firm under monopolistic competition faces a downward-sloping demand curve, as already noted. The difference is that under monopolistic competition it is assumed that there is free entry into the market, so that Figure 20.1 represents equilibrium only in the short run. This is because the firm shown in the figure is making supernormal profits, shown by the shaded area (which is $AR - AC$ multiplied by output).

The importance of free entry

This is where the assumption of free entry into the market becomes important. In Figure 20.1 the profits being made by the representative firm will attract new firms into the market. The new firms will produce differentiated products, and this will have two important effects on demand for the representative firm's product. First, the new firms will attract some customers away from this firm, so that its demand curve will tend to shift to the left. Second, as there are now more substitutes for the original product, the demand curve will become more elastic — remember that the availability of substitutes is an important influence on the price elasticity of demand.

Knowledge check 20.2

If a firm operating under monopolistic competition is making supernormal profits, what would you expect to happen to its demand curve?

Long-run equilibrium

This process will continue as long as firms in the market continue to make profits that attract new firms into the activity. It may be accelerated if firms are persuaded to spend money on advertising in an attempt to defend their market shares. The advertising may help to keep the demand curve downward sloping, but it will also affect the position of the average cost curve, by pushing up average cost at all levels of output.

Figure 20.2 shows the final position for the market. The typical firm is now operating in such a way that it maximises profits (by setting output such that $MR = MC$); at the same time, the average cost curve (AC) at this level of output is at a tangent to the demand curve. This means that $AC = AR$, and the firm is just making normal profit (i.e. is just covering opportunity cost). There is thus no incentive for more firms to join the market. In Figure 20.2 this occurs when output is at Q_1 and price is set at P_1.

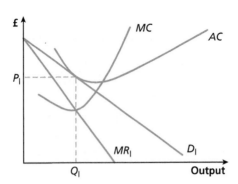

Figure 20.2 Long-run equilibrium under monopolistic competition

Efficiency

One way of evaluating the market outcome under this model is to examine the consequences for productive and allocative efficiency. It is clear from Figure 20.2 that neither of these conditions will be met. The representative firm does not reach the minimum point on the long-run average cost curve, and so does not attain productive efficiency; furthermore, the price charged is above marginal cost, so allocative efficiency is not achieved.

Evaluation of the model of monopolistic competition

If the typical firm in the market is not fully exploiting the possible economies of scale that exist, it could be argued that product differentiation is damaging society's total welfare, in the sense that it is the product differentiation that allows firms to keep their demand curves downward sloping. In other words, too many different products are being produced. However, this argument could be countered by pointing out that consumers may enjoy having more freedom of choice. The very fact that they are prepared to pay a premium price for their chosen brand indicates that they have some preference for it.

Another crucial difference between monopolistic competition and perfect competition is that under monopolistic competition firms would like to sell more of their product at the going price, whereas under perfect competition they can sell as much as they like at the going price. This is because price under monopolistic competition is set above marginal cost.

The use of advertising to attract more customers and to maintain consumer perception of product differences may be considered a problem with this market. It could be argued that excessive use of advertising to maintain product differentiation is wasteful, as it leads to higher average cost curves than needed. On the other hand, the need to compete in this way may result in less X-inefficiency than could arise under a complacent monopolist.

Knowledge check 20.3

Why are firms under monopolistic competition more keen to sell more output than firms under perfect competition?

Examples of monopolistic competition

The theory of monopolistic competition describes a market with some features of monopoly and some features of perfect competition. Entry barriers are low, so the market has many firms. However, firms in the market use product differentiation to influence consumers, and thus face downward-sloping demand curves. What sorts of market in the real world might typify this structure?

Road transport market

When you journey along a motorway or trunk road in the UK, observe the heavy goods vehicles (HGVs) and smaller vans that you pass. You will see HGVs and vans in a wide variety of liveries, from a wide range of countries and carrying a wide diversity of loads.

This is a market characterised by many competing firms, many of which operate in niche markets. Firms try to differentiate their offering by carrying particular categories of products — building materials, perhaps, or electronic goods. Some may trade between certain destinations. They advertise by broadcasting these specialisms on their vehicles, in the *Yellow Pages* or on the internet.

Another part of the road transport market that may typify monopolistic competition is local taxi markets. Count the local taxi companies in your local *Yellow Pages*. Again, firms may seek to differentiate their products through having a fleet livery, by advertising pre-booking only or by offering a limousine service. There may also be firms that specialise in longer-distance trips, say to airports.

Food outlets

Another example is food outlets. The number of restaurants and fast-food outlets has mushroomed in recent decades, and on many high streets in UK towns there is a proliferation of eating places and takeaways. One of the characteristics of a market operating under monopolistic competition is the product differentiation that takes place. Each individual seller sets out to be different from its competitors. This is certainly a characteristic of the fast-food sector, where outlets offer different styles of cuisine — burgers, pizza, Indian, Chinese, Thai, Mexican and so on. Before condemning such a market as being damaging to consumers because of the effect on productive and allocative efficiency, it is worth being aware that this market offers consumers a wide range of choice for fast food. If they value this choice, then this should be seen as a benefit that arises because of the market structure.

Exercise 20.1

Figure 20.3 shows a firm under monopolistic competition.

a Identify the profit-maximising level of output.

b At what price would the firm sell its product?

c What supernormal profits (if any) would be made by the firm?

d Is this a short-run or a long-run equilibrium? Explain your answer.

e Describe any subsequent adjustment that might take place in the market (if any).

f At what level of output would productive efficiency be achieved? (Assume that *AC* represents long-run average cost for this part of the question.)

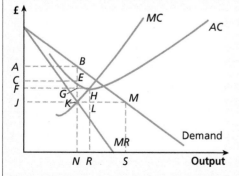

Figure 20.3 A firm under monopolistic competition

Summary: monopolistic competition

- The theory of monopolistic competition has its origins in the 1930s, when economists such as Edward Chamberlin and Joan Robinson were writing about markets that did not conform to the models of perfect competition and monopoly.
- The model describes a market where there are many firms producing similar, but not identical, products.
- By differentiating their product from those of other firms, it is possible for firms to maintain some influence over price.
- To do this, firms engage in advertising to build brand loyalty.
- There are no barriers to entry into the market.
- There are many firms operating in the market.
- Firms in the short run may make supernormal profits.
- In response, new entrants join the market, shifting the demand curves of existing firms and affecting their shape.
- The process continues until supernormal profits have been competed away, and the typical firm has its average cost curve at a tangent to its demand curve.
- Neither productive nor allocative efficiency is achieved in long-run equilibrium.
- Consumers may benefit from the increased range of choice on offer in the market.

Market concentration

Chapter 19 pointed out that the models of perfect competition and monopoly produce very different outcomes for productive and allocative efficiency. Perfect competition produces a 'good' allocation of resources, but monopoly results in a deadweight loss. In the real-world economy it is not quite so simple. In particular, not every market is readily classified as following either of these extreme models. Indeed, you might think that the majority of markets do not correspond to either of the models, but instead display a mixture of characteristics.

An important question is whether such markets behave more like a competitive market or more like a monopoly. There are many different ways in which markets with just a few firms operating can be modelled, because there are many ways in which the firms may interact. Some of these models will be explored later in the chapter.

It is helpful to have some way of gauging how close a particular market is to being a monopoly. One way of doing this is to examine the degree of concentration in the market. Later it will be seen that this is not all that is required to determine how efficiently a market will operate; but it is a start.

The concentration ratio

Concentration is normally measured by reference to the **concentration ratio**, which measures the market share of the largest firms in an industry. For example, the three-firm concentration ratio measures the market share of the largest three firms in the market; the five-firm concentration ratio calculates the share of the top five firms, and so on. Concentration can also be viewed in terms of employment, reflected in the proportion of workers in any industry that are employed in the largest firms.

Synoptic link

Being able to measure concentration in a market is important in deciding whether the authorities need to intervene in a market to protect consumers. This is explored further in Chapter 23.

Key term

n-firm concentration ratio a measure of the market share of the largest *n* firms in an industry

Quantitative skills 20.1

Calculating a concentration ratio

Consider the following example. Table 20.1 gives average circulation figures for the firms that publish national newspapers in the UK (with a circulation of more than 100,000 per day). In the final column these are converted into market shares.

Table 20.1 Concentration in the UK newspaper industry, January 2018

Firm	Newspapers	Average circulation	Market share (%)
dmg media	Daily Mail, Metro	2,818,514	34.6
News UK	Sun, Times	1,986,152	24.4
London Evening Standard	London Evening Standard	888,017	10.9
Northern & Shell	Daily Star, Daily Express	756,719	9.3
Trinity Mirror	Daily Mirror, Daily Record	717,279	8.8
Telegraph Group	Daily Telegraph	385,346	4.7
Johnston Press	i	257,223	3.2
Pearson	Financial Times	189,579	2.3
Guardian Media Group	Guardian	152,714	1.9
Total		**8,151,543**	**100.0**

Source: Audit Bureau of Circulations (www.abc.org.uk)

The market shares are calculated by expressing the average circulation for a firm as a percentage of the total. For example, the market share of the *Financial Times* is $100 \times 189,579/8,151,543 = 2.3\%$.

The three-firm concentration ratio is calculated as the sum of the market shares of the biggest three firms: that is, $34.6 + 24.4 + 10.9 = 69.9\%$.

Concentration ratios may be calculated on the basis of either shares in output or shares in employment. In the above example, the calculation was on the basis of output (daily circulation). The two measures may give different results because the largest firms in an industry may be more capital-intensive in their production methods, which means that their share of employment in an industry will be smaller than their share of output. For purposes of examining market structure, however, it is more helpful to base the analysis of market share on output.

This might seem an intuitively simple measure, but it is too simple to enable an evaluation of a market. For a start, it is important to define the market appropriately: for instance, in the above example are the *Financial Times* and the *Sun* really part of the same market?

There may be other difficulties too. Table 20.2 gives some hypothetical market shares for two markets. The five-firm concentration ratio is calculated as the sum of the market shares of the largest five firms. For market A this is $68 + 3 + 2 + 1 + 1 = 75$; for market B it is $15 + 15 + 15 + 15 + 15 = 75$. In each case the market is perceived to be highly concentrated, at 75%. However, the nature of likely interactions between the firms in these two markets is very different because the large relative size of firm 1 in market A is likely to give it substantially more market power than any of the largest five firms in market B. Nonetheless, the concentration ratio is useful for giving a first impression of how the market is likely to function.

Knowledge check 20.4

How would you calculate the four-firm concentration ratio for an industry in terms of sales?

Table 20.2 Market shares (% of output)

Largest firms in rank order	Market A	Market B
Firm 1	68	15
Firm 2	3	15
Firm 3	2	15
Firm 4	1	15
Firm 5	1	15

Figure 20.4 shows the five-firm concentration ratio for a number of industrial sectors in the UK. Concentration varies from 5% in construction and 12% in printing and publishing to 71% in cement and 99% in tobacco products. In part, the difference between sectors might be expected to reflect the extent of economies of scale, and this makes sense for many of the industries shown.

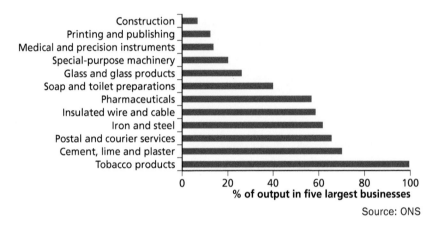

Source: ONS

Figure 20.4 Concentration in UK industry

Summary: market concentration

- It is important to be able to evaluate the degree of concentration in a market.
- While not a perfect measure, the concentration ratio is one way of doing this, by calculating the market share of the largest firms.

Oligopoly

Key term

oligopoly a market with a few sellers, in which each firm must take account of the behaviour and likely behaviour of rival firms in the industry

A number of markets seem to be dominated by relatively few firms — think of motor vehicle manufacturing or commercial banking in the UK, or the newspaper industry. A market with just a few sellers is known as an **oligopoly** market. An important characteristic of such markets is that when making economic decisions each firm must take account of its rivals' behaviour and reactions. The firms are therefore interdependent.

An important characteristic of oligopoly is that each firm has to act strategically, both in reacting to rival firms' decisions and in trying to anticipate their future actions.

There are many different ways in which a firm may take such strategic decisions, and this means that there are many ways in which an oligopoly market can be modelled, depending on how the firms are behaving. This chapter reviews just a few such models.

Oligopolies may come about for many reasons, but perhaps the most convincing concerns economies of scale. An oligopoly is likely to develop in a market where there are modest economies of scale — economies that are not substantial enough to require a natural monopoly, but are large enough to make it difficult for too many firms to operate at minimum efficient scale.

Within an oligopoly market, firms may adopt rivalrous behaviour or they may choose to cooperate with each other. The two attitudes have implications for how markets operate. Cooperation will tend to take the market towards the monopoly end of the spectrum, whereas non-cooperation will take it towards the competitive end. In either scenario, it is likely that the market outcome will be somewhere between the two extremes.

Knowledge check 20.5

What are the two key characteristics of an oligopoly market?

The kinked demand curve model

One such model revolves around how a firm *perceives* its demand curve. This is called the kinked demand curve model, and was developed by Paul Sweezy in the USA in the 1930s.

The model relates to an oligopoly in which firms try to anticipate the reactions of rivals to their actions. One problem that arises is that a firm cannot readily observe its demand curve with any degree of certainty, so it must form expectations about how consumers will react to a price change.

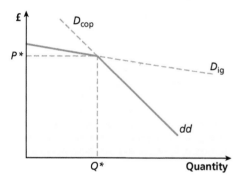

Figure 20.5 The kinked demand curve

Figure 20.5 shows how this works. Suppose the price is currently set at $P\star$; the firm is selling $Q\star$, and is trying to decide whether to alter price. The problem is that there is only one point on the demand curve that can be observed: that is, when price is $P\star$, the firm sells $Q\star$.

However, the firm is aware that the degree of sensitivity to its price change will depend on whether or not the other firms in the market will follow its lead. In other words, if its rivals ignore the firm's price change, there will be more sensitivity to this change than if they all follow suit.

Figure 20.5 shows the two extreme possibilities for the demand curve which the firm perceives that it faces. If other firms ignore its action, D_{ig} will be the relevant demand curve, which is relatively elastic. On the other hand, if the other firms copy the firm's moves, D_{cop} will be the relevant demand curve.

The question then is under what conditions will the other firms copy the price change, and when will they not? The firm may imagine that if it raises price there is little likelihood that its rivals will copy. After all, this is a non-threatening move that gives market share to the other firms. So for a price *increase*, it is D_{ig} that is the relevant section.

On the other hand, a price reduction is likely to be seen by the rivals as a threatening move, and they are likely to copy in order to preserve their market positions. For a price *decrease*, then, it is D_{cop} that is relevant.

Knowledge check 20.6

In the kinked demand curve model, is the price prevailing in the market likely to be volatile?

Study tip

Although the kinked demand curve is a popular model, remember that it is just one attempt to model strategic behaviour between firms. There are many ways in which firms may interact, so there are many different ways of trying to model the interactions.

Key terms

game theory a method of modelling the strategic interaction between firms in an oligopoly

prisoners' dilemma an example of game theory with a range of applications in oligopoly theory

Putting these together, the firm perceives that it faces a kinked demand curve (*dd*). The firm then faces a difficult choice. If it increases price, it will lose customers because rivals are not expected to react, and will continue to sell at the old price. On the other hand, if the firm reduces price, it will face intense competition from rivals, and will be unlikely to gain many customers. Its best strategy may thus be to do nothing. A key implication of this model is that price will remain relatively stable through time.

Game theory

An alternative approach in the economic theory of the firm has been in the application of **game theory**. This began as a branch of mathematics, but it became apparent that it had wide applications in explaining the behaviour of firms in an oligopoly.

Game theory itself has a long history, with some writers tracing it back to correspondence between Pascal and Fermat in the mid-seventeenth century. Early applications in economics were by Antoine Augustin Cournot in 1838, Francis Edgeworth in 1881 and J. Bertrand in 1883, but the key publication was the book by John von Neumann and Oskar Morgenstern, *Theory of Games and Economic Behaviour*, published in 1944. Other famous names in game theory include John Nash (played by Russell Crowe in the film *A Beautiful Mind*), John Harsanyi and Reinhard Selton, who shared the 1994 Nobel prize for their work in this area.

Russell Crowe playing the part of mathematician and game theorist John Nash in *A Beautiful Mind*

The prisoners' dilemma

Almost certainly, the most famous game is the **prisoners' dilemma**, introduced in a lecture by Albert Tucker (who taught John Nash at Princeton) in 1950. This simple example of game theory turns out to have a multitude of helpful applications in economics.

Two prisoners, Al Fresco and Des Jardins, are being interrogated about a major crime, and the police know that at least one of the prisoners is guilty. The two are kept in separate cells and cannot communicate with each other. The police have enough evidence to convict them of a minor offence, but not enough to convict them of the major one.

Each prisoner is offered a deal. If he turns state's evidence and provides evidence to convict the other prisoner, he will get off — *unless* the other prisoner also confesses. If both refuse to deal, they will just be charged with the minor offence. Table 20.3 summarises the sentences that each will receive in the various circumstances.

Table 20.3 The prisoners' dilemma: possible outcomes (years in jail)

		Des			
		Confess		Refuse	
Al	Confess	10	10	0	15
	Refuse	15	0	5	5

Quantitative skills 20.2

Reading and using a matrix of numerical data

In each case, Al's sentence (in years) is shown in red and Des's in blue. How do we read the matrix? Think about this from Al's perspective. If Al confesses, we look at the red entries in the first row of the table. This shows that the sentence that Al will receive depends on what Des chooses to do. If Des also confesses, then Al gets a sentence of 10 years, but if Des refuses to deal, then Al gets away scot-free.

Suppose Al instead refuses to confess. We then read across the second row, and see that Al gets a heavy sentence if he refuses to confess but Des confesses (i.e. testifies against Al), but if they both refuse to confess they both get off relatively lightly.

If both Al and Des refuse to deal, they will be convicted of the minor offence, and each will go down for 5 years. However, if Al confesses and Des refuses to deal, Al will get off completely free, and Des will take the full rap of 15 years. If Des confesses and Al refuses, the reverse happens. However, if both confess, they will each get 10 years.

Think about this situation from Al's point of view, remembering that the prisoners cannot communicate, so Al does not know what Des will choose to do and vice versa. You can see from Table 20.3 that, whatever Des chooses to do, Al will be better off confessing. John Nash referred to such a situation as a **dominant strategy**.

The dilemma is, of course, symmetric, so for Des too the dominant strategy is to confess. The inevitable result is that if both prisoners are selfish they will both confess — and both will then get 10 years in jail. If they had both refused to deal, they would *both* have been better off; but this is too risky a strategy for either of them to adopt. A refusal to deal might have led to 15 years in jail.

The prisoners' dilemma and economics

What has this to do with economics? Suppose there are two firms (Diamond Tools and Better Spades) operating in a duopoly market (i.e. a market with only two firms). Each firm has a choice of producing 'high' output or 'low' output. The profit made by one firm depends on two things: its own output, and the output of the other firm.

Table 20.4 shows the range of possible outcomes for a particular time period. Consider Diamond Tools: if it chooses 'low' when Better Spades also chooses 'low',

> **Key term**
>
> **dominant strategy** a situation in game theory where a player's best strategy is independent of those chosen by others

> **Knowledge check 20.7**
>
> Why does Des face a dominant strategy to confess?

it will make £2 million profit (and so will Better Spades); but if Diamond Tools chooses 'low' when Better Spades chooses 'high', Diamond Tools will make zero profits and Better Spades will make £3 million.

The situation that maximises joint profits is for both firms to produce low; but suppose you were taking decisions for Diamond Tools — what would you choose?

Table 20.4 Diamond Tools and Better Spades: possible outcomes (profits in £m)

		Better Spades			
		High		Low	
Diamond Tools	High	1	1	3	0
	Low	0	3	2	2

If Better Spades produces 'low', you will maximise profits by producing 'high', whereas if Better Spades produces 'high', you will still maximise profits by producing high! So Diamond Tools has a dominant strategy to produce high — it is the profit-maximising action whatever Better Spades does, even though it means that joint profits will be lower.

Given that the table is symmetric, Better Spades faces the same decision process, and also has a dominant strategy to choose high, so they always end up in the northwest corner of the table, even though southeast would be better for each of them. Furthermore, after they have made their choices and seen what the other has chosen, each firm feels justified by its actions, and thinks that it took the right decision, given the rival's move. This is known as a **Nash equilibrium**, which has the characteristic that neither firm needs to amend its behaviour in any future period. This model can be used to investigate a wide range of decisions that firms need to take strategically.

> **Key term**
>
> **Nash equilibrium**
> situation occurring within a game when each player's chosen strategy maximises payoffs given the other player's choice, so that no player has an incentive to alter behaviour

Exercise 20.2

Suppose there are two cinemas in a market, X and Y; you are taking decisions for firm X. You cannot communicate with the other firm; both firms are considering only the next period. Each firm is choosing whether to set price 'high' or 'low'. Your expectation is that the payoffs (in terms of profits) to the two firms are as shown in Table 20.5 (firm X in red, firm Y in blue):

Table 20.5 Cinemas X and Y: possible outcomes

		Firm Y chooses:			
		High		Low	
Firm X chooses:	High price	0	10	1	15
	Low price	15	1	4	4

a If firm Y sets price high, what strategy maximises profits for firm X?
b If firm Y sets price low, what strategy maximises profits for firm X?
c So what strategy will firm X adopt?
d What is the market outcome?
e What outcome would maximise the firms' joint profit?
f How might this outcome be achieved?
g Would the outcome be different if the game were played over repeated periods?

Collusion: cartels and price leadership

Look back at the prisoners' dilemma game in Table 20.4. It is clear that the requirement that the firms be unable to communicate with each other is a serious impediment from the firms' point of view. If both firms could agree to produce 'low', they would maximise their joint profits, but they will not risk this strategy if they cannot communicate.

If they could join together in a **cartel**, the two firms could come to an agreement to adopt the low–low strategy. However, if they were to agree to this, each firm would have a strong incentive to cheat because if each now knew that the other firm was going to produce low, they would also know that they could produce high and dominate the market — at least, given the payoffs in the table.

This is a common feature of a cartel, which is an agreement between firms on price (or on output). Collusion can bring high joint profits, but there is always the temptation for each of the member firms to cheat and try to sneak some additional market share at the expense of the other firm/s in the cartel.

Key term

cartel an agreement between firms on price and output with the intention of maximising their joint profits

Extension material: a two-firm cartel

You can see how a cartel might operate in Figure 20.6, which shows the situation facing a two-firm cartel (a duopoly). Panels (a) and (b) show the cost conditions for each of the firms, and panel (c) shows the whole market.

If the firms aim to maximise their joint profits, then they set $MR = MC$ at the level of the market (shown in panel (c)). This occurs at the joint level of output $Q_1 + Q_2$, with the price set at $P\star$. Notice that the joint marginal cost curve is the sum of the two firms' marginal cost curves.

The critical decision is how to divide the market up between the two firms. In the figure, the two firms have different cost conditions, with firm 1 operating at lower short-run average cost than firm 2. If the firms agree to set price at $P\star$, and each produces up to the point where marginal cost equals the level of

(market) marginal revenue at $MR\star$, then the market should work well. Firm 1 produces Q_1 and firm 2 produces Q_2. Joint profits are maximised, and there is a clear rule enabling the division of the market between the firms.

However, notice that firm 2 is very much the junior partner in this alliance, as it gets a much smaller market share. The temptation to cheat is obvious. If firm 2 accepts price $P\star$, it sees that its profits will be maximised at $Q_2\star$, so there is a temptation to try to steal an extra bit of market share.

Of course, the temptation is also there for firm 1, but as soon as either one of the firms begins to increase output the market price will have to fall to maintain equilibrium, and the cartel will be broken: the market will move away from the joint profit-maximising position.

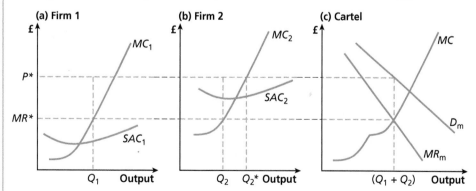

Figure 20.6 Market allocation in a two-firm cartel

Synoptic link

The operations of the Competition and Markets Authority are discussed in Chapter 23.

Knowledge check 20.8

Why should cartels be made illegal?

Key term

overt collusion a situation in which firms openly work together to agree on prices or market shares

Knowledge check 20.9

What factors might hinder collusion between firms?

There is another downside to the formation of a cartel. In most countries around the world they are illegal. For example, in the UK the operation of a cartel is illegal under the UK Competition Act, under which the Competition and Markets Authority is empowered to fine firms up to 10% of their turnover for each year the cartel is found to have been in operation.

This means that **overt collusion** is rare. The most famous example is not between firms but between nations, in the form of the Organisation of the Petroleum Exporting Countries (OPEC), which over a long period of time has operated a cartel to control the price of oil.

Conditions favouring collusion

Some conditions may favour the formation of cartels — or at least, some form of collusion between firms. The most important of these is the ability of each of the firms involved to monitor the actions of the other firms, and so ensure that they are keeping to the agreement.

In this context, it helps if there are a relatively small number of firms; otherwise it will be difficult to monitor the market. It also helps if they are producing similar goods; otherwise one firm could try to steal an advantage by varying the quality of the product. When the economy is booming it may be more difficult to monitor market shares, because all firms are likely to be expanding. If firms have excess capacity, this may increase the temptation to cheat by increasing output and stealing market share; on the other hand, it also makes it possible for the other firms to retaliate quickly. The degree of secrecy about market shares and market conditions is also important.

Collusion in practice

Although cartels are illegal, the potential gains from collusion may tempt firms to find ways of working together. In some cases, firms have joined together in rather loose strategic alliances, in which they may work together on part of their business, perhaps undertaking joint research and development or technology swaps.

For example, in 2018 Tesco joined with Carrefour in a strategic alliance to buy products for more than 19,000 stores. This was intended to consolidate its position relative to Amazon, Aldi and Lidl. It was hoped that the alliance would result in higher sales of wine, camembert and other French products being sold in Tesco stores — and more British products being sold in Carrefour's supermarkets in France. This could also be seen as a defence against the possible repercussions of Brexit.

The airline market is another sector where strategic alliances have been important, with the Star Alliance, Oneworld and SkyTeam effectively carving up the long-haul routes between them. Such alliances offer benefits to passengers, who can get access to a wider range of destinations, business-class lounges and frequent-flier rewards, and to the airlines, which can economise on airport facilities by pooling their resources. However, the net effect is to reduce competition, and the regulators have kept a close eye on behaviour. For example, in 2012 the European Commission launched an investigation into three members of the SkyTeam alliance to see whether they were operating against the interest of consumers.

Tacit collusion

Alternatively, firms may look for **tacit collusion**, in which the firms in a market observe each other's behaviour very closely and refrain from competing on price, even if they do not actually communicate with each other. Such collusion may emerge gradually over time in a market, as the firms become accustomed to market conditions and to each other's behaviour.

One way in which this may happen is through some form of *price leadership*. If one firm is a dominant producer in a market, then it may take the lead in setting the price, with the other firms following its example. It has been suggested that the OPEC cartel operated according to this model in some periods, with Saudi Arabia acting as the dominant firm.

Price leadership

An alternative is *barometric price leadership*, in which one firm tries out a price increase and then waits to see whether other firms follow. If they do, a new higher price has been reached without the need for overt discussions between the firms. On the other hand, if the other firms do not feel the time is right for the change, they will keep their prices steady and the first firm will drop back into line or else lose market share. The initiating firm need not be the same one in each round. It has been argued that the domestic air travel market in the USA has operated in this way on some internal routes. The practice is facilitated by the ease with which prices can be checked via computerised ticketing systems, so that each firm knows what the other firms are doing.

The frequency of anti-cartel cases brought by regulators in recent years suggests that firms continue to be tempted by the gains from collusion. The operation of a cartel is now a criminal act in the UK, as it has been in the USA for some time.

Non-price competition

Firms in a cartel may agree not to compete on price, but this is not the only way in which firms can compete, and there are other ways of trying to gain an advantage over rival firms — through **non-price competition**. This is an attempt by firms to differentiate their product by making it seem a less close substitute to the goods or services produced by rivals.

Firms may compete by seeking to develop brand loyalty among their customers. This could be done by advertising that sets out to distinguish a firm's product from those of its competitors. Launching a loyalty card system can also encourage customers to stick with a particular brand. The use of clever packaging, or the offering of discounts to return customers can also be effective. Products may also be differentiated through product development, adding new or improved features.

Monopsony

The discussion of market structure so far has focused on the number of sellers in a market, and the interrelationships between them. However, it is also important to consider the number of traders who are potential buyers in a market. An extreme situation would be where there is a single buyer of a good or service. Such a market structure is known as a **monopsony**.

Key terms

tacit collusion situation occurring when firms refrain from competing on price, but without communication or formal agreement between them

non-price competition steps that firms can take to compete with rival firms other than on price, such as advertising or product differentiation

monopsony a market in which there is a single buyer of a good, service or factor of production

Synoptic link

Policies introduced to promote competition and protect consumers are discussed in Chapter 23; alternative pricing strategies are discussed in Chapter 21.

Knowledge check 20.10

Give two examples of ways in which firms may indulge in non-price competition.

A single buyer may be able to exert substantial influence over the suppliers of the good when drawing up contracts on the price and quality of goods. Suppose that a firm is producing computer chips in competition with other similar firms, but enters into a contract to sell all of its output to a particular computer manufacturer. This may have advantages for the firm, which is assured of a secure market for its output. However, in return for this it may have to agree a competitive price and production schedule with the buyer, which is effectively acting as a monopsonist. The monopsonist gains by keeping its costs down and by being assured of regular supply of components. The consumer gains indirectly because of the monopsonist's low cost base.

Another example might occur in some labour markets. There may be towns in which there is a single large employer that employs a significant proportion of the local labour force. Again, such an employer might be seen to have market power within that local labour market.

Think about the supermarkets in the UK. It is possible that the sheer buying power of the large chains would leave the relatively fragmented suppliers in a weak bargaining position. The supermarkets would then be able to keep their costs down by using their bargaining strength. This has been a matter of concern for the competition authorities in the past. In this case, it might seem that there is not a single buyer, as this market is dominated by a few large supermarkets. This might be considered to be an **oligopsony**, rather than a monopsony, as there are a few buyers in the market. However, once a supplier enters into an exclusive contract to supply a particular firm, the relationship becomes more like a monopsony.

The dominance of the supermarkets in their product market has also had knock-on effects for other small retailers — the corner shops that find it difficult to match the low prices charged by the supermarkets. This has the effect of reducing consumer choice.

Evaluation of monopsony

Firms

The monopsonist gains by facing lower costs, which should increase profitability. However, its suppliers may be disadvantaged by receiving lower prices for their output — to the extent of facing the possibility of being forced out of business. On the other hand, suppliers may gain by knowing they have an assured regular buyer for their produce.

In the mid-2010s there was a high-profile campaign by dairy farmers, who argued that the supermarkets were forcing them to supply milk at an unsustainably low price. In the end, the supermarkets agreed to set a minimum price to be paid for milk supplies.

Consumers

From the consumers' point of view, they may gain by seeing lower prices, given that the monopsonist is minimising its costs. However, this of course depends on whether the monopsonist passes the lower prices on to consumers, or whether it is looking to increase its profits. There is also the question of whether the monopsonists' suppliers economise on quality in order to meet the demands of the monopsonist, which would mean that consumers are suffering.

Key term

oligopsony a market in which there are a few buyers of a good, service or factor of production

Knowledge check 20.11

What does a firm have to gain by being a monopsonist?

Employees

Workers employed by the monopsonist may or may not be better off. With the lower cost of raw materials, the monopsonist may be able to offer greater job security to its workers — or even higher wages, although whether it would do this rather than taking a higher profit margin is by no means clear.

Exercise 20.3

Discuss the extent to which consumers gain or lose as a result of supermarket buying power with their suppliers.

Exercise 20.4

For each of the following markets, identify the model that would most closely describe it (i.e. perfect competition, monopoly, monopolistic competition or oligopoly):

a a large number of firms selling branded varieties of toothpaste
b a sole supplier of postal services
c a large number of farmers producing cauliflowers, sold at a common price
d a situation in which a few large banks supply most of the market for retail banking services
e a sole supplier of rail transport
f a single employer of unskilled labour in a town

Study tip

In the context of this chapter, it is helpful to be ready with some examples of markets that conform to the various types of market structure. You need to think about this before the exam period, so that you are ready to use them.

Summary: oligopoly

- An oligopoly is a market with a few sellers, each of which takes strategic decisions based on likely rival actions and reactions.
- Because there are many ways in which firms may interact, there is no single way of modelling an oligopoly market.
- One model is the kinked demand curve model, which argues that firms' perceptions of the demand curve for their products are based on their views about whether or not rival firms will react to their own actions.
- This suggests that price is likely to remain stable over a wide range of market conditions.
- Game theory is a more flexible way of modelling interactions between firms.
- The prisoners' dilemma can demonstrate the potential benefits of collusion, but also shows that in some market situations each firm may have a dominant strategy to move the market away from the joint profit-maximising position.
- If firms could join together in a cartel, they could indeed maximise their joint profits — but there would still be a temptation for firms to cheat, and try to steal market share. Such action would break up the cartel, and move the market away from the joint profit-maximising position.
- However, cartels are illegal in most societies.
- Firms may thus look for covert ways of colluding in a market: for example, through some form of price leadership or through non-price competition.
- A monopsony is a market in which there is a single buyer of a good or service.

Competition in oligopolistic markets

An oligopolistic market is one in which firms engage in strategic competition. Strategic competition exists when the actions of one firm have an appreciable effect on its rival or rivals. Common textbook examples of oligopoly include the oil industry, motor manufacturing, soft drinks and airlines operating between particular city pairs. But oligopolists are not necessarily large firms. Close to the university campus in Southampton there is a road containing several small restaurants and takeaways. They are engaged in strategic competition because if one firm were to change its prices this would have an appreciable effect on the sales and thus profits of the others. So you can see that many firms will find themselves competing in oligopolistic markets and thus it is important that, as economists, we try to understand how such markets operate.

Modelling oligopoly

The defining characteristic of oligopoly is that the actions of one firm have an appreciable effect on its rival(s) and thus when modelling such a market it is natural to begin by assuming that each firm recognises this interdependence and takes it into account when formulating its strategy. To keep things simple, let's suppose there are just two firms in the market and each of them is thinking about what price to charge for its product. Again, just for simplicity, we will focus on two possibilities.

What is the highest price that they might conceivably choose? To answer this, consider the maximum aggregate profit that the two firms could theoretically generate. Figure 20.7 depicts the case of two firms producing identical products with identical horizontal marginal cost (average cost) curves.

The market demand curve is *D* and *MR* shows the (joint) marginal revenue accruing to the firms if they set the same price. This is the same marginal revenue curve that would have existed had the market been a monopoly.

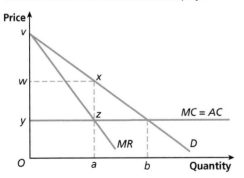

Figure 20.7 Maximising joint profits?

If the firms were producing different products (as is usually the case) then the analysis would be more complex but again we could take the monopoly price or prices to be the upper limit on possible choices.

An alternative option for each of our two firms would be to set a price below the monopoly level. If one firm were to choose the monopoly price and the other a lower price, then the latter would gain a larger market share and, provided the price was not too low, a larger profit. But if both chose the low price, each would earn less profit than if they had both chosen the monopoly price. The situation facing the firms is illustrated in Table 20.6.

Table 20.6 Profits of two firms

		Firm B chooses:			
		High price		Low price	
Firm A chooses:	High price	2	2	0	3
	Low price	3	0	1	1

The two firms, A and B must choose either a high price or a low price and the decisions are assumed to be made simultaneously, in the sense that each firm makes its decision without knowledge of the other firm's choice. The figures represent the profits of the two firms, with the first number in each cell denoting the profit of firm A and the second the profit of firm B. Thus, for example, if both opt for high (the monopoly price) then each will earn a profit of 2 (half the monopoly profit), but if, say, A chooses high and B chooses low, A will make a profit of 0 and B will make 3.

Follow-up questions

a What is the maximum joint profit that the firms could theoretically generate? Explain how this could be achieved.

b What prices will the two firms choose (high or low)?

c The passage described the situation close to the campus at the University of Southampton, in which there are several restaurants operating in close proximity. Discuss whether they would be able to maximise their joint profits through collaboration.

Case study 20.2

Theatre tickets

Arguably, the theatre scene in a large city such as London is an example of monopolistic competition, with many theatres offering different plays. Each theatre will have a partially differentiated product, in the sense that they will be mounting different productions.

If you decide to book a ticket for a play or the latest musical, you may pay a different price depending on when you buy it. Theatregoers who are anxious not to miss the latest hit production will be prepared to book early, and may have to pay a high price to be sure of getting a good seat. However, the theatres realise that the marginal cost of admitting extra people when not all the seats have been sold is very low. This can then appeal to consumers who are happy to be flexible in their plans. In other words, there may be people who are happy to queue for returned tickets and run the risk of missing out in order to get a cheaper seat.

Follow-up questions

a Discuss how this pricing policy by theatres is related to the elasticity of demand of different theatregoers.

b What are the characteristics of the theatregoers that enable this pricing policy to be implemented?

c What do the theatres gain from being able to adopt this pricing strategy?

21 Pricing strategies and contestable markets

Having examined a range of models of market structure, it is time to investigate the sorts of pricing strategy that firms may adopt, and how they decide which to go for. This chapter also discusses ways in which firms may try to prevent new firms from joining a market, in terms of both pricing and non-price strategies. The theory of contestable markets is investigated as well.

Learning objectives

After studying this chapter, you should:
- → be aware of the possible pricing rules that can be adopted by firms
- → understand the notion of cost-plus pricing, and how this may relate to profit maximisation
- → be familiar with the idea of predatory pricing
- → be aware of the concept of limit pricing
- → understand the notion of contestable markets and its implication for firms' behaviour
- → be familiar with other entry deterrence strategies

Synoptic link

Pricing strategies are needed by firms that operate under monopoly (covered in Chapter 19) and oligopoly (covered in Chapter 20).

Knowledge check 21.1

Explain why a firm under perfect competition faces a horizontal demand curve.

Synoptic link

Barriers to entry and their significance are discussed in Chapters 19 and 20.

Pricing rules

In the analysis of market structure, it was assumed that firms set out to maximise profits. However, Chapter 18 pointed out that sometimes they may set out to achieve other objectives. The price of a firm's product is a key strategic variable that must be manipulated in order to attain whatever objective the firm wishes to achieve.

Figure 21.1 illustrates the variety of pricing rules that are possible. The figure shows a firm operating under a form of market structure that is not perfect competition — because the firm faces a downward-sloping demand curve for its product shown by $AR (= D)$. Remember that under perfect competition the firm is a price-taker, so the only possible pricing rule is to accept the price prevailing in the market. However, in other forms of market structure, firms may have some power to influence the price of their product.

An important influence on the pricing strategies adopted by firms is the extent to which they face competition in their product markets. One of the key assumptions of the perfect competition model is that there is freedom of entry into and exit from the market. This chapter highlights the importance of *barriers to entry* in determining the pricing strategy adopted by firms. Such barriers may exist for several reasons, including the technology of production (as in the case of the natural monopoly discussed earlier), legal protection in the form of patent regulations, and other reasons that will emerge during the discussion.

Profit maximisation

If the firm chooses to maximise profits, it will choose output such that marginal revenue is equal to marginal cost, and will then set the price to clear the market. In terms of the figure, it will set output at Q_1 and price at P_1.

Knowledge check 21.2

Give an example of a barrier to entry.

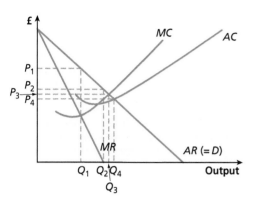

Figure 21.1 Possible pricing rules

Revenue maximisation

As noted in Chapter 18, the economist William Baumol argued that, if there is a divorce of ownership from control in the organisation of a firm, whereby the shareholders have delegated day-to-day decision making to managers (a principal–agent situation), the managers may find themselves with some freedom to pursue other objectives, such as revenue maximisation. A revenue maximiser in Figure 21.1 would choose to produce at the output level where total revenue is at a maximum, which occurs when marginal revenue is zero. This occurs at Q_2 in the figure, with the price set at P_2.

Sales maximisation

If instead managers set out to maximise the volume of sales subject to covering opportunity cost, they will choose to set output at a level such that price equals average cost, which will clear the market. In Figure 21.1 this happens at Q_4 (with price at P_4). Notice that the firm would make losses if it were to produce more than this, as it would have to sell at a price below average cost.

Allocative efficiency

It has been argued that allocative efficiency in an individual market occurs at the point where price is equal to marginal cost. In Figure 21.1 this is at Q_3 (with price P_3). However, from the firm's perspective there is no obvious reason why this should become an objective of the firm, as it confers no particular advantage.

> **Study tip**
>
> Figure 21.1 may be a useful figure for you to use if you are required to show how firms with differing objectives may take different decisions on their price–output combination. If you wish to use it, make sure that you know how to draw it correctly — and, of course, remember to label all the curves and axes correctly.

Chapter 18 noted that behavioural theories of the firm have suggested that firms may not always take decisions in the kind of mechanistic way that is implied by maximisation rules. For example, they may try to demonstrate a commitment to corporate social responsibility, by being seen to behave in the public interest. Might this affect their choice of pricing strategy?

Corporate social responsibility

One way of demonstrating such a commitment might be to refrain from setting the highest price that the market could stand. For example, a firm may announce that it is setting a 'fair' price for its products. For the firm, the question here is whether this will be the best way of demonstrating its commitment. It may consider that it will gain more publicity by maintaining its prices at the level it would normally have done, but then using some of the profits in various ways that benefit the community.

The notion of setting a fair price brings to mind the *fair trade* schemes that operate, whereby firms argue that they are acting in a way that ensures a fair price for their suppliers in developing countries. Perhaps ironically, this often entails setting a higher price for produce, providing opportunities for the consumers to make a contribution to the primary producers.

Synoptic link

Fair trade schemes are examined in Chapter 29.

Exercise 21.1

For each of the following situations, identify the pricing rule most appropriate to achieve the firm's objectives, and comment on the implications that this has for efficiency.

a A firm producing computers tries to achieve as high a market share as possible, measured in value terms.
b A firm producing tablet computers tries to make as high a surplus over costs as can be achieved.
c A national newspaper sets out to maximise circulation (subject to covering its costs), knowing that this will affect advertising revenues.
d A farmer producing cabbages finds that she cannot influence the price of her product.

▌ Pricing in practice

It seems clear that in practice most firms do not know the shape of their revenue and cost curves with any great precision. It might thus be argued that they cannot actually adopt any of these rules, and need to find alternative ways of devising a pricing strategy.

Cost-plus pricing

Key term

cost-plus pricing a pricing policy whereby firms set their price by adding a mark-up to average cost

One such approach would be to make a series of small (marginal) changes, and observe the effects each time, thereby moving gradually towards whatever objective the firm wishes to attain. However, if you were to ask managers how they decide on price, many of them would probably say that they use **cost-plus pricing** (sometimes known as mark-up pricing). In other words, they calculate average cost at their chosen output level, and then add on a mark-up to bring them some profit per unit. Indeed, when the Bank of England conducted a survey of British companies to see how they set their prices, 37% said that they set prices using a mark-up pricing rule.

Does this nullify the profit-maximising hypothesis? Not necessarily. Saying that a firm sets price as a mark-up on average cost leaves a very important question unanswered: namely, what determines the size of the mark-up that the firm can add to average cost?

The Bank of England survey also discovered that firms in markets in which there were few competitors set higher mark-ups than those in markets in which there were more firms. Mark-ups were also higher in markets where there were differentiated products than in markets producing homogeneous ones.

This pattern of behaviour is entirely compatible with the profit-maximisation hypothesis, where mark-ups are expected to be lower in the presence of a high degree of competition. In other words, cost-plus pricing may be a strategy used by firms to find the profit-maximising level of price and output, albeit through a process of trial-and-error. In other words, a firm may experiment with different prices in order to iterate towards the profit-maximising level.

Knowledge check 21.4

Why do so many firms rely on cost-plus pricing?

Summary: pricing rules in practice

- There are many pricing rules that a firm may choose to adopt, depending on the objectives it wishes to achieve.
- In practice, firms may not know their cost and revenue curves with any accuracy.
- By making marginal changes and observing the effects, they may be able to move towards the price that would achieve their chosen objective.
- Many firms use cost-plus pricing, adding a profit margin to average cost.
- The size of the mark-up may depend on the degree of competition in the market and the extent to which the product is differentiated.
- Cost-plus pricing is not inconsistent with profit maximisation.

Price wars

Another finding of the Bank of England's survey was that firms were very strong in saying that they wished to avoid price wars. This could be expected from the kinked demand curve model, where firms in an oligopoly realise that a price reduction is likely to be matched by rivals, leaving all firms with lower profits but having relatively little effect on market shares.

Synoptic link

The kinked demand curve model was discussed in Chapter 20.

Price wars: an example

And yet, price wars do break out from time to time. For example, in the early 2000s a price war broke out in the UK tabloid newspaper market. It was initiated by the *Express*, but the main protagonists were the *Mirror* and the *Sun*, which joined in after a couple of weeks. The *Mirror* cut its price from 32p to 20p, and the *Sun* from 30p to 20p.

After a week at these lower prices, the editor of the *Sun* was serving champagne in the newsroom in celebration. Their reading of the situation was that the *Mirror* had not expected the *Sun* to follow the price cut. Three weeks after the *Mirror's* price cut, it put its price back up again — followed by the *Sun*. Analysts and observers commented that the only gainers had been the readers, who had enjoyed three weeks of lower prices.

Why should firms act in this way? The *Mirror* argued that it was trying to re-brand itself, and capture new readers who would continue to read the paper even after the price returned to its normal level. This may hint at the reason for a price war — to affect the long-run equilibrium of the market. The *Sun*'s retaliation was a natural defensive response to an aggressive move.

A price war broke out in the UK tabloid market in 2002

Why initiate a price war?

Knowledge check 21.5

Why might firms not benefit from a price war in the long run?

In some cases a price war may be initiated as a strategy to drive a weaker competitor out of the market altogether. The motivation then is clear, especially if the initiator of the price war ends up with a monopoly or near-monopoly position in the market. It could be argued that this represents an attempt to maximise profits in the long run by establishing a monopoly position.

Price wars may also be initiated by firms wishing to break into a market. For example, the discount stores Aldi and Lidl launched low price offers on their range of products in an attempt to compete with UK supermarkets.

Exercise 21.2

Discuss the extent to which consumers benefit from a price war.

Predatory pricing

Key term

predatory pricing an anti-competitive strategy in which a firm sets price below average variable cost in an attempt to force a rival or rivals out of the market and achieve market dominance

Perhaps the most common context in which price wars have broken out is where an existing firm or firms have reacted to defend the market against the entry of new firms.

When the low-cost airlines such as easyJet first began to enter the market, some of the established airlines tried to counter their entry through **predatory pricing**, driving their prices down to low levels by cross-subsidising from other routes. This was countered by legal action — for example when easyJet took action against KLM in 1996. Since then, airlines have been accused of predatory pricing on a number of occasions — including British Airways in 2007 and Flybe in 2010, which were both investigated by the competition authorities. However, proven cases have been rare in recent years, perhaps because firms realise that they may be unlikely to escape prosecution.

So-called predatory pricing is illegal under English and EU law. But how could predatory pricing be proved in court? In practice, the legal definition is based on economic analysis.

Areeda–Turner principle

Chapter 18 defined the shut-down price for the firm, pointing out that if a firm was failing to cover average variable costs, its strategy should be to close down immediately, as it would be better off doing so. The courts have backed this theory, and state that a pricing strategy should be interpreted as being predatory if the price is set below average variable costs, as the only motive for remaining in business while making such losses must be to drive competitors out of business and achieve market dominance. This is known as the *Areeda–Turner principle* (after the case in which it was first argued in the USA).

Knowledge check 21.6

Why would setting a price below average variable cost be seen as proof of predatory pricing?

On the face of it, it would seem that consumers have much to gain from such strategies through the resulting lower prices. However, a predator that is successful in driving out the opposition is likely to recoup its losses by putting prices back up to profit-maximising levels thereafter, so the benefit to consumers is short lived.

In practice, clearly the low-cost airlines survived the attempts of the established airlines to hold on to their market shares. Indeed, in the post-9/11 period, which was a tough one for the airlines for obvious reasons, the low-cost airlines flourished while the more conventional established airlines went through a very difficult period indeed.

Threat of predatory pricing to deter entry

In some cases, the very threat of predatory pricing may be sufficient to deter entry by new firms, if the threat is a credible one. In other words, the existing firms need to convince potential entrants that they, the existing firms, will find it in their best interests to fight a price war, otherwise the entrants will not believe the threat. The existing firms could do this by making it known that they had surplus capacity, so that they would be able to increase output very quickly in order to drive down the price.

Whether entry will be deterred by such means may depend in part on the characteristics of the potential entrant. After all, a new firm may reckon that, if the existing firm finds it worth sacrificing profits in the short run, the rewards of dominating the market must be worth fighting for. It may therefore decide to sacrifice short-term profit in order to enter the market — especially if it is diversifying from other markets and has resources at its disposal. The winner will then be the firm that can last the longest; but, clearly, this is potentially very damaging for all concerned.

Study tip

Notice the importance of firms' perceptions in this analysis. Firms take decisions based on their perceptions of their own position in the market, and on their expectations of how rival firms will react. This is a key feature of oligopoly markets — and of economists' models that attempt to explain firms' behaviour.

Limit pricing

An associated but less extreme strategy is **limit pricing**. This assumes that the incumbent firm has some sort of cost advantage over potential entrants: for example, economies of scale.

Figure 21.2 shows a firm facing a downward-sloping demand curve, and thus having some influence over the price of its product. If the firm is maximising profits, it is setting output at Q_0 and price at P_0. As average revenue is comfortably above average cost at this price, the firm is making healthy supernormal profits.

Suppose that the natural barriers to entry in this industry are weak. The supernormal profits will be attractive to potential entrants. Given the cost conditions, the incumbent firm is enjoying the benefit of economies of scale, although producing below the minimum efficient scale.

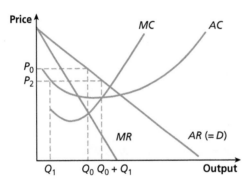

Figure 21.2 Limit pricing

If a new firm joins the market, producing on a relatively small scale, say at Q_1, the impact on the market can be analysed as follows. The immediate effect is on price, as now the amount $Q_0 + Q_1$ is being produced, pushing price down to P_2. The new firm (producing Q_1) is just covering average cost, so is making normal profits and feeling justified in having joined the market. The original firm is still making supernormal profits, but at a lower level than before. The entry of the new firm has competed away part of the original firm's supernormal profits.

Setting a lower price

One way in which the firm could have guarded against entry is by charging a lower price than P_0 to begin with. For example, if it set output at $Q_0 + Q_1$ and price at P_2, then a new entrant joining the market would push the price down to a level below P_2, and without the benefit of economies of scale would make losses and exit the market. In any case, if the existing firm has been in the market for some time, it will have gone through a process of learning by doing, and therefore will have a lower average cost curve than the potential entrant. This makes it more likely that limit pricing can be used.

Thus, by setting a price below the profit-maximising level, the original firm is able to maintain its market position in the longer run. This could be a reason for avoiding making too high a level of supernormal profits in the short run, in order to make profits in the longer term.

Notice that such a strategy need not be carried out by a monopolist, but could also occur in an oligopoly, where existing firms may jointly seek to protect their market against potential entry.

Contestable markets

It has been argued that in some markets, in order to prevent the entry of new firms, the existing firm would have to charge such a low price that it would be unable to reap any supernormal profits at all.

This theory was developed by industrial economist William Baumol, and is known as the theory of **contestable markets**. It was in recognition of this theory that the monopoly model in Chapter 19 included the assumption that there must be no substitutes for the good, *either actual or potential*.

For a market to be contestable, it must have no barriers to entry or exit and no sunk costs. *Sunk costs* refer to costs that a firm incurs in setting up a business and which cannot be recovered if the firm exits the market. Furthermore, new firms in the market must have no competitive disadvantage compared with the incumbent firm(s): in other words, they must have access to the same technology, and there must be no significant learning-by-doing effects. Entry and exit must be rapid.

Under these conditions, the incumbent firm cannot set a price that is higher than average cost, because as soon as it does it will open up the possibility of **hit-and-run entry** by new firms, which can enter the market and compete away the supernormal profits.

Consider Figure 21.3, which shows a monopoly firm in a market. The argument is that, if the monopolist charges the profit-maximising price, then if the market is contestable the firm will be vulnerable to hit-and-run entry — a firm could come into the market, take some of the supernormal profits, then exit again. The only way the monopolist can avoid this happening is to set price equal to average cost, so that there are no supernormal profits to act as an incentive for entry.

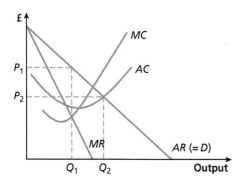

Figure 21.3 Contestability

Contestability in practice

On the face of it, the conditions for contestability sound pretty stringent. In particular, the firm in Figure 21.3 enjoys some economies of scale, so you would think that some sunk costs had been incurred.

However, suppose a firm has a monopoly on a domestic air route between two destinations. An airline with surplus capacity — that is, a spare aircraft sitting in

Knowledge check 21.7

Explain why setting a price equal to average cost could be a rational strategy.

Key terms

contestable market a market in which the existing firm makes only normal profit, as it cannot set a higher price without attracting entry, owing to the absence of barriers to entry and sunk costs

hit and run entry where a firm enters a market to take short-run supernormal profits knowing it can exit without incurring costs

Synoptic link

Sunk costs were first defined in Chapter 18, and now become critical as an essential ingredient of contestability.

Knowledge check 21.8

What are the four key conditions for a market to be contestable?

a hangar — could enter this route and exit again without incurring sunk costs in response to profits being made by the incumbent firm. This is an example of how contestability may limit the ability of the incumbent firm to use its market power.

Notice in this example that, although the firm only makes normal profits, neither productive nor allocative efficiency is achieved.

A moot point is whether the threat of entry will in fact persuade firms that they cannot set a price above average cost. If entry and exit are so rapid, perhaps the firms can risk making some profit above normal profits and then respond to entry very aggressively if and when it happens. After all, it is difficult to think of an example in which there are absolutely no sunk costs. Almost any business is going to have to advertise in order to find customers, and such advertising expenditure cannot be recovered.

This will be re-examined in the Chapter 23 when discussing competition policy, as it is an important issue in that context, and the degree of contestability may affect the perception of how much market power is in the hands of existing firms.

The impact of the internet on contestability

The growth of the internet has had a significant impact on the contestability of markets and hence on competitiveness. By making information more freely available, the internet has given consumers improved knowledge of market conditions and enabled them to make more informed choices. Furthermore, the growth of online sales has made it much easier for new firms to enter markets.

One good example of this is the travel industry. In 2016, UK residents made more than 70 million trips abroad, so this is a significant sector. In the past, many overseas trips, especially holidays, were arranged by the high-street travel agents. Although there were many retail outlets, the largest chains of travel agents were responsible for a significant market share. The internet has revolutionised this sector, with online firms competing effectively with the established firms, and individual consumers able to make their own travel arrangements much more effectively. This is an example of where increased contestability of a market has resulted in an increase in competitiveness.

Exercise 21.3

Discuss the extent to which the following markets may be considered to be contestable — or to have become more so in recent years:

a opticians
b travel agents
c financial services
d the postal service
e aircraft manufacture

Other entry deterrence strategies

Pricing is not the only strategy that firms adopt in order to deter entry by new firms. Another approach that has been used over a wide range of economic activities is to raise the fixed costs of being in the industry.

Advertising and publicity

Advertising can be regarded as a component of fixed costs because expenditure on it does not vary directly with the volume of output. If the firms in an industry typically spend heavily on advertising, it will be more difficult for new firms to become established, as they too will need to advertise widely in order to attract customers. If Apple launches a new iPhone, or Samsung releases a new version of their Galaxy phone, this is always accompanied by a high-profile television campaign designed to reinforce brand loyalty — and perhaps to attract new customers. By having a strong brand image and strong customer loyalty, new firms trying to break into the market face an enormous challenge in order to gain credibility in the market.

Notice that such costs are also sunk costs, and cannot be recovered if the new firm fails to gain a foothold. It has sometimes been suggested that the cost of excessive advertising should be included in calculations of the social cost of monopoly.

Knowledge check 21.9

Why could advertising be regarded as a deterrent to entry by new firms?

Research and development

A characteristic of some industries is the heavy expenditure undertaken on research and development (R&D). A prominent example is the pharmaceutical industry, which spends large amounts on researching new drugs — and new cosmetics.

This is another component of fixed costs, as it does not vary with the volume of production. Again, new firms wanting to break into the market know that they will need to invest heavily in R&D if they are going to keep up with the new and better drugs and cosmetics always coming on to the market.

The high costs of R&D in the pharmaceutical industry can deter new firms entering the market

Exercise 21.4

For each of the following, explain under what circumstances the action of the firm constitutes a barrier to entry and discuss whether there is a strategic element to it, or whether it might be regarded as a 'natural' or 'innocent' barrier.

a A firm takes advantage of economies of scale to reduce its average costs of production.
b A firm holds a patent on the sale of a product.
c A firm engages in widespread advertising of its product.
d A firm installs surplus capacity relative to normal production levels.
e A firm produces a range of very similar products under different brand names.
f A firm chooses not to set price at the profit-maximising level.
g A firm spends extensively on research and development in order to produce a better product.

Market structure and competitiveness

A good way of gaining insight into the way in which market structure can affect the intensity of competitiveness in a market is to look at examples of markets that have experienced a change in market conditions that has induced a change in market structure. The process of deregulation affords such an opportunity, and there have been several examples of this in recent years. The low-cost airlines have transformed the face of air travel. They show some of the effects of changing market structure, and how firms are able to become profitable by understanding some economic analysis.

The low-cost airlines appeared on the scene as long ago as 1971, with the advent of Southwestern in the USA, followed by Ryanair in 1985 and easyJet in 1995. There is now a plethora of such companies.

This market provides an illustration of how intensified competition can affect the operation of markets. Before the advent of the low-cost airlines, the market for air travel was dominated by large national carriers, in many cases either state-run or heavily subsidised by governments. As time went by, these large airlines began to join together in strategic alliances that enabled them to work together yet maintain their individual characters. The market seemed to be consolidating and was effectively becoming more concentrated.

Synoptic link

The effects of deregulation are discussed in Chapter 23.

Deregulation provided an opening for changes in the market structure, by reducing the barriers to entry of new firms. However, in order to exploit that opening, the budget airlines needed a good understanding of economic analysis. Their success has been built on a thorough understanding of cost structures and a recognition of the contestability of airlines, together with the judicious use of price discrimination.

Focus on costs

Profits depend on costs as well as revenue. EasyJet (not to mention other budget airlines, such as Ryanair and Flybe) took a close look at the structure of costs. By focusing on each individual item of costs and looking for ways of cutting costs to a minimum, the budget airlines were able to achieve profitability.

In part, this has been connected with the understanding of demand. As the budget airlines developed, they offered a 'no frills' approach, doing away with pre-assigned seats and pre-issued tickets, free in-flight catering, a separate business class and so on. They also used more remote airports, where charges were relatively low.

By paying careful attention to the various forms of costs, the budget airlines were able to expand, to make profits and to transform air travel.

The arrival of low-cost airlines transformed the market structure for air travel

Pricing strategy

The focus on costs was only part of the strategy. As far as its pricing strategy was concerned, easyJet claimed on its website that it 'operates a very simple fare structure…based on supply and demand'. The nature of the price structure is that passengers who book early pay the lowest prices, whereas those who book close to their travel time pay the highest prices. This is an illustration of how a firm can use price discrimination.

You might expect that in a competitive market, the price structure would be the opposite. If prices follow costs, the marginal cost to easyJet of carrying an extra passenger is likely to be pretty low, so the flight could be filled up by offering last-minute deals, with the price being driven close to marginal cost, as would happen in a perfectly competitive market. But this is clearly not happening at easyJet, as the later a passenger books, the higher the price that they face.

This suggests that easyJet took a different view, taking into account the nature of demand, and using price discrimination on its flights. People who book at the last minute are likely to be business travellers who need to fly urgently, perhaps for a business meeting or to clinch a deal. Such customers are likely to have low elasticity of demand, and thus be prepared to pay a higher price for their ticket.

This is in contrast to those who can book well in advance, who are more likely to be people travelling for pleasure — visiting relatives or going on holiday. For these travellers, the choice of when to fly is more flexible. This means there are more possible flights from which they can choose. And we know that when there are substitutes for a commodity, the price elasticity of demand is high. It is for these customers that easyJet can offer the low prices that we see being advertised. After all, at the prices that easyJet advertises, it probably costs some customers more to get to the airport than it costs for the flight! EasyJet can make use of this difference in demand elasticity to charge different prices to different customers, even if the product (such as the flight from London to Nice) is the same for all of them.

How competition transformed the market

The entry of the budget airlines caused the existing firms to reconsider the way in which they operate. Some reacted by setting up their own budget subsidiaries, with varying degrees of success. Others had to accept that they needed to focus on longer-haul flights. The budget airlines case therefore provides another example of how competition can transform a market, and how contestability can affect firms' behaviour.

It is also worth noting that the low-cost airlines flourished not only by taking customers away from the existing airlines, but also by tapping a new customer base. By offering low fares and easy accessibility, they have attracted passengers who would not otherwise have dreamed of flying. As these airlines became more established, and as competition among them intensified, they began to bring back some premium facilities, such as choice of seat, so non-price competition began to come into play.

Summary: pricing strategies and entry deterrence

- Although price wars are expected to be damaging for the firms involved, they do break out from time to time.
- They may occur when firms wish to increase their market shares, or when existing firms wish to deter the entry of new firms into the market.
- Predatory pricing is an extreme strategy that forces all firms to endure losses. It is normally invoked in an attempt to eliminate a competitor, and is illegal in many countries.
- Limit pricing occurs when a firm or firms choose to set price below the profit-maximising level in order to prevent entry. The limit price is the highest price that an existing firm can set without allowing entry.
- In some cases, the limit price may enable the incumbent firm or firms to make only normal profit. Such a market is said to be contestable.
- Contestability requires that there are no barriers to entry or exit and no sunk costs — and that the incumbent firm(s) have no cost advantage over hit-and-run entrants.
- Firms have adopted other strategies designed to deter entry, such as using advertising or R&D spending to raise the cost of entry by adding to required fixed costs.

Case study 21.1

Airline contestability

At the time of US deregulation, which began in 1978, a number of influential economists argued that an absence of actual competitors in airline markets did not indicate a lack of competition. Airline markets, they argued, are *contestable*, and therefore the mere threat of entry is sufficient to keep prices at or near competitive levels. To what extent is this a correct interpretation of these markets?

Aircraft are by nature, highly mobile ('capital with wings'). This is the basis of the argument that airline markets are contestable — if an aircraft can easily be moved between markets then there are no sunk costs associated with its use in any particular market. There have been many empirical studies of US airline markets in the 40 years since deregulation, and the particular question of whether the markets are contestable has been investigated in a number of ways.

One approach is to see whether prices depend on the number of actual competitors on a route. If the market is contestable, then there should be no relationship between the two. Many studies have found, however, that actual competition does matter. For example, some research by Weiher, Sickles and Perloff found that the average ratio of price to marginal cost was 3.3 on routes operated by a monopolist but 2.2 for routes with two airlines.

A second approach is to seek to compare the effect of actual and potential competitors. This, of course, raises the question of how to identify potential competitors. One method is to define a potential entrant to a city-pair as an airline that serves one or both of the endpoints but not the route itself. Studies of this type find that the impact of a potential entrant on prices is between one-tenth and one-third of the impact of an actual competitor.

Finally, there has been some analysis of the impact of actual entry onto or exit from a route. The evidence here suggests that both entry and exit have an impact on price, the former reducing price by about 9% on average and the latter causing price to rise by about 10%.

Taken together, the research provides strong evidence that airline markets are not contestable and that, while potential entrants do have some impact on prices, their effect is small in relation to that of actual competitors.

There are a number of reasons why airline markets are not contestable. First, in practice passengers do not respond instantaneously to price differentials, and so incumbents can react before an entrant is able to capture the entire market. Furthermore, entry typically does involve set-up costs that cannot be recovered if the firm subsequently exits the market. Thus hit-and-run entry is unlikely to be a profitable strategy. Second, experience has shown that incumbent airlines have a variety of means of deterring entry, in addition to price retaliation. For example, frequent flyer programmes increase the relative attractiveness of airlines with extensive networks over small entrants.

To what extent are airline markets contestable?

Follow-up questions

a Explain the key characteristics of a contestable market, and why economists initially thought that airline markets would be a good example.

b Explain and evaluate the evidence presented in the passage which suggests that contestability might not be as strong as had been thought.

The labour market

An important market in any economy is the market for labour, and no doubt you will one day be part of that market, if you are not already. Labour is a crucial factor of production for firms, so the demand for labour comes from firms wanting to hire workers. People need to work in order to earn income, which is done through the medium of supplying labour. In this chapter, you will see the way in which the demand for labour from firms and the supply of labour by workers come together in the labour market. The chapter also discusses the nature of equilibrium in the labour market, and some reasons why it might not always be possible to reach equilibrium.

Learning objectives

After studying this chapter, you should:
→ understand the factors which influence the demand for and supply of labour
→ appreciate that the demand for labour is a derived demand
→ understand the factors that influence the supply of labour to a particular occupation
→ be aware of how market failure can affect labour markets
→ be able to demonstrate labour market equilibrium
→ be able to use demand and supply analysis to examine the effects of government policies that affect the labour market
→ appreciate the significance of the elasticity of demand for and supply of labour

Synoptic link

This chapter builds on material that was contained in Theme 1, especially the early chapters that developed the demand and supply model. This chapter applies this analysis to the labour market. The concepts of elasticity, producer surplus and externalities are also drawn into the discussion.

The demand for labour

What do firms do and why do they demand labour? In Chapter 17, a firm was defined as 'an organisation that brings together factors of production in order to produce output'. The aim of a firm, therefore, is to produce output to sell in order to generate revenue and make profits. Labour is one of the key factors of production used by firms as part of this process.

This means that firms do not demand labour for its own sake, but for the sake of the revenue that is obtained from selling the output that labour produces. The demand for labour is thus an example of a **derived demand.** Understanding this is crucial for an analysis of the labour market.

Key term

derived demand demand for a good or service not for its own sake, but for what it produces, e.g. labour is demanded for the output that it produces

To illustrate this, consider a firm that manufactures cars. The firm hires workers to operate the machinery that is used in production. However, the firm does not hire a labourer because it is a nice organisation. The firm aims to make profit by selling the cars produced, and the worker is needed because of the labour services that he or she provides. This notion of derived demand underpins the analysis of labour markets.

As in any demand and supply analysis, the price is important: in the case of a labour market, we consider the wage rate as being the price of labour.

Study tip

There are two key things to realise here: that the wage rate is seen as the price of labour and that the demand for labour is a derived demand. Be clear in your mind about this notion of a derived demand, as it underpins much of the discussion of labour markets.

It is important to be aware that although there is a tendency to talk about 'the' labour market, or about 'unemployment' in the aggregate, in reality there is not a single labour market in the economy, but a multitude of sub-markets. This partly reflects the fact that individual workers differ from each other in terms of their characteristics and skills. There are different markets for different types of labour, such as lawyers, accountants, cleaners and bricklayers. There may also be geographic sub-markets, given that labour may be relatively immobile. An employer may perceive that it operates in a particular industry, so there may be a labour market for an industry, or for particular skills within an industry. Indeed, a firm may find itself operating in several different sub-markets.

This interlocking pattern of labour markets is likely to evolve over time, as technology changes, bringing with it the need for different skills, and a different balance of skills.

The demand curve for labour

Consider the demand for a particular type of labour — in other words, a particular labour market. Given that the demand for labour is a derived demand, the first factor that will determine the demand for labour is the output that labour produces (and the revenue that the firm will generate from selling it). Given the law of diminishing returns, the additional output produced by labour as more labour is deployed is expected to diminish, other things remaining equal. This is because capital becomes relatively scarcer as the amount of labour increases without a corresponding increase in capital.

If the firm faces a downward-sloping demand curve for its product, it has to reduce the selling price in order to sell more output. An important consideration is how much labour input to use. This decision is based partly on the productivity of labour, but it will also depend on the cost of labour (its price).

The main cost of using labour is the wages paid to the workers. There may be other costs — hiring costs and so on — but these can be set aside for the moment. We would expect the demand for labour to vary with the wage rate, and to be downward-sloping. If we assume that the firm is operating under perfect competition in the labour market, it must accept the wage rate set by the market. Figure 22.1 illustrates this, where D_L is the demand for labour and $W^\star$ is the market wage rate. The firm will employ workers up to $L^\star$.

Knowledge check 22.1

Explain why the demand for capital machinery is a derived demand.

Synoptic link

The law of diminishing returns was introduced in Chapter 18; it is especially important here in influencing the demand for labour.

Knowledge check 22.2

What is meant by the 'law of diminishing returns'?

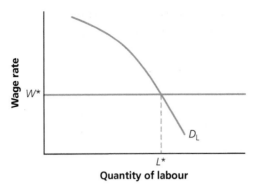

Figure 22.1 The labour input decision of a profit-maximising firm

Factors affecting the position of the demand for labour curve

There are a number of factors that determine the *position* of a firm's labour demand curve. Because the demand for labour is a derived demand, the amount of output that labour is able to produce will be an important factor. If labour becomes more productive for some reason, then this will lead to an increase in the demand for labour. For example, if a new technological advance raises the productivity of labour, it will also affect the position of the labour demand curve.

In Figure 22.2, you can see how the demand for labour would shift if there were an increase in the productivity of labour as a result of new technology. Initially, demand is at D_{L0}, but the increased technology pushes the curve to D_{L1}. If the wage remains at $W^\star$, the quantity of labour hired by the firm increases from L_0 to L_1. Similarly, in the long run, if a firm expands the size of its capital stock, this will also affect the demand for labour.

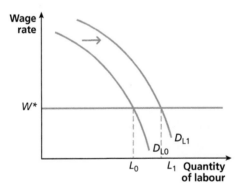

Figure 22.2 The effect of improved technology

It can also be seen that because the demand for labour is a derived demand, a change in the revenue that the firm receives from selling the output that labour produces will affect the demand for labour. For example, suppose that in a competitive product market, the equilibrium price of a good falls — perhaps as a result of a shift in the demand curve for the good. This will have a knock-on effect on the firm's demand for labour, as illustrated in Figure 22.3. Initially, the firm was demanding L_0 labour at the wage rate $W^\star$, but the fall in demand for the product leads to a fall in the revenue that the firm receives from selling the good (even though the productivity of labour has not changed), so the labour demand curve shifts from D_{L0}

to D_{L1}. Only L_1 labour is now demanded at the wage rate $W^\star$. This suggests that the demand for labour will tend to increase during a boom period, but fall during a recession.

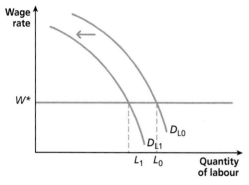

Figure 22.3 The effect of a fall in the demand for a firm's product on the demand for labour

Knowledge check 22.3

Identify three factors that influence the position of the labour demand curve.

Summary: the demand for labour

- The demand for labour is a derived demand, as the firm wants labour not for its own sake, but for the output that it produces.
- In the short run, a firm faces diminishing returns to increases in labour input if capital is held constant.
- The firm has a downward-sloping demand curve for labour.
- The position of the firm's labour demand curve depends on those factors that influence the productivity of labour, such as technology and efficiency, but also on the price of the firm's product.

Wage elasticity of the demand for labour

In addition to the factors affecting the *position* of the demand for labour curve, it is also important to examine its *shape*. In particular, what factors affect the firm's elasticity of demand for labour with respect to changes in the wage rate? In other words, how sensitive is a firm's demand for labour to a change in the wage rate (the cost of labour)?

Chapter 2 examined the influences on the price elasticity of demand, and identified the most important as being the availability of substitutes, the relative size of expenditure on a good in the overall budget, and the time period over which the elasticity is measured. In looking at the elasticity of demand for labour, similar influences can be seen to be at work.

- *Availability of substitutes:* one significant effect on the elasticity of demand for labour is the extent to which other factors of production, such as capital, can be substituted for labour in the production process. If capital or some other factor can be readily substituted for labour, then an increase in the wage rate (ceteris paribus) will induce the firm to reduce its demand for labour by relatively more than if there were no substitute for labour. The extent to which labour and capital are substitutable varies between economic activities, depending on the technology of production, as there may be some sectors in which it is relatively easy for labour and capital to be substituted, and others in which it is quite difficult.

Knowledge check 22.4

Consider a firm making designer jewellery. Would you expect it to be straightforward or difficult for the firm to substitute capital for labour?

■ *Size of expenditure:* the share of labour costs in the firm's total costs is important in determining the elasticity of demand for labour. In many service activities, labour is a highly significant share of total costs, so firms tend to be sensitive to changes in the cost of labour. However, in some capital-intensive manufacturing activities, labour may comprise a much smaller share of total production costs.

■ *Time period:* capital will tend to be inflexible in the short run. Therefore, if a firm faces an increase in wages, it may have little flexibility in substituting towards capital in the short run, so the demand for labour may be relatively inelastic. However, in the longer term the firm will be able to adjust the factors of production towards a more efficient overall balance. Therefore, the elasticity of demand for labour is likely to be higher in the long run than in the short run.

Knowledge check 22.5

Explain why the demand for labour will be more elastic in the long run than in the short run.

Whether capital can be substituted for labour varies, depending on the technology of production

These three influences closely parallel the analysis of what affects the price elasticity of demand. However, as the demand for labour is a derived demand, there is an additional influence that must be taken into account: the price elasticity of demand for the product. The more price elastic is demand for the product, the more sensitive will the firm be to a change in the wage rate, as high elasticity of demand for the product limits the extent to which an increase in wage costs can be passed on to consumers in the form of higher prices.

In order to derive an industry demand curve for labour, it is necessary to add up the quantities of labour that firms in that industry would want to demand at any given wage rate, given the price of the product. As individual firms' demand curves are downward sloping, the industry demand curve will also slope downwards. In other words, more labour will be demanded at a lower wage rate.

Summary: the elasticity of the demand for labour

- The elasticity of demand for labour depends partly on the degree to which capital may be substituted for labour in the production process.
- The share of labour in a firm's total costs will also affect the elasticity of demand for labour.
- Labour demand will tend to be more elastic in the long run than in the short run, as the firm needs time to adjust its production process following a change in market conditions.
- As the demand for labour is a derived demand, the elasticity of labour demand will also depend on the price elasticity of demand for the firm's product.

Exercise 22.1

Using diagrams, explain how each of the following will affect a firm's demand for labour:

a a fall in the selling price of the firm's product

b adoption of improved working practices, which improve labour productivity

c an increase in the wage (in a situation where the firm must accept the wage as market determined)

d an increase in the demand for the firm's product

Labour supply

On the supply side of the labour market, it is important to consider the factors that will influence the quantity of labour that workers wish to supply. Again, it may be supposed that this will depend partly on the wage rate.

So far, labour supply has been considered only as it is perceived by a firm, and the assumption has been that the firm is in a perfectly competitive market for labour, and therefore cannot influence the 'price' of labour. Hence the firm sees the labour supply curve as being perfectly elastic, as drawn in Figure 22.1 above.

However, for the industry as a whole, labour supply is unlikely to be flat. Intuitively, you might expect to see an upward-sloping labour supply curve. The reason for this is that more people will tend to offer themselves for work when the wage is relatively high. However, this is only part of the background to the industry labour supply curve.

An increase in the wage rate paid to workers in an industry will have two effects. On the one hand, it will tend to attract more workers into that industry, thereby increasing labour supply. However, the change may also affect the supply decisions of workers already in that industry, and for existing workers an increase in the wage rate may have ambiguous effects.

Individual labour supply

Consider an individual worker who is deciding how many hours of labour to supply. Every choice comes with an *opportunity cost*, so if a worker chooses to take more leisure time, he or she is choosing to forgo income-earning opportunities. In other words, the wage rate can be seen as the opportunity cost of leisure. It is the income that the worker has to sacrifice in order to enjoy leisure time.

Knowledge check 22.6

Explain why the supply of labour may be perfectly elastic for a firm operating under perfect competition in the labour market.

The effect of the wage rate on labour supply

Now think about the likely effects of an increase in the wage rate. Such an increase raises the opportunity cost of leisure. This in turn has two effects. First, as leisure time is now more costly, there will be a substitution effect against leisure. In other words, workers will be motivated to work longer hours.

However, as the higher wage brings the worker a higher level of real income, a second effect comes into play, encouraging the consumption of more goods and services — including leisure, if it is assumed that leisure is a *normal good*.

Notice that these two effects work against each other. The substitution effect encourages workers to offer more labour at a higher wage because of the effect of the change in the opportunity cost of leisure. However, the income effect encourages the worker to demand more leisure as a result of the increase in income. The net effect could go either way.

It might be argued that at relatively low wages the substitution effect will tend to be the stronger. However, as the wage continues to rise, the income effect may gradually become stronger, so that at some wage level the worker will choose to supply less labour and will demand more leisure. The individual labour supply curve will then be backward bending, as shown in Figure 22.4, where an increase in the wage rate above $W^\star$ induces the individual to supply fewer hours of work in order to enjoy more leisure time.

Knowledge check 22.7

Define the term 'normal good'.

Knowledge check 22.8

Explain how a fall in the wage rate affects the opportunity cost of leisure.

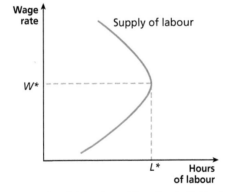

Figure 22.4 A backward-bending individual labour supply curve

Non-pecuniary benefits

It is important to realise that decisions about labour supply may also be influenced by job satisfaction. A worker who finds his or her work to be satisfying may be prepared to accept a lower wage than a worker who really hates every minute spent at work. Indeed, firms may provide other **non-pecuniary benefits** — in other words, firms may provide benefits that are not fully reflected in wages. These are sometimes known as *fringe benefits*. They might include a subsidised canteen or other social facilities. They could also include in-work training, better-than-average pension schemes or job security. If this is the case, then in choosing one job over another, workers may consider not only the wage rate, but the overall package offered by employers. In other words, by providing non-pecuniary benefits, firms may effectively shift the position of their labour supply curves, as workers will be prepared to supply more labour at any given wage rate. It may also be seen as a way in which firms can encourage loyalty, and thus hold on to workers when the job market is tight.

Key term

non-pecuniary benefits benefits offered to workers by firms that are not financial in nature

Industry labour supply

The labour supply curve for an industry can be expected to be upward sloping, as in Figure 22.5. The reason for this is that more people will tend to offer themselves for work when the wage is relatively high. People will join the market at a higher wage rate, either from outside of the workforce altogether or from other industries where wages have not risen. In this way, wages act as a signal to workers about which industries are offering the best returns to work. This is another example of the way in which the price mechanism operates to allocate resources within a society.

Figure 22.5 A labour supply curve

A number of factors may influence the position of the labour supply curve. An increase in the rate of unemployment benefits payable could mean that for some industries the number of people prepared to offer themselves for work may fall, resulting in a leftward shift of the labour supply curve. On the other hand, an increase in the rate of immigration to a country could shift the supply curve of labour to the right.

An important issue here concerns the decision of individuals about whether to participate in the workforce. The **participation rate** measures the proportion of the population of working age who are employed or looking for work. This excludes people such as students, those who have taken early retirement, and those who for other reasons are not looking for work. Those not looking for work may include parents undertaking childcare, but also *discouraged workers*: those who have failed to gain employment and are no longer seeking work.

The wage elasticity of supply

There are several factors that may influence the elasticity of labour supply: in other words, the extent to which an increase in the wage rate in a labour market will encourage an increase in the supply of labour. First, this may depend on whether there is unemployment, so that there are workers ready to take up jobs. However, there are also likely to be obstacles to flexibility in labour supply. For example, the unemployed workers available for work may not have the skills needed for the vacancies available, so that training may be needed. Labour supply may thus be relatively inelastic in the short run. The supply of labour for unskilled workers is likely to be more elastic than for occupations that require higher-level skills as there may be a larger pool of workers available.

In the long run if wage differentials persist, labour supply may be more elastic. More people may be attracted into high-paid occupations, industries or regions. Alternatively, firms may shift their locations to where labour is more plentiful.

> **Key term**
>
> **participation rate**
> the proportion of the population of working age who are in employment or seeking work

> **Knowledge check 22.9**
>
> Identify the influences on the position of the labour supply curve for an industry.

Knowledge check 22.10

If the economy is at full employment, is the supply of labour likely to be elastic or inelastic?

Summary: labour supply

- For an individual worker, a choice needs to be made between income earned from working and leisure.
- The wage rate can be seen as the opportunity cost of leisure.
- An increase in the wage rate will encourage workers to substitute work for leisure through a substitution effect.
- However, there is also an income effect, which may mean that workers will demand more leisure at higher income levels.
- If the income effect dominates the substitution effect, then the individual labour supply curve may become backward bending.
- At the industry level, higher wages will encourage more people into the industry, such that the industry supply curve is not expected to be backward bending.
- Labour supply is likely to be more elastic in the long run than in the short run.

Labour market equilibrium

Bringing demand and supply curves together for an industry shows how the equilibrium wage is determined. Figure 22.6 shows a downward-sloping demand curve (D_L) and an upward-sloping labour supply curve (S_L). Equilibrium is found at the intersection of demand and supply. If the wage is lower than $W^\star$ employers will not be able to fill all their vacancies, and will have to offer a higher wage to attract more workers. If the wage is higher than $W^\star$ there will be an excess supply of labour, and the wage will drift down until $W^\star$ is reached and equilibrium obtains.

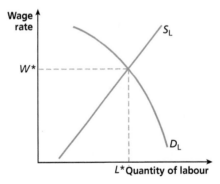

Figure 22.6 Labour market equilibrium

Synoptic link

Notice that in this chapter, labour market equilibrium is being discussed from a microeconomic perspective. Macroeconomic analysis sees unemployment in an overall context as it views the economy in aggregate. However, macroeconomics also takes into account 'the' labour market, and views unemployment as a total for the economy. It is important to make these links between microeconomic analysis of individual markets and macroeconomic analysis of the aggregates. Unemployment is discussed from a macroeconomic perspective in Chapter 10.

We can examine the effects of changes in market conditions. For instance, a change in the factors that determine the position of the labour demand curve will induce a shift of labour demand and an adjustment in the equilibrium wage. Suppose there is an increase in the demand for the firm's product. This will lead to a rightward shift in the demand for labour, say from D_{L0} to D_{L1} in Figure 22.7. This in turn will lead to a new market equilibrium, with the wage rising from W_0 to W_1.

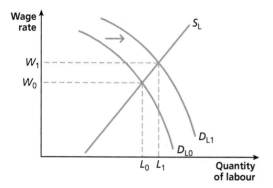

Figure 22.7 An increase in the demand for labour

Exercise 22.2

Using diagrams, explain how the market equilibrium will change for an industry if:

a there is an increase in the rate of immigration into a country

b new health and safety legislation raises the cost of labour

c there is an increase in the selling price of a firm's product

This may not be the final equilibrium position, however. If the higher wages in this market now encourage workers to switch from other industries in which wages have not risen, this will lead to a longer-term shift to the right of the labour supply curve. In a free market, the shift will continue until wage differentials are no longer sufficient to encourage workers to transfer.

Extension material: explaining wage differentials

A common topic of debate concerns why there should be such large differences in pay between people in different occupations. For example, why should footballers in the top teams get paid so much? Demand and supply in the labour market can provide part of the answer.

Consider an example of differential earnings — say, surgeons and butchers. First think about the surgeons. Surgeons are in relatively inelastic supply, at least in the short run. The education required to become a surgeon is long and demanding, and is certainly essential for entry into the occupation. Furthermore, not everyone is cut out to become a surgeon, as this is a field that requires certain innate abilities and talents. This implies that the supply of surgeons is limited, and does not vary a great deal with the wage rate.

The situation may be reinforced by the fact that, once an individual has trained as a surgeon, there may be few alternative occupations to which, if disgruntled, he or she could transfer. There is a natural limit to how many surgeons there are *and* to their willingness to exit from the market.

What about butchers? The training programme for butchers is less arduous than for surgeons, and

a wider range of people is suitable for employment in this occupation. Labour supply is thus likely to be more elastic than for surgeons. If butchers were to receive high enough wages, more people would be attracted to the trade and wage rates would eventually fall.

In addition, there are other occupations into which butchers can transfer when they have had enough of cutting up all that meat; they might look to other sections of the catering sector, for example. This reinforces the relatively high elasticity of supply.

Is this the whole of the story? The discussion so far has centred entirely on the supply side of the market. But demand is also important. Indeed, it is the position of the demand curve when interacting with supply that determines the equilibrium wage rate in a labour market. It may well be that the supply of workers skilled in underwater basket weaving is strictly limited; but if there is no demand for underwater basket weavers then there is no scope for that skill to earn high wages. In the above example, it is the relatively strong demand for surgeons relative to their limited supply that leads to a relatively high equilibrium wage in the market.

Summary: labour market equilibrium

- Labour market equilibrium is found at the intersection of labour demand and labour supply.
- This determines the equilibrium wage rate for an industry.
- Demand and supply analysis can be used to explore the effects of changes in market conditions.
- Changes in relative wages between sectors may induce movement of workers between industries.

Labour mobility

In some situations, labour markets in practice can be seen to be inflexible. One reason for this is that workers are not perfectly mobile. Mobility here can be seen in two important dimensions. First, there may be geographic immobility, where workers may be reluctant to move to a new region in search of appropriate employment. Second, there may be immobility between occupations. Both sorts of immobility can hinder the free operation of labour markets.

Geographic mobility

There are a number of reasons that help to explain why workers may not be freely mobile between different parts of the country. It could be that the workers who are available are located in areas remote from where the vacancies are appearing. If the available workers are living in Newcastle, but the vacancies are in London, then they may not respond to the higher wages on offer, given the costs of transport and moving house — or the difficulty of finding out that the jobs are available. There may also be social effects — people do not like to move away from their friends and relatives, or to leave the area that they know or where their favourite football team plays. Parents may not wish to disrupt their children's education.

The relatively high rate of owner-occupied housing in the UK means that workers who are owner-occupiers may need a strong inducement to move to another part of the country in search of jobs. For council house tenants, too, it may be quite difficult to relocate to a different area for employment purposes because they will have to return to the bottom of the waiting list for housing. Differences in house prices in different parts of the country add further to the problem of matching workers to jobs.

There may also be information problems, in that it may be more difficult to find out about job availability in other areas. The internet may have reduced the costs of job search to some extent, but it is still easier to find jobs in the local area, where the reputation of firms is better known to locals. Where both partners in a relationship are working, this may also make it more difficult to find jobs further afield that would suit both of them, and there is some evidence that females tend to be less mobile geographically than males.

International labour mobility

International mobility of labour has increased in recent years, especially since the expansion of the EU in 2004, with the addition of ten new member countries. One of the features of the Single Market measures of 1992 was to allow free movement of people, goods, services and capital within the EU. Not all of the existing EU members allowed free movement of labour from the new members, but the UK did. As a result, it experienced significant migration from eastern Europe, especially from Poland. This was partly a response to the wage differential between the countries. As the productivity of labour was higher in the UK than in Poland and other countries, wages in the UK were also relatively high. This wage differential acted as an incentive for workers to move to the UK. The process of Brexit would be likely to reverse this trend. Indeed, even in 2018 there were signs that the NHS was facing difficulties in recruiting staff.

Knowledge check 22.11

How would you expect the immobility of labour to affect the elasticity of supply of labour?

A Polish shop in London — higher wages attract Polish workers to the UK

Exercise 22.3

Draw two labour market diagrams to represent the demand and supply of labour in the UK and Poland before the EU expansion. Show on the diagrams how the two markets would adjust to a flow of workers from Poland to the UK.

Occupational mobility

The difficulty that people face in moving between occupations is an important source of labour market inflexibility, and may result in structural unemployment. Over time, it is to be expected that the pattern of consumer demand will change, and if the pattern of economic activity is to change in response, it is important that some sectors of the economy decline to enable others to expand. As the UK economy has moved away from manufacturing towards service sector activities, people have needed to be occupationally mobile to find work.

There are costs involved for workers switching between occupations. A displaced farm worker may not be able to find work as a ballet dancer without some degree of retraining! Firms may be expected to underprovide training to their workers because of the free-rider problem. There may therefore be a need for some government intervention to ensure that training is provided in order to combat the problem of structural unemployment and to facilitate occupational mobility.

Synoptic link

The notion of structural unemployment was discussed in Chapter 10 among other causes of unemployment.

Synoptic link

The free-rider problem
was discussed in Chapter
7 in the context of public
goods, but it also applies
here. Firms may poach
workers from other firms
that have invested in
training, thus free-riding on
the training costs.

As with geographic mobility, another factor that may impede occupational mobility is the question of information. Workers may not have enough information to enable them to judge the benefits from occupational mobility. For example, they may not be aware of their aptitude for different occupations, or the extent to which they may gain job satisfaction from a job that they have not tried. These arguments do not apply only to workers displaced by structural change in the economy. They are equally valid for workers who are in jobs that may not necessarily be the best ones for them.

Knowledge check 22.12

Suggest ways in which the information gap could be overcome.

Extension material: monopsony in a labour market

The previous chapter discussed the characteristics of a monopsony market. Suppose that one firm is the sole user of a particular type of labour, or is the dominant firm in a city or region, and thus is in a monopsony situation.

Such a monopsonist faces the market supply curve of labour directly, rather than simply accepting the equilibrium market wage. It views this supply curve as its average cost of labour because it shows the average wage rate that it would need to offer to obtain any given quantity of labour input.

Figure 22.8 shows a monopsonist's demand curve for labour and its supply curve of labour, seen by the firm as its average cost curve of labour (AC_L). If the market were perfectly competitive, equilibrium would be where supply equals demand, which would be with the firm using $L\star$ labour at a wage rate $W\star$.

From the perspective of the monopsonist firm facing the supply curve directly, if at any point it wants to hire more labour, it has to offer a higher wage to encourage more workers to join the market — after all, that is what the AC_L curve tells it. However, the firm would then have to pay that higher wage to all its workers, so the *marginal cost* of hiring the extra worker is not just the wage paid to that worker, but the increased wage paid to all the other workers as well. So the marginal cost of labour curve (MC_L) can be added to the diagram.

If the monopsonist firm wants to maximise profit, it will choose to operate where the demand for labour equals the MC_L. In other words, it will use labour up to the level L_m. In order to entice workers to supply this amount of labour, the firm need pay only the wage W_m. (Remember that AC_L is the supply curve of labour.) You can see, therefore, that a profit–maximising monopsonist will use less labour, and pay a lower wage, than a firm operating under perfect competition. From society's perspective, this entails a welfare loss, just as was seen in the comparison of monopoly and perfect competition in Chapter 19.

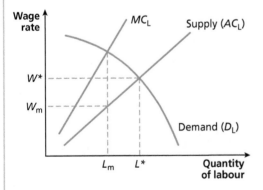

Figure 22.8 A monopsony buyer of labour

Summary: labour mobility

- Geographic immobility may impede the operations of the labour market, if workers are not readily able to move between different parts of the country.
- Occupational immobility may also contribute to the inflexibility of the labour market.

Effects of government intervention in the labour market

There are various ways in which governments intervene in labour markets, either in an attempt to protect vulnerable workers, or to improve the flexibility and effectiveness with which labour markets operate.

Unemployment benefits

An important influence on labour supply, particularly for low-income workers, is the level of unemployment benefit. If unemployment benefit is provided at too high a level, it may inhibit labour force participation, in that some workers may opt to live on unemployment benefit rather than take up low-skilled (and low-paid) employment. In such a situation, a reduction in unemployment benefit may induce an increase in labour supply.

However, such a policy needs to be balanced against the need to provide protection for those who are unable to find employment. It is also important that unemployment benefit is not reduced to such a level that workers are unwilling to leave their jobs to search for better ones, as this may inhibit the flexibility of the labour market.

Incentive effects

Similarly, there are dangers in making the taxation system too progressive. Most people accept that income tax should be progressive (i.e. that those on relatively high incomes should pay a higher rate of tax than those on low incomes) as a way of redistributing income within society and preventing inequality from becoming extreme. However, there may come a point at which marginal tax rates are so high that a large proportion of additional income is taxed away, reducing incentives for individuals to supply additional effort or labour. Again, however, it is important to balance these incentive effects against the distortion caused by having too much inequality in society.

Synoptic link

Progressive taxes may be used to influence the distribution of income in a country, and are discussed in Chapter 27.

Minimum wage

In its manifesto published before the 1997 election, the Labour Party committed itself to the establishment of the National Minimum Wage (NMW). This was the first time that such a measure had been used in the UK on a nationwide basis, although **minimum wages** had sometimes been set in particular industries.

A Low Pay Commission was set up to oversee the implementation of the policy, which came into force in April 1999. The level of the NMW depends on age. Initially, the NMW was set at £3.60 per hour for those aged 22 and over, and £3 for those aged 18–21. The rates are revised each year.

Key term

minimum wage a government-set minimum wage rate below which firms are not allowed to pay

The living wage

A twenty-first-century development has been the concept of the *living wage*. The UK Living Wage Campaign was launched by a community alliance in 2001 and grew into a national movement. The campaign began because it was seen that the NMW was not providing people with enough funds to live on. The living wage is thus based on a calculation of the basic cost of living in the UK. It is an estimate of how much income households need to afford an acceptable standard of living.

From April 2016, the government adopted a mandatory national living wage (NLW) that would apply to workers aged 25 and above. In 2018, the rate was set at £7.83, compared with the rates for the NMW, which were £7.38 for those aged 21–24, £5.90 for those aged between 18 and 20, and £4.20 for those under 18. Apprentices were guaranteed £3.70 per hour.

The Living Wage Foundation continues to argue that the mandatory level of the NLW is insufficient to cover the cost of achieving an adequate standard of living. In 2018, they recommended a UK living wage of £8.45 outside London, with a living wage of £9.75 needed to cover the higher costs of living in London.

Objectives of a minimum wage policy

The objectives of the minimum wage policy are threefold. First, it is intended to protect workers against exploitation by the small minority of bad employers. Second, it aims to improve incentives to work by ensuring that 'work pays', thereby tackling the problem of voluntary unemployment. Third, it aims to alleviate poverty by raising the living standards of the poorest groups in society.

The policy has been a contentious one, with critics claiming that it meets none of these objectives. It has been argued that the minority of bad employers can still find ways of exploiting their workers: for example, by paying them on a piecework rate so that there is no set wage per hour, or by offering zero-hours contracts. Another criticism is that the policy is too indiscriminate to tackle poverty, and that a more sharply focused policy is needed for this purpose: for example, many of the workers receiving the NMW may not in fact belong to poor households, but may be women working part time whose partners are also in employment. But perhaps most contentious of all is the argument that, far from providing a supply-side solution to some unemployment, a national minimum wage is causing an increase in unemployment because of its effects on the demand for labour.

> **Knowledge check 22.13**
>
> Identify the arguments in favour of a minimum wage policy.

A minimum wage in a perfectly competitive labour market

Consider a firm operating in a perfectly competitive market, so that it has to accept the wage that is set in the overall market of which it is a part. In Figure 22.9 the firm's demand curve is represented by D_L, and in a free market it must accept the equilibrium wage $W\star$. It thus uses labour up to $l\star$.

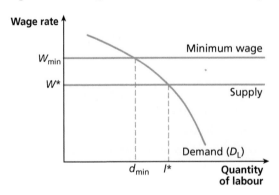

Figure 22.9 The effect of a minimum wage on a firm in a perfectly competitive labour market

If the government now steps in and imposes a minimum wage, so that the firm cannot set a wage below W_{min}, it will reduce its labour usage to d_{min}, since it will not be profitable to employ labour beyond this point.

This effect will be similar for all the other firms in the market, and the results of this can be seen in Figure 22.10. Now the demand curve is the combined demand of all the firms in the market, and the supply curve of labour is shown as upward sloping, as it is the market supply curve. In free market equilibrium the combined demand of firms in the market is $L^\star$, and $W^\star$ emerges as the equilibrium wage rate.

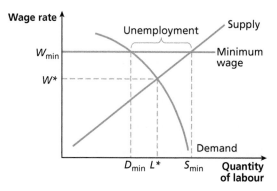

Figure 22.10 The effect of a minimum wage in a perfectly competitive labour market

When the government sets the minimum wage at W_{min}, all firms react by reducing their demand for labour at the higher wage. Their combined demand is now D_{min}, but the supply of labour is S_{min}. The difference between these $(S_{min} - D_{min})$ is unemployment. Furthermore, it is involuntary unemployment — these workers would like to work at the going wage rate, but cannot find a job.

Notice that there are two effects at work. Some workers who were formerly employed have lost their jobs — there are $L^\star - D_{min}$ of these. In addition, however, the incentive to work is now improved (this was part of the policy objective, remember?), so there are now an additional $S_{min} - L^\star$ workers wanting to take employment at the going wage rate. Thus, unemployment has increased for two reasons.

It is not always the case that the introduction of a minimum wage leads to an increase in unemployment. For example, in the market depicted in Figure 22.11 the minimum wage has been set below the equilibrium level, so will have no effect on firms in the market, which will continue to pay $W^\star$ and employ $L^\star$ workers. At the time of the introduction of the NMW, McDonald's argued that it was in fact already paying a wage above the minimum rate.

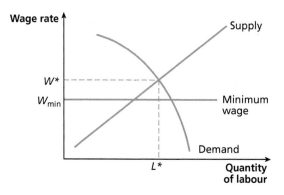

Figure 22.11 A non-binding minimum wage in a perfectly competitive labour market

Extension material: monopsony and the minimum wage

There is another situation in which a minimum wage would *not* lead to unemployment. Suppose that the labour market in question has a monopsony buyer of labour. The firm's situation is shown in Figure 22.12. In the absence of a minimum wage, the firm hires L_0 labour at a wage W_0. A minimum wage introduced at the level W_{min} means that the firm now hires more labour up to the point where demand equals supply and, as drawn in Figure 22.12, this takes the market back to the perfectly competitive outcome.

Notice that the authorities would have to be very knowledgeable to set the minimum wage at exactly the right level to produce this outcome. However, any wage between W_0 and W_{min} will encourage the firm to increase its employment to some extent as the policy reduces its market power. Of course, setting the minimum wage above the competitive equilibrium level will again lead to some unemployment. Thus, it is critical to set the wage at the right level if the policy is to succeed in its objectives.

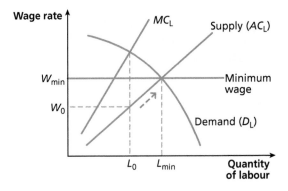

Figure 22.12 A minimum wage with a monopsony buyer of labour

It is important to remember that there is not just a single labour market in the UK. In fact, it could be questioned whether a single minimum wage set across the whole country could be effective, as it would 'bite' in different ways in different markets. For example, wage levels vary across the regions of the UK, and it must be questioned whether the same minimum wage could be as effective in, say, London as in Northern Ireland or the north of England.

Exercise 22.4

Sketch some diagrams to explore how the elasticity of demand for and the supply of labour influence the impact on market equilibrium of the imposition of a minimum wage.

Synoptic link

In discussing policy issues you should remain aware of the distinction between microeconomics and macroeconomics when discussing labour markets. However, in designing macroeconomic policy it is more natural to think in terms of the labour market as a whole, if only because the headline indicator is the overall level of unemployment. As with the minimum wage, a policy designed at the macro level may not have equal effects across the economy. Unemployment is discussed from a macroeconomic perspective in Chapter 10.

A maximum wage?

The controversy over the bonuses paid to bankers and other top executives has led some commentators to recommend that, in addition to setting a minimum wage, the authorities should set a **maximum wage**, or a wage ceiling. It is argued that this would stem the excesses that characterise executive pay. Indeed, Jeremy Corbyn called for a maximum wage in 2017, as being one solution to inequality in the UK.

An argument often put forward in this context is that high salaries and bonuses are needed to provide incentives for effort, but supporters of the maximum wage counter

Key term

maximum wage a policy under which employers face a wage ceiling, being prohibited from paying a wage above a set level

this by saying that the incentive effects are not strong at those levels of pay. This could reflect the diminishing marginal utility of income — the idea that additional increments of income provide less additional utility as incomes rise. It is also likely that attempts to introduce such a measure would be fraught with difficulties. For example, how would the level of the maximum wage be set? And, of course, the political pressures against such a policy would be enormous.

Figure 22.13 shows how a maximum wage might work. In the absence of the maximum wage, the equilibrium would occur when demand equals supply, with the wage at $W\star$ and the supply of labour at $L\star$. If employers cannot pay a wage above W_{max}, the supply of labour falls to S_{max}. Employers would like to employ more at this wage (up to D_{max}), but are unable to recruit as many as they would like.

Study tip

There is a useful reminder here that the design of policy must take into account the realities of the political context.

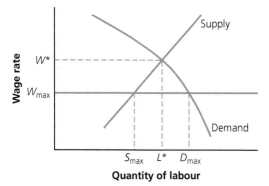

Figure 22.13 A maximum wage

If it is the case that employees at this level of income are relatively insensitive to pay, then the supply of labour would be relatively more inelastic than shown in the figure, so the fall in labour supply would not be as marked. However, it is possible that in the longer run, employees at this level would be internationally mobile, so might depart for jobs overseas where they could command a higher salary.

Synoptic link

An alternative approach to imposing a maximum wage to tackle inequality might be to raise the rate of income tax on higher levels of income. Inequality is discussed in Chapter 27.

Anger at banker's bonuses — should the authorities should set a maximum wage?

Public sector wages

One sector in which the government can intervene more easily is the public sector. After all, it determines and negotiates the wages that it pays to its employees. This can distort the overall labour market, if the private sector sets wages according to labour market conditions but the public sector offers wages that are significantly different.

If the public sector sets wages that are lower than equilibrium in the overall market, then it will have difficulty in recruiting, and may end up hiring the least well-qualified workers. In many developing countries, the opposite problem has been encountered, where public sector pay (and job security) is high, so all of the best workers gravitate into the public sector, leaving the private sector struggling to find employees.

Policies to improve the flexibility of the labour market

What steps could the government take to promote flexibility? A number of obstacles to flexibility have been identified. To what extent are these amenable to policy intervention?

Training, skills and information

The process of structural change in an economy may be impeded if the people looking for work, perhaps because they have been released from a declining sector, do not have the requisite skills needed for the sectors that are expanding. It is also important for unemployed workers to have good information about the jobs available.

Successive governments have been aware of this issue, and have introduced measures to provide opportunities for workers to undergo training and incentives for employers to provide it. The latest policy in this area is the apprenticeship levy, which was introduced in April 2017. This attempts to overcome the free-rider problem, and has set a target of having 3 million apprentices in place by 2020. Large employers are required to make a payment into an online service account, but can reclaim their levy payments (plus a subsidy) when they take on apprentices into approved schemes. Employers who benefit by recruiting trained workers from other firms will not be able to reclaim their levy payments. Smaller employers (with wage bills below £3 million) can claim subsidies towards the costs of taking on apprentices.

Trade union reform

Knowledge check 22.14

Explain why trade union pressure on wages could lead to unemployment.

A further question concerns the extent to which the trade unions have affected the operation of labour markets. By negotiating for a wage that is above the equilibrium level, trade unions may trade off higher wages for lower levels of employment. The potential disruption caused by strike action can also impede the workings of a labour market.

Some indication of this disruption can be seen in Figure 22.14. Clearly, compared with the 1970s and 1980s, the amount of disruption through strikes in recent years has been very low, although even the 1979 figure pales into insignificance besides the 162 million working days lost in the General Strike of 1926. In fact, however, the 1970s and 1980s were a tempestuous period, in which trade union action severely disrupted UK industry. So why has life become so much quieter?

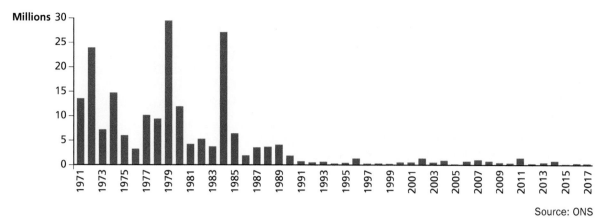

Figure 22.14 Working days lost in the UK through industrial action, 1971–2017

Source: ONS

It was perhaps no surprise that unions should have worked hard to protect their members during the 1980s, when unemployment was soaring and the Thatcher government was determined to control inflation — including inflation of wages. Legislation was introduced in the early 1980s to begin to reform the trade unions, and after the highly disruptive miners' strike ended in 1985, the government introduced a number of further reforms designed to curb the power of the trade unions, making it more difficult for them to call rapid strike action. For example, secret ballots were to be required before strike action could be taken. This may help to explain why trade union membership has been in decline since the 1980s. By weakening the power of trade unions in this way, some labour market inflexibility has been removed.

Another factor may have been changes in the structure of economic activity during this period. Manufacturing employment was falling, whereas the service sectors were expanding. Traditionally, union membership has been higher among workers in the manufacturing sector than in services.

It is worth being aware that strikes do not only occur in connection with wage claims, but also in relation to working conditions or job security. For example, there were some high-profile strikes by train workers on Southern Rail that started in 2016, which were concerned with the proposal to operate driver-only trains (trains without guards). Such action later spread to other rail companies.

Regional policy

There have always been differences in average incomes and in unemployment rates between the various regions of the UK. In broad terms, there are two possible responses to this — either persuade workers to move to regions where there are more jobs, or persuade the firms to move to areas where labour is plentiful. Each of these solutions poses problems. Housing markets limit the mobility of workers, and it is costly for firms to relocate their activities.

The regions most affected in the past have been those that specialised in industries that subsequently went into decline: for example, coal mining areas or towns and regions dominated by cotton mills. In a broad context, it is desirable for the economy to undergo structural change as the pattern of international comparative advantage changes, but it is painful during the transition period. Thus, successive governments have implemented regional policies to try to cope with the problems experienced in areas of high unemployment.

At the same time, the booming regions can be affected by the opposite problem — a shortage of labour. Thus, measures have been taken to encourage firms to consider relocating to regions where labour is available. These have included leading by example, with some civil service functions being moved out of London.

Funding and grants

EU funding has helped in this regard, with Scotland, Wales and Northern Ireland all qualifying for grants. Between 1999 and 2012, Regional Development Agencies (RDAs) set up by the Labour government had responsibility for promoting economic development in their regions. The RDAs were abolished as part of government efforts to reduce the budget deficit, and ceased operating in March 2012.

During the course of the 2010 Coalition government, George Osborne, the then chancellor of the exchequer, launched the concept of the 'Northern Powerhouse'. This was a strategy designed to provide funding to revitalise cities in the north of England, devolving powers from Westminster to local people, providing funds for locally determined projects, and spending £13 billion on improving transport infrastructure.

Technology and unemployment

One of the greatest fallacies perpetuated by non-economists is that technology destroys jobs. Bands of labourers known as Luddites rioted between 1811 and 1816, destroying textile machines, which they blamed for high unemployment and low wages. In the twenty-first century there is a strong lobbying group in the USA arguing that outsourcing and cheap labour in China are destroying US jobs. President Trump has reinforced this message in his tweets, and used this argument to justify the imposition of tariffs on imports of a range of products from China.

In fact, new technology and an expansion in the capital stock should have beneficial effects — so long as labour markets are sufficiently flexible. Consider a market in which new technology is introduced. If firms in an industry invest in technology and expand the capital stock, this affects the productivity of labour and hence the demand for labour, as shown in Figure 22.15, where demand shifts from D_1 to D_2. In this market, the effect is to raise the wage rate from W_1 to W_2 and the employment level from L_1 to L_2.

Synoptic link

The effect of tariffs is discussed in the context of trade protectionism in Chapter 25.

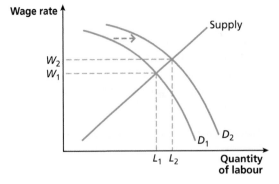

Figure 22.15 An increase in capital

However, it is important to look beyond what happens in a single market, as the argument is that it is all very well expanding employment in the technology sector — but what about the old industries that are in decline? Suppose the new industries absorb less labour than is discarded by the old declining industries? After all, if the effect of technology is to allow call centres to create jobs in India, does this not harm employment in the UK or USA?

Specialisation

The counter-argument to this lies in the notion of the gains from specialisation introduced briefly in Chapter 1. This argues that countries can gain from international trade through specialising in certain activities. Setting up call centres in India frees UK workers to work in sectors in which the UK can specialise efficiently.

There is one proviso, of course. It is important that the workers released from the declining sectors have (or can obtain) the skills that are needed for them to be absorbed into the expanding sectors. This recalls the question of whether the labour market is sufficiently flexible to allow the structure of economic activity to adapt to changes in the pattern of comparative advantage. However, it also serves as a reminder that policy should be aimed at enabling that flexibility, and not at introducing protectionist measures to reduce trade, which would be damaging overall for the economy.

Knowledge check 22.15

What type of unemployment is caused by a mismatch of skills?

Synoptic link

The arguments for and against protectionism in trade are set out in Chapter 25, which also examines the potential gains from specialisation in more detail than could be covered in Chapter 1.

Summary: government intervention in labour markets

- Governments have intervened in labour markets in various ways.
- This includes providing unemployment benefits and setting the National Minimum Wage.
- An important factor influencing the rate of unemployment is the degree of flexibility in labour markets.
- Trade union reforms were introduced during the 1980s and have contributed to flexibility in labour markets.
- Regional policy has attempted to reduce the differentials in unemployment rates between the regions of the UK.
- Adjustment in labour markets is needed in order to cope with the changing international pattern of specialisation.

Case study 22.1

Valuing professional footballers

The football transfer market was buoyant in the summer of 2017. Among the most prominent traders were the top English Premiership clubs such as Manchester United, Liverpool and Chelsea, and big-spending European clubs such as Paris Saint-Germain. The FA Premier League has the highest revenues of any domestic football league in the world, grossing more than £4.5 billion in revenues in the 2016/17 season, according to Deloitte. The top Premiership clubs also compete in the highly lucrative UEFA Champions League. The battle between television firms for broadcasting rights is a key factor in generating these revenues.

So not surprisingly, the top English Premiership clubs are able to outbid most of their rivals to attract the best players in the world. In 2017, it was reported that the average salary of a footballer playing in the English Premier League had reached

£2.6 million per year (£50,817 per week), comfortably more than footballers playing in the top leagues in Germany, Italy and Spain. These figures suggest that a high proportion of the television revenues goes into players' salaries — rather than into lower ticket prices.

But is there any economic justification for Paris Saint-Germain paying a transfer fee of £198 million to Barcelona for Neymar, or Juventus paying £99.2 million to Real Madrid to obtain the services of Cristiano Ronaldo?

From an economic and financial perspective, professional footballers are complex productive assets who are expected to provide a flow of services both on and off the field over the period of their employment contract. One way of valuing a professional footballer is to calculate the value of the expected flow of net benefits accruing to the holder of the asset — that is, the club. In other words, the value of a professional footballer should be related to the marginal revenue that the player brings to the club.

Calculating the productivity of a professional footballer requires estimating the expected additional cash flows accruing to the club as a consequence of signing that player. Broadly speaking, there are two types of revenue stream that a player can generate. First, there are the revenue streams associated with the player's on-the-field contribution to team performance. Team revenues tend to be 'win-elastic'. Winning teams tend to attract more spectators, generating higher match-day revenues. Media revenues can also be win-elastic with bigger viewing audiences for the more successful teams.

Sponsorship and merchandising revenues also tend to be higher for more successful teams. But a player's value will also depend on his expected image value off the field. Star players can generate greater revenues by virtue of being star players irrespective of their actual impact on team performance. Glamour as well as glory makes money in professional team sports, which when all is said and done are part of the entertainment industry. So from the economic perspective the fundamental value of a professional footballer can be stated as:

$$\text{marginal productivity} = (MPC \times MWR) + PIV$$

where MPC is the (expected) marginal playing contribution, MWR is the marginal win revenue and PIV is the player image value. Calculating a player's value requires an estimate of the incremental impact of the player on the team performance,

Cristiano Ronaldo — is he worth the transfer fee?

an estimate of the sensitivity of the team's revenues to team performance and an estimate of the off-the-field marketing value of the player.

Follow-up questions

a Explain what is meant by the 'marginal revenue' that a footballer brings to the club.

b What is meant by the statement that team revenues tend to be 'win-elastic'?

c Explain why 'glamour as well as glory makes money'.

d To what extent does the discussion of a footballer's marginal productivity help to explain why professional footballers command such high wages?

e How would you expect the market for footballers would be affected if the government were to impose a maximum wage?

Immigration and the labour market

During the Brexit referendum, one of the major issues of contention was that of immigration. One of the aspects of the Single European Market is the free movement of people between member states, and one of the main benefits claimed for leaving the EU was that the UK would no longer have to accept migrant workers, but could impose independent control.

The concerns about the free entry of migrant workers centred around two main arguments. On the one hand, it was claimed that migrant workers steal jobs from native workers, causing unemployment for UK workers. On the other hand, it was also claimed that migrants come to the UK in order to claim social security benefits, thus living on the taxes paid by native citizens. These two arguments conflict with each other.

The data show that since the enlargement of the Single Market in 2004, about 80% of migrant workers from the newly acceded countries have been in employment. This is a higher employment rate than people whose country of birth was the UK, the rest of the EU or the rest of the world. The last category shows significantly lower employment rates.

If immigrants and native workers compete for the same jobs (i.e. they are substitutes), the effect on the UK labour market is that wages would fall and employment would increase, following an extension of labour supply.

If migrant workers have different skills than native workers, the effect on the labour market is different, as the migrant and native workers are complements. In this case, the impact on the labour market is an extension of labour demand, resulting in higher wages and contributing to economic growth.

An additional effect occurs if the migrant workers bring with them new ideas and work practices. This can create an additional externality effect if these ideas rub off on native workers, raising their productivity.

Follow-up questions

a Why do the concerns raised in the second paragraph conflict with each other?

b Using an appropriate diagram, analyse the effects on the labour market in the cases where migrant workers are substitutes for native workers.

c Again using a diagram, analyse the effect of immigration when the migrants and native workers are complements.

d Discuss the impact of Brexit on the labour market.

Government intervention to promote competition

If resources are going to be allocated efficiently within a society, it is crucial that business organisations make the appropriate economic decisions. Previous chapters have shown that firms may sometimes be able to gain market dominance, giving them sufficient market power to take decisions that cause a distortion in resource allocation. This chapter explores the major policy areas in which authorities attempt to influence firms' economic decision making. It looks first at competition policy, through which the authorities attempt to encourage competition in markets and protect the interests of consumers. It then examines measures introduced to regulate privatised industries, most of which are natural monopolies posing particular problems for resource allocation.

Learning objectives

After studying this chapter, you should:

→ understand the economic underpinnings of competition policy
→ appreciate that there may be situations in which unremitting competition may not be in the best interests of society
→ be familiar with the role of the Competition and Markets Authority
→ be aware of the issues that may affect the judgements of a market under investigation
→ be familiar with the general institutional background of competition policy in the UK and the EU
→ be familiar with the process for investigating mergers
→ understand the need to regulate natural monopolies and some of the problems that may arise in attempting to do so

---

Competition and the government

Key term

competition policy a set of measures designed to promote competition in markets and protect consumers in order to enhance the efficiency of markets

An awareness of the market failure that can arise from imperfect competition has led governments to introduce measures designed to promote competition and protect consumers. Such measures are known as **competition policy**.

A key focus of such legislation in the past has been monopoly, as economic analysis highlighted the allocative inefficiency that can arise in a monopoly market if the firm sets out to maximise profit. In particular, policy has tended to focus on situations in which the merger of previously separate firms could potentially lead to market dominance. More recently, the scope of legislation has widened, and competition policy has been toughened significantly.

Underlying this aspect of government policy has been the growing belief that competition induces firms to eliminate X-inefficiency as well as encouraging better resource allocation. However, this must always be balanced against the possible sacrifice of economies of scale if competition can only be enabled by fragmentation of the production process. The question of contestability is also important, as it is possible that the very threat of competition may be sufficient to affect firms' behaviour.

The belief that competition benefits consumers by encouraging businesses to be efficient in their production has been the main driving force for competition policy. One facet of this branch of policy has been to control **merger** activity. A merger between firms (or the acquisition of one firm by another) can be seen as a move to reduce competition where the combined firm comes to control a significant share of a product market, or even become a monopoly.

X-inefficiency does not occur only in the private sector, and a further set of measures has tried to address the question of efficiency in the provision of public sector services by encouraging the private sector to be involved in partnership with the public sector in its economic activities.

Synoptic link

The notion of X-inefficiency was introduced as part of the discussion of the costs facing firms in Chapter 18.

Key term

merger where firms join together to form a single firm, potentially reducing competition in a market by increasing concentration

Why worry about monopoly?

Discussion in Chapter 19 undertook a comparison of perfect competition and monopoly, and it is this analysis that lies at the heart of competition policy. Figure 23.1 should remind you of the discussion.

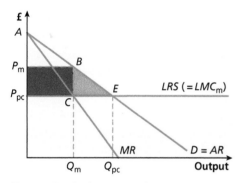

Figure 23.1 Perfect competition and monopoly compared

Here it is assumed there is an industry that can operate either under perfect competition, with a large number of small firms, or as a multi-plant monopolist. For simplicity, it is also assumed that there is no cost difference between the two forms of market structure, so that the long-run supply schedule (LRS) under perfect competition is perceived by the monopolist as its long-run marginal cost curve. In other words, in long-run equilibrium the monopoly varies output by varying the number of plants it is operating.

Under perfect competition, output would be set at Q_{pc} and market price would be P_{pc}. However, a monopolist will choose to restrict output to Q_m and raise price to P_m. Consumer surplus will be reduced by this process, partly by a transfer of the purple rectangle to the monopoly as profits, and partly by the red triangle of irretrievable deadweight loss. Competition policy is intended to alleviate this deadweight loss, which imposes a cost on society.

Knowledge check 23.1

Explain what is meant by a 'deadweight loss' in this context.

The structure–conduct–performance paradigm

Indeed, this analysis led to a belief in what became known in economics as the *structure–conduct–performance paradigm*. At the core of this belief, illustrated in Figure 23.2, is the simple idea that the structure of a market, in terms of the number

Synoptic link

Be sure that you understand why it is argued that structure, conduct and performance are linked in this way. If necessary look back at Chapters 19 and 20, which discuss alternative market structures and how the structure of the market influences decision making by firms.

of firms, determines how firms in the market conduct themselves, which in turn determines how well the market performs in achieving productive and allocative efficiency.

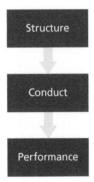

Figure 23.2 The structure–conduct–performance paradigm

Under perfect competition firms cannot influence price, and all firms act competitively to maximise profits, thereby producing good overall performance of the market in allocating resources. On the other hand, under monopoly the single firm finds that it can extract consumer surplus by using its market power, and as a result the market performs less well.

This point of view leads to a distrust of monopoly — or, indeed, of any market structure in which firms might be seen to be conducting themselves in an anti-competitive manner. Moreover, it is the structure of the market itself that leads to this anti-competitive behaviour.

If this line of reasoning is accepted, then monopoly is always bad, and mergers that lead to higher concentration in a market will always lead to allocative inefficiency in the market's performance. Legislation in the USA tends to presume that a monopoly will work against the interests of society. However, there are some important issues to consider before pinning too much faith on this assumption.

Cost conditions

The first issue concerns the assumption that cost conditions will be the same under perfect competition as under monopoly. This simplifies the analysis, but there are many reasons to expect economies of scale in a number of economic activities. If this assumption is correct, then a monopoly firm will face lower cost conditions than would apply under perfect competition.

Perfect competition versus monopoly

In Figure 23.3, LRS represents the long-run supply schedule if an industry is operating under perfect competition. The perfectly competitive equilibrium would be at output level Q_{pc} with the price at P_{pc}. However, suppose that a monopolist had a strong cost advantage, and was able to produce at constant long-run marginal cost LMC_m. It would then maximise profit by choosing the output Q_m, where MR_m is equal to LMC_m, and would sell at a price P_m. In this situation the monopolist could actually produce more output at a lower price than a firm operating under perfect competition.

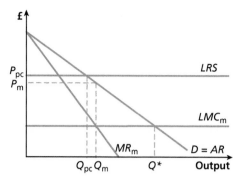

Figure 23.3 Suppose that monopoly offers much better cost conditions

Notice that in the monopoly situation the market does not achieve allocative efficiency, because with these cost conditions, setting price equal to marginal cost would require the firm to produce $Q^\star$ output. However, this loss of allocative efficiency is offset by the improvements in productive efficiency that are achieved by the monopoly firm. This is an example of dynamic efficiency, whereas allocative efficiency is a more static concept that considers the best use of existing resources with existing technologies.

It could be argued that the monopolist should be regulated, and forced to produce at $Q^\star$. However, what incentives would this establish for the firm? If a monopolist knows that whenever it makes supernormal profits the regulator will step in and take them away, it will have no incentive to operate efficiently. Indeed, Joseph Schumpeter argued that monopoly profits were an incentive for innovation, and would benefit society, because only with monopoly profits would firms be able to engage in research and development (R&D). In other words, it is only when firms are relatively large, and when they are able to make supernormal profits, that they are able to devote resources to R&D. Small firms operating in a perfectly competitive market do not have the resources or the incentive to be innovative.

Knowledge check 23.2

Explain why firms operating under perfect competition may not have an incentive to be innovative.

A less extreme case

Figure 23.4 illustrates a less extreme case. As before, equilibrim under perfect competition produces output at Q_{pc} and price at P_{pc}. The monopoly alternative faces lower long-run marginal cost, although with a less marked difference than before: here the firm produces Q_m output in order to maximise profits, and sets price at P_m.

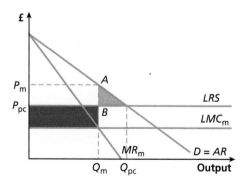

Figure 23.4 Cost conditions again – a less extreme example

Analysis of this situation reveals that there is a deadweight loss given by the red triangle; this reflects the allocative inefficiency of monopoly. However, there is also a gain in productive efficiency represented by the purple rectangle. This is part of monopoly profits, but under perfect competition it was part of production costs. In other words, production under the monopoly is less wasteful in its use of resources in the production process.

Is society better off under monopoly or under perfect competition? In order to evaluate the effect on total welfare, it is necessary to balance the loss of allocative efficiency (the red triangle) against the gain in productive efficiency (the purple rectangle). In Figure 23.4 it would seem that the rectangle is larger than the triangle, so society overall is better off with the monopoly. Of course, there is also the distribution of income to take into account — the area P_mABP_{pc} would be part of consumer surplus under perfect competition, but under monopoly becomes part of the firm's profits.

Contestability

Knowledge check 23.3

What price would a monopoly set to avoid competition if it faces perfect contestability?

A second important issue concerns contestability, which was introduced in Chapter 21. If barriers to entry into the market are weak, and if the sunk costs of entry and exit are low, the monopoly firm will need to temper its actions to avoid potential entry.

Thus, in judging a market situation, the degree of contestability is important. If the market is perfectly contestable, then the monopoly firm cannot set a price that is above average cost without allowing hit-and-run entry. In this case, the regulator does not need to intervene. Even without perfect contestability, the firm may need to set a price that is not so high as to induce entry. In other words, it may choose not to produce at the profit-maximising level of output, and to set a price below that level.

Concentration and collusion

The structure–conduct–performance argument suggests that it is not only monopolies that should be the subject of competition policy, but any market in which firms have some influence over price. In other words, oligopolies also need careful attention because of the danger that they will collude, and act *as if* they were a joint monopoly. After all, where a market has just a small number of sellers there may be a temptation to collude, either in a cartel or tacitly. Government authorities may therefore be wary of markets in which concentration ratios are simply high, even if not 100%.

For this reason, it is important to examine whether a concentrated market is *always* and *necessarily* an anti-competitive market. This is tantamount to asking whether structure necessarily determines conduct. A high concentration ratio may mean that there is a small number of firms of more or less equal size, or it could mean that there is one large firm and a number of smaller competitors. In the latter case you might expect the dominant firm to have sufficient market power to control price.

With a small number of equally sized firms, it is by no means certain that they will agree to collude. They may be very conscious of their respective market shares, and so act in an aggressively competitive way in order to defend them. This may be especially true where the market is not expanding, so that a firm can grow only at the expense of the other firms. Such a market could well display intense competition, causing it to drift towards the competitive end of the scale. This would suggest that the authorities should not presume guilt in a merger investigation, since the pattern of market shares may prove significant in determining the firms' conduct, and hence the performance of the market.

An example of this occurred in 2003, when a number of UK supermarkets attempted to take over Safeway. The judgement of the authorities then was that the takeover bids were unacceptable, except the bid from Morrisons. This was because the Morrisons bid created a more even balance in size among the largest supermarkets, which would be likely to intensify competition. A similar argument was made in 2018 when a merger between Sainsbury and Asda was proposed. The combined market share of these companies was 31.4%; arguably, this would allow the group to compete more effectively with Tesco, which had a market share of 27.6%.

Globalisation

Another significant issue is that a firm that comes to dominate a domestic market may still face competition in the broader global market. This may have been especially significant within the Single European Market.

In this regard, there has been a longstanding debate about how a domestic government should behave towards its large firms. Some economists believe that the government should allow such firms to dominate the domestic market in order that they can become 'national champions' in the global market. This has been especially apparent in the airline industry, where some national airlines are heavily subsidised by their national governments in order to allow them to compete internationally. Others have argued that if a large firm faces competition within the domestic market, this should help to encourage its productive efficiency, enabling it to become more capable of coping with international competition.

Synoptic link

This did not mean that the Sainsbury/Asda merger would necessarily be unproblematic, as concerns were expressed that the merger would provide added monopsony power over suppliers. This is discussed later in this chapter.

Knowledge check 23.4

Explain why competition may be intense in an oligopoly market in which the firms are all of similar size.

Exercise 23.1

Discuss the extent to which a firm's performance in terms of efficiency is dictated by the market environment in which it operates.

Summary: market structure and firms' performance

- Competition policy refers to a range of measures designed to promote competition in markets and to protect consumers in order to enhance the efficiency of markets in resource allocation.
- One view is that market structure determines the conduct of firms within a market, and this conduct then determines the performance of the market in terms of allocative efficiency.
- A profit-maximising monopolist will produce less output at a higher price than a perfectly competitive market, causing allocative inefficiency.
- However, there may be situations in which the monopolist can enjoy economies of scale, and thereby gain in productive efficiency.
- In a contestable market, a monopolist may not be able to charge a price above average cost without encouraging hit-and-run entry.
- In a concentrated market, the pattern of market shares may influence the intensity of competition between firms.
- A firm that is a monopoly in its own country may be exposed to competition in the international markets in which it operates.

Competition policy in the UK

In the UK, competition policy has tended to be less rigid than in the USA, where there has been a natural distrust of monopoly. Policy has therefore been conducted in such a way as to take account of the issues discussed above. This has meant that cases of monopoly or concentrated markets have been judged on their individual merits on a case–by–case basis.

This pragmatic approach was embedded in UK legislation from the start — which was the 1948 Monopolies and Restrictive Practices (Inquiry and Control) Act. This Act set up the Monopolies and Restrictive Practices Commission to investigate markets in which a single firm (or a group of firms in collusion) supplied more than one-third of a market. The commission was asked to decide whether such a market was operating in the public interest, although at that stage the legislation was not very precisely defined.

Since then the legislation has been steadily tightened through a sequence of acts, the most recent of which are the Competition Act of 1998 and the Enterprise Act of 2002. The Competition Act is in two sections ('chapters'), one dealing with anti-competitive agreements between parties (e.g. firms) and the other dealing with anti-competitive practices by one or more parties — that is, the abuse of a dominant position in a market.

Cartels

Synoptic link

Cartels were first introduced and defined in Chapter 3, and discussed more fully in Chapter 20. An example of a cartel is discussed later in this chapter.

Cartels are covered by Chapter 1 of the 1998 Act, but less formal agreements between firms are also within the scope of the act: for example, price fixing, agreements to restrict output and agreements to share a market. The Enterprise Act elevated the operation of a cartel to a criminal offence (as opposed to a civil offence).

The Competition and Markets Authority

Since April 2014, the conduct of the policy has been entrusted to the Competition and Markets Authority (CMA) (previously it was implemented by two agencies: the Office of Fair Trading (OFT) and the Competition Commission). The CMA investigates mergers and anti-competitive practices in markets. The expectation was that merging the OFT and the Competition Commission into a single body would simplify the implementation of competition policy in the UK, thus avoiding duplication and saving costs. The CMA would also be able to operate with shorter time frames for investigations, reducing the uncertainty faced by firms that find themselves under investigation.

The main functions of the CMA are:

- investigating mergers which could potentially give rise to a substantial lessening of competition (SLC)
- investigating markets to assess particular markets in which there are suspected competition problems
- antitrust enforcement by investigating possible breaches of UK or EU prohibitions against anti-competitive agreements and abuse of a dominant position
- criminal cartels: the CMA is able to bring criminal proceedings against individuals who commit the cartel offence
- consumer protection

Knowledge check 23.5

It has been relatively rare for the CMA to impose fines on firms for anti-competitive behaviour. Do you think this means that the policy is not working?

A merger is subject to investigation by the CMA if the firms involved in the proposed merger or acquisition have a combined market share in the UK of more than 25% and if the combined assets of the firms exceed £70 million worldwide.

The CMA has a wide range of powers that it can invoke should it find that a merger is likely to result in an SLC. However, there is no presumption that the CMA will find anything wrong with a market, and the result of an investigation may be that a proposed merger raises no concerns about there being an SLC. Indeed, on a number of occasions the CMA's predecessor, the OFT, launched a consumer awareness campaign, having found that the problem with a market lay in the way consumers understood its workings, and not with the market itself.

Probably the best way of understanding how competition policy operates is by exploring an example of how it has worked in practice. First, however, there is a very important issue to be examined.

The relevant market

The first step in any investigation is to identify the **relevant market**. Until the scope of the market has been defined, it is not possible to calculate market shares or concentration ratios.

How should the market be defined in this context? In other words, which products should be included? Or over which region should the market be defined? Take the market for sugar — is this defined as the market for all sugar, or just for granulated sugar? Is organic sugar a separate product? Or, regarding the market for rail travel in Scotland, do bus services need to be considered as part of the Scottish market for travel?

One way of addressing this question is to apply the *hypothetical monopoly test*. Under this approach, the product market is defined as the smallest set of products and producers in which a hypothetical monopolist controlling all such products could raise profits by a small increase in price above the competitive level.

Key term

relevant market a market to be investigated under competition law, defined in such a way that no major substitutes are omitted but no non-substitutes are included

Knowledge check 23.6

Why is it important to define the relevant market?

Extension material: the hypothetical monopoly test

The hypothetical monopoly test is effectively a question about substitution. If in a hypothetical market an increase in price will induce consumers to switch to a substitute product, then the market has not been defined sufficiently widely for it to be regarded as a monopoly. This is demand-side substitutability. One way of evaluating it would be to consult the cross-price elasticity of demand — if it could be measured. This would determine which products were perceived as substitutes for each other by consumers.

For example, in 2003 a number of supermarkets put in bids to take over the Safeway chain. The first step in the investigation was to define the relevant market. One issue that was raised was whether discount stores such as Lidl and Aldi, which sell a limited range of groceries, should be considered part of the same market as supermarkets selling a wide range of grocery products. In the south of the country, the cross-price elasticity of Sainsbury's demand was 0.05 with respect to Lidl's price, but 1.48 with respect to Tesco's price. This suggested that Sainsbury and Tesco were in the same market, but Lidl was not.

It is also important to consider the question of substitutes on the supply side: in other words, whether an increase in price may induce suppliers to join the market. Supply-side substitutability is related to the notion of contestability, in the sense that one way a market can be seen to be contestable is if other firms can switch readily into it — that is, if there are potential substitutes.

An example of an investigation: airports

BAA plc

In 1987 the British Airports Authority was privatised, and BAA plc was established. The new company was responsible for the airports that had previously been under the aegis of the British Airports Authority — namely, the three London airports (Heathrow, Gatwick and Stansted), plus airports in Scotland (Aberdeen, Edinburgh, Glasgow and Prestwick). Prestwick was sold in 1991, and Southampton was acquired in 1990. This meant that BAA plc had an effective monopoly on flights in and out of London and a stranglehold on flights in and out of Scotland.

One of the objectives in setting up BAA plc was to have a single enterprise that would be able to take strategic decisions to plan ahead, and to provide the airport capacity needed to meet the expected growth in demand. In addition, it was hoped that the provision of the infrastructure needed for air travel would help to encourage competition among the airlines providing the transport services.

In the event, things did not work out well, and after 20 years of operation, BAA plc was seen to have failed to provide sufficient capacity to meet demand in the South East region. There was also mounting criticism of the way that BAA was managing its airports — especially Heathrow. In March 2007, the OFT referred the case to the Competition Commission for investigation under the Enterprise Act 2002. The brief for the investigation was 'to investigate whether any feature, or combination of features, of the market or markets for airport services in the UK as exist in connection with the supply of airport services by BAA Limited prevents, restricts or distorts competition in connection with the supply or acquisition of any goods or services in the UK or a part of the UK. If so there is an "adverse effect on competition"' (Competition Commission, 2008).

In terms of market share, it was clear that BAA was in a very strong position. The Competition Commission noted that its seven airports accounted for more than 60% of all passengers using UK airports. In the South East, Heathrow, Gatwick, Stansted and Southampton between them accounted for 90% of air passengers; in Scotland, 84% of air passengers were accounted for by Edinburgh, Glasgow and Aberdeen. The key issue is whether this market position was damaging competition, and hence working against consumer interests.

BAA's dominant market position was found to be having an adverse effect on competition

Competition between airports

An important aspect of this is whether there is scope for competition between airports, and what effect such competition would have on the nature and quality of service that would be offered. In order to approach this question, the Competition Commission looked at evidence relating to non-BAA airports that could be regarded as being in potential competition with each other. Some evidence was found which suggested that there could be competition between airports, particularly in relation to the low-cost airlines. However, competition is most likely where there is spare capacity — which is not the case for Heathrow and Gatwick.

Competition also requires there to be the potential for substitution in demand. In other words, there needs to be some overlap in the potential catchment area for competing airports. In relation to BAA's airports in Scotland, it was found that there was some overlap in catchment between Glasgow and Edinburgh — but not with Aberdeen. In the South East, there was little evidence of competition between BAA's London airports and non-BAA airports (apart from some competition between Southampton and Bournemouth). However, there was significant overlap in the catchment areas of these airports, suggesting the possibility of some competition (subject to capacity constraints).

The Competition Commission came to the view that the shortage of capacity in the South East had partly arisen from the common ownership of the three BAA London airports, and that had these airports been under separate ownership, the incentives to expand capacity and improve the quality of service being offered would have been higher.

Having concluded that there was evidence that the market structure was having an adverse effect on competition, the Competition Commission in its provisional findings recommended that BAA should sell two of its three airports in the South East, and should not be allowed to continue to own airports in both Glasgow and Edinburgh.

Since that time, BAA has become Heathrow Airport Holdings Ltd, owning four airports: Heathrow, Southampton, Glasgow and Aberdeen. It sold Gatwick in 2009, Edinburgh and Prestwick in 2012, and Stansted in 2013. Southampton Airport was acquired by AGS Airports in 2014.

In May 2016, the CMA published an evaluation of the effectiveness of these measures. It found that passenger numbers had increased at Gatwick, Stansted and Edinburgh, with an additional 34 million passenger journeys in 2015 compared with 2009. Quantifiable benefits associated with the remedies were estimated to reach some £870 million by 2020.

Another investigation: media companies

More recently, the CMA has intervened in a proposed merger between 21st Century Fox and Sky plc. The European Commission had indicated that it was happy for this to go ahead, but concerns were raised that the merger would give Rupert Murdoch too much influence over the UK media, given his ownership of the *Times, Sunday Times* and *Sun* newspapers. The CMA issued its provisional findings report in January 2018, and found that the merger would 'be expected to operate against the public interest'. The situation became more complicated when Disney announced its intention to take over 21st Century Fox. This was put under review by the US regulator (although President Trump praised the companies for the merger).

Knowledge check 23.7

Why is competition more likely when there is spare capacity in the market?

Study tip

Although it is helpful to be aware of such examples, do not spend lots of time studying the details. What is important is that you understand the underlying economic analysis that underpins the work of the CMA.

Competition policy in the European Union

As a member of the European Union (EU), UK competition policy has been closely coordinated with EU legislation. This meant that cases of large-scale mergers and acquisitions that were handled by the European Commission (EC) could not also be considered by the CMA. The same applied to cartels if the EC chose to exercise its jurisdiction. This arrangement was sensible, as it allowed the EC to investigate potential abuse of market power where the effects transcend national boundaries. However, it does mean that the CMA has had to focus on cases that were either of mainly UK interest, or which the EC chose not to pursue. An example of an EC investigation was in July 2018, when the EC fined Google a record €4.34 billion for illegally using the Android operating system to cement its dominant position in search engines.

The structure of UK policy was designed to be consistent with the stance adopted by the EC. Brexit would offer the opportunity for the UK to adopt its own independent stance, but would also bring a substantially increased workload. The challenge would be to continue to coordinate action with EC investigations.

Such coordination problems are not new, given the way in which large corporations operate in global markets. For example, in one of the most famous of all competition investigations, Microsoft went on trial in the USA for alleged predatory action in the way that it had launched its internet browser; although initially the judgment went against it, there followed a lengthy appeal. The EU then launched its own court action against Microsoft, making similar allegations about the way it marketed its media player.

Summary: competition policy

- Competition policy in the UK is implemented through the Competition and Markets Authority, which replaced the Office of Fair Trading and the Competition Commission in April 2014.
- The main pillars of policy are legislation dealing with agreements between firms and the abuse of a dominant position.
- A key step in any investigation is to define the relevant market.
- The CMA carries out a preliminary investigation of mergers that meet the criteria in terms of market share and size of assets.
- It then decides whether to initiate a thorough investigation.
- Some mergers are allowed to proceed without referral.
- The CMA may permit the merger to go ahead, may impose conditions on the firm, or may prohibit it.
- Competition policy has been coordinated with that of the EU, but Brexit offers new opportunities/challenges.

Exercise 23.2

Consider the situation when a firm acquires a competitor in order to enhance its market share.

Suppose that Firm A is a brewing company, and it acquires a competitor brewer (Firm B). The acquisition makes the combined firm the largest brewer in Great Britain, with an overall market share of between 33% and 38% and a portfolio of leading beer brands. Suppose that the Competition and Markets Authority investigates the acquisition and finds the following:

- The two firms had a common interest in raising operating margins.
- Consumers are not price-sensitive in choice of brand.
- Firm A charged different prices according to the type of customer. Discounts were offered to multiple retailers.
- It was thought that an increase in non-price competition (advertising and marketing) was likely to follow the merger.
- Firm A argued that the merger would bring synergy benefits and cost savings.

Discuss the information provided, identify actual or potential sources of anti-competitive behaviour and make a judgement about whether the merger would lead to a substantial lessening of competition. If you were the Competition and Markets Authority, what would be your recommendation?

Regulation of monopoly

Natural monopolies pose particular problems with regard to allocative efficiency. Figure 23.5 involves an industry with substantial economies of scale relative to market demand — indeed, the minimum efficient scale is beyond the market demand curve. (In other words, long-run average cost is still falling beyond market demand.)

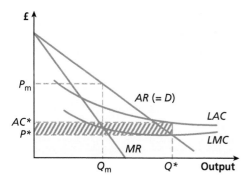

Figure 23.5 A natural monopoly

Synoptic link

The notion of a natural monopoly was first introduced in Chapter 19 as part of the discussion of monopoly markets.

This market is almost bound to end up as a monopoly because the largest firm is always able to dominate the market and undercut smaller competitors, as it has a natural cost leadership position. If the monopoly chooses to maximise profits, it will set marginal revenue equal to marginal cost, choose output Q_m and set price at P_m.

Such industries tend to have large fixed costs relative to marginal costs. Railway systems, water or gas supply and electricity generation are all examples of natural monopolies.

The key problem is that if such firms were forced to set a price equal to marginal cost, they would make a loss. If the firm in Figure 23.5 were required to set price equal to marginal cost (i.e. at $P^\star$) then it would not be viable: average cost would be $AC^\star$, with losses represented by the shaded area on the diagram.

Key term

nationalisation where a privately owned firm or industry is taken into public ownership

Knowledge check 23.8

Why would a government not regard it as appropriate for a nationalised industry to make supernormal profits?

Nationalisation

In the past, one response to this situation would have been to **nationalise** the industry (i.e. take it into state ownership), since no private sector firm would be prepared to operate at a loss, and the government would not allow firms running such natural monopolies to act as profit-maximising monopolists making supernormal profits.

In order to prevent the losses from becoming too substantial, many utilities such as gas and electricity supply adopted a pricing system known as a *two-part tariff system*, under which all consumers paid a monthly charge for being connected to the supply, and on top of that a variable amount based on usage. In terms of Figure 23.5, the connection charge would cover the difference between $AC\star$ and $P\star$, spread across all consumers, and the variable charge would reflect marginal cost.

However, as time went by this sort of system came to be heavily criticised. In particular, it was argued that the managers of the nationalised industries were insufficiently accountable. The situation could be regarded as an extreme form of the principal–agent problem, in which the consumers (the principals) had very little control over the actions of the managers (their agents), a situation leading to considerable X-inefficiency and waste.

Nationalisation has been much less used in the twenty-first century, but there have been some high-profile examples. These have occurred when the government has decided to intervene to bail out failing firms. The bailout of a number of banks during the financial crisis in the late 2000s is one prominent example, although the banks concerned have now been returned to the private sector. Another example occurred in 2018, when the Virgin Trains East Coast franchise failed. The company was taken into public hands, to be run by the Department for Transport until 2020, when a new public–private partnership is expected to be launched.

Privatisation

Key term

privatisation where an enterprise in public ownership is returned to private ownership

During the period of Margaret Thatcher's Conservative government in the 1980s there was widespread **privatisation** (i.e. the transfer of nationalised industries into private ownership), one central argument being that this would force the managers to be accountable to their shareholders, which would encourage an increase in efficiency.

However, this did not remove the original problem: that these industries were natural monopolies. Therefore, wherever possible, privatisation was also accompanied by measures to encourage competition, which was seen as an even better way to ensure efficiency improvements. This proved to be more feasible in some industries than in others because of the nature of economies of scale — there is little to be gained by requiring that there be several firms in a market where the economies of scale can be reaped only by one large firm. However, the changing technology in some of the industries did allow some competition to be encouraged, especially in telecommunications.

Knowledge check 23.9

Why did competition flourish more readily in telecommunications than in some other natural monopolies?

Royal Mail was privatised in October 2013, becoming a quoted company on the London Stock Exchange. The company has a 'Universal Service Obligation', under which it must continue to provide 6-days a week, a one-price-goes-anywhere postal service. It delivers to 30 million addresses in the UK, and is also subject to control on prices. These obligations are subject to regulation by Ofcom.

Price regulation

Where it was not possible, or feasible, to encourage competition, regulation was seen as the solution. Attention of the regulatory bodies focused on price, and the key control method was to allow price increases each year at a rate that was a set amount below changes in the retail price index (RPI). This became known as the $(RPI - X)$ rule, and was widely used, the idea being that it would force companies to look for productivity gains to eliminate the inefficiency that had built up. The X refers to the amount of productivity gain that the regulator believed could be achieved, expressed in terms of the change in average costs. For example, if the regulator believed that it was possible to achieve productivity gains of 5% per year, and if the RPI was increasing at a rate of 10% per year, then the maximum price increase that would be allowed in a year would be $10\% - 5\% = 5\%$.

There are problems inherent in this approach. For example, how does the regulator set X? This is problematic in a situation where the company has better information about costs than the regulator — another instance of the problems caused by the existence of asymmetric information. There is also the possibility that the firm will achieve its productivity gains by reducing the quality of the product, or by neglecting long-term investment for the future and allowing maintenance standards to lapse.

It is also important to realise that as time goes by, if the $(RPI - X)$ system is effective, the inefficiency will be gradually squeezed out, and the X will have to be reduced as it becomes ever more difficult to achieve productivity gains.

In the case of water supply, the regulator Ofwat adopted a variant of the rule. Water companies were required to set prices in accordance with $(RPI + k)$, where k is Ofwat's estimate of how much was needed for capital investment.

Profit regulation

An alternative method of regulation would be to place a limit on the rate of return the firm is permitted to make, thereby preventing it from making supernormal profits. This too may affect the incentive mechanism: the firm may not feel the need to be as efficient as possible, or may fritter away some of the profits in managerial perks to avoid declaring too high a rate of return.

Quality standards

In the mid-2010s, concerns rose about the effectiveness of price regulation. It was perceived that there was too strong a focus on cost-saving rather than output delivery, and that companies were looking for static rather than dynamic efficiency. There was increasing concern about environmental issues, and the quality of output that was being produced.

The regulators Ofwat (water) and Ofgem (gas and electricity) acted to phase out the $RPI - X$ controls, to be replaced by the RIIO ('**R**evenue using **I**ncentives to deliver **I**nnovation and **O**utputs') method. RIIO is a price control mechanism that specifies the outputs that companies are required to deliver and the revenue that they are able to earn for delivering these outputs efficiently. The aim of this change is to provide better incentives for companies to meet quality standards, rather than just focusing on costs.

Performance targets

Under RIIO, companies who can deliver their output targets under budget gain through the revenue generation. However, companies that fail to meet their performance targets are punished financially. Companies need to report to their regulator on an annual basis.

In the case of water supply, government strategy requires companies to provide social tariffs for customers who cannot afford to pay for water. This is also monitored as part of the performance approach.

Knowledge check 23.10

Explain why the presence of asymmetric information could limit the effectiveness of regulation.

Key term

regulatory capture a situation in which the regulator of an industry comes to represent the industry's interests rather than regulating it

Limits to the regulatory approach

Government intervention through direct controls has to be carefully designed to avoid introducing market distortions. This is reflected in the changing approaches over time that attempt to rectify flaws that became apparent.

Asymmetric information can also come into play, when the companies have better information about the way they are operating than their regulators.

In some cases, **regulatory capture** is a further problem. This occurs when the regulator becomes so closely involved with the firm it is supposed to be regulating that it begins to champion its cause rather than imposing tough rules where they are needed.

Exercise 23.3

How does the principal–agent argument help to explain why nationalised industries may become inefficient? How does privatisation (with regulation) attempt to remedy this situation?

Summary: regulation of natural monopolies

- Natural monopolies pose particular problems for policy, as setting price equal to marginal cost forces such firms to make a loss.
- In the past, many such industries were run by the state as nationalised industries.
- However, this led to widespread X-inefficiency.
- Many of these industries were privatised after 1979.
- Regulation was put into place to ensure that the newly privatised firms did not abuse their market positions.
- Prices were controlled through the application of the $(RPI - X)$ rule, although this has been replaced by the RIIO method.
- In some cases, regulatory capture was a problem, whereby the regulators became too close to their industries.

Other interventions to promote competition

There are other ways in which governments intervene in order to promote competition, reflecting the view that this is the best way of ensuring consumer protection and good resource allocation.

Anti-competitive behaviour

The CMA does not only deal with mergers and acquisitions, but also investigates cartels (price-fixing) and other forms of anti-competitive behaviour by firms.

Price-fixing by firms in a cartel is illegal in most countries in the world. In the UK it is potentially a criminal offence. An example of CMA action was in 2018, when two of the main suppliers of bagged household fuels to large supermarkets and petrol stations were found guilty of bid-rigging. The firms had colluded to rig competitive tenders to supply Tesco and Sainsbury's, agreeing to submit bids designed to lose out to the other firm, so that each could retain its existing customer. They were fined over £3.4 million.

An example of another form of anti-competitive behaviour was an investigation carried out into the pricing behaviour of the pharmaceutical company Pfizer. The company produced an anti-epilepsy drug that was supplied to the NHS. The CMA discovered that expenditure by the NHS on the drug had increased from about £2 million in 2012 to about £50 million in 2013, following a price increase. The price charged to the NHS was higher than the price at which Pfizer were selling the drug in any other European country. The CMA imposed a fine of £84.2 million on the company.

A similar case emerged in December 2016, when a CMA press release announced its *provisional* finding that Acatavis UK appeared to have contravened competition law in its pricing of hydrocortisone tablets to the NHS. For example, the price of 10 mg packs of the drug were seen to have increased from £0.70 in April 2008 to £88 per pack by March 2016.

Public–private partnerships

It has been recognised that the same arguments that apply to the impact of competition on private sector efficiency are also relevant for public sector activity. In the case of public goods, there has to be some sort of government involvement as a free market will not ensure the provision of these goods. However, this does not necessarily mean that the public sector has to provide these goods directly. A number of ways in which the public sector can ensure provision through some sort of engagement with the private sector have been developed.

The simplest form of this is **contracting out**. Under such an arrangement, the public sector issues a contract to a private firm for the supply of some good or service. One example is waste disposal, where a local authority may issue a contract for a firm to provide the necessary waste disposal service. Competition between firms can be encouraged by a **competitive tendering** process. In other words, the contract would be announced and firms invited to put in bids specifying the quality of service they are prepared to provide, and at what price. The local authority would then be in a position to look for efficiency in choosing the most competitive bid.

More complex models of cooperation between public and private sectors have been developed, involving various kinds of **public–private partnership** (PPP). A PPP is 'an arrangement by which a government service or private business venture is funded and operated through a partnership of government and the private sector' (National Audit Office). The most common partnership model is the **Private Finance Initiative** (PFI).

The Private Finance Initiative

The PFI was launched in 1992 as a way of trying to increase the involvement of the private sector in the provision of public services. This established a partnership

Knowledge check 23.11

Why is government intervention needed to ensure the supply of a public good?

Key terms

contracting out a situation in which the public sector places activities in the hands of a private firm and pays for the provision

competitive tendering a process by which the public sector calls for private firms to bid for a contract for provision of a good or service

public–private partnership (PPP) an arrangement by which a government service or private business venture is funded and operated through a partnership of government and the private sector

Private Finance Initiative (PFI, later PF2) a funding arrangement under which the private sector designs, builds, finances and operates an asset and associated services for the public sector in return for an annual payment linked to its performance in delivering the service

between the public and private sectors. The public sector specifies, perhaps in broad terms, the services that it requires, and then invites tenders from the private sector to design, build, finance and operate the scheme. In some cases, it may be that the project would be entirely free-standing — for example, the government may initiate a project such as a new bridge, which is then taken up by a private firm that will recover its costs entirely through user charges such as tolls. In some other cases, the project may be a joint venture between the public and private sectors. The public sector could get involved with such a venture in order to secure wider social benefits, perhaps through reductions in traffic congestion that would not be reflected in market prices, and thus would not be fully taken into account by the private sector. In other cases, it may be that the private sector undertakes a project and then sells the services to the public sector, often over a period of 25 or 30 years.

The aim of the PFI is to improve the financing of public sector projects. This is partly achieved by introducing a competitive element into the tendering process, but in addition it enables the risk of a project to be shared between the public and private sectors. This was intended to enable efficiency gains to be made.

The PFI has been much debated — and much criticised because of poor quality outputs and high costs to the taxpayer. A reformed process (PF2) was launched in December 2012, but enthusiasm for this approach has waned. The collapse of Carillon (which held a number of PFI contracts) in early 2018 fuelled the criticisms.

One effect of the PFI is to reduce the pressures on public finances by enabling greater private sector involvement in funding. However, it might be argued that this may in fact raise the cost of borrowing, if the public sector would have been able to borrow on more favourable terms than commercial firms. The introduction of a competitive element in the tendering process may be beneficial, but on the other hand it could be argued that the private sector may have less incentive than the public sector to give due attention to health and safety issues. In other words, there may be a concern that private firms will be tempted to sacrifice safety or service standards in the quest for profit. Achieving the appropriate balance between efficiency and quality of service is an inevitable problem to be faced in whatever way transport is financed and provided, for example, but it becomes a more critical issue to the extent that use of the PFI switches the focus more towards efficiency and lower costs.

PFI deals often involve major road construction projects

Encouragement of small businesses

There are measures in place to encourage small businesses. One example of this was in the wake of the financial crisis, a time when the UK government was keen to restore confidence in the economy.

The Department of Business Innovation and Skills (BIS) noted that small and medium-sized enterprises (SMEs) provide 'nearly 60% of our jobs and 50% of GDP'. A new set of measures to help small businesses was launched in 2010/11, including steps to improve access to finance for small businesses and to provide other forms of support. The underlying rationale for these measures was to help small businesses to compete more effectively, and to provide targeted support to small firms with high growth potential.

One of the features of the financial crisis was that banks became reluctant to lend, causing particular problems for small firms in need of funding for investment. Banks faced a severe crisis, and some needed government assistance to bail them out of trouble. This was perhaps one of the largest-scale interventions of recent decades. Its prime aim was not to promote competition, but this was one of its side-effects through the encouragement for banks to lend to small businesses.

Synoptic link

The roots of the financial crisis and its effects are discussed in Chapters 30 and 31.

Deregulation

Freeing firms from regulation may lead to more intensive competition. Until 2006, the Royal Mail held a monopoly in the postal service market in the UK, having held that position for 350 years. From the 1 January 2016, any licensed operator was able to deliver mail to business and residential customers. This led to a surge of new businesses providing delivery services.

Restrictions on monopsony power

The main focus of the work of the CMA is on mergers and markets in which there could potentially be problems with firms gaining a dominant position. In the past, the Competition Commission has also identified issues with competition involving a monopsony, rather than a monopoly position. A high-profile example involved UK supermarkets.

Large supermarkets form a major part of the food industry in the UK, providing consumers with low prices and a wide variety of products. However, issues were raised about the way in which some of the supermarkets were treating their suppliers and farmers. When small farmers are supplying supermarkets that have substantial buying power, there is a possibility of the exploitation of market power. In December 2012, the competition minister announced that the Groceries Code Adjudicator was to be given greater powers to enforce the Groceries Code, providing additional protection for farmers and other suppliers, including the ability to fine supermarkets that transgress the code. In February 2015 it was announced that the Adjudicator was launching an investigation into Tesco following allegations that it had delayed payments to some suppliers and treated payments for shelf promotions unfairly.

The proposed merger of Sainsbury with Asda in 2018 raised concerns that the combined group would have enhanced monopsony power over its suppliers. This echoed concerns that had been rising over a number of years, notably the controversy that arose over the pricing of milk in supermarkets. Farmers argued that the price they were receiving for milk at the farm gate was not covering their costs, and that the supermarkets were using the product as a loss leader — at the farmers' expense.

Synoptic link

Monopsony is a form of market structure in which buyers have market power to affect the prices they pay to their suppliers. It was discussed in Chapter 20.

The impact of government intervention

It is clear that successive UK governments have taken serious action to promote competition, using a variety of tools and approaches. The assumption underpinning this approach to intervention is that competition encourages firms to be efficient, as firms that fail to reach efficiency in their activities will lose out to their rivals, making lower profits and gaining lower market shares — and perhaps being forced out of the market altogether.

At the same time, competition should also ensure that consumers face reasonable prices, with good-quality products and variety of choice. Indeed, the whole basis of the market system is that the consumer is king, and firms only make profit when they are producing the products that consumers wish to buy.

How effective has all this intervention been in practice? This is difficult to evaluate, as it is not possible to observe how things would look in the absence of intervention. There have been instances where the CMA or its predecessors have stepped in to prohibit a merger or acquisition, or have set conditions that safeguard consumer interests. The number of merger cases that are brought to the attention of the CMA seems high, but many of these are ruled not to be contentious or not meeting the threshold rules for investigation. In any case, it might be argued that the very existence of the CMA with its powers to intervene may act as a deterrent to anti-competitive actions.

Is monopoly always bad? Microsoft reached a position in which it supplied 95% of the global market for operating systems for PCs. It was argued that this was not because of abusing a dominant market position, but because it was very good at what it did. Are firms like Amazon and Google reaching market dominance because they are building market power? Or because they are providing a service that consumers want?

Is competition always good? When a local shop goes out of business because it cannot compete with the prices and variety of choice offered by the supermarkets, do consumers end up with less choice, or with more choice?

There are no simple answers to these questions, but endless possibilities for debate and for watching how markets evolve into the future.

Exercise 23.4

Discuss why it is important for the government to intervene to promote competition. Do you regard the measures outlined in this chapter to be sufficient to protect consumers?

Summary: government intervention to promote competition

- Governments intervene in a variety of ways to promote competition.
- The authorities have also attempted to encourage efficiency through the establishment of public-private partnerships, such as the Private Finance Initiative.
- Support has been provided to help small businesses, particularly with access to finance.
- The Groceries Code Adjudicator holds a watching brief to ensure that supermarkets do not abuse their monopsony power.
- Evaluating the impact of intervention is not straightforward, but the existence of legislation and monitoring by the CMA may deter firms from acting against consumer interests.

Case study 23.1

Opticians

In August 2017, the CMA launched an inquiry into a proposed acquisition by Vision Express of Tesco Opticians. Both companies operated retail optician chains in the UK.

An early step in any inquiry of this sort is to identify the relevant market to be investigated. Optical services are provided through a range of outlets, including independent opticians, retail chains and supermarkets, with some differentiation in the types of products offered. For example, independent opticians tend to offer products towards the luxury end of the market, whereas supermarkets tend to provide cheaper frames and lenses. The CMA decided that all three categories of competitors should be included in the market, as they are seen to compete with each other to some extent.

At a national level, the CMA did not perceive there to be any competition concerns raised by the proposed merger, but recognised that there could be concerns at a more local level that could affect customers. The acquisition involved 206 Tesco stores that would pass into the ownership of Vision Express. The CMA looked at each of the stores and in each case identified the drive time that covered 80% of the stores' customers. Where the catchment area defined in this way would see a reduction in the number of outlets to 5 or 4 or fewer, a more detailed analysis of competitive conditions was undertaken. In most of these areas, the CMA regarded the remaining outlets as providing sufficient competitive constraints. However, in three areas (Barrow-in-Furness, Helston and Ryde) the catchment area would contain only three outlets, which could result in a 'realistic prospect of a substantial lessening of competition'. Furthermore, the CMA did not regard it as likely that entry and expansion would be able to mitigate the potential anti-competitive effects of the merger.

Under the procedures, the next step could have been to take the inquiry to a higher level, but the CMA gave the two parties to the merger the opportunity to offer undertakings that could demonstrate that customers in the three areas would be protected.

In the event, the undertakings offered by Vision Express was to divest itself of the outlets in the three affected areas, without transferring electronic or physical customer lists. This was accepted by the CMA, and the case was closed.

Follow-up questions

a Explain what is meant by 'relevant market' and why it is important for an investigation of this sort.

b What sort of anti-competitive measures might Vision Express have carried out in the three potentially affected areas if the CMA had not taken action to prevent it?

c How convincing do you find the undertakings to be?

d What decision would you have taken if you had been the CMA?

Theme 3 key terms

allocative efficiency achieved when society is producing the appropriate bundle of goods and services relative to consumer preferences; this occurs when price equals marginal cost

arbitrage a process by which prices in two market segments are equalised by the purchase and resale of products by market participants

average total cost total cost divided by the quantity produced

backward integration a process under which a firm merges with a firm that is involved in an earlier part of the production chain

barrier to entry a characteristic of a market that prevents new firms from readily joining the market

bounded rationality a situation in which a firm's ability to take rational decisions is limited by a lack of information or an inability to interpret the information that is available

cartel an agreement between firms on price and output with the intention of maximising their joint profits

competition policy a set of measures designed to promote competition in markets and protect consumers in order to enhance the efficiency of markets

competitive tendering a process by which the public sector calls for private firms to bid for a contract for provision of a good or service

conglomerate merger a merger between two firms operating in different markets

constant returns to scale found when long-run average cost remains constant with an increase in output, i.e. when output and costs rise at the same rate

contestable market a market in which the existing firm makes only normal profit, as it cannot set a higher price without attracting entry, owing to the absence of barriers to entry and sunk costs

contracting out a situation in which the public sector places activities in the hands of a private firm and pays for the provision

corporate social responsibility actions that a firm takes in order to demonstrate its commitment to behaving in the public interest

cost-plus pricing a pricing policy whereby firms set their price by adding a mark-up to average cost

derived demand demand for a good or service not for its own sake, but for what it produces, e.g. labour is demanded for the output that it produces

diseconomies of scale occur for a firm when an increase in the scale of production leads to higher long-run average costs

dominant strategy a situation in game theory where a player's best strategy is independent of those chosen by others

dynamic efficiency a view of efficiency that takes into account the effect of innovation and technical progress on productive and allocative efficiency in the long run

economies of scale occur for a firm when an increase in a firm's scale of production leads to production at lower long-run average cost

external economies of scale economies of scale that arise from the expansion of the industry in which a firm is operating

firm an organisation that brings together factors of production in order to produce output

forward integration a process under which a firm merges with a firm that is involved in a later part of the production chain

game theory a method of modelling the strategic interaction between firms in an oligopoly

hit and run entry where a firm enters a market to take short-run supernormal profits knowing it can exit with incurring costs

horizontal integration the result of a horizontal merger

horizontal merger a merger between two firms at the same stage of production in the same industry

industry long-run supply curve (*LRS*) under perfect competition, the curve that, for the typical firm in the industry, is horizontal at the minimum point of the long-run average cost curve

internal economies of scale economies of scale that arise from the expansion of a firm

law of diminishing returns law stating that if a firm increases its inputs of one factor of production while holding inputs of the other factor fixed, it will eventually derive diminishing marginal returns from the variable factor

limit price the highest price that an existing firm can set without enabling new firms to enter the market and make a profit

long run the period over which the firm is able to vary the inputs of all its factors of production

marginal cost the cost of producing an additional unit of output

marginal revenue the additional revenue gained by a firm from selling an additional unit of output

market structure the market environment within which firms operate

maximum wage a policy under which employers face a wage ceiling, being prohibited from paying a wage above a set level

merger where firms join together to form a single firm, potentially reducing competition in a market by increasing concentration

minimum efficient scale the level of output at which long-run average cost stops falling as output increases

minimum wage a government-set minimum wage rate below which firms are not allowed to pay

monopolistic competition a market that shares some characteristics of monopoly and some of perfect competition

monopoly a form of market structure in which there is only one seller of a good or service

monopsony a market in which there is a single buyer of a good, service or factor of production

***n*-firm concentration ratio** a measure of the market share of the largest *n* firms in an industry

Nash equilibrium situation occurring within a game when each player's chosen strategy maximises payoffs given the other player's choice, so that no player has an incentive to alter behaviour

nationalisation where a privately owned firm or industry is taken into public ownership

natural monopoly monopoly that arises in an industry in which there are such substantial economies of scale that only one firm is viable

non-pecuniary benefits benefits offered to workers by firms that are not financial in nature

non-price competition steps that firms can take to compete with rival firms other than on price, such as advertising or product differentiation

normal profit profit that covers the opportunity cost of capital and is just sufficient to keep the firm in the market

not-for-profit organisations organisations such as charities that operate on a non-profit-making basis

oligopoly a market with a few sellers, in which each firm must take account of the behaviour and likely behaviour of rival firms in the industry

oligopsony a market in which there are a few buyers of a good, service or factor of production

organic growth when a firm grows internally by reinvesting profits or borrowing from banks

overt collusion a situation in which firms openly work together to agree on prices or market shares

participation rate the proportion of the population of working age who are in employment or seeking work

perfect competition a form of market structure that produces allocative and productive efficiency in long-run equilibrium

perfect/first-degree price discrimination situation arising in a market whereby a monopoly firm is able to charge each consumer a different price

predatory pricing an anti-competitive strategy in which a firm sets price below average variable cost in an attempt to force a rival or rivals out of the market and achieve market dominance

price taker a firm that must accept whatever price is set in the market as a whole

principal–agent (agency) problem a problem arising from conflict between the objectives of the principals and those of the agents who take decisions on their behalf

prisoners' dilemma an example of game theory with a range of applications in oligopoly theory

Private Finance Initiative (PFI, later PF2) a funding arrangement under which the private sector designs, builds, finances and operates an asset and associated services for the public sector in return for an annual payment linked to its performance in delivering the service

private sector made up of firms that are privately owned

privatisation where an enterprise in public ownership is returned to private ownership

product differentiation a strategy adopted by firms that marks their product as being different from their competitors'

productive efficiency occurs when firms have chosen appropriate combinations of factors of production and produce the maximum output possible from those inputs, thus producing at minimum long-run average cost

public–private partnership (PPP) an arrangement by which a government service or private business venture is funded and operated through a partnership of government and the private sector

public sector made up of state-owned organisations, including those that run central and local government activities and some enterprises in public ownership

regulatory capture a situation in which the regulator of an industry comes to represent the industry's interests rather than regulating it

relevant market a market to be investigated under competition law, defined in such a way that no major substitutes are omitted but no non-substitutes are included

satisficing behaviour under which the managers of firms aim to produce satisfactory results for the firm, e.g. in terms of profits, rather than trying to maximise them

short run the period over which a firm is free to vary the input of one of its factors of production (labour), but faces a fixed input of the other (capital)

short-run supply curve for a firm operating under perfect competition, the curve given by its short-run marginal cost curve above the price at which $MC = SAVC$; for the industry, the horizontal sum of the supply curves of the individual firms

shut-down price the price below which a firm will cease production in the short run, as it is not covering its variable cost

static efficiency efficiency at a particular point in time

sunk costs short-run costs that cannot be recovered if the firm closes down

supernormal profits/abnormal profits/economic profit terms referring to profits that exceed normal profit

tacit collusion situation occurring when firms refrain from competing on price, but without communication or formal agreement between them

third-degree price discrimination situation in which a firm is able to charge groups of consumers a different price for the same product

total fixed costs costs that do not vary with the level of output

total variable costs the sum of costs that vary with the level of output

transnational company a firm that conducts its operations in a number of countries

vertical merger a merger between two firms in the same industry, but at different stages of the production process

X-inefficiency situation arising when a firm is not operating at minimum cost, perhaps because of organisational slack

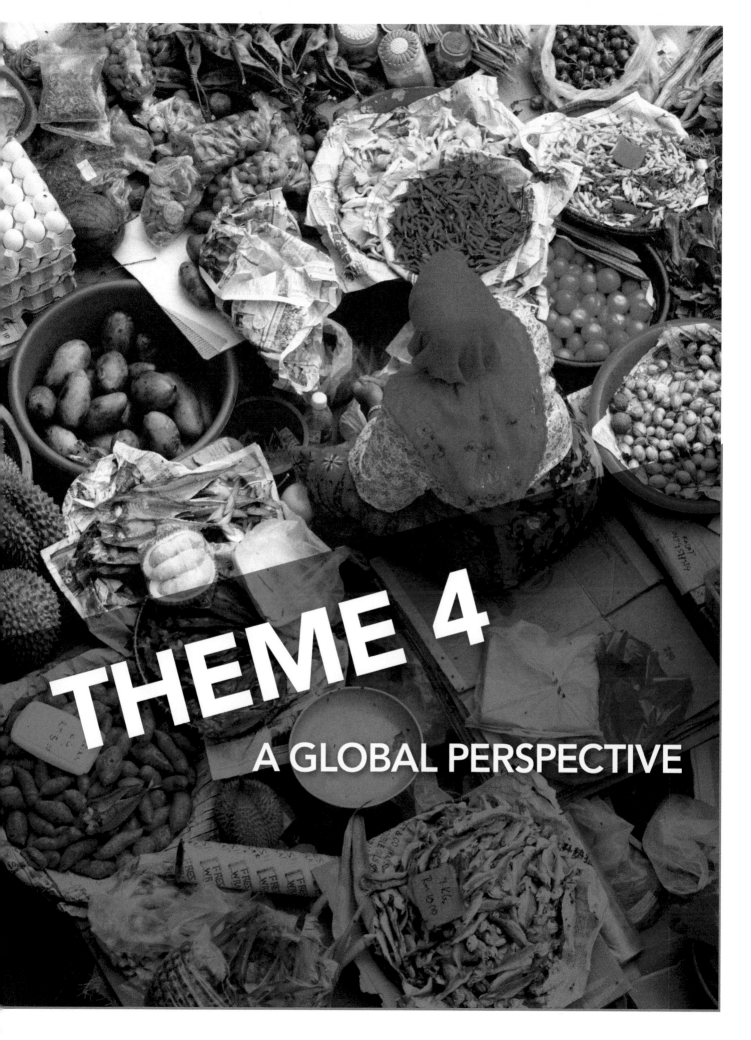

THEME 4

A GLOBAL PERSPECTIVE

Globalisation and trade

The world economy is becoming increasingly integrated, and it is no longer possible to think of any single economy in isolation. The UK economy is no exception. It relies on international trade, engaging in exporting and importing activity, and many UK firms are increasingly active in global markets. This situation has created opportunities for UK firms to expand and become global players, and for UK consumers to have access to a wider range of goods and services. However, there is also a downside: global shocks, whether caused by oil prices, financial crises or the emergence of China as a world economic force, can reverberate throughout economies in all parts of the world. These are some of the issues that will be explored in this chapter.

Learning objectives

After studying this chapter, you should:
→ understand what is meant by globalisation, and be aware of the factors that have given rise to this phenomenon
→ understand the importance of foreign direct investment and the role of transnational companies
→ be aware of the impact that external shocks can have within the global economy
→ appreciate the importance of trade and exchange between nations
→ be familiar with the meaning and importance of absolute and comparative advantage
→ appreciate the meaning and relevance of the terms of trade
→ be familiar with the general pattern of world trade and the trade of the UK

What is globalisation?

Key term

globalisation a process by which the world's economies are becoming more closely integrated

The term **globalisation** has been much used in recent years, not least by the protest groups that have demonstrated against it. It is therefore important to be clear about what the term means before seeking to evaluate its strengths and weaknesses.

Ann Krueger, the first deputy managing director of the IMF, defined globalisation as 'a phenomenon by which economic agents in any given part of the world are much more affected by events elsewhere in the world' than before. Joseph Stiglitz, the Nobel Laureate and former Chief Economist at the World Bank, defined it as follows:

> Fundamentally, [globalisation] is the closer integration of countries and peoples of the world which has been brought about by the enormous reduction of costs of transportation and communication, and the breaking down of artificial barriers to the flows of goods, services, capital, knowledge, and (to a lesser extent) people across borders.
>
> Source: *Globalization and its Discontents* (Penguin, 2004)

On this basis, globalisation is crucially about the closer integration of the world's economies. Critics have focused partly on the environmental effects of rapid global economic growth, and partly on the opportunities that powerful nations and large corporations have for exploiting the weak. Some of these arguments will be evaluated after a more careful exploration of the topic.

Foreign direct investment

An important aspect of globalisation has been the spread of **foreign direct investment (FDI)** by transnational companies. UNCTAD has identified three main reasons for such activity:

1 market seeking

2 resource seeking

3 efficiency seeking

Some transnational companies may engage in FDI because they want to sell their products within a particular market, and find it preferable to produce within the market rather than elsewhere: such FDI is *market seeking*. Second, transnational companies may undertake investment in a country in order to take advantage of some key resource. This might be a natural resource such as oil or natural gas, or a labour force with certain skills, or simply cheap unskilled labour: such FDI is *resource seeking*. Third, transnational companies may simply review their options globally, and decide that they can produce most efficiently in a particular location. This might entail locating just part of their production chain in a certain country. Such FDI is *efficiency seeking*.

Market-seeking FDI has been important in some regions in particular. The opening up of China to foreign investment has proved a magnet for transnational companies wanting to gain access to this large and growing market. In addition, non-European firms have been keen to gain entry to the EU's Single Market, which encouraged substantial flows of FDI into Europe (including the UK). For the UK, there has been a two-way flow of direct investment. In other words, foreign investors have invested in the UK, and UK investors have invested abroad. It remains to be seen how the pattern of FDI in the UK will be affected by the Brexit situation.

FDI can have positive and negative effects on the host country. On the positive side, it is hoped that FDI will bring potential gains in employment, tax revenue, capital and technology, with consequent beneficial impact on economic growth. This may be seen as especially important for developing countries that may especially lack capital and technology or the ability to raise tax revenue. However, there is a downside, as these potential benefits may not always be as strong as had been hoped. In particular, if profits are repatriated to shareholders elsewhere in the world, then the long-term impact of FDI may be diluted, rather than feeding back into economic growth. For developing countries, the tax concessions negotiated by foreign transnational firms may reduce the benefits, and the technology may not be appropriate, or not disseminated.

> **Key term**
>
> **foreign direct investment (FDI)** investment undertaken in one country by companies based in other countries

> **Knowledge check 24.1**
>
> Suppose a transnational company brings investment into a developing country. How would you expect this to affect employment in the host country?

Summary: globalisation and foreign direct investment

- Globalisation is a process in which countries have become increasingly interconnected.
- An important part of globalisation has been the spread of foreign direct investment (FDI) by transnational companies.
- Motivations for FDI include market-seeking, resource-seeking and efficiency-seeking reasons.

Factors contributing to globalisation

The quotation from the book by Joseph Stiglitz not only defines what is meant by globalisation, but also offers some reasons for its occurrence.

Transportation and communication costs

One of the contributory factors to the spread of globalisation has undoubtedly been the rapid advances in the technology of transportation and communications.

Improvements in transportation have enabled firms to fragment their production process to take advantage of varying cost conditions in different parts of the world. For example, it is now possible to site labour-intensive parts of a production process in parts of the world where labour is relatively plentiful, and thus relatively cheap. This is one way in which **transnational companies** thrive, in some cases operating across a wide range of countries.

> ### Key terms
>
> **transnational company** a company whose production activities are carried out in a number of countries
>
> **General Agreement on Tariffs and Trade (GATT)** the precursor of the WTO, which organised a series of 'rounds' of tariff reductions
>
> **World Trade Organization (WTO)** a multilateral body responsible for overseeing the conduct of international trade

> ### Knowledge check 24.2
>
> The internet allows knowledge to be shared across national boundaries. How would you expect this to facilitate globalisation?

Furthermore, communications technology has developed rapidly with the growth of the internet and e-commerce, enabling firms to compete more easily in global markets. The importance of email and other forms of communication such as video-conferencing and Skype should not be underestimated. It is now taken for granted that there can be instant communication across the globe. This has made it very much easier for firms to communicate within their organisations and with other firms, and has certainly fuelled the closer integration of firms and economies. The emergence of a global media presence also enables the rapid sharing of information and ideas, keeping consumers well-informed about new products coming to the market.

These technological changes have augmented the existing economies of scale and scope, enabling firms to grow. In the countries in which they operate, the sheer size of some transnational companies gives them political as well as economic power.

Reduction of trade barriers

A second factor that has contributed to globalisation has been the successive reduction in trade barriers during the period since the Second World War, first under the auspices of the **General Agreement on Tariffs and Trade (GATT)**, and later under the **World Trade Organization (WTO)** which replaced it.

> ### Synoptic link
>
> The operations of the WTO will be explored in Chapter 25, after we have examined the context provided by economic analysis.

In addition to these trade-liberalising measures, there has been a trend towards the establishment of free trade areas and customs unions in various parts of the world, with the European Union being just one example. The appearance of China on the world stage has also been of crucial importance. China has the largest population of any country in the world, and has experienced economic growth at an unprecedented and consistent rate in recent decades. It joined the WTO in 2001, and has had a major impact on global markets. By joining the WTO, China agreed to abide by its rules, thus affecting the confidence with which other countries could view trade with, and investment in, China.

By facilitating the process of international trade, such developments have encouraged firms to become more active in trade, and thus have added to the impetus towards globalisation.

Deregulation of financial markets

Hand in hand with these developments, there have been moves towards removing restrictions on the movement of financial capital between countries. Many countries have removed financial capital controls, thereby making it much easier for firms to operate globally. This has been reinforced by developments in technology that enable financial transactions to be undertaken more quickly and efficiently.

Migration

In Europe, the formation of the Single European Market enabled freer movement of people within Europe. The effects of this were reinforced by the ending of the Cold War, which affected global labour supply.

Synoptic link

The effects of migration on labour markets were discussed in Chapter 22, which noted the potential benefits and costs of such movement of labour.

The impact of globalisation

Globalisation and the growth of transnational companies have had significant effects on countries, governments, producers, consumers, workers and the environment. Not all of these effects have been positive. At the heart of the globalisation process has been the increased interdependence of economies, which has had profound effects.

Standards of living

By enabling increased specialisation and trade, globalisation has enabled economic growth to take place. This has enabled an increase in standards of living for people in many countries. Furthermore, it has allowed more consumer choice, as people may access a wider range of products than was previously possible. Notice that this may have a downside, as along with choice comes a danger that inappropriate products and lifestyles may spread at the expense of local cultures.

Structural change

Increased specialisation comes with a transitional cost. Countries have had to adjust to new patterns of economic activity. For example, many advanced countries have seen their economies go through a transition in which traditional sectors such as manufacturing have declined in the face of competition from developing countries. This process is known as **deindustrialisation**. The service sectors have expanded, but workers displaced from manufacturing occupations do not always find it easy to retrain for service sector jobs. Some producers have been unable to compete with lower-cost producers from elsewhere in the world, but others have flourished as service activity has expanded.

Synoptic link

The launch of Brexit and the 'America First' stance of President Trump seems to buck this trend, and will be examined in Chapter 25.

Knowledge check 24.3

How does in-migration to a country affect economic growth?

Key term

deindustrialisation a process whereby the structure of economic activity in a country shifts away from manufacturing activity towards the service sector

Synoptic link

Specialisation and the gains from trade are explored later in this chapter.

Synoptic link

This notion of structural unemployment was discussed in Chapter 10.

Interdependence of economies

One of the issues concerning a more closely integrated global economy is the question of how robust the global economy will be to shocks. In other words, globalisation may be fine when the world economy is booming, as all nations may be able to share in the success. But if the global economy goes into recession, will all nations suffer the consequences? There are a number of situations that might cause the global economy to take a downturn, which then affects countries and their governments around the world.

Oil prices

Oil prices seem to provide one possible threat. Historically, sudden changes in oil prices have caused widespread disruption — for example, in 1973–74 and in 1979–80.

Figure 5.2 on page 70 shows the historical time path of the price of oil from 1965 to 2016, measured in US dollars. In 1973–74 the sudden increase in the price of oil took most people by surprise. Oil prices had been steady for several years, and many economies had become dependent on oil as an energy source, not only for running cars but for other uses such as domestic central heating. The sudden increases in the price in 1973–74 and again in 1979–80 caused widespread problems because demand in the short run was highly inelastic, and oil-importing countries faced sudden deficits on their balance of payments current accounts. However, in time people switched away from oil for heating, firms developed more energy-efficient cars, and demand was able to adjust. Arguably, national economies in the twenty-first century are less vulnerable to changes in the price of oil than they were in 1973. However, volatility in the price of such a key commodity is significant. Figure 24.1 shows how the price of oil changed on a monthly basis after 2000, causing concern in late 2004 when it once more began to rise, accelerating in 2007–08.

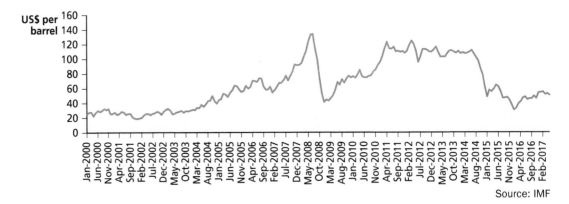

Source: IMF

Figure 24.1 The price of oil since 2000

Arguably, economies were better equipped to withstand the increase than they had been in the 1970s. The UK was partly able to weather the storm of the early 2000s because of its position as an oil producer, although by this time, reserves were becoming depleted.

Another difference was that the price rises in 1973–74 and 1979–80 had been primarily supply-side changes, caused by disruptions to supply following the actions of the OPEC cartel. In the 2000s part of the upward pressure on price was coming from demand, with China's demand for oil being especially strong. In the event, the pressures of falling demand as the global recession began to unfold brought the price of oil tumbling, only to rise again as the global economy began to recover. By 2011 oil prices were back well above $100 per barrel. Production of oil from shale increased in the USA after 2014, and prices again fell. In early 2017, OPEC started to curb production to support the price.

The price of oil is significant because of its importance to so many businesses as an energy source, so fluctuations in its price can have knock-on effects across the global economy. Higher oil prices have highlighted awareness of environmental issues, and stimulated the search for new sources of energy.

Knowledge check 24.4

Why would OPEC want to curb production in 2017?

Financial crises

Given the increasing integration of financial markets, a further concern is whether globalisation increases the chances that a financial crisis will spread rapidly between countries, rather than being contained within a country or region. The 1997 Asian financial crisis provides some evidence on this issue.

This crisis began in Thailand and South Korea. Both countries had been the recipients of large flows of FDI. In the case of Thailand, a significant part of this had been investment in property, rather than in productive investment. The Thai currency (the baht) came under speculative pressure early in 1997, and eventually the authorities had to allow a devaluation. This sparked a crisis of confidence in the region, and foreign investors began to withdraw funds, not only from Thailand but from other countries too. As far as globalisation was concerned, the key questions were how far the crisis would spread, and how long it would last.

In the event, five countries bore the main burden of the crisis: Indonesia, Malaysia, the Philippines, South Korea and Thailand. Beyond this grouping there were some knock-on effects because of trade linkages, but arguably these were not too severe, and were probably dominated by other events taking place in the period. At the time of the crisis, Indonesia and the Philippines had been at a somewhat lower stage of development than the other countries involved, and thus suffered more deeply in terms of recession. However, with the benefit of hindsight, it seems that the region showed resilience in recovering from the crisis. Indeed, it can be argued that South Korea and Thailand especially emerged as stronger economies, through the weeding out of some relatively inefficient firms and institutions, and through a heightened awareness of the importance of sound financial regulation.

China and the USA

An important question in the early to mid-2000s was how the global economy would cope with two seemingly distant but related phenomena: the rapid growth of the Chinese economy, and the deficit on the US current account of the balance of payments. The US current account deficit arose partly from the heavy public expenditure programme of the Bush administration. However, the deficit grew to unprecedented levels partly through the actions of China and other East Asian economies that had chosen to peg their currencies to the US dollar. Effectively, this meant that those economies were buying US government securities as a way of maintaining their currencies against the dollar, thereby keeping US interest rates relatively low and allowing the American public to borrow to finance high consumer spending.

Who gained from this situation? The USA was able to spend, and China was able to sell, fuelling its rapid rate of economic growth. In due course, China agreed to allow its currency to adjust towards its true equilibrium – albeit rather slowly. However, the events left a legacy of distrust between the USA (especially President Trump) and China.

The credit crunch

Another example of the dangers of close interdependence began to unfold in 2007–08, when the so-called 'credit crunch' began to bite, and commercial banks in several countries found themselves in financial crisis. This followed a period in which relatively low interest rates had allowed a bubble of borrowing. When house prices began to slide, many banks in several countries found that they had overextended themselves, and had to cut back on lending, in some cases threatening their viability. This affected a number of countries simultaneously, and there was a danger that the financial crisis would affect the real economy, leading to a recession. This was a recession that would affect countries all around the globe because of the new interconnectedness of economies. It became apparent that no single country could tackle the problem alone, as measures taken to support the banks in one economy had rapid knock-on effects elsewhere. Once this was realised, coordinated action was taken, and in October 2008 the central banks of several countries reduced their bank rates together. This was followed by action aiming to salvage the situation and avoid a full-blooded recession.

By early 2009, the UK economy was officially in recession, the bank rate had been driven down to an unprecedented 0.5%, and the Bank of England was introducing quantitative easing to try to stimulate the economy. One of the problems was that the commercial banks had become reluctant to lend, so firms that wanted to invest were finding it difficult to obtain funds. Attempts were made to coordinate the efforts of governments of key countries around the world — for example, at the G20 Summit held in London in April 2009. As time went by and the recession deepened, a number of countries in the eurozone faced crises with the level of public debt. This affected Ireland, Greece and Portugal in particular, all of which needed bailouts. The financial crisis will be discussed in Chapters 30 and 31.

The environment

Critics of globalisation have pointed to the impact that the increase in trade associated with globalisation may be having on the environment, especially in the context of climate change and global warming. This is bound up with the notion of **sustainable development**, which refers to the effect that economic growth and increased trade may have on future generations.

The core of the argument is that increased trade means increased emissions of greenhouse gases because of the need to transport goods over long distances. For example, if you check the country of origin of the fruit and vegetables in your local supermarket, you will find that these are imported from far and wide. This is the case even for some produce that can be grown in the UK. On this basis it is argued that increasing such trade damages the environment. However, the case is not fully accepted by everyone. For example, a study by DEFRA showed that importing tomatoes from Spain into the UK (especially by sea) causes less environmental damage than growing them domestically because of the difference in climate between the two countries. This enables tomatoes to be grown in a more environmentally friendly manner in Spain, where no heat is needed to encourage growth and ripening. Nonetheless, this is an aspect of globalisation that needs to be considered and taken into account.

> **Key term**
>
> **sustainable development** 'development which meets the needs of the present without compromising the ability of future generations to meet their own needs' (Brundtland Commission, 1987)

Summary: globalisation

- Although closer integration may bring benefits in terms of increased global production and trade, it may also create vulnerability by allowing adverse shocks to spread more rapidly between countries.
- Such shocks include oil price changes and financial crises. However, the integrated global economy may turn out to be more resilient in reacting to adverse circumstances.
- Globalisation facilitates and accelerates the process by which gains from trade may be tapped.
- However, the transitional costs for individual economies in terms of the need for structural change have encouraged politicians to turn to protectionist measures.
- Critics of globalisation have pointed to the environmental costs of rapid global economic growth and the expansion of trade, and have argued that it is the rich countries and the multinational corporations that gain the most, rather than the developing countries.

Exercise 24.1

Examine the economic arguments for and against globalisation.

Specialisation and international trade

The central importance of international trade for growth and development has been recognised since the days of Adam Smith and David Ricardo. For example, during the Industrial Revolution a key factor was that Britain could bring in raw materials from its colonies for use in manufacturing activity. Today, consumers in the UK are able to buy and consume many goods that simply could not be produced within the domestic economy. From the point of view of economic analysis, Ricardo showed that countries could gain from trade through a process of *specialisation*.

Absolute and comparative advantage

The notion of specialisation was briefly introduced in Chapter 1, where it was pointed out that the division of labour could enable efficiency gains. This analysis can now be extended to demonstrate the potential gains to be made from specialisation and trade.

Consider an example. Matthew and Sophie supplement their incomes by working at weekends. They have both been to evening classes and attended pottery and jewellery-making classes to sell at a local market. Depending on how they divide their time, they can make differing combinations of these goods; some of the possibilities are shown in Table 24.1.

Notice that Sophie is better than Matthew at both activities; if they each spend all of their time producing one of the goods, Sophie can make 18 pots to Matthew's 12,

Table 24.1 Matthew and Sophie's production

Matthew		Sophie	
Pots	**Bracelets**	**Pots**	**Bracelets**
12	0	18	0
9	3	12	12
6	6	6	24
3	9	3	30
0	12	0	36

Key terms

absolute advantage the ability to produce a good more efficiently (e.g. with less labour)

comparative advantage the ability to produce a good *relatively* more efficiently (i.e. at lower opportunity cost)

law of comparative advantage a theory arguing that there may be gains from trade arising when countries (or individuals) specialise in the production of goods or services in which they have a comparative advantage

or 36 bracelets to Matthew's 12. This illustrates **absolute advantage**. Sophie is simply better than Matthew at both activities. Another way of looking at this is that, in order to produce a given quantity of a good, Sophie needs less labour time than Matthew.

There is another significant feature of this table. Although Sophie is better at producing both goods, the difference is much more marked in the case of bracelet production than for pot production. So Sophie is relatively more proficient in bracelet production: in other words, she has a **comparative advantage** in making bracelets. This is reflected in differences in opportunity cost. If Sophie switches from producing pots to producing bracelets, she must forgo 6 pots for every 12 additional bracelets that she makes. The opportunity cost of an additional bracelet is thus 6/12 = 0.5 pots. For Matthew, there is a one-to-one trade-off between the two, so his opportunity cost of a bracelet is 1 pot.

More interesting is what happens if the same calculation is made for Matthew and pot making. Although Sophie is absolutely better at making pots, if Matthew increases his production of pots, his opportunity cost in terms of bracelets is still 1. But for Sophie the opportunity cost of making pots in terms of bracelets is 12/6 = 2, so Matthew has the lower opportunity cost. Although Sophie has an *absolute* advantage in pot making, Matthew has a *comparative* advantage. It is this difference in comparative advantage that gives rise to the gains from specialisation.

The **law of comparative advantage** states that overall output can be increased if individuals specialise in producing the goods in which they have a comparative advantage.

Knowledge check 24.5

Is the presence of absolute advantage sufficient to ensure that there are potential gains from specialisation and trade?

Gains from international trade

This same principle can be applied in the context of international trade. Suppose there are two countries, Anywhere and Somewhere, where Anywhere has an absolute advantage in the production of both agricultural and manufactured goods. Assume (for simplicity) that the two countries are of similar size in output terms, although Somewhere uses more resources in production than Anywhere because of the absolute advantage held by Anywhere. However, suppose that Anywhere faces lower opportunity cost in producing manufactured goods, and Somewhere has lower opportunity cost in producing agricultural goods. Their respective *PPF*s are shown in Figure 24.2.

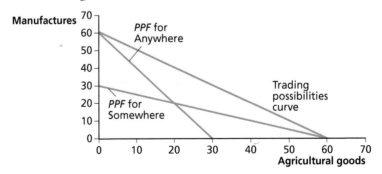

Figure 24.2 Trading possibilities for Anywhere and Somewhere

The pattern of comparative advantage held by the two countries is reflected in the different slopes of the countries' *PPFs*. In the absence of trade, each country is constrained to consume along its *PPF*. For example, if Somewhere wants to consume 20 units of manufactures, it can consume a maximum of 20 units of agricultural goods.

However, suppose that each country were to specialise in producing the product in which it has a comparative advantage. Anywhere could produce 60 units of manufactures and Somewhere could produce 60 units of agricultural goods. If each country were to specialise completely in this way, and if trade were to take place on a one-to-one basis (i.e. if one unit of manufactures is exchanged for one unit of agricultural goods), then it can be seen that this expands the consumption possibilities for both countries. The **trading possibilities curve** in Figure 24.2 shows the potential consumption points for each country in this situation.

Key term

trading possibilities curve shows the consumption possibilities under conditions of free trade

Quantitative skills 24.1

Calculating opportunity cost ratios

The key to comparative advantage is the difference in the opportunity costs faced by each country in the production of these goods. This can be calculated. First notice that if Anywhere chooses to increase output of agricultural goods by 10 units, it must sacrifice 20 units of manufactures, so the opportunity cost ratio is 2:1, meaning that for every unit of extra agricultural goods it must sacrifice 2 units of manufactures. However, for Somewhere 10 units of manufactures are sacrificed if 10 more units of agricultural goods are to be produced, so the opportunity cost ratio is 1:1. Similarly, the opportunity cost ratios for manufactured goods are 0.5 for Anywhere and 1 for Somewhere.

Exercise 24.2

Figure 24.3 shows production possibility curves for two countries, each of which produces both coats and scooters. The countries are called 'Here' and 'There'.

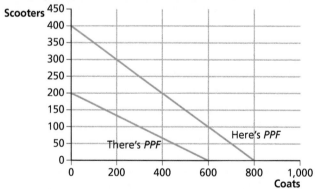

Figure 24.3 Coats and scooters

a Suppose that Here produces 200 scooters and There produces 100: how many coats are produced in each country?

b Now suppose that 300 scooters and 200 coats are produced by Here, and that There produces only coats. What has happened to the total production of coats and scooters?

Knowledge check 24.6

Country A's opportunity cost ratio for good X relative to good Y is 3:1, compared with a ratio of 2:1 for Country B. Which country should specialise in producing good X?

In the above examples and exercises, specialisation and trade are seen to lead to higher overall production of goods. Although the examples have related to goods, you should be equally aware that services too may be a source of specialisation and trade. This is potentially important for an economy such as the UK's, where there is a comparative advantage in the provision of financial services.

Who gains from international trade?

Synoptic link

Don't forget these three fundamental questions of economics that were introduced in Chapter 1: what, how and for whom. They underpin economic analysis.

Specialisation can result in an overall increase in total production. However, one of the fundamental questions of economics in Chapter 1 was 'for whom?' It is *possible* that exchange can take place between countries in such a way that both countries are better off. But whether this will actually happen in practice depends on the prices at which exchange takes place.

In particular, specialisation may bring dangers and risks, as well as benefits. One obvious way in which this may be relevant is that, by specialising, a country allows some sectors to run down. For example, suppose a country came to rely on imported food, and allowed its agricultural sector to waste away. If the country then became involved in a war, or for some other reason was unable to import its food, there would clearly be serious consequences if it could no longer grow its own foodstuffs. For this reason, many countries have in place measures designed to protect their agricultural sectors — or other sectors that are seen to be strategic in nature. This argument was key in the establishment of the Common Agricultural Policy in Europe.

Over-reliance on some commodities may also be risky. For example, the development of artificial substitutes for rubber had an enormous impact on the demand for natural rubber; this was reflected in falls in its price and caused difficulties for countries that had specialised in producing rubber.

The terms of trade

Key term

terms of trade the ratio of export prices to import prices

One of the key factors that determines who gains from international trade is the **terms of trade**, defined simply as the ratio of export prices to import prices.

Suppose that both export and import prices are rising through time, but import prices are rising more rapidly than export prices. This means that the ratio of export to import prices will fall — which in turn means that a country must export a greater volume of its goods in order to acquire the same volume of imports.

Quantitative skills 24.2

Calculating and interpreting the terms of trade

Export and import prices are expressed as index numbers, based on a particular year. Suppose we want to know how the terms of trade for a country have changed in October 2019 relative to 2000. This can be done using the data in Table 24.2, which shows price indexes for exports and imports based on 2011=100.

Table 24.2 The terms of trade

Date	Price index of exports	Price index of imports
2000	72.1	74.4
October 2019	94.8	95.7

First calculate the price index number for October 2019 based on 2000 =100. The rebased price index for exports is $100 \times 94.8/72.1 = 131.5$. For the price of imports, the index is 128.6 (check this calculation to make sure you understand how to do it). These calculations show that prices of both exported and imported goods have risen over the period.

The terms of trade represent the relative price change over the period, so for October 2019 we calculate the ratio of the price of exports to the price of imports. This is normally expressed as a percentage (i.e. as an index number), so the calculation is $100 \times 131.5/128.6 = 102.3$. The terms of trade increased by 2.3% between 2000 and October 2019. This indicates that the same volume of exports will purchase a greater volume of imports than in 2000.

A fall in the terms of trade indicates that the same volume of exports will purchase a smaller volume of imports than before. A downward movement in the terms of trade is thus unfavourable for an economy. Figure 24.4 shows the terms of trade for selected countries since 2000. You can see from this that different countries can experience changes in the terms of trade in very different ways in the same period of time. This depends strongly on the pattern of a country's exports and imports. For the countries shown, Uganda's exports are dominated by coffee, so coffee prices have a strong influence on the terms of trade. For Zambia, it is copper that dominates. The terms of trade for the UK varied very little over this period, relative to Zambia or Sierra Leone.

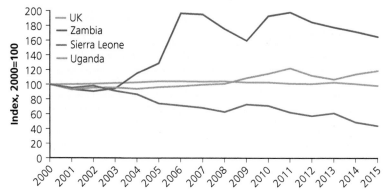

Source: World Development Indicators

Figure 24.4 The terms of trade in selected countries, 2000–2015 (2000 = 100)

Knowledge check 24.7

If the export prices for a country increase by 15% over a given period, but import prices rise by 20%, have the terms of trade improved or deteriorated?

The terms of trade are calculated purely with respect to prices, and take no account of changing volumes of trade. In other words, a deterioration in the terms of trade does not necessarily mean that an economy is worse off, so long as the volume of trade is increasing sufficiently rapidly.

Extension material: the terms of trade

The terms of trade described in the text are known more formally as the *net barter terms of trade*. As noted, the net barter terms of trade relate solely to the relative prices of exports and imports, so do not take into account changes in the volume of exports and imports. The *income terms of trade* take the volume of trade into account, being defined as the value of a country's exports divided by the price of imports. In other words, this measures the purchasing power of a country's exports in terms of the price of its imports. It is possible for all countries to experience an increase in the income terms of trade simultaneously.

Exercise 24.3

In 2015, the terms of trade index for United Arab Emirates was 192.6 (based on 2000 = 100). For Sierra Leone it was 44.1, and for Bolivia it was 99.7. Explain what is implied by these statistics.

In recent years, concerns have been raised about the effect of changes in the terms of trade for developing countries. One problem faced by developing countries that export primary products is that they are each too small as individual exporters to be able to influence the world price of their products. They must accept the prices that are set in world commodity markets.

Short-run volatility

In the case of agricultural goods, demand tends to be relatively stable over time, but supply can be volatile, varying with weather and climatic conditions from season to season. Figure 24.5 shows a typical market in two periods. In period 1 the global harvest of this commodity is poor, with supply given by S_1: equilibrium is achieved with price at P_1 and quantity traded at Q_1. In period 2 the global harvest is high at S_2, so that prices plummet to P_2 and quantity traded rises to Q_2.

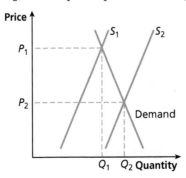

Figure 24.5 Volatility in supply

Notice that in this case the movement of prices is relatively strong compared with the variation in quantity. This reflects the price elasticity of demand, which is expected to be relatively inelastic for many primary products. From the consumers' point of view, the demand for foodstuffs and other agricultural goods will tend to be inelastic, as demand will not be expected to respond strongly to changes in prices.

For many minerals and raw materials, however, the picture is different. For such commodities, supply tends to be stable over time, but demand fluctuates with the economic cycle in developed countries, which are the importers of raw materials. Figure 24.6 illustrates this. At the trough of the business cycle, demand is low, at D_1, and so the equilibrium price will also be low, at P_1. At the peak of the cycle, demand is more buoyant, at D_2, and price is relatively high, at P_2.

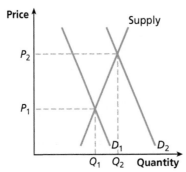

Figure 24.6 Volatility in demand

From an individual country's point of view, the result is the same: the country faces volatility in the prices of its exports. From this perspective it does not matter whether the instability arises from the supply side of the market or from the demand side. The problem is that prices can rise and fall quite independently of conditions within the domestic economy.

Instability of prices also means instability of export revenues, so if the country is relying on export earnings to fund its development path, to import capital equipment or to meet its debt repayments, such volatility in earnings can constitute a severe problem — for example, if export earnings fall such that a country is unable to meet its commitments to repaying debt.

Long-run deterioration

The nature of the demand for primary products may be expected to influence the long-run path of relative prices. In particular, the income elasticity of demand is an important consideration. As real incomes rise in the developed countries, the demand for agricultural goods can be expected to rise relatively slowly. Ernst Engel pointed out that at relatively high income levels, the proportion of expenditure devoted to foodstuffs tends to fall and the demand for luxury goods rises. This suggests that the demand for agricultural goods shifts relatively slowly through time.

In the case of raw materials, there have been advances in the development of artificial substitutes for many commodities used in manufacturing. Furthermore, technology has changed over time, improving the efficiency with which inputs can be converted into outputs. This has weakened the demand for raw materials produced by developing countries.

Furthermore, if some developing countries are successful in boosting output of these goods, there will be an increase in supply over time. Figure 24.7 shows the result of such an increase. Suppose that the market begins with demand at D_0 and supply at S_0. Market equilibrium results in a price of P_0 and quantity of Q_0. As time goes by, demand moves to the right a little to D_1, and supply shifts to S_1. The result is a fall in the price of the commodity to P_1.

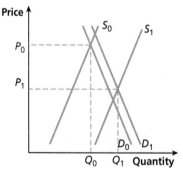

Figure 24.7 Long-term movements of demand and supply

It is thus clear that not only may developing countries experience short-run volatility in prices, but the terms of trade may also deteriorate in the long run.

Study tip

You might have thought that the demand and supply model was just useful in microeconomics, but notice that it can also be helpful in other contexts. Look for examples in the news where the model can help to interpret events.

Pattern of comparative advantage

In the light of these twin problems, it is perhaps no surprise that many developing countries see themselves as trapped by their pattern of comparative advantage, rather than being in a position to exploit it. They have therefore been reluctant to continue in such a state of dependency on primary products, but the process of diversification into a wide range of products has been difficult to achieve.

A potential change in this pattern was seen in 2007 and 2008, with food prices rising rapidly. This included the prices of some staple commodities such as maize and rice. The net effect of this on developing countries was mixed. Countries in a position to export these commodities benefited from the rise in prices — that is, an increase in their terms of trade. However, there are many developing countries that need to import these staple commodities and for them the terms of trade deteriorated. These trends were interrupted by the onset of recession in many developed countries in 2008.

Knowledge check 24.8

Explain why a long-run deterioration the terms of trade for primary products is a problem for many developing countries.

Dependence on trade

The degree to which a country or region engages in trade depends on several factors. One important influence is the extent to which a country has the resources needed to trade — in other words, whether it can produce the sorts of goods that other countries wish to buy. However, it also depends on the policy stance adopted by a country. Some countries have been very open to international trade. For example, a number of countries in South East Asia built success in economic growth on the basis of promoting exports. In contrast, there are countries such as India that in the past have been less eager to trade, and introduced policies that have hindered their engagement with trade.

Two Swedish economists, Eli Heckscher and Bertil Ohlin, argued that a country's comparative advantage would depend crucially on its relative endowments of factors of production. They argued that the optimal techniques for producing different commodities varied. Some commodities are most efficiently produced using labour-intensive techniques, whereas others could be more efficiently produced using relatively capital-intensive methods. This then suggests that if a country has abundant labour but scarce capital, then its natural comparative advantage would lie in the production of goods that require little capital but lots of labour. In contrast, a country with access to capital but facing a labour shortage would tend to have a comparative advantage in capital-intensive goods or services.

Changes in the price of staple commodities such as maize and rice could change the pattern of comparative advantage for many developing countries

Labour- or land-intensive techniques

Under these arguments, it would seem to make sense for developing countries to specialise in labour- or land-intensive activities such as agriculture or other primary production. Countries like the UK or the USA could then specialise in more capital-intensive activities such as manufacturing activity or financial services. By and large, this describes the way in which the pattern of world trade developed. However, the pattern is not static and there have been changes over time. For example, countries in South East Asia, such as Hong Kong, Singapore or Taiwan, encouraged the structure of their economies to change over time, switching away from labour-intensive activities as the access to capital goods improved over time. Their success then induced changes in the structure of activity in more developed countries as the availability of imported manufactured goods allowed the expansion of service sector activity. In more recent years, China's economy has been undergoing even faster structural change, with the rapid expansion of the manufacturing sector, supported by an exchange rate policy that made its exports highly competitive in global markets.

Whether it is good for countries to rely on this pattern of natural comparative advantage is a different matter — for example, in the light of the changing patterns of relative prices reflected in the evolution of the terms of trade over time. Over-specialisation can result in unbalanced development, which can create vulnerability.

This suggests that there may be potential for countries to seek to alter the pattern of their comparative advantage by diversifying their economies and developing new specialisms in the face of changing patterns of global consumer demand. This is not an easy path for an economy to travel, and it may be tempting to turn instead to a more inward-looking protectionist strategy. There is a choice to be made between seeking to exploit this natural comparative advantage, or diversifying the economy in an attempt to develop new specialisms.

There has been change over time, as shown in Figure 24.8, which shows the share of world exports of manufactured goods coming from high-income countries. You can see that this declined from about 63% in 1990, ending at about 47% in 2015. This may be seen as part of the process of deindustrialisation, with many developed economies moving away from manufacturing industries to focus more on service sector activities. This made it possible for some developing countries to take their place in producing manufactured goods.

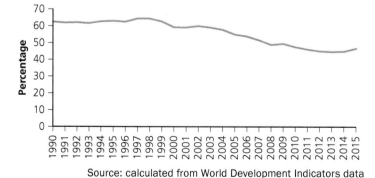

Source: calculated from World Development Indicators data

Figure 24.8 Share of manufactured exports from high-income countries

Summary: the gains from trade

- Specialisation opens up the possibility of gains from trade.
- The theory of comparative advantage shows that even if one country has an absolute advantage in the production of goods and services, trade may still increase total output if each country specialises in the production of goods and services in which it has a comparative advantage.
- Who gains from specialisation and trade depends crucially on the prices at which exchange takes place.
- The terms of trade are measured as the ratio of export prices to import prices.
- When the terms of trade deteriorate for a country, it needs to export a greater volume of goods to be able to maintain the same volume of imports.
- The terms of trade have tended to be volatile in the short run, and to deteriorate over the longer term for countries that rely heavily on non-fuel primary production.
- The pattern of comparative advantage that characterises a country may depend on the relative endowments of the factors of production.

The pattern of world trade

In order to provide the context for a discussion of the effect of globalisation on trade, and the place of the UK economy in the global economy, it is helpful to examine the pattern of world trade.

Table 24.3 presents some data on this pattern. It shows the size of trade flows between regions. The rows of the table show the exports from each of the regions to each other region, while the columns show the pattern of imports from each region. The numbers on the 'diagonal' of the table (in bold type) show the trade flows *within* regions. One remarkable feature of the table is the high involvement of Europe in world trade, accounting for 38.0% of imports and 37.7% of the exports. Of course, this includes substantial flows within Europe. In contrast, Africa shows very little involvement in world trade, in spite of the fact that, in population terms, it is far larger.

Table 24.3 Intra- and interregional merchandise trade, 2016 (US$bn)

Origin	Destination							
	North America	South and Central America	Europe	CIS	Africa	Middle East	Asia	World
North America	**1,105**	156	356	10	26	72	462	2,187
South and Central America	119	**115**	89	6	14	15	146	504
Europe	529	93	**4,106**	133	173	200	654	5,888
CIS	17	3	207	**77**	15	15	83	417
Africa	28	8	133	2	**68**	17	82	338
Middle East	56	5	99	4	24	**86**	314	588
Asia	1,028	138	847	87	160	238	**2,745**	5,243
World	2,882	518	5,837	319	480	643	4,486	**15,165**

Note: world totals have been calculated from the table.

Source: based on data from World Trade Organization

Indeed, trade flows between the developed countries — and with the more advanced developing countries — have tended to dominate world trade, with the flows between developing countries being relatively minor. This is not surprising, given that by definition the richer countries have greater purchasing power. However, the degree of openness to trade of economies around the world varies also as a result of conscious policy decisions. Some countries, especially in East Asia, have adopted very open policies towards trade, promoting exports in order to achieve export-led growth. In contrast, some countries (including a number in Latin America) have been much more reluctant to become dependent on international trade, and have adopted a more closed attitude towards trade. In more recent years, both China and India have been experiencing economic growth at a very high rate indeed, and have become significant trading nations. This has had repercussions for other countries around the world.

Knowledge check 24.9

Why do you think that the share of intraregional trade (that is, that is within a region, such as Europe trading with Europe) is much higher for Europe than for North America?

Quantitative skills 24.3

Using percentages

In Table 24.3, origin countries are shown in the rows, and destination countries in the columns. For example, to identify the exports from (say) Europe to Asia, you need to look in the Europe row and the Asia column, which is $654 bn. The world column shows total exports from each of the row regions, so the total of Europe exports is $5,888 bn. The share of Europe's exports going to Asia is thus $100 \times 654/5,888 = 11.1\%$. In similar fashion, the share of Europe's imports coming from Asia is $100 \times 847/5,837 = 14.5\%$. Make sure you understand why this is the case.

Knowledge check 24.10

What percentage of exports from the Middle East go to Asia?

UK trade

Figures 24.9(a) and (b) show the destination of UK exports of goods and services to major regional groupings in the world. The most striking feature of this graph is the extent to which the UK relies on Europe and the USA for more than 70% of its exports. Figures 24.10(a) and (b) reveal a similar pattern for the UK's imports of goods and services. Notice also that imports of goods from China (including Hong Kong) have become significant — and comprise a much larger share in imports than in exports.

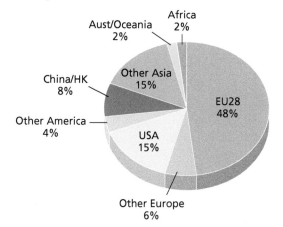

Figure 24.9(a) Destination of UK exports of goods, 2017

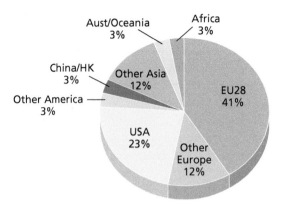

Figure 24.9(b) Destination of UK exports of services, 2017

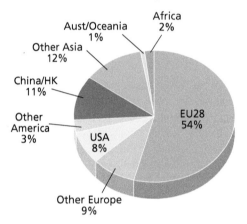

Figure 24.10(a) Source of UK imports of goods, 2017

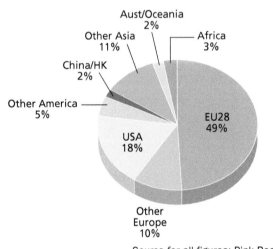

Source for all figures: Pink Book

Figure 24.10(b) Source of UK imports of services, 2017

The proportion of UK trade (both exports and imports) that is with Europe has undergone substantial change over the past 50 years. In 1960, when the Commonwealth was still thriving and the UK was ambivalent about the idea of European integration, less than a quarter of UK exports went to other European countries (23% of exports of goods in 1960). Figure 24.11 shows that, by 2000, the

EU was receiving about 60% of the UK's exports of goods, and more than half of the UK's imports of both goods and services were coming from the EU. This declined somewhat after then, but in 2017, 49% of UK exports were still going to the EU, and 55% of its goods imports were coming from the EU.

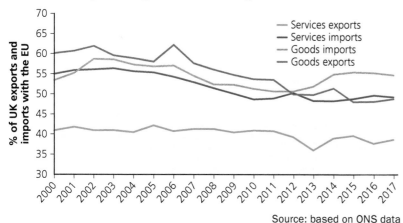

Source: based on ONS data

Figure 24.11 UK trade with the EU since 2000

Exercise 24.4

a Using the data provided in Table 24.3, calculate the share of each region in world exports and imports. Think about the factors that might influence the contrasting performance of the EU and Africa. Also, for each region calculate the share of exports and imports that are within the region and comment on any significant differences that you find.

b Are there any aspects of the pattern of world trade that took you by surprise? Can you find reasons for these?

The emerging economies

Industrialisation and economic growth began in the UK and other countries in Western Europe and North America, and by the 1960s there was a divide between those countries that had gone through the development and growth process and those that had not. Since the 1960s, relatively few countries have managed to bridge the gap in living standards.

There was a group of countries that became known as the *newly industrialised countries* (NICs) that made the transition. These included some countries in South East Asia, such as Singapore, South Korea, Taiwan and Hong Kong, and some Latin American countries, although the latter group fell foul of hyperinflation, which interrupted their progress.

Knowledge check 24.11

Why would hyperinflation in Latin America impede the process of economic growth?

More recently, some other countries have accelerated in terms of economic growth and human development; they have become known as the **emerging economies**. This group has included the so-called **BRIC** countries (Brazil, Russia, India and China), and a less defined group including Thailand, Malaysia, Turkey and South Africa, among others. These economies (especially China) have had a significant effect on the global economy.

Key terms

emerging economies economies that have experienced rapid economic growth with some industrialisation and characteristics of developed markets

BRIC countries a group of countries (Brazil, Russia, India, China and (later) South Africa who enjoyed a period of rapid economic growth and formed a political alliance

The BRIC countries

In the early 2000s, a group of countries — Brazil, Russia, India and China — were identified as experiencing rapid economic growth and closing the gap on the developed economies. The BRIC economies were originally just a set of countries identified as having some characteristics in common. However, they began forming a political group and having summit meetings, and in 2011 they invited South Africa to join them. At this point in time, the BRICs accounted for about 18% of world GDP and 15% of world trade, and contained about 40% of the world's population. If economic growth continues at current rates, the group will gain increasing economic and political influence relative to the G7.

Figure 24.12 shows economic growth in the BRICs since 2000, with the growth rate for the world as a whole to provide context. The consistency and rapidity of growth during the 2000s reveals why these countries were singled out for attention, although Brazil and South Africa were perhaps rather less successful in terms of their growth rates. What makes this performance more startling is the size of these economies, both in population and in the size of GDP. The achievements of the economies of China and India are especially impressive, in each case starting from a relatively low base — and for these two economies, the growth seemed relatively robust in the face of the global recession. China in particular showed very little sign of slowing down. However, the factors underlying the growth performance were different in each case, as these economies are all at very different stages in terms of average incomes and display different characteristics, both politically and economically.

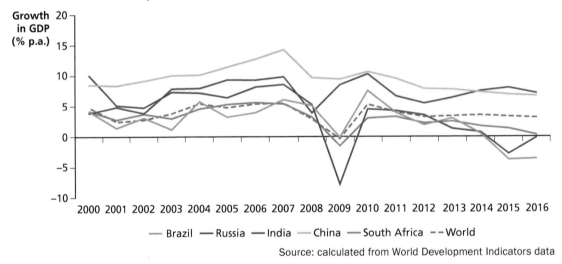

Source: calculated from World Development Indicators data

Figure 24.12 Growth in the BRIC countries since 2000 (PPP$)

These countries, together with some other rapid-growth economies, have had a significant impact on the global economy, most obviously in the case of China, which in 2014 overtook the USA as the world's biggest economy based on GDP in PPP$.

The impact on the global economy has been evident in many ways. China's growth was built on rapid growth of exports, which for at least part of the period was bolstered by China's exchange rate, maintained at a level that made China's exports highly competitive overseas. A number of the Asian emerging economies also accumulated reserves of US Treasury securities during the 2000s, which had the effect of allowing lower US interest rates than would otherwise have been.

This in turn encouraged consumer borrowing, and may have contributed to the financial crisis. Of course, China also needed to import goods that it needed to fuel its production process, with a consequent impact on commodity prices in global markets. The net effect of these factors is quite difficult to evaluate, but it could be argued that without China's continuing growth through the period of recession following the financial crisis, the slowdown would have been longer-lived.

China's exports are highly competitive in global markets

What factors influence the pattern of trade?

Comparative advantage

Different countries display different patterns of comparative advantage, which then determine the products in which they can specialise and reap potential gains from trade. Advanced countries will tend to have a comparative advantage in capital-intensive or hi-tech products, whereas developing countries are more likely to specialise in land- or labour-intensive production.

Emerging economies

The rise of the emerging economies (including the BRICS) has altered the pattern of trade between countries. These economies have moved into sectors that were previously the province of the advanced economies, while the advanced economies have shifted into service activities, especially in financial and professional services.

Trading blocs and trading agreements

The proliferation of trading blocs has also influenced the pattern of international trade. The moves made by the UK through Brexit, and President Trump's suspicion of NAFTA herald changes in the pattern of trade.

Synoptic link

The notion of comparative advantage and its effect on trade is discussed earlier in this chapter.

Relative exchange rates

Changes in relative exchange rates affect the prices at which products trade internationally, and influence the potential division of the gains from trade via the terms of trade. However, exchange rates will tend to adjust to maintain relative international competitiveness when countries operate a floating exchange rate system (as most countries do).

Synoptic link

The role of trading blocs will be explored in Chapter 25, and exchange rates will be examined in Chapter 26.

Summary: patterns of trade

- There are substantial differences in the degree to which countries trade: trade with and within the EU accounts for an appreciable proportion of world trade, whereas Africa shows very little involvement.
- About three-quarters of UK exports go to Europe and the USA.
- The share of UK trade with the rest of Europe has increased substantially over the past 40 years.
- The patterns of trade between countries are influenced by comparative advantage, the growth of trading blocs and the terms of trade.

Case study 24.1

More than just exports

The UK imports a great many products, from Audi cars to Hollywood blockbusters, from other European countries and overseas. At the same time, companies based in the UK, from Vauxhall to the BBC, sell their products to customers abroad.

As the Nobel prize-winning economist Paul Krugman argued in an interview to the BBC, international trade matters as it helps firms to specialise and produce in large quantities. At the same time, it expands everyone's choice. Indeed, if you walk down the biscuit aisle in a UK supermarket you will see that it has biscuits from Denmark, Britain and the United States, as people enjoy variety. This, of course, applies to both exports and imports: the BBC exports the *Dr Who* series to Europe and the USA, while BBC4 has taken to showing Scandinavian and other European subtitled crime drama; Cadbury exports chocolate to the USA and Germany, while British supermarkets import Milka from Germany and Belgian Godiva chocolate.

International trade in goods is an important and integral part of any economy. As well as material goods, firms may trade in services such as banking and consultancy, invest directly in other companies abroad or contract a foreign company to produce a specific good exclusively for them. Business people

understand the importance of these various international activities, while governments often focus on exports of goods. But why do governments focus on firms' export activities?

One reason is the ease of observation – income statements submitted by companies will detail revenues from domestic and foreign sources separately. Exports are simply revenues from abroad. However, observing other types of involvement in international markets, such as investments and outsourcing, is substantially more difficult.

The BBC exports the *Dr Who* series to Europe

Internationalisation

A recent survey of European firms allowed researchers to look into firms' international activities in seven European countries, including the UK. One observation is that it is very common for European manufacturing firms to have contacts with firms beyond country borders. Almost 80% of firms with at least ten employees engage in some form of international activity.

Exporting is the most frequent mode of internationalisation, with about two-thirds of firms shipping some products abroad. However, many other modes are also popular. About half the firms import directly — that is, they do not just buy foreign-made goods from an intermediary. Working with foreign customers based on contracts is quite widespread, as a quarter of firms have outsourced some of their production, using foreign inputs made specifically for them. Almost 40% of firms provide outsourcing for other firms. Foreign ownership is not rare, as about 10% of firms own or are owned by foreign firms. So, while exports are important, firms are likely to get involved in several modes of internationalisation at once.

Some of the most competitive companies are engaged in several modes of internationalisation. Consider Armstrong, a specialist mid-sized company making acoustic and metal ceilings in the UK. This company makes metal and glass ceilings for theatres, shopping malls and tube stations, and exports them worldwide. However, to be globally competitive, it uses a large amount of tools, materials and semi-finished products made in other countries. Part of the labour-intensive work is contracted out to eastern Europe. Moreover, it is part of a global network owned by a US global player designing and manufacturing floors and ceilings.

Often, several modes of internationalisation are interrelated, with one activity leading to another. For instance, when Kraft took over Cadbury, it started to produce Oreo biscuits, previously imported into the UK, at a plant in Sheffield and then exported the biscuits to other countries.

International activities are found to be related to overall firm performance: companies that are tied into global business are likely to be more efficient and do better in their home market. In some cases, this is the result of learning from foreign business practices. However, it is often the case that a higher level of performance has been achieved before starting to trade: due to fixed trade costs, only the most productive firms may be competitive on export markets.

Follow-up question

Discuss the range of ways in which firms engage in internationalisation, and whether this activity yields net benefits to economies.

Trading blocs and restrictions on trade

Although the economic analysis of specialisation suggests that there are potential gains to be made from engaging in international trade, there has been a continuing debate about trade liberalisation and protectionism. Furthermore, the economic landscape of Europe since the Second World War has been shaped by the move towards ever-closer economic integration. Regional trading blocs have also proliferated in other parts of the world. This chapter explores these issues.

Learning objectives

After studying this chapter, you should:

→ be familiar with the role and effectiveness of the World Trade Organization

→ be aware of the different forms that economic integration may take: free trade areas, customs unions, common markets and economic and monetary union

→ know the features of these alternative forms of integration and understand the distinction between them

→ understand the significance of the Single European Market (SEM)

→ evaluate the costs and benefits of membership of a single currency area

→ be aware of the role and effectiveness of monetary and fiscal policy within a single currency area

→ be aware of the ways in which protectionist policies have been implemented

→ be able to evaluate the case for and against protectionism

The World Trade Organization

The Great Depression of the 1930s had seen unemployment in the UK and the USA rise to more than 20% following a massive stock market crash on Wall Street. In an attempt to avoid any recurrence of this, a famous conference was held at Bretton Woods in the USA in 1944 to agree on a set of rules under which international trade would be conducted. This conference established an exchange rate system under which countries agreed to set the price of their currencies relative to the US dollar.

Synoptic link

The Great Depression was discussed in Chapter 16 (see Figure 16.7 in particular). Alternative exchange rate regimes are examined in Chapter 26, together with an evaluation of their strengths and weaknesses. The role of the institutions established by the conference is discussed in Chapter 29.

In addition, the conference set up three institutions to oversee matters. The International Monetary Fund (IMF) would provide assistance (and advice) to countries experiencing balance of payments difficulties and the World Bank would provide assistance (and advice) on long-term development issues. However, it was also recognised that the conduct of trade would need some oversight. Initially, this role was fulfilled by the General Agreement on Tariffs and Trade (GATT), under the auspices of which there was a sequence of 'rounds' of reductions in tariffs, together with a significant reduction in quotas and voluntary export restraints. The last of these was the Uruguay Round, which covered the period 1986–94 and led to the formation of the World Trade Organization (WTO), which replaced the GATT in 1995.

While continuing to pursue reductions in barriers to trade, the WTO has also taken on the role of providing a framework for the settlement of trade disputes. You will appreciate that, with all the moves towards regional integration and protectionism, such a role is very important. Since its formation in 1995 the WTO has received more than 500 dispute cases, and issued more than 350 rulings.

In 2000 new talks started, covering agriculture and services. The fourth WTO Ministerial Conference in Doha in November 2001 incorporated these discussions into a broader work programme, the Doha Development Agenda. According to the WTO website, this agenda includes:

work on non-agricultural tariffs, trade and environment, WTO rules such as anti-dumping and subsidies, investment, competition policy, trade facilitation, transparency in government procurement, intellectual property, and a range of issues raised by developing countries.

Progress on the Doha agenda has been far from smooth. This is partly because agriculture is an especially contentious area, with the USA, the EU and Japan having large-scale policies in place to support their agricultural sectors. In the case of the EU's Single Market, some moves have been made towards reforming the Common Agricultural Policy, but progress has not been as rapid as developing countries would like — remembering that agriculture is especially important for many of the developing countries. Reluctance on the part of the rich nations to provide concessions in these key areas, combined with determination on the part of developing countries to make genuine progress, resulted in a seeming deadlock.

Synoptic link

The particular challenges facing developing countries are discussed in Chapter 28.

Knowledge check 25.1

Why would rich nations be reluctant to provide concessions to developing countries on agriculture?

The so-called 'Bali package' of measures was agreed in 2013, amidst great optimism among ministers. This was followed by the 'Nairobi package' in December 2015, but crucial issues surrounding agriculture remain. President Trump's adversarial attitude towards the WTO before and after his election may have implications for the future of the WTO.

Activists protest against the WTO in Bali in 2013

Trading blocs and the WTO

There has been a proliferation of regional trade agreements in recent years — as at May 2018 the WTO's database had received 459 notifications of regional trade agreements, of which 287 were in force. There has been much debate as to whether these agreements are stepping stones to further global cooperation, or whether they may turn out to be obstacles to that process. If nations establish individual agreements with other nations or groups of nations, this may militate against reaching agreement on a more global scale, especially if the groupings of nations establish stronger barriers against trade with nations that are not part of the blocs. In other words, such regional agreements may be divisive rather than advancing globally freer trade.

The WTO monitors the establishment and operations of trading blocs, and performs an important role in arbitrating in the case of disputes between countries that arise in relation to the conditions under which trade takes place.

Summary: the World Trade Organization

■ The World Trade Organization (WTO) has a responsibility to promote trade by pursuing reductions in tariffs and other barriers to trade, and also discharges a role in dispute settlement between nations.

Trading blocs

An important influence on the pattern of world trade has been the establishment of **trading blocs** in different parts of the world. These are intended to encourage trade among groups of nations, normally on a regional basis, in order to tap the gains from

Key term

trading bloc where a group of countries in a region agrees to cooperate in international trade through some sort of free trade area or other form of association trade. Examples are ASEAN (an organisation of ten countries in South East Asia), MERCOSUR (five countries in Latin America), NAFTA (Canada, the USA and Mexico) and, of course, the European Union. These groupings are at very different stages of integration and cooperation.

Regional trade integration can take on a variety of forms, representing differing degrees of closeness. The underlying motivation for integration is to allow trading partners to take advantage of the potential gains from international trade, as illustrated by the law of comparative advantage. By reducing the barriers to trade, this specialisation can be encouraged, and there should be gains from the process. In practice, there may be other economic and political forces at work that affect the nature of the gains, and the extent to which integration will be possible — and beneficial.

Free trade areas

A **free trade area** is a group of countries that agree to trade without barriers between themselves, but maintain their own individual barriers with countries outside the area. The North American Free Trade Area (NAFTA) is one such grouping. The Association of South East Asian Nations (ASEAN) has the aim of establishing a free trade area by the year 2020.

Customs unions

A **customs union** goes further than a free trade area, not only eliminating barriers to trade between the member countries, but also having a common tariff barrier against the rest of the world. Notice that a customs union does not need to have a common currency.

Knowledge check 25.2

What is the key difference between a customs union and a free trade area?

Evaluation of trading blocs

An important question in evaluating both free trade areas and customs unions is the extent to which they are able to generate increased trade and improved efficiency in production.

By creating a free trade area or customs union (i.e. without or with common barriers against the rest of the world), it is possible that the member nations will trade with each other instead of with the rest of the world: in other words, it is possible that trade will simply be diverted from the rest of the world to the partners in the agreement. Such **trade diversion** does not necessarily mean that gains from trade are being fully exploited. Indeed, it is possible that trade could be diverted from an efficient producer outside the bloc to a less efficient producer within the bloc. If the bloc is to be successful, there needs to be **trade creation**, in which more expensive domestic production or imports would be replaced by cheaper output from a partner within the trading bloc.

Key terms

free trade area a group of countries that agrees to trade without barriers between themselves, but having their own individual barriers with countries outside the area

customs union a group of countries that agrees to trade without barriers between them, and with a common tariff barrier against the rest of the world

trade creation the replacement of more expensive domestic production or imports with cheaper output from a partner within the trading bloc

trade diversion the replacement of cheaper imported goods by goods from a less efficient trading partner within a bloc

Extension material: the effects of trade creation and trade diversion

Figure 25.1 illustrates the effects of trade creation. It shows the demand and supply of a good in a certain country that joins a customs union. Before joining the union, the price of the good is T, which includes a tariff element. Domestic demand is D_0, of which S_0 comes from domestic producers, and the remainder is imported. When the country joins the customs union, the tariff is removed and the domestic price falls to P. Consumers benefit from additional consumer surplus, given by the area $PTBG$. However, notice that not all of this is pure gain to the country. The area $PTAC$ was formerly part of producer surplus, so there has been a redistribution from domestic firms to consumers. $ABFE$ was formerly tariff revenue collected by the government, so this represents effectively a redistribution from government to consumers. The area ACE is a net gain for the country, as this represents resources that were previously used up in the production of the good, but which can now be used for other purposes. The area BFG also represents a welfare gain to the country.

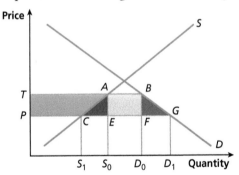

Figure 25.1 The effects of trade creation

Figure 25.2 helps to show the effects of trade diversion. Here, D represents the demand curve for a commodity that is initially imported from a country outside the customs union. It is assumed that the supply of the good from the non-member is perfectly elastic, as shown by S_n. However, the importing country imposes a tariff of the amount T, so the quantity imported is given by Q_n, and the price charged is $P_n + T$.

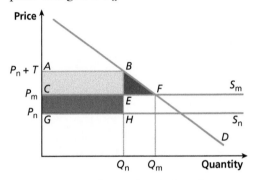

Figure 25.2 The effects of trade diversion

After the importing country joins the customs union, the tariff is removed, but the good is now imported from a less efficient producer within the union. The supply from this member country is assumed to be elastic at S_m, so the new price is P_m and the quantity is Q_m.

In examining the welfare effects, there are two issues to consider. First, notice that consumer surplus has increased by the area $ABFC$. However, this is not pure gain to the economy because, in the original position, the government was collecting tariff revenue of the amount $ABHG$. In other words, the increase in consumer surplus comes partly as a pure gain (the triangle BFE), but partly at the expense of the government ($ABEC$). This is not all, because the area $CEHG$ was also formerly part of tariff revenue, but now is a payment by domestic consumers to producers in the other (member) country. This means that whether the country is better or worse off depends on the relative size of the areas BFE (which is a gain) and $CEHG$ (which is a loss).

It is to be hoped that a trading agreement such as a free trade area or customs union would generate efficiency gains. If firms are able to service a larger overall market, it should be possible to exploit economies of scale, which would reduce average production costs. This may require countries to alter their pattern of specialisation to take full advantage of the enlarged market. For example, within the European Union there is a wide range of countries having different patterns of comparative advantage, ranging from countries like France and Germany to the more recent members from eastern Europe and the Baltic. The relative endowment of labour and capital among the member states can be expected to be very different.

This diversity is important for the success of a trade grouping. Remember that it is the *difference* in relative opportunity costs of production that drives the comparative advantage process and creates the potential gains from trade. However, it is clear that there also tends to be a strong political dimension affecting the outcome of such trade agreements.

Common markets

It may be that the countries within a customs union wish to move to closer integration, by extending the degree of cooperation between the member nations. A **common market** adds to the features of a customs union by harmonising some aspects of the economic environment between them. In a pure common market, this would entail adopting common tax rates across the member states, and a common framework for the laws and regulations that provide the environment for production, employment and trade. A common market would also allow for the free movement of factors of production between the member nations, especially in terms of labour and capital (land is less mobile by its nature!). Given the importance of the public sector in a modern economy, a common market would also set common procurement policies across member governments, so that individual governments did not favour their own domestic firms when purchasing goods and services. The Single European Market has encompassed most of these features, although tax rates have not been harmonised across the countries that are included.

Economic and monetary union

An alternative form of integration is where countries choose to share a common currency, but without the degree of cooperation that is involved with a free trade area or common market. Such an arrangement is known as a **monetary union** or a *currency union*. Full **economic and monetary union** combines the common market arrangements with a shared currency (or permanently fixed exchange rates between the member countries). This requires member states to follow a common monetary policy, and it is also seen as desirable to harmonise other aspects of macroeconomic policy across the union.

Knowledge check 25.4

Why must member states under economic and monetary union follow a common monetary policy?

The adoption of permanently fixed exchange rates is a contentious aspect of proposals for economic and monetary union, as governments are no longer able to use monetary policy for internal domestic purposes. This is because monetary variables become subservient to the need to maintain the exchange rate, and it is not possible to set independent targets for the rate of interest or money supply if the government has to maintain the value of the currency on the foreign exchange market. This is all very well if all countries in the union are following a similar economic cycle, but if one country becomes poorly synchronised with the others, there may be major problems.

Knowledge check 25.3

Suppose that when a country becomes part of a trading bloc, it finds that it can replace goods that it previously imported with lower priced goods produced within the bloc. Is this trade creation or trade diversion?

Key terms

common market a set of trading arrangements in which a group of countries removes barriers to trade among them, adopt a common set of barriers against external trade, establish common tax rates and laws regulating economic activity, allow free movement of factors of production between members and have common public sector procurement policies

monetary union a situation in which countries adopt a common currency

economic and monetary union a set of trading arrangements the same as for a common market, but in addition having a common currency (or permanently fixed exchange rates between the member countries) and a common monetary policy

For example, it could be that the union as a whole is enjoying a boom, and setting interest rates accordingly. For an individual member country suffering a recession, this could mean deepening and prolonging the recession, as it would not be possible to relax interest rates in order to allow aggregate demand to recover.

A successful economic and monetary union therefore requires careful policy coordination across the member nations. Notice that economic and monetary union involves fixed exchange rates between the member countries, but does not necessarily entail the adoption of a common currency, although this may follow at some stage.

Summary: trading blocs

- Economic integration can take a variety of forms, of differing degrees of closeness.
- A free trade area is where a group of countries agrees to remove restrictions on trade between them, but without having a common external tariff.
- A customs union is a free trade area with an agreed common set of restrictions on trade with non-members.
- A customs union can entail trade creation, in which member countries benefit from increased trade and specialisation.
- However, there may also be trade diversion, in which countries divert their trading activity from external trade partners to countries within the union.
- Trade diversion does not always bring gains, as the producers within the union are not necessarily more efficient than external producers.
- A common market is a customs union in which the member countries also agree to harmonise their policies in a number of key respects.
- Economic and monetary union entails fixed exchange rates between member countries, but not necessarily agreement to adopt a common currency.

The European Union

The European Union is one of the most prominent examples of regional trade integration, and has progressed further than most in evolving towards economic and monetary integration. Figure 25.3 shows the population size of EU member countries in 2016, and the dates at which they joined.

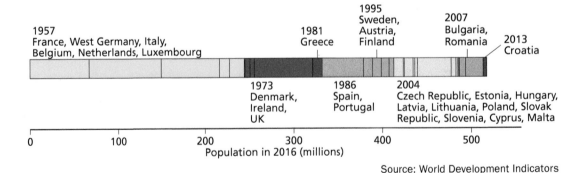

Source: World Development Indicators

Figure 25.3 Population of EU28

Bulgaria and Romania had been judged not to be ready to join in 2004, but joined in 2007; Croatia joined in 2013. Negotiations with Turkey began in 2005, but quickly ran into problems. If Turkey were to join, this would add a massive 79.5 million citizens to the EU.

Notice that the 15 pre-2004 member countries of the EU (the 'EU15') already contained more people than the USA; the combined population of the EU28 member states in 2016 was more than 510 million, compared with 323 million in the USA.

The Single European Market (SEM)

From the moment of formation of the European Economic Community (EEC) in 1957, the member countries began working towards the creation of a single market in which there would be free movement of goods, services, people and capital. In other words, the idea was to create a *common market* in which there would be no barriers to trade. The EEC was a *customs union* in which internal tariffs and non-tariff barriers were to be removed and a common tariff was to be set against the rest of the world.

A package of measures that came into effect in January 1993 might be seen as the final stages in the evolution of the Single European Market (SEM). The key measures were the removal (or reduction) of border controls and the winding down of non-tariff barriers to trade within the EU. In this way, physical, technical and fiscal barriers were removed. It has also become increasingly easy for people to move around within the EU, with passport and customs checks being abolished at most internal borders. Associated with these measures were a number of expected benefits.

The Single Market package came into effect in 1993, bringing a number of benefits to the EU countries

Transaction costs

Tariff barriers between EU countries were abolished under the Treaty of Rome, but a range of non-tariff barriers had built up over the years as countries sought to protect domestic employment. It was expected that the removal of these obstacles to trade, combined with the removal of border controls, would reduce the costs of trade within the EU. However, it is difficult to gauge the significance of these transaction cost savings, as it is not easy to quantify them.

Economies of scale

As trade increases, firms will find that they are operating in a larger market. This should allow them to exploit more fully the economies of large-scale production. From society's point of view, this should lead to a more efficient use of resources, as long as the resulting trade creation effects are stronger than any trade diversion that may take place.

The nature of technological change in recent years has favoured the growth of large-scale enterprises. Improved transport and communications have contributed to this process. The SEM has enabled firms in Europe to take advantage of these developments.

Knowledge check 25.5

Why is it important for society's efficient use of resources for trade creation effects in the SEM to be stronger than trade diversion?

Intensified competition

Firms will find that they are facing more intense competition within that larger market from firms in other parts of the EU. This then brings up the same arguments that are used to justify privatisation — that intensified competition will cause firms or their managers to seek more efficient production techniques, perhaps through the elimination of X-inefficiencies. This again is beneficial for society as a whole.

From the perspective of individual countries, there has been a divergence of views concerning the large firms that have been created through mergers and acquisitions. In some countries, large firms have been seen as 'national champions'. These have been protected (or even subsidised) by domestic governments, based on the argument that they will then be better prepared to compete in the broader European market. Elsewhere, governments have taken the view that the only way to ensure that domestic firms are lean enough to be competitive in overseas markets is to face intense competition at home, as an inducement to efficiency.

Who gains most from the SEM?

As trade within Europe becomes freer, two groups of countries stand to gain the most. First, the pattern of comparative advantage between countries will be important. Many EU countries are advanced industrial nations, where labour is expensive relative to capital. These countries tend to specialise in manufacturing or capital-intensive service activities, and already have fairly similar structures. It is thus possible that the relatively labour-abundant countries of southern Europe may gain more from closer integration and an expansion of trade. This is because they have a pattern of comparative advantage that is significantly different from existing members. This diversity was reinforced by the characteristics of the new entrants who joined in May 2004.

Second, if the main effect of integration is to remove barriers to trade, the countries with the most to gain may be those that begin with relatively high barriers.

Exercise 25.1

Explain why it might be the relatively labour-intensive countries of southern Europe — and the countries of eastern Europe and the Baltic that joined in 2004, 2007 and 2013 — that stand to gain most from the SEM.

The UK and Brexit

The UK relies heavily on trade with the EU. Figure 25.4 shows the percentage of UK exports and imports that is with countries in the EU, with data going back to 1960. Between 1960 and 1973 (when the UK became a member of the EU), exports and imports rose from about 30% of the total to about 45%. After entry, trade with the EU expanded further. By the 1990s, exports to the EU comprised around 60% of the UK's exports, and imports slightly lower. It is therefore difficult to consider the UK in isolation from its European trading partners.

Source: OECD

Figure 25.4 UK trade with the EU(27) since 1960

The referendum decision

In the referendum vote of 23 June 2016, the British electorate voted to leave the EU. For many economists, this seemed to fly in the face of the economic arguments about the benefits from trade and closer integration of economies. While the rest of the world was globalising and moving towards closer interrelationships between countries, here was the UK seemingly moving in the opposite direction.

Those in favour of leaving the EU argued that membership of the SEM imposed too many restrictions on the UK and prevented the formation of trade agreements with other countries. In other words, the UK could be better off by leaving the EU (even if this meant facing tariffs on exports to Europe), as this would then enable free trade with other trading partners.

In the event, the vote was not based solely on economic principles. Political considerations and unease about perceived growing inequality and immigration influenced voting behaviour, and the referendum result was a surprise to many. A further concern was about sovereignty, and whether the UK needed to be less tied to European regulations. Following the result, views became increasingly entrenched and negotiations were impeded by political infighting.

The UK's economic future

The economic future of the UK economy was seen to depend on the results of negotiations on the terms of exit, and on whether the UK would be able to reach trade deals with countries outside the EU. Whatever the outcome, many economists agreed that the long-term consequence of leaving the EU would be negative. Some estimates suggest that even with a 'soft' Brexit, in which the UK remains in the SEM (like Norway),

UK households would be some 1.3% worse off. A harder Brexit under which the UK trades with the EU under WTO rules could leave households some 2.7% worse off. Research at the Centre for Economic Performance points out that if the likely effect on productivity and foreign direct investment is taken into account, then the long-run impact could be between 6.3% and 9.5%.

There are strong arguments that there are potential gains from specialisation and trade. The challenge for the UK post-Brexit would be to find a way of preserving and creating trading relationships that allow the country to continue to gain from international trade.

Exercise 25.2

Review recent progress with the Brexit process. How has the UK economy responded to changes in the global environment?

The single currency area

The establishment of the SEM was seen by some as an end in itself, but others regarded it as a step towards full monetary integration, in which all member states would adopt a single currency, thereby reducing the transaction costs of international trade even more.

However, full monetary union and the adoption of a common currency is about much more than transaction costs and has raised considerable debate, not least because of the political dimension surrounding the loss of sovereignty by individual countries. This is partly an economic issue, focusing on the loss of separate currencies and (perhaps more significantly) the loss of control over national economic policy.

Treaty of Maastricht

The Maastricht Treaty created the European Union (EU). This treaty encompassed not only economic issues, such as the introduction of the single currency, but also aspects of social policy, steps towards creating a common foreign, security and defence policy, and the development of a notion of European 'citizenship'.

It was considered that, if a single currency was to be established, the participating nations would need to have converged in their economic characteristics. If the countries were too diverse in their economic conditions, the transition to a single currency would be costly. For example, if they had very different inflation rates, interest rates or levels of outstanding government debt, the tensions of union might be too great to sustain. Strong countries would be dragged down, and weak countries would be unable to cope. The Maastricht Treaty therefore set out the *convergence criteria* by which countries would be eligible to join the single currency area. These criteria covered aspects of both monetary and fiscal policy.

Monetary policy

This is obviously important, as monetary union entails the centralisation of monetary policy within the EU. If there is to be a single currency and a single central bank to control interest rates or money supply, the monetary conditions of the economies concerned need to be reasonably close before union takes place. It was thus important to evaluate whether countries were sufficiently close to be able to join with minimal tension.

Inflation

Could countries with widely different inflation rates successfully join in a monetary union? One view is that it would be unreasonable to expect a country with 10% or 20% inflation to join a monetary union along with a country experiencing inflation at just 1%. An alternative view is that it is equally unreasonable to expect a country to cure its inflation before joining a union when one of the alleged benefits of joining is that it will cure inflation by enforcing financial discipline and removing discretion over monetary policy from individual states. However, the first criterion specified by the treaty was that countries joining the union should be experiencing low and similar inflation rates — defined as inflation no more than 1.5% above the average of the three countries with the lowest rate.

Interest and exchange rates

Given that financial capital tends to follow high interest rates, it is argued that diversity of interest rates before union may be undesirable, as this would imply instability of capital movements. Similarly, it has been argued that a period of exchange rate stability before union would be some indication that countries have been following mutually consistent policies, and would indicate that union is plausible.

The criteria set out in the treaty required that long-term interest rates be no more than 2% above the average of the three countries with the lowest rate, and that each joining country should have operated for a period of 2 years without the need for realignment of their currency.

Fiscal policy

Should there also be conformity in fiscal stance between countries? Would there be severe problems if countries embarked upon union and policy coordination in conditions in which unemployment rates differed markedly? These are separate but related questions. If unemployment is high, this will be connected (via social security payments) with the fiscal stance adopted by the government — as judged in terms of the government budget deficit.

The reason why unemployment rates are relevant is that there may need to be fiscal transfers between member states in order to reduce the differentials. This will clearly be politically significant in the context of a monetary union, and is an issue that will affect the long-term viability of the union. However, although unemployment rates are potentially important for this reason, the convergence criteria did not refer to unemployment directly. Instead, the criteria included a reference to fiscal policy. In practice, the divergence in unemployment rates was substantial.

Two areas are critical in judging the distance between countries in terms of fiscal policy. First, there is the question of the short-term fiscal stance, which can be measured by the budget deficit. Second, it is important to consider some indication of a longer-term commitment to stability in fiscal policy, in terms of achieving sustainable levels of outstanding government debt. Thus, the treaty required that the budget deficit be no larger than 3% of GDP, and that the national debt be no more than 60% of GDP.

Knowledge check 25.6

Why would financial capital be expected to follow high interest rates in some countries?

Knowledge check 25.7

Why would divergence in unemployment rates be an issue for a monetary union?

Economic and monetary union

The final stage of the transition towards the single currency was European Economic and Monetary Union (EMU). Under EMU, exchange rates between participating countries were permanently locked together: in other words, no further realignments were allowed. Furthermore, the financial markets of the countries were integrated, with the European Central Bank setting a common interest rate across the union. This was achieved in 1999.

Formation of the euro area

In the event, 11 countries were judged to have met the Maastricht criteria (Belgium, Germany, Spain, France, Ireland, Italy, Luxembourg, the Netherlands, Austria, Portugal and Finland). Together with Greece, these countries formed the single currency area, which came into operation on 1 January 2002. Slovenia joined the eurozone in 2007, followed by Cyprus and Malta in 2008, Slovakia in 2009, Estonia in 2011 and Latvia in 2014.

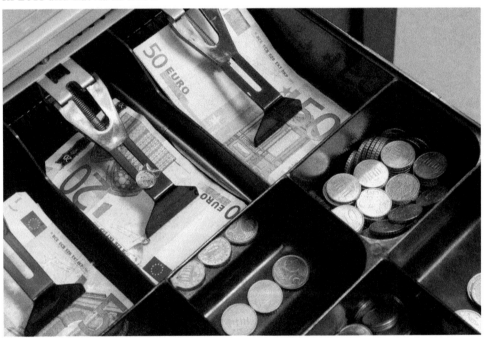

Euro notes and coins began to circulate in the eurozone in 2002

Costs and benefits of a single currency

Some of the arguments for and against a single currency area such as the eurozone are similar to those used in evaluating a fixed exchange rate system against a flexible one. This is because a common currency is effectively creating an area in which exchange rates between member nations are fixed for ever, even if that common currency varies relative to the rest of the world. The question of whether such an arrangement is beneficial overall for the member states rests on an evaluation of the benefits and costs of joining together. An **optimal currency area** occurs when a group of countries is better off with a single currency.

Benefits

The main benefits of a single currency area come in the form of a *monetary efficiency gain*, which has the effect of encouraging more trade between member countries.

Key term

optimal currency area a situation in which a group of countries is better off with a single currency

Synoptic link

The characteristics and operations of fixed and floating exchange rate systems are discussed in Chapter 26.

The hope is that this will bring further gains from exploiting comparative advantage between countries and enabling firms to reap the benefits of economies of scale.

The efficiency gain comes from two main sources. First, there are gains from reducing *transaction costs*, if there is no longer the need to convert from one currency into another. Second, there are gains from the *reduction in uncertainty*, in the sense that there is no longer a need to forecast future movements in exchange rates — at least between participating countries. This is similar to the gains from a fixed exchange rate system, but it goes further, as there is no longer a risk of occasional devaluation or revaluation of currencies.

The extent to which these gains are significant will depend on the degree of integration between the participating nations. If most of the trade that takes place is between the participants, the gains will clearly be much more significant than if member nations are also trading extensively with countries outside the single currency area.

Knowledge check 25.8

Why would a high level of uncertainty about exchange rate movements hinder economic growth?

Costs

The costs come in the conduct and effectiveness of policy. Within the single currency area, individual countries can no longer have recourse to monetary policy in order to stabilise the macroeconomy. As with the fixed exchange rate system, one key question then is how well individual economies are able to adjust to external shocks. Thus, it is important for each economy to have flexibility. In addition, individual countries have to be aware that, once in the single currency area, it is impossible to use monetary policy to smooth out fluctuations in output and employment.

In this context, it is very important that the economic cycles of participating economies are well synchronised. If one economy is out of phase with the rest, it may find itself facing an inappropriate policy situation. For example, suppose that most of the countries within the eurozone are in the boom phase of the business cycle, and are wanting to raise the interest rate in order to control aggregate demand: if one country within the zone is in recession, then the last thing it will want is rising interest rates, as this will deepen the recession and delay recovery. These arguments came to the fore during the recession of the late 2000s, as evidenced by the experience of Greece, which suffered a much deeper and long-lasting recession than some other countries such as Germany.

Evaluation of a single currency area

Paul Krugman suggested a helpful way of using cost–benefit analysis to evaluate these aspects of a single currency area. He argues that both the costs and the benefits from a single currency area will vary with the degree to which member countries are integrated. Thus the benefits from joining such a currency area would rise as the closeness of integration increased, whereas the costs would fall.

The balance between costs and benefits

Figure 25.5 illustrates the balance between costs and benefits. For countries that are not very closely integrated (that is, if 'integration' is less than t^*), the costs from joining the union exceed the benefits, so it would not be in the country's interest to join. However, as the degree of integration increases, so the benefits increase, and the costs decrease, so for any country beyond t^*, the benefits exceed the costs, and it is thus worth joining.

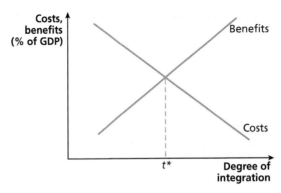

Figure 25.5 Costs and benefits of a single currency area

For an individual country considering whether or not to join the euro area, a first step is to reach a judgement on whether the country is to the left or to the right of $t^\star$. There may be other issues to consider in addition to the costs and benefits, but unless the country has at least reached $t^\star$, it could be argued that entry into the union should not be considered.

One way of viewing the situation is that the costs are mainly macroeconomic, but the benefits are microeconomic. This complicates the evaluation process. Some research published in 2006 argued that most of the boost to trade within the euro area occurred during the initial period, and would not continue to build up over time. It was also suggested that the EU countries that decided not to join the euro (the UK, Sweden and Denmark) gained almost as much as the countries that had joined.

The experience in Europe

The experience of some European countries during and in the aftermath of the financial crisis cast doubt on whether the eurozone could be viewed as an optimal currency area. In particular, some countries faced problems because they could not pursue independent monetary or fiscal policies.

From a UK perspective, the debate has shifted substantially. There was a time when a key issue was whether the UK should join the euro, and the 1997 Labour government went to great lengths to set out the conditions that would need to be met for this to be seen as the best way forward. This debate has now been supplanted by the Brexit vote.

Exercise 25.3

In the light of experience with the euro, discuss whether the eurozone is really an optimal currency area.

Study tip

Note that feelings can run high on issues like the euro and the EU, but you need to stay objective as far as possible, and advance economic arguments, not personal views.

Structural change

A feature that all of these forms of integration have in common is that they involve the removal of barriers to trade among member countries. It is important to be aware that this will not be perceived as a good thing by all the parties involved. In order to benefit from increased specialisation and trade, countries need to allow the pattern of their production to change. The benefits to the expanding sectors are apparent, but it is also the case that industries that formerly enjoyed protection from competition will become exposed to competition, and will need to decline in order to allow resources to be transferred into the expanding sectors. This can be a painful process for firms that need to close down, or move into new markets, and for workers who may need to undergo retraining before they are ready for employment in the newly expanding parts of the economy.

An especially contentious area of debate in the UK concerns the structural change that has taken place in recent decades, in which manufacturing activity has declined and financial services have expanded. This reflects the changing pattern of the UK's comparative advantage, in which banking, finance and insurance have become a major strength of the economy, whereas the manufacturing sector has found it more difficult to compete with the host of new entrants into this market from elsewhere in the world.

Summary: the European Union

- The Maastricht Treaty created the European Union (EU), and set out the route towards closer integration.
- The treaty also set out the convergence criteria, to be used to judge which countries were ready to join in monetary union. These criteria covered financial and fiscal aspects.
- Twelve countries adopted the euro as their common currency in January 2002.
- The main benefits of a common currency area are that it encourages trade by reducing transaction costs and reducing foreign exchange risk.
- However, the downside is that individual countries have less autonomy in controlling their macroeconomies. Adjusting to external shocks and smoothing short-term fluctuations in output and employment become more difficult with a common monetary policy that may not always be set in ways that are appropriate for all participating countries.
- There are many other examples of regional trade agreements that have reached various stages of integration, such as NAFTA and ASEAN.

Restrictions on free trade

Comparative advantage is just one of many reasons for countries to engage in international trade. Trade enables consumers in a country to have access to products that could not be produced at home, and enables producers to have access to new markets and resources. In some cases it allows producers to take advantage of economies of scale that would not be possible if they had to rely only on selling to the domestic market. From the country's perspective, export-led growth may be possible, and there are countries such as China and other countries in South East Asia that have benefited from this. It is also possible that exposure to competition from foreign firms provides a good incentive for domestic firms to become more efficient, raising the quality of their goods or the efficiency with which they are produced. Consumers may then gain from wider variety of available products, improved quality and lower prices.

Synoptic link

Comparative advantage was explained in Chapter 24.

Key term

protectionism measures taken by a country to restrict international trade

In spite of these potential gains from trade, countries have often seemed reluctant to open their economies fully to international trade, and have tended to intervene in various ways to protect their domestic producers: a process known as **protectionism**.

Key terms

infant industry an industry that needs protection from international competition in the short run so that it can learn to become competitive

sunset industry an industry in decline that needs protection for its displaced workers

Knowledge check 25.9

Why might over-protection of an infant industry be ineffective in allowing the industry to compete in global markets?

Reasons for protectionism

Many reasons have been given for this, not all of which have a grounding in economic analysis.

There may be political reasons for wanting to protect domestic industries. For example, there may be strategic arguments that a country should always maintain an agricultural sector so as not to be over-dependent on imported foodstuffs, as this could be disastrous in the event of war. Such arguments were used in setting up the Common Agricultural Policy in Europe. President Trump's arguments for imposing a levy on steel imports in 2018 similarly claimed that the USA's steel industry was suffering from unfair competition, which was a threat to national security.

Some have also argued that domestic industries should be protected because of the impact of high unemployment among workers displaced from declining sectors — so-called **sunset industries**. This is really an argument about the period of transition to more open trade, as it could also be noted that workers released from those declining sectors could, in time, be redeployed in sectors that are more efficient in comparative advantage terms.

A common line of argument is about the need to protect so-called **infant industries**. This may be especially important in the context of developing countries wanting to develop their manufacturing sectors. The argument is that protecting a domestic industry from international competition will allow firms engaged in the new activities to become familiar with the market so that in the longer term they will be able to compete. A problem with both infant and sunset industries is that once protection is put in place, it is difficult to remove. The infants may never grow up and declining sectors may never expire completely.

Free trade?

David Ricardo's theory of comparative advantage, developed in the early nineteenth century, formed the basis of the arguments for free trade, and still has some resonance today. However, the idea is not without its critics from economists such as Ha-Joon Chang.

One line of criticism is historically based. In the Industrial Revolution, Britain led the world in the development of manufacturing industry. Was this based on the principles of free trade? It can be argued that Britain's success was built on being able to import raw materials from its colonies, but although Britain was keen to import these materials under free trade conditions, it was also ready to restrict the ability of other nations to follow in its footsteps. For example, India was subjected to heavy tariffs on its textile workshops, forcing it to become a source of raw cotton rather than textiles. This protected the Lancashire textile mills.

The South Korean economy went through a period of rapid economic growth in the 1960s. Again, this was facilitated by high subsidies for firms and tariff barriers. There are other examples of the way in which industries have been protected to allow rapid economic growth to take place, often at the expense of potential competing nations.

A second line of argument notes that Ricardo's analysis rested on the assumption that capital and other factors of production were immobile, providing support for local specialisation. When factors of production are more mobile — as in today's world — this argument becomes less compelling.

There has been a tendency for institutions such as the World Bank and the International Monetary Fund to provide policy advice for developing countries based on becoming more open to international trade and promoting exports of goods in which developing countries may hold a comparative advantage. This advice has not always produced the expected results, partly because they are not in a position to take full advantage of trading opportunities in a hostile global market.

Forms of protectionism

When recession began to threaten in 2008, there was strong lobbying in several countries in favour of introducing protectionist measures. Indeed, in the lead-up to the G20 Summit in April 2009, the World Bank reported that the 17 members of that group had taken a total of 47 trade-restricting steps in the previous months. However, the drive towards globalisation had created a more integrated global economy, in which many firms relied on a global supply chain. With the production process fragmented between different parts of the world, the dangers of protectionism become more severe, and the possibilities of rapid contagion from a crisis become acute.

Tariffs

A policy instrument commonly used in the past to give protection to domestic producers is the imposition of a **tariff**. Tariff rates in the developed countries have been considerably reduced in the period since the Second World War, but nonetheless are still in place.

Key term

tariff a tax imposed on imported goods

The operation of a tariff

Figure 25.6 shows how a tariff is expected to operate. D represents the domestic demand for a commodity, and S_{dom} shows how much domestic producers are prepared to supply at any given price. The price at which the good can be imported from world markets is given by P_w. If dealing with a global market, it is reasonable to assume that the supply at the world price is perfectly elastic, especially for a small economy that is unable to influence the world price. Another way of thinking about this is that supply is perfectly elastic in the sense that the country can import as much as it wishes at the going world price. So in the absence of a tariff, domestic demand is given by D_0, of which S_0 is supplied within the domestic economy and the remainder $(D_0 - S_0)$ is imported. If the government wishes to protect this industry within the domestic economy, it needs to find a way of restricting imports and encouraging home producers to expand their capacity.

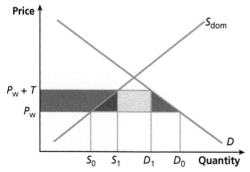

Figure 25.6 The effects of a tariff

By imposing a tariff, the domestic price rises to $P_w + T$, where T is the amount of the tariff. This has two key effects. One is to reduce the demand for the good from D_0 to D_1; the second is to encourage domestic producers to expand their output of this good from S_0 to S_1. As a consequence imports fall substantially, to $(D_1 - S_1)$. On the face of it, the policy has achieved its objective. Furthermore, the government has been able to raise some tax revenue (given by the yellow rectangle).

Negative effects of a tariff

However, not all the effects of the tariff are favourable for the economy. Consumers are certainly worse off, as they have to pay a higher price for the good; they therefore consume less, and there is a loss of consumer surplus, represented in the figure by the sum of the shaded areas. Some of what was formerly consumer surplus has been redistributed to others in society. The government has gained the tariff revenue, as mentioned. In addition, producers gain producer surplus, shown by the dark blue coloured area. There is also a deadweight loss to society, represented by the red and purple triangles. These areas were formerly part of consumer surplus, but are now lost. In other words, overall society is worse off as a result of the imposition of the tariff. Notice that the impact of the tariff will depend on the elasticity of demand and supply in the domestic market.

Effectively, the government is subsidising inefficient local producers, and forcing domestic consumers to pay a price that is above that of similar goods imported from abroad.

Some would defend this policy on the grounds that it allows the country to protect an industry, thus saving jobs that would otherwise be lost. However, this goes against comparative advantage and in the longer term it may delay structural change. For an economy to develop new specialisations and new sources of comparative advantage, there needs to be a transitional process in which old industries contract and new ones emerge. Although this process may be painful, it is necessary in the long run if the economy is to remain competitive. Furthermore, the protection which firms enjoy that allows them to reap producer surplus from the tariff may foster complacency and an inward-looking attitude. This is likely to lead to X-inefficiency, and an inability to compete in the global market.

Even worse is the situation that develops where nations respond to tariffs raised by competitors by putting up tariffs of their own. This has the effect of further reducing the trade between countries, and everyone ends up worse off, as the gains from trade are sacrificed. President Trump's decision to extend the tariffs on steel to Canada, the EU and Mexico in 2018 brought an immediate response from those countries, threatening a trade war that would leave all involved worse off as a result. Although the WTO is committed to reducing tariffs over time, retaliation in the form of 'countervailing duties' is permitted.

Synoptic link

Notice that the notions of consumer and producer surplus turn up again here. These were first discussed in Chapter 4.

Knowledge check 25.10

Identify the ways in which consumer surplus is reduced following the imposition of a tariff.

Quotas

An alternative policy that a country may adopt is to limit the imports of a commodity to a given volume. For example, a country may come to an agreement with another country that only a certain quantity of imports will be accepted by the importing country. Such arrangements are known as *voluntary export restraints (VERs)* or more commonly as **quotas**.

Key term

quota an agreement by a country to limit its exports to another country to a given quantity or quota

The effects of a quota

Figure 25.7 illustrates the effects of such a quota. D represents the domestic demand for this commodity, and S_{dom} is the quantity that domestic producers are prepared to supply at any given price. Suppose that without any agreement, producers from country A would be prepared to supply any amount of the product at a price P_a. If the product is sold at this price, D_0 represents domestic demand, of which S_0 is supplied by domestic producers and the remainder $(D_0 - S_0)$ is imported from country A.

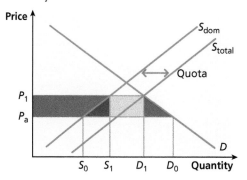

Figure 25.7 The effects of a quota

By imposing a quota, total supply is now given by S_{total}, which is domestic supply plus the quota of imports allowed into the economy from country A. The market equilibrium price rises to P_1 and demand falls to D_1, of which S_1 is supplied by domestic producers and the remainder is the agreed quota of imports.

> ### Study tip
> Notice that the diagram for a quota is very like the diagram for a tariff. Make sure you do not confuse the two, as they differ in terms of who gains and who loses from the measure.

Gainers and losers

Figure 25.7 shows who gains and who loses by this policy. Domestic producers gain by being able to sell at the higher price, so (as in the case of the tariff) they receive additional economic rent given by the dark blue area. Furthermore, the producers exporting from country A also gain, receiving the yellow rectangle (which, in the case of the tariff, was tax revenue received by the government). As in the case of the tariff, the two triangles (red and purple) represent the deadweight loss of welfare suffered by the importing country. Such an arrangement effectively subsidises the foreign producers by allowing them to charge a higher price than they would have been prepared to accept. Furthermore, although domestic producers are encouraged to produce more, the protection offered to them is likely to lead to X-inefficiency and weak attitudes towards competition.

There have been many examples of such agreements, especially in the textile industry. For example, the USA and China had long-standing agreements on quotas for a range of textile products. Ninety-one such quotas expired at the end of 2004 as part of China's accession to the WTO. As you might expect, this led to extensive lobbying by producers in the USA, especially during the run-up to the 2004 presidential election. Notice that it could be argued that the removal of the quotas would allow domestic consumers to benefit from lower prices, and would allow American textile workers to be released for employment in higher-productivity sectors, where the USA maintains a competitive advantage.

The USA has tried to curtail the growth of the highly competitive Chinese textile industry through the use of import quotas

A production subsidy

Another way in which a country may attempt to restrict trade is by subsidising domestic producers to enable them to compete more effectively with imports. Figure 25.8 illustrates a possible scenario.

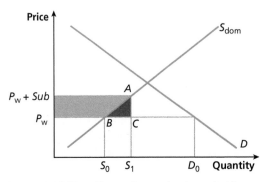

Figure 25.8 The effects of a production subsidy

This shows domestic demand and supply for a product that can be imported at the world price P_w. Without intervention, demand is D_0, of which S_0 is supplied by domestic producers, with the remainder being imported.

Assume that the country is too small a producer to affect the world price. If the government decides to pay a subsidy of an amount *Sub* to domestic producers, this affects the supply curve such that it is horizontal up to S_1 in Figure 25.8. This encourages domestic firms to increase production up to S_1, but unlike the case of the tariff, domestic consumers are still able to buy the good at the world price, so there is not the same impact on consumer surplus. Imports are $D_0 - S_1$, so this measure has reduced the country's dependence on imported goods.

Producers gain from this, receiving the additional producer surplus given by the blue shaded area. However, this needs to be covered by the government, as does the area ABC in the figure, which represents the production inefficiency that was a deadweight loss in the case of the tariff.

The total cost to the government of providing the subsidy is thus the sum of the shaded areas. The downside of this approach is that these funds need to be raised from elsewhere in the economy, thus distorting the allocation of resources in other markets. Although consumers are better off in respect of this product with the subsidy than with a tariff, as taxpayers they may pay the price in other ways. Furthermore, it is not clear that subsidising domestic production in this way provides any better incentives for efficiency than the tariff approach. If governments wish to encourage firms to become more efficient in order to compete, a better approach might be to subsidise education and training or research and development to improve production techniques, and thus tackle the problem more directly. Of course, this would depend on what was causing the inefficiency in the first place.

At the WTO ministerial summit in Nairobi in 2015, it was agreed that developed country members would eliminate all export subsidies immediately, and that developing country members would eliminate them by the end of 2018.

Knowledge check 25.11
How would the effectiveness of a subsidy or tariff be affected if domestic supply was highly inelastic?

Non-tariff barriers

Key term

non-tariff barriers measures imposed by a government that have the effect of inhibiting international trade

There are other ways in which trade can be hampered, one example being the use of what are known as **non-tariff barriers**. These often comprise rules and regulations that control the standard of products that can be sold in a country.

This is a grey area, as some of the rules and regulations may seem entirely sensible and apply equally to domestic and foreign producers. For example, laws that prohibit the sale of refrigerators that contain CFCs are designed to protect the ozone layer, and may be seen as wholly appropriate. In this case, the regulation is for purposes other than trade restriction. However, there may be other situations in which a regulation is more clearly designed to limit trade: for example, by making it more difficult for foreign firms to meet technical or quality standards.

Such rules and regulations may operate especially against producers in developing countries, who may find it especially difficult to meet demanding standards of production. This applies in particular where such countries are trying to develop new skills and specialisations to enable them to diversify their exports and engage more actively in international trade.

Knowledge check 25.12
Explain how trade would be affected if a country insisted that all imports of a particular product had to be imported through a single understaffed office.

The impact of protectionist policies
Protectionist policies have a number of effects on economic agents in a country. These effects differ according to which policy is in operation, but are most clearly

illustrated with reference to the imposition of a tariff, which is the most common form of protectionist policy.

- *Consumers:* in general, consumers are likely to be worse off as a result of protectionist measures. In the case of a tariff, consumer surplus is lower after a tariff, as consumers must pay a higher price for the good, and will consume less.
- *Producers:* producers in the domestic economy will gain from protection, as they will receive higher producer surplus (at the expense of consumers). However, their incentives to produce efficiently will be low, so in the long run they may never become able to compete effectively in world markets. The infant industry benefits are rarely delivered.
- *Governments:* when a government imposes a tariff, it gains by the revenue that it raises. This may be valuable for the government of a developing country that faces problems with raising revenue through other forms of taxation, because of the lack of an administrative structure.
- *Living standards:* for society as a whole, the imposition of a tariff carries a deadweight welfare loss, so overall well-being is lower with a tariff in place.
- *Equality:* protectionist measures entail a redistribution of resources, from consumers to producers, so there may be an increase in inequality in the society.

Exercise 25.4

Figure 25.9 illustrates the impact of a tariff. S_{dom} represents the quantity supplied by domestic producers, and D_{dom} shows the demand curve of domestic consumers. The world price is *OE*, and the country can import as much of the good at that price as it wishes.

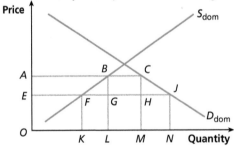

Figure 25.9 A tariff

a In the absence of government intervention, identify domestic demand and supply, and the quantity of imports.

b Suppose now that a tariff is imposed on imports of this product. Identify the price that will be charged in the domestic market.

c What will be the quantity demanded, the quantity supplied by home producers, and the quantity imported?

d Which area represents government revenue from the tariff?

e Identify the additional producer surplus received by domestic producers.

f Identify and explain the deadweight loss of the tariff.

g Discuss whether a tariff can be beneficial for society.

h Suppose that a tariff has been in place on this commodity, but that the government proposes to remove it. Discuss the effects that the removal of the tariff will have, and the difficulties a government might face in removing it.

Summary: trade protectionism

- The law of comparative advantage shows that countries can gain from international trade by specialising in the production of goods or services in which they have a lower opportunity cost of production.
- In spite of these possible gains, countries have often introduced protectionist measures to restrict trade, including tariffs, quotas and non-tariff barriers.

Case study 25.1

Tariff retaliation

Tariffs are the most common form of protectionist measure. In 2018, the USA was concerned about the effect that international trade was having on employment levels, and launched a series of tariff increases on a range of goods. A prisoners' dilemma game can be used to explore the possible implications of this situation.

Table 25.1 shows a pay-off matrix showing the gains that two countries could make under different tariff rates. The pay-offs for Country A are shown in red and those for Country B are shown in blue.

Table 25.1 A tariff pay-off matrix

		Country B					
		No tariff		Medium tariff		High tariff	
Country A	No tariff	100	100	50	125	30	80
	Medium tariff	125	50	70	70	20	90
	High tariff	80	30	90	20	40	40

To read the matrix, take the example of Country A first of all. If Country B imposes no tariff, then Country A receives a pay-off of 100 if it also imposes no tariff, but if Country B imposes a high tariff, Country A would only gain a pay-off of 30.

Follow-up questions

a Which combination of tariff levels would maximise the joint pay-off of the two countries?

b Which combination of tariff levels would represent the worst joint outcome for the two countries?

c Suppose that Country B imposes no tariff. What level of tariff would maximise the pay-off for Country A?

d If Country A goes ahead and imposes the tariff that would maximise its pay-off, what level of tariff would maximise the pay-off for Country B?

e If Country B imposes this level of tariff, what is Country A's best strategy?

f Discuss whether this situation is likely to apply in the event of a tariff war between the USA and its trading partners.

The North American Free Trade Agreement (NAFTA)

NAFTA is a trilateral agreement between the USA, Canada and Mexico that was launched on 1 January 1994, with the aim of removing tariff barriers between the countries. These provisions were fully implemented on 1 January 2008. Although NAFTA is primarily about trade in goods and services between the three countries, there are also side agreements dealing with environmental and labour issues.

The US Department of Agriculture claimed that NAFTA is 'one of the most successful trade agreements in history', having stimulated 'significant increases in agricultural trade and investment' between the three member countries.

Whether all partners have gained equally remains an open question. There is a strong protectionist lobby in the USA that has argued that jobs have been lost as a result of the agreement. Some commentators in Mexico have argued that NAFTA has damaged Mexico's agricultural sector, as it has faced subsidised imports from the USA. Labour issues have also been highly contentious, and the proposal from the USA to erect new fences to stem the flow of migrants from Mexico into the USA has aroused substantial debate.

It is important to treat these arguments with great care, as there are sensitive political issues that can sometimes override economic analysis. The law of comparative advantage suggests that there are potential gains from engaging in trade, but the process of liberalising trade entails short-run costs.

These may be expected to be transitional, especially for economic activities that are forced into decline in the face of expanding imports from partner countries. The existence of these costs should not prevent trade liberalisation if the long-term gains are sufficient to overcome them eventually. There must be a balancing of the costs against the benefits.

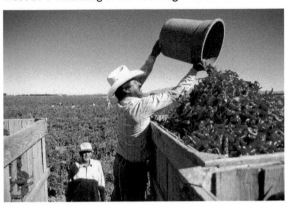

Whether Mexico's agricultural sector has benefited from NAFTA is open to debate

Follow-up questions

a What do you think might have motivated the members of NAFTA to join together in a free trade agreement?

b Which countries do you think would have most to gain from NAFTA?

c What factors would you need to take into account in evaluating the potential benefits of trade liberalisation in the context of an agreement such as NAFTA?

d In 2017, Canada accounted for about 77% of the USA's imports of steel, and Mexico accounted for a further 9%. What would you expect to be the result of the USA imposing a 25% tariff on imported steel?

The balance of payments and exchange rates

The balance of payments summarises transactions between the home country and the rest of the world. For any economy that is open to international trade, it is important to monitor these transactions. The exchange rate is also a crucial variable, as it influences the competitiveness of domestic firms in international markets, and is inextricably linked with the state of the balance of payments. The way in which the exchange rate is determined has wide-reaching effects on the conduct and effectiveness of macroeconomic policy. From the end of the Second World War until the early 1970s, a system of fixed exchange rates was in operation, whereby economies set the value of their currency relative to the US dollar. After this system broke down, most developed countries allowed their currencies to 'float', finding their own market levels, although at times governments have been tempted to intervene in this market. Some countries continue to peg their exchange rates to the US dollar. This chapter thus investigates why the exchange rate is so important, and how the various systems for determining its value work.

Learning objectives

After studying this chapter, you should:
→ understand the role and significance of the balance of payments and the need to maintain external balance in the long run
→ be familiar with the use of alternative policy measures to manage the balance of payments
→ understand what is meant by the market for foreign exchange
→ understand the operation of a fixed exchange rate system
→ be familiar with a floating exchange rate system
→ be aware of the major determinants of exchange rates within a floating exchange rate system
→ understand the way in which macroeconomic policy influences the exchange rate, and vice versa
→ understand how changes in exchange rates can affect the level of economic activity in a country
→ be familiar with measures of international competitiveness and their significance

---

The balance of payments

For an economy like the UK that is open to international trade, it is important to monitor the trade that takes place. The balance of payments is a set of accounts that monitors the transactions that take place between UK residents and the rest of the world. For an individual household it is important to monitor incomings and outgoings, as items purchased must be paid for in some way — either by using income or savings, or by borrowing. In a similar way, a country has to pay for goods, services or assets that are bought from other countries. The balance of payments accounts enable the analysis of such international transactions.

Key terms

current account of the balance of payments account identifying transactions in goods and services between the residents of a country and the rest of the world, together with income payments and international transfers

financial account of the balance of payments account identifying transactions in financial assets between the residents of a country and the rest of the world

capital account of the balance of payments account identifying transactions in (physical) capital between the residents of a country and the rest of the world

As with the household, transactions can be categorised as being either incoming or outgoing items. For example, if a car made in the UK is exported (i.e. purchased by a non-resident of the UK), this is an 'incoming' item, as the payment for the car is a credit to the UK. On the other hand, the purchase of a bottle of Italian wine (an import) is a debit item.

Knowledge check 26.1

A UK-based firm sells a machine tool to a company in the USA. Would this be a credit or a debit item in the balance of payments?

Similarly, all other transactions entered into the balance of payments accounts can be identified as credit or debit items, depending on the direction of the payment. In other words, when money flows into the country as the result of a transaction, that is a credit; if money flows out, it is a debit. As all items have to be paid for in some way, the overall balance of payments when everything is added together must be zero. However, individual components can be positive or negative.

In line with international standards, the accounts are divided into three categories: the **current account**, the **financial account** and the **capital account**.

Synoptic link

The key features of the balance of payments accounts were introduced in Chapter 10, and it would help you to look back and revise this. In this chapter we look at the components of the balance of payments more closely.

Figure 26.1 reminds you of the relative size of the balances on the main accounts since 2000, expressed as a percentage of GDP. As the total balance of payments must always be zero, the surplus (positive) components above the line must always exactly match the deficit (negative) items below the line. What this means is that any deficit on the current account must be matched by a surplus on the financial and other accounts. The relative magnitudes of the three major accounts vary through time.

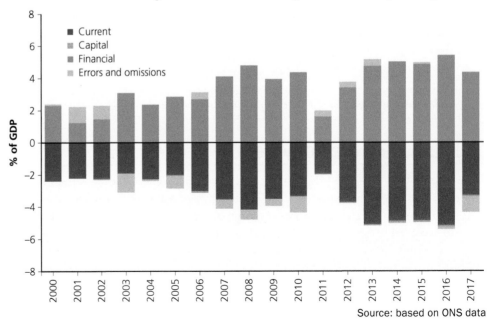

Source: based on ONS data

Figure 26.1 The UK balance of payments since 2000

Knowledge check 26.2

Why is it helpful to express the variables in Figure 26.1 as a percentage of GDP?

The current account

Figure 26.2 shows the components of the current account expressed as a percentage of GDP. The overall balance (CBAL) was in deficit throughout this period (the most recent surplus was in 1983, when North Sea oil was still bolstering the trade in goods). After 1997 the overall balance increased relative to GDP, with a slight improvement in the recession that followed the financial crisis in the late 2000s.

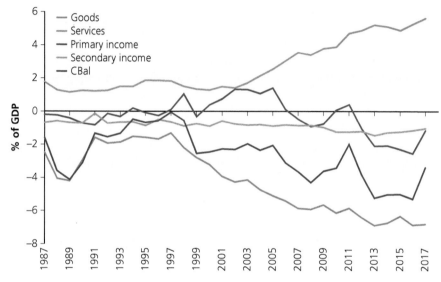

Source: calculated from ONS data

Note: primary income is income from direct, portfolio and other investments; secondary income includes taxes and transfers.

Figure 26.2 The composition of the current account since 1987 (balances)

Quantitative skills 26.1

Calculate the balance of an item in the balance of payments accounts

In 2017, the exports of goods were estimated as £338.9 billion and imports were £476.3 billion. The balance of trade in goods was thus total exports minus imports: that is, 338.9 − 476.3 = −£137.4 billion.

Trade in goods

Trade in goods (formerly known as **visible trade**) has traditionally shown a deficit for the UK — it has shown a surplus in only 6 years since 1950. As reserves of oil in the North Sea ran down, the UK became a net importer of oil, although up to 2004 the UK had been a net exporter: in other words, the oil part of the trade in goods was in surplus. However, imports of cars and other consumer goods have persistently exceeded exports, and you can see from Figure 26.2 that the deficit on trade in goods was already rising before 2004. By 2017 the deficit on goods had reached about 6.7% of GDP (£137.4 billion)

Key term

visible trade trade in goods

Key term

invisible trade trade in services

Trade in services

In contrast, trade in services has recorded a surplus in every year since 1966. This was formerly known as **invisible trade**.

In 2016, almost all items in services showed a surplus, the only significant deficit item being travel. The main reason for this is the increasing number of UK residents travelling aboard. Significant surplus items include financial services (a surplus of £50.8 billion), other business services (£22.7 billion) and insurance and pension services (£17.4 billion).

Investment income

An important item on the current account is investment income (known in the official accounts as *primary income*), which represents earnings accruing to domestic citizens on past investment abroad, less income earned by overseas residents who own assets in the UK. The largest item in this part of the account is earnings from direct investment, although there is also an element of portfolio investment — earnings from holdings of bonds and other securities. If UK assets are sold abroad, this generates a credit item on the financial account. However, the investment income that accrues in the future would be a debit item on the current account. For example, when SABMiller (a company with headquarters in the UK) was taken over by Anheuser-Busch in 2016, this generated a positive item on the financial account, but the profits subsequently generated by the company flow out of the UK, and constitute a negative item on the current account. You can see that primary income has shown a deficit in most years since 2006.

Current transfers

The final category is current transfers (*secondary income* in the official accounts). These include taxes and social contributions received from non-resident workers and businesses, bilateral aid flows and military grants. However, the largest item is transfers with EU institutions, which showed a deficit of £9.4 billion in 2016.

Knowledge check 26.3

Looking at Figure 26.2, which item contributed most clearly to the smaller current account deficit in 2011?

The financial account

The financial account shows transactions associated with changes in the ownership of the UK's foreign financial assets and liabilities. There are four categories of these transactions:

- *Foreign direct investment:* an important part of the financial account is where UK investors undertake investment overseas, and where overseas investors purchase assets in the UK. The net flows of such foreign direct investment are part of the financial account (although the income received in future years appears in the current account).
- *Portfolio investment:* this relates to equities and securities.
- *Other types of financial assets:* these have become increasingly important and include various forms of financial derivatives such as options and financial futures.

■ *Reserve assets:* these include gold and foreign exchange held by the Bank of England. These were important when the country was operating a fixed exchange rate system, but transactions are infrequent in a system of floating exchange rates.

Synoptic link

Financial instruments created through securitisation are discussed in Chapter 30, which examines the financial sector. Exchange rate systems are explored later in this chapter.

Surplus on the financial account

The trend towards globalisation means that both inward and outward investment increased substantially during the 1990s, although there was a dip after 2000. However, Figure 26.1 shows that the financial account has been in strong surplus in the early part of the twenty-first century. This is in part forced by the deficit on the current account. In other words, if an economy runs a current account deficit, it can do so only by running a surplus on the financial account. Effectively, what is happening is that, in order to fund the current account deficit, the UK is selling assets to foreign investors and borrowing abroad.

An important question is whether global trade imbalances like this are sustainable in the long run. Selling assets or borrowing abroad has future implications for the current account, as there will be outflows of investment income, and debt repayments in the future following today's financial surplus. It also has implications for interest rate policy. If the authorities were to hold interest rates high relative to the rest of the world, this would tend to attract inflows of investment, again with future implications for the current account.

Other problems may arise for countries that operate with persistent current account surpluses, which focuses resources on delivering exports. This may be at the expense of domestic consumption expenditure. This was an issue for China during the period when it was intent on maintaining a strong export position.

Knowledge check 26.5

If there is an increase in inward foreign direct investment in the present, how would the current account of the balance of payments be affected in the future?

Investment flows

Notice that the balance of payments summarises transactions in each period, so deals with flows. In the case of the financial account, the accumulated stocks of assets and liabilities is also important; this international investment position is monitored by the balance sheet of the stock of external assets and liabilities.

Figure 26.3 shows the time path of foreign direct investment in the UK since 1987, again expressed as a percentage of GDP. You can see that the flows in and out of the UK since the late 1990s have been quite volatile. This arises partly because the flows tend to be dominated by large-scale mergers and acquisitions, which cause sudden changes in the size of the flow.

Knowledge check 26.4

Would an increase in the income from portfolio investment be an item on the current, financial or capital account?

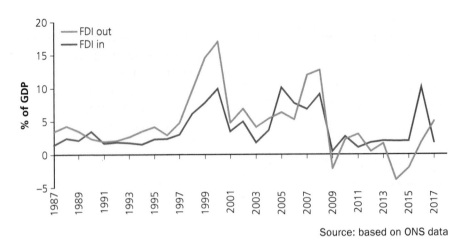

Source: based on ONS data

Figure 26.3 Foreign direct investment in the UK

Study tip

Remember that it is important to have a general feel for trends in the data over the recent past, but it is not necessary to spend time learning detailed data about the economy.

The capital account

The capital account is relatively small. The largest item relates to the flows of capital associated with migration. If someone migrates to the UK, that person's status changes from being a non-resident to being a resident. His or her property then becomes part of the UK's assets, and a transaction has to be entered in the balance of payments accounts. There are also some items relating to various EU transactions. This balance on this account is very small compared to the other components, and has never been greater than 0.1% of GDP.

Dealing with a current account deficit

There are several possible causes of a deficit on the current account of the balance of payments.

■ *Competitiveness:* the competitiveness of domestic production relative to other countries is important. If productivity at home is weak, or if domestic firms are producing poor quality products, then the demand for exports will be relatively low.
■ *Inflation:* if inflation in the home country is high relative to elsewhere, this will again discourage exports and encourage imports. With high inflation, rising labour costs can fuel this process.
■ *Rapid economic growth:* this can draw in imports and contribute to a current account deficit.

To some extent, these effects can be mitigated through exchange rate movements, as will be discussed shortly. However, given these potential problems, what can be done about it?

Expenditure-reducing

If the deficit stems from high demand for imports, then one possible remedy would be to reduce aggregate demand, inducing people to spend less on imported goods. The problem with adopting this approach is that this would hinder economic growth, and potentially lead to higher unemployment. This approach was enforced in the UK under fixed exchange rates.

Expenditure-switching

An alternative approach could be to find ways of encouraging domestic residents to switch their expenditure from imports towards domestically produced goods. This might be tackled through a 'Buy British' campaign, although this is likely to have limited effects. The more direct approach could be to introduce protectionist measures, such as tariffs or non-tariff barriers. As discussed in the previous chapter, this approach imposes welfare costs on the domestic economy, and runs the risk of provoking retaliation from other countries, thus imposing costs on all concerned.

Supply-side measures

If the root problem of the deficit is that domestic producers are operating at lower productivity levels, or are producing low-quality products, then this could be tackled at source, by providing incentives for producers to innovate and invest to improve the competitiveness of their goods.

Synoptic link

Supply-side policies were discussed in more detail in Chapter 16.

Summary: the balance of payments

- The balance of payments is a set of accounts that contains details of the transactions that take place between the residents of an economy and the rest of the world.
- The accounts are divided into three sections: the current, financial and capital accounts.
- The current account identifies transactions in goods and services, together with some income payments and international transfers.
- The financial account measures transactions in financial assets, including investment flows and central government transactions in foreign reserves.
- The capital account, which is relatively small, contains (physical) capital transfers.
- The overall balance of payments must always be zero.
- The current account has been in persistent deficit since 1984, reflecting a deficit in trade in goods that is partly offset by a surplus in invisible trade.
- The financial account has been in strong surplus — as is required to balance the current account deficit.
- Persistent trade imbalances may not be sustainable in the long run.

Exercise 26.1

Allocate each of the items in Table 26.1 to either the current, financial or capital accounts, and calculate the balances for each account. Check that (together with errors and omissions) the total is zero. All data refer to 2015, at current prices in £ billion.

Table 26.1

Item	Current prices, 2015 (£bn)
a Trade in goods	−118.6
b Net direct investment	−76.1
c Investment income	−42.8
d Current transfers	−22.8
e Transactions in reserve assets	−21.1
f Trade in services	+86.3
g Capital transfers	−2.0
h Compensation of employees	−0.1
i Total net portfolio investment	+139.0
j Other transactions in financial assets	−103.1
k Errors and omissions	+9.2

The foreign exchange market

Chapter 5 introduced the foreign exchange market, and argued that it could be regarded as involving demand and supply, just like any normal market. A foreign exchange transaction is needed whenever trade takes place. If, as a UK resident, you buy goods from abroad, you need to purchase foreign exchange — say, euros — and you have to supply pounds in order to buy euros. Similarly, if a French tourist in the UK buys UK goods or services, the transaction needs to be carried out in pounds, so there is a demand for pounds.

This market is shown in Figure 26.4. The demand curve is downward sloping because when the €/£ rate is low, UK goods, services and assets are relatively cheap in terms of euros, so demand is relatively high. On the other hand, when the €/£ rate is relatively high, Europeans receive fewer pounds for their euros, so the demand will be relatively low.

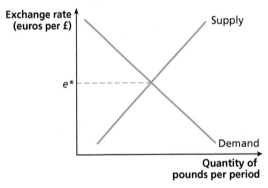

Figure 26.4 The market for pounds

The supply curve of pounds is upward sloping. When the €/£ rate is relatively high, the supply of pounds will be relatively strong, as UK residents will get plenty of euros for their pounds and thus will demand European goods, services and assets, supplying pounds in order to buy the foreign exchange needed for the transactions. When the €/£ rate is low, European goods, services and assets will be relatively expensive for UK residents, so fewer pounds will be supplied.

The market is in equilibrium at $e^\star$, where the demand for pounds is just matched by the supply of pounds. This position has a direct connection with the balance of payments. If the demand for pounds exactly matches the supply of pounds, this implies that there is a balance between the demand from Europeans for UK goods, services and assets and the demand by UK residents for European goods, services and assets. In other words, the balance of payments is in overall balance. The key question for consideration is how the market reaches $e^\star$ — in particular, do the authorities allow the exchange rate to find its own way to $e^\star$, or do they intervene to ensure that it gets there?

If the authorities agree to manage the exchange rate, by fixing the value of their currency relative to that of another country, they operate a **fixed exchange rate** system.

Key term

fixed exchange rate a system in which the government of a country agrees to fix the value of its currency in terms of that of another country

Knowledge check 26.6

How would the market for sterling be affected if Europeans were to find British goods less attractive?

Summary: the foreign exchange market

- The foreign exchange market can be seen as operating according to the laws of demand and supply.
- The demand for pounds arises when non-residents want to buy UK goods, services or assets.
- The supply of pounds arises when UK residents wish to buy foreign goods, services or assets.
- When the exchange rate is at its equilibrium level, this automatically ensures that the overall balance of payments is zero.

A fixed exchange rate system

In the Bretton Woods conference at the end of the Second World War, it was agreed to establish a fixed exchange rate system, under which countries would commit to maintaining the price of their currencies in terms of the US dollar. This system remained in place until the early 1970s. For example, from 1950 until 1967 the sterling exchange rate was set at $2.80, and the UK government was committed to making sure that it stayed at this rate. This system became known as the **Dollar Standard**. Occasional changes in exchange rates were permitted after consultation if a currency was seen to be substantially out of line — as happened for the UK in 1967.

> ### Key term
>
> **Dollar Standard** a system of fixed exchange rates established following the Bretton Woods conference, under which countries pegged their currencies to the US dollar; this lasted until the early 1970s

John Maynard Keynes played a leading role in the Bretton Woods conference

Figure 26.5 illustrates how this works. Suppose the authorities announce that the exchange rate will be set at e_f. Given that this level is set independently by the government, it cannot be guaranteed to correspond to the market equilibrium, and in Figure 26.5 it is set above the equilibrium level. At this exchange rate the supply of pounds exceeds the demand for pounds. This can be interpreted in terms of the overall balance of payments. If there is an excess supply of pounds, the implication is that UK residents are trying to buy more American goods, services and assets than

Americans are trying to buy British: in other words, there is an overall deficit on the balance of payments.

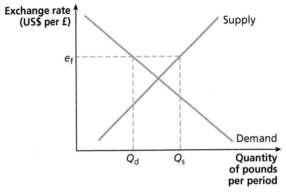

Figure 26.5 Maintaining a fixed exchange rate

In a free market, you would expect the exchange rate to adjust until the demand and supply of pounds came back into equilibrium. As the authorities are committed to maintaining the exchange rate at e_f, such adjustment cannot take place. However, the UK owes the USA for the excess goods, services and assets that its residents have purchased, so the authorities then have to sell **foreign exchange reserves** in order to make the books balance.

In terms of Figure 26.5, Q_d represents the demand for pounds at e_f and Q_s represents the supply. The difference represents the amount of foreign exchange reserves that the authorities have to sell to preserve the balance of payments. Such transactions are known as 'official financing', and are incorporated into the financial account of the balance of payments.

Key term

foreign exchange reserves stocks of foreign currency and gold owned by the central bank of a country to enable it to meet any mismatch between the demand and supply of the country's currency

Knowledge check 26.7

Under a fixed exchange rate regime, if the equilibrium level of the exchange rate is below the official rate, how would the authorities bring the market into line?

Notice that the *position* of the demand and supply curves depends on factors other than the exchange rate that can affect the demand for UK and American goods, services and assets in the respective countries. It is likely that, through time, these will shift in position. For example, if the preference of Americans for UK goods changes through time, this will affect the demand for pounds.

The effect of changes in the demand for pounds

Consider Figure 26.6. For simplicity, suppose that the supply curve remains fixed but demand shifts through time. Let e_f be the value of the exchange rate that the UK monetary authorities have undertaken to maintain. If the demand for pounds is at D_1, the chosen exchange rate corresponds to the market equilibrium, and no action by the authorities is needed. If demand is at D_0, then with the exchange rate at e_f there is an excess supply of pounds (as shown in Figure 26.5). The monetary authorities in the UK need to buy up the excess supply by selling foreign exchange reserves. Conversely, if the demand for pounds is strong, say because Americans have developed a preference for Scotch whisky, then demand could be at D_2. There is now excess demand for pounds, and the UK monetary authorities supply additional pounds in return for US dollars. Foreign exchange reserves thus accumulate.

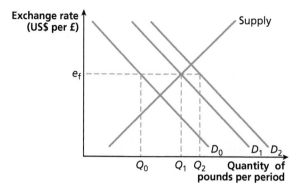

Figure 26.6 Maintaining a fixed exchange rate in the face of changing demand for pounds

In the long term, the system will operate successfully for the country so long as the chosen exchange rate is close to the average equilibrium value over time, so that the central bank is neither running down its foreign exchange reserves nor accumulating them.

A country that tries to hold its currency away from equilibrium indefinitely will find this problematic in the long run, as it will cause a persistent trade imbalance. For example, in the early years of the twenty-first century China and some other Asian economies were pegging their currencies against the US dollar at such a low level that they were accumulating foreign exchange. In the case of China, it was accumulating substantial amounts of US government stock. The low exchange rate had the effect of keeping the exports of these countries highly competitive in world markets. However, such a strategy relies on being able to continue to expand domestic production to meet the high demand; otherwise inflationary pressure will begin to build.

Under a fixed exchange rate system, a persistent disequilibrium may need to be addressed by realigning the value of the currency, either by reducing the price of its currency (a **devaluation**) to tackle persistent current account deficits, or by raising the price of the currency (a **revaluation**) to deal with persistent surpluses.

The Dollar Standard

During the period of the Dollar Standard, the pound was probably set at too high a level, which meant that UK exports were relatively uncompetitive, and in 1967 the UK government announced a devaluation of the pound from $2.80 to $2.40.

During the Dollar Standard period, the UK economy went through what became known as a 'stop–go' cycle of growth. When the government tried to stimulate economic growth, the effect was to suck in imports, as the marginal propensity to import was high. The effect of this was to generate a deficit on the current account of the balance of payments, which then needed to be financed by selling foreign exchange reserves.

This process has two effects. First of all, in selling foreign exchange reserves, domestic money supply increases, which then puts upward pressure on prices, threatening inflation. In addition, the Bank of England has finite foreign exchange reserves, and cannot allow them to be run down indefinitely. This meant that the government had to rein in the economy, thereby slowing the rate of growth again; hence the label 'stop–go'.

Key terms

devaluation process whereby a government reduces the price of its currency relative to an agreed rate in terms of foreign currency

revaluation process whereby a government raises the price of domestic currency in terms of foreign currency

Fixed exchange rates and monetary policy

An important point emerges from this discussion. The fact that intervention to maintain the exchange rate affects domestic money supply means that under a fixed exchange rate regime the monetary authorities are unable to pursue an independent monetary policy. In other words, money supply and the exchange rate cannot be controlled independently of one another. Effectively, the money supply has to be targeted to maintain the value of the currency. Governments may be tempted to use tariffs or non-tariff barriers to reduce a current account deficit, but this has been shown to be distortionary.

Synoptic link

The distortionary effects of tariffs were discussed in Chapter 25 as part of the explanation of protectionism.

The effects of devaluation

During the stop–go period there were many debates about whether there should be a devaluation. The effect of devaluation is to improve competitiveness. At a lower value of the pound, you would expect an increase in the demand for exports and a fall in the demand for imports, ceteris paribus.

However, this does not necessarily mean that there will be an improvement in the current account. One reason for this concerns the elasticity of supply of exports and import substitutes. If domestic producers do not have spare capacity, or if there are time lags before production for export can be increased, then exports will not expand quickly in the short run, and so the impact of this action on exports will be limited. Furthermore, similar arguments apply to producers of goods that are potential substitutes for imported products, which reinforces the sluggishness of adjustment. In the short run, therefore, it may be that the current account will worsen rather than improve, in spite of the change in the competitiveness of domestic firms.

> **Knowledge check 26.8**
>
> Explain why a devaluation may not lead to an immediate reduction in the current account deficit.

The J-curve effect

This is known as the **J-curve effect**, and is shown in Figure 26.7. Time is measured on the horizontal axis, and the current account is initially in deficit. A devaluation at time *A* initially pushes the current account further into deficit because of the inelasticity of domestic supply. Only after time *B*, when domestic firms have had time to expand their output to meet the demand for exports, does the current account move into surplus.

Key term

J-curve effect a situation following a devaluation, in which the current account deficit moves further into deficit before improving

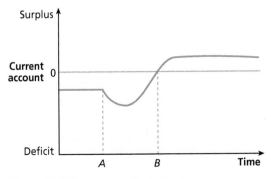

Figure 26.7 The J-curve effect of a devaluation

A second consideration relates to the elasticity of demand for exports and imports. Again, if competitiveness improves but demand does not respond strongly, there may be a negative impact on the current account. If the demand for exports is price inelastic, a fall in price will lead to a fall in revenue. There is reason to expect that the demand for exports is relatively inelastic in the short run. In many cases, exports may be supplied under contracts that cannot be immediately renegotiated. Furthermore, people and firms may wait to see whether the devaluation is permanent or temporary, and thus not revise their spending plans in the short run.

The Marshall-Lerner condition

The **Marshall–Lerner condition** states that devaluation will have a positive effect on the current account only if the sum of the elasticities of demand for exports and imports is negative and numerically greater than 1. If there is a devaluation, there will be a quantity effect and a price effect. At the new exchange rate, the quantity effect on the trade balance will be positive because exports tend to increase and imports to decrease. However, there is also a negative price effect, because export prices in terms of foreign currency have fallen and import prices in domestic currency have risen. The trade balance (measured in revenue terms) will improve only if the quantity effect fully offsets the price effect — in other words, if the Marshall–Lerner condition holds true.

The Bretton Woods Dollar Standard broke down in the early 1970s. Part of the reason for this was that such a system depends critically on the stability of the base currency (i.e. the US dollar). During the 1960s the USA's need to finance the Vietnam War meant that the supply of dollar currency began to expand, one result of which was accelerating inflation in the countries that were fixing their currency in terms of the US dollar. It then became increasingly difficult to sustain exchange rates at fixed levels. The UK withdrew from the Dollar Standard in June 1972.

Competitive devaluation

Under a fixed exchange rate regime, there may be a temptation for countries to improve their international competitive position by engineering a devaluation. The danger here is that other countries would respond by introducing a similar policy, thus negating the original effects. The eventual effect would be to reduce world trade overall.

> **Key terms**
>
> **Marshall-Lerner condition** the condition that devaluation will have a positive effect on the current account only if the sum of the elasticities of demand for exports and imports is negative and numerically greater than 1
>
> **competitive devaluation** a situation in which one country attempts to gain an advantage by devaluing its currency, inducing a response from other countries

Summary: fixed exchange rates

- After the Bretton Woods conference at the end of the Second World War, the Dollar Standard was established, under which countries agreed to maintain the value of their currencies in terms of US dollars.
- In order to achieve this, the monetary authorities engaged in foreign currency transactions to ensure that the exchange rate was maintained at the agreed level, accumulating foreign exchange reserves to accommodate a balance of payments surplus and running down the reserves to fund a deficit.
- Occasional realignments were permitted, such as the devaluation of sterling in 1967.
- Under a fixed exchange rate system, monetary policy can be used only to achieve the exchange rate target.
- A devaluation has the effect of improving international competitiveness, but the effect on the current account depends on the elasticity of demand for exports and imports.
- The current account may deteriorate in the short run if the supply response is sluggish.
- The Bretton Woods system broke down in the early 1970s.

Exercise 26.2

A firm wants to purchase a machine tool which is obtainable in the UK for a price of £125,000, or from a US supplier for $300,000. Suppose that the exchange rate is fixed at £1 = $3.

a What is the sterling price of the machine tool if the firm chooses to buy in the USA?

b From which supplier would the firm be likely to purchase?

c Suppose that, between ordering the machine tool and its delivery, the UK government announces a devaluation of sterling, so that when the time comes for the firm to pay up the exchange rate is £1 = $2. What is the sterling price of the machine tool bought from the USA?

d Comment on how the competitiveness of UK goods has been affected.

e Discuss the effects that the devaluation is likely to have on the economy as a whole.

Key terms

floating exchange rate
a system in which the exchange rate is permitted to find its own level in the market

Exchange Rate Mechanism (ERM) a system that was set up by a group of European countries in 1979 with the objective of keeping member countries' currencies relatively stable against each other

Floating exchange rates

Under a **floating exchange rate** system, the value of the currency is allowed to find its own way to equilibrium. This means that the overall balance of payments is automatically assured, and the monetary authorities do not need to intervene to make sure it happens. In practice, however, governments have tended to be wary of leaving the exchange rate entirely to market forces, and there have been occasional periods in which intervention has been used to affect the market rate.

An example of this was the **Exchange Rate Mechanism (ERM)**, which was set up by a group of European countries in 1979 with the objective of keeping member countries' currencies relatively stable against each other. This was part of the European Monetary System (EMS). Each member nation agreed to keep its currency within 2.25% of a weighted average of the members' currencies, known as the European Currency Unit (ECU). This was an *adjustable peg* system. Eleven realignments were permitted between 1979 and 1987.

The UK opted not to join the ERM when it was first set up, but started shadowing the Deutschmark in the mid-1980s, aiming to keep the rate at around DM3 to the pound, as you can see in Figure 26.8. The UK finally decided to become a full member of the ERM in September 1990. However, the rate at which sterling had been set against the Deutschmark was relatively high, and the situation was worsened by the effects of German reunification, which led to substantial capital flows into Germany, reinforcing the overvaluation of sterling. Once it became apparent that sterling was overvalued, speculative attacks began, and the Bank of England's foreign exchange reserves were depleted; in 1992 the pound left the ERM. You can see in Figure 26.8 that the value of the pound fell rapidly after exit.

Source: Bank of England

Figure 26.8 The nominal DM/£ exchange rate, 1987–95

Factors influencing floating exchange rates

If the foreign exchange market is left free to find its own way to equilibrium, it becomes important to consider what factors will influence the level of the exchange rate. In particular, will the exchange rate resulting from market equilibrium be consistent with the government's domestic policy objectives?

The key factors are:

- relative interest rates and monetary policy
- relative inflation rates
- net investment in the UK
- speculation

Interest rates and monetary policy

Financial flows into or out of the UK may be induced by the relative level of interest rates. If UK interest rates are high relative to elsewhere, this may attract an inflow of financial capital, thus putting upward pressure on the interest rate and leading to an appreciation of the exchange rate. Similarly, under quantitative easing, an increase in money supply could cause a depreciation (through its effect on interest rates).

Synoptic link

Quantitative easing and the monetary transmission mechanism were introduced in Chapter 16, and will be explored more fully in Chapter 31.

The significance of this is that changes in the stance of monetary policy will have an effect on the exchange rate under a floating exchange rate system. These become an important part of the transmission mechanism of monetary policy.

Relative inflation rates

Exchange rate equilibrium also implies a zero overall balance of payments. If the exchange rate always adjusts to the level that ensures this, it might be argued that the long-run state of the economy is one in which the competitiveness of domestic firms remains constant over time. In other words, you would expect the exchange rate to adjust through time to offset any differences in inflation rates between countries. The **purchasing power parity theory of exchange rates** argues that this is exactly what should be expected in the long run. The nominal exchange rate should adjust in such a way as to offset changes in relative prices between countries.

Key term

purchasing power parity theory of exchange rates theory stating that in the long run exchange rates (in a floating rate system) are determined by relative inflation rates in different countries

The trade balance

The exchange rate in a free market is determined by the demand and supply for the currency, as explained above. Thus, changes in the balance between exports and imports can affect the exchange rate. An increase in the demand for exports implies an increase in the demand for sterling, so would lead to an appreciation of the currency (ceteris paribus).

Net investment in the UK

An increase in foreign direct investment would have similar effects. If the UK becomes an attractive prospect for foreign investors, this could also lead to an appreciation — or at least upward pressure on the exchange rate.

Speculation

In the short run the exchange rate may diverge from its long-run equilibrium. An important influence on the exchange rate in the short run is speculation. So far, the discussion of the exchange rate has stressed mainly the current account of the balance of payments. But the financial account is also significant, especially since regulation of the movement of financial capital was liberalised. Some of these capital movements are associated with foreign direct investment, which was discussed in the previous chapter. However, sometimes there are also substantial movements of what has come to be known as **hot money**: that is, stocks of funds that are moved around the globe from country to country in search of the best return. The size of the stocks of hot money is enormous, and can significantly affect exchange rates in the short run. The returns to be gained from such capital flows depend on the relative interest rate in the country targeted, and on the expected exchange rate in the future, which in turn may depend on expectations about inflation.

Suppose you are an investor holding assets denominated in US dollars, and the UK interest rate is 2% higher than that in the USA. You may be tempted to shift the funds into the UK in order to take advantage of the higher interest rate. However, if you believe that the exchange rate is above its long-run equilibrium, and therefore is likely to fall, this will affect your expected return on holding a UK asset. Indeed, if investors holding UK assets expect the exchange rate to fall, they are likely to shift their funds out of the country as soon as possible — which may then have the effect of pushing down the exchange rate. In other words, this may be a self-fulfilling prophecy. However, speculators may react to news in an unpredictable way, so not all speculative capital movements act to influence the exchange rate towards its long-run equilibrium value.

Key term

hot money stocks of funds that are moved around the world from country to country in search of the best return

In financial markets, 'hot money' moves swifly around the world in search of the best return

Speculation was a key contributing factor in the unfolding of the Asian financial crisis of 1997. Substantial flows of capital had moved into Thailand in search of high returns, and speculators came to believe that the Thai currency (the baht) was overvalued. Outward capital flows put pressure on the exchange rate, and although the Thai central bank tried to resist, it eventually ran down its reserves to the point where it had to devalue. This then sparked off capital flows from other countries in the region, including South Korea.

A managed (dirty) float

Under a floating exchange rate system, the authorities do not intervene in the exchange market. However, exchange rates are notoriously volatile and there may be occasions in which the authorities may wish to intervene to try to stabilise the currency. When this happens, it represents a move away from a pure float to a managed floating exchange rate (sometimes known as a 'dirty' float).

One way in which the authorities could influence the exchange rate under this system would be by using the interest rate to influence international financial flows. This is difficult to implement under inflation targeting, where the prime use of the interest rate is to ensure that inflation remains within its target range.

A second way would be to buy or sell sterling in order to influence its price (i.e. the exchange rate). There may be a temptation for the authorities to intervene when the pound reacts to external shocks to the economy – for example, the depreciations that occurred at the outset of the financial crisis and following the Brexit referendum vote. However, the official financing item in the balance of payments accounts in the UK has been relatively minor, indicating that there has been little attempt to manage the exchange rate.

One rationale for attempting to manage the exchange rate would be to improve a country's competitiveness through a depreciation. This strategy would clearly have an impact on other countries, and could thus induce a response, becoming a form of competitive depreciation. This is likely to be counter-productive in the long run.

Key term

managed float where the authorities intervene in a floating exchange rate system occasionally in order to stabilise the currency

Summary: floating exchange rates

- Under a floating exchange rate system, the value of a currency is allowed to find its own way to equilibrium without government intervention.
- This means that an overall balance of payments of zero is automatically achieved.
- The purchasing power parity theory argues that the exchange rate will adjust in the long run to maintain international competitiveness, by offsetting differences in inflation rates between countries.
- In the short run, the exchange rate may diverge from this long-run level, particularly because of speculation.
- The exchange rate is thus influenced by relative interest rates and expected inflation, as well as by news about the economic environment.

Fixed or floating?

In evaluating whether a fixed or a floating regime is to be preferred, there are many factors to be taken into account; this section will consider three of them. First, it is important to examine the extent to which the respective systems can accommodate and adjust to external shocks that push the economy out of equilibrium. Second, it is important to consider the stability of each of the systems. Finally, there is the question of which system best encourages governments to adopt sound macroeconomic policies.

Adjustment to shocks

Every economy has to cope with external shocks that occur for reasons outside the control of the country. A key question in evaluating exchange rate systems is whether there is an effective mechanism that allows the economy to return to equilibrium after an external shock.

Under a floating exchange rate system, much of the burden of adjustment is taken up by changes in the exchange rate. For example, if an economy finds itself experiencing faster inflation than other countries, perhaps because those other countries have introduced policies to reduce inflation, then the exchange rate will adjust automatically to restore competitiveness.

However, if the country is operating a fixed exchange rate system, the authorities are committed to maintaining the exchange rate, and this has to take precedence. Thus, the only way to restore competitiveness is by deflating the economy in order to bring inflation into line with other countries. This is likely to bring with it a transitional cost in terms of higher unemployment and slower economic growth. In other words, the burden of adjustment is on the real economy, rather than on allowing the exchange rate to adjust.

The Bretton Woods system operated for more than 20 years in a period in which many economies enjoyed steady economic growth. However, in the UK the system brought about a stop–go cycle, in which the need to maintain the exchange rate hampered economic growth, because of the tendency for growth to lead to an increase in imports and thus to a current account deficit. The increasing differences between inflation rates in different countries led to the final collapse of the system, suggesting that it was unable to cope with such variation.

Knowledge check 26.10

Why would differences in inflation rates between countries create problems with operating a fixed exchange rate system?

Furthermore, a flexible exchange rate system allows the authorities to utilise monetary policy in order to stabilise the economy — remember that under a fixed exchange rate system, monetary policy has to be devoted to the exchange rate target.

Stability

When it comes to stability, a fixed exchange rate system has much to commend it. After all, if firms know that the government is committed to maintaining the exchange rate at a given level, they can agree future contracts with some confidence. Under a floating exchange rate system, trading takes place in an environment in which the future exchange rate has to be predicted. If the exchange rate moves adversely, firms then face potential losses from trading. This foreign exchange risk is reduced under a fixed rate regime.

In a climate where speculative activity creates volatility in exchange rates, international trade may be discouraged because of the exchange rate risk. The effects of such volatility can be mitigated to some extent by the existence of **futures markets**. In such a market, it is possible to buy foreign exchange at a fixed price for delivery at a specified future date.

Key term

futures market a market in which it is possible to buy a commodity at a fixed price for delivery at a specified future date; such a market exists for foreign exchange

For example, suppose a firm is negotiating a deal to buy component parts for a manufacturing process that will be delivered in 3 months' time. The firm can buy the foreign exchange needed to close the deal in the futures market, and then knows that the contract will be viable, having negotiated a price for the components based on the known exchange rate, rather than on the unpredictable rate that will apply at that future date. The firm may, of course, have to pay a price for the foreign currency that is below the current (*spot*) exchange rate, but as the future rate has been built into the terms of the contract, that will not affect the viability of the deal. The process by which a firm avoids losses by buying forward is known as *hedging*.

However, even with the use of hedging to reduce the risk, it is costly to engage in international trade when exchange rates are potentially volatile, so world trade is unlikely to be encouraged under such a system. Of course, it might be argued that the risk to firms is still present under a fixed exchange rate system, in the sense that a government may choose to realign its currency, with even greater costs to firms that are tied into contracts. However, such realignments were rare under Bretton Woods, and are more predictable than the volatility that can occur on a day-to-day basis in the foreign exchange market.

The exchange rate and foreign direct investment

It is important also to realise that flows of foreign direct investment may be influenced by the exchange rate — and by expectations about future movements of the exchange rate. This will be one of the key factors that a foreign firm takes into account when deciding where to locate its investment.

Macroeconomic policy

Critics of the flexible exchange rate system argue that it is too flexible for its own good. If governments know that the exchange rate will always adjust to maintain international competitiveness, they may have no incentive to behave responsibly in designing macroeconomic policy. Thus, they may be tempted to adopt an inflationary domestic policy, secure in the knowledge that the exchange rate will bear the burden of adjustment. In other words, a flexible exchange rate system does not impose financial discipline on individual countries.

An example of this was seen in the UK in the early 1970s when the country first moved to a floating exchange rate regime. Money supply was allowed to expand rapidly, and inflation increased to almost 25%, aided by the oil price shock. Other examples are evident in Latin America, where hyperinflation affected many countries during the 1980s and early 1990s. For the country itself, such policies are costly in the long run, as reducing inflation under flexible exchange rates is costly. If interest rates are increased in order to reduce domestic aggregate demand and thus reduce inflationary pressure (see Chapter 31), the high return on domestic assets encourages an inflow of hot money, thereby putting upward pressure on the exchange rate. This reduces the international competitiveness of domestic goods and services, and deepens the recession.

Synoptic link

You can see the path of inflation in the 1970s in the UK by looking back at Figure 10.2 on page 146.

Key terms

appreciation a rise in the exchange rate within a floating exchange rate system

depreciation a fall in the exchange rate within a floating exchange rate system

There may also be spillover effects on other countries. Suppose that two countries have been experiencing rapid inflation, and one of them decides to tackle the problem. It raises interest rates to dampen domestic aggregate demand, which leads to an **appreciation** of its currency. For the other country, the effect is a **depreciation** of the currency. (If one currency appreciates, the other must depreciate.) The other country thus finds that its competitive position has improved, and it faces inflationary pressure in the short run. It may then also choose to tackle inflation, which in turn will affect the other country. These spillover effects could be minimised if the countries were to harmonise their policy action.

Knowledge check 26.11

How does a depreciation of a country's currency affect the demand for its exports?

Study tip

Make sure that you can distinguish between a depreciation and a devaluation, and between an appreciation and a revaluation.

When a government under a fixed exchange rate system chooses to lower the exchange rate, this is known as a devaluation; if the exchange rate falls under a floating exchange rate system, it is known as a depreciation.

Similarly, an increase in the exchange rate initiated by the authorities under a fixed exchange rate system is known as a revaluation, whereas under a floating rate system a rise in the exchange rate is known as an appreciation.

The exchange rate and macroeconomic policy

The discussion above has shown that the relationship between the exchange rate and macroeconomic policy is an important one. Under a fixed exchange rate system, the need to maintain the value of the currency is a constraint on macroeconomic policy, and forces the economy to adjust to disequilibrium through the real economy. On the other hand, it does have the benefit of imposing financial discipline on governments.

Knowledge check 26.12

Why does a fixed exchange rate system impose financial discipline on a government?

Under floating exchange rates the relationship with policy is less obvious. With a flexible exchange rate, the authorities can use monetary policy to stabilise the economy, knowing that there will be overall balance on the balance of payments. Nonetheless, the government needs to monitor the structure of the balance of payments. When interest rates are set at a relatively high level compared with other countries, the financial account will tend to be in surplus because of financial inflows, with a corresponding deficit on the current account. This may not be sustainable in the long run. Viewed in another way, if the current account is in deficit, the financial account will need to be in surplus to ensure there is overall balance.

Summary: fixed vs floating exchange rates

■ There are strengths and weaknesses with both fixed and floating exchange rate systems.

■ A floating exchange rate system is more robust in enabling economies to adjust following external shocks, but it can lead to volatility and thus discourage international trade.

■ Under a floating exchange rate system, much of the burden of adjustment to external shocks is borne by changes in the exchange rate, rather than by variations in the level of economic activity, which may be affected more under a fixed exchange rate system.

■ A fixed exchange rate system offers stability, in the sense that firms know the future value of the currency, whereas under a floating rate regime there is more volatility.

■ A fixed exchange rate system imposes discipline on governments, and may facilitate international policy harmonisation.

Exercise 26.3

Critically evaluate the following statements, and discuss whether you regard fixed or floating exchange rates as the better system.

a A flexible exchange rate regime is better able to cope with external shocks.
b A fixed exchange rate system provides a more stable trading environment and minimises risk.
c Floating exchange rates enable individual countries to follow independent policies.
d A fixed exchange rate system may encourage governments to adopt distortionary policies, such as tariffs and non-tariff barriers, in order to control imports.

International competitiveness

In analysing the UK's position within Europe and with its other trading partners, the relative competitiveness of UK goods and services is an important issue. The UK has persistently shown a deficit on the current account over a long period of time, but especially in the 2000s. Does that imply that UK goods are uncompetitive in international markets? In order to investigate this, and to evaluate its importance, it is first necessary to examine how competitiveness can be measured, and the factors that affect it.

Competitiveness of UK goods

The demand for UK exports in world markets depends on a number of factors. In some ways, it is similar to the demand for a good. In general, the demand for a good depends on its price, on the prices of other goods, and on consumer incomes and preferences. In a similar way, you can think of the demand for UK exports as depending on the price of UK goods, on the price of other countries' goods, and on incomes in the rest of the world and foreigners' preferences for UK goods over those produced elsewhere. However, in the case of international transactions the exchange rate is also relevant, as this determines the purchasing power of UK incomes in the rest of the world. Similarly, the demand for imports into the UK will depend on the relative price of domestic and foreign goods, incomes in the UK, preferences for foreign and domestically produced goods and the exchange rate. These factors will all come together to determine the balance of demand for exports and imports.

The exchange rate plays a key role in influencing the levels of both imports and exports. Figure 26.9 shows the time path of the US$/£ exchange rate since 1971. It shows some fluctuations between 1971 and the late 1980s, although around a declining trend. However, since then the exchange rate seems to have remained fairly steady — but you can see the falls that occurred during the financial crisis and after the Brexit vote.

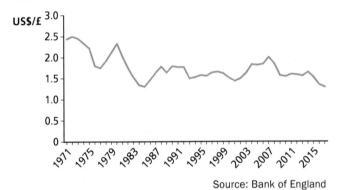

Source: Bank of England

Figure 26.9 The nominal exchange rate, US$/£, 1971–2017

Nonetheless, there was a fall from a peak of $2.50 to the pound in 1972 to $1.53 in 2015 (before the Brexit vote). Other things being equal, this would suggest an improvement in the competitiveness of UK products. In other words, Americans wanting to buy UK goods got more pounds for their dollars in 2015 than in 1972, and thus would tend to find UK goods more attractive.

Nominal exchange rate

However, some care is needed because other things do not remain equal. In particular, remember that the competitiveness of UK goods in the US market depends not only on the exchange rate, but also on movements in the prices of goods over time, so this needs to be taken into account — which is why Figure 26.9 refers to the *nominal exchange rate*. In other words, if the prices of UK goods have risen more rapidly than prices in the USA, this will partly offset the downward movement in the exchange rate.

Figure 26.10 shows the nominal exchange rate again, but also the ratio of UK/US consumer prices. This reveals that between 1971 and 1977 UK prices rose much more steeply than those in the USA, and continued to rise relative to the USA until the 1990s. Thus, the early decline in the nominal exchange rate was offset by the movement in relative prices.

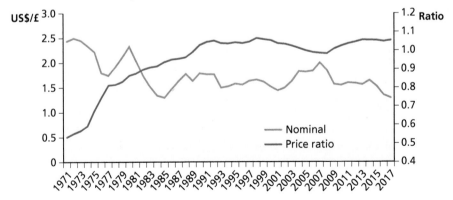

Sources: calculated from Bank of England, IMF, OECD data

Figure 26.10 The nominal exchange rate, US$/£, and the ratio of UK/US prices since 1971

Real exchange rate

In order to assess the overall competitiveness of UK goods compared with the USA's, it is necessary to calculate the **real exchange rate**, which is defined as the nominal exchange rate multiplied by the ratio of relative prices.

The real exchange rate is shown in Figure 26.11. The real exchange rate also shows some fluctuations, especially between about 1977 and 1989. However, there does not seem to be any strong trend to the series, and the real rate was at a similar level at the end of the period than at the beginning, having fallen slightly since 2015.

Key term

real exchange rate the nominal exchange rate adjusted for differences in relative inflation rates between countries

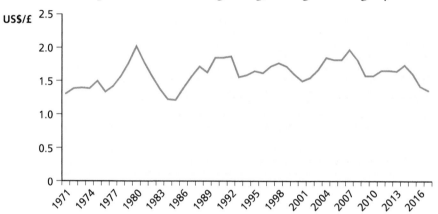

Source: calculated from data in Figure 26.10

Figure 26.11 The real exchange rate, US$/£

Sterling effective exchange

Notice that this series relates only to competitiveness relative to the USA, as it is the real US$/£ exchange rate. An alternative measure is the *sterling effective exchange rate*, shown in Figure 26.12. This shows the strength of sterling relative to a weighted average of exchange rates of the UK's trading partners. Notice the fall in the effective rate that occurred towards the end of 2008 at the time of the financial crisis, and the further fall in 2016 after the Brexit vote.

Knowledge check 26.13

To what extent does the time path of the real exchange rate provide support for the purchasing power parity theory?

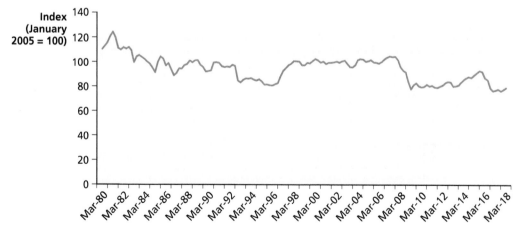

Source: Bank of England

Figure 26.12 The sterling effective exchange rate since 1980 (2005 = 100)

Quantitative skills 26.2

The real exchange rate

Table 26.2 provides data for the €/£ exchange rate, together with the consumer price index for the euro area and for the UK for the period from 2005 to 2017. These data can be used to calculate the real exchange rate.

Table 26.2 Competitiveness of the UK compared to the eurozone

	Nominal exchange rate (€/£)	Consumer price index (2005 = 100)	
		UK	Eurozone
2005	1.4629	100.0	100.0
2006	1.4670	102.4	102.2
2007	1.4619	104.8	104.4
2008	1.2588	108.6	107.8
2009	1.1233	110.9	108.1
2010	1.1664	114.5	109.9
2011	1.1527	119.7	112.9
2012	1.2337	123.0	115.7
2013	1.1776	126.1	117.3
2014	1.2411	128.0	117.7
2015	1.3782	128.0	117.7
2016	1.2233	128.9	118.0
2017	1.1413	132.4	119.7

Sources: based on data from OECD and Bank of England

To calculate the real exchange rate for 2017, the nominal exchange rate must be multiplied by the ratio of prices in the UK to the euro area. This is $1.1413 \times 132.4 \div 119.7 = 1.262$. Thus the real exchange rate had not fallen by as much as the nominal rate, because prices in the UK had risen by more than in the eurozone over the period.

Exercise 26.4

Use the data in Quantitative skills 26.2 to calculate the real exchange rate for each year in the period, plot the results against time and comment on the effect that any movement will have had on the competitiveness of UK goods and services relative to the eurozone.

Study tip

The distinction between real and nominal values is important, not only in relation to the exchange rate but in many other macroeconomic variables. Make sure that you are clear about the difference between real and nominal, and why it matters (see Chapter 9).

Summary: international competitiveness

■ Relative prices and the exchange rate are an important influence on the competitiveness of goods and services in the international market.
■ The real exchange rate adjusts the nominal exchange rate to allow for differing inflation rates between countries.

International differences in productivity

From a different angle, competitiveness also depends on relative costs of production in different countries, which influence the prices that firms can charge. In particular, if UK firms face higher unit labour cost than their trading partners, this puts them at a disadvantage in terms of costs. This reflects different levels of productivity across countries. Remember that productivity is a measure of productive efficiency: for example, **labour productivity** is output per unit of labour input. Different countries show appreciable differences in efficiency by this measure.

Key term

labour productivity a measure of output per worker, or output per hour worked

Measures of productivity

However, international comparisons of productivity are not straightforward, as measurements are subject to differences in data collection and differences in work practices. One approach might be to compare data on GDP per head of population. As a measure of productivity levels, however, this is a misleading indicator. In particular, working hours are longer in the UK than in many other countries (especially within Europe), so differences in GDP per head partly reflect differences in the quantity of labour input. Defining relative to population would also be misleading if there are differences in participation rates between countries.

GDP per hour worked

For this reason, GDP per hour worked is often seen as a more reliable indicator of relative productivity levels. This measure is graphed in Figure 26.13. The UK does not perform especially well on this measure, with only Japan in particular showing lower productivity. It can be dangerous to look at selected countries: in a different study, the UK was seen to be ranked 20th out of 35 countries on the basis of GDP per hour worked.

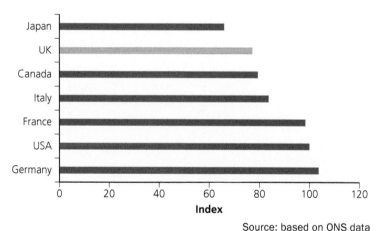

Source: based on ONS data

Figure 26.13 GDP per hour worked 2015 (Index, USA = 100)

Figure 26.14 gives the time path for an index of GDP per hour worked, based on 1990 = 100. Notice that this focuses not on absolute levels of productivity, but on changes through time, comparing with 1990 as the base. The UK fares rather better here, increasing by 50% compared with its 1990 level. In Germany productivity increased by 49% over the same period. The figure also highlights the problems that Greece faced in the recession that started in the late 2000s. Productivity went into decline at that time, and had not recovered by the end of the period.

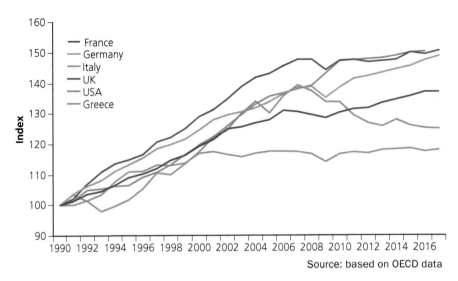

Source: based on OECD data

Figure 26.14 Index of GDP per hour worked (1990 = 100)

Knowledge check 26.14

Which country in Figure 26.14 showed the least increase in productivity over this period?

Key term

total factor productivity
the average productivity of all factors, measured as the total output divided by the total amount of inputs used

Total factor productivity

It is also important to realise that labour productivity is not the only relevant measure, as countries may also differ in their use of capital. **Total factor productivity** is more difficult to measure, as the measurement of capital stock is especially prone to error and misinterpretation. However, some estimates of multifactor productivity growth are shown in Figure 26.15.

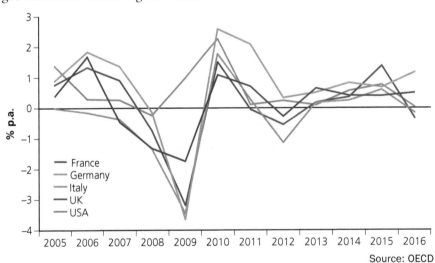

Source: OECD

Figure 26.15 Multifactor productivity growth

Unit labour costs

A strong reason for wanting to compare productivity levels and changes across countries is because of its influence of international competitiveness. However, this does not only reflect differences in productivity, but also needs to take account of differences in rates of pay, which affect the relative costs of producing across countries. **Unit labour costs** measure the average cost of labour per unit of output produced. If a country experiences higher increases in unit labour costs over time, this will affect the competitiveness of the goods produced. Figure 26.16 shows how unit labour costs have increased in selected countries since 2000.

Key term

unit labour costs the average cost of labour per unit of output produced

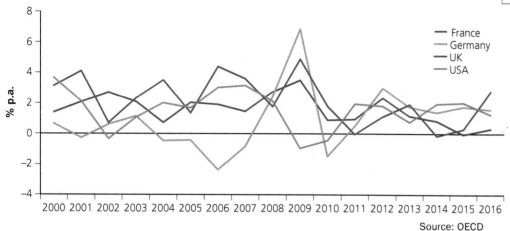

Source: OECD

Figure 26.16 Unit labour costs

You can see that Germany enjoyed a period in the early 2000s when unit labour costs were falling. However, notice also how the European countries saw large increases in unit labour costs at the time of the financial crisis. This is what we would expect to see if output is falling, but firms are keeping workers in employment rather than reducing their workforce.

Exercise 26.5

Table 26.3 provides data on real GDP per person employed for a range of countries, measured in PPP$, which is a possible measure of productivity.

a Which countries experienced the largest and smallest percentage growth in productivity on this measure during this period?

b How does the UK's performance compare with that of the other countries?

c Discuss the strengths and weaknesses of this indicator compared with the other indicators discussed in the text.

Table 26.3 Real GDP per person employed, selected countries

	UK	Germany	Greece	Japan	USA
2005	76,486	86,456	73,635	68,472	101,026
2006	77,731	88,137	76,277	69,356	101,934
2007	79,220	88,980	78,121	70,454	102,856
2008	78,054	88,878	77,082	69,896	102,690
2009	75,859	83,901	74,545	66,971	103,595
2010	76,840	86,484	72,754	69,916	106,690
2011	78,115	87,603	71,369	70,294	107,456
2012	78,122	87,412	72,689	71,626	108,103
2013	78,605	86,838	74,185	72,141	109,330
2014	79,003	87,612	74,650	71,513	110,100
2015	79,720	88,481	73,369	72,119	111,131
2016	80,371	89,805	72,584	72,619	111,712

Source: World Development Indicators

Productivity and competitiveness

Countries gain from trade by exploiting their comparative advantage, so maintaining that comparative advantage seems desirable. If productivity in the UK grows more slowly than in countries such as the USA or Germany, this implies a loss of competitiveness over time. This in turn may mean that the UK gains less strongly from its exporting activity in world markets. International competitiveness may also be lost if the UK experiences inflation at a more rapid rate than its trading rivals.

These arguments seem to suggest that there are significant benefits to be gained from maintaining international competitiveness by improving productivity and keeping inflation under control.

If the UK finds that its exports have become less competitive, and that imports have become more competitive with domestic goods, then this could result in a fall in aggregate demand, and a possible increase in unemployment, magnified by multiplier effects.

Furthermore, if the UK experiences a deficit on the current account of the balance of payments, there will also be a corresponding surplus on the financial account, so essentially the UK funds the deficit by selling financial assets to economic agents overseas. In the long run, the income paid out on foreign investment feeds through to reinforce the deficit on the current account.

The benefits of engaging in trade have been widely discussed, but is there a downside to this? When world trade is booming, the gains from trade can help to maintain the economy at or close to full employment. However, suppose there is a global recession? If the economy is committed to trade, and reliant on export revenues, a sudden fall in export demand could deepen the recession in the domestic economy, and this is the risk of being export-biased in economic activity. However, in normal times, it seems better to be competitive in international markets than to be uncompetitive.

Summary: productivity

- Competitiveness can depend on the relative costs of production in different countries, which in turn partly reflects differences in productivity.
- Data for international comparison of productivity differences need to be treated with some care, but GDP per hour worked is a helpful indicator.
- Labour productivity is not a sufficient measure, given that countries differ in their relative endowments of labour, capital and other factors of production.
- International competitiveness also depends on the costs of labour.

Balancing the balance of payments

There are many ways in which the overall 'balance' of the balance of payments can be achieved – which sometimes becomes controversial. An example of this was the way that China's exchange rate policy in the early 2000s facilitated its rapid economic growth, but left a legacy of distrust between China and other countries (especially the USA).

One way in which the balance of payments is made to balance is through allowing the exchange rate to respond to the relative levels of supply and demand in the foreign exchange market. In other words, if the exchange rate is free to find its market level, it will tend to move to equalise the demand and supply of currency.

However, the balance of payments depends not only on trade in goods and services, but also on transactions in financial assets. The demand for a country's financial assets depends not only on the exchange rate, but also on the relative rate of interest in different countries. If UK interest rates are high compared with those elsewhere in the world, there will tend to be an inflow of financial capital. The resulting financial surplus will tend to cause the exchange rate to appreciate. This in turn affects the competitiveness of domestic goods and services, so the net result may be that the financial account surplus will be offset by a deficit on the current account.

Some countries have chosen to treat the balance of payments in a different way, by fixing the exchange rate in terms of some other currency, such as the US dollar. What this means is that any surplus or deficit on current or financial accounts must be offset by the purchase or sale of reserve assets (that is, financial assets denominated in terms of US dollars) in order to maintain the price of the currency.

The choice between fixing the exchange rate and allowing it to find its market value has a major effect on the structure of the balance of payments. This is illustrated in Figure 26.17, which shows the structure of the balance of payments for the USA and China in 2003.

In the USA, where the exchange rate is allowed to find its own market value, the accounts reveal a substantial current account deficit (amounting to nearly 5% of GDP), balanced by

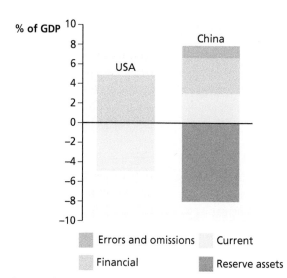

Figure 26.17 The balance of payments, USA and China, in 2003

a financial account surplus. In contrast, China shows surpluses on both the current and the financial account, balanced by substantial transactions in reserve assets, indicating that the Chinese authorities were artificially holding the value of their currency away from its equilibrium value.

Why should they want to do this? One reason is that the policy allowed China to maintain rapid growth in exports, by keeping its goods highly competitive in international markets, while at the same time attracting flows of inward foreign direct investment. In order to do this, it had to purchase US dollar-denominated assets – such as US Treasury bills. In turn, this allowed the USA to maintain its current account deficit, funded partly by the sale of Treasury bills.

A by-product of this strategy is that interest rates in the USA were lower than they would otherwise have been. This may have contributed to the financial crisis that followed.

Follow-up questions

a Discuss this from the perspective of China. What are the benefits of this strategy – and what are the risks?

b Now view the strategy from the USA's viewpoint. Why do you think that the USA tried to persuade China to revalue its currency?

c Why might China's strategy have contributed to the financial crisis?

d Comment on how the strategy adopted by China may have left a legacy in its relationship with the USA?

The UK's productivity puzzle

Productivity is crucial for any economy for a number of reasons. For one thing, relative productivity levels across countries influence the international competitiveness of an economy's output. If the products that a country seeks to export are lacking in quality and/or design, and if they are inefficiently produced then it will always be difficult to compete abroad. For another thing, it is increases in productivity through time that allow living standards to increase. If productivity is stagnant, then workers will not see their earnings increasing over time.

Figure 26.18 shows the time path of output per worker since the first quarter of 2000. The 'actual' series is an index based on 2000 Q1 = 100. The 'trend' series is based on calculating the average rate of change between 2000 Q1 and 2008 Q2, then extrapolating this forward to the first quarter of 2018. In other words, the trend shows how productivity would have changed had it continued to increase at its previous average rate. This shows the extent to which productivity has stagnated since the onset of recession in 2008.

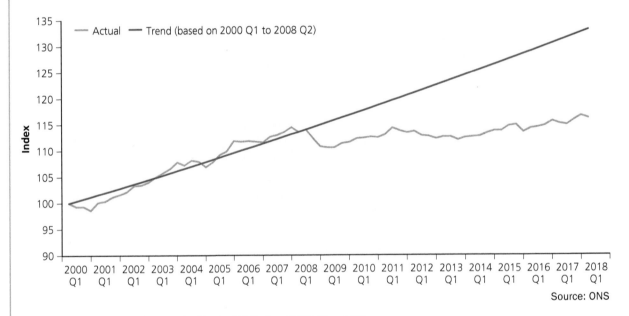

Figure 26.18 Output per hour worked in the UK (Index, 2000 Q1 = 100)

This is not a new story. UK has attracted criticism for its poor productivity performance for many years. The consensus often appears to be that the UK's performance on this key variable has been dismal, and that the UK is near the foot of the productivity league table.

The way in which productivity was affected by the recession (and continued to stagnate afterwards) was shared by many of the UK's trading partners, but this is little consolation if the UK is really at the bottom of the league table. In fact, this is not completely true, as the UK's relative international position is middle-of-the-table rather than bottom. However, the UK does lag behind key trading partners such as France, Germany and the USA (see Figure 26.13).

The impact of globalisation should be positive for productivity, as the increasing interconnectedness of economies should

make it easier for technology transfer to take place. Furthermore, the mobility of labour within the EU should allow the spread of good working practices and human capital. These effects should bring productivity levels closer across countries.

So what can the UK do about its position? The economy performs well in some areas — in particular in terms of new start-up companies and investment in research and development. However, Andy Haldane (Chief Economist at the Bank of England) argues that one of the key factors that the UK is not getting right is in the dissemination of new techniques. In other words, the UK does well in terms of having some world-class companies at the cutting edge of technology and efficiency — but a long tail of companies that have been slow to come up to speed.

This would suggest that encouraging the dissemination of best practice techniques — and investment in human capital — is what is needed if the UK is to close the productivity gap.

Follow-up questions

a What are the links between productivity and international competitiveness?

b If firms decided to hold on to workers during the recession instead of making them redundant, how would this affect the productivity measures?

c If globalisation facilitates convergence of productivity levels across countries, how would the UK be likely to perform following Brexit?

d Why would investment in human capital be beneficial for productivity growth?

27 Poverty and inequality in developed and developing countries

One of the gravest economic challenges facing the world today is the global inequity in the distribution of resources. In 2016, the world population was estimated to have reached 7.4 billion and 6.2 billion of these people lived in so-called 'developing countries'. In 2013, it was estimated that 10.7% of the world's population (767 million people) lived in absolute poverty, of whom more than a half were in sub-Saharan Africa. In addition to this global inequality, there is inequality in the distribution of income and wealth in all societies, although the extent of inequality varies between countries. This chapter explores ways of measuring inequality and poverty in both developed and developing countries, looks at some of the causes of inequality and discusses some of the policies that are used to affect the distribution of income and wealth.

Learning objectives

After studying this chapter, you should:
- be aware of significant differences between regions of the world in terms of their level and pace of development
- recognise the strengths and limitations of economic and social indicators in providing a profile of a country's stage of development
- be familiar with ways of identifying and monitoring inequality, including Lorenz curves and the Gini coefficient
- be familiar with ways of measuring relative and absolute poverty
- be aware of the changing pattern of inequality in the UK
- understand the main causes of inequality and poverty
- be familiar with policies designed to affect the distribution of income and wealth

Developed and developing countries

In considering the global economy, it is apparent that there is a divide; there are some countries that have gone through a process of economic and human development to reach a high standard of living, but there are many other countries that have failed to make progress in this way. Historically, inequality between nations rose from the 1820s until the 1990s, but began to fall after then. In seeking to analyse inequality, there are two crucial dimensions that need to be taken into account. On the one hand, it is important to be aware of inequality between nations, and the gap in living standards that exists between different regions of the world. However, it is also important to be aware that there is inequality within societies — even within the most developed economies in the world. The first step in examining these issues is to identify the developed and developing countries in the world.

Defining development

What is meant by 'development'? You might think that it is about economic growth — if a society can expand its productive capacity, surely that is development? But development means much more than this. Economic growth may well be an *essential* ingredient, since development cannot take place without an expansion of the resources available in a society; however, it is not a *sufficient* ingredient, because those additional resources must be used wisely, and the growth that results must be the 'right' sort of growth.

Wrapped up with development are issues concerning the alleviation of poverty — no country can be considered to be 'developed' if a substantial portion of its population is living in absolute poverty. Development also requires structural change, and possibly changes in institutions and, in some cases, cultural and political attitudes.

Summary: growth and development

- Economic growth is one aspect of economic development, in that it provides an increase in the resources available to members of society in developing countries.
- However, in addition, development requires that the resources made available through economic growth are used appropriately to meet development objectives.

Which are the developing countries?

It is difficult to find an agreed definition of what constitutes a developing country. It cannot be defined solely in terms of average incomes because the notion of development encompasses a wide variety of different dimensions. A country may have relatively high average incomes, but yet be characterised by high poverty or inequality, or be weak in the provision of education or healthcare. In the discussion that follows, a wide range of countries will be referred to as *developing,* and the discussion will be illustrated by examples from a selection of countries from different regions of the world.

In broad terms, the countries regarded as developing are concentrated in four major regions: sub-Saharan Africa, Latin America, South Asia and South East Asia. This excludes some countries in the 'developing' range, but relatively few. For some purposes it may be necessary to treat China separately, rather than including it as part of South East Asia, partly because of its sheer size, and partly because it has followed a rather different development path.

It is very important when discussing economic development to remember that there is wide diversity between the countries that are classified as developing, and although it is tempting to generalise, you need to be a little wary of doing so. Different countries have different characteristics, and face different configurations of problems and opportunities. Therefore, a policy that works for one country may fail totally in a different part of the world.

Inequality between countries

One measure of the level of development is GNI per capita — the average level of income per person in the population. Although this is not an ideal indicator, it can help to illustrate the inequality that exists between countries around the world.

Synoptic link

Chapter 9 discussed some of the problems associated with using GNI per capita as an indicator of development, and you may find it helpful to refer back to this. In Chapter 28 there is discussion of alternative ways of trying to measure development.

The measure used here to look at inequality between countries is GNI per capita, measured in *purchasing power parity dollars* (PPP$). This is important because using official exchange rates to convert from local currency into US dollars can be misleading. The US$ measure understates the *real* purchasing power of income in developing countries, but what is of interest is exactly that — the relative command over resources that people in different countries have.

Knowledge check 27.1

Give reasons why GNI per capita measured in US$ may be misleading as a measure of relative living standards across countries.

Figure 27.1 shows the relative size of GNI per capita in PPP$ for regional groupings of countries around the world in 2016. It includes data for developing countries, compared with developed countries (represented by the members of the OECD). The gap in income levels between the developing countries and the OECD countries shows very clearly in the figure; equally, the gap between the developing countries of sub-Saharan Africa and South Asia and those in East Asia and Latin America is apparent.

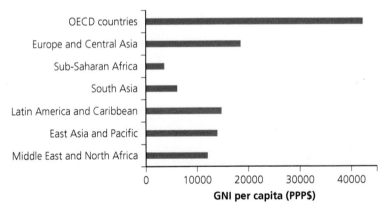

Note: the data for the Middle East and North Africa are for 2014.

Source: World Development Indicators

Figure 27.1 GNI per capita, regional groupings, 2016 (PPP$)

Study tip

In this and the following chapter, you will find data relating to selected countries around the world. The main source for these data is the World Bank, which publishes data about most countries in its *World Development Indicators*. If you want to follow up data on individual countries, visit https://data.worldbank.org/. Also useful is the United Nation's *Human Development Report*, which you can access at http://hdr.undp.org/en.

Not all data are available on a regional basis, so in discussing the developing countries, a selected group of countries has been chosen as a focus, with three countries from each of the four major regional groupings, and three developed economies. The GNI per capita (PPP$) levels in 2016 are shown in Figure 27.2. Because of the diversity of countries in each of the regions, such a selection must be treated with some caution. Malaysia, (South) Korea and China have been chosen to represent East Asia and the Pacific in order to highlight three of the countries that have been successful in achieving economic growth over a sustained period, and the following discussion will highlight some of the factors that have enabled this to take place.

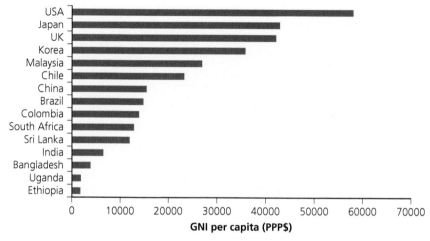

Source: World Development Indicators

Figure 27.2 GNI per capita, selected countries, 2016 (PPP$)

As has been discussed, GNI has some limitations as a measure of living standards, even when measured in PPP$. One limitation that is especially important when considering low-income countries is that in many developing countries there is much *informal economic activity*, which may not be captured by a measure like GNI, based on monetary transactions. Such activity includes subsistence agriculture, which remains important in many countries, especially in sub-Saharan Africa. In other words, GNI may not capture production that is directly used for consumption.

However, the informal sector also encompasses many other forms of activity in both rural and urban areas, from petty traders, shoe-shiners and wayside barbers to small-scale enterprises operating in a wide range of activities. The International Labour Organization (ILO) has estimated that the informal economy comprises more than half of the global labour force. This suggests the need for some caution in the use of GNI per capita data as a measure of the gap in living standards between countries.

Knowledge check 27.2

Give an example of an activity carried on in the UK that would be classified as being 'informal' in the sense of being excluded from the GNI calculations.

Inequality within a country

It will always be the case that individuals and groups in a society will have less income and/or wealth than others. However, the degree of inequality varies from one country to another; and before exploring the causes of inequality, and the policies that might be used to influence how income and wealth are distributed within society, it is necessary to be able to characterise and measure inequality. This is important in order to be able to judge relative standards of living in different countries or different periods.

Income distribution and inequality

Synoptic link

You may find it helpful to look back at Chapter 13, which explained the important distinction between income and wealth (see page 182).

GNI per capita is an average measure, and so does not reveal information about how income is distributed among groups in society. One way of presenting data on this topic is to rank households in order of their incomes, and then calculate the share of total household income that goes to the poorest 10%, the poorest 20% and so on.

Quantitative skills 27.1

Deciles and quintiles

When the groups are divided into tenths in this way, they are referred to as *deciles*; thus, the poorest 10% is the first decile, the next 10% is the second decile and so on. Similarly, the poorest 20% is the first *quintile*. This is useful in trying to explore the pattern of the distribution of income because it quantifies the difference between income going to low-income and high-income households.

According to the World Bank, the top decile (richest 10%) of households in Brazil receive 55.8 times higher income than the lowest decile (poorest 10%). In Belarus, on the other hand, the ratio is only 5.5. These are extreme examples of the degree of inequality in the distribution of income within countries. The degree of inequality is important in international comparisons of living standards across countries.

Table 27.1 presents some data for three developed countries. Notice that the unit of measurement is normally the household rather than the individual, on the presumption that members of a household tend to share their resources — a millionaire's life-partner may not earn any income, but he or she is not usually poor.

Table 27.1 Distribution of income in the USA, the UK and Norway, by quintiles (%)

	UK, 2012	USA, 2013	Norway, 2012
First decile	2.9	1.7	3.6
First quintile	7.5	5.1	9.3
Second quintile	12.3	10.3	14.4
Third quintile	17.0	15.4	18.1
Fourth quintile	23.1	22.7	22.9
Top quintile	40.1	46.4	35.3
Top decile	24.7	30.2	20.9
Ratio top quintile: first quintile	5.3	9.1	3.8

Source: World Development Indicators

It can be seen that in the UK households in the top quintile receive 5.3 times more income than those in the poorest quintile. On the basis of these data, inequality in the UK is lower than that in the USA, but higher than that in Norway.

Knowledge check 27.3

Calculate the decile ratio for each of the countries in Table 27.1. Do these give the same ranking as for the quintile ratios in the table?

The Lorenz curve

The structure of such income distribution information is quite different from the sorts of data that economists normally encounter, and it is helpful to find an appropriate type of diagram to allow the data to be presented visually. The **Lorenz curve** is one such method — some Lorenz curves are shown in Figure 27.3.

Key term

Lorenz curve a graphical way of depicting the distribution of income within a country

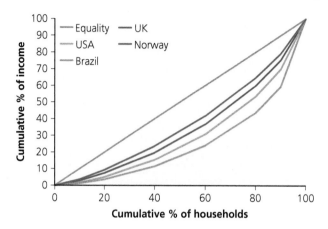

Figure 27.3 Lorenz curves

Lorenz curves are constructed as follows. The curves for the UK, USA and Norway are based on the data in Table 27.1. The first step is to convert the numbers in the table into *cumulative* percentages. In other words (using the UK as an example), the data show that the poorest 20% receive 7.5% of total household income, the poorest 40% receive 7.5% + 12.3% = 19.8%, the poorest 60% receive 19.8% + 17.0% = 36.8%, and so on. It is these cumulative percentages that are plotted to produce the Lorenz curve, as in Figure 27.3. (The figure also plots the lowest and highest deciles.)

Suppose that income were perfectly equally distributed between households. In other words, suppose the poorest 10% of households received exactly 10% of income, the poorest 20% received 20% and so on. The Lorenz curve would then be a straight line going diagonally across the figure.

To interpret the country curves, the closer a country's Lorenz curve is to the diagonal equality line, the more equal is the distribution. You can see from the figure that Norway comes closest to the equality line, bearing out the earlier conclusion that income is more equally distributed in that country. The UK and the US curves are closer together, but there seems to be slightly more inequality in the USA, as its Lorenz curve is further from the equality line. Brazil has also been included on the figure, as an example of a society in which there is substantial inequality.

Knowledge check 27.4

Explain why Figure 27.3 suggests that income inequality is more pronounced in Brazil than in the USA.

Exercise 27.1

Use the data provided in Table 27.2 to calculate the ratios of top decile income to bottom decile income, and of top quintile income to bottom quintile income. Then draw Lorenz curves for the two countries, and compare the inequalities shown for Belarus and South Africa with each other and with the countries already discussed.

Table 27.2 Income distribution in Belarus and South Africa

	Percentage share of income or consumption	
	South Africa	Belarus
Lowest decile	0.9	3.9
Lowest quintile	2.5	9.3
Second quintile	4.7	14.0
Third quintile	8.0	17.7
Fourth quintile	15.9	22.4
Highest quintile	68.9	36.7
Highest decile	51.3	22.6

Source: *World Development Indicators*

Key term

Gini coefficient a measure of the degree of inequality in a society

Study tip

In data published by the World Bank and United Nations (and sometimes the ONS), the Gini coefficient is known as the Gini index.

The Gini coefficient

The Lorenz curve is fine for comparing income distribution in just a few countries. However, it is also helpful to have an index that could summarise the relationship in a numerical way. The **Gini coefficient** does just this. It is a way of trying to quantify the equality of income distribution in a country, and is obtained by calculating the ratio of the area between the equality line and the country's Lorenz curve (area A in Figure 27.4) to the whole area under the equality line (area $A + B$ in Figure 27.4).

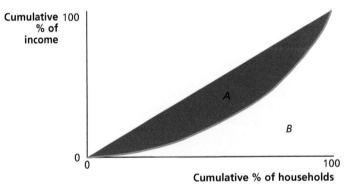

Figure 27.4 The Gini coefficient and the Lorenz curve

In published data, the Gini coefficient is expressed as a percentage (i.e. multiplied by 100). The closer the Gini coefficient is to 100, the further the Lorenz curve is from equality, and thus the more unequal is the income distribution. The Gini coefficient values for the countries in Figure 27.3 (and those in Exercise 27.1) are shown in Table 27.3.

Table 27.3 The Gini coefficient

Country	Gini coefficient
USA	41.1
UK	32.6
Norway	25.9
Brazil	51.5
Belarus	27.2
South Africa	63.4

Source: *World Development Indicators*

Some measurement issues

When measuring income inequality, some important measurement issues need to be borne in mind. For example, in talking about the 'poorest' and 'richest' households, you need to be aware that absolute income levels per household may be a misleading indicator, given that households are of different sizes and compositions. Thus, when looking at the income distribution in the UK, it is important to make adjustments for this.

The way this is done is by the use of *equivalence scales*. These allow a household to be judged relative to a 'reference household' made up of a childless couple. It can then be decided that a household with a husband, wife and two young children rates as 1.18 relative to the childless couple with a rating of 1. So if the couple with two children had an income of, say, £40,000 per year, this would be the equivalent of 40,000/1.18 = £33,898. In order to examine the inequality of income, it is these equivalised incomes that need to be considered.

A further question is whether income is the most appropriate indicator. People tend to smooth their consumption over their lifetimes, and it has been argued that it is more important to look at consumption (expenditure) than income when considering inequality.

Then there is the question of housing costs. In the short run, households have no control over their spending on housing. Some measures of inequality therefore choose to exclude housing costs from the calculations in order to focus on the income that households have at their disposal for other expenditures. As housing tends to constitute a higher proportion of the budgets of poor households, measures of inequality that exclude housing costs tend to show greater levels of inequality.

It is also important to bear in mind that the standard of living that households can achieve depends partly on government-provided services, such as health and education. Remember that rich as well as poor households may benefit from these.

Finally, in considering inequality in a society, it may be important to examine inequalities in the distribution of wealth as well as income. Wealth can be regarded as the accumulated stock of assets that households own, and in the UK wealth is more unequally distributed than income.

Synoptic link

Inequality in the distribution of wealth is one cause of inequality in income, which is discussed later in the chapter.

It is interesting to note that many people remain unaware of where they fit into the income distribution of their country. A survey in the USA found that 19% of Americans believed that they were in the top 1% of earners.

Summary: developing countries and inequality

- Developing countries are largely located in four major regions: sub-Saharan Africa, Latin America, South Asia and South East Asia.
- These regions have shown contrasting patterns of growth and development.
- Different countries have different characteristics, and face different configurations of problems and opportunities.
- GNI per capita is one measure of the standard of living in a country, but it has a number of shortcomings for developing countries.
- In particular, it neglects the importance of the informal sector, and fails to take into account inequality in the distribution of income.
- Some degree of inequality in income and wealth is present in every society.
- Inequality is measured by ranking households in order of income, then comparing the income received by the richest decile (or quintile) with that received by the poorest.
- The Lorenz curve gives a visual impression of the income distribution; this can be quantified into the Gini coefficient as a single statistic representing the degree of income inequality.
- Calculations of the income distribution are normally undertaken using equivalised incomes, taking into account the size and composition of households.
- In some cases, consumption (expenditure) provides a more reliable measure of inequality, as people tend to smooth their consumption over time.

Measuring poverty

One aspect of inequality is poverty. If there is a wide gap between the richest and poorest households, it is important to evaluate just how poor those poorest households are, and whether they should be regarded as being 'in poverty'. This requires a definition of poverty.

Absolute poverty

One way of defining poverty is to specify a basket of goods and services that is regarded as the minimum required to support human life. Households that are seen to have too low an income to allow them to purchase everything in that basic bundle of goods would be regarded as being in **absolute poverty**.

A common way of measuring the poverty rate in a country is to estimate the percentage of the population living below a poverty line, known as a **headcount ratio**. The poverty line in this context is an estimate of the income needed to ensure basic human survival. People living below this level are perceived to be in absolute poverty. To enable international comparisons of poverty levels, the World Bank have defined an **International Poverty Line**. This is based on 2011 PPP prices, and from October 2015 it was set at PPP$1.90. The line has to be reset every few years in line with changing prices over time. The World Bank estimated that around 700 million people worldwide were living beneath this level in 2015. Some individual countries set their own national poverty line to reflect local conditions.

Key terms

absolute poverty situation of a household whose income is insufficient to allow it to purchase the minimum bundle of goods and services regarded as necessary for survival

headcount ratio a measure of the percentage of a country's population living below a poverty line

International Poverty Line an agreed measure that defines the absolute poverty line based on international prices, set at PPP$1.90 from October 2015

Knowledge check 27.5

Explain why it is necessary to recalibrate the poverty line on a regular basis.

Figure 27.5 shows the percentage headcount ratio for a range of countries. Notice that countries in the figure are ranked from top to bottom in ascending order of GNI per capita in PPP$.

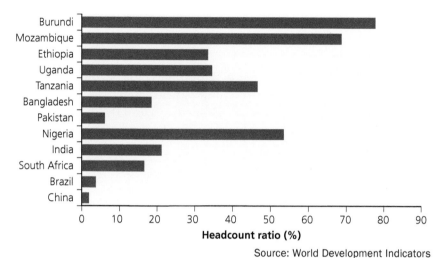

Source: World Development Indicators

Figure 27.5 Percentage of population living below the International Poverty Line in selected countries

Quantitative skills 27.2

More about interpreting graphs

When you are faced with a graph such as that in Figure 27.5, where the countries are ranked in order of another variable, you can learn about the relationships between variables from observing the pattern of the bars. In this case, we have the headcount ratio shown for a number of countries that are ranked in order of GNI per capita. If there had been a perfect correlation between relative poverty levels and GNI per capita, then the pattern of the bars would be smooth. However, this is not the case. Bangladesh and Pakistan show relatively low headcount ratios relative to some countries with a higher GNI per capita, such as Nigeria and Tanzania. Watch for this jagged pattern in some of the figures in Chapter 28, as this (or its absence) could be helpful.

Relative poverty

For a country like the UK, this absolute poverty line is not helpful, as so few people fall below it. Thus poverty is defined in *relative* terms. If a household has insufficient income for its members to participate in the normal social life of the country, it is said to be in **relative poverty**. This too is defined in terms of a threshold poverty line, set at 60% of the median adjusted household disposable income. (The median is the income of the middle-ranked household.)

In Europe (including the UK), estimates of poverty are based on a regular survey of households conducted in EU member states and some other selected countries. In 2015, the UK's threshold for poverty was set at £12,567. Households with income below this are described as being in relative poverty (or being 'at risk of poverty'); households that experience this in the current year and at least two of the three preceding years are said to be in **persistent poverty**.

Key terms

relative poverty situation obtaining if household income falls below 60% of median adjusted household disposable income

persistent poverty where a household is currently in relative poverty and has also been in this state in at least two of the preceding three years

Knowledge check 27.6

Calculate the median income level for the UK in 2015.

Study tip

This distinction between absolute and relative poverty is an important one. Absolute poverty is almost entirely confined to the developing countries, but relative poverty can exist in any society, even the advanced nations, because some individuals may be excluded from normal society.

Figure 27.6 presents some data for a range of European countries in 2015. The proportion of people below the relative poverty line varies substantially across these countries, from 9.6% in Iceland to 25.4% in Romania. The UK shows relative income poverty that is below, but close to, the EU average — and persistent poverty that is well below the average. Indeed, the UK's persistent poverty rate was the fifth-lowest among the EU member states.

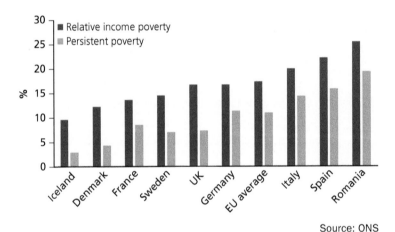

Source: ONS

Figure 27.6 Relative and persistent poverty 2015, selected countries

The percentage falling below the poverty line is not a totally reliable measure on its own: it is also important to know *how far* below the poverty line households are falling. The *income gap* (the distance between household income and the poverty line) is a useful measure of the intensity of poverty as well as of its incidence.

Exercise 27.2

Imagine that you are the Minister for Poverty Alleviation in a country in which the (absolute) poverty line is set at $500. Of the people living below the poverty line, you know that there are two distinct groups, each made up of 50 individuals. The people in group 1 have an income of $450, whereas those in group 2 have only $250. Suppose that your budget for poverty alleviation is $2,500.

a Your prime concern is with the most needy: how would you use your budget?
b Suppose instead that your prime minister instructs you to reduce the percentage of people living below the poverty line: do you adopt the same strategy for using the funds?
c How helpful is the poverty line as a strategic target of policy action?

Changes in inequality and poverty over time

Although the distribution of income does not change rapidly from one year to the next, there have been changes over time. Figure 27.7 graphs the Gini coefficient, calculated for income (post-tax equivalised) in the UK since 1977.

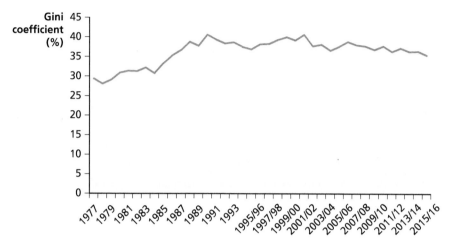

Source: based on ONS data

Figure 27.7 The Gini coefficient for the UK since 1977

Because people can be expected to smooth their consumption through time, expenditure inequality is seen to have been a little steadier than income inequality. However, both show a noticeable increase in inequality during the 1980s, since when there seems to have been no discernible trend.

It is worth noting that this has been a common feature for the developed countries overall. A study by OECD found no generalised trend in the distribution of household incomes since the mid-1970s, although about half of the countries studied did show an increase between the mid-1980s and mid-1990s.

Another study, undertaken by the Institute for Fiscal Studies, analysed trends and noted that there were very different trends identifiable over some 'periods of political interest'. In particular, between 1979 and 1990, with Margaret Thatcher as prime minister, income growth was higher for each successive quintile.

However, you should not read too much into these differences. The causes of change in income distribution reflect not only the political stance of the government in power, but other changes occurring in society, and in the pattern of employment over time.

Summary: poverty

- Absolute poverty measures whether individuals or households have sufficient resources to maintain a reasonable life.
- Relative poverty measures whether individuals or households are able to participate in the life of the country in which they live: this is calculated as 50% of median adjusted household disposable income.
- Income distribution and poverty levels change relatively slowly over time.
- In the UK there has been little change since the mid-1990s, following a decade of increasing inequality.

Causes of inequality and poverty

Inequality arises from a variety of factors, some reflecting patterns in wealth (through the ownership of assets), some relating to the operation of the labour market and some arising from the actions of governments. Changes in the demographic structure of the population can also be important.

The distribution of wealth

Perhaps the most obvious way in which wealth influences inequality and its changes through time is through inheritance. Wealth that accumulates in a family over time and is then passed down to succeeding generations constitutes a source of inequality that does not arise from the current state of the economy or the operations of markets.

As explained earlier, you need to be aware that income and wealth are not the same. Income is a 'flow' of money that households receive each period, whereas wealth is a 'stock': that is, the accumulation of assets that a household owns. During 2012–14 people in the highest decile were estimated to own 45% of identified wealth in the UK, and were 5.2 times wealthier than the bottom 50% of households. The Gini coefficient for total wealth in 2014 was 63, which is much higher than that for income, indicating that wealth is much less evenly distributed than income.

Notice that, although wealth and income are not the same thing, inequality in wealth can *lead to* inequality in income, as wealth (the ownership of assets) creates an income flow — from interest, rents and profits — which then feeds back into a household's income stream.

A significant change in the pattern of ownership of assets in recent decades has been the increase in home ownership and the rise in house prices. For those who continue to rent their homes, and in particular for those who rent council dwellings, this is a significant source of rising inequality.

For developing countries, there is also considerable inequality in the distribution of ownership of assets. Financial markets in developing countries are much less well developed than in developed countries, and many people, especially in the rural areas, do not have access to the formal financial institutions. This inevitably means a concentration in the ownership of financial assets. Furthermore, the ownership of land is highly concentrated in some countries. This is notably the case in much of Latin America and has contributed to the relatively high levels of inequality that have characterised that region. The situation is further complicated by the fact that property rights are weak in many developing countries, so that even if a household has farmed a piece of land for generations, it may not be able to demonstrate ownership rights over that land. Such inequality in the ownership of assets leads also to inequality in income distribution.

Labour market explanations

As explained in Chapter 22, there are several ways in which the labour market is expected to give rise to inequalities in earnings. Inequality could arise from demand and supply conditions in labour markets, which respond to changes in the pattern of consumer demand for goods and services, and changes in international comparative advantage between countries. Furthermore, differences between different occupations and economic sectors reinforce income inequalities.

Knowledge check 27.7

In a period of rising house prices, is the main impact on income or on wealth inequality?

Synoptic link

Notice that when we talk about the labour market in the aggregate, we tend to ignore the fact that at the microeconomic level, there are significant differences between individual labour markets. This was discussed in Chapter 22.

Structure of employment

However, a by-product of changes in the structure of the economy may be an increase in inequality between certain groups in society. For example, a change in the structure of employment, away from unskilled jobs and towards occupations requiring a higher level of skills and qualifications, can lead to an increase in inequality, with those workers who lack the skills to adapt to changing labour market conditions being disadvantaged by the changes. In other words, if the premium that employers are prepared to pay in order to hire skilled or well-qualified workers rises as a result of changing technology in the workplace, then those without such skills are likely to suffer.

The decline in the power of the trade unions may have contributed to this situation, as low-paid workers may find that their unions are less likely to be able to offer employment protection. It has been argued that this is a *good* thing if it increases the flexibility of the labour market. But again, a balance is needed between worker protection and free and flexible markets.

Synoptic link

The impact of trade unions of the labour market was explored in Chapter 22.

Wage gap

The difference in earnings between female and male workers has also been highlighted. In the UK, female workers on average earn 16.8% lower wages than males (based on the male median wage). This is a smaller gap than in the USA where females receive wages 18.1% below males. However, this is a much greater gap than in some other countries such as Italy (5.6%) or Denmark (5.8%). Research by the Institute for Fiscal Studies showed that the wage gap in the UK has fallen for female workers whose highest educational attainment was at GCSE level, but has remained more or less constant for women with A-level or degree-level qualifications since the 1990s. Some of the earnings differences between men and women can be explained by the fact that when women have to take time out from working to look after children, they lose human capital by missing out on work experience. However, such market explanations may not suffice to explain all the differences in earnings that are observed.

Knowledge check 27.8

Does the existence of a persistent wage gap between male and female workers necessarily mean that there is discrimination in the workplace?

Underdeveloped labour markets

Many developing countries are characterised by inefficient and underdeveloped labour markets, which may give rise to income inequalities. This may in particular contribute to inequality between rural and urban areas. In many countries, rural areas are still highly dependent on subsistence agriculture, with relatively little wage labour. In contrast, the modern sector, located primarily in the urban areas, demonstrates higher wage levels and a more formal sector — but with limited job opportunities. This can create a situation in which there is substantial migration from the rural to the urban areas, attracted by the high wage differentials between the regions.

However, given limited job opportunities in the formal urban sector, the result may be high levels of urban unemployment, together with congestion and overcrowding. The high rate of migration may also give rise to the development of an urban informal sector, so that the labour market is effectively structured in three segmented sections — rural, urban informal and urban formal. The limited linkages between them may then perpetuate inequality.

Demographic change

A feature of many developed countries in recent years has been a change in the age structure of the population. Improved medical drugs and treatments have meant that people are living longer, and this has combined with low fertility rates to bring about an increase in the proportion of the population who are in the older age groups. This has put pressure on the provision of pensions, and increased the vulnerability of this group in society. State pensions have been funded primarily by the contributions of those in work, but if the number of people of working age falls as a proportion of the whole population, then this funding stream comes under pressure.

Many developed countries have seen a change in the age structure of the population

▌Government intervention

In the developed countries, there are a number of ways in which government intervention influences the distribution of income in a society, although not all of these interventions are expressly intended to do so. Most prominent is the range of transfer payments and taxation that has been implemented.

The overall effect of these measures has a large effect on income distribution. This can be shown using a Lorenz curve, as in Figure 27.8. ('Original income' is income before any adjustment is made for the effect of taxation or benefits.) You can see the extent to which tax and benefit measures bring the Lorenz curve closer to the equality line.

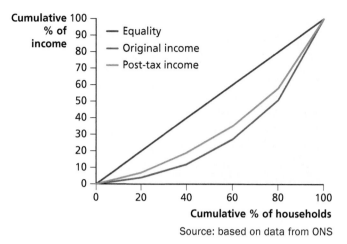

Figure 27.8 Lorenz curves for income in the UK, 2015/16

Benefits

There are two forms of benefit that households can receive to help equalise the income distribution. First, there are various types of cash benefit, such as income support, child benefit, incapacity benefit and working tax credit. These are designed to protect families whose income in certain circumstances would otherwise be very low. Second, there are benefits in kind, such as health and education. These accrue to individual households depending on the number of members of the household and their age and gender. Of these, the cash benefits are far more important in influencing the distribution of income. For the lowest quintile such benefits make up about three-fifths of growth in income; they are also significant for the second quintile.

Taxation

Direct taxes

Direct taxes (taxes on incomes) tend to be progressive. In other words, higher income groups pay tax at a higher rate.

In the UK the main direct taxes are income tax, corporation tax (paid by firms on profits), capital gains tax (paid by individuals who sell assets at a profit), inheritance tax and petroleum revenue tax (paid by firms operating in the North Sea). There is also the council tax, collected by local authorities and National Insurance contributions (NIC).

With a tax such as income tax, its progressive nature is reflected in the way the tax rate increases as an individual moves into a higher income range. In other words, the **marginal tax rate** increases as income increases. The **progressive** nature of the tax ensures that it does indeed help to reduce inequality in income distribution — although its effects are less than those of the cash benefits discussed earlier.

Figure 27.9 shows average direct tax rates for households by quintile group in 2015/16. Notice that the figure shows *average* rather than *marginal* tax rates. When average rates are rising, marginal tax rates are higher than the average. Exercise 27.3 illustrates this.

Key terms

direct tax a tax levied directly on income

marginal tax rate tax on additional income, defined as the change in tax payments due divided by the change in taxable income

progressive tax a tax in which the marginal tax rate rises with income, i.e. a tax bearing most heavily on the relatively well-off members of society

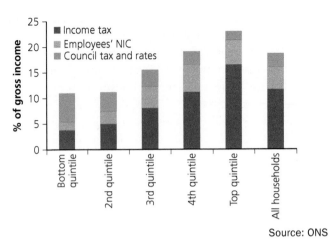

Source: ONS

Figure 27.9 Average direct taxes by quintile households 2015/16

Figure 27.9 shows how income tax is progressive, as the average tax rate increases from 3.8% in the bottom quintile to 16.5% in the top quintile. However, it also shows that council tax is certainly not progressive, as it takes a higher percentage from the bottom quintile than from the top.

Exercise 27.3

Table 27.4 shows the amount of tax paid by an individual as income increases. Calculate the average and marginal tax rates at each of the income levels. (*Remember the definition of the marginal tax rate provided above.*)

Table 27.4

Income	Tax paid
£1,000	£100
£2,000	£300
£3,000	£600
£4,000	£1,000

Knowledge check 27.9

Looking at Figure 27.9, would you say that employees' NIC payments are progressive or regressive?

Indirect taxes

The effect of **indirect taxes**, on the other hand, can sometimes be **regressive**: in other words, indirect taxes may impinge more heavily on lower-income households. Indirect taxes are taxes that are paid on items of expenditure, rather than on income.

Examples of indirect taxes are value added tax (VAT), which is charged on most goods and services sold in the UK, tobacco taxes, excise duties on alcohol and oil duties. These specific taxes are levied per unit sold. When demand is price inelastic, producers are able to pass much of an increase in the tax rate on to consumers, whereas if demand is price elastic they have to absorb most of the increase as part of their costs.

Key terms

indirect tax a tax on expenditure, e.g. VAT

regressive tax a tax bearing more heavily on the relatively poorer members of society

Synoptic link

Indirect taxes were discussed in Chapter 8 and in Case Study 8.1.

Knowledge check 27.10

Explain why producers are more able to pass on an increase in indirect taxes to consumers when demand is relatively price-inelastic.

Why should some of these taxes be regressive? Take the tobacco tax. In the first place, the number of smokers is higher among lower-income groups than among the relatively rich — research has shown that only about 10% of people in professional groups now smoke compared with nearly 40% of those in unskilled manual groups. Second, expenditure on tobacco tends to take a lower proportion of income of the rich compared with that of the poor, even for those in the former group who do smoke. Thus, the tobacco tax falls more heavily on lower-income groups than on the better-off. It is estimated that for households in the bottom quintile of the income distribution in 2015/16, indirect taxes accounted for 27.0% of their disposable income, compared with 14.4% for households in the top quintile. The largest share of indirect tax was VAT, which accounted for 11.4% of disposable income of households in the bottom quintile, compared with 7.1% for the top quintile.

Notice that a tax that is simply **proportional** to income would be neither regressive nor progressive, but would be charged at the same percentage rate to all taxpayers.

Key term

proportional tax a tax that is proportional to income, being neither regressive nor progressive

The balance of taxation

Achieving a balance of taxation between direct and indirect taxes is an important aspect of the government's redistributive policy. A switch in the balance from direct to indirect taxes will tend to increase inequality in a society.

There may be reasons why such a switch is seen as desirable. When Margaret Thatcher came to power back in 1979, one of the first actions of her government was to increase indirect taxes and introduce cuts in income tax. An important part of the rationale was that high marginal tax rates on income can have a disincentive effect: if people know that a large proportion of any additional work they undertake will be taxed away, they may be discouraged from providing more work. In other words, cutting income tax can encourage work effort by reducing marginal tax rates.

This is yet another reminder of the need for a balanced policy, one that recognises that while some income redistribution is needed to protect the vulnerable, disincentive effects may arise if the better-off are over-taxed. It is also important to be aware that disincentives may also affect low-paid workers, if after-tax pay falls below the level of available social security benefits.

Long-term policy

An economic analysis of the causes of inequality suggests that there are some long-term measures that can be taken to reduce future inequality, although they may take quite a while to become effective. Policies that encourage greater take-up of education, and provide skills retraining, may be important in the long run if the unskilled are not to be excluded from the benefits of economic growth.

Capitalism and inequality

To some extent it could be argued that some inequality is inevitable within a free market capitalist society. Indeed, it could be argued that without some inequality, capitalism could not operate, as it is the pursuit of gain that provides firms with the incentive to maximise profits, workers with the incentive to provide labour effort, and consumers with the incentive to maximise their utility. It is the combination of these efforts by economic agents that leads to good resource allocation, through the working of Adam Smith's 'invisible hand'. In a world in which every individual was guaranteed the same income as everyone else, there would be no incentive for anyone to strive to do better. However, few would argue for complete equality of income. More important is that there should be equality of opportunity.

The impact of economic growth on inequality

Weak institutions and poor governance in developing countries mean that measures such as taxation and transfers to influence the distribution of income are largely untried or ineffective. The economist and Nobel laureate Simon Kuznets argued that there is expected to be a relationship between the degree of inequality in the income distribution and the level of development that a country has achieved. He claimed that in the early stages of economic development income is fairly equally distributed, with everyone living at a relatively low income level. However, as development begins to take off there will be some individuals at the forefront of enterprise and development, and their incomes will rise more rapidly. So in this middle phase the income distribution will tend to worsen. At a later stage of development, society will eventually be able to afford to redistribute income to protect the poor, and all will begin to share in the benefits of development.

This can be portrayed as a relationship between the Gini coefficient and the level of development. The thrust of the Kuznets hypothesis is that this should reveal an inverted U-shaped relationship, as shown in Figure 27.10.

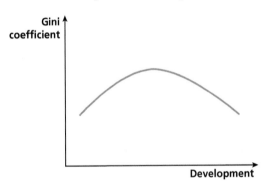

Figure 27.10 The Kuznets curve

Figure 27.11 shows the Gini coefficient for the range of countries used earlier in the chapter which, remember, are ranked in order of GNI per capita. The pattern shown by this figure suggests that there may be some evidence that countries in the middle range of GNI per capita have higher Gini values, but the evidence is not strong.

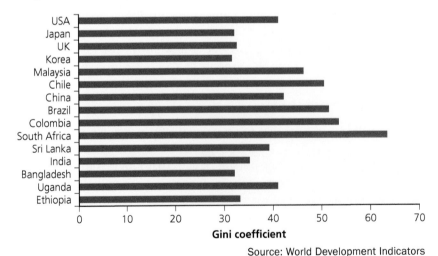

Source: World Development Indicators

Figure 27.11 The Gini coefficient

Extension material: the Kuznets curve: empirical evidence

One reason why the empirical support for the Kuznets hypothesis is rather weak is that the relationship may not show up clearly in *cross-section* data — in other words, when the evidence is based on looking at how the relationship varies across countries at a single point in time. Looking at how the relationship changes through time for individual countries might be more revealing, but unfortunately data on inequality is expensive to compile and not collected on a regular basis. Such data would be known as *time series* data.

It is also worth noting that there are substantial regional variations in the degree of inequality. Latin America has been known for wide inequality between groups in society, whereas eastern Europe has shown much lower levels of inequality, partly because inequality was low across the Soviet bloc. This may also conceal the underlying Kuznets relationship.

Exercise 27.4

Using appropriate economic analysis, discuss the various policy measures available to a government wishing to ensure an equitable distribution of income without damaging incentives to work.

Exercise 27.5

Discuss the extent to which developing countries would benefit from introducing policies attempting to reduce income inequality.

Summary: causes of inequality

- Inequality arises from a range of factors.
- The distribution of wealth is strongly influenced by the pattern of inheritance, but in recent years changing patterns of home ownership, coupled with rises in house prices, have also been significant.
- The natural operation of labour markets gives rise to some inequality in income.
- The skills premium resulting from technological change has widened the wage gap between skilled and educated workers on the one hand, and the unskilled on the other.
- Gender differences in pay persist, in spite of successive policies intended to root out discrimination.
- Government action influences the pattern of income distribution, with the net effect being a reduction in inequality.
- Most effective in this is the provision of cash benefits to low-income households.
- Income tax is progressive, and helps to redistribute income towards poorer households.
- Some indirect taxes, however, can be regressive in their impact.
- It is important to keep a balance between protecting the low-paid and providing incentives for those in work.

Inequality and economic growth

If you visit Rio de Janeiro, you may be surprised to see high metal fences in front of many of the luxurious multi-storey buildings along the lovely beaches of Copacabana. However, it is not really surprising, given that Rio has one of the highest crime rates in Brazil, exacerbated by the high level of income inequality. It is not uncommon to find a substantial gap between the rich and the poor in many societies. Inequality exists in both developing and developed countries. For example, Nobel laureate Paul Krugman has noted that the 13,000 richest families in the USA have almost as much income as the 20 million poorest households; those 13,000 families have incomes 300 times that of average families. Thus, it is important to examine the effects of such income inequality not only on crime rate and social behaviour, but also on the economy.

Level of income inequality

The level of income inequality depends primarily on the distribution of assets and wages as well as on government policy. First, an important factor is the distribution of productive assets such as land. If land ownership is concentrated among a few owners, which is typical of many agriculture-dominated developing economies, then income inequality tends to be high in such countries. In addition, if the ownership of minerals and natural resources is concentrated among the elite, then countries well endowed with natural resources — especially mineral resources such as oil, diamonds, copper and so on — tend also to have higher asset and income inequality than other types of economy. Another factor that explains variations across countries is the rural–urban inequality within developing countries, which is the result of urban bias.

Overall, income inequality depends to a large extent on earnings inequality, as in many countries earnings account for 60–70% of total income. In some countries, rising wage inequality has often been ascribed to technological change. New technologies generate a demand for skills. This favours higher-skilled workers over lower-skilled ones and leads to increasing wage differentials between skilled and unskilled workers. In addition, education tends to play an important role in reducing income inequality.

Thus, if some groups in a society do not have access to education, this leads to higher earnings inequality and therefore higher income inequality. Thus, earnings inequality is clearly an important contributor to the increases in overall income inequality witnessed in many countries recently.

Economic performance and output

But how does inequality influence economic performance and output? More unequal societies tend to develop larger groups of people who are excluded from opportunities that others enjoy. Poor people may not have the same chances in life as richer people, and may thus never quite realise their full productive potential. This may be because they do not get as good an education as those afforded by richer families, or because they can't get loans to start up a business as easily, or because they can't afford the insurance they would require to undertake some risky — but productive — venture. An income distribution with lots of poor people, or unequally distributed opportunities, would under-utilise its aggregate productive potential to a greater degree than a distribution with relatively fewer poor people, or one where opportunities were more equitably distributed. Both theory and empirical evidence suggest that these incomplete realisations of economic potential are not of concern only to those who care about equity as such. They also affect aggregate economic potential, and therefore aggregate output and its rate of growth.

The impact on growth may also be negative when the gap between the rich and the poor widens excessively. For instance, rural economies with very high land concentration in a few hands and landlessness for the majority face very high shirking and supervision costs. For these reasons, these economies tend to be less efficient (e.g. to have lower yields per hectare) than more equitable agrarian systems, even when accounting for the economies of scale in marketing, processing and shipping which benefit larger farms.

Political instability and social problems

Finally, high levels of income inequality can also create political instability and social problems and very negatively affect growth over both the short and long term. There is increasing evidence of a strong relation between inequality and the crime rate. Income differences between households create *psychological stress* for the relatively poor that may explain higher morbidity, mortality and violence rates. Social tensions, in turn, erode the security of property rights, augment the threat of expropriation, drive away domestic and foreign investment and increase the cost of business security and contract enforcement.

In Rio de Janeiro, the slum areas or 'favelas' sit alongside middle-class districts reflecting the high level of income inequality in Brazil

Follow-up questions

a Identify the key causes of inequality in a society.

b Discuss how inequality in wealth can affect inequality in income.

c Why should inequality create political instability?

d In your own words, outline the main ways in which inequality may have an impact on economic growth.

28 Emerging and developing economies

One of the greatest challenges faced by the world economy is the enormous gap in living standards that has built up as the process of economic growth and development has left many countries far behind. Development is not about economic growth alone, but growth is a vital prerequisite if progress in development is to be achieved. This chapter evaluates some of the factors that may be thought to contribute to the process of economic growth — and some of the obstacles to growth that have hindered progress, especially in sub-Saharan Africa. This will be illustrated with reference to the experience of some economies that have begun to close the gap in living standards.

Learning outcomes

After studying this chapter, you should:
→ be familiar with ways of measuring and monitoring human development
→ understand the importance of economic growth for developing countries
→ be familiar with the Harrod–Domar model of economic growth, and its relevance for developing countries
→ understand the importance of factors that can contribute to economic growth, such as capital, technology and human capital
→ be familiar with the contrasting patterns of development in different regions of the world
→ understand the causes and significance of rapid population growth
→ appreciate the importance of missing markets, especially financial markets
→ be aware of the importance of social capital in promoting long-term development

Key terms

development process by which real per capita incomes are increased and the inhabitants of a country are able to benefit from improved living conditions, i.e. lower poverty and enhanced standards of education, health, nutrition and other essentials of life

tiger economies a group of economies in South East Asia (Hong Kong, South Korea, Singapore and Taiwan) that enjoyed rapid economic growth from the 1960s

Measuring development

Chapter 27 noted that the notion of 'development' goes beyond economic growth. It encompasses many more aspects of the quality of people's lives. In other words, although expanding the resources available to a society through economic growth is an essential ingredient of development, the way in which those resources are used is also crucial.

How do we recognise that a country is undergoing development? The discussion in this chapter will be illustrated using indicators for a selection of countries from different regions of the world, but try to remember the wide diversity among the countries that are classified as developing. There are some countries that have undergone a process of economic growth, and have started to close the gap on the developed countries. This group includes the **tiger economies** of South East Asia (Hong Kong, South Korea, Singapore and Taiwan) and more recently a group of emerging economies, including the BRIC countries (Brazil, Russia, India and China plus South Africa). However, there are also developing countries, especially in sub-Saharan Africa, that have made relatively little progress.

How can the developing countries be identified? An obvious first indicator to consider would be GNI per capita, but the problems entailed in using this measure for international comparisons are well known.

Synoptic link

GNI per capita was introduced in Chapter 9, which also investigated some of the problems in its use. This was further explored in Chapter 27. You may find it helpful to review this material.

Figure 27.2 on page 463 shows levels of GNI per capita (measured in PPP$) for selected countries from different regions of the world. Recall that the countries here have been ranked in descending order of GNI per capita in PPP$. The figure underlines the gap in income levels between countries, but there are other dimensions of development that need to be taken into account.

Study tip

Do not be tempted to learn by heart lots of statistics about individual countries, as this will not be expected of you. Being aware of the general differences in the stage of development reached by countries in different regions may be helpful, but the detail is not necessary.

The Human Development Index

Key term

Human Development Index a composite indicator of the level of a country's development, varying between 0 and 1

To deal with the criticism that GNI per capita fails to take account of other dimensions of the quality of life, in 1990 the United Nations Development Programme (UNDP) devised an alternative indicator, known as the **Human Development Index** (HDI). This was designed to provide a broader measure of the stage of development that a country had reached. It has since become a widely used indicator.

Health, education and standard of living

The basis for this measure is that there are three key aspects of human development: resources (living standards), knowledge of how to make good use of those resources (education), and a reasonable life span in which to make use of those resources (health) (see Figure 28.1). The three components are measured by, respectively, GNI per capita in PPP$, indicators of education (mean years of schooling and expected years of schooling) and life expectancy. The measurements are then combined to produce a composite index ranging between 0 and 1, with higher values reflecting higher human development.

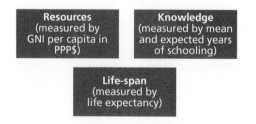

Figure 28.1 Components of the Human Development Index

You may wonder why education is represented by two different variables. The key to this is that the two measures reflect two contrasting (but important) aspects of education. Mean years of schooling is a variable that informs us about the effectiveness of past education, as it is based on the mean number of years of schooling that adults aged 25 or above had received. If you like, it is a measure of the output of the education system. Expected years of schooling, on the other hand, is an input measure, as it tells us how many years of schooling a child entering education can expect to receive.

Knowledge check 28.1

In Ethiopia in 2017, mean years of schooling were 2.6 whereas expected years of schooling were 8.4. What does this imply for changes in the education system?

Values of the HDI for 2016 are charted in Figure 28.2 for the selected countries. The countries are still ranked in ascending order of GNI per capita, but the gap between low and high human development is less marked here. Exceptions are South Africa and Malaysia, which are ranked lower on the basis of the HDI than on GNI per capita: what this suggests is that these countries have achieved relatively high income levels, but other aspects of human development have not kept pace. There are other countries in the world that share this feature. You will see that there are also countries that seem to perform better on HDI grounds than on GNI per capita — for example, Chile and Sri Lanka.

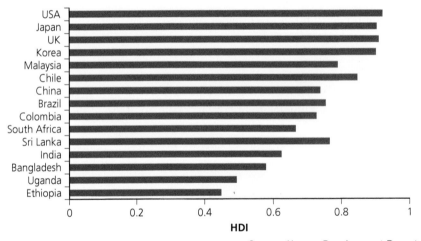

Source: Human Development Report

Figure 28.2 The Human Development Index, selected countries

Figures 28.3 and 28.4 show the levels of two of the measures that enter into the HDI: life expectancy and mean years of schooling. It would seem that life expectancy is primarily responsible for the low ranking of South Africa in the HDI, as its level of life expectancy is out of kilter with its average income level and mean years of schooling. In contrast, Bangladesh performs quite well in terms of lifespan, but relatively poorly in terms of education. By comparing these data, you can get some idea of the diversity between countries that was mentioned earlier.

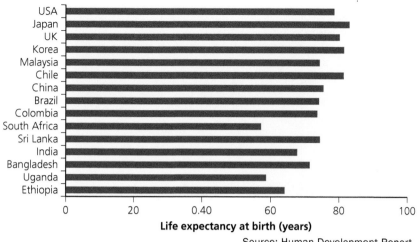

Figure 28.3 Life expectancy at birth (years), selected countries

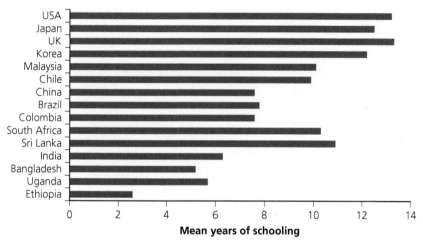

Source: Human Development Report

Figure 28.4 Mean years of schooling, selected countries

In part, this diversity reflects differing priorities that governments have given to different aspects of development. Countries such as Brazil have aimed primarily at achieving economic growth, while those such as Sri Lanka have given greater priority to promoting education and healthcare.

Knowledge check 28.2

Looking at Figures 28.3 and 28.4, did India perform relatively better on knowledge or or health provision?

Quantitative skills 28.1

A development diamond

Another way of putting a country into perspective is to construct a *development diamond*. An example is shown in Figure 28.5 This compares Ethiopia's performance with the average for countries in its region: sub-Saharan Africa. On each axis, the value of the variable achieved by Ethiopia is expressed as a proportion of the value for sub-Saharan Africa. In this instance, Ethiopia is seen to have life expectancy slightly above the average for sub-Saharan Africa, but performs less well on GNI per capita and mean years of schooling. These combined with other indicators contribute to the HDI value, which is lower than the average for sub-Saharan Africa.

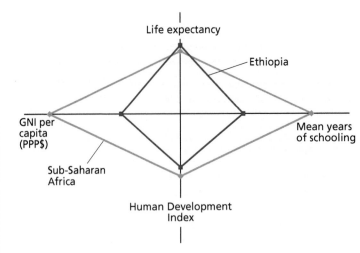

Figure 28.5 A development diamond for Ethiopia compared with all countries in sub-Saharan Africa

Growth vs development

There is a view that growth should be the prime objective for development, since by expanding the resources available, the benefits can begin to trickle down through the population. An opposing view claims that, by providing first for basic needs, more rapid economic growth can be facilitated. The problem in some cases is that growth has not resulted in the trickle-down effect, and inequality remains. It may be significant that countries such as Brazil and South Africa, where the GNI per capita ranking is high relative to the HDI ranking, are countries in which there remain high levels of inequality in the distribution of income.

> **Synoptic link**
>
> Inequality was discussed in Chapter 27, where the experience of Brazil and South Africa was noted.

The HDI may be preferred to GNI per capita as a measure of development on the grounds that it reflects the key dimensions of development as opposed to growth. However, it will always be difficult to reduce a complex concept such as development to a single statistic. The diverse characteristics of developing countries demand the use of a range of alternative measures in order to identify the configuration of circumstances and problems facing a particular country. In the area of healthcare it is useful to look at the number of doctors relative to population, or levels of infant mortality. Access to improved water, sanitation or electricity is informative about the level of infrastructure, as is the access to a mobile phone.

Other indicators of development

Although the HDI is a useful composite indicator that is more informative about relative living standards across countries, it still neglects some important dimensions of development. The UNDP has recognised this, and has produced a number of other indicators designed to complement the HDI, notably in respect of inequality, gender and poverty.

Exercise 28.1

Collect data on a country of your choice from the *Human Development Report* (at http://hdr.undp.org/; go to the 'Data' tab), and construct a development diamond to compare your country with the average for the region in which it is located. Discuss what you learn from this. Note that you can choose any indicators that you think would be useful, you do not need to be restricted to the ones shown in Figure 28.5.

The Inequality-adjusted HDI

Inequality in the three components of the HDI (health, education and standard of living) are used to adjust the HDI to try to estimate the extent to which potential human development is lower because of inequalities. For example, the previous chapter noted the relatively high inequality that persists in South Africa. In terms of the Inequality-adjusted HDI (IHDI), the conclusion drawn is that the loss in potential human development due to inequality in South Africa amounts to 34.7%.

Gender inequality

The situation of women in many countries has been a major concern. Women tend to receive less education, are exposed to greater health risks and receive lower incomes. The UNDP has produced two ways of exploring gender inequality across countries. One approach is simply to calculate the HDI separately for females and males. In more developed countries, female life expectancy is often significantly higher than for males, so the difference in HDI levels between females and males is not great, even where females face lower GNI per capita. Indeed, there are some countries (e.g. Estonia) where females have a higher HDI than males. Elsewhere the picture is very different: for example, in Pakistan, female HDI is more than 25% lower than for males. A second measure focuses on the key gender issues of health, empowerment and the labour force.

Knowledge check 28.3

In the UK in 2015, females enjoyed higher life expectancy and were expected to receive more years of schooling than males. Mean years of schooling were more or less the same. Why was the HDI for females only 0.894 compared with 0.924 for males?

The Multidimensional Poverty Index

In the previous chapter, poverty was seen in relation to income or consumption levels. However, poverty is not just about income, it is also about deprivation — lack of access to key resources. The Multidimensional Poverty Index (MPI) attempts to reflect the number of deprivations faced by households. These deprivations are grouped into the three key components of the HDI (health, education and standard of living). They include school attainment and attendance (for education) and nutrition and child mortality (for health). In terms of resources, deprivations cover a range of things, such as access to electricity, clean water, sanitation, good cooking fuels, a floor that is not dirt, sand or dung, and assets related to information (e.g. radio, television, phone), mobility or livelihood. These multiple deprivations are combined into an index that reflects both the number of people regarded as being poor in terms of deprivations, and the number of deprivations that they suffer. A headcount ratio is published showing the percentage of the population who are poor under this definition. Some results are shown in Figure 28.6.

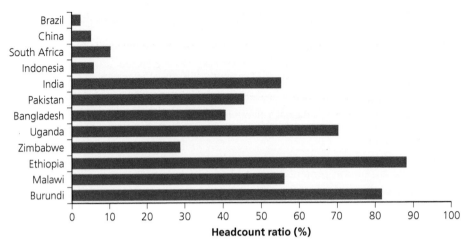

Source: Human Development Report

Note: the countries are in descending order of GNI per capita (PPP$)

Figure 28.6 People in multidimensional poverty

Knowledge check 28.4

Why would lack of access to a radio, television or phone be seen as a significant deprivation as part of a poverty indicator?

Notice from the jagged pattern of the bars that there does not appear to be a strong association between poverty and average incomes.

Characteristics of developing countries

There are many other indicators that can be used to capture the varied characteristics of developing countries that may contribute to their progress in achieving development. For example, the pattern of economic activity may be important, as heavy dependence on low productivity agriculture may hinder economic growth. Access to good infrastructure can be captured by data on access to electricity, sanitation or clean water. Transport and communications are also vital for development, so access to the internet or mobile phones, or the quality of roads are all important indicators that can provide clues to the problems faced by particular countries.

Exercise 28.2

Table 28.1 presents data for three countries on a range of indicators. Can you identify which of these countries is likely to have the lowest and highest GNI per capita (PPP$)?

Table 28.1 Indicators of development

Indicator	Country A	Country B	Country C
Life expectancy at birth (years)	65.5	62.2	48.9
Expected years of schooling	10.3	11.1	11.4
FDI inflow (% of GDP)	5.3	2.3	0.8
Mobile cellular subscriptions (per 100 people)	41.8	81.3	76.4
Unemployment (% of total labour force)	2.1	11.0	25.3
HIV/AIDS prevalence (% population aged 15–49)	0.6	5.4	27.2
Infant mortality (aged under 5 per 1000 births)	49.6	49.4	60.7
Agriculture valued added (%GDP)	24.4	35.6	9.9

Source: World Bank

Summary: indicators of development

- Developing countries are largely located in four major regions: sub-Saharan Africa, Latin America, South Asia and South East Asia.
- These regions have shown contrasting patterns of growth and development.
- The Human Development Index (HDI) recognises that human development depends on resources, knowledge and health, and therefore combines indicators of these key aspects.
- Other composite indicators have been produced to encompass different dimensions of the standard of living.
- Different countries have different characteristics, and face different configurations of problems and opportunities.

Factors influencing growth and development

Although development is about more than economic growth, growth is a crucial part of any process of economic and human development. It provides the increase in resources necessary to enable a country to provide for the basic needs of its citizens and to expand its choices in the future, and it lays the foundations for future development.

The following sections build on our previous discussion about economic growth, extending the analysis to incorporate the particular problems faced by developing countries.

Synoptic link

Economic growth was discussed in Chapter 14.

Primary product dependency

Many developing countries, especially in sub–Saharan Africa, continue to rely heavily on the agricultural sector to provide employment and incomes. Because labour productivity in agriculture tends to be relatively low, this may keep rural incomes low.

It is worth remembering that one of the driving forces behind the Industrial Revolution in Britain was an increase in agricultural productivity, enabling more workers to shift into manufacturing activity. In the context of a developing country, this transition may run into a number of problems. It is thus important to examine if there are obstacles to increasing agricultural productivity.

In some developing countries the problem stems from the form of land tenancy agreements, which can lead to inefficiency. In other cases, problems arise because of insecure property rights and the inheritance laws that pertain.

Knowledge check 28.5

In some developing countries, many farmers do not own the land that they farm, with the landlord receiving a share of the crop as payment. Why might this result in inefficiency?

The difficulty of improving agricultural productivity does not make it easy for developing countries to engage in active international trade, but in practice some have little choice but to rely on primary production in their export activity. For many developing countries, the share of primary goods in exports remains extremely high.

In developing countries, even small enterprises may be involved in exporting activity. For example, many small farmers even in remote villages in Uganda grow some coffee for export. However, they rely on traders travelling around the rural areas to buy the coffee and sell it on to the exporters. This creates difficulties for the farmers, who may not be able to check up readily on the prices being charged in the cities, and who do not have the storage or market facilities to produce on a larger scale. If they do not have the communication links with which to determine what a good price for their crop is, the traders have an information advantage that may be exploited. The spread of mobile phones is helping to tackle this issue, by enabling farmers to keep in touch with market conditions, thus improving the information available to them in negotiating a fair price for their produce, and in taking decisions about what crops they should produce.

Small coffee farmers in Uganda may not have access to up-to-date market information

Synoptic link

The dangers of depending on primary products for export revenues were discussed in Chapter 24 in exploring the potential gains from trade.

Volatility of commodity prices

Relying on primary exports can create vulnerability. In the short run, many primary product prices tend to be volatile, thus creating uncertainty. This volatility may arise on the supply-side due to variations in the weather, or on the demand-side if demand varies with the business cycle.

Knowledge check 28.6

Consider a good where output is highly dependent on weather conditions, which vary from year to year. Would the resulting volatility in price be greater or lower if the demand for the good is relatively price inelastic?

In the long run, there may be a tendency for the terms of trade to move against primary producers in favour of manufactured goods. The **Prebisch and Singer hypothesis** argued that this would result partly because of the relatively low income elasticity of demand for primary products (especially food) compared with manufactured goods. In addition, the production of primary goods faces diminishing returns to scale, whereas manufacturing activity enjoys economies of scale. This suggests that the technology of production can influence relative prices, although this may be counterbalanced by the prevalence of imperfect competition in manufacturing.

Key term

Prebisch–Singer hypothesis an observation that the terms of trade for primary products relative to manufactures will tend to deteriorate in the long run

Savings and investment

For a developing country, one important problem is the inability to produce capital goods. In many developing countries the capacity to produce capital goods is limited because they lack the necessary technical knowledge and resources. Furthermore, a country in which there are high levels of poverty, and in which many households face low income-earning opportunities, needs to devote much of its resources to consumption. The question for developing countries is thus how to overcome this problem in order to kick-start a process of economic growth.

Figure 28.7 illustrates the problem. A shortage of capital means low per capita income, which means low savings, which in turn means low investment, limited capital, and hence low per capita incomes. In this way a country can get trapped in a *low-level equilibrium* situation.

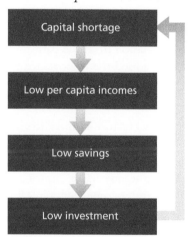

Figure 28.7 A low-level equilibrium trap

Knowledge check 28.7

Explain why a shortage of capital means low per capita income.

One view of economic growth sees it in terms of a shift in the aggregate supply curve (as in Figure 14.1 on page 191).

Synoptic link

Chapter 14 argued that investment is critical to the process of expanding the productive capacity of the economy, which suggests that the first focus for developing countries must be on savings and investment.

For both developed and developing countries, the potential productive capacity of the economy depends fundamentally on two things: the quantity of factors of production available within the economy, and the efficiency with which they are utilised. By increasing the quantity and/or quality of the factors of production and their productivity, the aggregate supply curve can be shifted to the right.

For the developing countries, the problem is magnified because of lack of resources. In many cases, human capital is low, and there are limited resources to devote to education, training and improving health. Capital tends to be scarce, and the flows of foreign direct investment — especially to the poorest developing countries — are relatively low. Markets do not operate effectively to allocate resources efficiently. There are thus many obstacles to be overcome in seeking to promote growth and development. So, how can savings be mobilised to enable investment?

The Harrod–Domar model

The idea that the initial focus for developing countries should be on savings and investment is supported by the **Harrod–Domar model** of economic growth, which first appeared in separate articles by Roy Harrod in the UK and Evsey Domar in the USA in 1939. This model was to become significant in influencing developing countries' attitudes towards the process of economic growth. It was developed in an attempt to determine how equilibrium could be maintained in a growing economy.

The basic finding of this model was that an economy can remain in equilibrium through time only if it grows at a particular rate, given by the ratio of the savings rate to the capital–output ratio (s/k). This unique stable growth path is thus seen to depend on the savings ratio and the productivity of capital. Any deviation from the path will cause the economy to become unstable. This finding emphasised the importance of savings in the process of economic growth, and led to the conclusion that a country wishing to achieve economic growth must first increase its flow of savings.

Figure 28.8 illustrates the process that leads to growth in a Harrod–Domar world. Savings are crucial in enabling investment to be undertaken — always remembering that some investment will have to be used to replace existing capital that has worn out. Investment then enables capital to accumulate and technology to be improved. The accumulation of capital leads to an increase in output and incomes, which leads to a further flow of savings, and the cycle is back to where it started.

Figure 28.8 The Harrod-Domar process of economic development

> ### Key term
>
> **Harrod-Domar model** a model of economic growth that emphasises the importance of savings and investment

> ### Study tip
>
> This is quite a useful schematic diagram describing the process of economic growth, as long as you remember all the ways in which it may fail to work smoothly.

Extension material: the algebra of the Harrod–Domar model

The algebra of the Harrod–Domar model can be revealing.

Suppose there is a closed economy with no government. If there is equilibrium in the goods market, then planned saving (S) equals planned investment (I):

$$S = I$$

Assume that there is no depreciation, so investment results in capital accumulation (ΔK, where Δ means 'change in'):

$$I = \Delta K$$

Assume also that the capital–output ratio (k) remains constant over time. Then:

$$k = \Delta K / \Delta Y$$

where Y is income and/or output.

If savings are a proportion (s) of income, then for equilibrium to be maintained:

$$sY = \Delta K = k\Delta Y$$

Rearranging, this implies that the growth rate of output ($\Delta Y / Y$) must be equal to s/k.

This then provides a simple rule. If a government wishes to achieve a growth rate of, say, 5%, and knows that the capital–output ratio is 3, then the saving ratio needs to be $3 \times 5 = 15\%$. This is a simple rule, but deceptive. There are many reasons why it is not enough to generate a flow of saving and then sit back and wait for results, especially in the context of developing countries.

The key question is whether this process can allow a developing country to break out of the low-level equilibrium trap. Figure 28.8 can be used to identify a number of problems that may prevent the Harrod–Domar process from being effective for developing countries.

A savings gap

It has already been argued that generating a flow of savings in a developing country may be problematic. When incomes are low, households may have to devote most of their resources to consumption, and so there may be a **savings gap**.

Some savings have proved possible for some countries in some circumstances. For example, in the early 1960s South Korea had an average income level that was not too different from that of countries like Sudan or Afghanistan, but it managed to build up the savings rate during that decade. Now, it is a high-income country and a member of OECD.

Can savings be mobilised?

Even if there are savings, there is no guarantee that these can be mobilised for productive investment, so the savings gap is not only about the ability to save, but to do so in a way that funds can be channelled to where they are needed.

Some important preconditions must be met if savings are to be transformed into investment. If the funds that have been saved are to be mobilised for investment, there must be a way for potential borrowers to get access to the funds. In developed countries this takes place through the medium of financial markets. For example, it may be that households save by putting their money into a savings account at the bank; then with this money the bank can make loans to entrepreneurs, enabling them to undertake productive investment.

> **Key term**
>
> **savings gap** a situation in which a country cannot generate a sufficient flow of savings for investment

In developing countries in 2014, only 53.1% of people aged 15 and above had an account with a financial institution. In sub-Saharan Africa, the figure was only 28.9% and in some countries it was even lower — for example, only 3.5% of people in Niger had an account and only 6.9% in Burundi. Any savings are therefore in the form of fixed assets or as cash stored in a pot, and cannot readily be transformed into productive investment.

In addition, governments in some periods have made matters worse by holding down interest rates in the hope of encouraging firms to borrow. The idea here is that a low interest rate means a low cost of borrowing, which should make borrowing more attractive. However, this ignores the fact that if interest rates are very low there is little incentive to save. In this case, firms may wish to invest but may not be able to obtain the funds to do so.

> **Knowledge check 28.8**
>
> Why would low interest rates deter saving?

The other prerequisite for savings to be converted into investment is that there must be entrepreneurs with the ability to identify investment possibilities, the skill to carry them through and the willingness to bear the risk. Such entrepreneurs are in limited supply in many developing countries.

A foreign currency gap

For investment to be productive in terms of raising output and incomes in the economy, some further conditions need to be met. In particular, it is crucial for firms to have access to physical capital, which will raise production capacity. Given the limited capability of producing capital goods in many developing countries, they have to rely on capital imported from the developed countries. This may be beneficial in terms of upgrading home technology, but such equipment can only be imported if the country has access to the foreign currency to pay for it.

One of the most pressing problems for many developing countries is that they face such a **foreign currency gap** — in other words, they find it difficult to earn sufficient foreign currency with which to purchase the crucial imports required to allow manufacturing activity to expand. In order to do this, physical capital is needed, together with key inputs to the production process. Indeed, many developing countries need to import food and medical supplies in order to develop their human capital. A shortage of foreign currency may therefore make it difficult for the country to accumulate capital.

Capital flight

Another problem in mobilising savings generated domestically is that potential investors may perceive that they can get a higher return by investing in foreign companies abroad rather than domestically. This process is known as **capital flight**. This process may be reinforced if the country has encouraged foreign direct investment by transnational companies. These companies may attract funds from domestic investors. Furthermore, the capital flight may often be augmented when transnational companies repatriate their profits to overseas shareholders.

Key terms

foreign currency gap a situation in which a developing country is unable to import the goods that it needs for development because of a shortage of foreign exchange

capital flight a situation in which savings generated in a developing country are invested abroad

The tiger economies were all very open to international trade, and focused on promoting exports in order to earn the foreign exchange needed to import capital goods. This strategy worked very effectively, and the economies were able to widen their access to capital and move to higher value-added activities as they developed their capabilities.

Harrod–Domar and external resources

Figure 28.9 extends the earlier schematic presentation of the process underlying the Harrod–Domar model of economic growth. This has been amended to underline the importance of access to technology and human capital.

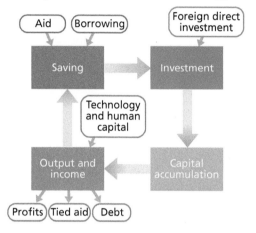

Figure 28.9 The Harrod-Domar process of economic development augmented

The discussion above has emphasised the difficulty of mobilising domestic savings, both in generating a sufficient flow of savings and in translating such savings into productive investment.

The question arises as to whether a developing country could supplement its domestic savings with a flow of funds from abroad. Figure 28.9 identifies three possible injections into the Harrod–Domar process. First, it might be possible to attract flows of overseas assistance from higher-income countries. Second, perhaps the amount of investment could be augmented directly by persuading transnational companies to engage in foreign direct investment. Third, perhaps the country could borrow on international capital markets to finance its domestic investment. It is worth noting that the tiger economies took full advantage of these external sources of funds.

Each of these ways of attracting external resources has a downside associated with it. As far as overseas assistance is concerned, in the past such flows have been seen by some donor countries as part of trade policy, and have brought less benefit to developing countries than had been hoped. For example, a country may provide aid to a developing country only on condition that it use the funds to buy goods from the donor country (often at an inflated price!). In the case of the transnational companies, there is a tendency for the profits to be repatriated out of the country, rather than recycled into the economy. Finally, international borrowing has to be repaid at some future date, and many developing countries have found themselves burdened by debt that they can ill afford to repay.

Knowledge check 28.9

Under what conditions could international borrowing be successful in raising economic growth in a developing country?

Summary: factors influencing growth and development

- Although development is a broader concept than economic growth, growth is a key ingredient of development.
- Economic growth can be seen in terms of a shift in long-run aggregate supply.
- Continued reliance on primary production is a high-risk strategy as productivity levels tend to be low in agriculture.
- The volatility of commodity prices causes problems in the short run.
- The Harrod–Domar model of economic growth highlights the importance of savings, and of transforming savings into productive investment.
- However, developing countries may face a savings gap such that funds are insufficient to finance investment.
- Developing countries may also face a foreign currency gap, and be unable to import needed capital equipment.
- Capital flight may also impede the growth process.
- If resources cannot be generated within the domestic economy, a country may need to have recourse to external sources of funding.

Demographic factors

Early writers on development were pessimists. For example, Thomas Malthus argued that real wages would never rise above a bare subsistence level. This was based on his ideas about the relationship between population growth and real incomes.

Malthus, having come under the influence of David Ricardo, believed that there would always be *diminishing returns to labour*. This led him to believe that as the population of a country increased, the average wage would fall, since a larger labour force would be inherently less productive. Furthermore, Malthus argued that the birth rate would rise with the real wage, because if families had more resources they would have more children; at the same time, the death rate would fall with an increase in the real wage, as people would be better fed and therefore healthier.

Extension material: population growth and real wages

Figure 28.10 shows one way of looking at the relationship between population growth and real wages. The left-hand panel illustrates the relationship between population size and the real wage rate, reflecting diminishing returns to labour in agriculture. The right-hand panel shows the birth rate (B) and death rate (D) functions. When the wage is relatively high, say at W_1, the birth rate (B_1) exceeds the death rate (D_1), which in turn means that the population will grow. However, as population grows, the real wage must fall (as shown in the left-hand panel), so eventually the wage converges on $W\star$, which is an equilibrium situation.

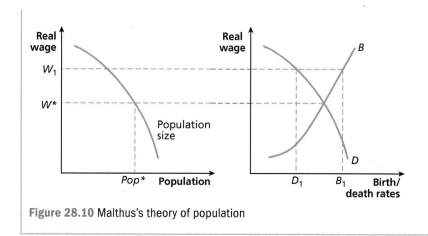

Figure 28.10 Malthus's theory of population

For these reasons, Malthus believed that it was not possible for a society to experience sustained increases in real wages, basically because the population was capable of exponential growth, while the food supply was capable of only arithmetic growth because of diminishing returns.

Although he was proved wrong (he had not anticipated the improvements in agricultural productivity that were to come), the question of whether population growth constitutes an obstacle to growth and development remains. At the heart of this is the debate about whether people should be regarded as key contributors to development, in their role as a factor of production, or as a drain on resources, consuming food, shelter, education and so on. Ultimately, the answer depends on the quantity of resources available relative to the population size.

Rapid population growth

In global terms, world population is growing at a rapid rate, by more than 80 million people per year. In November 1999 global population went through the 6 billion mark, and in October 2013 it reached 7 billion — that is, about seven times as many people as in 1800. But the growth is very unevenly distributed: countries like Germany and Japan are expected to experience declining populations in the period 2015–25, while sub-Saharan Africa's population continues to grow by 2.5% per annum. A country whose population is growing at 2.5% per annum will see a doubling in just 28 years, so the growing pressure on resources to provide education and healthcare is considerable. The proportion of the population aged below 15 is very high for much of sub-Saharan Africa.

The demographic transition

Demographic transition in developed countries
It has been observed that developed countries seem to have gone through a common pattern of population growth as their development progressed. This pattern has become known as the **demographic transition**, and is illustrated in Figure 28.11 for England and Wales between 1750 and 2000. This shows the birth rate and death rate for various years over this period. Remember that the natural rate of increase in population is given by the difference between these: the birth rate minus the death rate. (This ignores net migration.)

Key term

demographic transition process through which many countries have been observed to pass whereby improved health lowers the death rate, and the birth rate subsequently also falls, leading to a low and stable population growth

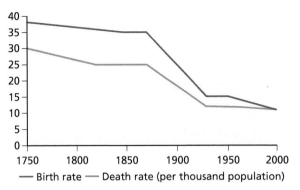

Source: D. Perkins et al., *The Economics of Development*, Norton/World Bank

Figure 28.11 The demographic transition in England and Wales, 1750–2000

Notice that between 1750 and 1820 the death rate fell more steeply than the birth rate, which means that the population growth rate accelerated in this period. This was the time when Britain was embarking on the Industrial Revolution, and corresponds to the early 'take-off' period of economic growth. At this stage the birth rate remains high. However, after 1870 there is a further fall in the death rate, accompanied by an even steeper fall in the birth rate, such that population growth slows down. You can see that by 2000 the natural population growth had shrunk to zero.

This demographic transition process has been displayed in most of the developed countries. The supporting story is that when the development process begins, death rates tend to fall as incomes begin to rise. In time families adapt to the change, and new social norms emerge in which the typical family size tends to get smaller. For example, as more women join the workforce, the opportunity cost of having children rises — by taking time out from careers to have children, their forgone earnings are now higher. This process has led to stability in population growth.

Demographic transition in developing countries

For countries that have undergone the demographic transition in a later period, things have not been so smooth. Figure 28.12 shows the pattern of the demographic transition for Sri Lanka, which is one of the countries that have achieved some stability in the rate of population growth. Here, it is not until after about 1920 that the death rate begins to fall — and it falls more steeply than it did in the early stages of economic growth in England and Wales. After 1950 it falls even more steeply, partly because methods of hygiene and modern medicine were able to bring the death rate down more rapidly.

Perhaps more crucially, the birth rate in Sri Lanka remained high for much longer — in other words, households' decisions about family size do not seem to have adjusted as rapidly as they did in England and Wales. This led to a period of relatively rapid population growth, before population stabilised.

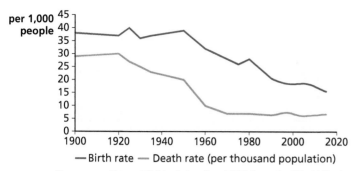

Source: as Figure 28.11; data after 1990 from the World Bank

Figure 28.12 The demographic transition in Sri Lanka, 1900–2015

For a number of countries in sub-Saharan Africa, death rates have fallen, but birth rates remain high, so the natural rate of population growth is also high. For example, in Malawi, the death rate fell from 8.9 per 1,000 people in 1990 to less than 7.5 in 2015, while the birth rate fell from 50 per 1,000 to 37.1, meaning that the natural population growth rate at the end of the period was 3% per annum.

Extension material: the microeconomics of fertility

To some extent, a household's choice of family size might be viewed as an externality issue. Figure 28.13 illustrates this. MPB (= MSB) represents the marginal benefit that the household receives from having different numbers of children (which is assumed to equal the marginal social benefit), and MPC represents the marginal private costs that are incurred. If education is subsidised, or if the household does not perceive the costs inflicted on society by having many children, then the marginal social cost of children (MSC) is higher than the marginal private cost.

Households will thus choose to have C_1 children, rather than the $C\star$ that is optimal for society. In other words, a choice of large family size might be interpreted as being a market failure. Note that this

discussion assumes that the household has the ability to choose its desired family size by having access to, and knowledge of, methods of contraception.

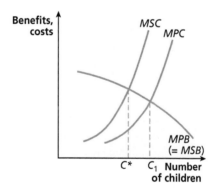

Figure 28.13 The microeconomics of fertility

Figure 28.14 shows fertility rates for the group of countries used earlier. Remember that the countries are in rank order of GNI per capita measured in PPP$. The fertility rate records the average number of births per woman. Thus, in Uganda the average number of births per woman is 5.7. Of course, this does not mean that the average number of children per family is so high, as not all the babies survive.

This pattern of high fertility has implications for the age structure of the population, leading to a high proportion of young dependants in the population. For example, in 2016, 48% of Uganda's population were aged 15 or less. This creates a strain on a country's limited resources, because of the need to provide education and healthcare for so many children, and in this sense high population growth can prove an obstacle to development.

Knowledge check 28.10

In Mali in 2016, 48% of the population were aged 15 years or less. What does this mean for the size of the workforce?

This argument might be countered by pointing out that people themselves are a resource for the country. However, it is a question of the balance between population and the availability of resources.

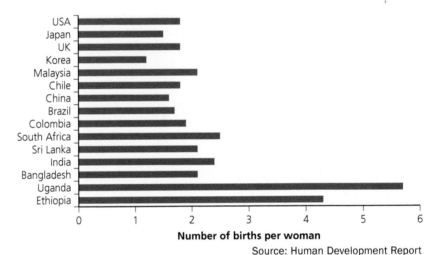

Source: Human Development Report

Figure 28.14 Total fertility rates, selected countries

Summary: demographic factors

- Early writers such as Malthus were pessimistic about the prospects for sustained development, believing that diminishing returns to labour would constrain economic growth.
- Globally, population is growing rapidly, with most of the increase taking place in developing countries.
- Developed countries and some developing countries have been seen to have passed through a demographic transition, such that population growth stabilises following decreases in death and birth rates.
- However, many developing countries have not completed the transition, remaining in the rapid population growth phase.
- Coupled with the age structure of the population, rapid population growth can create difficulties for developing countries because of the pressure on resources.

Exercise 28.3

Discuss the way in which the age structure of a population may influence the rate of economic growth and development.

Debt

For some developing countries, a major problem that had to be faced was that by the 1990s they had accumulated substantial amounts of outstanding international debt. This constituted a severe drain on resources, as export revenues had to be side-lined in order to keep up with debt repayments. This position became unsustainable for many countries, especially in sub-Saharan Africa.

> **Synoptic link**
>
> The measures introduced to cope with unsustainable debt levels are discussed in Chapter 29.

Access to credit and banking

For many developing countries, a particular problem has been the provision of finance for small (but important) projects in rural areas. Where a large portion of the population lives in the rural areas, the difficulty of raising funds for investment has been an impediment to improving agricultural productivity — in spite of the significance of this sector in many developing countries.

There are elements of market failure in rural credit markets. In particular, there is an information failure. In the absence of branch banking, people in the rural areas do not have access to the formal financial sector. The commercial banks based in the urban areas do not have the information needed to be able to assess loan applications for rural projects. Furthermore, property rights are not secure, so it may be difficult to provide collateral against loans when ownership of land cannot be proved.

> **Synoptic link**
>
> Information as a form of market failure was discussed in Chapter 7.

This means that many people in the rural areas are forced to depend on informal markets for credit, borrowing from local moneylenders or merchants at high, sometimes punitive, interest rates. The rates of interest in the informal sector tend to be much higher than are available in the formal sector, partly because of the risk premium, with it being difficult to assess the probability of default. In addition, local moneylenders may have monopoly power as people in a village may not be able to access other sources of finance.

Access to credit and banking is not only an issue in rural areas. Firms in urban areas also face problems in starting up new businesses, with lack of access to commercial banks and, in many cases, the lack of a stock market.

Infrastructure

Infrastructure covers a range of important facilities needed to support the development process. Transport and communications networks are needed to allow trading activity, as are market facilities. Schools, clinics and hospitals are needed if education and healthcare are to be provided to the population. The public good aspects of some types of infrastructure need to be borne in mind. The provision of transport and communications systems, or the improvement of market facilities to enable trading to take place, may be crucial for the smooth development of a country, but will be under-provided if left to the free market.

> **Key term**
>
> **infrastructure** the complex of physical capital goods needed to support development in the form of roads, communication networks, market, education and healthcare facilities etc.

Synoptic link

Public goods as a form of market failure were discussed in Chapter 7.

The lack of good infrastructure will be especially important for a developing country wanting to attract transnational companies to bring foreign direct investment. Such companies will not be prepared to operate in an economy where the transport and communications infrastructure is inadequate to allow efficient and effective trade to take place.

Knowledge check 28.11

Explain why some infrastructure facilities may be regarded as public goods.

Education and skills

For a developing country wishing to develop its manufacturing activity, there is then a need for skilled labour with which to operate capital goods. In other words, human capital in the form of skilled, healthy and well-trained workers is as important as physical capital if investment is to be productive.

In principle, it could be thought that today's developing countries have an advantage over the countries that developed in earlier periods. In particular, they can learn from earlier mistakes, and import technology that has already been developed, rather than having to develop it anew. This suggests that a convergence process should be going on, whereby developing countries are able to adopt technology that has already been produced, and thereby grow more rapidly and begin to close the gap with the more developed countries.

However, by and large this has not been happening, and a lack of human capital has been suggested as one of the key reasons for the failure. This underlines the importance of education in laying the foundations for economic growth as well as contributing directly to the quality of life.

In the case of the tiger economies, their education systems had been well established, either through the British colonial legacy (in the case of Singapore and Hong Kong) or through past Japanese occupation periods (in Taiwan and South Korea). In all of these countries, education received high priority, and cultural influences encouraged a high demand for education. The tiger economies thus benefited from having highly skilled and well-disciplined labour forces that were able to make effective use of the capital goods that had been acquired.

A problem for many developing countries is that people do not fully perceive the future benefits to be gained from educating their children, so they will demand less education than is desirable for society. In many rural areas, it is common for education to be undervalued in this way, and for drop-out rates from schooling to be high. This may arise both from a failure to perceive the potential future benefits that children will derive from education, and from the high opportunity cost of education in villages where child labour is widespread.

Knowledge check 28.12

What form of market failure is present when people do not send their children to school?

The situation in many countries has been worsened by poor curriculum design, whereby the legacy of colonial rule was a school system and curriculum not well directed at providing the sort of education likely to be of most benefit within the context of a developing country. Furthermore, there tended to be a bias towards providing funds to the tertiary sector (which benefits mainly the rich elites within society) rather than trying to ensure that all children received at least primary education.

The benefits from developing people as resources may overflow into other component areas: for example, through an increase in labour productivity — if healthy and educated people are able to work better — or by ensuring that products are better able to meet international standards, thereby reinforcing linkages with the rest of the world.

The impact of HIV/AIDS

The HIV/AIDS epidemic had a major impact on developing countries, especially those in sub-Saharan Africa. There, the prevalence of the disease became unimaginably high during the epidemic: for example, in Botswana it was estimated that in 2003 some 37.3% of the population aged 15–49 were affected; and in Swaziland the prevalence rate was 38.8%. The repercussions of the disease are especially marked because of its impact on people of working age. This affected the size of the labour force, and left many orphans with little hope of receiving an education, which in turn has implications for the productivity of future generations. Even after the height of the epidemic had passed, the effects lingered: in 2016 Botswana was still showing a prevalence rate of 21.9% and in Swaziland the rate was 27.2%.

Governments reacted to the disease in very different ways. In countries where the government was open about the onset of the disease and has striven to promote safe sex, the chances of keeping the disease under control are much higher. For example, in 1990, the incidence of HIV/AIDS among adults in Thailand and South Africa was similar, at about 1%. Thailand confronted the problem through a widespread public campaign such that, by 2001, the incidence was still about 1%. South Africa did little to stop the spread of the disease, with the president choosing to downplay the problem and the minister of health recommending beetroot as a treatment.

> **Synoptic link**
>
> Thailand's approach here could be seen as an illustration of the application of behavioural economics via nudge theory, which was discussed in Chapter 5.

In 2005, the incidence of the disease in South Africa was estimated to be nearly 20%. Some other governments have also kept silent, perhaps not wanting to admit that it is a problem, and here the disease has run rampant. There may also have been problems in measuring the incidence of HIV/AIDS accurately, as individuals may be hesitant to seek treatment or to report that they have the disease for fear of social stigma. The incidence of the disease has been in decline, but in 2016 the incidence of HIV/AIDS among adults aged 15–49 in the developing countries of sub-Saharan Africa was still 4.3%.

Property rights

It has been noted that the lack of property rights may prevent individuals from obtaining credit, as commercial banks tend to insist on collateral to safeguard their loans. The legal framework that ensures secure rights over property is undeveloped in many developing countries. This not only creates difficulty in gaining credit, but also affects the incentives that people have to invest. For example, if an individual has no established ownership over a piece of land, there is no incentive to invest in improving its productivity.

Non-economic factors

In addition to the economic issues discussed, developing countries face a variety of challenges and circumstances that can help or hinder growth and development.

Governance and corruption

For many reasons, good governance is vital for growth and development. For a developing country to make the best use of its resources, there needs to be a framework in which a responsible government is able to provide an environment for growth, allowing markets to work effectively wherever possible, but being able to intervene where necessary to correct market failures.

Where governments have raised funds for development purposes, through borrowing or from aid donors, it has sometimes been the case that such funds have been employed for prestige projects, which impress lenders (or donors) but do little to further development. Other funds have been diverted into private use by government officials, and there are well-documented examples of politicians, officials and civil servants who have accumulated personal fortunes at the expense of the development of their countries. Figure 28.15 presents a Corruption Perception Index, produced regularly by the non-governmental organisation Transparency International since 1995. Notice again how Singapore and South Korea, the tiger economies, score as being 'highly clean' — indeed, on this index Singapore was the sixth least corrupt nation in the world.

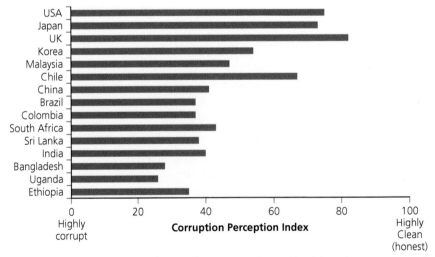

Source: Transparency International (www.transparency.org)

Figure 28.15 Perceptions of corruption, selected countries, 2017

There is a need to be careful with such indicators, for by its nature corruption is difficult to identify and to measure. Corruption may be disguised more successfully in some countries than in others. Nonetheless, the way in which firms and governments perceive the relative state of corruption in different countries may affect their decisions on where to locate foreign direct investment or provide overseas assistance.

Tendencies towards corruption are likely to be more significant in countries where there is relatively little political stability, so that the government in power knows it will not remain in power for long. Even in the absence of corruption, this discourages such governments from taking a long-term perspective and encourages short-termism.

The lack of effective tax collection infrastructure may make it difficult for the government to raise funds. Even with sound governance, there is a tendency for bureaucracy to impede the development process. For example, Figure 28.16 shows the time that is needed to set up a new business in our sample of countries. Brazil is clearly an outlier in this figure, but notice the observations for the lower-income countries shown.

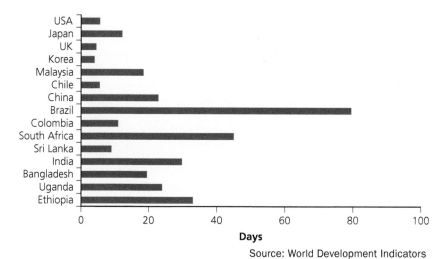

Source: World Development Indicators

Figure 28.16 Time required to set up a business (days)

Economic instability

It is argued that stability in the macroeconomy is important in order to encourage investment. If the macroeconomic environment is unstable, firms will not be sufficiently confident of the future to want to risk investing in projects. In addition, if the government becomes overactive in the economy, this may starve the private sector of resources.

A key aim for a developing country should be to ensure that prices can act as effective signals in guiding resource allocation. If overall inflation is allowed to get out of hand, then allocative efficiency cannot be expected. On the other hand, a stable macroeconomy should serve to improve the operation of microeconomic markets. An economy that is stable should also be better able to withstand external shocks.

Synoptic link

The potential problems caused by hyperinflation were discussed in Chapter 15. Some issues relating to financial markets in emerging and developing economies are discussed in Chapter 30.

Knowledge check 28.13

Why might a government intervene to fix food prices in urban areas?

If prices can act as signals this can then create a climate for enterprise, enabling people to exploit their capabilities. In the past, many governments in developing countries have tended to intervene strongly in markets, distorting prices away from market equilibrium values — especially food prices, which were often kept artificially low in urban areas, thus damaging farmers' incentives. In addition, it is important to encourage the development of financial markets that will act to channel savings into productive investment.

Civil and international conflict

In sub-Saharan Africa, in particular, there have been further problems resulting from civil or international conflicts. These have often had the effect of diverting resources away from development priorities. If the government of a country does not expect to be in power for very long, it has little incentive to develop policies to stimulate development in the long term, but will concentrate on gaining short-run popularity in the hope of hanging onto power. In some cases in Africa, civil conflict has lasted for decades, and this also may discourage firms and individuals from undertaking much-needed investment.

Political stability

Political stability can promote development by encouraging leaders to take a long-term view. This was the case for Singapore, where Lee Kuan Yu, who was prime minister from 1957 until 1991, guided the economy through a period of rapid growth and development. However, political stability by itself does not guarantee success — as demonstrated by the case of Zimbabwe, where Robert Mugabe enjoyed a long period of rule until 2018, but demolished rather than built up the economy.

In the case of the tiger economies, the government did have a strong influence — although less so in the case of Hong Kong. In Singapore the government kept a tight rein on the macroeconomy, encouraged savings, nurtured the education system, guided the development of key strategic sectors in the economy and provided good infrastructure for trade and industry, as well as maintaining an open economy. In South Korea the government subsidised the development of large conglomerate firms that provided the foundations for economic growth.

Geography

It is important to remember that developing countries vary considerably in many ways, not least in their geographic location and character. Land-locked economies such as Uganda face challenges with transport and trading. Some countries are dominated by adverse conditions such as arid desert lands or mountainous terrain. Others may have fertile and favourable climatic conditions, or advantageous strategic locations. These natural disadvantages and advantages may of course influence the prospects for growth and development.

Summary: other factors influencing development

- Some developing countries found themselves facing unsustainable levels of international debt that they could not repay without hindering development.
- In many developing countries, the provision of credit and banking in rural areas has been a major challenge.
- Infrastructure is important to enable growth and development to take place.
- Education and skills training is crucial in enabling the development of human capital.
- The HIV/AIDS epidemic hindered development in many countries, especially in sub-Saharan Africa.
- Inadequate property rights can also hinder the growth process.
- Non-economic factors have also been a challenge, including problems of weak governance, corruption and economic and political instability.

Exercise 28.4

Which of the following can be seen as impediments to growth?

a A lack of savings resulting from low per capita incomes
b Underdeveloped financial markets
c Lack of confidence in financial assets and institutions
d Low real interest rates
e Shortage of entrepreneurs
f Inadequate infrastructure
g Low levels of human capital
h Foreign exchange shortage
i Limited government resources
j Weak governance and civil conflict

Which of these factors are likely to be present in developing countries?

Contrasting patterns of development

The East Asian experience

The rapid growth achieved by the East Asian tiger economies was undoubtedly impressive, and held out hope that other developing countries could begin to close the gap in living standards. Indeed, the term 'East Asian miracle' was coined to describe how quickly these economies had been able to develop. At the heart of the success were four countries: Hong Kong, Singapore, South Korea and Taiwan; others, such as Malaysia and Thailand, were not far behind.

How was their success achieved?

None of these countries enjoys a rich supply of natural resources. Indeed, Hong Kong and Singapore are small city-states whose only natural resources are their excellent harbours and strategic locations; they both have small populations.

The tigers soon realised that to develop manufacturing industry it would be crucial to tap into economies of scale. This meant producing on a scale that would far outstrip the size of their domestic markets — which meant that they would have to rely on international trade.

export-led growth
situation in which economic growth is achieved through the exploitation of economies of scale, made possible by focusing on exports and so reaching a wider market than would be available within the domestic economy

By being very open to international trade and focusing on export markets, the tigers were able to sell to a larger market, and thereby improve their efficiency through economies of scale. This enabled them to enjoy a period of **export-led growth**. In other words, the tiger economies expanded by selling their exports to the rest of the world, and building a reputation for high-quality merchandise. This was helped by their judicious choice of markets on which to focus: they chose to move into areas of economic activity that were being vacated by the more developed nations, which were moving up to new sorts of product.

The export-led growth hypothesis explains part of the success of the tiger economies, but there were other contributing factors. The tiger economies nurtured their human capital and attracted foreign investment. Their governments intervened to influence the direction of the economies but also encouraged markets to operate effectively, fostering macroeconomic and political stability and developing good infrastructure. Moreover, these countries embarked on their growth period at a time when world trade overall was buoyant.

Hong Kong harbour — by being open to international trade and focusing on export markets, the tiger economies were able to sell to a larger market

Sub-Saharan Africa

The experience of countries in sub–Saharan Africa is in total contrast to the success story of the tiger economies. Even accepting the limitations of the GNI per capita measure, the fact that GNI per capita was lower in the region as a whole in 2000 than it had been in 1975 (or even earlier) paints a depressing picture. Can sub–Saharan Africa learn from the experience of the tiger economies?

Part of the explanation for the failure of growth in this region lies in the fact that sub-Saharan Africa lacks many of the positive features that enabled the tiger economies to grow. Export-led growth is less easy for countries that have specialised in the production of goods for which demand is not buoyant. Furthermore, it is not straightforward to develop new specialisations if human and physical capital levels are low, the skills for new activities are lacking and poverty is rife. Encouraging development when there is political instability, and when markets do not operate effectively, is a major challenge.

Latin America

Countries in Latin America followed yet another path. There was a period in which the economies of Argentina, Brazil and Mexico, among others, were able to grow rapidly, enabling them to qualify as 'newly industrialised economies'. However, such growth could not be sustained in the face of the high rates of inflation that afflicted many of the countries in this region, especially during the 1980s. Indeed, many of them experienced bouts of hyperinflation, inhibiting economic growth.

In part this reflected fiscal indiscipline, with governments undertaking high levels of expenditure which they financed by printing money. In many cases, countries in this region have tended to be relatively closed to international trade. International debt reached unsustainable levels, and continued to haunt countries such as Argentina, which in 2005 offered its creditors about 33% of the value of its outstanding debt. Around three-quarters of the creditors accepted the deal, knowing that otherwise they would probably get nothing at all.

Synoptic link

The BRIC countries were discussed in the context of globalisation in Chapter 24.

Summary: contrasting patterns of development

- A small group of countries in South East Asia, known as the East Asian tiger economies, underwent a period of rapid economic growth, closing the gap on the more developed countries.
- This success arose from a combination of circumstances, including a high degree of openness to international trade, which was seen as crucial if economies of scale were to be reaped.
- However, the tigers are also characterised by high levels of human capital and political and macroeconomic stability.
- In contrast, countries in sub-Saharan Africa have stagnated; in some cases, real per capita incomes were lower in 2000 than they had been in 1975.
- Countries in Latin America began well, experiencing growth for a period, but then ran into economic difficulties.
- The BRIC countries have enjoyed recent success in economic growth.

Exercise 28.5

Looking back over the nature of the economic growth process and the obstacles to growth that have been outlined, discuss the extent to which countries in sub-Saharan Africa may be able to use the pattern of development that was used so successfully in East Asia to promote growth.

Study tip

This chapter has outlined some of the common obstacles to economic growth and development. However, always remember that all countries are different, so you need to avoid making broad generalisations that assume that all developing countries are the same. Each faces a different profile of problems and characteristics.

HIV/AIDS and the macroeconomy

Since the beginning of the HIV/AIDS epidemic, the World Health Organization (WHO) has estimated that more than 70 million people has been infected with the virus — and some 35 million people have died from HIV. At the end of 2016, there were 36.7 million people (including 2.1 million children) living with HIV, with 1.8 million people becoming newly infected in 2016 globally, including 160,000 children.

The overall number of people living with HIV continued to increase, partly because of the ongoing number of new infections, but also because antiretroviral therapy was having beneficial effects in keeping those infected alive for longer. However, only about 25% of pregnant women living with HIV in low- and middle-income countries received medicine to prevent transmission of HIV to their babies.

The geographic concentration of the disease was high, with some two-thirds of all people living with HIV in sub-Saharan Africa. As many as 67% of new infections are in Africa.

HIV has a number of macroeconomic effects, and it has been estimated that the disease is likely to reduce growth in high-prevalence countries by between 0.5% and 1.5% over 10–20 years. It can also widen economic inequality.

In part, this reflects the fact that HIV/AIDS reduces life expectancy, which in turn may reduce economic growth, through its effects on education, saving and fertility.

There are also likely to be direct effects. Most obviously, there is an effect on the productivity of those affected, especially on unskilled workers in labouring jobs. The disease also affects the rate of absenteeism. Furthermore, HIV/AIDS does not affect all age groups in society equally, which has an effect on the dependency ratio (that is, the percentage of the population who depend on those who are in work). If productivity falls, then this reduces the rate of return on investment in both human and physical capital, and a high prevalence rate may deter foreign investment.

A concern for the future is that in 2013 young people between the ages of 15 and 24 accounted for some 33% of all new HIV infections, and survey data from 64 countries indicated that only 40% of males and 38% of females had accurate and comprehensive knowledge about HIV and how to avoid its transmission. This information failure may be viewed as a form of market failure, but all too often the policy response in some countries has failed to address it.

An AIDS awareness billboard in Malawi

Follow-up questions

a The passage indicates that HIV/AIDS reduces life expectancy, and that this has three economic effects. Using the following hints, explain how these effects occur.
Hint 1 (education): the decision to invest in education depends partly on the expected rate of return in terms of future expected income. What effect does a fall in life expectancy have on the expected future stream of income?
Hint 2 (saving): think about the motivation to save. This may include precautionary saving for old age.
Hint 3 (fertility): one of the main ways in which HIV is transmitted is from mother to child; if more children are expected not to survive, how would this affect fertility?

b Explain the macroeconomic effects of lower education and savings, and higher fertility.

c Explain why a fall in productivity may have detrimental economic effects.

d Explain how policy could be better designed to combat information failure.

29 Strategies influencing growth and development

Strategies influencing growth and development

The previous chapter dealing with economic development referred to the limited resources that are available within developing countries, which have constrained attempts to stimulate economic growth and development. A key question in this context is whether the government of a developing country can rely on market-oriented strategies, or whether a more interventionist stance may be needed. This chapter explores strategies of each of these types.

Learning outcomes

After studying this chapter, you should:
→ be familiar with possible market-oriented strategies for growth and development
→ understand the benefits and costs associated with foreign direct investment
→ be familiar with possible interventionist strategies for growth and development
→ appreciate the potential use of overseas assistance for promoting development, and the effectiveness of such flows of funds in the past
→ be aware of the possible use of borrowing to obtain funds for development and its dangers
→ understand the role of the Bretton Woods institutions in international development
→ be familiar with the HIPC Initiative

▌ Market-friendly growth?

The World Bank has promoted the notion that policies for growth should be market-friendly. The core idea of this is that markets should be allowed to work without government intervention wherever this is possible, but that governments should intervene when there is a need to correct market failure. One way of looking at this is that **market-oriented strategies** should be adopted in situations when it is possible for markets to work effectively. However, there may be situations in which markets cannot be expected to be effective, and in such circumstances **interventionist strategies** will be required.

In all of this discussion, it is important to remember that developing countries have diverse characteristics, so that a one-size-fits-all approach is not likely to be successful. Different countries face different configurations of obstacles and opportunities, so need different policies and strategies.

The shortage of resources in many developing countries has been a severe obstacle to their economic growth and development. This was emphasised by the Harrod–Domar model of economic growth, depicted in Figure 28.9 on page 495.

The underlying process by which growth can take place requires the generation of a flow of savings that can be transformed into investment in order to generate an increase in capital, which in turn enlarges the productive capacity of the economy. This then enables output and incomes to grow, which in turn feeds back into savings

Key terms

market-oriented strategy a strategy for encouraging development that relies on enabling markets to work effectively

interventionist strategy a strategy for stimulating development that focuses on addressing market failure

and allows the process to become self-sustaining. However, the process will break down if savings are inadequate, or if markets do not operate sufficiently well to maintain the chain.

Knowledge check 29.1

Give two reasons why markets may fail to allow savings to be transformed into investment in the Harrod–Domar model.

Market-oriented strategies for growth and development

Many markets in developing countries are seen to be missing or underdeveloped. These include some parts of the economy, such as financial markets, which are crucial in ensuring a flow of funds to the sectors that need to invest in order to allow economic growth to take place. Internal product markets may also be ineffective, not to mention the markets that facilitate international trade, which allow a developing country to earn much-needed foreign exchange.

Trade liberalisation

A contentious issue over many years has been that of trade liberalisation — whether countries should remove barriers to international trade in order to look for potential gains.

Synoptic link

Chapter 25 discussed the relative merits of free trade and protectionism and examined the effects of a tariff.

It is important for developing countries to be able to adopt an appropriate trade policy if they are to reap these potential gains. In turn, trade is important because developing countries need to be able to obtain foreign exchange with which to import the capital and technology that is needed to transform the structure of the domestic economy.

Tariffs impose a welfare cost on the country that imposes them, but will liberalising trade by removing tariff and non-tariff barriers benefit developing countries? In spite of the arguments in favour of free trade, developing countries may not always gain by opening up to global competition. A developing producer seeking to sell in a global market is likely to find itself facing stiff competition from well-established producers, often with market power as well as superior experience of trading globally.

Knowledge check 29.2

Give an example of a non-tariff barrier that may make it difficult for a developing producer to compete in the global market.

Foreign direct investment

One possible source of external funding that has been attractive to many developing countries is foreign direct investment (FDI). This entails encouraging transnational companies (TNCs) to set up part of their production in a developing country.

Synoptic link

Transnational companies were introduced during the discussion of globalisation in Chapter 24.

In evaluating the potential impact of TNCs operating in developing countries, it is important to consider the characteristics of such companies. Many operate on a large scale, often having an annual turnover that exceeds the less developed country's GDP. They tend to have their origins in the developed countries, although some developing countries are now beginning to develop their own TNCs.

TNCs are in business to make profits, and it can be assumed that their motivation is to maximise global after-tax profits. While they may operate in globally oligopolistic markets, they may have monopoly power within the developing countries in which they locate. They operate in a wide variety of different product markets — some are in primary production (Geest, Del Monte, BP), some are in manufacturing (General Motors, Mitsubishi) and some are in tertiary activity (McDonald's). These characteristics are important in shaping the analysis of the likely benefits and costs of attracting FDI into a developing country.

Chapter 24 identified three basic motivations for TNCs to locate in another country: looking for markets, resources or efficiency — or some combination of the three, of course.

Potential benefits

Perhaps the prime motivation for developing countries in seeking to attract FDI inflows is the injection they provide into the Harrod–Domar chain of development.

Synoptic link

The Harrod–Domar model was discussed in Chapter 28.

In addition to providing investment, TNCs are likely to supply capital and technology, thereby helping to remedy the country's limited capacity to produce capital goods. They may also assist with the development of the country's human capital, by providing training and skills development for the workers they employ, together with management expertise and entrepreneurial skills, all of which may be lacking in the country.

Developing countries may also hope that the TNC will provide much-needed modern sector jobs by employing local workers. Given the rate of migration to the urban areas discussed in Chapter 27, such employment could be invaluable to the country, where employment cannot keep up with the rapid growth of the labour force.

The government may also expect to be able to collect tax revenues, both directly from the TNC in the form of a tax on profits and indirectly from taxes on the workers' employment incomes. Moreover, the TNC will export its products, and thus generate a flow of foreign exchange for the country.

In time, there may also be spillover effects. As local workers learn new skills and gain management expertise and knowledge about technology, they may be able to benefit local firms if at some stage they leave the TNC and take up jobs with local companies — or use their new-found knowledge to start their own businesses. These effects can be significant in some cases.

Potential costs

In evaluating the potential benefits of FDI, however, developing countries may need to temper their enthusiasm a little, as there may be some costs associated with attracting TNCs to locate within their borders. This is certainly the case if the anti-globalisation protesters are to be believed, as they have accused the TNCs of exploiting their strength and market power in order to damage the developing countries in various ways.

In examining such costs, it is important to try to reach a balanced view and to be aware that some of the accusations made by the critics of globalisation may have been overstated. On the other hand, it is also important to remember that TNCs are profit-making firms, and not humanitarian organisations seeking to promote justice and equality.

> ### Study tip
>
> Be careful not to confuse FDI by TNCs with overseas assistance — TNCs are not charitable organisations!

Employment effects

An important consideration is whether the TNC will make significant use of local labour. It might hire local unskilled labour, but use expatriate skilled workers and managers. Some TNCs may in any case be relatively capital-intensive in their production methods. This would tend to reduce the employment and spillover effects of the TNC presence. Another possibility is that the TNC may pay wages that are higher than necessary in order to maintain a good public image, and to attract the best local workers. This is fine for the workers lucky enough to be employed at a high wage, but it can make life difficult for local firms if they cannot hold on to their best workers.

Tax revenue

In addition, the government's desire for tax revenue may not be fully met. In seeking to attract TNCs to locate within their borders, developing countries may find that they need to offer tax holidays or concessions as a 'carrot'. This will clearly limit the tax revenue benefits that the country will receive. It is also possible for TNCs to manipulate their balance sheets in order to minimise their tax liability. A high proportion of the transactions undertaken by an TNC are internal to the firm. Thus, it may be possible to set prices for internal transactions that ensure that profits are taken in the locations with the lowest tax. This process is known as transfer pricing. It is not strictly legal, but is difficult to monitor.

> ### Knowledge check 29.3
>
> Why might it be difficult to monitor the practice of transfer pricing?

Foreign exchange earnings

As far as the foreign exchange earnings are concerned, a key issue is whether the TNC will recycle its surplus within the country or repatriate its profits to its shareholders elsewhere in the world. If the latter is the case, this will limit the extent to which the country will benefit from the increase in exports. However, at least the TNC will be able to market its products internationally, and if the country becomes better known as a result then, again, there may be spillovers for local firms. Gaining credibility and the knowledge to sell in the global market is problematic for developing countries, and this is one area in which there may be definite benefits from the TNC presence.

TNCs' market power

The country should also be aware that the TNC may use its market power within the country to maximise profits. Local competitors will find it difficult to compete, and the TNC may be able to restrict output and raise price. In addition, TNCs have been accused of taking advantage of more lax environmental regulations, polluting the environment to keep their costs low. The actions of the anti-globalisation protesters in this area may have influenced TNCs to clean up their act somewhat by encouraging an awareness of corporate social responsibility.

Location

Finally, TNCs tend to locate in urban areas in developing countries — unless they are purely resource seeking, in which case they may be forced to locate near the supply of whatever natural resource they are seeking. Locating in the urban areas may increase inequality between the rural and urban areas, which has been a problem in some developing countries.

Exercise 29.1

Draw up a list of the benefits and costs of TNC involvement in a developing country, and evaluate the benefits relative to the costs. Remember that many developing countries are enthusiastic about attracting TNCs to locate in their countries. Try to identify which are the most important benefits that they are seeking.

Given the need to evaluate the benefits and costs of FDI flows, it is important that governments can negotiate good deals with the TNCs. For example, countries such as Indonesia have negotiated conditions on the proportion of local workers who will be employed by the TNC after a period of years. This helps to ensure that the benefits are not entirely dissipated. Of course, it helps if the country has some key resource that the TNC cannot readily acquire elsewhere. There is some recent evidence that high levels of human capital help to attract FDI flows, which may help to explain why East Asia and China have been recipients of more FDI inflows than countries in sub-Saharan Africa.

Summary: foreign direct investment

- Transnational companies (TNCs) are companies whose production activities are carried out in more than one country.
- Foreign direct investment (FDI) by TNCs is one way in which a developing country may be able to attract external resources.
- TNCs may be motivated by markets, resources or cost effectiveness.
- Developing countries hope to benefit from FDI in a wide range of ways, including capital, technology, employment, human capital, tax revenues and foreign exchange. There may also be spillover effects.
- However, TNCs may operate in ways that do not maximise these benefits.

Reducing government involvement

Attracting foreign TNCs to bring investment into a country is one way of giving a boost to the working of markets within developing countries. It is also important to ensure that governments themselves do not intervene in ways that distort the working of markets — for example, by subsidising firms in some sectors or controlling prices. This has been a failing in many countries, reflecting the way that governments in the past have tended to intervene inappropriately. For example, many governments have been tempted to try to fix prices of goods, rather than allowing market forces to dictate prices. This can then have unintended effects on incentives. If a government decides to hold food prices down in the urban areas, in order to help the urban poor (or to keep their electorates happy), this then distorts the market and provides insufficient incentive for farmers.

In some developing countries, the government has intervened through subsidising firms or operating state-owned enterprises that have become inefficient and rent-seeking. Removal of subsidies may encourage firms to become more competitive. Privatisation of state-owned enterprises could be one way of improving incentives towards efficiency.

Knowledge check 29.4

Why would the removal of subsidies encourage firms to become more competitive?

Synoptic link

Notice that the arguments set out in Chapter 5 concerning subsidies and in Chapter 23 relating to privatisation are pertinent here in the context of developing countries.

Liberalising exchange rates

Some developing countries have operated a fixed exchange rate system, fixing the value of the currency, usually against the US dollar. Although this may reduce uncertainty and enforce fiscal discipline, there may be distortionary effects if the country fixes the currency at a level that is away from its equilibrium.

Synoptic link

The advantages and disadvantages of a fixed exchange rate system are discussed in Chapter 26.

A country that has held its exchange rate above its equilibrium value may benefit from adopting a floating exchange rate regime, and allowing the exchange rate to find its own value in international markets. As the rate moves towards equilibrium, the country should experience an increase in demand for its exports, which will have become more competitive with devaluation. However, in the short run, problems could arise if supply is inelastic — in other words, if domestic producers cannot respond quickly to the increase in demand, the result could be inflationary pressure and a rising deficit on the current account of the balance of payments. Hopefully, this should improve in the long run, but the short-run costs could damage the credibility of the policy.

Microfinance schemes

Chapter 28 noted that the provision of rural credit is a particular problem in many developing countries. Attempts have been made to remedy this situation through **microfinance** schemes. This approach was pioneered by the Grameen

Key term

microfinance schemes that provide finance for small-scale projects in developing countries

Bank, which was founded in Bangladesh in 1976. The bank made small-scale loans to groups of women who otherwise would have had no access to credit, and each group was made corporately responsible for paying back the loan. The scheme has claimed great success, both in terms of the constructive use of the funds in getting small-scale projects off the ground and in terms of high pay-back rates.

The Grameen Bank

In 1974 a severe famine afflicted Bangladesh, and a flood of starving people converged on the capital city, Dhaka. Muhammad Yunus was an economics professor at Chittagong University. He tells how he was struck by the extreme contrast between the neat and abstract economic theories that he was teaching, and the plight and suffering of those surviving in bare poverty, and suffering and dying in the famine.

He also tells how he decided to study the problem at first hand, taking his students on field trips into villages near to the campus. On one of these visits they interviewed a woman who was struggling to make a living by making bamboo stools. For each stool that she made, she had to borrow the equivalent of 15p for the raw materials. Once she had paid back the loan, at interest rates of up to 10% per week, her profit margin was just 1p. The woman was never able to escape from her situation because she was trapped by the need to borrow, and the need to pay back at such punitive rates of interest. Her story was by no means unique, and Yunus was keen to find a way of enabling women like her to have access to credit on conditions that would allow them to escape from poverty. He began experimenting by lending out some of his own money to groups in need.

Muhammad Yunus launched the Grameen Bank experiment in 1976. The idea was to provide credit for small-scale income-generating activities. Loans would be provided without the need for collateral, with borrowers being required to form themselves into groups of five with joint responsibility for the repayments. The acceptance of this joint responsibility and the lack of collateral helped to minimise the transaction costs of making and monitoring the loans.

On any criteria, the project proved an enormous success. The repayment record has been impressive, although the Grameen Bank charges interest rates close to those in the formal commercial sector, which are much lower than those of the informal moneylenders. Since the initial launch of the bank, lending has been channelled primarily to women borrowers, who are seen to invest more carefully and to repay more reliably — and to be most in need.

By the end of May 1998 more than $2.4 billion had been loaned by Grameen Bank, including more than 2 million loans for milch cows, nearly 100,000 for rickshaws, 57,000 for sewing machines and many more for processing, agriculture, trading, shop keeping, peddling and other activities. Grameen-type credit programmes are now operating in 59 countries in Africa, Asia, the Americas, Europe and Papua New Guinea. By 2011, Grameen had 8.349 million borrowers (97% of whom were women), covering 81,379 villages.

As for the impact of Grameen loans in economic terms, the loans are seen to have generated new employment, to have reduced the number of days workers are inactive, and to have raised income, food consumption and living conditions of Grameen Bank members — not to mention their social impact on the lives of millions of women. Muhammad Yunus and the Grameen Bank were awarded the Nobel Peace Prize in 2006.

A member from the Grameen bank collects money from the borrowers

ROSCAS

Other schemes have involved groups of households coming together to pool their savings in order to accumulate enough funds to launch small projects. Members of the group take it in turns to use these joint savings, paying the loan back in order for the next person to have a turn. These are known as *rotating savings and credit schemes* (ROSCAS), and they have had some success in providing credit on a small scale. In spite of assisting some successful enterprises, however, such schemes have been found to be less sustainable than Grameen-style arrangements, and have tended to be used to obtain consumer durable goods rather than for productive investment and innovation.

In the absence of such schemes, households may be forced to borrow from local moneylenders, often at very high rates of interest. In part this may reflect a high risk of the borrower's defaulting, but it may also reflect the ability of local moneylenders to use market power. The absence of insurance markets may also deter borrowing for productive investment, especially in rural areas.

There is limited arbitrage between the formal and informal sectors, and institutions in the formal sector may find it difficult to gain information that they would need to make loans available.

Knowledge check 29.5

What is meant by 'arbitrage' in this context? (Hint: the concept of arbitrage was introduced in Chapter 19, in the context of price discrimination.)

Study tip

Notice that it may be useful to be able to relate these problems in providing credit for small projects in rural areas to issues of market failure.

How successful has the microfinance movement been? The Grameen Bank has provided finance to many people in many parts of the world. Attempts to replicate the Grameen model have also had some success, but in many cases have struggled to be sustainable in funding terms, needing support from governments or non-governmental organisations (NGOs).

Privatisation

In many developing countries state-owned enterprises are common. These are often inefficient and poorly-run, so countries have often been advised to privatise such enterprises so that they can be managed more effectively. This policy remains controversial, given the relative lack of managerial and entrepreneurial expertise in many developing countries. Furthermore, many countries lack the administrative infrastructure that would allow monitoring and regulation of privatised enterprises.

Summary: rural credit and privatisation

- The provision of credit in developing countries is problematic, especially in rural areas.
- This is partly due to forms of market failure.
- Microfinance is one way in which attempts have been made to provide credit for small projects in developing countries.
- The Grameen Bank in Bangladesh pioneered such schemes, using group-lending schemes focusing on women.
- Other schemes have included rotating savings and credit schemes.
- In the absence of access to formal credit arrangements, the informal market operates, charging high interest rates relative to the formal sector.
- Privatisation has often been recommended to many developing countries with large numbers of state-owned enterprises, but the effectiveness of this strategy is unproven.

Interventionist strategies

Where markets cannot be made to work effectively, governments may need to adopt a more interventionist approach.

Development of human capital

The importance of human resources in the process of growth and development has already been highlighted. For many developing countries, labour is relatively abundant — at least relative to physical capital — but in many cases the potential is not being realised. Investment in human capital is crucial in many developing countries in order to facilitate development.

Education, training and healthcare

Education and training is needed in order to raise agricultural productivity, and to provide a skilled labour force that enables the growth of modern sector economic activity such as manufacturing industry — and for the increased utilisation of technology. Certainly the absence of skilled labour is a substantial obstacle to economic growth. However, human capital does not only involve education and training, important as that is. For many developing countries, improved provision of nutrition and healthcare can be equally important in raising the productivity of workers — and in contributing directly to the quality of life.

An important question in the context of a market-friendly approach to growth and development is whether markets can be relied on to ensure the appropriate provision of education and healthcare, or whether there is some form of market failure that requires government intervention.

In the case of both education and healthcare, it can be argued that there are significant externality effects. In the case of education, it has been shown that there are spillover effects, in the sense that a group of educated workers cooperating together becomes more productive because the members of the group interact with each other. This implies that the marginal social benefits of education exceed the marginal private benefits — because society gains from the way in which workers are able to work together.

In terms of healthcare, consider the example of a vaccination programme against a communicable disease. An individual may perceive that the marginal benefit of having their child vaccinated is relatively low, because the probability of becoming infected may be low. However, if everyone thinks in the same way, this increases the likelihood of there being an epidemic of the disease. Thus the social benefits that arise from a vaccination programme may exceed the private benefits — so in the absence of intervention, too few individuals will invest in vaccination.

> **Synoptic link**
>
> Externality effects were discussed in Chapter 6; other forms of market failure were discussed in Chapter 7.

Information failures

There may also be information failures in education and healthcare. A poor rural household may not perceive the full benefits of education — especially where uneducated parents are taking decisions on behalf of their children. They may then decide to keep their children out of school, perhaps believing that the benefits to the household from child labour exceed the benefits of sending their children to school. In many developing countries, there has been a tendency to keep female children away from school, as the household may not see any benefit from female education. In healthcare, there may also be situations in which households do not understand the potential benefits from medical treatment (especially preventative treatment), or may not perceive the value of good nutrition.

> **Knowledge check 29.6**
>
> How might a government encourage higher take-up of education by females?

Given these arguments about market failure, there may be a case for some form of intervention in order to ensure better take-up of education and healthcare. This might take the form of subsidising education, perhaps by providing free primary school education, or it might be through regulation — enforcing a minimum school-leaving age.

The question then arises of how a government can raise the finances needed in order to improve education and healthcare, especially given the problems associated with tax collection systems. For many developing countries, this has proved a major stumbling block.

Exercise 29.2

Using appropriate diagrams, explain how the provision of education and healthcare may be subject to externality effects. Discuss possible policies to ensure improved healthcare provision in developing countries.

Trade policy

Protectionism

If a country faces a foreign exchange gap, there are two broad approaches that it can take in drawing up its trade policy to deal with the problem. One is to reduce its reliance on imports in order to economise on the need for foreign currency — in other words, to produce goods at home that it previously imported. This is known as an import substitution policy, which depends on introducing protectionist measures. An alternative possibility is to try to earn more foreign exchange through export promotion.

Import substitution

The import substitution strategy has had some appeal for a number of countries. The idea is to boost domestic production of goods that were previously imported, thereby saving foreign exchange. A typical policy instrument used to achieve this is the imposition of a tariff.

Synoptic link

Issues surrounding the use of protectionism and tariffs were discussed in Chapter 25. In particular, you may find it helpful to look back at the effects of imposing a tariff (see Figure 25.6 on p. 421).

However, not all the effects of a tariff are favourable for the economy. Consumers are certainly worse off, as they have to pay a higher price for the good, and there is a deadweight loss to society. However, some governments may find this a handy way of raising tax revenue.

Knowledge check 29.7

If a government of a developing country imposes a tariff on an imported good, who benefits?

Some would defend this policy on the grounds that it allows the country to protect an infant industry. In other words, through such encouragement and protection, the new industry will eventually become efficient enough to compete in world markets.

There are two key problems with this argument. First, unless the domestic market is sufficiently large for the industry to reap economies of scale, local producers will never be in a position to compete globally. Second, because of such protection, domestic firms are never exposed to international competition, and so will not have an incentive to improve their efficiency. In other words, tariff protection fosters an inward-looking attitude among local producers that discourages them from trying to compete in world markets. They remain happy with the protection that provides them with producer surplus.

Export promotion via primary industries or new activities

Export promotion requires a more dynamic and outward-looking approach, as domestic producers need to be able to compete with producers already established in world markets. The choice of which products to promote is critical, as it is important that the country develops a new pattern of comparative advantage if it is to benefit from an export promotion strategy.

For primary producers, a tempting strategy is one that begins with existing products and tries to move along the production chain. However, this relies on producers being able to gain entry to markets that may already be dominated by experienced producers, or may face quality control regulations that they find it difficult to match.

Given the difficulty of developing new primary industries, is it possible to encourage the development of new economic activities that could fuel exports?

The East Asian tiger economies pursued export promotion strategies, making sure that their exchange rates supported the competitiveness of their products and that their labour was appropriately priced. However, it must be remembered that the tiger economies expanded into export-led growth at a time when world trade itself was booming, and when the developed countries were beginning to move out of labour-intensive activities, thereby creating a niche to be filled by the tigers. If many other countries had expanded their exports at the same time, it is not at all certain that they could all have been successful.

As time goes by, it becomes more difficult for other countries to follow this policy. It is particularly difficult for countries that originally chose import substitution, because the inward-looking attitudes fostered by such policies become so deeply entrenched.

Exercise 29.3

Discuss the possible effects on developed countries if developing countries characterised by low-wage labour become more active in world markets.

It should also be remembered that there will always be dangers in trying to develop new kinds of economic activity that may entail sacrificing comparative advantage. This is not to say that developing countries should remain primary producers for ever, but it does suggest that it is important to select the new forms of activity with care in order to exploit a potential comparative advantage.

Exercise 29.4

Discuss the relative merits of import substitution and export promotion as trade strategies. Under what conditions might import substitution have a chance of success?

Summary: trade policy

- In designing a trade policy, a developing country may choose to go for import substitution, nurturing infant industries behind protectionist barriers in order to allow them to produce domestically goods that were formerly imported.
- However, such infant industries rarely seem to grow up, leaving the country with inefficient producers which are unable to compete effectively with world producers.
- Export promotion requires a more dynamic and outward-looking approach, and a careful choice of new activities.

Buffer stock schemes

In some commodity markets, prices can exhibit volatility over time. This could arise, for example, when the supply of a good varies from period to period because of the varying state of the harvest. In such a market, the supply curve will shift to the right when the harvest is good, but shift to the left in a period when the weather is poor or where crops are affected by some disease or blight. It may also be that the demand curve tends to shift around through time, with demand for some goods reflecting fluctuations in the performance of economies. In other words, demand may shift to the left when recession bites, but to the right in times of boom and prosperity.

Suppose that Figure 29.1 represents a market in which demand is relatively stable between periods, but in which supply varies between S_{poor} when the harvest is poor and S_{glut} when the harvest is good. The price varies between P_p and P_g. This creates a high level of uncertainty for producers, who find it difficult to form good expectations about the future prospects for the commodity. This means that they are less likely to invest in ways of improving productivity because of uncertain future returns. If a way could be found of stabilising the price of the good, then this could encourage producers.

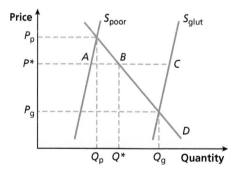

Figure 29.1 A buffer stock

A **buffer stock** is a way of attempting to do this. A scheme is set up whereby excess supply is bought up by the buffer stock in glut years to prevent the price from falling too low. In periods when the harvest is poor, stocks of the commodity are released on to the market in order to maintain the price at the agreed level. In terms of Figure 29.1, suppose that it is agreed to maintain the price at P^*. When there is a glut year, with the supply curve located at S_{glut}, there is excess supply at the agreed price of the amount BC, so this amount is bought up by the buffer stock and stored. If the supply is at S_{poor} because of a poor harvest, there is excess demand, so the buffer stock releases the quantity AB on to the market, maintaining the price.

Key term

buffer stock a scheme intended to stabilise the price of a commodity by buying excess supply in periods when supply is high, and selling when supply is low

Although this does have the effect of stabilising the price at $P\star$, there is a downside. If the members of the buffer stock scheme agree to maintain the price at too high a level, relative to the actual average equilibrium price over time, then it will run into difficulties. Notice in Figure 29.1 that to maintain price at $P\star$, the buffer stock buys up more in the glut year than it has to sell in the poor harvest year. If this pattern is repeated, then the size of stocks to be stored will rise over time. This is costly and will eventually become unsustainable.

Knowledge check 29.8

What would happen if a buffer stock sets price below the average long-run equilibrium level?

Exercise 29.5

Discuss why prices in some markets may be unstable from year to year and evaluate ways in which more stability might be achieved. How effective would you expect such measures to be? What would be the benefits to economic agents of having greater stability in prices?

Other interventionist strategies

There are other ways in which governments have adopted an interventionist approach to promote growth and development.

Infrastructure

Potentially more effective is intervention to provide social infrastructure, by improving transport and communication, or providing market facilities that enable domestic and international markets to work more effectively. One obvious drawback to this approach is that governments rarely have the resources to finance such investment, and have to rely on external sources of funds.

Managed exchange rates

Having seen the success of export-led growth strategies in some economies, another possible strategy to promote economic growth is to manipulate the exchange rate in order to improve the competitiveness of a country's exports. This was a path followed by China in its period of rapid export-led growth. The downside of this approach is that resources need to be diverted into the export sector to enable exports to expand. This could work for China as a centrally planned economy, as exports could be encouraged at the expense of domestic consumption. This would not work everywhere, and even in China it could not be sustained indefinitely.

Promoting joint ventures with global companies

Could growth be stimulated by promoting joint ventures between local companies and TNCs? This has been attempted, but such a marriage of unequals faces severe challenges. In particular, the TNC partner is likely to be able to hold a dominant position in the partnership, and to be wary of divulging too much information about its technology to local firms.

Industrialisation

Looking at the countries that have succeeded in becoming developed, it is noticeable that very few have managed to achieve this by continuing to specialise in primary production, a possible exception being Chile. So, can a developing country develop through a process of **industrialisation**?

In an influential paper in 1954, Sir Arthur Lewis argued that agriculture in many developing countries was characterised by surplus labour. Perhaps farms were operated on a household basis, with the work and the crop being shared out between members of the household. If there was not enough work to be done by all the members of the household, then, although all seemed to be employed, there would in fact be hidden unemployment, or under-employment. Given the size of the rural population and its rapid growth, there could be almost unlimited surplus labour existing in this way.

Lewis then pointed out that because the labour at the margin in agriculture was not contributing to output, it would be possible to transfer such surplus labour into the industrial sector without a loss of agricultural output, as the remaining labour would be able to take up the slack. All that would be necessary is for the industrial sector to set a wage sufficiently higher than the rural wage to persuade workers to transfer. Industry could then reap profits that could be reinvested to allow industry to expand, without any need for the industrial wage to be pulled upwards to cause inflation.

Unfortunately, the process did not prove to be as smooth as Lewis suggested. One reason relates to human capital levels. Agricultural workers do not have the skills or training that prepares them for employment in the industrial sector, so it is not straightforward to transfer them from agricultural to industrial work, especially if it is the least productive workers who choose to migrate. Furthermore, if migration to the cities is rapid, the urban infrastructure may not be able to cope, perhaps resulting in the development of shanty towns, which might be seen as a form of negative externality.

Key term

industrialisation a process of transforming an economy by expanding manufacturing and other industrial activity

Knowledge check 29.9

Explain why the development of shanty towns might be seen as an externality.

A shanty town on the outskirts of Cape Town — urban infrastructure often cannot cope with rapid migration to the cities

Key term

Lewis model a model developed by Sir Arthur Lewis which argued that less developed countries could be seen as being typified by two sectors, traditional and modern, and that labour could be transferred from the traditional to the modern sector in order to bring about growth and development

It is also the case that the expanding industry did not always reinvest the surplus in order to enable continuous expansion of the industrial sector. Foreign firms tended to repatriate the profits, and in any case tended to use modern, relatively capital-intensive technology that did not require a large pool of unskilled labour.

Perhaps more seriously, the **Lewis model** encouraged governments to think in terms of industry-led growth, and to neglect the rural sector. This meant that agricultural productivity often remained low, and inequality between urban and rural areas grew.

Tourism

The analysis so far suggests that developing countries need to diversify away from primary production and into new activities that do not require large amounts of capital, preferably involving the production of goods or services that can earn foreign exchange and that have a high income elasticity of demand. On the face of it, tourism would seem to fit the bill.

In the first place, the income elasticity of demand for tourism is strongly positive. This means that, as real incomes rise in the more developed countries, there will be an increase in the demand for tourism. Within the domestic economy, the development of the tourist sector will have an impact on employment. In the early stages there will be a demand for construction workers, and later there will be jobs in hotels and in transport and other services. Tourism is also the sort of activity that is likely to have large multiplier effects on the domestic economy. The World Bank has reported that visitor expenditures outside the hotel sector can range from half to nearly double the in-hotel spending. In addition, there is likely to be scope for small labour-intensive, craft-based activities to sell goods to foreigners without actually having to go into the export business — because the tourists come to the producers. Tourism may also attract foreign direct investment if international hotel chains move in to cater for the visiting tourists.

Knowledge check 29.10

Explain what is meant by the 'multiplier effects' of tourism.

Tourism will require an improvement in the country's infrastructure. For example, it may require road improvements, and upgraded transport and communications facilities. However, such facilities not only help the tourist sector, but also generate externality effects, in the sense that local businesses (and residents) benefit from the improvements as well.

Another potentially important aspect of tourism from the government's perspective is that it may generate a flow of tax revenue. This may come partly from taxes on goods and services, but also from airport taxes and landing fees.

As usual, however, there is a potential downside as well. Tourists will also demand goods that cannot be produced locally, so there may be a need to increase imports, adding to the current account deficit on the balance of payments. This may be reinforced by the outflow of profits from the foreign direct investment. In addition, there may be negative externality effects arising from the erosion of the environment. And tourists exhibit different lifestyles, which may alter the aspirations of the local population, and encourage the consumption of inappropriate (and perhaps imported) products.

It is also important to keep opportunity costs in mind. The development of any new activity entails the sacrifice of some alternative. In deciding to develop tourism, some other option will have to be forgone. For example, resources that are used to improve the transport and communications infrastructure cannot be used to improve education or healthcare. Of course, tourism may prove to be so successful that it will generate resources that can be devoted to education or healthcare, but opportunity costs are not an issue that can be ignored in the present.

Fair trade

Given the relatively weak position that developing countries hold when they try to compete in global markets, there has been increasing interest in the notion of **fair trade schemes**. These had small beginnings, with a number of charities campaigning for small producers in developing countries to be given a 'fair' price for their products. This has flourished and proliferated, to the extent that most supermarkets now stock items labelled as being 'fair trade' — often with a premium price, although this can be difficult to judge because of quality differences between products. If consumers in the rich countries are prepared to pay more for produce in the knowledge that a larger amount goes to the producer, then this may be a way of giving better incentives to farmers in developing countries.

Key term

fair trade schemes
schemes that set out
to ensure that small
producers in developing
countries receive a fair
price for their products

However, it is important also to consider the economic arguments that underlie this sort of scheme. There are two key issues. First, are there good economic grounds for intervening by providing subsidies in fair trade schemes? Second, what would be the effect of those subsidies?

The market failure argument in this case is based on the abuse of market power, under which small producers in developing countries are unable to receive a 'fair' price for their output. This may partly reflect information failure as well, as small producers may not always be in a position to discover the going market price for the crops that they produce. The increased use of mobile phones in some countries is helping to overcome this information failure, but there is a long way to go before it is eliminated. The problem is made worse by the time lags involved in responding to changes in market conditions. It takes 3 to 4 years for a newly planted coffee plant to produce marketable coffee, so it is impossible to respond quickly to an increase in price. Indeed, given that prices are set in world markets, and are subject to fluctuations, it is possible that a farmer may manage to increase output only to find that prices have plummeted.

If the issue is one of market power, then using the power of the consumer to affect the bargaining power of the small producer could potentially improve the distribution of the gains from production and provide improved incentives for the producer. If the issue is one of information failure, then the appropriate targeted response would be to take steps to resolve that failure by providing better information to the producers. A fair trade scheme may be able to help by providing advice and guidance to farmers. If the issue is with price fluctuations, then it is not clear how a fair trade scheme by itself can deal with the problems of gestation lags.

In the longer term, there are a number of unanswered questions to be addressed. Some critics have argued that providing subsidies to small producers can produce some anomalous and unintended effects. One danger is that farmers may be subsidised to continue production in a market in which prices may already be on a downward spiral, rather than switching to alternative commodities with better long-term prospects.

Exercise 29.6

Discuss the economic arguments for and against fair trade schemes, and come to a view about whether you regard them as benefiting developing producers.

Overseas aid

If developing countries could enter a phase of economic growth and rising incomes, one result would be an increase in world trade. This would benefit nations around the world, and the more developed industrial countries would be likely to see an increase in the market for their products. This might be a reason for the governments of more developed countries to help developing countries with the growth and development of their economies. Of course, there may also be a humanitarian motive for providing assistance — to reduce global inequality.

Indeed, there may be market failure arguments for providing aid. For example, it may be that governments have better information about the riskiness of projects in developing countries than private firms have. In relation to the provision of education and healthcare, it was argued earlier that there may be externality effects involved. However, governments may not have the resources needed to provide sufficient education for their citizens. Similarly, some infrastructure may have public good characteristics that require intervention.

Official aid is known as **Official Development Assistance** (ODA), and is provided through the Development Assistance Committee of the Organisation for Economic Co-operation and Development (OECD).

At a meeting of the United Nations in 1974, the industrial countries agreed that they would each devote 0.7% of their GNP to ODA. This goal has been reiterated regularly since then. Progress towards this target has not been impressive. Figure 29.2 shows the performance of donor countries relative to this target, and you can see that only five countries achieved the 0.7% UN target in 2017. The USA's share looks modest in this figure, but it should be borne in mind that in terms of US dollars, the USA is by far the largest contributor.

Key term

Official Development Assistance aid provided to developing countries by countries in the OECD

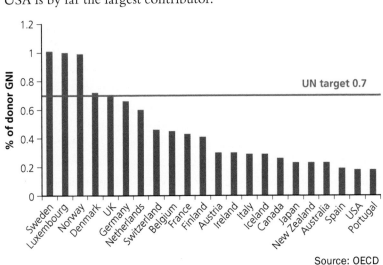

Source: OECD

Figure 29.2 Official Development Assistance in 2017

Figure 29.3 shows the relative size of financial flows into low-income countries since 1990. You can see that ODA flows declined in the second half of the 1990s, but increased in the early years of the twenty-first century. This was partly because ODA at this time included funds devoted to debt forgiveness, as brokered by the World Bank under the Heavily Indebted Poor Countries (HIPC) Initiative, which is discussed later in the chapter. The flows have declined since, perhaps associated with the onset of global recession.

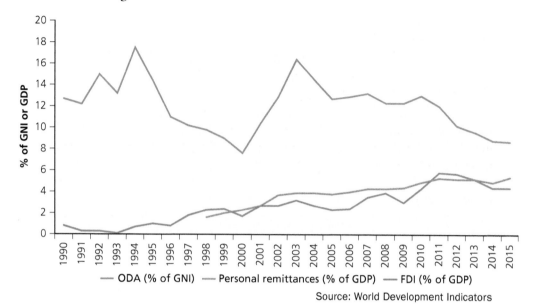

Source: World Development Indicators

Figure 29.3 Financial flows into low-income countries, 1990–2015

The effectiveness of aid

There has been much criticism of overseas aid, and its effectiveness has been questioned. There are many possible reasons for the ineffectiveness of aid. It may simply be that providing aid to the poorest countries reduces its effectiveness, in the sense that the resources of such countries are so limited that the funding cannot be efficiently utilised. In some cases it may be related to the fact that aid flows are received by governments, which can be inefficient or corrupt, so there are no guarantees that the funds are used wisely by these governments. Or it might simply be that the flows of aid have not been substantial enough to have made a difference.

There are other explanations, however. For example, some donor countries in the past have regarded aid as part of their own trade policy. By tying aid to trade deals, the net value of the aid to the recipient country is much reduced: for instance, offering aid in this way may commit the recipient country to buying goods from the donor country at inflated prices.

In other cases, aid has been tied to use in specific projects. This may help to assure the donor that the funds are being used for the purpose for which they were intended. However, it is helpful only if appropriate projects were selected in the first place. There may be a temptation for donors to select prestige projects that will be favourably regarded by others, rather than going for a developing country's top-priority development projects.

Knowledge check 29.11

Do you think that a project to provide hydro-electric power would necessarily be an appropriate project for overseas aid?

Bilateral and multilateral aid

Another distinction is between overseas assistance that is given by one country to another (bilateral aid), and funds that are channelled through organisations such as the World Bank or the United Nations (multilateral aid). Multilateral aid is less likely to be tied to trade agreements, but in some cases may be made conditional on the recipient country implementing certain policies.

The effect on incentives

An important issue for all sorts of aid is that it should be provided in a way that does not damage incentives for local producers. For example, dumping cheap grain into developing markets on a regular basis would be likely to damage the incentives for local farmers by depressing prices.

Dutch disease

A final issue to notice is that in some cases, the acceptance of foreign aid by a country may result in a phenomenon known as *Dutch disease*. The discovery of a large natural gas field in the Netherlands in the late 1950s resulted in a revaluation of the currency, causing a loss of competitiveness in the manufacturing sector and an acceleration of the deindustrialisation process. It has been argued that a flow of foreign aid into a country can have a similar effect, if the receipt of aid causes the exchange rate to rise, thus reducing the competitiveness of the country's exports.

Aid is not always effective — dumping cheap grain into developing country markets is likely to depress local prices

Summary: other interventionist strategies

- Buffer stock schemes may help to stabilise prices.
- Industrialisation may be seen as an essential step towards achieving productivity gains and economic growth, but can lead to rural neglect.
- Tourism may be a valuable route to economic growth and to earning foreign currency.
- Fair trade schemes may be able to provide incentives for small producers.
- Official Development Assistance (ODA) comprises grants and concessional funding provided from the OECD countries to developing countries.
- The countries most in need of ODA may not be in a position to use it effectively.
- In some cases the direction of ODA flows is influenced by the political interests of the donor countries.
- The developed countries have pledged to devote 0.7% of their GNPs to ODA, but few have reached this target.
- Some evidence suggests that aid has been ineffective except in countries that have pursued 'good' economic policies.
- The tying of aid to trade deals or to specific projects can limit the aid's benefits to recipient countries.

Exercise 29.7

Examine the arguments for and against providing assistance to those countries in most need of it, as opposed to those best equipped to make good use of it.

Study tip

The giving (and receiving) of overseas aid can become quite an emotive topic with some people. If it is a topic on which you feel strongly, try to remember in the exam that you are supposed to be analysing the issue based on economic arguments, so don't let your personal views overcome your economic analysis.

Personal remittances

Figure 29.3 shows that the other important source of external financial flows into low-income countries is personal remittances. This has shown a steady increase throughout the period since 1990. Personal remittances here are defined as personal transfers and compensation of employees. In other words, this includes current transfers in cash or in kind to residents of an economy from non-residents, together with incomes of workers who are employed in an economy in which they are not residents. For example, a worker may take a job abroad, but send part of the earnings back to the family in the home country.

The steady increase in such remittances may reflect the effects of globalisation, with more workers being more able to migrate to work abroad and more people being forced to migrate as a result of violence and conflict in the home economy. The World Bank has estimated that more than 215 million people live outside the country of their birth. The extent to which such financial flows can contribute to the process of economic growth and human development is hard to monitor.

International borrowing and the debt crisis

Another option for developing countries is to borrow the funds needed for development. This may be on concessional terms from the World Bank or the International Monetary Fund (IMF), or on a commercial basis from international financial markets.

Loan conditionality

It is important to notice that when countries borrow from the World Bank or the IMF, the loans come with strings attached. In other words, these bodies impose conditions on countries wanting to borrow, typically in relation to the sorts of economic policy that should be adopted. Such policy programmes will be considered below.

The beginnings of the debt crisis

As with other forms of external finance, problems have arisen for some countries that have tried to borrow internationally. These problems first became apparent in the early 1980s, when Mexico announced that it could not meet its debt repayment commitments. The stock of outstanding debt has been a major issue for many developing countries, especially in sub-Saharan Africa.

Figure 29.4 presents some data about this. It can be seen that in 1990 the debt position for many of these countries was serious indeed. In the case of Uganda, in 1990 more than 80% of the value of exports of goods and services was needed to service the outstanding debt. For a country with limited resources, this leaves little surplus to use for promoting development. The encouraging aspect of Figure 29.4 is that for most of these countries the situation had considerably improved by 2015 — in some cases dramatically so, as in Uganda, for example.

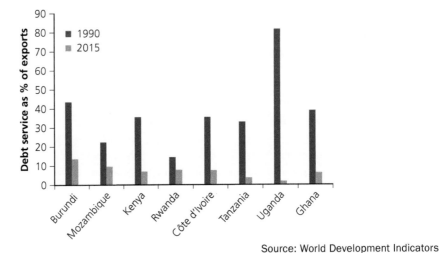

Source: World Development Indicators

Figure 29.4 Debt servicing in selected countries in sub-Saharan Africa, 1990 and 2015

With so high a proportion of export revenues needed to service outstanding debt, it is to be expected that resources to stimulate economic growth and development would be very limited. But how did countries accumulate such high levels of debt? The story begins in the mid-1970s with the first oil price crisis. In 1973–74 oil prices quadrupled. Countries that were not oil producers were suddenly faced with a deficit on the current account of the balance of payments, as the demand for oil in the short run was highly inelastic.

For developing countries, this was a major problem. They knew that if they went to the IMF for a loan, they would be forced to accept onerous conditions, so they were reluctant to do this. On the other hand, the oil producers were enjoying windfall gains, and their surpluses were lodged with the banks, which were thus keen to lend. Developing countries were therefore drawn in to borrowing from the banks rather than the IMF, and they took out loans at variable interest rates.

The second oil price crisis came in 1979–80, when prices tripled. Many countries were now in deep trouble, carrying a legacy of past debts and needing to borrow still more. Furthermore, countries like the USA and the UK were adopting macroeconomic policies that were pushing interest rates to high levels, making it more difficult for developing countries to meet their existing commitments.

The threat of default

This resulted in the debt crisis of the 1980s, when a number of countries were threatening to default on their debts. A number of plans (including the Baker and Brady Plans) were introduced to safeguard the international financial system, but from the developing countries' viewpoint these entailed mainly a rescheduling of existing debt: in other words, they were given longer to pay. A consequence was that debt levels continued to grow.

Unwise use of funds

The problems were made worse because in some countries the borrowed funds were not used wisely. Development through borrowing is sustainable only if the funds are used to enable exports to grow, so that the funds can be repaid. When they do not lead to increased export earnings, repayment problems will inevitably result.

Today, the problem of debt is much reduced. Before looking at how this was brought about, it is helpful to explore the role of the so-called Bretton Woods institutions — the World Bank, the International Monetary Fund and the World Trade Organization.

Summary: international borrowing

- Another way for developing countries to obtain external funds is through borrowing.
- Loans provided by the World Bank and the IMF have conditions attached that are not always palatable for developing countries.
- Many developing countries have borrowed in the past, but have then been unable to meet the repayments.
- In some cases this was because the funds were not well used.

Exercise 29.8

Discuss the extent to which good government within a developing country is a necessary condition for the successful mobilisation of internal and external resources.

The Bretton Woods institutions

Synoptic link

The launch of the Dollar Standard following the Bretton Woods conference was discussed in Chapter 26.

Key terms

International Monetary Fund (IMF) multilateral institution that provides short-term financing for countries experiencing balance of payments problems

World Bank multilateral organisation that provides financing for long-term development projects

General Agreement on Tariffs and Trade (GATT) precursor of the WTO, GATT organised a series of 'rounds' of tariff reductions

World Trade Organization (WTO) multilateral body responsible for overseeing the conduct of international trade

Synoptic link

The role of the WTO was discussed in the context of international trade in Chapter 25.

At the end of the Second World War in 1945, a conference was held at Bretton Woods, New Hampshire, USA, at which John Maynard Keynes was an influential delegate. In addition to establishing the exchange rate system that operated until the early 1970s, the conference set up three key institutions with prescribed roles, in support of the international financial system.

International Monetary Fund

The **International Monetary Fund (IMF)** was set up with a specific brief to offer short-term assistance to countries experiencing balance of payments problems. Thus, if a country were running a deficit on the current account, it could borrow from the IMF in order to finance the deficit. However, the IMF would insist that, as a condition of granting the loan, the country put in place policies to deal with the deficit — typically, restrictive monetary and fiscal policies.

World Bank

The International Bank for Reconstruction and Development was the second institution established under the Bretton Woods agreement. It soon became known as the **World Bank**. The role of the World Bank is to provide longer-term funding for projects that will promote development. Much of this funding is provided at commercial interest rates, as the role of the bank was seen to be the channelling of finance to projects that normal commercial banks would perceive as being too risky. However, some concessional lending is also made through the International Development Association (IDA), which is part of the World Bank.

World Trade Organization

Initially, Bretton Woods set up the **General Agreement on Tariffs and Trade (GATT)**, with a brief to oversee international trade. This entailed encouraging countries to reduce tariffs, but the GATT also provided a forum for trade negotiations and for settling disputes between countries. The GATT was replaced by the **World Trade Organization (WTO)** in 1995. Between them, these organisations have presided over a significant reduction in the barriers to trade between countries — not only tariffs, but other forms of protection too.

Heavily Indebted Poor Countries (HIPC) Initiative

By the late 1990s it was clear that many countries' international debt burdens had become unsustainable. Pressure was put on the World Bank and the UN to offer debt forgiveness to developing countries to herald the millennium.

The World Bank was reluctant to consider this route. One of the reasons for its reluctance concerns moral hazard. It is argued that if a country expects to be forgiven its debt, it will have no incentive to behave responsibly. Furthermore, a country that has been forgiven its debt may have no incentive to be more responsible in the future — and other countries too will have less of an incentive to pay off their debts.

Synoptic link

The concept of moral hazard was first introduced in Chapter 7, and will also be important in Chapter 30.

The response was the **HIPC Initiative**, which allows for debt forgiveness on condition that the country demonstrates a commitment to 'good' policies over a period of time. The HIPC Initiative was first launched in 1995, but the conditions were so restrictive that few countries were able to benefit. Thus, a number of pressure groups, including Jubilee 2000, lobbied the World Bank to allow the initiative to be more accessible. The original HIPC measures required countries to follow the policy package for a period of 6 years before they would qualify for any debt relief.

Key term

HIPC Initiative an initiative launched in 1995 to provide debt relief for heavily indebted poor countries

The HIPC policy package incorporated four main steps:

1 Successful implementation of policies to enhance economic growth

2 Development of a Poverty Reduction Strategy Paper (PRSP)

3 Encouragement of private enterprise

4 Diversification of the export base

In July 2005 government leaders from the G8 countries met at a summit meeting in Gleneagles. At this meeting the countries present pledged to cancel the debt of the world's most indebted countries — which effectively meant those countries that had qualified under the HIPC initiative. Jubilee 2000 continued to argue that HIPC remained overly restrictive, and pointed out that some countries facing heavy debt burdens were excluded from HIPC, and were therefore also excluded from the Gleneagles statement. This included such countries as Bangladesh, Cambodia, the Philippines, Nigeria and Peru.

What is not entirely clear is the extent to which improvements in debt service levels can be attributed to the HIPC Initiative. A number of commentators have pointed out that it is not only the HIPC countries that witnessed a reduction in debt service levels.

The Washington Consensus

The influence of the Bretton Woods institutions on economic growth and development has been considerable. In particular, the World Bank and the IMF have tended to impose conditions on countries in return for lending or debt forgiveness. These conditions were based on the prevailing views about how economies would respond to policy changes.

At a conference in 1989, John Williamson drew up a set of ideas about economic policy that he then believed represented accepted views. These ideas became known as the *Washington Consensus*. The ten core policies were:

- fiscal discipline
- reordering public expenditure priorities
- tax reform
- liberalising interest rates
- a competitive exchange rate
- trade liberalisation
- liberalising inward foreign direct investment
- privatisation
- deregulation
- secure property rights

Knowledge check 29.13

To what extent are these measures market-oriented as opposed to being interventionist?

It was argued that countries that adopted these measures would be able to initiate a process of economic development, and the list formed the basis of the conditions imposed on countries. The measures reflect a market-oriented view of how economies operate. Although many countries did adopt some or all of these policies, it became clear that the consensus was not a complete solution. For example, China offered an alternative model, blending the introduction of market reforms with continuing state control.

It has also been argued that the set of measures neglects a number of key issues surrounding governance and the need to establish reliable and robust institutions to underpin the economy. In addition to the consensus measures, successful development also needs attention to be given to improving the way that markets work, especially in terms of the need for flexible labour markets, and there needs to be targeted poverty reduction and social safety nets to bring together macro and micro aspects of the economy. This has led to initiatives centred on the notion of inclusive growth. Under this approach, it becomes important to ensure that growth provides genuine benefits for the populace.

Non-governmental organisations (NGOs)

Key term

non-governmental organisations non-profit, voluntary citizens' groups (including charities) organised on a local, national or international level

Also active in promoting and supporting development in developing countries are charities and other non-profit, voluntary citizens' groups organised on a national or international level. These are known as **non-governmental organisations** (NGOs). Examples include charities such as Oxfam or Médecins sans Frontières that raise funds through public giving for development projects in developing countries. These have made an impact not only through direct donations to fund development projects, but also through pressure on governments and multilateral organisations.

NGOs have been active in supporting projects that operate at a local level and are tailored for the needs of those local communities, encouraging self-help and sustainability. While not having the financial power of governments or the Bretton Woods institutions, NGOs have demonstrated how focused projects can have a genuine impact on people's lives, and have encouraged institutions to recognise the importance of inclusivity in growth, and that one-size-fits-all solutions will not always be the best way forward for countries or communities.

Summary: institutions

- The Bretton Woods conference in 1945 set up three major multilateral organisations: the IMF, the World Bank and the GATT (which later became the WTO).
- The IMF has the role of providing short-term finance for countries experiencing balance of payments problems.
- The World Bank provides longer-term financing for development projects.
- The WTO oversees the conduct of international trade.
- The HIPC Initiative was designed to address the problems of debt in the poorest countries.
- Under the HIPC Initiative, debt relief is provided to countries that have shown a commitment to World Bank-approved policies and that have implemented a Poverty Reduction Strategy Paper (PRSP).
- The World Bank and IMF encouraged the adoption of policies known as the Washington Consensus, although this proved to be oversimplified in practice.
- NGOs support projects at a local level and have encouraged institutions to recognise the importance of inclusivity in growth.

Prospects for the future

This analysis of the situation facing developing countries does not seem to give many grounds for optimism, especially in sub-Saharan Africa, where so many countries seem to have stagnated, and where the combination of problems to be overcome seems so great. The early years of the twenty-first century showed more promise, with signs of economic growth. The global recession that afflicted many of the industrial economies may have interrupted the progress that developing countries had begun to enjoy. However, it is to be hoped that this will just be a temporary interruption, so that countries around the world and their citizens can become full partners in the global economy.

Case study 29.1

Ugandan coffee

The World Bank offers the story of Martha Wamatabu, who farms an acre of land in the Bududa district of Uganda. In a good season she harvests about 600 kilograms of coffee, but faces challenges in marketing the produce and in improving the productivity of her land.

The Ugandan economy depends heavily on its agriculture, which employs 71.7% of the population (but only 24.4% of GDP) and makes up 72.6% of exports, coffee being the most important crop.

Coffee production in Uganda is mainly carried out by small farmers, who intercrop coffee with bananas and subsistence crops such as beans (the bananas provide shade that is needed for the coffee trees). It has been estimated that there are some 500,000 producers of coffee in the country.

The farmers typically sun-dry the coffee beans and sell to traders who visit by bicycle, motorcycle or, in some cases, donkeys. The traders then consolidate the crop, which is then processed and sold to the exporters. Competition among the traders helps to ensure that the farmers receive a good price for their coffee. However, the transport infrastructure is poor.

Farmers face a number of problems. They typically face low productivity and unpredictable weather. Fertiliser use is low, and there is a shortage of agricultural extension officers. For many, there is insecurity over land ownership.

The Ugandan Coffee Development Agency (UCDA) provides advice for farmers in an attempt to raise productivity levels, but communicating with so many small producers is a challenge. Only 21.9% of Ugandans have access to the internet, and only 10.1% of the rural population have access to electricity. A promising development is that 55.1% of the population have mobile phones (from only 0.5% in 2000).

Follow-up questions

a Before 1992, the state-controlled coffee trading had a monopsony position on purchasing coffee from farmers. Why would farmers benefit from privatisation of this activity?

b Discuss the importance of transport infrastructure in the coffee production supply chain.

c Why would insecurity over land ownership be seen as a problem for farmers?

d Why would the increasing access to mobile phones be a benefit to farmers?

e Discuss the challenges facing the UCDA in attempting to raise productivity in coffee production.

Wildlife tourism in Tanzania

Tanzania is among the lowest-income countries in the world, with GNI per capita of US$900 in 2016. It is located in sub-Saharan Africa, and relies heavily on agriculture for employment, income and export earnings. In 2015, agriculture made up 68% of employment and 31% of GDP by value-added; 58% of its merchandise exports consisted of agricultural goods. Could Tanzania benefit from tourism?

In its favour, Tanzania has a rich wildlife and the potential to offer safari holidays, so there are resources that could attract foreign visitors. But can promoting tourism be achieved without doing damage to the environment and to biodiversity?

The internet has raised awareness of the variety of wildlife around the globe — it is easy to learn about animals and their habitats, which can then encourage people to want to visit and see the animals in their natural surroundings. At the same time, rising real incomes fuel the demand for tourism, and many active retirees have the income and the leisure time available to travel.

At the same time, habitats are shrinking, affecting the supply side of the tourism market. Some destinations have become overcrowded. Indeed, it is said that to visit the Masi Mara in Kenya is to find tourists looking at other tourists, rather than at wildlife.

The challenge is thus to reconcile the need for protecting nature with the need to stimulate economic growth and development.

Another key objective of encouraging tourism in a country like Tanzania is to ensure that local communities benefit, and are not alienated by the visitations of rich tourists. If local communities are to benefit, they need to be involved in projects and to understand the need to manage local ecosystems.

An example in Tanzania is the Ruaha Carnivore Project, launched in 2009 in association with Oxford University. This is based in the Ruaha National Park, which is home to significant populations of lions, cheetahs and African wild dogs. It is also home to local people who do not always see the value of cohabiting with carnivores that are prone to attacking their livestock. The project has therefore needed to work closely with local communities to reduce human–carnivore conflict.

In 2015, international tourism accounted for 23.8% of Tanzania's total exports.

Follow-up questions

a Discuss why promoting wildlife tourism could damage the environment and biodiversity.
b Why might the expansion of tourism impose costs on local communities?
c What benefits might there be for local communities if tourism increases?
d Would Tanzania be better off industrialising rather than promoting international tourism?

The modern economy relies heavily on the effective working of financial markets. In particular, it is important that a sufficient flow of money and credit is available if product markets are to operate and transactions are to be smooth. In this chapter, we explore the roles that the financial sector needs to fulfil and identify forms of market failure that may hinder this.

Learning objectives

After studying this chapter, you should:
→ appreciate the importance of the financial sector in the macroeconomy and the roles that it fulfils
→ be able to evaluate the role of the financial sector in the real economy
→ be familiar with ways in which market failure may hinder the operation of the financial sector

The role of the financial sector

The financial sector provides the environment in which economic activity takes place, which entails a number of key roles.

Facilitating saving

Individuals need to undertake saving, and businesses and individuals need to be able to borrow. This was highlighted in the discussion of the Harrod–Domar model in the context of developing countries, but is equally important for an advanced economy. It is through financial markets that savings can be mobilised for the investment.

Synoptic link

The Harrod–Domar model was explained in Chapter 28.

Knowledge check 30.1

Why is investment so important for the economy?

Individuals (and firms) wish to save for various reasons. It may be that a household needs to accumulate funds for future spending. This may partly depend on where an individual is in the life cycle. When young, there may be a need to save in order to have a deposit on a house. Savings may also be needed to support people in retirement. The financial sector offers opportunities for people to earn a return through saving, and thus have funds for later purposes. At current rates of interest, the returns may not provide a strong incentive for this.

Facilitating borrowing

The other side of the coin is that firms — and households — wish to borrow. Financial markets thus provide opportunities to obtain loans. This was seen in the circular flow model, where the savings behaviour of households enables firms to borrow in order to finance their investment.

> ### Synoptic link
>
> A simple version of the circular flow model was introduced in Chapter 13.

Again, the rate of interest is important, as this represents the cost of borrowing. Firms will borrow for investment as long as the rate of return on the investment exceeds the cost of borrowing. Households will borrow in order to undertake expenditures, but will also need to be aware of the cost of borrowing.

Facilitating the exchange of goods and services

On a practical level, financial markets need to facilitate the transactions that take place, with the exchange of goods and services. The importance of this can be seen by observing behaviour in countries that have experienced hyperinflation. When inflation reaches very high levels, people begin to try to avoid using money for transactions. Firms have to keep changing their prices, and people go frequently to the bank rather than keeping cash in their pockets. The transaction costs of this behaviour are high, and underlines the importance of having stable financial systems in order to facilitate transactions.

> ### Synoptic link
>
> Barter as a means of undertaking transactions was discussed in Chapter 1 — it is not a practicable way of allowing an economy to operate. Hyperinflation and the costs of inflation were discussed in Chapter 15.

> ### Knowledge check 30.2
>
> What is the term used by economists to describe the situation in which individuals visit the bank frequently in order to minimise their cash holdings?

Forward markets

Financial markets that operate in the modern economy also enable transactions to be conducted on the basis of contracts for future delivery — these are known as *forward* or *futures markets*. These are especially important in relation to transactions in certain commodities and in foreign exchange. Such arrangements are a way in which economic agents can minimise the risk of transactions.

An example is a where a manufacturing enterprise needs to buy commodities as inputs to its production process. Given the volatility of some commodity prices, there is uncertainty about the prices that will hold in future periods. Futures markets can help by allowing firms to contract forward to buy the commodities they know they will need at a future period at an agreed price at that agreed future date.

Synoptic link

Futures markets were discussed in Chapter 26 in the context of mitigating exchange rate risk. Futures markets for commodities are designed for similar purposes.

Knowledge check 30.3

Why might commodity prices be volatile?

The market for equities

The market for equities is also an important part of the modern financial system, by which firms can obtain funds through the stock market for their investment plans. The whole business of insurance and pension funds is based on the existence of stock markets. This allows investors to buy a stake in businesses that they see as offering the potential for future profits.

Summary: role of the financial sector

- Financial institutions provide the key link between borrowers and lenders, thus facilitating saving and borrowing.
- The exchange of goods and services is an important role for the financial system.
- At times, it is useful for economic agents to agree transactions which are to be undertaken at a future date, so the existence of forward markets is a role for the financial system.
- The market for equities is also an important part of a modern financial system.

The financial sector and the macroeconomy

Monetary policy is a key way in which the authorities seek to stabilise the macroeconomy, but it cannot be implemented without there being an efficient and effective financial sector. If there was any doubt about the importance of the financial sector, this was dispelled by the financial crisis that hit the global economy in the late 2000s. The crisis had far-reaching effects on the stability of the financial system, and worked through into the real economy, resulting in recession and rising unemployment. The recovery from this crisis was slow. In order to understand the reasons for the financial crisis, and the steps needed to deal with it, it is important first to understand how the financial system works, and the extent to which it may be subject to market failure.

Synoptic link

Monetary policy was discussed in Chapter 16.

Knowledge check 30.4

What are the key instruments of monetary policy?

The macroeconomy depends heavily on the financial sector to operate effectively. Lending and borrowing underpin the way in which the economy works: firms need to borrow in order to finance their investment, and households borrow for their spending. Insurance markets and pension funds are key features of the financial landscape. The process of globalisation enhances the importance of having an efficient foreign exchange market.

The credit crunch and financial crisis, with their impact on economic growth and unemployment, highlighted the importance of an effective financial sector for the

To understand how this came about, it is necessary to explore the ways in which the banking sector has developed over time, against a backdrop of deregulation and innovation in types of financial asset.

Financial institutions

Financial institutions provide the key link between borrowers and lenders, and are often referred to as **financial intermediaries**. This term covers banks, building societies and a range of other specialist institutions that provide financial services. Traditionally, the banking sector has been seen as being divided into two main sectors, made up of the **retail banks** and the **wholesale banks**.

Retail and wholesale banks

The retail banks include the high-street banks that provide banking services to households and small firms, accepting deposits and making loans, mainly on a relatively small scale, and providing a distributed branch banking service. The rise of internet banking has led to the closure of many high-street branches, but the underlying process remains unchanged.

Wholesale banks operate on a larger scale, taking deposits and making loans to companies and other banks. These include the investment banks and other specialist financial institutions. Building societies in the past were distinct institutions providing a specific service, accepting deposits from a range of small depositors and making long-term loans for house purchase, with the property acting as collateral on the debt.

One of the developments of recent years has been the blurring of these distinctions. Deregulation has allowed most building societies to rebrand themselves as retail banks, and the high-street banks have diversified into wholesale banking, becoming **universal banks**, operating in large-scale lending and investment as well as fulfilling their traditional high-street functions.

Key terms

financial intermediaries institutions such as banks and building societies that channel funds from lenders to borrowers

retail banks banks that provide high-street services to depositors

wholesale banks banks that deal with companies and other banks on a large scale

universal banks banks that operate in both retail and wholesale markets

High-street banks have diversified into wholesale banking, becoming universal banks

How banks operate

Banks operate in order to make profits. They take deposits and make loans, making profit from the return on the loans that they make. The more loans they make, the more profit, but this must be balanced against the need to carry enough liquid assets to meet the demands of depositors who wish to withdraw funds for use in transactions. There is thus a trade-off that the banks need to get right, between making loans and holding enough liquidity to service their customers. The **liquidity ratio** is the ratio of liquid assets to total assets.

Knowledge check 30.5

What is meant by 'liquidity'?

In the short run, banks can borrow from each other in order to maintain their liquidity ratio. Such **interbank lending** takes place at a rate of interest that depends on the amount of liquidity in the market and on the period over which the loan is required. The average rate of interest on loans made in the London interbank market is known as the **LIBOR**, which is set daily. Under normal circumstances, such lending ensures that banks have sufficient liquidity on a day-by-day basis, but problems emerged during the financial crisis.

Another way of accommodating a short-run shortage of funds is to sell financial assets to the central bank (or to other banks), then repurchase them at an agreed date — perhaps two weeks later. These sale and repurchase agreements are known as **repos**, and act like a loan.

Forms of borrowing

Borrowing takes place for various reasons and takes different forms. The nature and characteristics of the borrowing determine the conditions under which borrowing takes place, including the rate of interest to be charged.

Mortgages

The mortgage market is an important form of borrowing. These are long-term loans taken out for house purchase, in which the loan is secured against the value of the property. If the borrower defaults on the loan, the lender takes the property in lieu of the debt. The size of the loan is partly based on the lender's assessment of the ability of the borrower to maintain payments over the life of the loan. This may be related to the income and expected income of the borrower, but also to the expectation that house prices will rise in the future.

Unsecured borrowing

Borrowing may also take place without such collateral to cover default. Such unsecured borrowing will carry a higher rate of interest. In recent years, there has been an increase in very short-run loans to provide households with funds to tide them over until the next pay-day. Such *pay-day lending* comes at a very high rate of interest.

Exercise 30.1

Discuss whether the authorities should intervene to regulate the pay-day lending market.

Key terms

liquidity ratio the ratio of liquid assets to total assets

interbank lending borrowing and lending between banks to manage their liquidity and other requirements for short-term funds

LIBOR the average rate of interest on interbank lending in the London interbank market

repo a sale and repurchase agreement, whereby one financial institution sells a financial asset to another with an agreement to buy it back at an agreed future date

Another form of borrowing comes in the form of overdrafts, an arrangement whereby a bank's customer can spend more than is covered by current deposits at a pre-announced rate of interest. Such borrowing is limited to an amount agreed in advance. Credit cards also allow borrowers to incur debt, and allow ready payment for everyday transactions.

Interest rates

Interest rates reveal substantial variation. This can be explained with reference to some key characteristics of the form of borrowing to which they relate, particularly the risk involved with lending. The security and length of the loan contribute to the risk. It would be expected that lending with no collateral would carry a risk premium, as the cost of default is high for the lender. It is also the case that risk may be higher for a long-term loan because of the uncertainty attached to the future. This may be balanced by the nature of collateral — for example, in the case of mortgage lending, where the asset providing the collateral is expected to appreciate in value over time. This was especially true in periods when house prices were rising at a fast rate.

Unsecured loans, such as overdrafts and credit cards, carry significantly higher interest rates than the secured loans such as mortgages, or government securities, which may be perceived as much less risky.

> ### Knowledge check 30.6
>
> Why do credit card companies charge such a high rate of interest when balances are not paid off at the end of the month?

Financial instruments

The development of new financial instruments in recent decades has had a major influence on the way that financial markets operate. Shares are issued by firms in need of finance. Shareholders become part-owners of the company, and may receive dividends from the profits made by the firm. Those holding a large portion of a firm's shares can have a major say in how the firm operates.

> ### Synoptic link
>
> Notice, however, that when firms are owned by a large and fragmented number of shareholders, the managers who run the firm may not face great accountability, thus giving rise to the principal-agent problem, which was discussed in Chapter 17 (page 249).

When the government needs to borrow, it can do so by issuing bonds. A bond is a financial asset that pays a fixed amount each year and also carries a fixed value payable at a fixed date in the future when the bond matures. Bonds can be bought and sold, and the price of the bond varies with the market valuation at any point in time. The price of a bond varies inversely with the rate of interest.

Certificates of deposit (CDs) are one way in which a financial institution can extend its borrowing. These are certificates issued by banks to customers in return for deposits for a fixed term. For example, a large firm may agree to deposit a sum of money for a fixed period, receiving a CD in return. The CD can be sold on in the secondary market, so if the firm needs liquid funds, it can obtain them in spite of having agreed to the long-term deposit. From the bank's point of view, it knows it does not have to repay the deposit until a fixed point in the future.

Securitisation

Banks have also devised ways of selling some of their assets to other financial institutions. For example, suppose a bank has a stock of assets in the form of residential mortgages that generate a regular cash flow. It is possible for the bank to bundle these together and sell them on. This process is known as **securitisation**. This is a device that effectively turns future cash flows into a bond.

One effect of this is that banks find that they need not maintain such a high liquidity ratio in order to meet their obligations, and can thus expand their lending. This is what happened in the lead-up to the financial crisis of the late 2000s. Securitisation altered the balance of bank assets, with a higher proportion now being in the form of bonds rather than equity/shares. There is a key difference between the two, because firms can suspend dividends in a hard year, but the return on bonds has to be paid. It also turned out that some of the securitisation that had taken place had involved assets and cash flows that were less secure and more risky than had been thought — for example, the so-called sub-prime mortgage market, where some households began to default on their debts.

The seeds of the financial crisis

This laid the seeds of the financial crisis, when some banks had difficulty in meeting their obligations. Furthermore, with the banks holding lower liquidity ratios, the interbank lending system also came under pressure. In the UK, the government had to step in to bail out banks that were in difficulties.

As public debt rose, the government cut back on spending at the same time that banks were cutting down on lending. In this way, the crisis spread to the real sector of the economy. Recession was here. Chapter 31 explores the way in which the Bank of England responded to the situation.

> ### Knowledge check 30.7
> What is meant here by the 'real sector'?

The impact was also felt through the stock market, where falling share prices put pressure on insurance and pension funds. It also became apparent that it is not only the liquidity ratio that is important. Partly through securitisation, banks were holding a wider variety of financial assets, carrying varying amounts of risk. Their ability to meet all demands from their depositors and to cover loan defaults would depend on a bank's capital relative to its current liabilities and assets (weighted by the risk). This is measured by the **capital adequacy ratio**, defined as the ratio of a bank's capital to the value of its risk-weighted assets.

Market failure?

To what extent did market failure contribute to the financial crisis?

Information gap

As securitisation became widespread, there may well have been an information gap, in the sense that the banks were accumulating assets about which they had less than full knowledge. There was information asymmetry here, as the banks had less knowledge about the assets that they were acquiring than the original lenders. This applied in particular to mortgages that were being recycled. They were therefore

Key terms

securitisation process whereby future cash flows are converted into marketable securities

capital adequacy ratio the ratio of a bank's capital to its current liabilities and risk-weighted assets

Key term

asymmetric information
a situation in which some participants in a market have better information about market conditions than others

not in a position to come to an accurate estimate of the risk to which they were becoming exposed.

An information gap in the form of **asymmetric information** may also arise where regulators have incomplete and insufficient knowledge of banks' behaviour, and cannot therefore safeguard the stability of the financial system.

Synoptic link

The notion of asymmetric information was first introduced in Chapter 7 in the context of market failure.

Speculation

The trend towards securitisation tended to spread through the financial system, building into a sort of speculative bubble, in which increasing numbers of financial institutions sought to join the profit spree in anticipation of future profitability. The problem with such bubbles is that once they burst, all suffer together, and problems spread rapidly through the system.

Moral hazard

The banks perceived that securitisation meant their risks were covered, and they were thus prepared to expand their lending beyond what turned out to be reasonable. In other words, the banks thought that they could take on more risk because they were confident that their position was secure. They may even have realised that their position in financial markets meant that if anything did go wrong, they would be bailed out by governments who perceived them to be too big to fail — which, of course, is exactly what transpired. This could also create problems in the future if the financial institutions believe that they will always be bailed out if they get into difficulties.

Knowledge check 30.8

Explain what is meant by 'moral hazard'.

Synoptic link

The concept of moral hazard was explained in Chapter 7.

Externality effects

Once one bank is seen to be failing, the reputation of the whole banking system comes into question, and other banks initially unaffected also come under pressure through externality effects. In this way, contagion can affect the whole financial system and cause lines of credit to dry up as banks become increasingly unwilling to become further exposed by lending.

In the context of pensions schemes, people may buy insufficient insurance, or accumulate insufficient savings for their retirement, which imposes costs on society when they need to be supported in old age. The UK government tackled this using the behavioural economics concept of nudge theory, which suggests that people are less likely to opt out of a pension in which they are automatically registered, than to opt in to one that is provided. This approach has been very successful in making sure that more people are enrolled in a pension scheme.

Exercise 30.2

Discuss what effect the rise of internet banking is having on the financial system.

Market rigging

Market failure can also happen through the deliberate (and illegal) actions of individual economic agents. There have been allegations that some bankers have operated to distort interest rates or exchange rates in order to make illegal profits. For example, in 2016 four city traders who had worked for Barclays were jailed for rigging the LIBOR rate.

Extension material: the financial sector in emerging and developing countries

Developing countries face particular problems in relation to the financial sector. Formal financial institutions are less well equipped to provide financial services, as was discussed in Chapter 29. Stock markets may not exist, or may not function effectively. The provision of banking services to rural areas is fraught with difficulties. The banks are not readily able to assess the credit-worthiness of potential borrowers. There is a situation of asymmetric information here, as the borrowers have much better information about the riskiness of proposed projects than the banks can obtain, so are likely to be charged high interest rates. Property rights may be weak, so that borrowers cannot provide collateral that the banks would accept. This forces borrowers into the informal market, where local moneylenders have monopoly power, and can charge exorbitant rates of interest.

The Harrod–Domar approach suggests that saving and investment are crucial ingredients for a strategy to promote economic growth and human development. If funds cannot be raised domestically, then an injection of funds from abroad will be necessary, in the form of foreign direct investment, overseas assistance or borrowing on international financial markets.

Whichever approach is adopted, the financial sector is vital as a way of channelling the resources to where they are needed. This needs to be accomplished in a way that addresses areas of market failure. Rural credit markets may need specific attention, but funds also need to be provided for improvements in physical and social infrastructure that will then enable markets to operate effectively. In other words, funds are needed for road and communication links, market facilities and so on. In addition, it is important to be able to invest in human capital, by providing education and healthcare and ensuring adequate nutrition for the population.

All this is challenging for developing countries with limited resources. Where the financial sector has been able to work effectively, countries have been able to show progress on many fronts. This has been evident in the emerging economies. The economies that entered a period of rapid growth in the 1960s found ways of mobilising funds. For example, both South Korea and Singapore laid the foundations for rapid growth by finding ways of encouraging saving, the funds from which were then channelled into productive investment and infrastructure. More recently, China's success in mobilising foreign direct investment has been one of the key factors enabling growth.

In sub-Saharan Africa, economic growth has been more elusive. Financial markets have not developed to the same extent as in East Asia, nor have stock markets flourished. Such funds as have been generated — for example, through overseas assistance or international borrowing — have not always been used effectively.

Summary: the financial sector and the macroeconomy

- The banking sector covers retail and wholesale banking, but the distinction has become blurred over time.
- Banks aim to make profits, and face a trade-off between making loans and retaining sufficient liquidity to service their customers.
- Short-term liquidity requirements are managed through the interbank market.
- Borrowing takes a variety of forms.
- Interest rates payable on loans reflect risk and security.
- New financial instruments developed in recent decades through securitisation have increased the importance of the secondary market.
- Some banks found themselves in difficulties for a variety of reasons.

The history of insurance

Modern insurers charge a premium in exchange for a promise to pay out a larger sum of money if necessary. A risk-averse person will often prefer to pay a small sum today instead of incurring a larger cost later on. Some types of insurance are even mandatory by law. For example, car owners have to buy the basic type of insurance. They are not obliged to buy fully comprehensive insurance. Some choose not to, or 'self-insure'. They undertake to cover certain costs themselves. The insurance industry is now an important part of all developed economies.

The basic idea behind an insurance scheme is the pooling of risk. If a number of individuals enter the scheme, then hopefully only a few of them will need to make a claim. As long as the payments into the scheme cover the claims, then the scheme is viable in the long run. The idea of pooling risks predates private insurers. Many early communities used some form of cooperation (or social insurance) to deal with risks. There was always the possibility that an individual would become unable to work and fall into poverty. There were social and religious reasons to give charity to these people, but there was no guarantee.

The Poor Laws

Under the Elizabethan Poor Laws, communities were obliged to help poor people who were too infirm to support themselves. Taxes were used to raise funds. The Poor Laws required poor people to claim help in the community which they came from. There were good reasons for this, which are also important for private insurance. In a small community, people knew each other very well. They knew who had worked hard and followed social rules, such as attending church. They also knew who had not behaved themselves. Frequently, communities wanted to support only those who followed their rules. Traditionally, these people were called 'the deserving poor'. Other people, who broke social rules, might not be helped. The Poor Laws therefore forced paupers to go to the place where they were known. If they could go anywhere, then liars might claim relief that they were not entitled to. This problem is called an *asymmetry of information*. It means that one party has private information that others do not have. Elizabethan law-makers did not want lazy or deceitful people to exploit others.

Insurers also face the problem of *moral hazard*. This means that after someone has gained insurance, they have an incentive to change their behaviour and take less care. Early social insurance schemes, such as the Poor Laws, took moral hazard problems very seriously. Law-makers worried that people would not be motivated to avoid poverty if they thought they could claim handouts. Society would be less productive as a result. Strict rules were used to prove that paupers were not merely lazy. If they could work in any way, they were forced to do so or they would not be given anything. Payments were kept at a very low level. There was also a social stigma to receiving handouts. These factors helped to minimise the claims on the community.

The shipping industry

The Poor Laws only dealt with the very poorest. Most people had to self-insure. They built up as much wealth as possible and also relied on their relatives to provide for them in old age. Self-insurance was not as easy for merchants, especially those who operated on a large scale. For example, a shipwreck meant the loss of an entire cargo. If a merchant put his entire capital into that one cargo, he was running an enormous risk. But he could spread the risk by sending the cargo by several different ships. Each ship would carry the cargoes of several different merchants. The next step was the development of underwriting. Specialist brokers would offer insurance contracts on ships in exchange for a fee. The marine insurance sector developed well before other types of insurance. One of the most famous insurers, Lloyds of London, initially started as a group of marine underwriters based at the Lloyds coffeehouse in the City of London.

Over time, underwriters began to gather a great deal of information about the shipping industry. They could then assess the risks involved and charge premiums accordingly. Insurers had to worry about going bankrupt if they could not cover all the claims. However, competitive pressures pushed premiums downwards. The problem of setting the right premiums reappeared with the development of both fire and life insurance. Insurers lacked detailed data about the risks of fire or mortality. Without sufficient information, the early firms had trouble estimating the sums needed to cover their claims. In addition, early schemes used a variety of different financial structures. Initially, they did not even charge different premiums to different customers.

The Lloyds of London building in the City of London

Fire insurers

A number of fire insurance schemes were created after the Great Fire of London of 1666. During the massive rebuilding programme, great efforts were made to use stone and other fireproof materials instead of wood. The risks of fire were reduced and fire insurance schemes became more viable. It was not clear whether the government, a monopolist or several private firms should control fire insurance. In the end, a variety of firms competed for customers. Several of the early schemes were mutual funds. In this business model, the insured parties would agree to cover all legitimate claims made. The amount they were charged depended on the total sum of the claims in any one time period, plus running costs. The firm could always call on its members to provide more funds. This was not the case with firms which charged premiums. The premium was fixed in any one time period, even if the firm had to settle large claims. Early firms often set the premium rates far too low. They then found that their outgoings were larger than forecast. The earliest schemes went bust.

The fire insurers tended to restrict their activities to London. They found it very difficult to assess risks outside of the capital because they had less information about provincial areas. Life insurers also had difficulties in judging risks. They had to contend with other problems. Their critics sometimes argued that life insurance was immoral and encouraged gambling. These criticisms might seem surprising today, but there was a link between life insurance and betting. Some people placed bets on events such as the outcome of a war, or whether the king would die that year.

It was not only the famous who might be insured. People could insure their servants, neighbours or even complete strangers. Many contracts were not an attempt to reduce risks, but to gamble. People were speculating on how long their acquaintances might live and hoping to benefit from guessing correctly. Life insurance faces the same problems that plague other types of insurance: asymmetric information, adverse selection and moral hazard. Insurers found that many of the people covered by their policies were in worse health than had been expected. Second, many worried that after insurance had been issued there was an incentive to kill the insured party. Certainly, there have been plenty of cases of murderers insuring their victims in advance. For example, in the early twentieth century there were the 'Brides in the Bath' murders. George Smith was convicted of murdering three of his wives and claiming on their life insurance policies. Fire insurers also face fraud by deliberate acts of arson. A less dramatic example of moral hazard is the householder who takes less care of the insured property than before. Companies deal with moral hazard by putting clauses into their contracts forcing people to take due care. Otherwise, the contract is void.

Today, insurers charge different premiums to different individuals. However, some early schemes charged the same fee to all. If a single premium is charged then it must be high enough to cover the average claim per person. This is likely to be too high for some who are in good health. They will self-insure. Then too high a proportion of clients will be bad risks (unhealthy) and the scheme may be bankrupted.

Adapted from an article by Helen Paul in Economic Review, Vol. 33, No. 2, pp. 12–15.

Follow-up questions

a Why is the 'pooling of risk' so important in the insurance market?

b Explain the meaning of asymmetric information, adverse selection and moral hazard, and why these are examples of market failure.

c George Smith claimed on the life insurance of his victims. Was this an example of moral hazard or of adverse selection?

d If you take less care of your smartphone because you know that it is insured, is that an example of moral hazard or of adverse selection?

e Discuss how modern insurance companies address the issues of adverse selection and moral hazard.

This chapter explores the role of the central bank in the financial system, looking at the functions of the central bank, and the measures it has available to carry out those functions. Of particular importance are the provision of liquidity to the banking system and the role of an independent central bank in meeting targets set by the government. The need for regulation is examined, and the way in which changes in the regulatory framework may have contributed to the financial crisis and its resolution.

Learning objectives

After studying this chapter, you should:
- → be familiar with the core functions of the central bank
- → be aware of the operations of the Bank of England and their significance
- → be able to explain the rationale for inflation targeting and an independent central bank
- → be familiar with the way in which interest rates can be influenced through open market operations in normal periods
- → appreciate the factors that contributed to the financial crisis that began in the late 2000s
- → understand quantitative easing and why it was necessary to introduce it
- → be able to explain the need for financial regulation
- → be familiar with the way in which financial regulation is administered by the Bank of England
- → be aware of the roles of the BIS and IMF in coordinating global financial policies

Synoptic link

Notice that this chapter builds on material presented in earlier chapters. In particular, you will need to be familiar with the instruments and operation of monetary policy, which were introduced in Chapter 16.

Key term

central bank the banker to the government, performing a range of functions, which may include issue of coins and banknotes, acting as banker to commercial banks and regulating the financial system

The functions of the central bank

All developed and most developing countries have a **central bank** that fulfils a range of roles, including having the responsibility for issuing currency (banknotes and coins). For example, the UK has the Bank of England to act as the country's central bank. Being the body responsible for issuing notes and coins, the central bank has a direct impact on the quantity of money in circulation in the country. It has also been given responsibility for using monetary policy to keep inflation under control.

The central bank has other important roles to fulfil. The central bank acts as banker to the government, and may manage the government's programme of borrowing and the country's foreign exchange reserves. Furthermore, the central bank may act as a banker for the commercial banks and other financial institutions that operate in the economy. In addition, the central bank may act as the regulator of the financial system, monitoring the behaviour of the commercial banks and financial institutions. In some countries, the central bank has independent authority delegated from the government to pursue targets for inflation through the setting of interest rates or to promote growth and development. However, not all central banks perform all of these various functions.

The Bank of England operates in sterling money markets — known as the Sterling Monetary Framework (SMF). The Bank's responsibilities include ensuring an adequate supply of liquidity to the SMF participants — that is, the banks and other financial institutions that operate in sterling money markets.

Knowledge check 31.1

What would be the principal effect of rise in interest rates in the economy?

The central bank in the UK is the Bank of England

In developing countries, the central bank may have an important role in establishing and consolidating the domestic financial system in order to build confidence in the currency and financial institutions. It is worth being aware that in parts of sub-Saharan Africa less than 20% of households have an account with a financial institution. This is not only because of the lack of bank branches (although this is clearly important), but is partly due to a lack of confidence in financial institutions. There may also be a developmental role in ensuring that credit can be made available for key development priorities.

Synoptic link

The problems in providing credit in rural areas in developing countries was discussed in Chapter 28.

In some cases, the central bank may be given responsibility for roles that support other objectives of the government. An example here would be the State Bank of Pakistan, which also has a responsibility for the 'Islamisation' of the banking system, to recognise the importance to the country of developing Islamic forms of financial instrument.

Extension material: Islamic banking

The key difference between banking as it is known in western countries and Islamic banking is that Islam prohibits the use of interest (or usury, as it is known). This means that Islamic banks cannot charge interest on loans or pay interest on savings. Gambling is also prohibited.

A variety of financial instruments have been developed to allow banks to lend to firms or to households without charging interest. For example, a bank may agree a profit-sharing deal with a firm. The bank lends to the firm and then shares in the profits of the project. An alternative is a cost-plus-margin agreement. The bank purchases a given property at an agreed price, and immediately sells it to the buyer, stating the cost plus profit margin. The property is then treated as a commodity sold for money rather than an interest-based loan. The client pays in agreed termly instalments.

The core activities of the Bank of England, the UK's central bank, include acting as banker to the government and financial institutions, managing the country's exchange reserves and supply of currency, and regulating the financial system. These have strong implications for the supply of money and credit in the economy.

Issuing notes and coin

The issuing of notes and coin has long been a core function of the Bank of England, although it does not have a monopoly in the UK (only in England and Wales). Commercial banks in Scotland and Northern Ireland can also issue banknotes, but the issue is regulated by the Bank of England. It is still important to control the issue of banknotes in order to make sure that demands are met without leading to inflation. However, issuing notes and coin does not mean having control of the money supply because of the wide variety of other financial assets that are near-money.

Banker to the government

Knowledge check 31.2

Who sets the target for inflation, and what is the target that the Bank needs to meet?

The Bank of England acts as banker to the government, in the sense that tax revenues and items of government expenditure are handled by the Bank, as are items of government borrowing and lending. In the past, the Bank of England also had responsibility for managing government debt by issuing Treasury bills, but this was transferred to the Debt Management Office (an executive office within the Treasury) when the Bank was given independence to control the interest rate in order to meet the inflation target.

Banker to the commercial banks

The commercial banks and other SMF participants hold deposits at the Bank of England in the form of reserve balances and cash ratio deposits. The reserve balances are used as a stock of liquid assets, but also fulfil a clearing role, in the sense that they are used to equalise any imbalance in transactions between the major banks on a day-by-day basis. In normal times, the Bank agrees an average level of overnight reserves that SMF participants expect to require in the month ahead. If any institution holds reserves out of their agreed range, this attracts a charge. In other words, if a bank needs to borrow beyond its agreed average reserve level, it must pay a rate that is above the bank rate. Deposits above the agreed average are remunerated below bank rate. This encourages institutions to meet their requirements in the interbank market, which helps to keep the interbank rate close to the bank rate.

Managing the exchange rate

The Bank of England manages the UK's gold and foreign currency reserves on behalf of the Treasury. However, interventions have been rare in recent years, with the pound being allowed to find its own level in the foreign exchange market.

Monetary and financial stability

Apart from the functions outlined, the Bank's main mission is 'to promote the good of the people of the United Kingdom by maintaining monetary and financial stability'. **Monetary stability** is interpreted in terms of stability in prices (relative to the government's inflation target). **Financial stability** means an efficient flow of funds in the economy and confidence in UK financial institutions.

Study tip

Be clear about the core activities of the Bank of England and their relative importance for financial markets.

The efficient flow of funds requires that there is sufficient liquidity in the economy. In other words, there must be enough liquidity for the financial institutions to conduct their business. The traditional way in which this was done was by the Bank of England acting as the **lender of last resort**, being prepared to lend to banks if they could not obtain the funds that they needed elsewhere, albeit at a penalty rate. Although this was traditionally seen as a key role, events during the financial crisis made it untenable.

Inflation targeting

In 1997 a significant change in the conduct of monetary policy was introduced by the incoming Labour administration. The Bank of England was given independent responsibility to set interest rates in order to achieve the stated inflation target set by the government. This represented a major change by taking discretion for monetary policy away from the government. An important motivation for this change was to increase the credibility of government policy, in the sense that it could no longer try to use short-run policy measures to create a 'feel-good' factor in the economy. Instead, it was declaring a pre-commitment to controlling inflation, which it hoped would improve expectations about the future course of the macroeconomy.

Synoptic link

Make sure that you are familiar with the way in which a change in bank rate eventually feeds through to affect aggregate demand and the rate of inflation. This was explained in Chapter 16.

The **Monetary Policy Committee (MPC)** of the Bank of England has as its primary responsibility the maintenance of monetary stability by meeting the inflation target. However, it also has a secondary responsibility, as meeting the target for inflation is subject to supporting the economic policy of the government, including the objectives for economic growth and employment. In other words, the MPC cannot pursue the inflation target if this excessively endangers growth or employment.

Key terms

monetary stability a situation in which there is stability in prices relative to the government's inflation target

financial stability a situation in which there is a sufficient and efficient flow of liquidity in the economy

lender of last resort the role of the central bank in guaranteeing sufficient liquidity is available in the monetary system

Monetary Policy Committee (MPC) body within the Bank of England responsible for the conduct of monetary policy

The challenge of the period of inflation targeting has thus been to balance the needs of monetary stability (meeting the inflation target) with ensuring financial stability (by ensuring the efficient and adequate provision of liquidity).

The advantage of having an independent central bank to pursue the inflation target is to reinforce the credibility of the government's commitment to monetary stability, but the danger is that this could be pursued at the expense of the government's target for economic growth.

Exercise 31.1

Discuss the advantages and disadvantages of having an independent central bank dedicated to meeting an inflation target.

Summary: roles of the central bank

- The central bank of a country fulfils a number of important roles within the financial system to create monetary and financial stability.
- The central bank takes responsibility for issuing notes and coins — or at least for controlling the quantity in circulation.
- It may act as banker to the government and to other financial institutions.
- It also has a role in regulating the foreign exchange market.
- It may manage the government's debt position.
- In some countries, the central bank has been given independent responsibility for meeting a government target — for example, the Bank of England has responsibility for meeting the inflation target.

Policy measures available to the Bank of England

The financial crisis highlighted the need for central banks to enhance their roles in maintaining monetary and financial stability. This is well illustrated by exploring how the role of the Bank of England has evolved over time. In particular, there have been significant changes to the operations of the Bank of England in response to the introduction of inflation targeting and the financial crisis that began in the late 2000s. The crisis highlighted the need for closer monitoring of the financial system in order to ensure financial stability.

The pre-crisis period, 1997–2007

In 1997, the incoming Labour government delegated to the Bank of England the responsibility for meeting its inflation target. Specifically, the Bank was to keep inflation within 1 percentage point of the target, which was initially set at 2.5%, as measured by the retail price index (RPIX). From January 2004, the target was reset in terms of the consumer price index (CPI), with its rate of change falling within 1 percentage point of 2%. The performance relative to the target from 1997 to 2007 is shown in Figure 31.1.

In the pre-crisis period, the Bank targeted inflation by using the interest rate. As was explained in Chapter 30, there are many different interest rates on financial assets, varying with the degree of risk associated with the asset, the length of loans and so on. However, they are interconnected, so the Bank can influence the rates of interest by changing the rate that it charges on short-term loans to domestic banks. This is known as **bank rate**. You can see how this moved around in Figure 31.1. These changes in bank rate affect the interest rates on other financial assets.

Key terms

bank rate the rate of interest charged by the Bank of England on short-term loans to other banks

open market operations intervention by the central bank to influence short-run interest rates by buying or selling securities

Sources: ONS, Bank of England

Figure 31.1 UK bank rate and the inflation target, 1997–2007

Rates of interest also move around in response to market conditions, and the Bank of England can intervene to make sure that short-run interest rates are kept in line with bank rate. It does this by using **open market operations**, buying or selling securities in order to influence short-run interest rates.

Suppose there is a shortage of liquidity in the financial system. Financial institutions will need to borrow in order to improve their liquidity position. This puts upward pressure on interest rates, so there is a danger that interest rates will move out of line with bank rate. The Bank of England can intervene to prevent this, providing liquidity in the system by buying securities (Treasury bills or gilts) in the open market. Conversely, if there is excess liquidity in the system, interest rates may tend to fall, and the Bank can prevent this by selling securities in the open market.

This was a period in which policy appeared to be working effectively. Inflation remained within the specified one percentage point of its target, apart from one month when it rose to 3.1% (March 2007). Economic growth was steady during this period, and there were no obvious problems with liquidity. This period is sometimes known as the 'Great Moderation'.

Knowledge check 31.3

If the Bank of England were to buy securities in the open market, in which direction would this affect interest rates?

Exercise 31.2

Suppose there is excessive liquidity in the economy. Explain how open market operations would be used to deal with the situation.

Monetary policy from 2008

This period of stability was not to last. Figure 31.2 shows bank rate and inflation (measured by the percentage change in the CPI) from the beginning of 2008. You can see that the pattern is very different from that in the period 1997–2007. Inflation moved out of its target range, and bank rate plummeted to an all-time low.

Sources: ONS, Bank of England

Figure 31.2 UK bank rate and the inflation target since 2008

Knowledge check 31.4

Looking at Figure 31.2, was the MPC correct in thinking that inflation would fall in late 2008?

During 2008, inflation accelerated. This partly reflected increases in food and commodity prices world-wide. The Monetary Policy Committee took the view that this acceleration would not persist. Economic growth was expected to slow, and inflation was expected to move back below 2% per annum. Rather than increasing bank rate in order to put downward pressure on aggregate demand and inflation, the MPC reduced bank rate in August in anticipation of falling growth and inflation. In the following months, the financial crisis began to unfold.

Banks in difficulty

Even in 2007, it was becoming clear that a number of banks were facing difficulties, having expanded their borrowing substantially relative to their capital base. The response was to reduce lending, sell assets and look for new capital. Borrowing against property was one of the root causes, as the expectation that house prices would continue to rise had encouraged mortgage lending. When house prices in the USA stalled in 2005/06, defaults began to rise, putting pressure on lenders. The failure of some institutions prompted fears of recession, and one of the side-effects of globalisation was that financial markets were interconnected across national boundaries.

Knowledge check 31.5

Explain why large-scale bank failures would be damaging to the economy.

A problem with bank failures is the effect they have on confidence in the financial system. As the crisis developed, it was perceived that some of the banks that were in danger were 'too large' to be allowed to fail. The demise of a large financial institution would have such an effect on expectations that the whole financial system might be called into question. Hence the moves by the UK and other governments to bail out banks that were in difficulties, in spite of the effect that this had on public finances, as was shown in Figure 15.5 on page 214.

Shortage of liquidity

In the UK, the crisis showed up in the interbank market, where a shortage of liquidity put upward pressure on the interbank rate. By March 2009, bank rate had been reduced to 0.5%, and this was seen as being the lowest possible, although it was subsequently reduced to 0.25% in late 2016 for a period. The Bank of England suspended the reserves averaging regime in 2009, as it could no longer be effective. Instead, it introduced **quantitative easing**, a policy under which it created central

Key term

quantitative easing process by which liquidity in the economy is increased when the central bank purchases assets from the commercial banks

bank reserves electronically, which were used to purchase high-quality financial assets such as government bonds in order to provide additional liquidity. This allowed the Bank to continue to influence interest rates.

Notice that the sudden fall in the public sector net debt (including financial sector interventions) in 2014 resulted from the reclassification of Lloyds Banking Group from the public to the private sector, following sales by the UK government of part of its shareholdings in the group. By early 2017, the divestment was complete, although net debt remained at a relatively high level.

Quantitative easing

Quantitative easing is essentially a way of increasing money supply. The foundations for this had been set in January 2009 by establishing the Asset Purchase Facility (APF), a subsidiary company of the Bank of England that carries out the necessary transactions. By mid-2018, the APF had purchased £435 billion of assets by the creation of central bank reserves. The level of quantitative easing is decided by the MPC as a joint decision with that on bank rate.

The problem faced by the Bank in this situation was that the rate of inflation had to be kept under control, but at the same time, the reluctance of banks to lend would affect investment and the growth of the real economy, which was heading into recession. Expectations were weak, threatening to prolong the recession. The UK was not alone in facing this combination of circumstances, and other central banks were adopting similar strategies to deal with the growing crisis.

Recovery was slow

Figure 31.3 shows the extent to which some other countries were following a common path for economic growth. Having badged the financial turmoil as being the worst since the 1930s, governments were anxious to avoid a repetition of the mass unemployment that had happened then. This was avoided, but you can see in the figure that the recovery was not rapid. It is difficult to disentangle the extent to which the recovery was a consequence of the policy stance adopted by the government and the Bank of England.

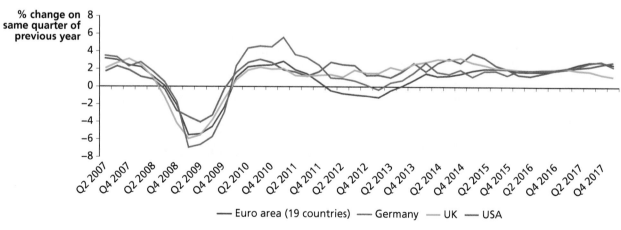

Source: OECD (2018), Quarterly GDP (indicator).
doi: 10.1787/b86d1fc8-en (accessed on 19 June 2018)

Figure 31.3 Annual growth rate of GDP since 2007 (quarterly data)

Key terms

Prudential Regulation Authority (PRA) the decision-making body in the Bank of England responsible for microprudential regulation of deposit-takers, insurers and major investment firms

microprudential regulation financial regulation intended to set standards and supervise financial institutions at the level of the individual firm

Financial Policy Committee (FPC) the decision-making body of the Bank of England responsible for macroprudential regulation

macroprudential regulation financial regulation intended to mitigate the risk of the financial system as a whole

Financial Conduct Authority (FCA) a body separate from the Bank of England responsible for conduct regulation of financial services firms

Knowledge check 31.6

Compare the performance of the UK economy with the EU19 in Figure 31.3. In which periods were there appreciable differences in performance?

Financial regulation

A commonly held view was that one of the key factors leading to the crisis had been the inadequate regulation of financial institutions, which had allowed banks to build up portfolios of lending that carried risk beyond what could be covered by their capital. One way of viewing this is that, although central banks such as the Bank of England had structures to enable them to achieve monetary stability, the regulatory framework had not allowed the same degree of control over financial stability.

A new regulatory framework came into operation in April 2013 to try to remedy this situation, and to avoid repetition of the financial crisis in the future. Two new statutory decision-making bodies were created that are part of the Bank of England. The **Prudential Regulation Authority (PRA)** is responsible for **microprudential regulation**, working at the level of the individual firm to promote the safeness and soundness of deposit-takers, insurers and major investment firms. The **Financial Policy Committee (FPC)** became responsible for **macroprudential regulation**:

> responsible for identifying, monitoring and taking action to remove or reduce systemic risks with a view to protecting and enhancing the resilience of the UK financial system. And, subject to that, supporting the economic policy of the Government, including its objectives for growth and employment.
> 'Changes to the Bank of England', Bank of England Quarterly Bulletin, 2013 Q1

In addition, the **Financial Conduct Authority (FCA)** was given responsibility for ensuring that relevant markets function well, and has responsibility for financial services firms that are not supervised by the PRA, including asset managers, hedge funds, many broker-dealers and independent financial advisers.

The intention of these arrangements is to improve the resilience and stability of the financial system by filling a perceived regulatory gap that had allowed the seeds of the crisis to develop. The USA and other countries in the EU have also established new bodies to perform similar tasks. This is crucial given the interconnectedness of financial markets following globalisation.

Knowledge check 31.7

Which body would be responsible for investigating allegations of market rigging by bankers?

Notice that the FPC has primary responsibility for financial stability, but (like the MPC) it also has secondary responsibility for supporting the government's economic policy. This means that it must keep a balance between taking steps to stabilise the financial system and facilitating economic growth and employment.

The FPC has the power to make recommendations. For example, it can make recommendations to the PRA and FCA to take action to safeguard financial stability. The PRA and FCA need to comply, or to explain why this is not seen to be appropriate. The FPC can use the *countercyclical capital buffer*, under which banks, building societies and large investment firms can be required to hold additional loss-absorbing capital. The FPC can also impose *sectoral capital requirements*, under which firms need to meet additional capital requirements where the FPC perceives a risk to the stability of the financial system as a whole. A further power held by the FPC concerns the scope of regulation, in that it can recommend changes to the boundary between regulated and non-regulated activities.

The aim of these measures is to reduce the likelihood of future financial crises by monitoring activity more closely and having early warning of where problems may be building up. The FPC and PRA between them can then take action to mitigate the risks of a crisis. Given the impact of globalisation, it is recognised that there is a need for international coordination of financial regulation. This is discussed shortly.

Evaluation of the response to the crisis

The financial crisis highlighted the importance of the financial system for the real economy. Monetary stability is important because low and predictable inflation helps economic agents to form expectations about the future. This encourages firms to invest and allows households to plan their consumption. This in turn can promote economic growth and improvements in the standard of living. However, the crisis demonstrated that financial stability is also crucial, as this enables the flow of funds needed for firms to finance their investment.

The period before the crisis was characterised by monetary stability, with the inflation target being met, and economic growth proceeding at a steady rate. However, the inadequacy of regulation led to a build-up of pressure which finally erupted in financial instability. This disrupted the financial system and had spillover effects for the real economy, resulting in recession and rising unemployment.

The main manifestations of this were in the failure of liquidity. The interbank market was unable to deliver the liquidity that was needed, and the Bank of England's role as lender of last resort could not be sustained with bank rate at 0.5%. In this situation, the Bank resorted to expansion of the money supply through the process of quantitative easing to supply liquidity while still keeping inflation within its target range.

The need for financial stability was tackled by the creation of new decision-making bodies with the responsibility for maintaining financial stability through enhanced regulation of the financial system and by monitoring developments in financial markets.

In seeking to maintain its primary objectives of both monetary and financial stability, the Bank needs also to maintain balance with its secondary objective of supporting the government's overall macroeconomic policy stance. This is no mean feat when the need to bail out failing banks has left a legacy of high public debt.

Study tip

Be clear in your mind about the distinction between monetary stability (low and predictable inflation) and financial stability (the efficient flow of liquidity). You should also be aware of the primary and secondary objectives of the Bank of England in terms of both monetary and financial stability.

Summary: the financial crisis and the response

- There have been significant changes to the operations of the Bank of England since the financial crisis.
- The Bank had been given independent responsibility for the conduct of monetary policy in 1997 with a brief to meet the government's inflation target.
- This was to be accomplished through the Monetary Policy Committee (MPC) setting bank rate.
- By setting bank rate, the rates of interest in other segments of the money market would also be affected.
- Open market operations were used to keep short-term interest rates in line with bank rate.
- In the financial crisis, banks faced shortages of liquidity and the interbank market could not cope.
- With bank rate at the lowest level that could be sustained, quantitative easing was introduced to supply liquidity to the financial sector.
- The crisis highlighted the need for greater regulation to maintain financial stability.

The international context

It is important to remember that the financial crisis was not only a problem for the UK, but affected most advanced economies. Indeed, some European countries faced more severe conditions than the UK. The actions of the Bank of England should thus be seen in the context of the oversight of the international financial system by the Bretton Woods institutions.

Along with globalisation has come the need to provide coordination of financial markets across countries. Deregulation increased the interconnectedness of financial markets, and the runaway advances in technology and the internet allowed financial transactions to take place smoothly and instantaneously. This improved the efficiency with which markets could operate, but also heightened the possibility for contagion — in other words, it increased the probability that crises could spread rapidly between countries.

There are three key organisations that contribute to international coordination of financial markets and regulation: the Bank for International Settlements (BIS), the International Monetary Fund (IMF) and the World Bank. Each fulfils a specific function in the global financial system. The BIS was established in 1930 and acts as a banker to central banks. It has also played a key role in financial regulation by brokering international agreements.

The Bank for International Settlements

The **Bank for International Settlements (BIS)** was originally set up in 1930 to settle the then-controversial issue of the reparation payments imposed on Germany at the end of the First World War. The onset of the Great Depression changed the focus, which switched to activities involving technical cooperation between central banks. The Bretton Woods conference called for the abolition of the BIS on the grounds that it would be rendered redundant by the IMF and World Bank. However, instead it refocused on European monetary and financial issues, becoming a forum for European monetary cooperation.

Synoptic link

The roles of the World Bank and the IMF, and the Bretton Woods conference that established them, were discussed in Chapter 29.

Key term

Bank for International Settlements (BIS) an institution that acts as a bank for central banks and sets standards for regulation of banks that are accepted globally

After the collapse of the Dollar Standard in the early 1970s, the need for international cooperation in the operation of financial markets became apparent, and in 1982 G10 central bankers created the Basel Committee on Banking Supervision, which was to play a key role in financial regulation. The debt crisis that affected a number of Latin American countries in the early 1980s highlighted the need to have measures in place to provide regulation and avoid the possibility of sovereign default (that is, where nations fail to meet their obligations in international debt).

The Basel Committee established a credit risk measurement framework that became a globally accepted standard. This has since been refined, the latest agreement being the Basel III agreement, which specifies internationally agreed capital adequacy requirements for banks. These are administered by central banks, so in the UK these Basel III capital requirements are built into the Bank of England's regulatory framework. The requirements, which are being phased in, are due to be complete by 2019. This gradual phasing in of the new regulations is intended to avoid slowing the recovery.

In this way, it is hoped that the likelihood of financial instability spreading across countries will be reduced, as central banks will be imposing similar regulation on their respective financial systems.

The International Monetary Fund

In the world of the twenty-first century, the IMF continues to play an important role in maintaining the stability of the interconnected global financial system. In particular, it has provided loans to prevent sovereign default. An example is the loan provided to Greece in 2010 (which is discussed in Case study 31.1 at the end of this chapter). The IMF has also provided loans to governments needing to bail out private banks that had become insolvent because of exposure to risky loans. Recent examples include loans to the governments of Ireland, Latvia and Hungary.

Christine Lagarde, managing director of the IMF

Evaluation of the international context

Globalisation has increased the interdependence of countries. This allows people around the world to share in economic success and gain mutual advantage through trade. However, it also allows financial crisis to spread more rapidly, and there is a need for international cooperation in regulating financial markets to reduce the likelihood of financial problems occurring.

The BIS, IMF and World Bank have contributed by providing a global framework within which financial markets can be coordinated, and common regulations agreed. However, this has not been not enough to prevent crises from occurring, such as the Asian financial crisis of 1997 and the global credit crunch of the late 2000s. In earlier years, the debt crisis of the 1980s gave warning that serious problems could occur when markets are not carefully monitored.

At the time of the 1980s debt crises, there was much criticism that the steps taken in response, such as the rescheduling of the debt of developing countries, were designed to safeguard the global financial system, but not designed to provide a permanent remedy to that debt. It was only with the HIPC Initiative that the World Bank agreed to allow debt forgiveness for developing countries — and even then under strict conditions. This may have impeded the development of countries, especially in sub-Saharan Africa, where debt was putting such a strain on their resources. It is encouraging that some progress has now been made towards promoting growth and development in developing countries, and that measures are now being put in place to improve the stability of the global financial system in the future.

Summary: the international context

- The process of globalisation has brought with it the need to coordinate the regulation and operation of financial markets around the world.
- The financial crisis of the late 2000s showed how rapidly a crisis could spread through global markets.
- The Bank for International Settlements has produced standards for the conduct of financial markets that are accepted internationally.
- The IMF has moved on from its traditional role in providing loans for balance of payments purposes, and has made loans to prevent sovereign default.

Case study 31.1

The bailout of Greece in 2010

In May 2010 the EU and the IMF announced a €110 billion bailout loan for Greece. Traditionally, the IMF made loans to help a country to overcome a balance of payments problem or to stabilise its currency. But does that apply to this example?

In this case there was only one reason for the IMF to lend money to Greece and that was to prevent a Greek sovereign default. Prior to the credit crunch, highly indebted governments could borrow cheaply. Governments such as the one in Greece took advantage of low borrowing costs by using debt to finance better public services. The recession that followed the crash of 2008 dented confidence. This led to an increase in the cost of borrowing. In Greece, the government debt servicing costs climbed, which created an even bigger fiscal deficit. The government was in a debt spiral, and a Greek sovereign default seemed imminent.

So, this was not a bailout for the people of Greece. Ordinary Greeks did not receive their share of the loan to blow recklessly on imported German BMWs. Instead, the money borrowed was used by the Greek government to pay its bondholders. These bondholders were French and German banks. According to research carried out by the Bank for International Settlements at the end of 2010, 96% of Greek government bonds were held by European banks. German

A protester in front of the Greek parliament — the bailout was used by the Greek government to pay its bondholders

banks alone held €22.7 billion of Greek debt. The Greek 'rescue package' was really designed to save the German and French banking system, which would have collapsed in the event of a Greek sovereign default. Most of the money lent to Greece spent no time in Greece; instead it was paid straight to French and German bankers.

Follow-up question

Discuss why it is so important to prevent sovereign default by a country such as Greece.

This final chapter focuses on the role of the state in the macroeconomy, especially looking at the relative size of the public and private sectors, and how this depends on a range of factors, including the stance adopted by the government in its fiscal policy. The chapter draws together material from earlier chapters to explore issues relating to the design of macroeconomic policy, and how this has been handled in different types of economy. After all, the priorities for the government of the UK may be very different from those of a developing country needing to deal with high levels of poverty and inequality.

Learning objectives

After studying this chapter, you should:
→ be familiar with the main categories of public expenditure (current and capital) and the role of transfer payments
→ appreciate the importance of the fiscal deficit and its significance for the national debt
→ understand the nature and uses of taxation and be aware of the Laffer curve
→ be able to use the *AD/AS* model under differing assumptions about the long-run aggregate supply curve
→ know what is meant by crowding out and how this affects the relative size of the public and private sectors
→ appreciate the significance of automatic stabilisers and the limitations of discretionary fiscal policy
→ be aware of the arguments surrounding the sustainability of fiscal policy
→ understand that different governments may face different challenges and have differing priorities
→ be familiar with the policy objectives that governments may have at the macroeconomic level and the policy instruments available to them
→ be familiar with problems that may complicate the process of policy design

Government and the economy

What is the role of the state in the modern macroeconomy?

Synoptic link

This chapter sets out to draw together material from across the themes that are pertinent to the design of macroeconomic policy. You may therefore find it helpful to reflect on different parts of the analysis that has been presented, so that you can see linkages between the themes.

At the macroeconomic level, the government has a number of key objectives. The most fundamental of these objectives is economic growth, as this allows improvements in the standard of living. However, in order to achieve economic growth, it is crucial to maintain economic stability, thus providing the economic environment within which economic growth can take place. It is also important to be aware of international competitiveness — and to achieve an acceptable distribution of income and wealth. Furthermore, there is a need to ensure that economic growth is sustainable. The government has a range of policy instruments with which to attempt to meet these and other macroeconomic objectives, including fiscal, monetary and supply-side policies.

Fiscal, monetary and supply-side policies

The term 'fiscal policy' covers a range of policy measures that affect government expenditures and revenues through the decisions made by the government on its expenditure, taxation and borrowing. Fiscal policy may be used to influence the level and structure of aggregate demand in an economy. The effectiveness of fiscal policy depends crucially on the whole policy environment in which it is utilised.

Monetary policy entails the use of monetary variables such as money supply and interest rates to influence aggregate demand, and has been discussed earlier. In recent years, the prime use of monetary policy has been in seeking to create a stable macroeconomic environment. By delegating the targeting of inflation to the Bank of England, the UK government has effectively yielded the active use of monetary policy.

Supply-side policies comprise a range of measures intended to have a direct impact on aggregate supply — specifically, on the potential capacity output of the economy. These measures are often microeconomic in character and are designed to increase output and hence economic growth.

Knowledge check 32.1

Give two examples of supply-side policies.

Public expenditure

Governments undertake expenditure in a number of key areas. **Government consumption expenditure** is spending on goods and services for current use, such as day-to-day expenditure on the wages and salaries of civil servants, and on education and healthcare. The government also undertakes **capital expenditure**, which is spending on infrastructure such as roads or hospitals. This is spending for the future. In addition, the government makes **transfer payments**, such as social security payments. These are payments designed to provide protection for vulnerable households, and may be cash benefits or payments in kind — for example, in the form of education or healthcare provision. These may be universal (paid to everyone) or means-tested (paid to people with low income and capital).

Knowledge check 32.2

How would spending on building a tunnel under Stonehenge be classified?

Figure 32.1 shows the time path of UK government current expenditure (known in the national accounts as *general government final consumption expenditure*) as a share of GDP since 1970; it shows minor fluctuations around a downward trend, suggesting that the public sector has been gradually reducing its share of the economy. The

Key terms

government consumption expenditure (current expenditure) spending by the government on goods and services

government capital expenditure spending by government on capital projects

transfer payments occur when the government provides benefits (in cash or in kind) to poor households

figure highlights which of the political parties was in power at different periods. In particular, notice the rather more marked downward trend during the 1980s, which will be discussed later in the chapter.

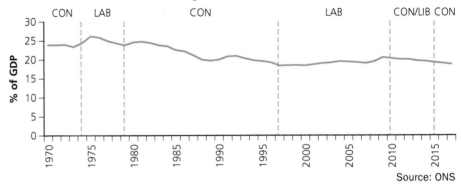

Figure 32.1 Government current expenditure, 1970–2017

Figure 32.2 provides an international perspective, showing the share of current and capital expenditure by governments in a range of countries. This reveals something of a contrast between, on the one hand, Ireland and Switzerland, and on the other hand, many other countries where governments have been more active in the economy. In part this reflects the greater role that government plays in some countries in providing services such as education and healthcare, whereas in other countries (e.g. the USA) the private sector takes a greater role, often through the insurance market.

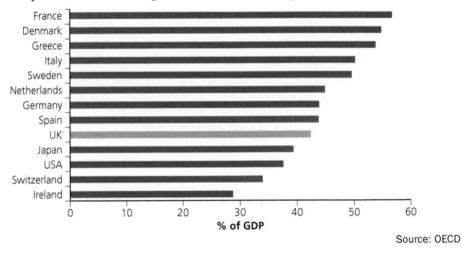

Figure 32.2 General government spending as a percentage of GDP, selected countries, 2015

The changing size and composition of public expenditure

Over time, both the size and composition of public expenditure has changed in many developed countries, as events have unfolded. Many countries have seen demographic changes, with people living for longer. This has resulted in ageing populations, and an increase in the dependency rate. This has had an appreciable impact on the demand placed on healthcare systems, including the NHS in the UK.

Knowledge check 32.3

What is meant by the 'dependency rate', and why is it important?

The NHS has also come under pressure because of new treatments that have been developed, raising people's expectations of improved healthcare, which cannot always be accommodated given the pressures on resources. Changes in technology have also raised expectations in other areas as well, requiring investment in infrastructure such as equipment in schools and colleges.

The financial crisis also had a dramatic effect on public expenditure, when governments had to intervene to bail out failing financial institutions. Such bailouts were not confined to the UK, and large expenditures were needed in Greece and other EU countries.

> **Synoptic link**
>
> In the UK, these bailouts caused a sudden increase in public sector net debt, as shown in Figure 15.5 and discussed in Chapter 31.

The significance of high public expenditure

Why does it matter if government expenditure is high relative to GDP? After all, there are some essential services that the government delivers through its spending. The question of what is the ideal balance of public and private sectors is discussed later in the chapter, but for now let's consider the key issues.

If the public sector becomes larger because of the need to meet increasing obligations, the natural result is that the private sector must become smaller. There is a number of ways in which this might happen.

Crowding out

If the economy is operating at full employment, then an increase in the size of the public sector can only occur at the expense of the private sector. If employment in the public sector increases, then there will be fewer workers available to take jobs in private enterprises. In addition, if an increase in government expenditure is financed through borrowing, the result would be an increase in interest rates, raising the cost of borrowing for private firms and reducing the supply of funds available for productive investment.

> **Synoptic link**
>
> The impact of crowding out is seen in the context of the *AD/AS* model later in the chapter.

> **Knowledge check 32.4**
>
> How would a fall in government expenditure affect the private sector if the government reduces its borrowing?

Productivity

A second consideration is whether the public sector will be more or less efficient than the private sector. The public sector does not need to maximise profits nor face competition, so the incentives to become efficient may not be strong. This suggests that the public sector will be less efficient in its use of resources than private enterprise. A switch in the balance of activity towards the public sector may therefore reduce the overall level of productivity in the economy.

National debt

An increase in the stock of public sector debt means an increase in the future interest payments on that debt, so this means that resources that could have been devoted to spending on public services must be used for repaying debt.

> ### Synoptic link
>
> The issue of the national debt will be explored more thoroughly later in this chapter.

The upside

With all these criticisms, it is important to remember that there may also be an upside to government expenditure. If the spending is on projects that improve the country's infrastructure, then this will promote efficiency and economic growth of the private sector in the longer term. Improved transport and communication links can reduce vital parts of the costs faced by firms. Similarly, spending on healthcare and education not only has beneficial effects on the standard of living as well as on productivity — and may improve the distribution of income and welfare and thus reduce inequality.

Taxation

Public expenditure must be financed in some way, and the overall position of the public sector relative to the private sector is not only determined by expenditure. The revenue side is also significant. Notice that taxation is not only needed in order to finance expenditure. In addition, taxation remains an important weapon against some forms of market failure, and it also influences the distribution of income. In this context, the choice of using direct or indirect taxes is important.

Direct and indirect taxes

Direct taxes are taxes levied on income of various kinds, such as personal income tax. Such taxes are designed to be progressive and so can be effective in redistributing income: for example, a higher income tax rate can be charged to those earning high incomes. In contrast, *indirect taxes* — taxes on expenditure, such as VAT and excise duties — tend to be regressive. As poorer households tend to spend a higher proportion of their income on items that are subject to excise duties, a greater share of their income is taken up by indirect taxes. Even VAT can be regressive if higher-income households save a greater proportion of their incomes.

> ### Synoptic link
>
> The characteristics of alternative forms of taxation were discussed in Chapter 27 in the context of the discussion of inequality, which explained the distinction between progressive, regressive and proportional taxes.

The effects of changes in taxes

Incentive effects

When Margaret Thatcher came to power in 1979, one of her first actions was to introduce a switch away from direct taxation towards indirect taxes. VAT was increased and the rate of personal income tax was reduced. In support of this move, it was pointed out that if an income tax scheme becomes too progressive, it can provide a disincentive towards effort. If people feel that a high proportion of their income is being taken in tax, their incentives to provide work effort are weak. Indeed, a switch from direct to indirect taxation is regarded as a sort of supply-side policy intended to influence the position of aggregate supply.

Knowledge check 32.5

Explain how reducing the rate of income tax can affect the position of the aggregate supply curve.

Margaret Thatcher introduced a switch away from direct taxation towards indirect taxation

Taxes and inequality

Perhaps the most important effect of a direct tax such as income tax is that it redistributes income from those on relatively high incomes to those on lower incomes, so long as the revenue raised is used in such a way as to benefit lower-income groups. For example, revenues may be used in the provision of education and healthcare, or in providing social security for those in need.

Synoptic link

The use of taxation to influence inequality by affecting the distribution of income was discussed in Chapter 27.

Foreign direct investment

The relative level of corporation tax in the domestic economy compared with elsewhere may influence the direction of flows of foreign direct investment (FDI), as transnational companies may be looking to minimise their tax liabilities. Having a high rate of corporation tax may thus deter foreign firms from investing in the domestic economy, or encourage domestic firms to invest elsewhere.

Real output, employment and the balance of trade

High taxation may also influence aggregate demand, by reducing disposable income of consumers. This could benefit the current account of the balance of payments by reducing the demand for imports, but the potential multiplier effects of a reduction in income may result in lower real output and employment. This is a costly way of tackling a current account deficit.

Synoptic link

The ideas of aggregate demand and the multiplier were introduced in Chapter 13, so you might want to glance back at that discussion.

The rate of indirect taxes such as VAT can also have an impact on the economy. When the UK economy was faced with recession in 2008, one of the steps taken to mitigate its effects was to reduce the rate of VAT (albeit temporarily). This was seen as one way of stimulating the economy.

Knowledge check 32.6

What effect would an increase in VAT have on prices?

Key terms

Laffer curve a curve showing the relationship between the tax rate and the amount of revenue raised as a consequence

government budget deficit (surplus) the difference between government expenditure and government revenue

fiscal deficit occurs when government outlays exceed government receipts

Tax revenue and the Laffer curve

Does an increase in the tax rate necessarily lead to a rise in tax revenue? Arthur Laffer argued that the answer to this was 'no'. He pointed out that changes in tax rates have two effects on tax revenue. The arithmetic says that an increase in the tax rate will increase the tax revenue. However, there is also an economic effect. As tax rates rise, incentive effects come into play, tending to work against the arithmetic effect, as people have less incentive to supply effort at the higher tax rates. The relationship can be captured in the so-called **Laffer curve**, an inverted U-shaped relationship between the tax rate and the amount of revenue raised, as shown in Figure 32.3.

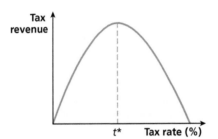

Figure 32.3 The Laffer curve

At low rates of tax, revenue increases as the tax rate increases, but beyond $t^\star$, the revenue begins to fall. If an economy has been operating with a tax rate above $t^\star$, then a reduction in the tax rate would actually increase the revenue raised by the tax. It is worth noting that Laffer himself pointed out that he had not invented the concept, as it can be found in the writings of Keynes, not to mention Ibn Khaldun, a fourteenth-century Muslim philosopher.

Public sector finances

In terms of the impact that fiscal policy can have on aggregate demand, both expenditure and revenue are important, the difference between them being the **government budget deficit (surplus)**. A deficit in this context occurs when expenditure exceeds revenue.

A fiscal deficit and the national debt

The way in which fiscal policy is conducted has implications for the overall size of the public sector in the economy. Traditionally, fiscal policy was used to affect the level of aggregate demand in the economy, under the influence of Keynesian thinking. The overall balance between government receipts and outlays affects the position of the aggregate demand curve, which is reinforced by multiplier effects. When government outlays exceed government receipts, the result is a **fiscal deficit**. This occurs when the revenues raised through taxation are not sufficient to cover the government's various types of expenditure. The **national debt** is the accumulation of past borrowing.

Structural and cyclical deficits

Notice that as the economy goes through a business cycle, the deficit will tend to fluctuate. During the downturn, there will be an increase in the fiscal deficit, as spending on benefits will rise, and tax revenues will fall. In other words, there will be a cyclical element to the size of the deficit. Such a **cyclical deficit** would fade away as the economy returns to its trend. Of more concern would be a situation in which the budget remains in deficit even with the economy at full employment. Such a **structural deficit** would need to be addressed, as it would not be sustainable in the long run.

Key terms

national debt the total amount of government debt, based on accumulated previous deficits and surpluses

cyclical deficit a budget deficit that occurs during the downturn of the business cycle, but disappears in the upturn

structural deficit a deficit that persists even when the economy is at full employment

Knowledge check 32.7

Explain why a structural deficit would be unsustainable if it was not addressed.

Study tip

Be very careful not to confuse the fiscal deficit with the national debt. The fiscal deficit is a 'flow' concept — the excess of government expenditure over revenues in the current period. The national debt is the 'stock' of accumulated past borrowing.

The fiscal deficit and fiscal policy

The overall size of the fiscal deficit may act as a constraint on the government's actions in terms of fiscal policy. In addition, the overall pattern of revenue and expenditure has a strong effect on the overall balance of activity in the economy. A neutral government budget can be attained either with high expenditure and high revenues, or with relatively low expenditure and revenues. Such decisions affect the overall size of the public sector relative to the private sector. Over the years, different governments in the UK have taken different decisions on this issue — and different countries throughout the world have certainly adopted different approaches.

In part, such issues are determined through the ballot box. In the run-up to an election, each political party presents its overall plans for taxation and spending, and typically they adopt different positions as to the overall balance. It is then up to those voting to give a mandate to whichever party offers a package that most closely resembles their preferences.

Extension material: limitations of the ballot box

Notice that there is a limit to how effective this process can be. The policies adopted by a government during its term of office cover a wide range of different issues, and individual voters may approve of some but not others — but they only get to vote once every 5 years or so, and then only on the whole package of measures. When the election comes round, the debates may be dominated by issues that happen to be contentious at the time, rather than the overall ideology of the parties. Furthermore, if the election turns out to be indecisive, so that the result is a coalition across parties with differing manifestos, the resulting policies may turn out to be a mixture. Another pertinent issue is whether voters will be fooled by being offered (or given) tax cuts just before an election, as they may know that the reality will be different in the long term.

Aggregate demand and supply and the government budget deficit

An important question concerns the extent to which a government budget deficit can be used to stabilise the macroeconomy by influencing aggregate demand. In order to explore this, it is important to revisit the aggregate supply curve.

Synoptic link

The *AD/AS* model was first introduced in Chapters 11–13; the *AS* curve was discussed in Chapter 12. We will now build on that analysis, and show how it is important in considering the effectiveness of fiscal policy.

To analyse the impact of public expenditure on aggregate demand, return to the model of aggregate supply and aggregate demand (*AS/AD*). Figure 32.4 shows how a shift in aggregate demand from AD_0 to AD_1 results in an increase in real output and the price level as the economy moves to a new equilibrium — a movement along the short-run aggregate supply curve (*SRAS*). However, the *SRAS* is called a *short-run* aggregate supply curve for a reason, and there is no guarantee that the equilibrium shown in Figure 32.4 can be sustained. For example, notice that the new equilibrium entails a higher overall price level. In time this will feed back into the costs faced by firms, causing the *SRAS* to shift back to the left. Of more importance, therefore, is the long-run aggregate supply curve.

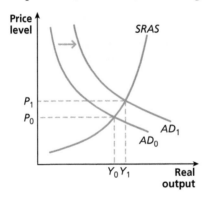

Figure 32.4 A shift in aggregate demand

Knowledge check 32.8

What factors other than an increase in government expenditure could cause a rightward shift in *AD*?

In this connection, it is important to recall the debate that developed over the shape of the long-run aggregate supply curve: this is important because it has implications for the conduct and effectiveness of policy options. This was discussed in Chapter 12.

The monetarist/classical view was that there was a natural rate of output, corresponding to full employment, The economy would adjust rapidly to this equilibrium position, so the authorities would not need to intervene. This was in contrast to the Keynesian position, which was that the economy could get caught in an equilibrium position below full employment, and that adjustment back to full employment could be slow. This difference of opinion was reflected in the shape of the long-run aggregate supply curve.

Knowledge check 32.9

How would a fall in aggregate demand affect real output with a Keynesian *LRAS* curve?

Summary: public expenditure and the *AD/AS* model

- Governments pursue a range of policy objectives, including low inflation and low unemployment, a favourable balance of payments position, economic growth, maintenance of a good environment, income redistribution and the correction of market failure.
- In order to pursue these objectives, governments have recourse to fiscal, monetary and supply-side policies.
- In using the *AD/AS* model to analyse policy options, it is useful to distinguish between monetarist and Keynesian views about the shape of aggregate supply.
- Monetarist economists have argued that the economy always converges rapidly on equilibrium at the natural rate of output, implying that policies affecting aggregate demand have an impact only on prices, leaving real output unaffected. Aggregate supply in this world is vertical.
- The Keynesian view is that the economy may settle in an equilibrium that is below full employment, and that there is a range over which aggregate supply slopes upwards.

The impact of a budget deficit

Shifting the aggregate demand curve affects only the overall price level in the economy when the aggregate supply curve is vertical — and the monetarist school of thought argued that it would always be vertical. With a Keynesian aggregate supply curve, a key issue for a government considering the use of fiscal policy is knowing whether there is spare capacity in the economy, because otherwise an expansion in aggregate demand from increased government spending will push up prices but leave real output unchanged.

Study tip

It is important to remember that it is not just spending that influences the position of aggregate demand, but the budget deficit — i.e. the balance between expenditure and revenue.

Under the multiplier, any increase in autonomous spending leads to a multiplied increase in equilibrium output. The idea of the multiplier is that, if there is an increase in (say) government expenditure, this provides income for workers, who will then spend that income and create further expenditure streams. The size of these induced effects will depend on the marginal propensity to withdraw.

In terms of the *AD/AS* diagram, the existence of the multiplier means that if there is an increase in government expenditure, the *AD* curve moves further to the right than it otherwise would have done, because of the multiplier effects. However, this does not mean that equilibrium income will increase by the full multiplier amount. Looking more closely at what is happening, you can see that there are some forces at work that are acting to weaken the multiplier effect of an increase in government expenditure.

Knowledge check 32.10

What forces act to weaken the effect of an increase in government expenditure?

Fiscal policy and crowding out

One way in which this happens is through interest rates. If the government finances its deficit through borrowing, a side-effect is to put upward pressure on interest rates, which then may cause private sector spending — by households on consumption and by firms on investment — to decline, as the cost of borrowing has been increased. As mentioned earlier, this process is known as the **crowding out** of private sector activity by the public sector. It limits the extent to which a government budget deficit can shift the aggregate demand curve, especially if the public sector activity is less productive than the private sector activity that it replaces. In principle, there could also be a **crowding in** effect if the government runs a surplus and thus puts downward pressure on interest rates.

When crowding out occurs, the public sector is effectively displacing private sector activity, so it affects the relative size of the public and private sectors.

Automatic and discretionary fiscal policies

It is important to distinguish between automatic and discretionary changes in government expenditure. Some items of government expenditure and receipts vary automatically with the business cycle. They are known as **automatic stabilisers**. For example, if the economy enters a period of recession, government expenditure will rise because of the increased payments of unemployment and other social security benefits, and revenues will fall because fewer people are paying income tax, and because receipts from VAT are falling. This helps to offset the recession without any active intervention from the government.

More important, however, is the question of whether the government can or should make use of discretionary fiscal policy in a deliberate attempt to influence the course of the economy. As already mentioned, the key issue is whether or not the economy has spare capacity, because attempts to stimulate an economy that is already at full employment will merely push up the price level.

There are many examples of how excessive government spending can create problems for the economy. Such problems arose in a number of Latin American economies during the 1980s. In Brazil, a range of policies were brought to bear in an attempt to reduce inflation — including direct controls on prices. However, with no serious attempt to control the fiscal deficit, inflation continually got out of control — reaching almost 3,000% in 1990. Only when the deficit was reduced did it become possible to bring inflation to a more reasonable level. More recently, the collapse of the economy of Zimbabwe was accompanied by inflation at such a high level that the printing presses could not keep up with the need for banknotes.

Extension material: the Barber boom

The UK has not been immune from this sort of effect. After the collapse of the Dollar Standard and at the time of the first oil price crisis of 1973–74, the then-chancellor of the exchequer, Tony Barber, launched a fiscal expansion, backed by a monetary expansion. This was to stem the rise in unemployment that was taking place. However, the result was that inflation soared to around 25%.

Balance between the public and private sectors

Both economic analysis and the UK experience support the view that fiscal policy should not be used as an active stabilisation device. However, this does not mean

---

Key terms

crowding out process by which an increase in government expenditure 'crowds out' private sector activity by raising the cost of borrowing

crowding in process by which a decrease in government expenditure 'crowds in' private sector activity by lowering the cost of borrowing

automatic stabilisers process by which government expenditure and revenue varies with the business cycle, thereby helping to stabilise the economy without any conscious intervention from government

that there is no role for fiscal policy in a modern economy. Earlier, it was pointed out that decisions about the size of government expenditure and revenue influence the overall balance between the public and private sectors. The balance that is achieved can have an important influence on the overall level of economic activity, and on economic growth, so the importance of designing an appropriate fiscal policy should not be underestimated. An important theme that runs through much economic analysis is that governments may be justified in intervening in the economy in order to correct market failure. Some of this intervention requires the use of fiscal policy: for example, taxes to correct for the effects of externalities, or expenditure to ensure the provision of public goods. In other words, fiscal policy can be an instrument that operates at the microeconomic level, as well as having macroeconomic implications.

Take infrastructure as an example. Infrastructure covers a range of goods that are crucial for the efficient operation of a market economy. Businesses need good transport links and good communication facilities. Households need good healthcare, education and sanitation facilities, not only in order to enjoy a good standard of life, but also to be productive members of the labour force. This may be especially important for developing countries.

Knowledge check 32.11

Explain why externality effects may come into play in relation to the provision of infrastructure.

Both public goods and externality arguments come into play in the provision of infrastructure, so there needs to be appropriate government intervention to ensure that such goods are adequately provided. The consequence of failing to do this will be to lower the productive capacity of the economy below what would otherwise have been possible. In other words, the aggregate supply curve will be further to the left than it need be.

On the other hand, too much government intervention may also be damaging. One of the most compelling arguments in favour of privatisation was that when the managers of public enterprises are insufficiently accountable for their actions, X-inefficiency becomes a major issue, so public sector activity tends to be less efficient than private sector enterprise. By this argument, too large a public sector may have the effect of lowering aggregate productive capacity below its potential level.

These arguments suggest that an important role for fiscal policy is in affecting the supply side of the economy, ensuring that markets operate effectively to make the best possible use of the economy's resources.

Income distribution and inequality

The other key role for fiscal policy is in affecting the distribution of income within society. Taxes and transfers can have a large effect on income distribution and inequality. This in turn may have effects on the economy by affecting the incentives that people face in choosing their labour supply.

Achieving a balance of taxation between direct and indirect taxes is an important aspect of the government's redistributive policy. A switch in the balance from direct to indirect taxes will tend to increase inequality in a society. The incentive effects must also be kept in mind. High marginal tax rates on income can have a disincentive effect: if people know that a large proportion of any additional income from work they undertake will be taxed away, they may be discouraged from providing more work.

Synoptic link

Public goods were discussed in Chapter 7.

Synoptic link

X-inefficiency in public enterprises was discussed in Chapter 23.

Synoptic link

The use of taxation to influence the inequality by affecting the distribution of income was discussed in Chapter 27.

In other words, cutting income tax can encourage work effort by reducing marginal tax rates. This is yet another reminder of the need for a balanced policy — one that recognises that, while some income redistribution is needed to protect the vulnerable, disincentive effects may arise if the better-off are over-taxed.

The role of the government in different countries

In an international context, there are significant differences between countries in relation to the role of the government in the economy. Political ideology plays a part in this, countries with socialist governments tending to see a stronger role for the state in intervening in the economy. However, this is not the only important factor.

For many developing countries, tax collection is a challenge, with no effective administrative system in place. The situation is compounded when many people in the country are living on low incomes or in absolute poverty. Furthermore, where subsistence activity is significant, taxation cannot be effectively implemented. As a consequence, governments may have to play a relatively limited role in the economy, or try to raise finance for government expenditure by other means, perhaps by levying taxes on international trade. Another possibility is to fund expenditure by printing money, but this has been seen to have disastrous consequences for inflation, and was certainly a major factor in one of the most extreme episodes of hyperinflation, which took place in Zimbabwe in the late 2000s.

Figure 32.5 shows tax revenue as a percentage of GDP for selected countries around the world — notice that these are ranked in descending order of GDP per capita in PPP$. In interpreting these data, it is important to remember that tax revenue in a particular country may be low because the country does not have an effective tax collection system, or it may be that the government in power does not wish to take an active role in the economy — at least in the form of imposing high taxes in order to finance high expenditure. This is well illustrated by the difference between the UK and the USA. Nonetheless, there is a tendency for the lower-income countries to display relatively low tax revenue relative to GDP. This is important because if the government has a limited capacity to raise tax revenue, this may limit the extent to which it is able to introduce policies to combat poverty, or to provide social infrastructure needed to encourage economic growth.

Knowledge check 32.12

What sorts of factors lie behind the difference between the UK and the USA in Figure 32.5?

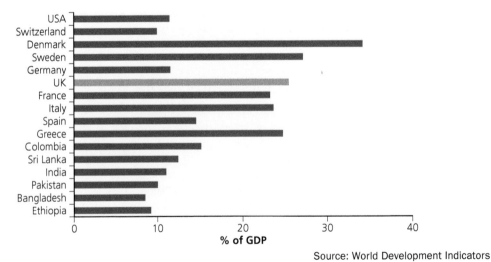

Source: World Development Indicators

Figure 32.5 Tax revenue as a percentage of GDP, selected countries, 2015

Governments have also been aware that foreign firms may take account of relative tax rates in different countries when deciding where to locate their investment. Countries that are keen to attract foreign direct investment may thus feel pressured to keep corporate tax rates relatively low in the hope of attracting inflows of investment. Indeed, many transnational companies have been able to negotiate tax holidays, leaving them free of taxation for a period after they bring their investment.

Sustainability of fiscal policy

Another important issue that came to the fore during the 1990s concerned the sustainability of fiscal policy. This is wrapped up with the notion that current taxpayers should only have to fund expenditure that benefits their own generation, and that the taxpayers of the future should make their own decisions, and not have to pay for past government expenditure that has been incurred for the benefit of earlier generations.

In this context, what is significant is the overall balance between receipts and outlays through time. If outlays were always larger than receipts, the spending programme could be sustained only through government borrowing, thereby shifting the burden of funding the deficit to future generations. This could also be a problem if it made it more difficult for the private sector to obtain funds for investment, or if it added to the national debt. The Labour governments of 1997–2010 introduced a so-called '**Golden Rule' of fiscal policy**, which stated that, on average over the economic cycle, the government should borrow only to invest and not to fund current expenditure. This was intended to help achieve equity between present and future generations. It should perhaps be noted that this was a self-imposed guideline, so there was no penalty for breaking the rule other than loss of political credibility. The Coalition government that followed was less committed to the concept of the Golden Rule, and the onset of the financial crisis — and the need to bail out commercial banks in order to safeguard the financial system — rendered the Golden Rule impossible to follow.

> **Key term**
>
> **Golden Rule of fiscal policy** rule stating that over the economic cycle net government borrowing will be for investment only, and not for current spending

If receipts and outlays more or less balance over the economic cycle, the economy is not in a position whereby the current generation is forcing future generations to pay for its consumption. However, as the economy does go through a business cycle, it is not practical to impose this rule at every point in time, so the so-called Golden Rule was intended to apply over the cycle as a whole.

There was also a commitment to keep public sector net debt below 40% of GDP — again, on average over the business cycle. Figure 15.5 showed data for this on a quarterly basis since 1997. The financial support offered to Northern Rock and other banks in the bailout of 2008 had a noticeable effect on public sector net debt, as is clear in the figure. Even without the financial sector interventions, net debt rose over the 40% mark in the last quarter of 2008 and kept rising thereafter. This reflected other measures taken by the government to try to mitigate the effects of the recession. One example was the reduction in the rate of VAT from 17.5 to 15%. This is tantamount to a fiscal expansion, but when it was introduced, it was made clear that it was intended as a temporary boost for a specified period. This statement enabled the government to maintain that it was not breaching its long-term fiscal commitment. The rate of VAT returned to 17.5% in January 2010, and was increased to 20% in January 2011.

Exercise 32.1

Discuss the extent to which the major British political parties adopt differing stances towards establishing a balance between the private and public sectors: that is, the extent to which each is 'high tax/high public spending' or 'low tax/low public spending'. Analyse the economic arguments favouring each of the approaches.

Summary: fiscal policy

- Fiscal policy concerns the use of government expenditure and taxation to influence aggregate demand in the economy.
- If the economy is in a state in which the aggregate demand curve cuts the vertical segment of aggregate supply, demand-side policy affects only the overall price level, and not real output.
- If the government funds its expenditure by borrowing, higher interest rates may crowd out private sector activity.
- The stance of the government budget varies with the business cycle, as a result of the operation of automatic stabilisers.
- The overall balance between private and public sectors varies through time and across countries.
- Direct taxes help to redistribute income between groups in society, but if too progressive they may dampen incentives to provide effort.
- The Golden Rule for fiscal policy was that the government should aim to borrow only for investment, and not for current expenditure (averaged over the economic cycle).
- There was also a commitment to keep public sector net debt below 40% of GDP; this commitment did not survive the financial crisis and recession that began in the late 2000s.

Macroeconomic policies in a global context

Governments have a range of policies available to them, but also a range of possible objectives that they wish to achieve. Different countries face their own configurations of resources and challenges, and may set their own priorities. It is therefore no surprise to find that there is no unique approach that has been adopted to the design of macroeconomic policy.

Objectives of policy

First consider the range of policy objectives that a government may need to take into account when designing a policy mix.

Economic growth

It is through economic growth that the productive capacity of the economy is raised, and this in turn allows the living standards of the country's citizens to be progressively improved over time. In a sense, therefore, this is the most fundamental of the policy objectives, and has been pursued by governments all around the world. Although there are some policy measures that may be thought to affect growth directly, many other policy objectives may need to be met as a precondition for creating the environment in which growth may flourish.

Alleviating poverty and inequality

For developing countries, economic growth may be seen as a prerequisite for the alleviation of poverty and inequality. Without increasing the quantity of resources available, it may be impossible to improve living conditions for those living in poverty. A counter argument to this is that addressing basic needs may be a prerequisite for growth to be possible. However, developing countries are likely to give higher priority to this objective than the developed countries.

Nonetheless, inequality in the distribution of income is a concern of governments that wish to influence the distribution of income within a society. This may entail transfers of income between groups — that is, from the rich to the poor — in order to protect the vulnerable. Such transfers may take place through progressive taxation (whereby those on higher incomes pay a greater proportion of their income in tax) or through a system of social security benefits such as the Jobseeker's Allowance or Universal Credit.

Poverty needs to be tackled to enable economic growth

Macroeconomic stability

It is widely accepted that instability in the macroeconomy impedes the process of economic growth, so another key objective for governments is to provide a stable macroeconomic environment that will facilitate growth. This is important for countries at all stages of development.

Macroeconomic stability can be interpreted in different ways. For a long period from the 1970s onwards, the focus was primarily on monetary stability, seen in terms of achieving a low and stable rate of inflation. The underlying argument here was that a low and stable inflation rate would improve confidence in the future course of the economy, and thus encourage firms to invest. This would then increase the productive capacity of the economy, resulting in economic growth.

The financial crisis that began in the late 2000s has drawn attention to the need to focus also on financial stability. In other words, there needs to be a sufficient and efficient flow of liquidity in the economy.

The need to safeguard the financial system by the bailout of failing banks further highlighted the need for fiscal stability. The sudden increase in public sector borrowing, and the consequent rise in debt, raised awareness of the need to prioritise measures to reduce fiscal deficits and national debt. For countries like Greece, this became the dominant priority in policy design.

Yet another element in reaching stability in the macroeconomic environment is the need to accommodate external shocks. These can come from many different sources, whether it be changes in the price of oil, or financial crisis spreading through globalised financial markets. Domestic policy may be needed to ensure macroeconomic stability is maintained in the face of such external shocks.

Full employment

Full employment is another objective for the macroeconomy. Unemployment imposes costs on society and on the individuals who are unemployed. From society's point of view, the existence of substantial unemployment represents a waste of resources and indicates that the economy is working below full capacity.

International competitiveness

As the world becomes increasingly interconnected through globalisation, it is increasingly important to maintain international competitiveness. This is partly about achieving productivity growth in line with international competitors. One way of viewing this is that it is about maintaining comparative advantage.

Balance of payments

Under a flexible exchange rate system, the overall balance of payments will always be zero because the exchange rate adjusts to ensure that this is so. Nevertheless, the balance of payments remains an objective, not so much to ensure overall balance as to maintain a reasonable balance between the current account and the financial account. If the current account is in persistent deficit, this could cause problems in the long run, as the implication is that the country is selling off its assets in order to obtain goods for present consumption. Under a fixed exchange rate system, the need to maintain the exchange rate acts as a constraint on economic growth, which tends to lead to an increase in imports and creates a current account deficit.

Maintaining a balanced budget

Even after having returned the bailed-out banks to the private sector, UK public sector net debt at the end of 2017 was about 85% of GDP, which is not sustainable in the long run, and involves large interest payments on the government. This cuts into the resources available for spending. A long-run objective is thus to bring down the level of national debt, but this may be a challenge in a period when economic growth remains below trend and in the face of uncertainty about the Brexit process.

To help to see the UK economy in perspective, Figure 32.6 shows the levels of government debt in a range of OECD countries in 2015, expressed as a percentage of GDP. At this point in time, UK's debt amounted to more than 100% of GDP. This was still below that of countries such as Japan, Greece or Italy — but well above the 40% that was considered acceptable under the Golden Rule.

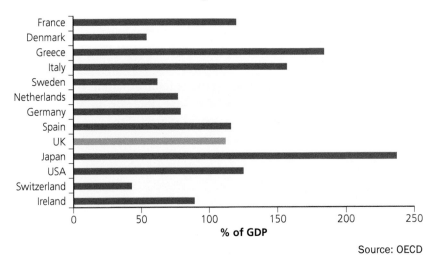

Source: OECD

Figure 32.6 General government debt as a percentage of GDP 2015

Environmental considerations

It must be recognised that it is not only resources that contribute to living standards: conserving a good environment is also important. Sustainable growth and development means growth that does not prejudice the consumption possibilities of future generations, and this consideration may act as a constraint on the rate of economic growth. Another policy priority is therefore to look for sustainability in economic growth.

Correcting market failure

At the *microeconomic* level there are policy measures designed to deal with various forms of market failure. Competition policy is one example of this; it is designed to prevent firms from abusing monopoly power, and to improve the allocation of resources. Although such policies operate at the microeconomic level, they have consequences for macroeconomic objectives such as economic growth.

Knowledge check 32.13

Explain how competition policy influences economic growth.

For developing countries, dealing with market failure is a high priority, if only because so many markets are underdeveloped or missing. For example, attention has been drawn to the need to improve the operation of financial markets in developing countries, in order to improve the flow of finance for investment. Measures may also be needed to ensure that inflows of external finance to developing countries can be effectively marshalled. This may entail improving the effectiveness with which flows of overseas assistance or international borrowing are utilised. It may also entail negotiating better deals with transnational companies that bring foreign direct investment into developing countries, to ensure that the country can retain more of the benefits of such investment.

Policy options

Previous chapters have identified a range of policy options that governments can bring to bear in order to address these various objectives. Each has its own strengths and weaknesses, and is suited to the achievement of different sets of objectives. Governments will thus choose the range of policies most appropriate to the objectives that they are trying to achieve, which may in turn depend on the particular challenges that are faced by economies in different circumstances.

Monetary and financial policy

Monetary policy entails the use of monetary variables such as money supply and interest rates to influence aggregate demand. The main objective of monetary policy in recent times has been to meet inflation targets, which is seen as a crucial part of macroeconomic stability. In the UK, the Bank of England used interest rates to keep inflation within its target range, while in Europe the European Central Bank (ECB) performed this role. In the USA, the Federal Reserve was also using interest rates to create a stable environment.

Money plays an important role in the modern economy, but the monetary authorities find it difficult to measure and monitor the amount of money in the economy — let alone trying to control it directly. Why should this be? Part of the explanation is that there are many sources of money in a modern, open economy. In other words, it is not simply a question of measuring, monitoring and controlling the quantity of banknotes and coins in circulation. For this reason, the authorities have turned to interest rates as the main instrument of monetary policy.

As explained in Chapter 31, the period of relative calm (the 'Great Moderation') in the late 1990s and early 2000s was interrupted by rising commodity prices and financial crisis. The need to safeguard the financial system without plunging economies into deep recession switched the focus from monetary stability to financial stability. In the

UK, inflation was allowed to rise above its target range while interest rates fell as far as they could fall. Quantitative easing (expansion of the money supply) was brought in to try to ensure an adequate flow of liquidity as some banks seemed reluctant to lend.

In the developing countries, the priorities for monetary policy have been rather different. With financial institutions being relatively underdeveloped, and many rural communities lacking access to formal financial markets, monetary policy has partly been used to improve the coverage of financial markets and to boost confidence in the financial system. The provision of microfinance is one way in which attempts have been made to provide access to credit in rural areas, but this still has a long way to go.

This is not to say that monetary stability is not also important for developing countries. Countries in Latin America experienced hyperinflation in the 1980s, setting back progress with economic growth. Countries such as Zimbabwe have also seen bouts of extreme instability. This is a reminder that maintaining stability is an important precondition for achieving economy growth.

Fiscal policy

The term 'fiscal policy' covers a range of policy measures that affect government expenditures and revenues through the decisions made by the government on its expenditure, taxation and borrowing. Fiscal policy may be used to influence the level and structure of aggregate demand in an economy, but is also utilised to affect the distribution of income within a society. It also plays a role in addressing issues of market failure.

Using discretionary fiscal policy to combat unemployment by stimulating aggregate demand has been largely discredited, as it was seen to be ineffective, especially in the context of a floating exchange rate regime. Nonetheless, fiscal policy plays a key role in the economy through its impact on the balance between the public and private sectors.

For many developed countries, the privatisation of nationalised industries has reduced the size of the public sector. The presumption is that exposing such industries to competitive forces would improve accountability and efficiency, and thus result in improved allocation of resources. This rests on the assumption that the private sector tends to be more efficient than the public sector.

The development of fiscal rules was intended to ensure that current taxation would be used primarily for the present generation, and public borrowing for investment that would benefit future generations. The need to provide bailout funding for banks considered too big to fail led to the abandonment of such a rule-based system, given that public sector borrowing could not be maintained within the agreed limits. The bailouts also led to a sharp rise in public sector net debt. Fiscal policy thus had to be redirected towards reducing the debt, the danger being that this would deepen and prolong the recession.

For developing countries, the challenges of raising revenue through taxation make it difficult to use fiscal policy to try to alleviate poverty and inequality, which leads to over-reliance on flows of overseas assistance from abroad.

Exchange rate policy

Since the collapse of the Dollar Standard in the early 1970s, floating exchange rates have become the norm. In other words, the policy towards the exchange rate has been to allow it to find its own equilibrium level in the foreign exchange market.

This has implications for other policy approaches, making fiscal policy less effective but strengthening the impact of monetary policy on aggregate demand.

The implication of a floating exchange rate system is that a country is not able to use changes in the exchange rate in order to influence the competitiveness of its goods relative to the rest of the world. If a country does wish to improve its competitiveness, a more effective approach is to find ways of improving productivity.

China has been accused of intervening to improve the competitiveness of its exports by manipulating its exchange rate. During the early 2000s, this caused controversy. By undervaluing its currency, it was claimed that China was giving itself an unfair advantage, allowing exports to grow rapidly and thus fuelling its economic growth.

Such a policy has significant side-effects. Within China itself, this meant that resources were being diverted into the export sector, potentially at the expense of domestic consumption. Elsewhere, China's accumulation of US Treasury bills pushed up their prices. This implies lower interest rates than would otherwise have prevailed. It may have contributed to the housing bubble in the USA, which was one of the triggers for the financial crisis. This culminated in international pressure, to which China succumbed after 2005. The real value of China's currency (the yuan/renminbi) rose by some 30% between 2005 and 2014, suggesting that the exchange rate was moving closer to its equilibrium value.

China has been accused of manipulating its exchange rate

Knowledge check 32.14

Why does having a common interest rate make it difficult for individual countries to respond to their own domestic economic problems?

The establishment of the eurozone could be seen as an example of a drastic form of exchange rate policy, under which the eurozone members agreed to adopt the euro, thereby adopting a common exchange rate against the rest of the world, and a common monetary policy alongside it. With the ECB setting a common interest rate across all of the eurozone members, it became difficult for individual countries to adopt differential responses to the financial crisis, with some members suffering much more severe recessions than others as a result.

Supply-side measures

Supply-side policies are measures intended to have a direct impact on aggregate supply — specifically, on the potential capacity output of the economy. These measures are often microeconomic in character and are designed to increase output and hence economic growth.

For the UK, such policies have included measures intended to increase the provision of education and training, measures to improve the flexibility with which markets operate, the promotion of competition and attempts to improve the incentives faced by economic agents. All these are intended to affect the position of the long-run aggregate supply curve, and expand the productive capacity of the economy. These policies were discussed in Chapter 16.

For developing countries, supply-side policies are crucial for growth and development. In particular, it is vitally important for developing countries to be able to invest in human capital. Improved provision of education and skills and enhanced healthcare delivery with better nutrition can have a dramatic impact on long-run growth by raising the productivity of the workforce. Markets can be made to work more effectively if transport and communication can be improved, or if such infrastructure as market facilities can be provided.

Notice that measures that lead to improvements in health, nutrition and education of the population also have direct effects on the alleviation of poverty and (potentially) inequality, so are doubly important for developing countries.

Regulation and control

This assembly of policy measures may not be enough. There may be situations in which the authorities may see the need to intervene directly through regulation or control. In particular, there may be a need to provide a legal and regulatory framework within which the behaviour of firms can be monitored in order to protect consumers.

A regulatory framework to promote competition may be needed, as was noted in Chapter 23 under Theme 3. The Competition and Markets Authority fulfils this role in the UK, and other countries have similar bodies.

For developing countries, it is important to establish an appropriate legal framework within which a system of secure property rights can be put in place. This is an essential underpinning for any economy to operate effectively. It was noted earlier that financial markets may fail to provide rural credit for potential investors, who may not be able to provide collateral against loans because of the lack of property rights. This is just one example of where a legal framework becomes important.

For developing countries, it is also important for them to be in a position to negotiate with more experienced partners. For example, when a transnational company (TNC) decides to locate in a country, it must agree terms with the host government. Given the economic (and perhaps political) power of the TNC compared with the host government, the country can all too easily find itself making too many concessions in order to attract the investment of the TNC.

There are also circumstances in which an international body may be needed to regulate markets at a global level. For example, it has been noted that there may be externalities that cross national boundaries, and a worldwide agreement may be needed to combat global warming. The World Trade Organization (WTO) exists partly to arbitrate on disputes between trading partners, and to enforce agreements on tariffs and the conditions under which trade takes place.

Transfer pricing

One particular example is the need to regulate a process known as **transfer pricing**. There are TNCs that spread their supply chain around the world, with different stages of the production process being located in different countries. In such circumstances, the TNC undertakes a lot of internal transactions between its own branches in different countries, and can set the prices at which those transactions take place. It becomes possible for the company to minimise its tax liability by manipulating those internal prices in such a way as to take the profit in a country with a low tax rate.

There is widespread agreement that such practices should be prohibited, but the controversy surrounding the activities of companies such as Google, Starbucks and Amazon shows that it is no easy matter to intervene. Part of the problem is that the TNCs are operating globally, but governments only operate nationally.

Problems in designing and implementing policy

Information inaccuracy

Policymakers face many problems when seeking to implement their chosen policies. For a start, they need information on which to base their policy design. A key problem here is that it takes time to collect data, so real-time data are not available. The policymaker only has data about how the economy was performing at some date in the past. And even this may be inaccurate, provisional or incomplete. Given the time that elapses in designing a policy and getting it approved, and then in it working its way through the system, a policy may only become effective after the need for it has passed.

Even when the data become available, there is no guarantee that they will be accurate, as some data series often get updated after first publication as inaccuracies or omissions become apparent.

Risk, uncertainty and external shocks

The economic environment is always changing. Policymakers must take policy decisions based on their best forecasts (or guesses!) about the future, knowing that this is characterised by high levels of risk and uncertainty. In addition, the economy is open to the impact of sudden and unanticipated shocks that may render forecasts unreliable.

Conflict between policies and objectives

Furthermore, a government needs to adopt a combination of policies that will enable it to achieve its objectives. One of the problems with this is that conflicts may arise, both between policies and between objectives. The policy adopted to deal with one objective may endanger achievement of another.

Indeed, the adoption of one policy measure may rule out the use of some other measure. For example, the authorities cannot adopt independent targets for money supply and the interest rate if they want the money market to remain in equilibrium. Targeting the exchange rate may mean that it is not possible to use monetary policy to influence aggregate demand. Introducing fiscal austerity in order to reduce public sector debt may prevent the achievement of economic growth. For a developing country, investing in healthcare or education may leave no funds available for spending on infrastructure such as roads and communications.

Key term

transfer pricing process by which a transnational company can minimise its global tax liability by manipulating the internal prices for transactions between its branches in different countries

Study tip

Keep alert for examples of contentious issues that arise in the media, which could be useful to you as examples.

Exercise 32.2

Given the following list of policy objectives, discuss the possible conflicts that may arise between them, and discuss how these might be resolved:

- low inflation
- low unemployment
- high economic growth
- a low deficit on the current account of the balance of payments
- maintenance of a high environmental quality
- equity in the distribution of income
- a balanced government budget

Summary: policy design and implementation

- Governments have several possible policy objectives — and a range of possible instruments to bring to bear.
- Economic growth is often seen as taking a high priority among objectives, but other targets of policy may be necessary for growth to take place.
- Developing countries may have different priorities compared with more advanced economies.
- Approaches to policy include monetary and fiscal policy, together with supply-side measures.
- Other policies such as regulation may sometimes be required.
- Regulation may sometimes need to be coordinated to address concerns that cross national boundaries.
- Policymakers need to take decisions on the basis of inadequate information, and under conditions of risk and uncertainty.
- Conflicts may arise both between policy objectives and between policy measures.

Case study 32.1

The UK's national debt

In March 2018, the ONS reported that the UK's national debt amounted to £1,763.8 billion (85.8% of GDP), an increase of £43.8 billion over the previous year. Figure 32.7 shows the time path of the national debt since 2000.

The data depicted here omit the effects of the bailout of banks during the financial crisis. (You can see the impact that this had in Figure 15.5 on page 214.) Even without the bailouts, it is clear that the level of public sector net debt has increased substantially since the financial crisis of the late 2000s.

In part, this reflects the cyclical deficit caused by the recession of 2008–13. However, the increase in the structural deficit cannot be ignored, in particular caused by the demographic impact of an ageing population, which has long-term effects on the government budget deficit.

The key question is whether the increase in the national debt is sustainable in the long run. One effect of the higher level of debt is that it brings with it the need to pay higher interest payments on the debt into the future. A stated objective is therefore to bring the level of national debt back to a sustainable level. However, there is no consensus on what is a desirable long-term ratio of debt to GDP. In the days of the

1997 Labour government, the target rate was set at 40%, but that no longer appears a feasible objective; the European protocol on what is excessive in this context is that the national debt should not exceed 60% — but even this seems challenging.

If the debt ratio is to be reduced, it is necessary either to reduce spending or to increase tax revenues. In June 2018, Theresa May pledged to increase spending on the NHS by £20 billion a year by 2023. There are other factors that will increase spending. New arrangements for student loan repayments mean an increase in spending, and the demographics of the population will lead to future increases in spending on pensions and adult social care. In July 2018, the Office for Budgetary Responsibility (OBR) noted that unless these issues were addressed, the national debt could reach 282.8% of GDP in 2067–68.

Follow-up questions

a Explain the distinction between 'cyclical' and 'structural' deficits.

b How does an increase in the national debt affect future government budget deficits?

c What measures could be introduced to bring the national debt to a level that would be sustainable in the long run?

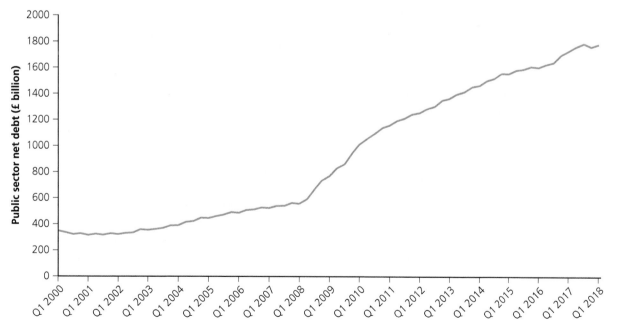

Source: ONS

Figure 32.7 The UK's national debt since 2000

Theme 4 key terms

absolute advantage the ability to produce a good more efficiently (e.g. with less labour)

absolute poverty situation of a household whose income is insufficient to allow it to purchase the minimum bundle of goods and services regarded as necessary for survival

appreciation a rise in the exchange rate within a floating exchange rate system

asymmetric information a situation in which some participants in a market have better information about market conditions than others

automatic stabilisers process by which government expenditure and revenue varies with the business cycle, thereby helping to stabilise the economy without any conscious intervention from government

Bank for International Settlements (BIS) an institution that acts as a bank for central banks and sets standards for regulation of banks that are accepted globally

bank rate the rate of interest charged by the Bank of England on short-term loans to other banks

BRIC countries a group of countries (Brazil, Russia, India, China and (later) South Africa who enjoyed a period of rapid economic growth and formed a political alliance

buffer stock a scheme intended to stabilise the price of a commodity by buying excess supply in periods when supply is high, and selling when supply is low

capital account of the balance of payments account identifying transactions in (physical) capital between the residents of a country and the rest of the world

capital adequacy ratio the ratio of a bank's capital to its current liabilities and risk-weighted assets

capital flight a situation in which savings generated in a developing country are invested abroad

central bank the banker to the government, performing a range of functions, which may include issue of coins and banknotes, acting as banker to commercial banks and regulating the financial system

common market a set of trading arrangements in which a group of countries removes barriers to trade among them, adopt a common set of barriers against external trade, establish common tax rates and laws regulating economic activity, allow free movement of factors of production between members and have common public sector procurement policies

comparative advantage the ability to produce a good *relatively* more efficiently (i.e. at lower opportunity cost)

competitive devaluation a situation in which one country attempts to gain an advantage by devaluing its currency, inducing a response from other countries

crowding in process by which a decrease in government expenditure 'crowds in' private sector activity by lowering the cost of borrowing

crowding out process by which an increase in government expenditure 'crowds out' private sector activity by raising the cost of borrowing

current account of the balance of payments account identifying transactions in goods and services between the residents of a country and the rest of the world, together with income payments and international transfers

customs union a group of countries that agrees to trade without barriers between them, and with a common tariff barrier against the rest of the world

cyclical deficit a budget deficit that occurs during the downturn of the business cycle, but disappears in the upturn

deindustrialisation a process whereby the structure of economic activity in a country shifts away from manufacturing activity towards the service sector

demographic transition process through which many countries have been observed to pass whereby improved health lowers the death rate, and the birth rate subsequently also falls, leading to a low and stable population growth

depreciation a fall in the exchange rate within a floating exchange rate system

devaluation process whereby a government reduces the price of its currency relative to an agreed rate in terms of foreign currency

development process by which real per capita incomes are increased and the inhabitants of a country are able to benefit from improved living conditions, i.e. lower poverty and enhanced standards of education, health, nutrition and other essentials of life

direct tax a tax levied directly on income

Dollar Standard a system of fixed exchange rates established following the Bretton Woods conference, under which countries pegged their currencies to the US dollar; this lasted until the early 1970s

economic and monetary union a set of trading arrangements the same as for a common market, but in addition having a common currency (or permanently fixed exchange rates between the member countries) and a common monetary policy

emerging economies economies that have experienced rapid economic growth with some industrialisation and characteristics of developed markets

Exchange Rate Mechanism (ERM) a system that was set up by a group of European countries in 1979 with the objective of keeping member countries' currencies relatively stable against each other

export-led growth situation in which economic growth is achieved through the exploitation of economies of scale, made possible by focusing on exports and so reaching a wider market than would be available within the domestic economy

fair trade schemes schemes that set out to ensure that small producers in developing countries receive a fair price for their products

financial account of the balance of payments account identifying transactions in financial assets between the residents of a country and the rest of the world

Financial Conduct Authority (FCA) a body separate from the Bank of England responsible for conduct regulation of financial services firms

financial intermediaries institutions such as banks and building societies that channel funds from lenders to borrowers

Financial Policy Committee (FPC) the decision-making body of the Bank of England responsible for macroprudential regulation

financial stability a situation in which there is a sufficient and efficient flow of liquidity in the economy

fiscal deficit occurs when government outlays exceed government receipts

fixed exchange rate a system in which the government of a country agrees to fix the value of its currency in terms of that of another country

floating exchange rate a system in which the exchange rate is permitted to find its own level in the market

foreign currency gap a situation in which a developing country is unable to import the goods that it needs for development because of a shortage of foreign exchange

foreign direct investment (FDI) investment undertaken in one country by companies based in other countries

foreign exchange reserves stocks of foreign currency and gold owned by the central bank of a country to enable it to meet any mismatch between the demand and supply of the country's currency

free trade area a group of countries that agrees to trade without barriers between themselves, but having their own individual barriers with countries outside the area

futures market a market in which it is possible to buy a commodity at a fixed price for delivery at a specified future date; such a market exists for foreign exchange

General Agreement on Tariffs and Trade (GATT) the precursor of the WTO, which organised a series of 'rounds' of tariff reductions

Gini coefficient a measure of the degree of inequality in a society

globalisation a process by which the world's economies are becoming more closely integrated

Golden Rule of fiscal policy rule stating that over the economic cycle net government borrowing will be for investment only, and not for current spending

government budget deficit (surplus) the difference between government expenditure and government revenue

government capital expenditure spending by government on capital projects

government consumption expenditure (current expenditure) spending by the government on goods and services

Harrod–Domar model a model of economic growth that emphasises the importance of savings and investment

headcount ratio a measure of the percentage of a country's population living below a poverty line

HIPC Initiative initiative launched in 1995 to provide debt relief for heavily indebted poor countries

hot money stocks of funds that are moved around the world from country to country in search of the best return

Human Development Index a composite indicator of the level of a country's development, varying between 0 and 1

indirect tax a tax on expenditure, e.g. VAT

industrialisation a process of transforming an economy by expanding manufacturing and other industrial activity

infant industry an industry that needs protection from international competition in the short run so that it can learn to become competitive

infrastructure the complex of physical capital goods needed to support development in the form of roads, communication networks, market, education and healthcare facilities etc.

interbank lending borrowing and lending between banks to manage their liquidity and other requirements for short-term funds

International Monetary Fund (IMF) multilateral institution that provides short-term financing for countries experiencing balance of payments problems

International Poverty Line an agreed measure that defines the absolute poverty line based on international prices, set at PPP$1.90 from October 2015

interventionist strategy a strategy for stimulating development that focuses on addressing market failure

invisible trade trade in services

J-curve effect a situation following a devaluation, in which the current account deficit moves further into deficit before improving

Keynesian school a group of economists who believed that the macroeconomy could settle in an equilibrium that was below full employment

labour productivity a measure of output per worker, or output per hour worked

Laffer curve a curve showing the relationship between the tax rate and the amount of revenue raised as a consequence

law of comparative advantage a theory arguing that there may be gains from trade arising when countries (or individuals) specialise in the production of goods or services in which they have a comparative advantage

lender of last resort the role of the central bank in guaranteeing sufficient liquidity is available in the monetary system

Lewis model a model developed by Sir Arthur Lewis which argued that less developed countries could be seen as being typified by two sectors, traditional and modern, and that labour could be transferred from the traditional to the modern sector in order to bring about growth and development

LIBOR the average rate of interest on interbank lending in the London interbank market

liquidity ratio the ratio of liquid assets to total assets

Lorenz curve a graphical way of depicting the distribution of income within a country

macroprudential regulation financial regulation intended to mitigate the risk of the financial system as a whole

managed float where the authorities intervene in a floating exchange rate system occasionally in order to stabilise the currency

marginal tax rate tax on additional income, defined as the change in tax payments due divided by the change in taxable income

market-oriented strategy a strategy for encouraging development that relies on enabling markets to work effectively

Marshall-Lerner condition the condition that devaluation will have a positive effect on the current account only if the sum of the elasticities of demand for exports and imports is negative and numerically greater than 1

microfinance schemes that provide finance for small-scale projects in developing countries

microprudential regulation financial regulation intended to set standards and supervise financial institutions at the level of the individual firm

monetarist school a group of economists who believed that the macroeconomy always adjusts rapidly to the full-employment level of output, and that monetary policy should be the prime instrument for stabilising the economy

Monetary Policy Committee (MPC) body within the Bank of England responsible for the conduct of monetary policy

monetary stability a situation in which there is stability in prices relative to the government's inflation target

monetary union a situation in which countries adopt a common currency

national debt the total amount of government debt, based on accumulated previous deficits and surpluses

natural rate of output the long-run equilibrium level of output to which monetarists believe the macroeconomy will always tend

natural rate of unemployment the unemployment rate that exists when the economy is in long-run equilibrium

non-governmental organisations non-profit, voluntary citizens' groups (including charities) organised on a local, national or international level

non-tariff barriers measures imposed by a government that have the effect of inhibiting international trade

Official Development Assistance (ODA) aid provided to developing countries by countries in the OECD

open market operations intervention by the central bank to influence short-run interest rates by buying or selling securities

optimal currency area a situation in which a group of countries is better off with a single currency

persistent poverty where a household is currently in relative poverty and has also been in this state in at least two of the preceding three years

Prebisch–Singer hypothesis an observation that the terms of trade for primary products relative to manufactures will tend to deteriorate in the long run

progressive tax a tax in which the marginal tax rate rises with income, i.e. a tax bearing most heavily on the relatively well-off members of society

proportional tax a tax that is proportional to income, being neither regressive nor progressive

protectionism measures taken by a country to restrict international trade

Prudential Regulation Authority (PRA) the decision-making body in the Bank of England responsible for microprudential regulation of deposit-takers, insurers and major investment firms

purchasing power parity theory of exchange rates theory stating that in the long run exchange rates (in a floating rate system) are determined by relative inflation rates in different countries

quantitative easing process by which liquidity in the economy is increased when the central bank purchases assets from the commercial banks

quota an agreement by a country to limit its exports to another country to a given quantity or quota

real exchange rate the nominal exchange rate adjusted for differences in relative inflation rates between countries

regressive tax a tax bearing more heavily on the relatively poorer members of society

relative poverty situation obtaining if household income falls below 60% of median adjusted household disposable income

repo a sale and repurchase agreement, whereby one financial institution sells a financial asset to another with an agreement to buy it back at an agreed future date

retail banks banks that provide high-street services to depositors

revaluation process whereby a government raises the price of domestic currency in terms of foreign currency

savings gap a situation in which a country cannot generate a sufficient flow of savings for investment

securitisation process whereby future cash flows are converted into marketable securities

structural deficit a deficit that persists even when the economy is at full employment

sunset industry an industry in decline that needs protection for its displaced workers

sustainable development 'development which meets the needs of the present without compromising the ability of future generations to meet their own needs' (Brundtland Commission, 1987)

tariff a tax imposed on imported goods

terms of trade the ratio of export prices to import prices

tiger economies a group of economies in South East Asia (Hong Kong, South Korea, Singapore and Taiwan) that enjoyed rapid economic growth from the 1960s

total factor productivity the average productivity of all factors, measured as the total output divided by the total amount of inputs used

trade creation the replacement of more expensive domestic production or imports with cheaper output from a partner within the trading bloc

trade diversion the replacement of cheaper imported goods by goods from a less efficient trading partner within a bloc

trading bloc where a group of countries in a region agrees to cooperate in international trade through some sort of free trade area or other form of association

trading possibilities curve shows the consumption possibilities under conditions of free trade

transfer payments occur when the government provides benefits (in cash or in kind) to poor households

transfer pricing process by which a transnational company can minimise its global tax liability by manipulating the internal prices for transactions between its branches in different countries

transnational company (TNC) a company whose production activities are carried out in a number of countries

unit labour costs the average cost of labour per unit of output produced

universal banks banks that operate in both retail and wholesale markets

visible trade trade in goods

wholesale banks banks that deal with companies and other banks on a large scale

World Bank multilateral organisation that provides financing for long-term development projects

World Trade Organization (WTO) a multilateral body responsible for overseeing the conduct of international trade

Practice questions

Paper 1: Markets and business behaviour

Section A

1 Figure 1 shows a production possibility frontier for an economy.

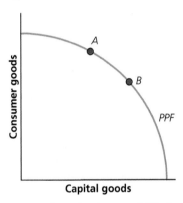

Figure 1 A production possibility frontier

a Which of the following are true about the points shown on the
   production possibility frontier above? **(1)**

   A A movement from *A* to *B* incurs no opportunity cost

   B Both *A* and *B* are currently unobtainable

   C A movement from *A* to *B* will lead to economic decline

   D Both *A* and *B* are economically efficient

b Explain the impact on future living standards of moving from
   point *A* to *B*. **(2)**

c The production possibility frontier is an economic model of the
   economy. The model assumes the frontier is for certain period of time.
   Explain why assumptions are made in economic models. **(2)**

2 Sainsbury's has cut the price of a pint of milk from 49p to 45p to compete
with low-cost supermarkets, such as Lidl. Following the milk price cut there
was a 1% increase in the demand for tea in Sainsbury's stores.

a Calculate the cross elasticity of demand for tea in Sainsbury's stores. **(2)**

b Tetley Tea is a normal good but Sainsbury's own-brand tea is an inferior
   good. Explain the difference between a normal and an inferior good. **(2)**

c Tea is most likely to have price elastic supply: **(1)**

   A When barriers to entry in the industry are high

   B If tea can be stockpiled

   C When consumers can easily switch to substitute products

   D If tea is a perishable product

3 The price mechanism can lead to the under-provision of public goods, such as national defence.

  a With reference to national defence, explain why public goods are under-provided by the price mechanism. **(4)**

  b Karl Marx, Adam Smith and Frederick Hayek all had different views on free market economies. Karl Marx predicted that free market economies would: **(1)**

   A Be replaced by command economies

   B Lead to a reduction in income inequality

   C Be the optimal economic system

   D Lead to government failure

4 Many schools in Outer London find it difficult to recruit teachers. It is estimated that around a third of schools in the area report at least one vacancy.

  a Explain how geographic immobility can lead to market failure in the labour market for teachers. **(4)**

  b The most appropriate form of government intervention to reduce geographic immobility of teachers is: **(1)**

   A The removal of relocation subsidies for teachers moving to London

   B A wage freeze for teachers in the public sector

   C The introduction of a maximum rental price scheme in London

   D An increase in funding for teacher training

5 A small-scale nickel producer is assumed to be operating under the conditions of perfect competition. The producer is currently making short-run supernormal profits, due to a high world price of nickel.

  a In the short-run, the small nickel producer will always be: **(1)**

   A Productively efficient

   B X-inefficient

   C Allocatively efficient

   D Dynamically efficient

  b Explain **one** impact on the small-scale nickel producer in the long-run as a result of low barriers to entry and exit. Illustrate your answer with an appropriate cost and revenues diagram. **(4)**

Section B

Read the following extracts before answering question 6.

Extract A: Minimum price for alcohol

Over the last five decades alcohol consumption in the UK has more than doubled, in part due to alcohol becoming more affordable over time. Each year the average adult in the UK will consume the equivalent of 500 pints of beer, which equates to only the eight highest in Europe on a per capita basis. However, in the UK, there is a higher number of non-drinkers and a habit of binge-drinking rather than consuming little and often.

These trends in UK alcohol consumption are imposing significant external costs. For one, alcohol-related admissions to hospital are on the rise, such as those relating to cirrhosis, a disease of the liver, which is falling elsewhere in Europe. More than 7,000 will die annually from alcohol-related illnesses. Moreover, anti-social behaviour and crime as a result of drinking is much higher compared to other European countries.

The announcement of a minimum price for alcohol in Scotland was therefore welcomed by medical professionals and the police. It is set at 50p per unit of alcohol and came into effect in May 2018. Other countries have also used minimum prices to deter alcohol consumption, such as Russia and in some Canadian provinces, causing significant drops in demand, crime and admissions to hospital, with the biggest impact being on long-term heavy drinkers.

However, its impact on the drinks industry may not be as damaging as initially thought. First, while 70% of alcohol bought in local shops and supermarkets is below the minimum price, drinks in pubs are already above the 50p per unit and are therefore unaffected. This could make the pub a more attractive alternative to drinking at home following a shop at Tesco. Second, even those drinks that are affected by the floor price could see little change in demand and therefore could see revenues rise too. Alcohol is a habit-forming good for many with few available substitutes. Indeed, a cross-country study by Florida University found that a 10% rise in alcohol prices led to only a 4.6% drop in demand for alcohol.

Governments could instead target all alcohol consumption using indirect taxation, such as a specific tax. This would also raise tax revenue which could be spent on tackling many of the external costs on public services, such as the NHS and the police. However, Scotland does not have the political power to do this and Westminster has been reluctant to put up indirect taxes when real incomes have been falling.

Extract B: The beer industry

In November 2015, the brewery company Anheuser-Busch took over its rival SABMiller in a deal thought to be worth in excess of £70 billion — amounting to £44 per share. At that time, Anhesuer-Busch produced famous brands such as Stella Artois, Becks and Corona, employed 155,000 people and earnt global revenues of over $47 billion. SABMiller's main brands included Peroni and Grolsch, it employed 70,000 people in 80 countries, and its revenues across the world were $26 billion. The deal brought together the two largest beer manufacturers in the world, producing 30% of the world's beer with potential cost savings of over £1 billion a year.

However, more recently, there have been issues with overt collusion in the beer manufacturing and retailing sector in Germany. In 2016, following a 6-year investigation, the German Cartel Office imposed fines of €90.5 million on several supermarkets found guilty of fixing prices for beer, coffee and sweets. The investigation found evidence of formal agreements between retailers and manufacturers during dawn raids. These agreements gave details of the exact scale and date of the price increases, which allowed a coordinated hike in prices for consumers.

German retailers Edeka, Metro and Netto fixed the price of Beck's beer (owned by Anheuser-Busch), while Lidl was involved in colluding over the price of Haribo sweets. However, Anheuser-Busch and retailer REWE Zentral were not fined due to their cooperation with the investigations.

6 The alcohol industry

a Explain the impact of a specific tax on alcohol on consumer surplus. Illustrate your answer with a demand and supply diagram. **(5)**

b With reference to Extract A, examine the significance of **two** external costs of alcohol consumption. **(8)**

c Discuss the likely economic effects of the minimum price for alcohol introduced in Scotland. **(12)**

d With reference to Extract B, assess the benefit of overt collusion for German retailers. Refer to game theory in your answer. **(10)**

e With reference to Extract B and your own knowledge, discuss the possible advantages for Anheuser-Busch from taking over SABMiller. Illustrate your answer with an appropriate diagram. **(15)**

Section C

EITHER

7 Amazon has significant market power over publishers, selling 9 out of 10 e-books in the UK.

Evaluate the economic effects of monopsony power in the e-book market. **(25)**

OR

8 The UK water industry has been regulated by Ofwat since its privatisation in the 1980s. It was announced that deregulation of the industry would begin in April 2018.

Evaluate the effectiveness of government intervention at promoting economic efficiency in the UK. Refer to an industry of your choice in your answer **(25)**

Paper 2: The national and global economy

Section A

1 China has overtaken the US as the top destination for foreign direct investment (FDI), for the first time since 2003. China currently runs a financial account deficit on their balance of payments.

a Explain the impact of increased FDI into China on their financial account of the balance of payments. **(2)**

b Foreign-owned companies send profits back to their home countries from China. What will be the impact on China's current account of the balance of payments? **(1)**

	Current account surplus	Component of current account
A	Decrease	Investment income
B	Decrease	Trade in services
C	Increase	Investment income
D	Increase	Trade in services

c Explain the impact of foreign companies sending profits home on China's gross national income (GNI). **(2)**

2 The marginal propensity to withdraw in the UK is estimated to be 0.55. The UK government has announced an extra £230 million for road improvements in the north of England.

a The total increase in national income as a result of the £230 million road improvement scheme is equal to: **(1)**

A £126.5 million

B £365.5 million

    C £418.2 million

    D £511.1 million

  b With reference to the multiplier effect, explain the impact of the road improvement scheme on UK aggregate demand. **(4)**

3 The UK's productivity performance against other countries is shown in Figure 2.

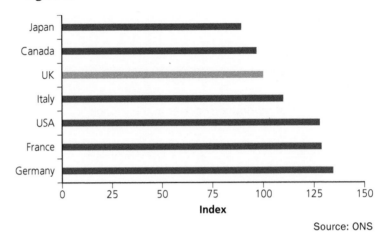

Source: ONS

Figure 2 GDP per hour worked in selected countries (Index, UK = 100)

  a It can be inferred from Figure 2 that UK productivity in 2016: **(1)**

    A Has risen by 10%

    B Is over 20% below Germany

    C Has fallen by 10%

    D Is over 20% above Canada

  b Explain **one** market-based supply-side policy the UK government could use to boost productivity. **(4)**

4 Figure 3 shows the UK unemployment rate in recent years.

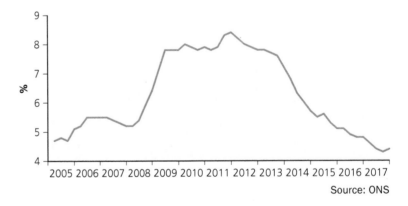

Source: ONS

Figure 3 UK Unemployment rate, 2005–2017

  a From Figure 3, it can be inferred that: **(1)**

    A More people are in employment in 2016 than in 2015

    B The rate of unemployment peaked at the start of the financial crisis

    C Fewer people are unemployed in 2016 than in 2015

    D The rate of unemployment is back to around pre-crisis levels

  b With reference to Figure 3, explain the impact of a fall in UK unemployment on the budget deficit. **(4)**

5 Mario Draghi, the President of the European Central Bank, said in 2016 that he would back a bailout of Italian banks in 'exceptional circumstances'.

  a Explain **one** role of central banks, such as the ECB. **(2)**

  b Explain why bank bailouts could lead to moral hazard in financial markets. **(2)**

  c Following the Italian government support for the bank Monte Dei Paschi di Siena, many investors began to purchase its shares, allowing the bank's share price to recover. Which role of financial markets is best illustrated in this example? **(1)**

  A Provision of a market for equities

  B Provision of forward markets

  C Provision of a market for commodities

  D Provision of loans to individuals

Section B

Read the following figures and extracts before answering question 6.

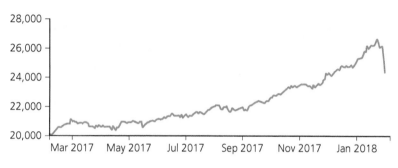

Source: Yahoo Finance

Figure 4 US share prices 12-month history (Dow Jones Index closing prices)

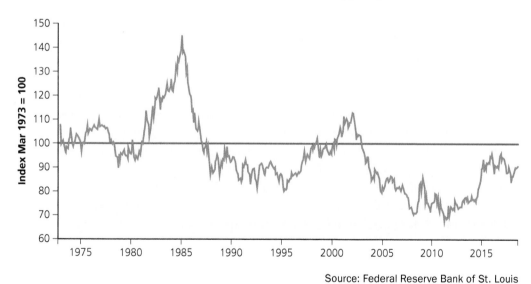

Source: Federal Reserve Bank of St. Louis

Figure 5 US exchange rate, 1973–2018 (Index, March 1973 = 100)

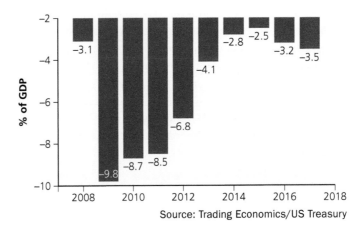

Source: Trading Economics/US Treasury

Figure 6 US budget deficit, 2008-2018

Extract C: Trump, tariffs and the WTO

Ever since Donald Trump was elected to 'Make America Great Again' there have been fears that his presidency could lead to a shift away from free trade and towards protectionism. One example of this is in the aluminium and steel market. The Trump administration has steel and aluminium imports in its sights with a 25% tariff on steel and 10% on aluminium, although together the two industries only account for 0.2% of US GDP. Mr Trump introduced these measures on the grounds of national security but also in an attempt to protect US jobs in key states and correct the 'bad deal' he claims the US gets from world trade, as shown by their trade deficit.

There could be significant implications for the US economy as a result of the tariffs. The tariffs will mean higher prices of steel and aluminium for other industries in the country, such as car manufacturing and construction, where more workers are employed. Moreover, there has already been retaliation against this form of US protectionism from both China and the EU.

The markets reacted badly to the announcement of the tariffs. While US steel producers saw their share price rise significantly, share prices fell overall with the Dow Jones Index down 1.6%, including falls for manufacturers Boeing and Caterpillar. This is in stark contrast to the rising share prices seen post Trump's election due to his pro-business stance.

The biggest damage could be on the global trading system itself. The World Trade Organization (WTO) has overseen the reduction of trade barriers over eight trade rounds since the Second World War. However, it faces the prospect of its courts being overrun by trade disputes following US protectionism and the coming retaliation. Worse still, with global trade talks having collapsed in Doha in 2015, the rise of regional trade agreements and the prospect of an angry Trump pulling the US out of the WTO altogether, it faces its biggest fight for survival it has ever known.

Extract D: The fall of the dollar

The beginning of 2018 has seen a fall in the value of the dollar against other major currencies. So far, the decline has only restored the currency to the same level as around a year ago. There are several factors, which have driven the dollar's decline.

First, there is better news for growth in Europe and for global growth in general. With rising stock markets, investors are starting to look beyond America for their chances to gain a return. Second, monetary policy conditions are changing.

America was the first major economy to start raising interest rates, which fuelled the 2014 dollar rise but the Federal Reserve is preaching caution on further increases. However, in contrast, interest rates have been increased in Canada and Britain recently and quantitative easing scaled back in the eurozone and in Japan, as their economies pick up. Finally, there is the Trump factor and political uncertainty over the Russia investigation and tensions with North Korea. There are also concerns that despite getting his tax reforms and tariffs passed, Mr Trump's political agenda may be stalling.

The future of the dollar is uncertain. Some commentators forecast a modest decline in the dollar's value over the year rather than an appreciation. Much will depend on the future economic performance and monetary policy decisions in the US and abroad, as well as Mr Trump's actions. However, during the global financial crisis many investors continued to purchase dollars despite falling economic growth and confidence. Maybe investors will be more resilient to Mr Trump than expected.

Extract E: US macroeconomic policy

Donald Trump finally flexed his economic muscles when he managed to pass his coveted tax reform bill, which came into effect in 2018. In the first year, the reforms were estimated to boost consumption and investment, equating to an increase of 0.3% in GDP. However, longer term, the reforms are expected to double the budget deficit to $1 trillion or 5% of US GDP. This is the largest peacetime deficit outside of major recessions. Despite the initial boost, the US will eventually need to deal with its rising national debt if it wants to prevent borrowing costs rising and significant crowding out from occurring.

The expansionary fiscal policy brought in by the reforms specifically includes a cut in corporation tax from 35% to 21%, income tax cuts for the wealthiest and some lower income workers, and cuts in inheritance tax. This will lead to lower tax bills for most taxpayers, but possibly rising income inequality. Also included were plans for public expenditure on childcare, defence and infrastructure (possibly the wall with Mexico).

The future of the US economy could now hinge on future monetary policy decisions. The Federal Reserve must decide on future interest rates and may have little choice but to raise rates if the US economy overheats and Trump's fiscal plan leads to significant inflationary pressure.

6 The US economy and Donald Trump

  a With reference to Extract C, explain the role of the World Trade
     Organization. **(5)**

  b With reference to Extract C, examine **two** economic effects of the US
     imposing tariffs on steel and aluminium imports. **(8)**

  c With reference to the information provided, discuss the causes
     of the fall in the dollar exchange rate **(12)**

  d Assess the impact on US real GDP of the recent fall in share prices.
     Illustrate your answer with an aggregate demand and supply diagram. **(10)**

  e With reference to Extract E, discuss the extent to which expansionary
     fiscal policy will allow the US to meet its macroeconomic objectives. **(15)**

Section C
EITHER

7 Economic growth in Africa slowed to just 1.4% in 2016, the slowest pace for two decades. However, this masks differences between African countries, with Nigeria in a recession but the Ivory Coast growing at 8%. Similar contrasts are found across the continent.

Evaluate the economic factors constraining economic growth and development in developing countries. Refer to a developing country of your choice in your answer. **(25)**

OR

8 The UK's Gini coefficient rose from 24 in 1979 to 36 during the global financial crisis, before falling to 34 recently. China saw an increase from 30 in the 1980s to 61 in 2010, before falling back to 46 over the past 7 years.

Evaluate the causes of an increase in income inequality within a country. Refer to the UK or a country of your choice in your answer. **(25)**

Paper 3: Microeconomics and macroeconomics

Section A
Read the following figures and extracts before answering question 1.

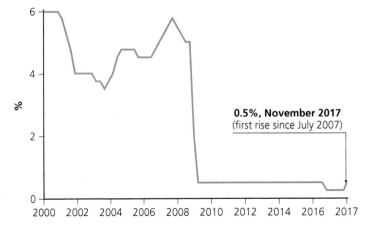

Source: Bank of England

Figure 7 UK base rates, 2000–2017

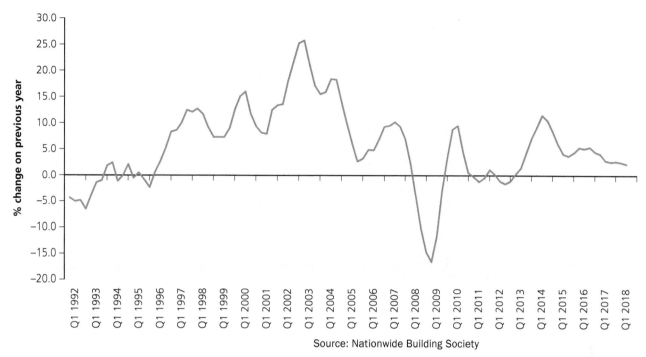

Figure 8 UK house prices over time (percentage change)

Source: Nationwide Building Society

Extract F: The buy-to-let sector

Buy-to-let involves buying a property, often with a mortgage, in order to rent it to tenants. The phenomenon started in 1996 and there are now over a million people who are buy-to-let investors.

For many years the buy-to-let sector has been extremely profitable but recent changes have meant that healthy profits have turned into losses. First, stamp duty has been increased by 3% for those buying second homes. Stamp duty is a tax that you have to pay the government when you buy a house. Second, house prices have been rising faster than rents. Britain's ratio of house prices to rents is now 50% above its long-run average. Finally, the recent interest rate increase to 0.5% have will have a big impact on people with buy-to-let mortgages who often have interest-only mortgages.

Some buy-to-let investors will remain profitable, especially those who are able to operate multiple properties in order to gain economies of scale, but many first-time landlords are now leaving the market.

A reduction in buy-to-let investors could be a positive development for UK financial markets. It has been argued that buy-to-let investors may have caused greater volatility in house prices and can exacerbate speculative bubbles as they purchase when prices are rising and sell when they are falling. Moreover, buy-to-let investors are four times more likely to default on their mortgages. This impacts on financial stability as 15% of mortgage debt is for buy-to-let mortgages, which further underlines the importance of the greater regulation of banks since the global financial crisis.

Extract G: Interest rates rise to 0.5%

For the first time in over a decade the Bank of England has raised the base rate, increasing it from 0.25% to 0.5%. This reverses the cut in interest rates in August 2017 following the Brexit vote. A further two rate rises are expected in the next 3 years.

The Monetary Policy Committee believed a rate rise was necessary given rising demand–pull inflation from stronger global growth and record low unemployment, despite uncertainty over Brexit. Inflation had previously risen to 3% due to temporary cost–push inflation from a weakened pound. However, it was decided that higher rates were needed to prevent the inflation target being missed in the medium term and to prevent inflation expectations rising.

The governor of the Bank of England, Mark Carney, believes that savers will be the first to benefit from the rate rise, with banks increasing rates to savers almost immediately. However, there may be a time lag for loans and credit cards rates to change.

Higher interest rates will have a significant impact on the 46% of homeowners who have a variable rate mortgage, and who will now face higher repayment costs of on average £12 a month. Due to historically low interest rates, over two million households have never experienced such an interest rate rise on their mortgage. However, the majority of the 8.1 million UK households have fixed rate mortgages and so there will be a time lag before any rate change will be felt.

With interest rates still at almost record lows, the impact on the UK economy is unlikely to be large for now. However, the Bank of England is certainly signalling to the markets that more contractionary monetary policy is on its way.

Extract H: House prices could fall by 40%

House prices are falling, at least according to the Nationwide building society in February 2018. This is the first time that house prices have fallen month on month since August the previous year and has meant that on an annual basis house price rises have slowed to a rate of just 2.2%. This is mainly due to falls in incomes, confidence and therefore demand.

Housing plays a key role in the economy, as it is the main source of wealth for many individuals. During the 1990s recession, house price falls led to homeowners to experience negative equity, where the price of their house was below the cost of their mortgage. This affected over a million households. It is also only a decade on from the collapse in the US housing market which contributed to the global financial crisis.

Paul Cheshire of the London School of Economics has forecast a fall in house prices by over 40% due to the over-valuation of UK housing. He believes that house price falls often begin in London before becoming more widespread across the country and therefore it is worrying that prices in London have dropped this month.

If prices do fall, it is likely to be those who have just got onto the housing ladder that will be affected most, and most at risk of negative equity, as seen in previous drops. It could take several years for prices to recover to current levels, should a dramatic housing market collapse occur.

1 UK housing market and interest rates

a With reference to Extract G, explain the concept of 'demand–pull inflation'. Illustrate your answer with an aggregate demand and supply diagram. **(5)**

b With reference to Extract F, examine **two** factors that could turn profits into losses for buy-to-let investors. **(8)**

c Discuss the potential risk posed to UK financial markets by the growth of buy-to-let investments. **(12)**

d Evaluate the microeconomic and macroeconomic impact on the UK economy of a '40% fall in house prices'. **(25)**

OR

e Evaluate the microeconomic and macroeconomic effects of a rise in interest rates from 0.25% to 0.5%. **(25)**

Section B

Read the following figures and extracts before answering question 2.

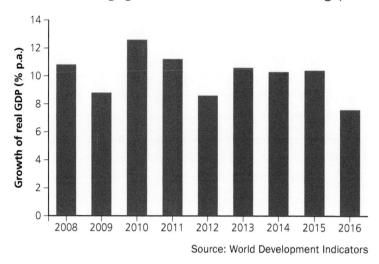

Source: World Development Indicators

Figure 9 Ethiopian economic growth, 2008–2016

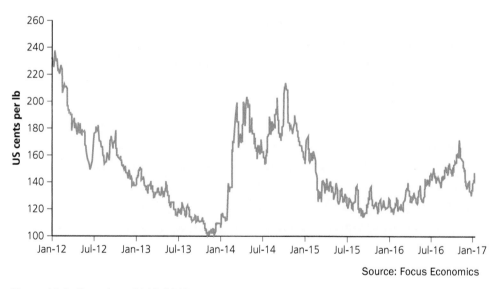

Source: Focus Economics

Figure 10 Coffee prices, 2012–2017

Extract I: Ethiopia's economy

Ethiopia has experienced rapid economic growth since 2008 (see Figure 9). Real GDP grew at an average rate of 10% between 2008 and 2016, making it one of the fastest-growing economies in the world.

Faster economic growth can help boost living standards and help reduce absolute poverty, while providing the government with significant tax revenue to promote economic development. For example, government spending on education rose from 11% of total spending in 1999–2000 to more than 25% in 2012–13. Ethiopia has made rapid progress in getting more children in school and is on track to achieve gender parity in education. There is still a lot more to be done to ensure all children are in school and are learning. Enrolment still lags in certain regions, with about 3 million primary school children not enrolled. Repetition and drop-out rates at all levels are still high.

Like many African nations, there is still a large reliance on the primary sector. Ethiopia is Africa's biggest coffee exporter and the world's fourth largest exporter of sesame. There have been no price controls in the global coffee trade since 1989, when the buffer-stock system run by the International Coffee Agreement broke down. Since then prices have been determined by market supply and demand. Over the last 10 years coffee prices have been volatile. A new international buffer stock scheme for coffee could therefore be hugely beneficial for coffee farmers in the country.

However, available evidence suggests that economic growth in Ethiopia has been accompanied by signs of a structural shift away from such traditional and primary sectors and towards the secondary sector. This has led to the reallocation of jobs and labour from the low-productive agriculture sector to the more productive manufacturing sector. Historical evidence shows that this type of labour reallocation is vital for more secure employment and higher living standards for Ethiopia in future.

Extract J: Ethiopian manufacturing

Ethiopia has the second-biggest population in Africa, standing at 100 million. Finding employment for its citizens is a key aim for the Ethiopian government. Given that the population is rising by 5% a year, that means that another million jobs are needed annually. The government therefore set out a target, called Vision 2025, to be the leading manufacturing hub in Africa. This will allow economic growth of 11% a year, with the manufacturing sector growing by 25% itself.

In order to promote manufacturing, a major infrastructure plan has been put in place, including more than a dozen industrial parks, affordable accommodation and better transport links, such as roads and electrified railways.

One example of an industrial park is Hawassa Industrial Park which is said to be the biggest in Africa, covering 350 acres. The park has already provided 10,000 jobs, such as in textiles, with the capacity for 50,000 more in the future.

Ethiopia is also attracting major global companies, including the American clothing company PVH, which owns brands such as Calvin Klein and Tommy Hilfiger. It now manufactures its clothes at the Hawassa Industrial Park. It is easy to see the attraction of Ethiopia for such a company. First, there is a relatively stable government. Second, Ethiopia is a low-cost location, due to its large, cheap workforce and expanding infrastructure. Finally, Ethiopia itself represents a growing market due to its rapid economic growth and rising population.

Industrialisation is not the only strategy for countries like Ethiopia to grow and develop. Indeed, it will be difficult for some firms in Ethiopia to compete internationally, as profits from global companies may be repatriated, and whether enough jobs can be created to match the country's ever-growing population remains to be seen.

2 Ethiopia

a With reference to Figure 9 and the information provided, explain one benefit of 'rapid economic growth' for Ethiopia **(5)**

b With reference to the information provided, examine the reasons why global companies are setting up in Ethiopia. **(8)**

c Discuss the potential benefit of a buffer stock scheme for coffee producers in Ethiopia. Illustrate your answer with an appropriate diagram. **(12)**

EITHER

d Evaluate the microeconomic and macroeconomic effects on Ethiopia's economy of increased education spending. **(25)**

OR

e Evaluate the microeconomic and macroeconomic effects of industrialisation on Ethiopia's economy. **(25)**

Acknowledgements

Photo credits

Cover and pp1, 123, 243, 279 Chee-Onn Leong/Adobe Stock; **p3** Christopher Dodge/Fotolia; **p6** Fototrm12/Fotolia; **p13** DPA Picture Alliance/Alamy; **p18** Renate W/Fotolia; **p21** Kaspars Grinvalds/Adobe Stock; **p24** KC Hunter/Alamy; **p33** Anjelagr/Fotolia; **p44** Gyula Gyukli/Fotolia; **p49** Costin79/Fotolia; **p54** DPA Picture Alliance/Alamy; **p66** TopFoto; **p71** TopFoto; **p74** Ingram; **p80** Galina Barskaya/Fotolia; **p83** Kingan/Fotolia; **p89** Sean Gladwell/Fotolia; **p93** Dmitry Naumov/Fotolia; **p98** BE&W Agencja Fotograficzna Sp. z o.o./Alamy; **p102** David Pearson/Alamy; **p107** Monkey Business/Fotolia; **p113** JEP News/Alamy; **p117** Pressmaster/Fotolia; **p126** 06photo/Fotolia; **p133** NLPhotos/Fotolia; **p140** ImageBroker/Alamy; **p143** Keith Morris/Alamy; **p150** Geoffrey Robinson/Alamy; **p155** Agencja Fotograficzna Caro/Alamy; **p162** TopFoto; **p164** RAM/Fotolia; **p172** think4photop/Fotolia; **p177** LianeM/Fotolia; **p182** 67photo/Alamy; **p186** Justin Kase Zninez/Alamy; **p195** Jake Lyell/Alamy; **p206** Robert Stainforth/Alamy; **p210** Desmond Kwande/Stringer/Getty Images; **p216** Bjanka Kadic/Alamy; **p220** Alan D. West/Alamy Live News; **p225** AFP/Pool; **p231** Christopher Furlong/Getty Images; **p246** Julio Etchart/Alamy; **p251** Bloomberg/Getty Images; **p254** Dragon Images/Fotolia; **p259** qaphotos.com/Alamy; **p272** Dinodia Photos/Alamy+J58:J108; **p276** Stephen Brashear/Getty Images; **p291** txakel/Fotolia; **p295** Ana Malin/Fotolia; **p300** Mark Richardson/Alamy; **p308** TopFoto; **p322** Keith Morris/Alamy; **p327** somkanokwan/Fotolia; **p329** easyJet; **p331** HappyAlex/Fotolia; **p336** wellphoto/Fotolia; **p343** Gregory Wrona/Alamy; **p349** Jeffrey Blackler/Alamy; **p354** dpa/Alamy Live News; **p364** Kumar Sriskandan/Alamy; **p372** Lev/Fotolia; **p394** Mariusz Prusaczyk/Fotolia; **p401** Kadmy/Fotolia; **p402** PjrStudio Alamy; **p406** Sonny Tumbelaka/AFP/Getty Images; **p411** VanderWolf Images/Fotolia; **p416** Robert Hoetink/Fotolia; **p424** SC Photos/Alamy; **p428** Universal Images Group Limited/Alamy; **p437** Hulton Archive/Stringer/Getty Images; **p444** Xinhua/Alamy; **p474** Tyler Olson/Fotolia; **p481** Thakala/Fotolia; **p490** Andrew Aitchison/Alamy; **p508** leeyiutung/Fotolia; **p510** Alan Gignoux/Alamy; **p518** Georg Kristiansen/Alamy; **p525** F Geoffroy/Fotolia; **p530** Morane/Fotolia; **p542** Greg Balfour Evans/Alamy; **p549** Lloyds of London; **p551** Chris Dorney/Fotolia; **p561** Stephen Jaffe/IMF via Getty Images; **p563** Kostas Pikoulas/Alamy; **p569** Tim Graham/Alamy; **p579** poco_bw/Fotolia; **p583** Margit Power/Fotolia

Index

Page numbers in **bold** refer to **key term definitions**.

A

abnormal profits **265**
absolute advantage **388**
absolute poverty **468**
accuracy of data 132–33, 585
acquisitions *see* mergers and acquisitions
actual economic growth **129**, **190**
ad valorem tax **77**
adverse selection **100**
  insurance case study 548
advertising, entry deterrence strategy 327
aggregate demand (*AD*) **160** *see also* government
  expenditure
  and the budget deficit 572–74
  components of 160–61
  consumption 161–64
  curve 167–68
  and economic growth 196
  government expenditure 166, 219
  increase in, short run impact 184
  and inflation 208–09
  investment 164–66, 169
  macroeconomic equilibrium 183–86
  monetary policy affecting 222–23
  multiplier effects 188
  net trade 166–67
  quantitative easing boosting 226
aggregate demand (*AD*) curve **167**–68
aggregate supply 170
  and the budget deficit 572–73
  case study 177
  curve 170
  and economic growth 190–91
  external shocks affecting 184–85
  and fiscal policy 219–20
  long run 173–76
  macroeconomic equilibrium 183–86
  policies affecting 229
  short run 170–73
  short-run aggregate supply (*SRAS*) curve 171
agricultural sector 68–69
  dependence on in developing countries 489–90
  NAFTA case study 428
  protectionism 420
  rises in food prices 394
  transfer of surplus labour, Lewis model 525–26
  Ugandan coffee case study 537
  volatility in supply 392

  vs manufacturing 64–65, 388–89, 491
  WTO talks 405
aid *see* Official Development Assistance (ODA)
airline industry
  CMA investigation into BAA airports 363–65
  competitiveness of budget airlines 322–23, 328–30
  contestability case study 331
  strategic alliances 312
Akerlof, George 99
alcohol, minimum price for 114
allocative efficiency **65**, **274**
  monopoly market 292, 359–60
  and pricing strategy 319–20
  under monopolistic competition 302
  under perfect competition 285
anti-competitive behaviour 322–23, 358, 362, 370–71
appreciation (of a currency) **448**
arbitrage **295**–96
  formal and informal sectors 518–19
Areeda–Turner principle 323
asymmetric information **97**, **546**
  insurance market 100, 549
  limiting regulation 370
  second-hand car example 99–100
  tackling 116–17
automatic stabilisers **574**
autonomous expenditure 166
  multiplier effects 187, 188, 228, 573
average propensity to consume **161**, 162
average revenue (*AR*) 263–65
  elasticity and total revenue 287–88
  limit pricing 324
  and the shut-down price 267–68
average total cost (*ATC*) **255**

B

backward integration **247**
balance of payments **154**, 429–30
  capital account 155, 434
  case study 457
  current account 155, 431–32
  economic growth 236
  financial account 155, 432–34
  and fixed exchange rate 437–38
  monitoring components of 156–58
  overall balance 156, 431
  policy objective 211–13
ballot box limitations 221, 571

Bank of England **223**, 550–51
  banker to commercial banks 552
  banker to the government 552
  core activities of 552–54
  exchange rate management 553
  independence of 225, 238
  inflation targeting 553–54
  issuing of notes and coin 552
  lender of last resort 553
  Monetary Policy Committee (MPC) 223–24, 553–54
  policy measures available to 554–58
  pricing survey 320–21
  quantitative easing 226, 556–57
  regulatory framework 558–59
  reserve assets held by 433
Bank for International Settlements (BIS) **560**–61
bank rate **223**–24, 552, **555**
  and monetary policy 225–27, 555–57
banking sector
  access to credit 501
  bank bailouts 214, 556, 567, 577, 587
  Grameen Bank 516–18
  Islamic banking 552
Barber, Tony, fiscal expansion 574
barometric price leadership 313
barriers to entry **277** see also freedom of entry
  monopoly markets 276, 288, 290
  other entry deterrence strategies 326–27
  and pricing strategies 318, 324
barter economy 14–15
Basel Committee 561
Baumol, William 268–69, 319, 325
bauxite, market for 69–70
behaviour of consumers 19–20, 78–79
behavioural theories 270
benefit system
  cash benefits 475
  payments in kind 475, 565
  reforming 230
  unemployment benefits 149, 152–53, 230, 345
bonds 544, 545
boom 197
borrowing 543–44
  cost of, rate of interest 163, 165, 222–23, 540, 544
  financial sector facilitating 540
  by firms for investment expenditure 165–66
  government 214, 544, 563, 567, 574, 577
  interbank lending 543
  international 532–33
  microfinance 516–19
  mortgages 543
  unsecured 543–44
bounded rationality **79**, **270**
Brazil 399–400
  case study 480–81
  development 509
  hyperinflation 574
  income inequality 465
Bretton Woods institutions 534–36
Bretton Woods system 437–38

breakdown of 441, 446
Brexit 413–14
BRIC countries **399**–401
broadcasting market, case study 102
budget deficit see government budget deficit
buffer stock schemes **523**–24
burden of taxation 77, 118
  sales taxes 107
business cycle **129**, **197** see also recession
  GDP fluctuations 198–99
business growth 244–52
  case studies 251–52
  constraints on firm growth 249–50
  growth of firms 245–49
  sizes and types of firms 244–45
business objectives 265–70
  behavioural theories 270
  long-term view 269–70
  profit maximisation 265–68, 270–71
  revenue maximisation 268–69
  sales maximisation 269

C

capital see also investment
  as a factor of production 6
  depreciation of 164
  source of economic growth 193–94
capital account of the balance of payments **155**, **430**, 434
capital adequacy ratio **545**
capital expenditure, government **565**
capital flight **494**–95
capital goods **10**
capital productivity **193**
capitalism and inequality 477
cartels **44**, **70**, **311**, 312–13, 362
central bank **223**, **550** see also Bank of England
  functions of 550–54
  international context 560–62
  policy measures 554–59
certificates of deposit (CDs) 544
ceteris paribus **3**
Chamberlin, Edward 299
Chang, Ha-Joon 420
China 399–400
  carbon dioxide emissions 237
  economic growth 136–37, 140, 201–02
  exchange rate policy 583
  export-led growth 196, 400–01
  membership of WTO 382
  trade war 167
  and the USA 385–86, 423–24
  vs USA, balance of payments 457
circular flow model 178–**79**
  injections into 180–81
  three measures of 179–80
  withdrawals from 181
claimant count of unemployment **149**
  unreliability of 151
classical/monetarist school **173**, 174, 572
Coase Ronald 112

cocaine, prohibition 115–16
collusion 311–13
   and concentrated markets 360–61
command economy **16**
commercial banks 223–24
   Bank of England as banker to 550, 552
commodity markets 69–71
   buffer stock schemes 523–24
   forward markets 540–41
   and terms of trade 392–94
   volatility of prices 490–91
common land 103
common market **409**
communications
   infrastructure 501–02
   technological advances 382
comparative advantage **388**
   and free trade restrictions 419–22
   and gains from trade 388–89
   influence on pattern of trade 401
   pattern of 393–94
   reliance on pattern of natural 394–95
competition
   EU policy 366
   government intervention to promote 232, 356–74
   and the internet 280
   in oligopolistic markets 316
Competition and Markets Authority (CMA) 362–63
   and anti-competitive behaviour 370–71
   merger investigations 365, 374, 375
competition policy **356–57**
   in the EU 366
   and monopoly 357–61
   in the UK 361–63
competitive devaluation **441**
competitive market **40**
competitive tendering **371**, 372
competitiveness
   international 462, 499–580
   and productivity 456
   of UK goods 449–52
complements **26**–27
   and cross elasticity of demand 36
concentration ratio 304–06
   and collusion 360–61
congestion charge, London 88–89, 108
conglomerate mergers **247**–48
   evaluation of 249
conspicuous consumption effect 24
constant returns to scale **261**–62
consumer goods **10**, 11
consumer income
   and demand for a good 24–26
   income elasticity of demand (*YED*) 35–36
consumer preferences
   change in, market equilibrium 53–54
   and demand for a good 27
   and prices 61, 62
consumer price index (CPI) **142**, 143
   and inflation 147, 554, 555

   versus the retail price index 144
consumer spending *see* consumption
consumer surplus **57**–58, 59, 60
   after a subsidy 78
   loss of after a tariff 422, 426
   perfect competition vs monopoly 292–93
   and price discrimination 294
   and sales taxes 107
consumption 10–11, **161**
   calculation 162
   factors influencing 161–63
   hypotheses 162
   and income 163
consumption externality **83**
contestability 325–26
   airline markets 331
   and price setting by monopoly 360
contestable markets **325**
contracting out **371**
coordination problem 15–17, 56–57
corporate social responsibility (CSR) **270**, 320
corruption 504–05
cost-plus pricing **320**–21
cost-push inflation 207–**08**
costs facing firms 253–58
   average and marginal costs 255–57
   differing cost conditions 284, 358–60
   law of diminishing returns 254
   long run costs 257–58
   short run costs 254–55
CPIH **142**, 143, 144
'credit crunch' 386
cross elasticity of demand (*XED*) **36**
crowding in **574**
crowding out 567, **574**
current account of the balance of payments **155**, **430**
   components of 431
   constraint on economic growth 236
   current transfers 432
   investment income 432
   trade in goods 431
   trade in services 432
current account deficit 212
   causes of 213, 434
   dealing with 434–35
current expenditure, government **565**
customs union **407**
cyclical deficit **571**
cyclical unemployment **152**

D

data 125
   inaccuracy of 132–33, 585
   sources of 125
debt *see also* borrowing
   debt forgiveness 562
   developing countries 501, 532–33
   government 214, 220, 580
   HIPC Initiative 534–35
   national debt, UK 568, 570–71, 587

deciles 464
decision making, rational 19–20, 270
deflation **145**
deindustrialisation **383**, 395, 530
demand **20**–28
  case studies 37–38
  and consumer incomes 24–26
  consumer preferences and other influences on 27–28
  and the effect of time 28
  elasticities 28–37
  individual and market 20–21
  and the price of other goods 26–27
demand curve **22**
  and consumer incomes 24–26
  downward sloping 22
  and elasticity 30–33
  horizontal 33
  kinked demand curve model 307–08
  for labour 333–35
  and the law of demand 21–22
  movements along and shifts of 23
demand-deficient unemployment **152**
demand for labour 332–35
  and equilibrium in the labour market 340–41
  and an increase in capital 352
  and the minimum wage 346, 347
  wage elasticity 335–37
  and wage levels 152
demand for money 75, 222
demand-pull inflation **208**
demand-side policies see also fiscal policy; monetary policy
  and design of policy mix 238, 239
  evaluation of 227–28
demergers 250
demerit goods 101 see also tobacco
demographic transition **497**
  in developed countries 497–98
  in developing countries 498–99
demographics
  ageing population and pension provision 474
  and labour input 175
  population growth 496–97
  and public expenditure 566
depreciation (of capital equipment) **164**
depreciation (of currency) 445, **448**
deregulation 230, 328, 373, 383
derived demand **332**–33
  demand for labour 332–35
  foreign exchange as 74
devaluation **439**
  effects of 440–41
developing countries 461
  access to credit and banking 501, 551
  capital flight 494–95
  characteristics 488
  comparative advantage 394, 395
  corruption 504–05
  debt and borrowing 501, 532–33
  demographic transition in 498–99
  economic growth vs basic needs 200, 578

economic instability 505–06
education 502–03, 520
fair trade schemes 320, 527
FDI 381, 512–15
financial sector 547
foreign currency gap 494
future prospects 537
health issues, impact of HIV/AIDS 503
HIPC initiative 534–35, 562
identifying 482–83
income inequality 462–63, 578–79
industrialisation 524–26
informal sector 132–33, 463
international trade 195–96
investment in human capital 195
lack of good infrastructure 502
market failure, correcting 581
microfinance schemes 516–18
NGO support for 536
overseas aid 528–30
primary product dependency 489–91, 537
privatisation 519
problems of measuring unemployment in 151
property rights 504, 584
and protectionism 420, 421
public sector wages 350
savings and investment 491–96
supply-side policies 584
tax revenue 576
terms of trade 392, 393, 394
tourism 526–27, 538
trade flows 397
trade policy 512, 521–23
underdeveloped labour markets 473
wealth inequality 472
WTO and agriculture trade concessions 405–06
development 461, **482** see also economic growth
  contrasting patterns of 507–09
  demographics 496–500
  factors influencing 489–96
  Human Development Index (HDI) 483–86
  measuring 482–89
  non-economic factors 504–07
differentiation, product **300**
diminishing marginal utility **21**
direct taxes 221, **475**–76, 568
  change to indirect taxation 568–69
discouraged workers **148**, 339
diseconomies of scale **260**, 261
disincentive effect 477, 568–69, 575–76
disinflation **145**
disposable income **161**
  and indirect taxes 477
  and real consumption 163
  and relative poverty 469
diversification 246, 249, 395, 542
division of labour **13**
  advantages and disadvantages 13
  economies of scale 258
Dollar Standard **437**, 439

dominant strategy **309**, 310
drugs
   anti-competitive behaviour 371
   effect of prohibition 115–16
Dutch disease, effect of foreign aid 530
dynamic efficiency **274**–75

E

earnings *see also* income
   differential 341
   export 393, 533
   foreign exchange 514–15
   wage gap 473
Easterlin paradox **138**
Easterlin, Richard 138
economic activity, three measures of 179–80
economic agents 5
economic growth 128–31, 190–91
   actual 129–30, 190
   and aggregate demand 196
   benefits of 200–01
   capital contributing to 193–94
   case studies 140, 203
   costs of 201–03
   and happiness/well-being 137–39
   Harrod–Domar model 492–93, 495
   and inequality 478–81
   international experience 136–37
   and international trade 195–96
   labour as main driver of 194–95
   and the output gap 191–92
   policy objective 205, 578
   potential 11, 128–29, 190
   sources of 193–97
   trade (business) cycle 197–200
   trade-offs with other objectives 202–03
   vs basic needs in developing countries 200, 486
economic and monetary union (EMU) **409**, 416
economic performance measures 124–28
   balance of payments 154–58
   economic growth 128–37
   employment and unemployment 148–54
   inflation 141–47
economic problem 4–5
economic profit **265**
economic statements, positive and normative 3–4
economic variables, measurement of 126–28
economically inactive **148**
economically irrational behaviours 78–79
economies of scale **258**
   external and internal 260–61
   finance and procurement 260
   and fixed costs (overheads) 259
   and limit pricing 324
   long-run average cost curve (*LAC*), shape of 261–62
   management and marketing 260
   of natural monopoly 290–91
   oligopoly markets 306–07
   technology of production 258–59

economies of scope 261
education
   component of Human Development Index 483–86
   developing countries 502–03
   externality effects 90–91, 99
   indicator of living standards 135
   information gap 99
   interventionist policy 231–32
efficiency 64–65, 273–75
   monopolistic competition 302
   monopoly market 292
   perfect competition vs monopoly 359–60
   and pricing rules 319–20
   under perfect competition 285
   X-inefficiency 268
elastic **29**
elasticity 28–37
   cross elasticity of demand (*XED*) 36
   definition **28**
   income elasticity of demand (*YED*) 35–36
   price elasticity of demand (*PED*) 29–35
   price elasticity of supply (*PES*) 46–48
   and total revenue 287–88
   using elasticities 37
emerging economies **399**
   influence on pattern of trade 401
emissions 237
   from increased trade 386
   and pollution trading systems 110–11
   reduction of 109
employment 148–54 *see also* full employment;
   unemployment
   measuring 149–51
   structural change 473
   in the UK 148
Engel, Ernst 393
entry and exit of firms 62–64
environmental issues 202
   biodiversity, loss of 88, 203
   deforestation 203
   and economic growth 140, 203, 237, 580–81
   effect of a disaster on GNI 135
   globalisation and emissions 386
   international externalities 87–88, 214–15
   plastic in the oceans 93
   pollution control using permits 110–11
   and wildlife tourism 538
equilibrium
   balance of payments equilibrium 211–13
   labour market 340–42
   low-level equilibrium trap 491, 493
   macroeconomic equilibrium 183–86
   market 52–56
   monopoly in 287–88
   Nash equilibrium **310**
   perfect competition 282–84
   under monopolistic competition 301, 302
equities market 541
equivalence scales 467
EU Emissions Trading System (EU ETS) 111

euro area/eurozone 414–18
  exchange rate policy 583
  real exchange rate 452
  recovery from financial crisis 557
European Union (EU) 410–11
  competition policy 366
  and the single currency area 414–18
  Single European Market (SEM) 411–12
  and structural change 418–19
  the UK and Brexit 413–14
exchange rate **158**
  and the balance of payments 211–12, 457, 580
  evaluation of fixed vs floating 446–49
  fixed exchange rates 437–41
  floating exchange rates 442–45
  foreign exchange market 73–74, 436–37
  influence on pattern of trade 401
  liberalising 516
  and macroeconomic policy 448
  manipulation of, China 583
  nominal 450
  policy approaches 582–83
  and purchasing power parity 134–35, 443, 462–63
  real exchange rate 451–52
  and short run aggregate supply curve 172
Exchange Rate Mechanism (ERM) **442**
expectations
  about future demand 164–65
  case study 177
  expected prices, effect on supply decisions 43–44
  of future price inflation 28, 235
  stock market 74–75
export-led growth **196**
export promotion 522
external benefit **83**
external cost **83**
external economies of scale **260–61**
external shocks
  adjustment to 446
  financial crisis as 227
  oil price shocks 71, 147, 199, 207
  supply shock, effect of 184–85
externalities **81**, 82–92
  case study 93
  dealing with 108–11
  and education 90–91
  and the environment 87–88
  and the financial crisis 546
  global warming 111
  and health 90
  pollution 108–11
  tackling 104–05
  and tourism 91
  and transport 88–89
  waste disposal and recycling 91

F

factors of production **6**–7 *see also* capital; labour (workers); productivity

and the circular flow model 178–79
  the environment as 202
fair trade schemes **527**
fertility rates 499–500
financial account of the balance of payments **155**, **430**
  investment flows 433–34, 444
  monitoring 157
  and overall balance of payments 156
  sustained surplus on 212, 213, 433
  transaction categories 432–33
Financial Conduct Authority (FCA) **558**
financial crisis 541–42
  in Asia (1997) 385
  bank bailouts 214, 556, 567, 577, 587
  and bank lending 373
  and the 'credit crunch' 386
  evaluation of response to 559
  and government budget 214, 220
  international context 560–63
  investment expenditure 169
  market failure contributing to 545–46
  pre-crisis period (1997–2007) 554–56
  seeds of 545, 583
  slow recovery from 557
financial intermediaries **542**
financial markets 75–76
  deregulation of 383
Financial Policy Committee (FPC) **558**
financial sector 539–49
  borrowing and loans 543–44
  emerging and developing countries 547
  financial crisis and market failure 545–46
  futures and equities markets 540–41
  institutions 542–43
  instruments 544–45
  and monetary policy 541
  role of 539–41
  saving and borrowing 539–40
financial stability **553**, 559
  regulation to ensure 558–59
  switch to 581–82
firms 39, 244
  case studies 271–72
  constraints on growth of 249–50
  costs facing 253–58
  as an economic agent 5
  economies of scale 258–63
  growth of 245–49
  objectives 265–71
  private and public sector 244–45
  revenues of 263–65
  scale of operations 245
first-degree price discrimination **294**
fiscal deficit **570**–71 *see also* government budget deficit
  and fiscal policy 571
fiscal policy 218, **219**–21, 565, 582
  and aggregate supply 219–20
  automatic stabilisers 574
  and crowding out 574
  and design of policy mix 238–39

discretionary 574
evaluation of 227
and the fiscal deficit 571
global context 582
'Golden Rule' of 577
government expenditure 219
income distribution 575–76
private and public sector balance 20–21, 574–75
and the single currency area 415–16
sustainability of 577
taxation 220, 221, 570, 576
in the UK 220
fixed costs
advertising 327
of natural monopoly 259, 290–91
R&D spending 327
short-run 254–56
and the shut-down price 267
fixed exchange rate system **436**, 437–38
during the Dollar Standard period 439
effect of changes in demand for pounds 438–39
effects of devaluation 440–41
monetary policy under 440
vs floating 445–49
flexibility of labour, policies to improve 230, 350–53
floating exchange rate **442**
factors influencing 443–45
versus fixed system 445–49
foreign aid see Official Development Assistance (ODA)
foreign currency gap **494**
foreign direct investment (FDI) **381**, 512–13
and corporation tax 569
and the exchange rate 447
and the financial account 432
potential benefits 513
potential costs 514–15
in the UK 433–34, 444
foreign exchange market 73–74, 436–37
foreign exchange reserves **438**
forward integration **247**
forward markets 540
free market economy **15**
free-rider problem **95**–96
and occupational mobility 343–44
free trade areas **407**, 408–10
free trade restrictions 419–27
freedom of entry see also barriers to entry
in different market structures 275
importance of 301
monopolistic competition 300
perfect competition 276, 281
frictional unemployment **151**
full employment **149**
and fiscal policy 219
and long-run aggregate supply 173–74
and macroeconomic equilibrium 185–86

macroeconomic policy goal 205–07, 579
and monetary policy 223
and the multiplier and aggregate demand 188
and the output gap 191, 192
funding for UK regions 352
futures market **446**, 540–41

G

game theory **308**
prisoners' dilemma 308–10
GDP see gross domestic product
gender differences 473, 487
General Agreement on Tariffs and Trade (GATT) **382**, **534**
geographic mobility of labour 342–43
Giffen goods 26
Gini coefficient **466**–67, 471, 478
global warming 87, 111
globalisation **380**–81 see also international trade
and competition 361
factors contributing to 382–83
and foreign direct investment 381
impact on environment 386
interdependence of economies 384–86
transnational companies 248
GNI per capita **132**, 483
calculating 132
growth of 136–37
and happiness 138
and inequality between countries 461–63
inequality in distribution 132
measurement issues 132–33
and purchasing power parity 134–35
using HDI in preference to 483–86
Golden Rule of fiscal policy **577**
government borrowing 214, 544, 563, 567, 574, 577, 582
government budget
balancing 214, 580
and taxation 220, 570
government budget deficit see also fiscal deficit
and the AD/AS model 572–73
cyclical 571
impact of 573–74
government budget deficit (surplus) **220**, **570**
government capital expenditure **565**
government consumption expenditure **565**–66
government expenditure 112–13, 166, 565–66
and the AD/AS model 570–73
automatic and discretionary changes 574
changing size and composition of 566–67
fiscal policy 219
multiplier effect 186
and revenue, balancing 220–21
significance of high 567–68
government failure **105**
costs of intervention 117–18
from sales taxes 106–07

government intervention
  competition policy 356–67
  costs of 117–18
  in the labour market 345–50
  redistribution of income 474–77
  reducing 515–16
  regulation of monopolies 367–70
  and short run aggregate supply curve 172
  to promote competition 370–74
Great Depression 228, 404
Greece, bailout of 563
gross domestic product (GDP) **12**, **129** see also real GDP
  and actual economic growth 129–30
  government debt as percentage of 580, 587
  nominal GDP 126, 127
  and the output gap 191
  per hour worked 453–54
  vs GNI 131–32
gross investment **164**, 193
gross national happiness (GNH) 138
gross national income (GNI) **129**
  advantages of 131–32
  cross-country differences in 461–63
  exchange rate and PPP 133–35
  informal sector 132–33
  and standard of living 135
growth see business growth; economic growth; population
  growth

H

habitual behaviour **78**
happiness, measurement of 137–39
Harrod–Domar model **492**–93
  and external resources 495
HDI see Human Development Index
headcount ratio **468**
health
  component of HDI 483–85
  externalities 90
  fast-food sector 37
  gender inequality 487
  indicator of living standards 135
  organic foods case study 67
healthcare
  asymmetric information 97–98, 520–21
  developing countries 195
  externality effects 90, 520
  and market failure 93
  vaccination 90, 520
Heavily Indebted Poor Countries (HIPC) Initiative 534–**35**
Heckscher, Eli 394
hedging 447
herding behaviour **78**
HIPC Initiative 534–**35**
hit-and-run entry **325**
HIV/AIDS
  hindering development 503
  impact on capacity output 195
  and the macroeconomy 510

horizontal equity 215
horizontal integration **247**
horizontal mergers **247**
  evaluation of 248
hot money **444**
household spending see consumption
housing market 72–73
  and the financial crisis 227, 386, 583
  and geographic mobility 342
  house prices and consumption 162
  house prices and wealth 182, 472
  inequality measures excluding 467
  mortgage lending 543, 544, 556
  rent controls 114–15
human capital **195**
  development of 519–21
  education and training 175–76, 231, 502
Human Development Index (HDI) **483**
  components of 483–86
  inequality-adjusted 487
hyperinflation 209–10, 399, 509, 540, 574

I

ILO unemployment rate **149**–50
IMF see International Monetary Fund
imperfect market information see information gaps
import substitution 521–22
in employment **148**
incentives
  capitalism and inequality 477
  effect of aid on 530
  of firms to invest, government providing 165
  and government intervention 516
  price mechanism 61–62
  and progressive taxation 229–30, 345, 568–69, 575–76
  to innovate, monopolist 359
  to meet quality standards 369
  to reduce pollution 110
incidence of a tax **77**
income **182** see also GNI per capita
  diminishing marginal utility of 349
  effect on labour supply 338
  and happiness 138
  redistribution of 215–17, 578–79
  unequal distribution of 461–68, 575–76
  and wage policies 345–50
income elasticity of demand (YED) **35**–36
index numbers **127**–28, 140–41
  export and import prices 390
  GDP per hour worked 453–54, 458
  price indices 142–45, 369
indirect taxes **76**, **106**, 221, **476**
individual labour supply curve 337–38
industrial action 350–51
industrialisation 524–**25**
industry long-run supply curve (LRS) **283**
inelastic **29**
inequality
  between countries 461–63

causes of 215–16, 472–74
changes in over time 471
costs of 216–17
and economic growth 478–81
in income distribution 132, 182, 463–67
long-term policies 477–79
ownership of assets 182, 472
and taxation 569
in wealth 182
within a country 463–67
infant industry **420**
inferior good **25**
inflation **141**
and a current account deficit 434
adjustment to shocks 446
case study 159
causes of 207–09
consumer price index (CPI) 142
costs of 209–11
CPI–RPI differences 143
deflation 145
hyperinflation 209–10, 399, 509, 540, 574
influence on floating exchange rate 443, 445
and macroeconomic policy 447–48
and monetary policy 223–27, 415, 555–56
retail price index (RPI) 142–43
targeting 553–55
UK and worldwide 146–47
and unemployment 233–36
informal sector 132–33, 463, 473
information gaps 81–82, 97
education 99
and the financial crisis 545–46
healthcare 97–98
insurance market 100
in labour market 232
merit and demerit goods 101
pensions 100
and principal–agent problem 250
second-hand cars 99–100
tackling 105, 116–17
tobacco 98
infrastructure 232, **501**–02, 524, 575
injections into circular flow **180**–81
multiplier effect 187
instability, macroeconomic 505–06
insurance 100
asymmetric information problem 100, 117
history of, case study 548–49
interbank lending **543**
interdependence of economies 384–86
interest rate 222–23 *see also* bank rate; monetary policy
Bank of England intervention 555
cost of borrowing 72, 543–44
and the demand and supply of money 75
and investment 165–66
and speculation 444
internal economies of scale **260**
internalising an externality 88, **108**, 112
international competitiveness 449–52

international externalities 87–88, 214–15
International Monetary Fund (IMF) **534**, 561
bailout of Greece (2010) 563
loan to Greece to prevent sovereign default 563
International Poverty Line **468**
international trade 387 *see also* protectionism
absolute and comparative advantage 387–88
case study 402–03
dependence on 394–95
and economic growth 195–96
gains from 388–90
impact on environment 386
net trade 166–67
patterns of world trade 396–402
terms of trade 390–94
internationalisation 403
internet 280, 326
interventionist policies **229**, 231–32
interventionist strategies **511**
buffer stock schemes 523–24
fair trade 527–28
human capital development 519–21
other strategies 524–26
overseas aid 528–30
tourism 526–27
trade policy 521–23
investment 10–11, **164**, **193** *see also* foreign direct
investment (FDI)
developing countries 491–93
expectations about future demand 164–65
and government incentives 165
and the rate of interest 165–66
in the UK from abroad, decline in 213
investment income 432
'invisible hand', Adam Smith 15, 66, 477
invisible trade **432**
involuntary unemployment **153**, 347
irrational behaviours 78–79

J

J-curve effect **440**

K

Keynes, John Maynard 16, 161, 162, 228, 437, 534
Keynesian school **173**–74, 572–73
kinked demand curve model 307–08
Krugman, Paul 402, 417, 480
Kuznets curve 478–79
Kuznets, Simon 478

L

labour market 332–55
case studies 353–55
demand for labour 332–37
and economic growth 194–95
equilibrium 340–42
flexibility of, improving 230, 350–53
government intervention 345–50
and inequalities in income 472–73

and long run aggregate supply 174, 175–76
    mobility of 232, 342–44
    supply of labour 337–40
labour mobility 342–44
labour productivity **193, 453**
  case study 458–59
labour supply 337–40
  and a maximum wage policy 349
  individual 337–38
  industry 339
  and unemployment benefit 230, 345
labour (workers) *see also* workforce; unemployment
  as a factor of production 6
  effect of increase in costs 55–56
  source of economic growth 194–95
Laffer curve **570**
land, factor of production 6
Latin America *see also* Brazil
  development pattern 509
law of comparative advantage **388**
law of demand **21**
law of diminishing returns **254**
  influencing the demand for labour 333
leakages (withdrawals) **180**
legislation *see also* regulation
  competition policy 361–62, 366
  limiting trade union powers 351
  prohibiting hard drugs 115–16
lender of last resort **553**
lending 226 *see also* borrowing
  by the central bank 553
  interbank 543
  mortgage 543, 544, 556
  'pay-day' 543
Lewis model **526**
LIBOR **543**, 546
life expectancy
  component of HDI 483–86
  gender inequality in 487
  HIV/AIDS reducing 510
lighthouse services, financing of 103
limit pricing **324–25**
liquidity ratio **543**, 545
liquidity shortage 555, 556–57, 559
living standards *see* standard(s) of living
living wage 345–46
loans
  bank 542–43
  IMF 561, 563
  and interest rates 544
  microfinance schemes 516–19
  mortgages 543
  unsecured 543–44
long run **253**
long run aggregate supply 173–76
  vertical (monetarist) *LRAS* curve 173, 174, 185–86, 192, 219, 236, 573
long-run average cost curve (*LAC*), shape of 261–62
long run costs 257–58

long-run supply (*LRS*) curve 283–84, 292–93, 357, 358–59
Lorenz curve **465**
  and the Gini coefficient 466
  for income in the UK 474–75
low-level equilibrium trap 491, 493
luxury good **35**

M

Maastricht Treaty 414
macroeconomic equilibrium 183–86
  below full employment level 185–86, 206
  effect of a supply shock 184–85
  effect of increase in aggregate demand 184
  at full employment 185
  long-run 185–86
  short-run 183, 184
macroeconomic policies 218
  case studies 239
  conflicts in implementation of 233–38
  design of policy mix 238–39
  evaluation of demand-side policies 227–28
  evaluation of supply-side policies 233
  and the exchange rate 447–48
  fiscal policy 219–21
  global context 581–86
  interventionist policies 231–32
  market-based policies 229–30
  monetary policy 222–27
  supply-side policies 229
macroeconomic policy objectives 204–17
  balance of payments equilibrium 211–13
  balanced government budget 214
  conflict between policies and objectives 585
  distribution of income 215–17
  global context 578–81
  increased economic growth 205
  inflation control 207–11
  protection of the environment 214–15
  unemployment reduction 205–07
macroeconomics **17, 124**
macroprudential regulation **558**
Malthus, Thomas 496–97
managed (dirty) float **445**
  China 524
marginal analysis **5**
marginal cost (*MC*) **62, 255**
  graphing 256–57
  MR = MC rule 266
marginal propensity to consume (MPC) **161**
  calculating 162
  interpreting 164
marginal propensity to import (MPM) **187**, 203, 219, 439
marginal propensity to save (MPS) **161**
marginal propensity to tax (MPT) **187**
marginal propensity to withdraw (MPW) **187**, 573
marginal revenue (*MR*) 264–65, **266**
  MR = 0, revenue maximisation 268–69
  MR = *MC* rule, profit maximisation 266–67
marginal social benefit (*MSB*) **58**

and externalities 84–85, 88, 90
 and family size 499
 reducing pollution 108, 109
marginal social cost (*MSC*) **84**
 and family size 499
 and pollution reduction 108
 of transport congestion 88–89
marginal tax rate **475**
market-based policies **104, 229**, 229–30
market concentration 304–06
 and collusion 360–61
market equilibrium 51–**52**
 effect of changes to 53–56
market failure **81**
 case study 93
 causes of 81–82
 correcting 104–05, 581
market operation 51–67
 case studies 67, 80
 consumer behaviour 78–79
 efficiency 64–65
 entry and exit of firms 62–64
 indirect taxes 76–77
 market equilibrium 51–56
 the price mechanism 61
 prices and preferences 61
 prices and resource allocation 56–61
 signalling and incentives 61–62
 subsidies 77–78
 working of a market economy 66
market-oriented strategies 512–19
 foreign direct investment (FDI) 512–15
 liberalising exchange rates 516
 microfinance 516–19
 privatisation 519
 reducing government involvement 515–16
 trade liberalisation 512
market power
 exploitation of, supermarkets 373
 and fair trade 527
 influence of cartels on supply 44
 third-degree price discrimination 295
market share 245–46, 304–06
 and collusion 312, 360–61
 competition for, case study 272
market structure **275**
 barriers to entry 277
 case studies 298, 316–17
 collusion 311–13
 and competitiveness 328–30
 market concentration 304–06
 monopolistic competition 277, 299–304
 monopoly 276, 286–97
 monopsony 313–15
 oligopoly 277, 306–10
 perfect competition 275–76, 278–86
 structure–conduct–performance paradigm 357–58
markets **14**
 agricultural markets 68–69
 commodity markets 69–71

effectiveness of 209–10
 financial markets 75–76
 foreign exchange market 73–74
 housing market 72–73
 stock market 74
Marshall–Lerner condition **441**
Marx, Karl 15
maximum wage **348**–49
measurement issues
 economic activity 179–80
 happiness 137–38
 income inequality 467–68
 real and nominal 126–27
 unemployment 149–51
media companies, CMA intervention 365
menu costs of inflation 209
mergers and acquisitions 246–48
 case studies 251–52, 375
 evaluation of 248–49
 investigation of by the CMA 362–65
 merger defined **357**
merit goods 101
microeconomics **17**
microprudential regulation **558**
migration 342–43, 383
 and the capital account 434
 expanding the workforce 174–75, 194
 and financial flows 531
 migrant workers 355
 rural–urban 473, 525
 and unemployment 153
minimum efficient scale **261**
minimum prices 114
minimum wage **345**
 in a perfectly competitive labour market 346–47
 and the living wage 345–46
 monopsony buyer of labour 348
 objectives of 346
 and public sector wages 350
mixed economy **16**
mobility of labour 342–44
models **2**
monetarist school **173**, 174, 572, 573
monetary policy 218, **222**–27, 565, 581–82
 and aggregate demand 222–23
 conflicting with fiscal policy 237–38
 evaluation of 227–28
 fixed exchange rate system 440
 from 2004 to 2007 225
 from 2008 to the late 2010s 226–27
 global context 581–82
 and interest rates 443
 Monetary Policy Committee (MPC) 223–24
 in the policy design mix 238–39
 and the single currency area 414–15
 transmission mechanism of **224**
 in the UK 223
Monetary Policy Committee (MPC) **223**–24, **553**–54
monetary stability **553**, 554, 559
 switch to financial stability 581–82

monetary union **409**
money
  demand and supply of 75
  functions of 14–15
  and the interest rate 222
money supply **208**–09
  and monetary policy 222, 226–27, 440
  and quantitative easing 226, 557
monopolistic competition **299**, 304
  case study 317
  characteristics of 300
  and efficiency 302
  evaluation of model 302
  examples of 302–03
  importance of free entry 301
  long-run equilibrium under 301–02
  short-run equilibrium under 301
monopoly 276, **286**, 293
  assumptions of model 286–87
  barriers to entry 288
  comparison with perfect competition 292–93, 357–59
  and competition policy 357–61
  competitive monopoly 291–92
  contestability 360
  cost conditions 358–59
  creation of 290
  distrust of 358
  and efficiency 292
  in equilibrium 287–88
  evaluation of 297
  and an increase in demand 289
  natural monopoly 259, 290–91, 367
  and price discrimination 294–97
  regulation of 367–70
monopsony **313**–14
  in a labour market 344
  evaluation of 314–15
  and the minimum wage 348
  restrictions on power of 373
moral hazard **100**
  and debt forgiveness 534
  and the financial crisis 546
  insurance market 100, 548, 549
MPC *see* Monetary Policy Committee
Multidimensional Poverty Index (MPI) 487–88
multiplier **186**
  and aggregate demand 188–89
  autonomous (government) spending 187, 188, 219, 228, 573
  calculating 187
  withdrawals and injections 187

N

n-firm concentration ratio **304**
NAFTA (North American Free Trade Area) 407, 428
Nash equilibrium **310**
Nash, John 308, 309
national debt 570–**71**
  of the UK, case study 587
national income

circular flow model 178–80
  income and wealth 182–83
  injections and withdrawals 180–82
National Minimum Wage (NMW) 345–48
nationalisation **368**
natural monopoly **259**
  regulation of 367–70
natural rate of output **173**, 572
natural rate of unemployment **173**, 236
nature of demand 19–38
  case studies 37–38
  demand 20–28
  elasticity 28–37
  rational decision making 19–20
nature of economics 2–18
  consumption and investment 10–11
  coordination problem 15–17
  economic agents 5
  economic growth or decline 11
  economic problem 4–5
  economic statements, positive and normative 3–4
  factors of production 6–7
  markets 14
  microeconomics and macroeconomics 17–18
  money, functions of 14–15
  production possibility frontier (*PPF*) 8–10
  social science, economics as 2–3
  specialisation and the division of labour 13–14
  three key economic questions 7–8
  total output in an economy 12
nature of supply 39–50
  case studies 49–50
  factors influencing supply 41–45
  price elasticity of supply (*PES*) 46–48
  supply curve 40–41
necessity **35**
negative production externalities
  global warming 87
  pollution 108
  toxic fumes 83–85
net debt, public sector 214, 220, 557, 577, 580
net investment **164**
  influence on floating exchange rates 444
net trade 166–67
NIMBY (not in my back yard) syndrome **111**
nominal exchange rate 450
nominal GDP **126**, 127
non-excludability **94**, 96
non-governmental organisations (NGOs) **536**
non-pecuniary benefits **338**
non-price competition **313**
non-renewable resources **7**
non-rivalry **94**
non-tariff barriers **425**
normal good **24**, 25, 35, 338
normal profit **265**, 281, 324
normative judgements 86, 101
normative statement **3**
not-for-profit organisations **244**
nudge theory **79**

O

occupational mobility of labour 343–44
Official Development Assistance (ODA) **528**
    bilateral and multilateral 530
    and 'Dutch disease' 530
    effectiveness of aid 529
    financial flows into low-income countries 529
Ohlin, Bertil 394
oil prices 70–71, 384–85
    debt crises caused by rise in 532–33
    impact on short-run aggregate supply 171, 172
    supply shocks 184–85, 199
oligopoly 277, **306**–07
    competition in, case study 316
    kinked demand curve model 307–08
    modelling using game theory 308–10
oligopsony **314**
OPEC 70–71, 312, 313, 384–85
open market operations **555**
opportunity cost **4**–5
    calculating ratios 389
    of leisure 338
    tourism 527
optimal currency area **416**
organic growth 245–**46**
output
    circular flow model 178–80
    and costs 256
    per unit of capital 193
    per worker 193, 453
output gap **191**–92, 197, 198
overseas aid see Official Development Assistance (ODA)
overt collusion **312**
owner-occupier market 72–73
ownership of assets and inequality 182, 472

P

participation rate **339**
pensions
    funding of state pensions 474
    inflation costs 209
    information problems 100
    and nudge theory 79, 546
percentage change calculation 127
perfect competition 275–76, **278**, 286
    assumptions of model 278–79
    comparison with monopoly 292–93, 357–60
    efficiency under 285
    evaluation of 285–86
    long-run equilibrium under 282–84
    in the short run 279–82
perfect knowledge assumption, perfect competition 279, 280
perfect price discrimination **294**
perfectly elastic supply **48**
perfectly inelastic supply **48**
performance targets 370
persistent inflation 208–09
persistent poverty **469**–70

PFI (Private Finance Initiative) 371–72
Phillips, Bill 233–34
Phillips curve **234**
    in the short and long run 236
    trade-off 234–35
policy targets see macroeconomic policy objectives
political instability and income inequality 480
political stability and development 506
'polluter pays' principle **108**
pollution externality 108–11
    emissions reduction 109
    measuring costs and benefits 109–10
    permit schemes 110–11
    plastics in the oceans 93
    tax imposition 108
Poor Laws 548
population growth 497–500
    age structure of a population 474, 499–500
    demographic transition 497–99
    fertility rates 499–500
    and real wages 496–97
positive consumption externalities see also education
    Christmas lights 85–86
    recycling 91
    vaccination 90
positive statement **3**
potential economic growth **11**, **128**, **190**
poverty 460 see also inequality
    causes of 472–74
    changes in over time 471
    economic growth vs basic needs 200, 578
    and indebtedness, HIPC initiative 534–35
    measuring 468–70
    Multidimensional Poverty Index (MPI) 487–88
    policies to alleviate 346, 578–79
    vs scarcity 4
Prebisch and Singer hypothesis **491**
predatory pricing **322**–23
price of a good
    and demand 21–24
    and supply 40, 41
price controls 113–15
price discrimination 294–97
    and ability to resell 295–96
    low-cost airlines 329–30
    perfect/first-degree 294
    rail travel case study 298
    third-degree 295
price elasticity of demand (*PED*) **29**, 29–35
    calculating 30
    influences on 33–34
    mathematical relationship between AR and
        MR 265
    and total revenue 31–32
    two extreme case of 33
    variation along a straight-line demand curve 30
price elasticity of supply (*PES*) **46**–48
    the short run and the long run 47
    two special cases 48
price-fixing by cartels 311–13, 370–71

price mechanism **61**
  incentives and signalling 61–62
  and labour supply 339
price of other goods
  effect on demand 26–27
  effect on supply 43
price regulation 369
price signal **62**
  unreliable for resource allocation 210–11
price stability *see* inflation
price taker **279**
price wars 321–22
prices and resource allocation 56–61
pricing rules 318–20
primary products *see also* agricultural sector
  dependence on 489–90
  deterioration in terms of trade 393, 491
  export promotion strategies 522
  fair trade schemes 527
  volatility in supply 392, 490
principal–agent (agency) problem **249**–50
  influence on the motivations of firms 270
  and revenue maximisation 269
  and X-inefficiency 268
prisoners' dilemma **308**–09
  and economics 309–10
private benefit **83**
private cost **83**
Private Finance Initiative (PFI) **371**–72
private goods **94**
private sector **244**
privatisation 230, **368**, 519
producer surplus **58**–60
  effect of a subsidy 78
  gains from protectionism 422, 426
  perfect competition vs monopoly 292–93
  and sales taxes 107
product differentiation **300**, 302
production costs 41–42
production externality **83**
production possibility frontier (*PPF*) **8**–10
production subsidies 424–25
productive efficiency 64–65, **261**, **274**
  monopoly market 292
  perfect competition vs monopoly 359–60
  under monopolistic competition 302
  under perfect competition 285
productivity **193**
  agricultural, in developing countries 489, 537
  and competitiveness 456
  international differences in 453–56
  measures of 453–55
  of the UK, case study 458–59
profit maximisation 265–68
  assumption of 270–71, 278
  behavioural theories 270
  and cost-plus pricing 320–21
  long run 269–70
  by monopoly 287–90
  MR = MC rule 266–67

pricing rules 319
  and the shut-down price 267–68
  X-inefficiency 268
profit regulation 369
progressive tax **475**
prohibition **115**–16
property rights 66, 111–12
  lack of in developing countries 504, 584
proportional tax **477**
protectionism **419**
  case studies 427–28
  export promotion 522
  forms of 421–25
  impact of 425–26
  import substitution 521–22
  reasons for 420
  summary 427
Prudential Regulation Authority (PRA) **558**
public expenditure *see* government expenditure
public goods 82, **94**–95
  examples of 95, 96
  extension material 95
  free-rider problem 95–96, 105
  tackling problem of 96–97
public–private partnership (PPP) **371**
public sector **244**
  crowding out private sector 567, 574
  finances 570–71
  wages 350
public sector net cash requirement (PSNCR) 214
public sector net debt 214, 220, 557, 577, 580
purchasing power parity dollars (PPP$) 134–35, 462–63
purchasing power parity (PPP) exchange rates **134**
purchasing power parity (PPP) theory of exchange rates **443**

Q

quality of life *see* standard(s) of living
quantitative easing **226**–27, 386, **556**–57, 559, 582
quintiles 464, 466
quotas 422–24
  effects of 423
  gainers and losers 423–24

R

rate of interest *see* interest rate
rational decision making 19–20
rationality 19–20, 78–79
real balance effect **168**
real exchange rate **451**, 452
real GDP **126**–27
  and actual economic growth 129–30, 190
  expenditure-side breakdown of 160–61
  fluctuations in, trade cycle 197–200
  and the output gap 191–92
real income effect 22, 26
real wage inflexibility **152**
real wages and population growth 496–97
recession **198** *see also* financial crisis
  and the business cycle 197–99

and close integration of global economy 384–86
and expectations about future demand 164–65
and fall in demand for labour 152, 335
Great Depression 228, 404
in the late 2000s 200–01, 226–27
and single currency area 417
recycling 91
redistribution of income 215–17, 575–76
regional policy and labour market flexibility 351–52
regional trade agreements see trading blocs
regressive tax **476**
regulation **104**
financial 558–59
of prices 113–14
profit regulation 369
prohibition 115–16
rent controls 114–15
regulatory capture **370**
relative poverty **469**
relevant market **363**
remittances 531
renewable resources **7**
rent controls 114–15
repos **543**
research and development (R&D) 327, 359
resources 6, 7
retail banks **542**
retail price index (RPI) **142**–43
price control (*RPI – X*) 369
versus the CPI 144
revaluation **439**
revenue see also average revenue (*AR*); marginal revenue (*MR*)
of firms 263–65
maximisation 268–69, 319
tax revenue 514, 570, 576
Ricardo, David 387, 420, 496
RIIO ('Revenue using Incentives to deliver Innovation and Outputs') 369
Robinson, Joan 299
ROSCAS (rotating savings and credit schemes) 518
RPIX (retail price index) 143, 211, 223, 554
Russia 399–400

S

sales maximisation 269
pricing rules 319
sales taxes 106–07
Samuelson, Paul 7–8
satisficing behaviour **270**
saving(s)
and circular flow model 180–81
financial sector facilitating 539
Harrod–Domar model 492–93, 495, 511–12
low-level equilibrium trap 491
marginal propensity to save (MPS) **161**
mobilisation of 493–94
and rate of interest 163, 166, 494
ROSCAS (rotating savings and credit schemes) 518

savings gap **493**
scale of operations 245
scarcity **4**
schooling see also education
component of HDI 483–86
mean vs expected years 484, 485
seasonal adjustment **130**
seasonal unemployment **152**
securities, open market operations 555
securitisation **545**, 546
shipping industry 548
shocks see external shocks
shoe-leather costs of inflation 209
short run **253**
short run aggregate supply 170–73
short-run aggregate supply curve (*SRAS*) **171**–72, 183, 185, 192, 572
short-run cost curves 256–57
short-run supply curve **281**
shut-down price **267**–68
signalling and incentives price mechanism 61–62
single currency area 414–18
benefits 416–17
costs 417
Europe experience 418
evaluation of 417–18
fiscal policy 415–16
formation of euro area 416
monetary policy 414–15
Treaty of Maastricht 414
SMEs, measures to encourage 373
Smith, Adam 13, 15, 66, 387, 477
smoking see tobacco
snob effects 24
social benefit **83**
social cost **83**
social science, economics as 2–3
specialisation 13
between firms and nations 14
and comparative advantage 387–88, 401
gains from 353, 390
labour- or land-intensive activities 395
transitional cost of 383
specific tax **76**
speculation 444–45, 546
stagflation **235**
standard(s) of living
and the environment 237
and globalisation 383
HDI as indicator of 483–86
limitations of GNI as measure of 131–32, 461–63
and minimum wage policy 346
and purchasing power parity 134–35
social indicators 135–36
and tariffs 426
state see under government...
static efficiency **274**
sterling effective exchange rate 451
Stiglitz, Joseph 380, 382
stock market 74, 541

strategies influencing growth and development
511–12
   Bretton Woods institutions 534–36
   case studies 537–38
   future prospects for developing countries 537
   interventionist strategies 519–33
   market-oriented strategies 512–19
street lighting, example of a public good 82, 95
strike action 350–51
structural change 383, 418–19
structural deficit **571**
structural unemployment **151**, 343
structure–conduct–performance paradigm 357–58
sub-Saharan Africa
   debt servicing 532
   development 485–86, 508–09
   wildlife tourism 538
subsidies **77**–78
   effect on supply 42–43
   production 424–25
substitutes **26**
   change in price of 54
   and cross elasticity of demand (*XED*) 36
   hypothetical monopoly test 363
   and price elasticity of demand 33–34
   supply side 43, 363
   and wage elasticity of demand for labour 335
substitution effect 22, 26, 338
sunk costs **254**, 325, 326, 327
sunset industry **420**
supernormal profits **265**, 277, 324, 325
supply **39**–50 *see also* labour supply
   case studies 49–50
   elasticity 46–48
   factors influencing 41–44
supply curve **40**–41
   movement along and shift of 41, 44–45
supply of money 75, 208–09, 222, 226–27, 440, 557
supply shocks 71, 184–85, 207
supply-side policies 218, **229**, 565, 584
   deregulation 230
   and design of policy mix 238, 239
   education and training 231–32
   evaluation of 233
   labour market flexibility 230
   to deal with a current account deficit 435
surplus *see also* consumer surplus; producer
   surplus
   on the financial account 430, 433, 457
sustainable development 7, **202**, **386**, 580–81
symmetric information **97**

T

tacit collusion **313**
tariffs 166–67, **421**
   impact of 426
   import substitution 521–22
   negative effects of 422
   operation of 421–22

reducing/removing 411, 512, 534
retaliation, case study 427
trade creation and diversion 408
tax revenue 514
   in different countries 576–77
   and the Laffer curve 570
taxes
   balance of taxation 477
   case studies 118–19
   collection issues in developing countries 505, 521, 576
   direct 221
   effect of changes in 568–70
   effect on supply 42–43
   and income distribution 475–77
   indirect taxes 76, 106, 221, 476
technology (of production)
   effect on employment 352–53
   effect on supply 42
   and long-run aggregate supply 175
   market equilibrium 55
   source of economies of scale 258–59
terms of trade **390**
   long-run deterioration 393
   pattern of comparative advantage 393–94
   short-run volatility 392–93
Thaler, Robert 79
Thatcher, Margaret 368, 471, 477, 568–69
third-degree price discrimination **295**
three key economic questions 7–8
tiger economies **482**
   development pattern 507–08
   export promotion strategies 522
time
   influence on demand 28
   and supply decisions 47
TNCs *see* transnational companies
tobacco
   information gaps 98, 117
   opportunity cost case study 18
   regressive taxation 476–77
   specific tax on 76–77
total factor productivity **193**, **454**
total fixed costs (*TFC*) **254**, 255
total output in an economy 12
total variable costs (*TVC*) **254**–55
tourism
   developing countries 526–27
   externalities 91
   Tanzania wildlife tourism 538
toxic fumes
   negative production externality 83–84
   reducing emission of 109
tradable pollution permit system **110**
trade *see also* international trade
   barriers, reducing/removing 382–83, 407,
      411, 412
   interventionist policy, developing countries
      521–23
trade balance 155, 159, 441, 443–44

trade creation **407**
    effects of 408
trade cycle **129**, **197** *see also* recession
    GDP fluctuations 198–99
trade diversion **407**
    effects of 408
trade in goods 159, 431
trade in services 402, 432
trade union reform 230, 350–51
trading blocs **406**–07
    common markets 409
    customs unions 407
    economic and monetary union 409–10
    evaluation of 407–09
    free trade areas 407
    influence on pattern of trade 401
    and the WTO 406
trading possibilities curve **389**
traffic congestion 88–89
training
    developing countries 502–03, 520
    interventionist policy 231–32
    and labour market flexibility 350
    and long run aggregate supply 175–76
    and occupational mobility 343
transfer payments **565**
transfer pricing **585**
transmission mechanism of monetary policy
    224, 443
transnational companies (TNCs) **248**, **382**
    and capital flight 494–95
    employment effects 514
    foreign direct investment by 381, 512–15,
      569
    foreign exchange earnings 514–15
    location of 515
    market power of 515
    potential benefits 513
    potential costs 514
    regulation and control 584
    tax holidays 514, 577
    transfer pricing 585
transport
    externalities 88–89
    HS2 project, case study 189
    monopolistic competition in road transport
      303
    technological advances 382

U

underemployment **151**
unemployed **148**
    ILO definition of 149
unemployment
    causes of 151–53
    costs of 153
    during the Great Depression 228
    and fiscal policy 415
    and inflation, Phillips curve 233–36

    measurement of 149–51
    and the minimum wage 347
    natural rate of 173
    reduction in (full employment) 205–06
    summary 154
    and technology 352–53
    in the UK, case study 159
unemployment benefits 149, 152–53, 230, 345
    effect of increase in 339
unit labour costs 454–**55**
unitary elastic **29**
universal banks **542**
urban areas, developing countries 473, 501, 515,
    525

V

vaccination against disease 90, 93, 520
value judgement **3**
variable costs **254**–55
VAT (value added tax) 76, 106, 221, 476, 477,
    568, 570
Veblen effect 24
vertical mergers **247**
    evaluation of 248
visible trade **431**
volatility
    in commodity prices 69–71, 384, 392–93, 490–91,
      523, 540
    exchange rate 446–47
    in inflation 210
voluntary export restraints (VERs) 422–23
voluntary unemployment **152**–53
von Hayek, Friedrich 16, 286

W

wage differentials 341, 343
wage elasticity
    demand for labour 335–37
    supply of labour 339
wage rate/wages
    and demand curve for labour 333–34
    effect on labour supply 338
    effect of minimum wage 345–48
    gender wage gap, UK 473
    and investment in new technology 352
    maximum wage policy 348–49
    and population growth 496–97
    and unemployment 152–53
Washington Consensus 535–36
waste disposal 91, 371
wealth **182**
    distribution of 467–68, 472
    versus income 182, 472
wealth effects **162**
welfare loss 85, 107
well-being, measurement of 138
wholesale banks **542**
withdrawals from the circular flow **180**, 181
    diluting the multiplier effect 187

workforce **148** *see also* human capital; labour (workers); labour market
   ILO unemployment rate 150
   and long-run aggregate supply curve 174–75
   size of, migration affecting 194–95
World Bank **534**
World Trade Organization (WTO) **382**, 404–06, **534**
world trade patterns 396–97
   case study 402–03
   emerging economies 399–401

   factors influencing 401–02
   UK exports and imports 397–99

X

X-inefficiency **268**
   competition eliminating 356–57, 412

Y

Yunus, Muhammad, Grameen Bank 517, 518